# SUPERVISION TODAY!

## SECOND EDITION

### STEPHEN P. ROBBINS
San Diego State University

### DAVID A. DE CENZO
Towson State University

PRENTICE HALL
Upper Saddle River, NJ 07458

*Library of Congress Cataloging-in-Publication Data*
Robbins, Stephen P.,
    Supervision today! / Stephen P. Robbins, David A.
De Cenzo.—2nd ed.
        p.    cm.
    Includes index.
    ISBN 0-13-608630-6
    1. Supervision of employees.    I. DeCenzo, David A.
II. Title.
HF5549. 12.R628   1998
658.3'02—dc21                                    98-3146
                                                        CIP

Acquisitions editor:  *Elizabeth Sugg*
Editorial/production supervision:  *Barbara Marttine
    Cappuccio*
Director of manufacturing and production:  *Bruce
    Johnson*
Managing editor:  *Mary Carnis*
Manufacturing buyer:  *Ed O'Dougherty*
Design director:  *Marianne Frasco*
Marketing manager:  *Danny Hoyt*
Associate editor:  *Judith Casillo*
Editorial assistant:  *Emily Jones*
Interior design:  *Eileen Burke*
Cover design:  *Bruce Kenselaar*
Cover photograph:  *Shoji Sato*
Image permission coordinator:  *Michelina Porrino*
Photo researcher:  *Teri Stratford*

©1998, 1995 by PRENTICE-HALL, INC.
Simon & Schuster/A Viacom Company
Upper Saddle River, New Jersey 07458

Printed in the United States of America

10  9  8  7  6  5  4  3  2  1

ISBN 0-13-608630-6

Prentice Hall International (UK) Limited, *London*
Prentice Hall of Australia Pty. Limited, *Sydney*
Prentice Hall Canada Inc., *Toronto*
Prentice Hall Hispanoamericana, S.A., *Mexico*
Prentice Hall of India Private Limited, *New Delhi*
Prentice Hall of Japan, Inc., *Tokyo*
Simon & Schuster Asia Pte. Ltd., *Singapore*
Editora Prentice Hall do Brasil, Ltda., *Rio de Janeiro*

**PHOTO ILLUSTATION CREDITS:**

| Page | Source |
|---|---|
| 2 | Charles Gupton/Charles Gupton Photography |
| 4 | Gary Moss/Gary Moss Photography |
| 18 | Ree DeDonato |
| 23 | Bruce Ayres/Tony Stone Images |
| 36 | Lukens Inc. |
| 39 | Jay Dickman |
| 56 | John Abbott/John Abbott Photography |
| 61 | Mason Morfit/FPG International |
| 65 | Bruce Byers/FPG International |
| 78 | Teri Stratford |
| 80 | Greg Girard/Contact Press Images |
| 83 | Chris Corsmeier/Chris Corsmeier Photography |
| 99 | Kim Blake/London Life Insurance Company |
| 108 | Michael Barley/Michael Barley Photography |
| 110 | Steve Rubin/The Image Works |
| 117 | Kea Motor Car Corporation |
| 122 | Dave Murray |
| 129 | IBM |
| 138 | Bob Daemmrich/Uniphoto Picture Agency |
| 140 | Frederick Charles/Frederick Charles Photography |
| 148 | Bettye Lane/Photo Researchers, Inc. |
| 150 | Charles Gupton/Tony Stone Images |
| 153 | Harris Corporation |
| 162 | IBM |
| 172 | Bob Daemmrich/Stock/Boston |
| 178 | Phil Schofield Photography |
| 186 | R. Lord/The Image Works |
| 188 | Hank Morgan/Photo Researchers, Inc. |
| 200 | Xerox Corporation |
| 207 | Dick Luria Photography, Inc./FPG International |
| 224 | Bob Daemmrich/Stock Boston |
| 226 | Ralph Mercer/Tony Stone Images |
| 236 | Kim Blake/London Life Insurance |
| 241 | Frank LaBua/Simon & Schuster/PH College |
| 247 | Manpower |
| 253 | Robert Scott |
| 264 | Terry Parke/Terry Parke Photography |
| 266 | Kitch Kezar/Tony Stone Images |
| 270 | Kim Blake/London Life Insurance Company |
| 280 | James Schnepf Photography, Inc. |
| 288 | Jose L. Pelaez/The Stock Market |
| 292 | Tim Defrisco/Allsport Photography (USA), Inc. |
| 306 | Gary Laufman Photography |
| 308 | Roppe Corporation |
| 316 | Lawrence Migdale/Stock Boston |
| 322 | Jenny Ogborne/Lincoln Electric Co. |
| 327 | Walt Ennis/W.L. Gore & Associates, Inc. |
| 332 | Susan S. Starr |
| 346 | Phil Huber/Black Star |
| 349 | Bonnie Sue/Photo Researchers, Inc. |
| 353 | Andy Sacks/Tony Stone Images |
| 360 | Pat McDonogh |
| 364 | UPI/Corbis-Bettmann |
| 377 | Terry Parke/Terry Parke Photography |
| 386 | Doug Plummer/Photo Researcher, Inc. |
| 387 | George Disario/The Stock Market |
| 394 | Rhoda Sidney/Stock Boston |
| 412 | Bruce Ayres/Tony Stone Images |
| 424 | Kevin Horan |
| 426 | Neal Peters/Neal Peters Collection |
| 438 | Charles Gupton/The Stock Market |
| 446 | Brian Smith |
| 451 | Molly Roberts |
| 460 | Mark Wagner/Tony Stone Images |
| 463 | Will van Overbeek |
| 466 | Honda of America Mfg., Inc. |
| 474 | David Stoecklein/The Stock Market |
| 489 | J. Griffin/The Image Works |
| 500 | Joe Sohm/UNICEF Photo |
| 502 | Richard Gardner/The Commercial Appeal |
| 512 | Kim Blake/London Life Insurance Company |
| 518 | UPI/Corbis-Bettmann |
| 526 | Marrin Rogers/Uniphoto Picture Agency |
| 528 | David Graham |
| 547 | Bill Denison/Uniphoto Picture Agency |
| 553 | Jonathan Nourok/Tony Stone Images |
| 568 | Nassau Community College |
| 570 | Bob Sacha/Bob Sacha Photography |
| 591 | Ron Scherman/Stock Boston |

# BRIEF CONTENTS

# CONTENTS

## PART SIX

## PERSONAL DEVELOPMENT 567

## 16 Building Your Career 568

# from the desks of
# Steve Robbins and
# Dave De Cenzo

Welcome to the second edition of *Supervision Today!* We think you will find this revised edition exciting. In our quest to make this the most complete supervision text currently available, we've taken into account a lot of feedback from readers of the first edition. We've developed a book that focuses on the basic elements of supervision—one that covers the essential and traditional concepts in effectively supervising employees; that has a strong applied, practical and skill focus; and that is user friendly. This new edition is also rich in instructional aids and experiential opportunities. Let's highlight some of these elements: specifically, the basis for the contents, the new features, the "student friendly" approach of this edition.

## THE FOUNDATIONS OF THE SECOND EDITION

Most of us understand concepts better when we can relate them to our everyday lives. We help the reader build an understanding of supervising through "real life" concepts, examples, and practice. We believe that when learners have an opportunity to apply what they are learning—in a classroom setting where risk-taking can be encouraged—they will perform more effectively on the job. Moreover, in the process they are building their supervisory portfolio!

We recognize that the supervisor's job has changed dramatically in recent years. Supervisors now work with a more diverse workforce in terms of race, gender, and ethnic background. Supervisor's jobs are also being affected by technological changes, a more competitive marketplace, and corporate restructuring and workflow redesign. Despite all of these changes, supervisors still need to understand the traditional elements of directing the work of others and the specific skills they need: goal-setting, budgeting, scheduling, delegating, interviewing, negotiating, handling grievances, employee counseling, and evaluating employees' performance.

**Traditional and contemporary**

**Real people**

**Full-color format**

**Lively writing style**

A good supervision text captures **traditional and contemporary** issues. We believe we've done this by focusing on issues that are relevant to the reader, and by including lots of examples and visual stimuli to make concepts come alive. We've included a **full-color** design format to visually capture the reality and the excitement of the supervisor's job. We've also spent years developing a **writing style** that has been called "lively, conversational, and interesting." That's just another way of saying our readers can understand what we are saying and feel as if we're actually in front of them giving a lecture. Of course, only you can judge this text's readability. We ask you to pick a few pages at random in the text and read them. We think you'll find the writing style both informative and lively.

*Question format.* Many headings address specific questions. Each of these questions was carefully chosen to reinforce understanding of very specific information. After reading a chapter (or a section, for that matter), you should be able to return to these headings and "respond" to the question. If you can't answer a question or are unsure of your response, you'll know exactly what sections need to be reread, reviewed, or where more of your effort needs to be placed. All in all, this format provides a self-check on your reading comprehension.

*Critical thinking as an important outcome.* Several years ago, training organizations began taking a hard look at themselves. What they typically found was that their programs needed to expand language-based skills, knowledge, and abilities across the curriculum. This has also been reinforced in another forum, as the Secretary of Labor published a report from the *Secretary's Committee on Acquiring Necessary Skills* (SCANS). What did these two activities have in common? Both highlighted the need for all training programs to cover the basic skill areas of communications, critical thinking, computer technology, globalization, diversity, and ethics and values.

This edition of *Supervision Today!* has been designed to facilitate the acquisition of these key skills by increasing levels of thinking from knowledge to comprehension and, finally, to application. We convey relevant supervisory knowledge to learners, give them an opportunity to reinforce their comprehension, and demonstrate how they can apply the concepts. The table on the inside cover of this book summarizes how this book covers critical skills.

**Job-task organization**

*Organization.* The book is **organized** to help the reader learn the role of the supervisor. It is divided into six parts—Part One: Introduction; Part Two: Planning and Control; Part Three: Organizing, Staffing, and Employee Development; Part Four: Stimulating Individual and Group Performance; Part Five: Coping with Workplace Dynamics, and Part Six: Personal Development.

FROM THE DESKS OF STEVE ROBBINS AND DAVE DE CENZO

# AN INVITATION

Now that we've explained the ideas behind the text, we'd like to extend an open invitation to you. If you'd like to give us some feedback, we encourage you to write. Send your correspondence to Dave De Cenzo at the Department of Management, Towson State University, Towson, Maryland 21252. Dave is also available on E-mail. His address is *decenzo@towson.edu.*

We hope you enjoy reading this book as much as we enjoyed preparing it for you.

Steve Robbins

Dave De Cenzo
decenzo@towson.edu

# VALUABLE FEATURES

The first edition contained a number of topics and features that readers considered unique, useful, and were particularly popular with them. We've retained these, and they include the following:

## CHAPTER OBJECTIVES

To make learning more efficient, each chapter of this book opens with a list of objectives that describe what you should be able to do after reading the chapter. These objectives are designed to focus your attention on the major issues within each chapter.

## CHAPTER SUMMARIES

Just as objectives clarify where on is going, chapter summaries remind you where you've been. Each chapter of this book concludes with a concise summary organized around the opening learning objectives.

## REVIEWING YOUR KNOWLEDGE

Every chapter in this book ends with a set of review and discussion questions. If you have read and understood the contents of a chapter, you should be able to answer the review questions. These review questions are drawn directly from the material in the chapter.

The discussion questions go beyond comprehending chapter content. They're designed to foster higher-order thinking skills. The discussion questions will allow you to demonstrate that you not only know the facts in the chapter, but that you can also use those facts to deal with more complex issues.

## CLASS EXERCISES

This portion of the *Performing Your Job* section allows you to learn and practice relevant supervisory skills introduced in the chapter. By combining your new knowledge and natural talents, you will be able to "practice" a supervisory activity and assess your own progress.

## CASE APPLICATIONS

Each chapter contains two case applications within the *Performing Your Job* section. Their focus allows you to apply your knowledge to solve real problems faced by real supervisors—most often in real companies.

## VIDEO CASES

Each part ends with Building A Portfolio, cases that work with a stop-action video and give the learner an opportunity to work with real supervisors solving real problems.

## MARGIN NOTES

Key terms are identified at the beginning of each chapter. When they first appear in this chapter, they appear in bold; and the bold term is defined in the margin for quick reference.

## SUPPLEMENTS PACKAGE

This book is accompanied by the full complement of support materials. For example, instructors who use this text can obtain the following classroom aids:

**Instructor's Manual with Transparency Masters**—written by Jerry Thomas, Chairman, Management Program, at Arapahoe Community College, it provides detailed lecture notes referenced to the more than 60 transparency masters at the end of the manual. In addition to suggested classroom activities and readings, it includes a guide to the videos and guidelines for evaluating case responses.

**Study Guide**—new to this edition, this study tool for students was written by F. Barry Barnes of the Organizational Leadership & Supervision Program at Purdue University School of Engineering and Technology. The guide provides a review of the learning objectives, outlines, key terms and concepts, and review questions for each chapter, with an answer key referenced to the textbook pages.

**Test Item File**—prepared by Thomas W. Lloyd of Westmoreland County Community College's Business Department, this provides over 950 multiple choice, true/false, short answer, and essay questions on three difficulty levels.

**Prentice Hall CUSTOM TEST**—offers the complete Test Item File in a powerful computerized testing program designed to operate on the WINDOWS platform. It provides full mouse support, complete question editing capabilities, random test generation, and printing capabilities. This software package is free with every adoption of the textbook.

**ABC News/Prentice Hall Video Library**—brings into the classroom four relevant news stories that pertain to supervisors from ABC's *World News Tonight* and *Nightline*.

**Stop Action Video**—contains six video cases that were specifically chosen to accompany every major section of the textbook: Introduction, Planning and Control, Organizing, Staffing, Employee Development, Stimulating Individual and Group Performance, Coping with Workplace Dynamics, Labor Relations, and Career Planning.

**PowerPoint Transparencies**—with over 80 visuals created from the textbook exhibits, this software is free with every adoption of the textbook.

**World Wide Web Site**—Prentice Hall's dedicated Web Site for SUPERVISION is the best way to introduce this new technology into your classroom. It allows instructors and students access to NewsLink, our electronic study guide, and provides links to other relevant sites on the Web. Visit our site at **www.prenhall.com/business_studies.**

# NEW IN THE SECOND EDITION

There are several new features and content topics that are included in this revision. First, we made a significant effort to "reengineer" this edition. That meant refocusing chapter material to better reflect the traditional elements regarding what a supervisor needs to know to be effective. With suggestions from several expert reviewers, we were able to eliminate three chapters and integrate their content within the new framework.

Topic coverage aside, we've also added several features which are designed specifically to assist both the reader and the instructor. These include:

# BUILDING A SUPERVISORY SKILL

*Supervisory skills.* We've included skill boxes throughout the text, which provide step-by-step guidelines for handling specific elements of a supervisor's job. These skills can make you a more effective supervisor once you have practiced and mastered them. They include skills such as developing budgets, conducting a performance evaluation, and managing your time.

# ASSESSING YOURSELF

*Self-assessment exercises.* Individuals like to get feedback about themselves that they then can use in their development. So, we've included a self-assessment in each chapter. Some examples include: How much do you know about diversity? (Chapter 2). Are you willing to delegate? (Chapter 6). Are you effective at disciplining? (Chapter 14).

## SOMETHING TO THINK ABOUT *(and to promote class discussion)*

*Class discussion.* These vignettes are designed to get readers thinking about an issue that affects supervisors on the job. For example, in Chapter

3, we look at criticism of planning; Chapter 7 involves hiring employees in an environment that is heavily influenced by federal legislation; and Chapter 12 focuses on gaining power in an organization. The write-ups are designed to have readers think about both sides of an issue, and build a case (verbally in class or in a written assignment) to support their position.

*The traditional supervisor.* In several places in the text, we've presented an issue that highlights a distinction between traditional and contemporary supervisors. For example, in Chapter 1, we address the traditional supervisor as one who was authoritative, then introduce a more contemporary view of the supervisor as an "empowering coach."

## DEALING WITH A DIFFICULT ISSUE

*Ethical issues.* No matter where supervisors work, at some point in their careers, they will be faced with a difficult issue—one that goes beyond just following the law. These sections are designed to have learners think about what they may face, and begin to develop a "plan of action" for handling ethical and moral dilemmas. For example, in Chapter 4, we focus your attention on the issue of control and its effect on employee privacy; in Chapter 9, the issue is rewarding appropriate behaviors; in Chapter 15, replacing striking workers.

*Reinforcement.* Each chapter also includes two pop quizzes. Our experience indicates that you need more practice for tests you will take on these subjects. These questions are actual test questions we've used before, and can serve as reinforcement for the learner. In each set, there are four questions: two multiple choice, one true/false, and one open-ended question. We've also provided the answer to each question at the end of each chapter, and we explain the correct response.

# ACKNOWLEDGMENTS

We'd like to thank the people who helped make this book possible. Many individuals provided some special assistance and we'd like to recognize them at this time.

First is Professor Al Crispo from Purdue University. Professor Crispo provided a thorough critique of the first edition of *Supervision Today!* His input played a major role in helping us to make significant changes for the new edition. The tone, flavor, and essential elements of this edition now more accurately reflect what is needed by those in supervisory positions. Al, thank you for your assistance.

A very special note of appreciation also goes to Sharon Lund O'Neil at the University of Houston. She helped with the pedagogy that is a critical element of this book.

We would also like to acknowledge the following companies, whose supervisors either participated in the preparation of these materials or allowed their illustrative material to be used:

Abbott-Northwestern Hospitals
ABC News
Advanced Filtration Systems Incorporated
Alliant Techsystems
American Express
Atlanta's Hatsfield Int'l Airport
Basler Electric Company
Boeing Company
Burger King Corporation
Business Week Magazine
CBS Television Production
Compaq Computer Corporation
Della Femina McNamee
Dialog Information Services
Digital Equipment Corporation
Falcone Catering Service
Ford Motor Company
Gerber Life Insurance
GoodYear
Harris Corporation
Hershey Pasta Group

Honda of American Manufacturing
Hong Kong Airport
Insight Magazine
Johnson & Johnson
Jostens
Kea Motor Car Corporation
Kelly Temporary Services
Lan Tech Incorporated
London Life Insurance Company
Manpower Incorporated
Metropolitan Transit Commission
Nassau Community College
New Alternatives Incorporated
New York University Library
Northwestern University Library
Orange Glen Post Office
Perimeter Productions
Pitney-Bowes
River Communications
Sara Lee Bakery
Saturn
Sears

Sikorsky Aircraft
Southwest Airlines
Southwest Door Company
Survival Skills Institute—Star Center
Travis County Tax Office
Tri-Ford Mercury
Tucson Police Department
U.S. Army Aviation Systems Command
U.S. Department of Defense
U.S. Figure Skating Association
University of Arizona
University of California–San Diego Library
University of Southern California Library
W.L. Gore & Associates Incorporated
Western Bank
Xerox Corporation

Finally, we'd like to add a personal note. Both of us would like to recognize individuals who are important in our lives.

From Steve: Special appreciation goes to my new life partner, Laura. Thanks, honey, for being so supportive and tolerating those daily trips into the office at 5 a.m.

From Dave: No person can truly survive in isolation. To be happy, you need the love and comfort of others. For me, these things come from my family—my wife of 15 years, Terri; and my children—Mark, who's starting high school; Meredith, who's such a beautiful middle-schooler; Gabriella, the mouse—my effervescent, active, and unbelievably caring first grader; and Natalie—my three-year old supervisor! Each of you are very special in your own way. Always remember that you are special to me—and unquestionably are my inspiration.

# PART ONE

# INTRODUCTION

Part One introduces you to work organizations and the functions of a supervisor. Emphasis is placed on the role of supervisors and the skills they need. Supervisory positions are being influenced by a number of environmental factors. These factors are explored with respect to their effect on the supervisory function.

Part One contains two chapters:

1. THE SUPERVISOR'S JOB

2. SUPERVISORY CHALLENGES FOR THE 21ST CENTURY

# 1

# THE SUPERVISOR'S JOB

# LEARNING OBJECTIVES

# KEY TERMS

After reading this chapter, you should be able to

1. Define what is meant by the term *supervisor*.
2. Explain the difference between supervisors, middle managers, and top management.
3. Identify the four functions in the management process.
4. Explain why the supervisor's role is considered ambiguous.
5. Describe the four essential supervisory competencies.
6. Explain why the supervisor's job will be increasingly important and complex in the future.

You should be able to define these supervisory terms.

conceptual competence

controlling

effectiveness

efficiency

first-level managers

interpersonal competence

leading

management

management functions

middle managers

operative employees

organization

organizing

planning

political competence

process

skill

supervisors

supervisory competencies

technical competence

top management

Meet Ray Morgan. Ray is a shipping and production supervisor at the Granite Rock Company in Watsonville, California. Ray has been with the company for more than 23 years—serving as a union employee for 20 years. Ray's desire and experience, plus specialized training he received, lead to him being offered the supervisory position about three years ago. To help prepare him for his promotion, Granite Rock sent Ray to about a dozen training seminars, which helped him focus his attention on supervisory responsibilities. For example, two seminars dealt with safety issues in the department and quality control. Because as a supervisor Ray must constantly deal with people, he also completed a 15-week Dale Carnegie program on effectively managing employees.

What does Ray do? Ray is responsible for meeting specific goals in his work unit. He works toward and meets these objectives through and with

## INTRODUCTION

This book is about the millions of Ray Morgans out there in organizations and the job they do. This book will introduce you to the challenging and rapidly changing world of *Supervision Today!*

## ORGANIZATIONS AND THEIR LEVELS

**Organization**
a systematic grouping of people brought together to accomplish some specific purpose.

Supervisors work in places called organizations. Before we identify who supervisors are and what they do, it's important to clarify what we mean by the term *organization*.

An **organization** is a systematic grouping of people brought together to accomplish some specific purpose. Your college or university is an organization. So are sororities, charitable agencies, churches, your neighborhood convenience store, the Los Angeles Lakers Basketball team, the Home Depot Corporation, the Australian Dental Association, and Cedars-Sinai Hospital. These are all organizations because each is comprised of three common characteristics.

his shipping and production employees—individuals who have varied backgrounds, skills, and experiences. Ray is responsible for scheduling employee work assignments. He needs to ensure that adequate staff are available on any given day, and that they know precisely what work they are to perform. Ray also participates in productivity-improvement meetings with his employees. He wants to make sure that the job is done right the first time and is a quality job at that. Furthermore, Ray is responsible for motivating his employees and evaluating their work. At times, when problems arise, he has to handle interpersonal conflicts. In summary, Ray advises, coaches, and provides feedback to the employees he supervises. ■

## WHAT THREE COMMON CHARACTERISTICS DO ALL ORGANIZATIONS HAVE?

First, every organization has a purpose. The distinct purpose of an organization is typically expressed in terms of a goal or set of goals. For example, the Rubbermaid Corporation set a goal of achieving 15 percent annual growth in revenues.[1] Second, no purpose or goal can achieve itself. It takes people to establish the purpose, as well as perform a variety of activities to make the goal a reality. Third, all organizations develop a systematic structure that defines the various roles of members, and which often sets limits on their work behaviors. This may include creating rules and regulations, giving some members supervisory control over other members, forming work teams, or writing job descriptions so that organizational members know what their responsibilities are.

In most traditional organizations, we can depict this structure as a pyramid containing four general categories (see Exhibit 1–1).

## WHAT ARE THE ORGANIZATIONAL LEVELS?

Generally speaking, organizations can be divided into four distinct levels. These are: operative employees, supervisors, middle managers, and top management. Let's briefly look at each level.

[1]L. Smith, "Rubbermaid Goes Thump," *Fortune,* October 2, 1995, p. 91.

## EXHIBIT 1–1

Levels in the traditional organizational pyramid.

Top Management

Middle Managers

Supervisors

Operative Employees

**Operative employees**
employees who physically produce an organization's goods and services by working on specific tasks.

The bottom level in the pyramid is occupied by **operative employees.** These are the employees who physically produce an organization's goods and services by working on specific tasks. The counter clerk at McDonald's, the claims adjuster at AllState Insurance, the assembly-line worker at the Saturn auto plant, and the postal carrier who delivers your mail are examples of operative employees. This category may also include many professional people: doctors, lawyers, accountants, engineers, and computer specialists. The common feature these operative workers share is that they generally don't manage or oversee the work of any other employee.

Now turn your attention to the top two levels in Exhibit 1–1. These are traditional management positions. **Top management** reflects a group of people responsible for establishing the organization's overall objectives and developing the policies to achieve those objectives. Titles of typical top management positions in business firms include chairman of the board, chief executive officer, president, and senior vice-president. Among nonprofit organizations, top management may have such titles as museum director, superintendent of schools, or the governor of a state.

**Top management**
a group of people responsible for establishing an organization's overall objectives and developing the policies to achieve those objectives.

**Middle managers**
all employees below the top-management level who manage other managers. These managers are responsible for establishing and meeting specific departmental or unit goals set by top management.

**Middle managers** include all employees below the top-management level who manage other managers. These individuals are responsible for establishing and meeting specific goals in their particular department or unit. Their goals, however, are not established in isolation. Instead, the objectives set by top management provide specific direction to middle managers regarding what they are expected to achieve. Ideally, if each middle manager met his or her goals, the entire organization would meet its objectives. Examples of job titles held by middle managers include vice president for finance, director of sales, division manager, group manager, district manager, unit manager, or high school principal.

Let's return to Exhibit 1–1. The only category that we haven't described is **supervisors.** Like top and middle managers, supervisors are also part of an organization's management team. What makes them unique is that they oversee the work of operative employees. Supervisors, then, are the only managers who don't manage other managers. Or another way to think of supervisors is as **first-level managers.** That is, counting from the bottom of the traditional pyramid-shaped organization, supervisors represent the first level in the management hierarchy.

What kinds of titles are likely to tell you that someone is a supervisor? Though names are sometimes deceiving, people with job titles like assistant manager, department head, department chair, head coach, foreman, or team leader are typically in supervisory positions. In the United States, about 4 million individuals have the job of supervisor.[2] The bulk of these people are employed in overseeing skilled and semi-skilled workers in industry and managing employees in retail sales and in offices.

Another interesting aspect of supervisors is that they may engage in operating tasks with their employees. The counter clerk at McDonald's may also be the shift foreman. Or the claims supervisor at AllState may also process claim forms. It is important to recognize that even though they perform operative tasks, supervisors are still part of management. That was made clear in 1947, when the U.S. Congress passed the Taft-Hartley Act. This act specifically excluded supervisors from the definition

**Supervisors**
part of an organization's management team, supervisors oversee the work of operative employees and are the only managers who don't manage other managers. *See also* First-level managers.

**First-level managers**
managers that represent the first level in the management hierarchy.

Fred Price of Northeast Tool in Charlotte, North Carolina, is typical of many supervisors today. He not only has supervisory responsibilities, he also performs a variety of "operative employee tasks" as a metal worker.

[2]G. T. Silvestri and J. M. Lukasiewicz, "A Look at Occupational Employment Trends to the Year 2000," *Monthly Labor Review,* September 1987, pp. 46–63.

of *employee*. Moreover, the Taft-Hartley Act stated that any person who can "hire, suspend, transfer, lay off, recall, promote, discharge, assign, reward, or discipline other employees while using independent judgment is a supervisor." Since first-level managers usually have this authority, the fact that they also engage in the same kind of work that their subordinates perform in no way changes their management status. In reality, they are still expected to perform the duties and responsibilities associated with the management process.

## THE MANAGEMENT PROCESS

Just as organizations have common characteristics, so, too, do managers at all levels of the organization. In spite of the fact that their titles vary widely, there are several common elements to their jobs—regardless of whether the supervisor is a head nurse in the intensive care unit of Cedars-Sinai Hospital who oversees a staff of eleven critical care specialists, or the president of the 115,000-member Boeing Corporation, the Seattle-based aircraft manufacturer.[3] In this section we'll look at these commonalities as we discuss the management process and what managers do.

### WHAT IS MANAGEMENT?

**Management**
the process of getting things done, effectively and efficiently, through and with other people. *See also* Process; Efficiency; Effectiveness

**Process**
the primary activities supervisors perform.

**Efficiency**
doing a task right; also refers to the relationship between inputs and outputs.

**Effectiveness**
doing a task right; goal attainment.

The term **management** refers to the process of getting things done, effectively and efficiently, through and with other people. There are several components in this definition that warrant some discussion. These are the terms *process, effectively,* and *efficiently*.

The term **process** in the definition of management represents the primary activities supervisors perform. In management terms, we call these the *functions of management*. The next section will describe these functions.

**Efficiency** means doing the task right and refers to the relationship between inputs and outputs. If you get more output for a given input, you have increased efficiency. You also increase efficiency when you get the same output with fewer resources. Since supervisors deal with input resources that are scarce—money, people, equipment—they are concerned with the efficient use of these resources. Consequently, supervisors must be concerned with minimizing resource costs.

While minimizing resource costs is important, it isn't enough simply to be efficient. A supervisor must also be concerned with completing activities. We call this **effectiveness**. Effectiveness means doing the right task. In an organization, we call this *goal attainment*.

[3]A. Taylor, III, "Boeing: Sleepy in Seattle," *Fortune*, August 7, 1995, p. 92.

Exhibit 1–2 shows how efficiency and effectiveness are interrelated. The need for efficiency has a profound impact on the level of effectiveness. It's easier to be effective if you ignore efficiency. For instance, you could produce more sophisticated and higher-quality products if you disregard labor and material input costs. Yet, that would probably create problems. Consequently, being a good supervisor means being concerned with both attaining goals (effectiveness) and doing so as efficiently as possible.

## WHAT ARE THE FOUR MANAGEMENT FUNCTIONS?

In the early part of this century, a French industrialist by the name of Henri Fayol wrote that all managers perform five management functions. They plan, organize, command, coordinate, and control.[4] In the mid-1950s, two professors at UCLA used the functions of planning, organizing, staffing, directing, and controlling as the framework for their management textbook.[5] The most popular textbooks still continue to be organized around **management functions,** though these have generally been condensed to the basic four: planning, organizing, leading, and controlling (see Exhibit 1–3).

Since organizations exist to achieve some purpose, someone has to define that purpose and the means for its achievement. A manager is that someone. The **planning** function encompasses defining an organization's goals, establishing an overall strategy for achieving these goals, and devel-

**Management functions**
planning, organizing, leading, and controlling.

**Planning**
defining an organization's goals, establishing an overall strategy for achieving these goals, and developing a comprehensive hierarchy of plans to integrate and coordinate activities.

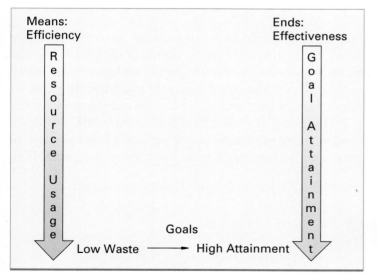

Means:
Efficiency

Ends:
Effectiveness

Resource Usage

Goal Attainment

Goals

Low Waste ⟶ High Attainment

### EXHIBIT 1–2

Efficiency vs. Effectiveness.

[4] H. Fayol, *Industrial and General Administration* (Paris: Dunod, 1916).

[5] H. Koontz and C. O'Donnell, *Principles of Management: An Analysis of Managerial Functions* (New York: McGraw-Hill, 1955).

## EXHIBIT I–3

Management functions.

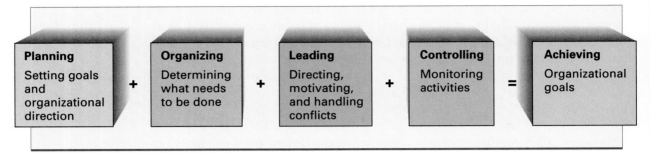

| Planning | | Organizing | | Leading | | Controlling | | Achieving |
|---|---|---|---|---|---|---|---|---|
| Setting goals and organizational direction | + | Determining what needs to be done | + | Directing, motivating, and handling conflicts | + | Monitoring activities | = | Organizational goals |

**Organizing**
determining what tasks are to be done, who is to do them, how the tasks are to be grouped, who reports to whom, and when decisions are to be made.

**Leading**
motivation of employees, direction of activities of others, selection of the most effective communication channel, and resolution of conflicts among members.

**Controlling**
monitoring an organization's performance and comparing performance with previously set goals. If significant deviations exist, getting the organization back on track.

oping a comprehensive hierarchy of plans to integrate and coordinate activities. Setting goals keeps the work to be done in its proper focus and helps organizational members keep their attention on what is most important.

Managers also have to divide work into manageable components and coordinate results to achieve objectives. This is the **organizing** function. It includes determining what tasks are to be done, who is to do them, how the tasks are to be grouped, who reports to whom, and where decisions are to be made.

We know that every organization contains people, and that part of a manager's job is to direct and coordinate these people. Performing this activity is the **leading** function of management. When managers motivate employees, direct the activities of others, select the most effective communication channel, or resolve conflicts among members, they're engaging in leading.

The final function managers perform is **controlling.** After the goals are set, the plans formulated, the structural arrangements determined, and the people hired, trained, and motivated, something may still go amiss. To ensure that things are going as they should, a manager must monitor the organization's performance. Actual performance must be compared with the previously set goals. If there are any significant deviations, it's the manager's responsibility to get the organization back on track. This process of monitoring, comparing, and correcting is what comprises the controlling function.

## DO MANAGEMENT FUNCTIONS DIFFER BY ORGANIZATIONAL LEVELS?

A manager's level in an organization will affect how these management functions are performed. A supervisor in the accounting department at Dell Computer won't do the same kind of planning as Dell's president. That's because, while all managers perform the four management functions, there are important differences relating to their level. Typically, top management focuses on long-term, strategic planning such as determining what overall business a company should be in. Supervisors focus on short-term, tactical planning such as scheduling departmental workloads for the next month. Similarly, top management is concerned with structuring the overall organization, while supervisors focus on structuring the jobs of individuals and work groups.

Not only does the type of planning, organizing, leading, and controlling tend to differ by level in the organization, so does the emphasis that managers give to the various functions. As Exhibit 1–4 illustrates, supervisors spend the majority of time on leading-related activities. More specifically, a study of more than 650 first-level managers asked them to identify the specific tasks they felt were very important to perform their jobs successfully.[6] Exhibit 1–5 lists tasks that at least 50 percent of these supervisors considered very important.

## CHANGING EXPECTATIONS OF SUPERVISORS

Forty years ago, if you asked a group of top executives what they thought a supervisor's or foreman's job was, you'd get a fairly standard answer. They would describe a man (which it was likely to be back then) who forcefully made decisions, told employees what to do, closely watched over those employees to make sure they did as they were told, disciplined them when they broke the rules, and fired those that didn't "shape up." Supervisors were the bosses "on the operating floor" and their job was to keep the employees in line and get the work out.

If you ask top executives that same question today, you'll find a few who still hold to the "supervisor-as-boss" perspective (see The Traditional Supervisor). But you'll also hear executives describe today's supervisor using terms like *trainer, adviser, mentor, facilitator,* or *coach.* In this section, we want to look at some of these changing expectations of supervisory managers.

### WHAT ROLES DO SUPERVISORS PLAY?

The supervisor's job is unique in that it bridges the management ranks with the operating employees. No one else in the organization can make that claim. Yet, because of this uniqueness, supervisors have an ambig-

[6]A. I. Kraut, "The Role of the Manager: What's Really Important in Different Management Jobs," *Academy of Management Executive*, November 1989, pp. 286–293.

EXHIBIT I–4

Distribution of time per function by organizational level. (*Source:* Adapted from T. A. Mahoney, T. H. Jerdee, and S. J. Carroll, "The Job(s) of Management," *Industrial Relations,* Vol. 4, No. 2 (1965), p. 103.)

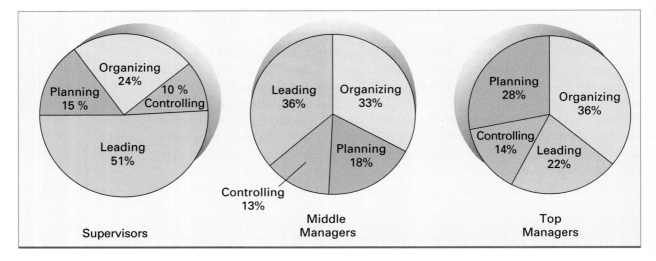

Supervisors — Organizing 24%, Planning 15%, Controlling 10%, Leading 51%

Middle Managers — Leading 36%, Organizing 33%, Planning 18%, Controlling 13%

Top Managers — Planning 28%, Organizing 36%, Controlling 14%, Leading 22%

EXHIBIT I–5

Key supervisory tasks. (Based on a survey of more than 650 supervisors). (*Source:* Based on A. J. Kraut, "The Role of the Manager: What's Really Important in Different Management Jobs," *Academy of Management Executive,* November 1989, p. 287.)

- Motivate employees to change or improve their performance.

- Provide ongoing performance feedback to employees.

- Take action to resolve performance problems in your work group.

- Blend employees' goals with organization's work requirements.

- Identify ways of improving communications among employees.

- Inform employees about procedures and work assignments.

- Keep track of employees' training and special skills as they relate to job assignments to aid their growth and development.

Are supervisors changing their roles in organizations today? By and large, the answer is *Yes*. But that's not true in all cases. Traditional supervisors—those who rule from an authoritative position—are alive and thriving in today's organizations.

It is important to recognize that the supervisor-as-boss model dominated organizations for the first eighty-five years of this century. In this capacity, supervisors were expected to know everything about the jobs their employees did. The boss, in fact, was assumed to be able to do every worker's job as well as, or better than, the worker could. Because the supervisor was more knowledgeable and skilled, employees looked to him or her for direction. Supervisors responded by giving orders. Employees expected to be told what to do and supervisors did just that. Moreover, these supervisors "demanded" that their orders be followed. All told, they ensured compliance with stated rules, regulations, and production goals.

Traditional supervisors were mainly held accountable for and expected to emphasize the technical or task aspects of the job. Their major concern was getting the job done—at all costs. As long as employees did what they were told, supervisors and their bosses were happy. That's how they got the title of *taskmaster*.

These individuals left no doubt as to who was in charge, and who had the authority and power in the group. He or she made all the decisions affecting the group and told others what to do. This "telling" frequently happened in the form of orders—mandates that were expected to be followed. Failure to "obey" these orders usually resulted in some negative reinforcement—like being fired for insubordination—at the hands of the traditional supervisor.

This traditional supervisor can still be found in all types of organizations—business, government, and the military. In some of these places, they have found that traditional supervision is most effective. In one organization, Warnaco and Authentic Fitness,[7] (makers of intimate apparel like Christian Dior,

*(cont'd)*

[7]Based on M. Mallory, "*What Do Women Want?*" Warnaco's Linda Wachner Knows, *U. S. News & World Report*, November 6, 1995, p. 75; S. Caminiti, "America's Most Successful Businesswoman," *Fortune*, June 15, 1992, pp. 102–108; M. Mahar, "The Measure of Success," *Working Woman*, May 1992, pp. 70–77; and D. W. Johnson, "Leaders of Corporate Change," *Fortune*, December 14, 1992, pp. 106–107.

uous role. Each of the following offers a different viewpoint of the supervisor's role:[8]

*Key person.*   Supervisors serve as the critical communication link in the organization's chain of authority. They are like the hub of a wheel around which all operating activities revolve.

*Person in the middle.*   Because they are "neither fish nor fowl," supervisors must interact and reconcile the opposing forces and competing expectations from higher management and workers. If unresolved, this conflicting role can create frustration and stress for supervisors.

*Just another worker.*   To some, particularly among upper-level managers, supervisors are often seen as "just another worker," rather than as management. This is reinforced when their decision-making authority is limited, when they're excluded from participating in upper-level decisions, and when they perform operating tasks alongside the same people they supervise.

*Behavioral specialist.*   Consistent with the belief that one of the most important abilities needed by supervisors is strong interpersonal skills, they are looked at as behavioral specialists. To succeed in their jobs, supervisors

[8]Based on J. W. Newstrom, and K. Davis, *Organizational Behavior: Human Behavior at Work,* 9th ed. (New York: McGraw-Hill, 1993), p. 239.

must be able to understand the varied needs of their staff and be able to listen, motivate, and lead.

While each of these four role descriptions has some truth to it, each also offers a slanted view of the supervisor's job. Our point is that different people hold different perceptions of this job, which can create ambiguity and conflicts for today's supervisor.

## ARE SUPERVISORS MORE IMPORTANT IN TODAY'S ORGANIZATIONS?

Regardless of what people think and the different role perceptions they hold, the fact is that the supervisor's job has, and will continue to become, increasingly important and complex in the future.[9] Why? There are at least three reasons.

[9]R. E. Crandall, "First-Line Supervisors: Tomorrow's Professionals," *Personnel*, November 1988, pp. 24–31.

First, organizations are universally implementing significant change programs to cut costs and increase productivity. Examples of these programs include quality improvement, introduction of work teams, group bonus plans, flexible work hours, accident prevention, and stress-reduction programs. These programs tend to focus on the work activities of operating employees. As a result, supervisors have become increasingly important because they typically assume responsibility for introducing and implementing these change efforts at the operations level.

Second, organizations are making extensive cutbacks in their number of employees. Boeing, Citicorp, Eastman Kodak, General Motors, IBM, U.S. West, Chevron, Sears, Westinghouse Electric, United Technologies, General Dynamics, and American Express are just a few of the major companies that have cut anywhere from a thousand to fifty-thousand jobs. Organizations are particularly thinning their ranks among middle managers and staff-support personnel. "Lean and mean" continues to be a major theme for the best American corporations. The implications of these cutbacks for supervisors are clear. Fewer middle managers will mean that supervisors will have more people directly reporting to them. Moreover, many of the tasks previously performed by people in support units—like work design, process flow, scheduling, and quality control—will be reassigned to supervisors and their employees. The net effect will be significantly expanded responsibilities for supervisors.

Finally, employee training is becoming more important than ever as organizations seek to improve productivity. New employees—many of them poorly prepared for work or who have language or communication deficiencies—require basic training in reading, writing, and mathematics. Changes in jobs brought about by computers, automation, and other technological advances require additional skill training among current employees in order to prevent their skills from becoming obsolete. It will be supervisors who will carry the primary burden for identifying these skill deficiencies, designing appropriate training programs, and in some cases even for providing the training itself.

## DOES A SUPERVISOR NEED TO BE A COACH?

Rick Carpenter has been a supervisor at the Hershey Pasta Group for more than twenty years. When asked how his leadership style has changed over this period, he says, "I've become a facilitator rather than a direction giver." This transition is not unique to Rick Carpenter. Supervisors are moving away from the authoritative style toward that of a facilitating coach.

Today's supervisors are far less likely to be able to do all aspects of their employees' jobs. Supervisors need to know what their employees are doing, but are not necessarily expected to be as skilled at specific job tasks as each employee. Moreover, employees don't need an authority figure to tell them what to do or to "keep them in line." Instead, they may need a coach who can listen, guide, train, and assist them. In their coaching role, supervisors are expected to ensure that their employees have the resources they need to do a first-class job. They must also develop their employees, clarify the responsibilities and goals, motivate employees to higher levels of performance, and represent their work group's interests within the organization.

## THE TRANSITION FROM EMPLOYEE TO SUPERVISOR

*It wasn't easy making the move from being one of the quality control specialists in the department to being the supervisor. On Friday I had been one of them. The next Monday I became their boss. Suddenly, people that I had joked around and socialized with for years were distancing themselves from me. I could see that they were apprehensive. They weren't sure, now, if I could be trusted. I didn't think our relationship was going to be much different. Hey, we were friends. We went out together every Friday after work. But I'm management now. I still think I'm like them, part of the group. But they don't see me that way. Even when I join them for drinks, it's not like it used to be. They have their guard up now. It's been a hard adjustment for me.*

The above comments from a recently promoted quality control supervisor at Monsanto captures the dilemma many new supervisors face when they're promoted from the ranks. In this section, we'll look at the primary roads people take to becoming supervisors and the challenges they face in mastering a new identity.

### WHERE DO SUPERVISORS COME FROM?

The majority of new supervisors are promoted from within the ranks of their current employer. The second major source of supervisory personnel is new college graduates. Occasionally, employees from other organizations are hired to become first-line supervisors; however, this is increasingly rare. The reason is that if employers have an open supervisory position, they often prefer to fill it with someone they know and who knows the organization. That favors promoting from within.

Employers tend to promote operative employees to first-line management jobs for several reasons. They know the operations function. They understand how things are done in the organization. They typically know the people they'll be supervising. Another advantage is that the organiza-

Ree Donato supervises reference, interlibrary loan, collection development, and instructional services at New York University's main library. She has a bachelor's degree in American Studies and a Masters of Library Science. She mostly supervises professional librarians who also hold advanced degrees.

tion knows a lot about the candidate. When management promotes "one of their own" into a supervisory position, they minimize risk. When they hire from the outside, they have to rely on limited information provided by previous employers. By promoting from within, management can draw on its full history with a candidate. Finally, and very importantly, promoting from within acts as an employee motivator. It provides an incentive for employees to work hard and excel.

What criteria does management tend to use in deciding whom to promote into first-line managerial positions? Employees with good work records and an interest in management tend to be favored. Ironically, not all "good" operative employees make good supervisors. The reason is that people with strong technical skills don't necessarily have the skills needed to manage others. Those organizations that successfully promote from the ranks select employees with adequate technical skills and provide them with supervisory training early in their new assignments.

Recent college graduates provide the other primary source of candidates for supervisory positions. Two-year and four-year college programs in supervision and management provide a basic foundation for preparing for the supervisor's job. When coupled with some additional organizational training, many new college graduates are equipped to step into first-line management.

## IS THE TRANSITION TO SUPERVISOR DIFFICULT?

Moving from one middle-management job to another or from a middle-management position to one in top management rarely creates the anxiety that comes when one moves from being an employee to a supervisor. It's a lot like being a parent. If you already have three kids, the addition of one more isn't too big a deal. Why? Because you already know quite a bit about parenting—and you've been "through it" before. The trauma lies in the transition from being childless to being a parent for the first time. The same applies here. The trauma is unique when one moves into first-line management and it is unlike anything managers will encounter later in their rise up the organizational ladder.

A recent study of what nineteen new supervisors experienced in their first year on the job helps us to better understand what it's like to become a first-line manager.[10] The people in this study were fourteen men and five women. All worked in sales or marketing. However, what they experienced would seem relevant to anyone making the employee-supervisor transition.

Even though these new supervisors had worked in their respective organizations as salespeople for an average of six years, their expectations of

[10]This section based on L. A. Hill, *Becoming a Manager: Mastery of New Identity* (Boston, MA: Harvard Business School Press, 1992).

a supervisory position were incomplete and simplistic. They didn't appreciate the full range of demands that would be made on them. Each had previously been a star salesperson. They were promoted, in large part, as a reward for their good performance. But "good performance" for a salesperson and "good performance" for a supervisor are very different—and few of these new supervisors understood that. Ironically, their previous successes in sales may actually have made their transition to management harder. Because of their strong technical expertise and high motivation, they depended on their supervisors less than the average salesperson for support and guidance. When they became supervisors and suddenly had to deal with low performing and unmotivated employees, they weren't prepared for it.

The nineteen new supervisors actually encountered a number of surprises. We'll briefly summarize the major ones because they capture the essence of what many supervisors encounter as they attempt to master their new identity.

*Their initial view of the manager as "boss" was incorrect.* Before taking their supervisory jobs, these managers-to-be talked about the power they would have and of being in control. As one put it, "Now, I'll be the one calling the shots." After a month, they spoke of being a "trouble-shooter," "a juggler," and a "quick-change artist." All emphasized solving problems, making decisions, helping others, and providing resources as their primary responsibilities. They no longer conceived of their jobs as being "the boss."

*They were unprepared for the demands and ambiguities they would face.* In their first week, these supervisors were surprised by the unrelenting workload and pace of being a manager. On a typical day, they had to work on many problems simultaneously and were met with constant interruptions.

*Technical expertise was no longer the primary determinant of success or failure.* They were used to excelling by performing specific technical tasks and being individual contributors, not by acquiring managerial competence and getting things done through others. It took four to six months on the job for most to come to grips with the fact that they now would be judged by their ability to motivate others to high performance.

*A supervisor's job comes with administrative duties.* These supervisors found that routine communication activities such as paperwork and exchange of information was time consuming and interfered with their autonomy.

*They weren't prepared for the "people challenges" of their new job.* The supervisors unanimously asserted that the most demanding skills they had to learn in their first year dealt with managing people. They expressed be-

Becoming a supervisor is a challenging opportunity. Some individuals look forward to "taking the helm" of a crew of workers, while others are put into this situation with little advance notice—or training. As you consider going into a supervisory position—or making yourself a more effective supervisor than you are today—think about the following two areas.

1. List five reasons why you want to be a supervisor.

   _____

   _____

   _____

   _____

   _____

2. Identify five potential problems or difficulties that you may encounter when you become a supervisor.

   _____

   _____

   _____

   _____

   _____

ing particularly uncomfortable in counseling employees and providing leadership. As one stated, "I hadn't realized . . . how hard it is to motivate people or develop them or deal with their personal problems."

Given this, and similar issues that arise when one becomes a supervisor, what does it take to be an effective supervisor? What competencies or general categories of skills does one need? Are these the same, regardless of one's level in the organization? We'll answer these questions in the next section.

## DO YOU REALLY WANT TO BE A SUPERVISOR?

The fact that you're learning about supervision indicates that you're interested in understanding how to supervise people. What is it about supervising people that excites you? Is it the fact that you can help an organization achieve its goals? Is it the challenge of supervising others—directing their work—that interests you? Is it the fact that supervision may lead to a management position and hopes of climbing the career ladder? Whatever your reasons, you need a clear picture of what lies ahead.

Supervisory positions are not easy. Even if you've been a superstar as an employee, this is no guarantee that you'll succeed as a supervisor. The fact that you are capable of doing excellent work is a big plus, but there are many other factors to consider. You need to recognize that supervising others may mean longer work hours. You're often on the job before your employees and leave after they do. Supervising can literally be a 24-hour, seven-day-a-week job. Now, that's not to be interpreted as being on the job every hour of every day. But when you accept the responsibility of supervising others, you really never can "get away" from the job. Things happen, and you'll be expected to deal with them—no matter when they happen, or where you are. It's not unheard of to get a call while you're on vacation, if problems arise. How did someone in the organization get your vacation phone number? You probably gave it to that individual—either as required by an organizational policy, or when you "called in" to see how things were going.

You also need to recognize that, as a supervisor, you may have a seemingly endless pile of paperwork to complete. Although organizations are continually working to eliminate paperwork, a lot still remains. This may include employee work schedules, production cost estimates, inventory documentation, or budget and payroll matters.

Another matter of importance that you should consider is the effect the supervisor's job may have on your pay! In many organizations, a raise in your base pay when you become a supervisor, does not translate into higher annual earnings. How so? Consider that, as a supervisor, you are no longer eligible for overtime pay. Instead, in most companies, you get compensatory (comp) time (time off). As an operative employee, your organization is legally required to pay you a premium rate (typically time and one-half) for overtime work. That may not be true when you become a supervisor. If you get a $3000 raise when you become a supervisor, but earned $3500 last year in overtime, you're actually earning less as a supervisor. This is something that you'll need to discuss with your organization before making your decision to become a supervisor.

What are the previous paragraphs really saying? They're telling you to think about why you want to supervise. Managing others can be rewarding. The excitement is real—and so are the headaches. You need to understand exactly what your motives are for becoming a supervisor—and what tradeoffs you're willing to make to become the best supervisor you can be.

# COMPETENCIES OF SUPERVISORS

**Supervisory competencies** conceptual, interpersonal, technical, and political capabilities.

Over thirty years ago, professor Robert Katz began a process of identifying essential **supervisory competencies.**[11] What Katz and others have found is that successful managers must possess four critical competencies. These are: conceptual, interpersonal, technical, and political capabilities. They are as relevant today as when Katz originally described them.

## WHAT IS TECHNICAL COMPETENCE?

Top management is composed of generalists. Louis Gerstner, Jr. was able to successfully move from CEO of RJRNabisco to CEO of IBM. It wasn't necessary for him to know a great deal about the manufacturing of cookies, cigarettes, or computers in order to do these jobs. The activities that consume top managers—strategic planning; developing the organization's overall structure and culture; maintaining relations with major customers, bankers, and the like—are essentially generic in nature. The technical demands of top management jobs tend to be related to knowledge of the industry and a general understanding of the organization's processes and products. This isn't true for managers at other levels.

**Technical competence** the ability to apply specialized knowledge or expertise.

Most managers manage within areas of specialized knowledge: the vice-president for human resources; the director of computer systems; the regional sales manager; the supervisor of health claims. These managers require **technical competence**—the ability to apply specialized knowledge or expertise. It's difficult, if not impossible, to effectively supervise employees with specialized skills if you don't have an adequate understanding of the technical aspects of their jobs. While the supervisor need not be able to perform certain technical skills, understanding what each worker does is part of every supervisor's job. For example, the task of scheduling work flow requires technical competence to determine what needs to be done.

## WHY ARE INTERPERSONAL COMPETENCIES CRITICAL?

**Interpersonal competence** the ability to work with, understand, communicate with, and motivate other people, both individually and in groups.

The ability to work well with people, understand their needs, communicate well, and motivate others—both individually and in groups—describes **interpersonal competence.** Many people are technically proficient, but interpersonally incompetent. They might be poor listeners, unconcerned with the needs of others, or they may have difficulty in dealing

[11]R. L. Katz, "Skills of an Effective Administrator," *Harvard Business Review,* September-October 1974, pp. 90–102.

Being a successful supervisor means having sound interpersonal competencies. In some cases, that may mean knowing how to deal effectively with employees who are having a serious disagreement.

with conflicts. Supervisors get things done through other people. They must have good interpersonal skills to communicate, motivate, negotiate, and delegate.

## What is Conceptual Competence?

**Conceptual competence** is the mental ability to analyze and diagnose complex situations. Strong conceptual abilities allow a supervisor to see that the organization is a complex system of many interrelated parts; and that the organization itself is part of a larger system that includes the organization's industry, the community, and the nation's economy. This gives the supervisor a broad perspective and contributes to creative problem solving. On a more practical level, strong conceptual abilities help managers make good decisions.

**Conceptual competence**
the mental ability to analyze and diagnose complex situations.

## Do Supervisors Need To Be Political?

The answer to this question is "Yes." Supervisors need to possess **political competence.** This refers to the supervisor's ability to enhance his or her power, build a power base, and establish the "right" connections in the organization. Politics is something supervisors engage in when they attempt to influence the advantages and disadvantages of a situation.[12] It goes beyond normal work activities. Whenever two or more people come together for some purpose, each has some idea of what should occur. If one person tries to influence the situation such that it benefits him or her more than

**Political competence**
a supervisor's ability to enhance his or her power, build a power base, and establish the "right" connections in the organization.

[12]D. Farrell and J. C. Petersen, "Patterns of Political Behavior in Organizations," *Academy of Management Review* (July 1982), p. 405.

the others, or keeps others from gaining some advantage, then politics is "being played." But all political behavior is not negative. It doesn't have to involve manipulating a series of events, complaining about fellow supervisors, or sabotaging the work or reputation of another to further one's career. There's a fine line between appropriate political behavior and negative politics. We'll come back to organizational politics in Chapter 12.

## COMPETENCIES AND MANAGERIAL LEVEL

While managers need to possess all four competencies, the importance each competency plays in the manager's job varies with the manager's level in the organization. As Exhibit 1–6 illustrates: (1) technical competence declines in importance as individuals rise in the organization; (2) interpersonal competencies are a constant to success, regardless of level in the organization; and (3) conceptual and political competencies increase in importance as managerial responsibility rises.

Technical abilities typically have the greatest relevance for first-level managers. This is true for two reasons. First, many supervisors perform technical work as well as managerial work. In contrast to other levels of management, the distinction between individual contributor and first-line manager is often blurred. Second, supervisors spend more time on training and developing their employees than do other managers. This requires

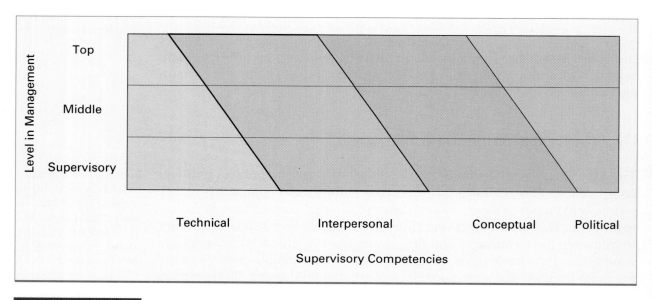

## EXHIBIT 1–6

How competency demands vary at different levels of management.

them to have a greater technical knowledge of their employees' jobs than that needed by middle- and top-level managers.[13]

There is overwhelming evidence that interpersonal abilities are critical at all levels of management. This shouldn't come as a shock since we know that managers get things done through other people. Supervisors are particularly in need of interpersonal competencies because they spend so much of their time in leading-function activities. Deni Sargol, a district sales manager for American Express in Florida, made this point when she compared her current job with her previous one as a regional retail manager with Richardson-Vicks, Inc. "The managerial aspects are pretty similar because it's basically people management." In talking with dozens of practicing supervisors, the one common viewpoint they shared was the importance of people skills to the successful achievement of their unit's objectives.

The importance of conceptual competence increases as managers move up in the organization. This is due to the type of problems managers encounter and the decisions they make at higher levels. Generally speaking, the higher a manager rises in an organization, the more the problems he or she faces tend to be complex, ambiguous, and ill-defined. These problems require custom-made solutions. In contrast, supervisors generally have more straightforward, familiar, and easily defined problems which lend themselves to more routine decision making. Ill-structured problems and custom-made solutions make greater conceptual demands on managers than do structured problems and routine decision making.

Finally, the higher one climbs in the organization's hierarchy, the more critical political competence becomes. Because resource allocation decisions are made at higher levels in an organization, middle and top managers are "fighting" for their piece of the organizational pie. Their need to develop alliances, support one project over another, or influence certain situations, involves higher level political skills. But don't interpret this to imply that politics are less important for supervisors. Because so much of the supervisor's job is well-defined, they need strong political skills to get their unit's work completed, and to survive (see Self-Assessment)!

---

[13]S. Baker and L. Armstrong, "The New Factory Worker," *Business Week*, September 30, 1966, pp. 59–68.

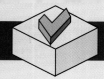
## DO YOU HAVE WHAT IT TAKES TO BE POLITICAL?

Are you an individual who likes to play politics? Is it something that you have the ability to do? Even if you prefer not to, can you "play" to protect yourself? Undoubtedly, politics exists in every organization. Therefore, one of the first steps is understanding your political temperament. Listed below are several statements. Check True or False based on how you feel about the statement most of the time.

|  |  | True | False |
|---|---|:---:|:---:|
| **1.** | I stay late just to impress my boss. | ☐ | ☐ |
| **2.** | I do not tell others how I do things, so they don't know what I do. | ☐ | ☐ |
| **3.** | I do not use gossip to my advantage. | ☐ | ☐ |
| **4.** | I rarely express my opinion about my organization if my opinions are negative. | ☐ | ☐ |
| **5.** | I go out of my way to make friends with powerful people. | ☐ | ☐ |
| **6.** | I would not raise concerns about someone's ability to do a job, even if we were competing for a promotion. | ☐ | ☐ |
| **7.** | I won't take credit for the work of someone else. | ☐ | ☐ |
| **8.** | I'd tell my boss if a coworker was actively looking for a new job. | ☐ | ☐ |
| **9.** | I would want my name on a group project, even though my effort was minimal. | ☐ | ☐ |
| **10.** | I see nothing wrong in tooting my own horn. | ☐ | ☐ |
| **11.** | I like having decorations all around my work area. | ☐ | ☐ |
| **12.** | I take action only after I am sure it's ethical to do so. | ☐ | ☐ |
| **13.** | I'd be foolish to publicly correct a mistake my boss made. | ☐ | ☐ |
| **14.** | I'd purchase stock in my company even if it's a financial risk. | ☐ | ☐ |
| **15.** | I would not play the role of "hatchetman," even if it meant a promotion for me. | ☐ | ☐ |
| **16.** | I want others to fear me more than like me. | ☐ | ☐ |
| **17.** | I would not join in with coworkers making fun of the boss. | ☐ | ☐ |
| **18.** | Getting ahead means promoting my self-interest. | ☐ | ☐ |
| **19.** | I would not want to help a coworker who makes my performance look bad. | ☐ | ☐ |

**20.** I think it's important to be friendly with everyone at work—especially those I don't like. ☐ ☐

## SCORING

Give yourself one point for each response that matches those given below.

| | | | |
|---|---|---|---|
| **1.** True | **6.** False | **11.** False | **16.** True |
| **2.** True | **7.** False | **12.** False | **17.** True |
| **3.** False | **8.** True | **13.** True | **18.** True |
| **4.** True | **9.** True | **14.** True | **19.** True |
| **5.** True | **10.** True | **15.** False | **20.** True |

## MAKING SENSE OF THE ASSESSMENT

Your political score on this assessment indicates how likely you are to use politics to gain an advantage in a situation. Scores greater than 14 indicate you have an above average willingness to use politics to get what you want. Scores from 10 to 13 indicate you use politics mainly to protect yourself—especially from your boss and those you perceive as having power. Scores from 6 to 9 indicate you have a true belief in others—that they are fair, honest, and not likely to mistreat you. Although noteworthy, this score may indicate you don't understand organizational politics, and you may be somewhat naive in assessing the effect politics may have on you. Finally, scores less than 5 indicate an absence of ability to play politics in an organization. Remember, politics isn't always destructive—there's a constructive component that you must use to your advantage.

Source: WINNING OFFICE POLITICS by Andrew Dubrin. Copyright © 1990. Reprinted with permission of Prentice Hall.

# FROM CONCEPTS TO SKILLS

Knowledge about a subject is important, but just as important is whether you can do anything with that knowledge. Can you put it into practice? Just as you wouldn't want a surgeon who had never operated on anyone taking a knife to you, it's not enough for you to just "know" about supervision. You should be able to actually supervise! You can learn to be an effective supervisor! No one is born with supervisory skills, although some people have a headstart.

It's true that supervision comes easier to some people than to others. Individuals who are fortunate enough to have parents, relatives, or friends who are managers have role models to emulate and give them insights into what the job entails. Similarly, individuals whose parents helped them set realistic goals, provided positive feedback, encouraged autonomy, practiced open communication, and fostered the development of a strong self-concept have learned behaviors that will help them as managers. Also, those who have had the fortune to work for a good manager have a role model to imitate. However, those without these advantages can improve their supervisory abilities.

This book will help you to be an effective supervisor by focusing on both conceptual knowledge and practical skills. In one chapter, for example, we'll discuss the importance of planning to a supervisor's success and show how setting goals is a key part of planning. Then we'll present specific techniques for helping employees set goals and provide you with an opportunity to practice and develop your goal-setting skills.

## WHAT IS A SKILL?

**Skill**
the ability to demonstrate a system and sequence of behavior that is functionally related to attaining a performance goal.

A **skill** is the ability to demonstrate a system and sequence of behavior that is functionally related to attaining a performance goal.[14] No single action constitutes a skill. For example, the ability to write clear communications is a skill. People who have this skill know the particular sequence of actions to be taken to propose a project or summarize a report. They can separate primary from secondary ideas. They can organize their thoughts in a logical manner. They can simplify complex ideas. None of these actions is by itself a skill. A skill is a system of behavior that can be applied in a wide range of situations.

What are the key skills related to supervisory effectiveness? While there is no unanimous agreement among teachers and trainers of supervision, certain skills have surfaced as being more important than others. Exhibit 1–7 lists key supervisory skills, organized as they will be presented in this text. In aggregate, they form the competency base for effective supervision.

## WHAT ELSE IS CRITICAL FOR ME TO KNOW ABOUT SUPERVISING?

If by now you're somewhat amazed by what a supervisor has to do and the skills he or she must have to succeed in an organization, let us add several other elements that you should consider. Specifically, what are the personal issues that you should address? Let's look at these.

[14]R. E. Boyatzis, *The Competent Manager: A Model for Effective Performance* (New York, NY: John Wiley & Sons, 1982), p. 33.

EXHIBIT 1–7

Key supervisory
skills.

Related to Planning and Control
- Goal setting
- Budgeting
- Creative problem solving
- Developing control charts

Related to Organizing, Staffing, and Employee Development
- Empowering others
- Interviewing
- Providing feedback
- Coaching

Related to Stimulating Individual and Group Performance
- Designing motivating jobs
- Projecting charisma
- Listening
- Conducting a group meeting

Related to Coping with Workplace Dynamics
- Negotiation
- Stress-reduction
- Counseling
- Disciplining
- Handling grievances

One of the first things you'll need to do is to recognize that you are part of management as a supervisor. This means that you support the organization and the wishes of management above you. Although you might disagree with those wishes, as a supervisor, you must be *loyal* to the organization. You must also develop a means of *gaining respect* from your employees, as well as your peers and boss. If you're going to be effective as a supervisor, you'll need to develop their trust and build credibility with them. One means of doing this is to continually keep your *skills and competencies* up-to-date. You must continue your "education," not only because it helps you, but also because it sets an example for your employees. It communicates that learning matters.

You'll also have to understand what legitimate power you have been given by the organization because you direct the activities of others. This legitimate power is your *authority* to act and expect others to follow your directions. Yet, ruling with the iron fist may not work. Accordingly, you'll need to know when to assert your authority and how to get things done without resorting to "because I told you so." In this latter case, you need to develop interpersonal skills that help you *influence* others. This is particularly true when dealing with organizational members that you don't supervise.

Finally, you'll need to recognize that organizational members are different—not only in their talents, but as individuals. You'll need to be *sensitive to their needs, tolerate and even celebrate their differences,* and *be empathetic* to them as individuals. Success, in part, will begin with the understanding of what being flexible means.

Throughout this text, we'll be addressing each of these areas. For instance, in the next chapter, we'll introduce you to the diversity of the work force and what that may mean for you. In Chapter 10 on leadership, we'll introduce trust and credibility and their role in your leadership effectiveness.

---

## POP QUIZ   (Are You Comprehending What You're Reading?)

**5.** Supervisors in contemporary organizations are less likely to be able to do their employees' jobs. True or False?

**6.** Interpersonal competence involves
   **a.** the ability to enhance one's power base
   **b.** the ability to analyze and diagnose complex situations
   **c.** the ability to motivate, negotiate with, and delegate to others
   **d.** the ability to apply specialized knowledge

**7.** Why do technical abilities frequently have the greater relevance for supervisors than for middle or top managers?

**8.** The ability to demonstrate a system and sequence of behavior related to achieving a goal is
   **a.** a conceptual competence
   **b.** a political competence
   **c.** a technical competence
   **d.** none of the above

---

## SUMMARY

After reading this chapter, I can:

1. **Define what is meant by the term supervisor.** A supervisor is a first-level manager who oversees the work of operative or non-management employees.

2. **Explain the difference between supervisors, middle managers, and top management.** While all are part of the managerial ranks, they differ by their level in the organization. Supervisors are first-level managers—they manage operative employees. Middle managers encompass all managers from those who manage supervisors up to those in the vice-presidential ranks. Top management is composed of the highest level managers—those responsible for establishing the organization's overall objectives and developing the policies to achieve those objectives.

3. **Identify the four functions in the management process.** Planning, organizing, leading, and controlling comprise the management process.

4. **Explain why the supervisor's role is considered ambiguous.** Because a supervisor is: (1) a key person (critical communication link in the organization); (2) a person in the middle (interacting and reconciling opposing forces and competing expectations); (3) just another worker (decision-making authority is limited and supervisors may perform operating tasks alongside the same people they supervise); and (4) a behavioral specialist (able to listen, motivate, and lead).

5. **Describe the four essential supervisory competencies.** Technical, interpersonal, conceptual, and political competence.

6. **Explain why the supervisor's job will be increasingly important and complex in the future.** There are more programs that focus on the work activities of operating employees; middle-management cutbacks have increased supervisory responsibilities; increased attention to training employees will be substantially implemented at the supervisory level.

## REVIEWING YOUR KNOWLEDGE

1. What differentiates supervisory positions from all other levels of management?
2. Is the owner-manager of a small store, with three employees, an operative, supervisor, or top manager? Explain.
3. What specific tasks are common to all managers?
4. Contrast time spent on management functions by supervisors versus top management.
5. "The best rank-and-file employees should be promoted to supervisors." Do you agree or disagree with this statement? Explain.
6. Why is conceptual competence more important for top managers than for first-level supervisors?
7. How can a supervisor be a "key person" and "just another worker"? Explain.

## ANSWERS TO THE POP QUIZZES

1. **d. All organizations make a profit.** While almost all organizations need to make money to survive, making a profit is not a characteristic of an organization.

2. **False.** Organizational members who are responsible for establishing and meeting specific goals in a department are called middle-level managers.
3. Efficiency involves a relationship between inputs and outputs. It focuses on doing things right. Effectiveness implies goal attainment. It focuses on doing the right things. If all things are equal, effectiveness is more important because it supports reaching the goals of the organization. [Note: Don't interpret this to mean that efficiency doesn't matter. It does!]
4. **b. organizing.** The question addresses part of the definition of the organizing function.
5. **True.** Today's employees have less need for an authority figure to tell them what to do. Instead, employees need a supervisor who can listen, guide, train, and assist them.
6. **c. the ability to motivate, negotiate with, and delegate to others.** The question addresses the definition of interpersonal competence.
7. Technical abilities frequently have greater relevance for supervisors because unlike higher-level managers, many supervisors perform technical work as well as managerial work. Also, supervisors spend more time training and developing their employees, which requires greater technical knowledge of their employees' jobs.
8. **d. none of the above.** The ability to demonstrate a system and sequence of behavior related to achieving a goal is a **skill.** ■

## A CLASS EXERCISE

When you begin a new course, do you have specific expectations of what you want from the class? You probably do, but how often do you communicate them to the instructor?[15] This information is important to both of you. As a supervisor, you will need to get accustomed to sharing and receiving information about your expectations and the expectations of others. You can begin by defining your expectations for this course. First, take out a piece of paper and place your name at the top; then respond to the following:

1. What do I want from this course?
2. Why are these things important to me?
3. How does this course fit into my career plans?
4. How do I like an instructor to "run" the class?
5. What is my greatest challenge in taking this class?

When you have finished answering these questions, pair up with another class member (preferably someone you do not already know) and exchange papers. Get to know one another (using the information on these sheets as a starting point). Prepare an introduction of your partner, and share your partner's responses to the five questions with the class and your instructor.

## THINKING CRITICALLY

### CASE 1.A

## The Transition to Supervisor

Byron Michaels is an up-and-comer. After graduating from Clemson University in 1993 with a degree in marketing, he joined Procter & Gamble as a sales representative in North Carolina.[16] Through the years, Byron made his sales goals, often exceeding them by 10 to 15 percent. Although he felt good about his early success, Byron wasn't always happy about how things were going. Frequently, he and a few of his colleagues met for lunch to share what they called their "bash the idiots in management" buffet. It was during these lunches that the group vented about their supervisors, changes in company policy, and the company's new incentive program. Although these were issues of interest to this group, nothing appeared so upsetting that it affected any of their work.

Then, late last year, Byron Michaels was promoted and transferred to a sales supervisory position. He was going to be responsible for the nonfood product line in the mid-west region. In their excitement, Byron's colleagues gave him a "send-off" party, which ended with one request—when you're in town, let's get together and "do lunch."

[15] The idea for this exercise came from Barbara Goza, "Graffiti Needs Assessment: Involving Students in the First Class Session," *Journal of Management Education*, Vol., 17, No. 1, February 1993, pp. 99–106.

[16] Concepts for this case were adapted from Fran McGovern, "Coffee with the Boss," *U.S. Air Magazine*, October 1993, pp. 132–133.

Six months have passed since Byron has seen his friends. On a trip back to North Carolina for a meeting, Byron sends advance notice of his pending arrival. Anxious to see him, the "bash the idiots in management" gang plans their reunion. On Thursday afternoon, they all meet. Prying Byron for the details of his new job, the discussion quickly reverts back to their favorite topic—supervisors. But this time is different. Byron, while previously vocal at these lunches, is silent. He listens attentively, nodding his head a few times, but says nothing. His friends, noticing his behavior, ask Byron if anything is wrong. "No, Byron says. "But, you guys gotta remember, I represent management now. For me to complain about the organization, its policies, or my fellow supervisors could jeopardize my job." "Great," his friends laugh, "we got ourselves a new addition to the bashing list."

## RESPONDING TO THE CASE

1. One of the more difficult situations a new supervisor will face is interacting with former operative colleagues. Once someone becomes a member of management, do you think he or she should stop socializing (e.g., having lunch or going to parties) with those who are not in supervisory positions? Why or why not?

2. If you were Byron Michaels, how would you react to your former colleagues who have now placed you on the "bashing" list?

3. Interview someone in a sales management position. Have them compare their job functions and competencies with someone who is a salesperson. How closely do their functions and competencies compare with those discussed in the text?

## CASE 1.B

### Leading the J-Team

Janet Simmons is a day supervisor for a local Jiffy Lube shop in Sioux City, Iowa. Janet is responsible for 12 employees. Her job responsibilities include planning the daily activities of these employees, certifying that all work has been done properly, and handling all money transactions. When Janet is not "supervising," she serves as an under-hood J-team crew member. In this capacity, she checks a variety of fluids, adds fluids as necessary, and inspects such things as the air filter, fuel filter, and the car's lights. Frequently, as supervisor, she has to move an employee from one task to another during the day— sometimes to complete a part of a job and other times because of specialized tasks to be done. For instance, only two of her employees are certified to handle transmission servicing.

Janet is in contact with her boss—the owner, Cara Ingalls—on a daily basis at the close of business. She discusses with her boss how many cars were serviced that day, what those services were, and the amount of money that is being deposited. Janet keeps Cara informed on the status of inventories and what orders need to be placed. She also keeps Cara apprised of any customer or employee issues that may arise.

Because of the nature of this business, it's imperative that employees are at work on time and get their work completed quickly. Janet knows that the key to this business is a happy work force that, in turn, satisfies customers. Accordingly, she takes special care to make sure her employees are enjoying their work, and she keeps them apprised of changes that may affect them. Every once in a while, Janet "springs" for an after work pizza party just to say thanks to her employees for doing a good job.

## RESPONDING TO THE CASE

1. List as many of Janet's responsibilities as you can. Prioritize the list. Write a paragraph about your list of priorities, telling why you placed certain items at the top of the list and others at the bottom.

2. Describe the supervisory functions that Janet is performing. Do you believe some functions are more important than others? Explain.

3. How can Janet avoid problems she may face in terms of supervising her employees while still pleasing her boss? What can she do to foster good relationships with her boss? With her employees? ■

# 2

# SUPERVISORY CHALLENGES FOR THE 21ST CENTURY

# LEARNING OBJECTIVES

# KEY TERMS

After reading this Chapter, you will be able to:

1. Explain how globalization affects supervisors.
2. Describe how technology is changing the supervisor's job.
3. Identify the significant changes that have occurred in the composition of the work force.
4. Explain why corporations downsize.
5. Understand the concept of Total Quality Management and identify its goals.
6. Describe why supervisors must be able to "thrive on chaos."
7. Define ethics.

You should also be able to define these supervisory terms.

baby-boomers

baby-busters

code of ethics

cultural environments

downsizing

ethics

mature workers

parochialism

reengineering

social obligation

social responsibility

social responsiveness

technology

telecommuting

total quality management (TQM)

workforce diversity

# PERFORMING EFFECTIVELY

Consider how hard it is sometimes to get your message across to others. At times, the hectic pace, the noise surrounding you, or the unavailability of others simply keeps you from sending your message. Yet, in most cases, if you keep trying, you succeed. Now, add another element to this scenario. What would happen if your boss couldn't hear? Imagine that because of a physical disability, your supervisor is deaf. Talking as you're accustomed to doesn't work very effectively. Under this condition, what do you do? If you're not sure, ask John Martinez.

John Martinez (pictured left) is a supervisor at Exabyte, a Boulder, Colorado manufacturer of computer disk drives. John supervises five employees. What's unusual in John's department is that John is deaf. His em-

## INTRODUCTION

It has been said often that the only thing that remains constant is change—and it's true! Supervisors like John Martinez must always be prepared for changing events that may have a significant effect on their lives. Changing events have always helped shape the interactions between supervisors and their employees, and undoubtedly will continue to do so. Some of the more recent changes include global market competitiveness, technology enhancements, workforce diversity, total quality management, downsizing, and the issue of ethics. Let's look at how these changes are affecting supervisors in organizations.

## GLOBAL COMPETITIVENESS

Many North American companies grew large and powerful following World War II, because they faced modest competition. For instance, in the 1950s and 1960s, General Motors became the world's largest and most profitable corporation. Was it because GM efficiently produced first-rate products that were carefully matched to the needs of auto consumers? Not really. GM's success was more due to the fact that its only major competition came from two other relatively inefficient American producers—Ford and Chrysler. Now, look at General Motors in the 1990s. It has drastically reduced costs, improved quality, and cut the time it takes from designing a

ployees, however, can hear. Surprisingly, this disability hasn't stopped John, or his employees from being very productive. Rather than dwell on John's differences, employees in John's unit have learned key phrases in sign language so that they can communicate effectively with John. From all accounts, the work goes on without a hitch.

Companies like Exabyte have recognized that quality workers aren't cut from a preestablished mode. Rather, they embrace the differences that each brings to the workplace. In fact, John Martinez is just one of six employees at Exabyte who are hearing impaired. To meet this challenge, and to effectively bring all workers together, the company hires a translator for meetings and offers sign language classes for employees. ■

car to having it in dealer showrooms. Did GM make these changes voluntarily? Absolutely not! It was forced to do this to meet changing global competition. Ford and Chrysler significantly improved their quality, developed innovative products like the minivan, and began selling imported cars under their brand name. Meanwhile, aggressive competition from foreign companies like Honda, Toyota, Nissan, BMW, and Volvo increased pressure on GM to change if it was going to survive.

## IS THERE SUCH A THING AS "BUY AMERICAN?"

The GM example illustrates that organizations are no longer constrained by national borders. Consider, for instance, that Burger King is owned by a British firm, and McDonald's sells hamburgers in China. Exxon, a so-called American company, receives almost 75 percent of its revenues from sales outside the United States. Honda makes cars in Ohio, and Toyota and General Motors jointly own a plant that makes cars in California. Parts for Ford Motor Company's Crown Victoria come from all over the world: Mexico (seats, windshields, and fuel tanks); Japan (shock absorbers); Spain (electronic engine controls); Germany (antilock brake systems); and England (key axle parts).

It is important to point out that, while organizations have become increasingly global in their perspectives and have accepted the reality that national borders no longer define corporations, the public has been slower to accept this fact. An example is the controversy over fair trade with Japan, which often leads to some backlash against Japanese products being sold in the United States. Many people feel that the sale of Japanese products takes jobs from Americans. The cry often is "Buy American." The irony is that many of the so-called Japanese products were made in the United States. For example, most Sony televisions sold in the United States are made in California, while "American" manufacturer Zenith's TVs are made in Mexico. The message from this example should be obvious: A company's national origin is no longer a very good gauge of where it does business or the national origin of its employees. Such companies as Sony and Samsung employ thousands of people in the United States. At the same time, such firms as Coca-Cola, Exxon, and Citicorp employ thousands in places like India, Hong Kong, and the United Kingdom. So phrases like "Buy American" represent old stereotypes that fail to reflect the changing global village.

## HOW DOES GLOBALIZATION AFFECT SUPERVISORS?

A boundaryless world introduces new challenges for supervisors. These range from how supervisors view people from foreign lands, to how they develop an understanding of these immigrating employees' cultures. A specific challenge for supervisors is to recognize the differences that might exist and find ways to make their interactions with all employees more effective. One of the first issues to deal with, then, is the perception of "foreigners."

**Parochialism**
seeing things solely through one's own eyes and within one's own perspectives; believing that what we do is best.

Americans in general hold a rather parochial view of the world. **Parochialism** means we see things solely through our own eyes and from our uniquely American perspective.[1] This translates into: we believe what we do is best. We simply do not recognize that other people have valid, though different, ways of thinking and doing things. Parochialism causes us to view our practices as being better than practices in other cultures. Obviously, we know that cannot be the case. However, changing this perception first requires us to understand the different cultures and their environments.

**Cultural environments**
values, morals, customs, and laws of countries.

All countries have different values, morals, customs, and laws. While cultural issues are much more involved than this and go beyond the scope of this book, we will look at some basic cultural issues that supervisors need to undestand. For example, in the United States we have laws that guard against discriminatory hiring and employment practices. Similar laws do not exist in many other countries. Understanding **cultural environments,** then, is critical to the success of supervising others in the global village.

[1]N. Adler, *International Dimensions of Organizational Behavior,* 2nd ed. (Boston, Mass: PWS-Kent, 1991), p. 11.

One of the better known studies about cultural environments was done by a researcher, Geert Hofstede.[2] Hofstede analyzed various aspects of different countries cultures. He found that a country's culture has a major effect on employees' work-related values and attitudes. By analyzing various dimensions, Hofstede developed a framework for understanding cultural differences. Countries that share similar cultures are represented in Exhibit 2–1.

Hofstede's findings group countries according to such cultural variables as status differences, societal uncertainty, and assertiveness. These variables indicate a country's means of dealing with its people and how the people see themselves. For example, in an individualistic society, people are primarily concerned with their own family. On the contrary, in a col-

| | |
|---|---|
| **Latin America** | Argentina |
| | Chile |
| | Columbia |
| | Mexico |
| | Peru |
| | Venezuela |
| **Anglo-American** | Australia |
| | Canada |
| | Ireland |
| | New Zealand |
| | South Africa |
| | United Kingdom |
| | United States |
| **Central European** | Austria |
| | Germany |
| | Switzerland |
| **Latin European** | Belgium |
| | France |
| | Italy |
| | Portugal |
| | Spain |
| **Nordic** | Denmark |
| | Finland |
| | Norway |
| | Sweden |

## EXHIBIT 2–1

Countries with similar cultural characteristics. (*Source:* Adapted from S. Ronen and A. I. Kranut, "Similarities Among Countries Based on Employee Work Values and Attitudes," *Columbia Journal of World Business* Summer 1977, p. 94.)

[2]G. Hofstede, *Culture's Consequences: International Differences in Work-Related Values* (Beverly Hills, Calif: Sage Publications, 1980).

lective society (the opposite of individualistic), people care for all individuals that are part of their group. The United States is a strongly individualistic society. Therefore, a supervisor may have difficulties relating to people from Pacific Rim countries, where collectivism dominates, unless he or she is aware of this cultural difference.

When working with people from different cultures, we informally learn the differences that exist between their culture and ours. Many companies also provide formal training in this area. An organization like the Mars Company (the candy maker), for example, builds on informal learning by providing formalized training to employees that focuses on the "major differences which may lead to problems."[3] Supervisors learn that they must be flexibile and adaptable in their dealings with employees. Recognizing differences in employees' backgrounds and customs fosters appreciation and even celebration of those differences.[4] Organizations like Digital, Honeywell, and Xerox have found that extensive training to "change the way supervisors think about people different from themselves"[5] has positive outcomes (see News Flash).

## NEWS FLASH! THE CULTURAL VARIABLES

To date, the most valuable framework to help managers better understand differences between national cultures has been developed by Geert Hofstede.[6] He surveyed over 116,000 employees in forty countries, all of whom worked for IBM. What did he find? Hofstede found that supervisors and employees vary in four dimensions of national culture: (1) individualism versus collectivism; (2) power distance; (3) uncertainty avoidance; and (4) quantity versus quality of life.[7]

*Individualism* refers to a loosely knit social framework in which people are supposed to look after their own interests and those of their immediate family. This is made possible because of the large amount of freedom that

*(cont'd)*

[6]Geert Hofstede, *Culture's Consequences: International Differences in Work-Related Values.*

[7]Hofstede called this last dimension masculinity-femininity. We've changed it because of the strong sexist connotation in his choice of terms.

[3]*HRMagazine*, January 1991, pp. 40–41.
[4]W. H. Wagel, *Personnel* (January 1990), p. 12.
[5]"Riding the Tide of Change," *The Wyatt Communicator* (Winter 1991), p. 11.

such a society allows individuals. Its opposite is *collectivism*, which is characterized by a tight social framework. People expect others in groups to which they belong (such as a family or an organization) to look after them and protect them when they are in trouble. In exchange for this, they feel they owe absolute allegiance to the group.

*Power distance* is a measure of the extent to which a society accepts the fact that power in institutions and organizations is distributed unequally. A high power-distance society accepts wide differences in power in organizations. Employees show a great deal of respect for those in authority. Titles, rank, and status carry a lot of weight. In contrast, a low power-distance society plays down inequalities as much as possible. Supervisors still have authority, but employees are not fearful or in awe of the boss.

A society that is high in *uncertainty avoidance* is characterized by an increased level of anxiety among its people, which manifests itself in greater nervousness, stress, and aggressiveness. Because people feel threatened by uncertainty and ambiguity in these societies, mechanisms are created to provide security and re-duce risk. Their organizations are likely to have more formal rules, there will be less tolerance for deviant ideas and behaviors, and members will strive to believe in absolute truths. Not surprisingly, in organizations in countries with high uncertainty avoidance, employees demonstrate relatively low job mobility, and lifetime employment is a widely practiced policy.

*Quantity versus quality of life*, like individualism and collectivism, represents a dichotomy. Some cultures emphasize the quantity of life, and value things like assertiveness and the acquisition of money and material goods. Other cultures emphasize the quality of life, placing importance on relationships and showing sensitivity and concern for the welfare of others.

With which cultures are U.S. supervisors likely to best fit? Which are likely to create the biggest adjustment problems? All we have to do is identify those countries that are most and least like the United States on the four dimensions. The United States is strongly individualistic, but low on power distance. This same pattern is exhibited by Great Britain, Australia, Canada, the Netherlands, and New Zealand.

*(cont'd)*

*(cont'd)*

Those least similar to the United States on these dimensions are Venezuela, Columbia, Pakistan, Singapore, and the Philippines.

The United States scored low on uncertainty avoidance and high on quantity of life. This same pattern was shown by Ireland, Great Britain, Canada, New Zealand, Australia, India, and South Africa. Those least similar to the United States on these dimensions are Chile and Portugal.

The study supports what many suspected—that the American supervisor transferred to London, Toronto, Melbourne, or a similar Anglo city would have to make the fewest adjustments. The study further identifies the countries in which "culture shock" is likely to be the greatest, resulting in the need to radically modify the American supervisory style.

## TECHNOLOGY ENHANCEMENTS

Change, newness, uncertainty? What do they mean for tomorrow's supervisors? Although making predictions can be viewed as an exercise in futility, evidence supports that supervisors need to concern themselves with change. The key to success, if it can be narrowed down to one statement is: Be prepared to make adjustments. Opportunities will abound for those prepared to accept and deal with the Information Age. Realize that as little as 20 years ago, almost no one had a fax machine, cellular phone, or personal pager. Computers were still too large to fit on desks. E-mail, modems, and the Internet weren't everyday words spoken by the general public. Sophisticated gadgetry was pretty much left to the *James Bond* movies!

Today, information technology, supported by the creation of the silicon chip, has permanently altered a supervisor's life forever. Electronic communications, optical character and voice recognition, and storage and retrieval data bases, among others, are significantly influencing how information is created, stored, and used.[8]

[8]J. Teresko, "Data Warehouses: Build Them for Decision-Making Power," *Industry Week* (March 18, 1996), pp. 43–45.

Technology has enabled workers to become more efficient and more customer oriented. At this Lukens Steel Company control room, a supervisor monitors production and checks to ensure that production quality is maintained. With technology Lukens can produce a variety of customized steel products at significantly lower cost than a decade ago.

Equally important are the constantly evolving skills and competencies supervisors must possess. Those who embrace knowledge and continuously learn new skills will be the ones who survive in the high-tech world. Imagine needing information on how well your unit is meeting production standards. Thirty years ago, getting that information may have taken as long as a month to obtain. Today, a few keystrokes on the keyboard of the computer on your desk can get you that same information almost instantaneously!

In the past two decades, American companies like General Electric, Wal-Mart, and 3M have witnessed automated offices, robotics in manufacturing, computer-assisted-design software, integrated circuits, microprocessors, and electronic meetings. These technologies combined have made these organizations more productive and, in some cases, helped them to create and maintain a competitive advantage.[9]

## WHAT IS TECHNOLOGY?

**Technology** is any high-tech equipment, tools, or operating methods that are designed to make work more efficient. Technological advances involve integrating technology with any process for changing inputs (raw materials) into outputs (goods and services). In years past, most processing opera-

**Technology**
any high-tech equipment, tools, or operating methods that are designed to make work more efficient.

[9]See for example, J. C. Collins and J. I. Porras, "A Theory of Evolution," *Audacity* (Winter 1996), pp. 5–11.

tions were performed by human labor. Technology has made it possible to enhance most production processes by replacing human labor with sophisticated electronic and computer equipment. An example is the assembly operation at Chrysler Corporation, which relies heavily on robotics. These robots perform repetitive tasks—like spot welding and painting—much faster than humans can. In addition, the robots aren't subject to the health problems caused by exposure to chemicals or other hazardous materials.

The use of technology goes far beyond application to mass production manufacturing processes. Technology is making it possible to better serve customers in many industries. The banking industry, for instance, has replaced thousands of bank tellers by installing ATM machines and electronic bill-paying systems. At the Lukens Steel Company, state-of-the-art technology enables them to customize customer orders, such that "making one-of-a-kind products" can be done as efficiently as producing a whole shipload of the same product.[10]

Technological advancements are also used to provide better, more useful information. Most cars built in the 1990s, for example, have a built-in computer circuit which a technician can plug into to diagnose problems with the automobile—saving countless diagnostic hours for a mechanic. At Frito-Lay, sales representatives record inventory and sales data into a hand-held computer, which is then transmitted daily to company headquarters. As a result, company officials have complete information on 100 product lines in more than 400,000 stores within 24 hours.[11]

## How Does Technology Change the Supervisor's Job?

Few jobs today are unaffected by advances in computer technology. Whether it is automated robotics on the production floor, computer-aided design in the engineering department, or automated accounting systems, these new technologies are changing the supervisor's job. Mary Jean Giroux, who oversees a retirement planning department at London Life Insurance Co., finds that advances in computer technology make her job considerably more complex. "We're expected to find ways to make our people more productive. The added complexity comes with learning all of the software programs and technical capabilities of the computers."

Undoubtedly, technology has had a positive effect on internal operations within organizations. How, specifically, has it changed the supervisor's job? To answer that question we need only to look at how the typical office is set up. Organizations today have become integrated communications centers. By linking computers, telephones, fax machines, copiers,

---

[10]J. H. Sheridan, "Betting on a Smart Mill," *Industry Week* (February 5, 1996), p. 39.

[11]J. Rothfeder and J. Bartimo, "How Software is Making Food Sales a Piece of Cake," *Business Week* (July 2, 1990), pp. 54–55.

printers, and the like, supervisors can get more complete information more quickly than ever before. With that information, supervisors can better formulate plans, make faster decisions, more clearly define the jobs that workers need to perform, and monitor work activities on an "as-they-happen" basis. In essence, technology today has enhanced supervisors' ability to more effectively and efficiently perform their jobs!

Technology is also changing where a supervisor's work is performed. Historically in organizations, the supervisor's work site was located close to the operations site. As a result, employees were in close proximity to their bosses. A supervisor could observe how the work was being done, as well as easily communicate with employees face-to-face. Through the advent of technological advancements, supervisors are now able to supervise employees in remote locations (see Something to Think About). Face-to-face interaction has decreased dramatically. Work, for many, occurs where their computers are. **Telecommuting** capabilities—linkage of a remote worker's computer and modem with coworkers and management at an office—have made it possible for employees to be located anywhere in the global village. Communicating effectively with individuals in remote locations, and ensuring that their performance objectives are being met, are some of the supervisor's new challenges.[12]

**Telecommuting** linking a worker's remote computer and modem with coworkers and management at an office.

---

## SOMETHING TO THINK ABOUT *(and to promote class discussion)*

### THE OFF-SITE EMPLOYEE

If you were to go back some 150 years in U.S. history, you'd find that it was not uncommon for most workers to be performing their jobs at home. Most goods were not mass produced. Individuals produced a finished product and took it to a market to sell. The along came the Industrial Revolution, which changed how work was done. Now we may be coming full circle—once again working at home. It is estimated that about one-fourth of the U.S. work force today are off-site employees, and that number is expected to rise. The majority of these workers are in such professions as sales, medicine, law, accounting, and a wide range of service occupations.[13]

What benefits do you see for organizations that have work done off site? What benefits do you believe exist for employees who work at home? What are the potential problems a supervisor may face in supervising off-site workers?

[13]T. Roberts, "Who are the High-Tech Home Workers?" *Inc. Technology,* 1994, p. 31.

---

[12]S. E. O'Connell, "The Virtual Workplace Moves at Warp Speed," *HRMagazine* (March 1996), pp. 51–53; and "Managing the Reinvented Work Place Becomes a Hot Topic," *The Wall Street Journal* (March 20, 1996), p. A-1.

## WORKING IN A DIVERSE ORGANIZATION

Forty years ago, workers were strikingly alike. In the 1950s, for example, the U.S. workforce consisted primarily of white males employed in manufacturing, who had wives who stayed at home tending to the family's two-plus children. Today's workforce is far more diverse, and it will continue to change.

### WHAT IS WORKFORCE DIVERSITY?

The single most important human resource issue in the coming decade may be adapting organizational policies and practices in light of increasing **workforce diversity**. This diverse workforce is made up of "males, fe-

**Workforce diversity**
the composition of the workforce to include males, females, whites, blacks, Hispanics, Asians, Native Americans, the disabled, homosexuals, heterosexuals, the elderly, and so on.

males, whites, blacks, Hispanics, Asians, native Americans, the disabled, homosexuals, straights, and the elderly" [sic].[14] There are some excellent predictors available to indicate exactly what the composition of this workforce will look like in the future.

In 1990, there were 124.7 million people in the overall U.S. workforce. By 2005, the U.S. Labor Department projects that figure will increase to 150.7 million. What is important is the makeup of those 26 million new workers. A full 85 percent of them will be women, immigrants, and members of minority groups.[15] A preview of the future can be seen today at a Digital Equipment Corporation plant in Boston. This factory's 350 employees include men and women from 44 countries who speak 19 languages. When plant management issues written announcements, they are printed in English, Chinese, French, Spanish, Portuguese, Vietnamese, and Haitian Creole.

Exhibit 2–2 briefly summarizes what is going on in the American labor force. In essence, along almost any dimension you choose, the workforce is becoming more diverse. Unfortunately, many company policies and practices were designed to deal with the relatively standardized employee of the past: a white male with a wife and several children at home. The only generalization that you can legitimately make about today's work force is that you can't generalize!

| Characteristic | 1950's | 1990's |
|---|---|---|
| Gender | Predominantly male | Male and Female |
| Race | Caucasian | Caucasian, African-American, Hispanic, Asian-American |
| Ethnic Origin | European descent | European descent, Mexican, Japanese, Vietnamese, African |
| Age | 20 to 65 | 16 to 80+ |
| Family Status | Single or married with children | Single, married with children, married with no children, co-habitating, dependent elders, dual-career couple, commuter relationship |
| Sexual Orientation | Heterosexual | Heterosexual, gay, lesbian, bi-sexual |
| Physical Abilities | Abled | Abled and disabled |

**EXHIBIT 2–2**

The diversifying of the American work force.

[14]S. Nelton, "Winning with Diversity," *Nation's Business* (September 12, 1992), p. 18.
[15]These figures are from L. Williams, "Scrambling to Manage a Diverse Workforce," *New York Times*, December 15, 1992, pp. A1, C2.

# How Does Diversity Affect Supervisors?

The implications of workforce diversity for supervisors are widespread. Employees don't set aside their cultural values and lifestyle preferences when they come to work. Therefore, supervisors must remake organizations to accommodate these different lifestyles, family needs, and work styles. They must be flexible enough in their practices to be accepting of others—others who are unlike them in terms of what is wanted and needed from work (see Assessing Yourself). This will require a broad range of new policies and practices. A few examples will make this point. Work schedules will need to be more flexible to accommodate working parents and couples maintaining commuter relationships (living in different locations). Companies will need to provide child care and elder care so employees will be able to give full attention to their work. Benefit programs will need to be redesigned and individualized to reflect more varied needs. Career-planning programs will need to be reassessed to deal with employees who are less willing to physically relocate for broadened job experience or promotions. All employees will need training, so they can learn to understand and appreciate people who are different from themselves. And, of course, supervisors will need to rethink their motivation techniques to respond to a widening range of employee needs.

In addition to the diversity brought about by such things as lifestyle, gender, nationality, and race, supervisors must be aware of the age differences they'll encounter. Today, there are three distinct age groupings.[16] Studies have shown that their views of each other vary widely and are often negative. First, there is the **mature worker,** those born prior to 1946. This group of workers, born shortly after the Great Depression, is security oriented and has a committed work ethic. While mature workers had been viewed as the foundation of the workforce, they may be regarded by the other generational groups as having obsolete skills and being inflexible in their ways. The **baby-boomers,** born in the late 1940s to early 1960s, are the largest group in the workforce. They are regarded as the career climbers—at the right place at the right time. Their careers advanced rapidly, as organizational growth during their initial years of employment was unsurpassed. Yet, the view of them by mature workers is that they are unrealistic in their views and tend to be workaholics. Finally, there are the Generation Xers, those born between 1964 and 1975. These "twentysomething **baby-busters"** are bringing a new perspective to the workforce—less commitment, less rule-bound, more into their own gratification, and with an intolerance of the baby-boomers and their attitudes.[17] As a result, they are viewed as selfish and not willing to play by the rules.

**Mature workers**
a group of workers born prior to 1946 who are security oriented and have a committed work ethic.

**Baby-boomers**
the largest group in the workforce; they are regarded as the career climbers—at the right place at the right time. Mature workers view them as unrealistic in their views and workaholics.

**Baby-busters**
a group of workers less committed, less rule-bound, and more into self-gratification, with an intolerance of baby-boomers and their attitudes. They are viewed as selfish and not willing to play by the rules.

[16]Adapted from C. M. Solomon, "Managing the Baby Busters," *Personnel Journal* (March 1992), p. 56.

[17]See, for example, S. Ratan, "Why Busters Hate Boomers," *Fortune* (October 4, 1993), pp. 56–70.

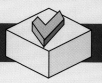

## HOW MUCH DO YOU KNOW ABOUT DIVERSITY?

Today's workforce is more diverse than ever before. Success for both supervisors and employees depends on being able to address issues of cultural diversity effectively. How aware are you of the following issues? Circle the correct answer.

1. The "Glass Ceiling" in corporations refers to:
   a. The feeling that many minorities and women experience of being constantly watched and supervised by those above them
   b. The hiring of female entry-level employees with the clear opportunity for future promotions based upon performance
   c. The high expectations, but frustrating limits, that women and minorities experience in promotions
   d. The effect of indirect lighting on employee motivation
2. You can tell who is gay or lesbian by
   a. Their mannerisms
   b. Whom they associate with at work
   c. The jobs they prefer
   d. The kind of personal stories they share
   e. None of the above
3. Provisions of the Disabilities Act prohibit an employer from inquiring into a job applicant's disability with questions concerning
   a. Mental illness          b. Age
   c. Past work experience     d. Religious affiliation
4. As of October 1994, women constituted 46 percent of the total U.S. workforce. The percentage of women occupying top executive-level jobs is
   a. 40                      b. 25
   c. 12                      d. 5
5. By the year 2000, which one of the following ethnic minority groups is predicted to be the largest in the U.S.?
   a. African-Americans       b. Hispanics
   c. Native Americans        d. Asian-Americans
6. Among full-time workers 25 and older, whites earn more than blacks at all levels, and the difference is greater than the wage disparities between men and women, regardless of race.
   a. True                    b. False
7. For every dollar men earn, women earn approximately
   a. 50 cents                b. 90 cents
   c. 60 cents                d. 70 cents

*(continued)*

8. Women in blue-collar, male-dominated occupations are physically sexually harassed more often than their female white-collar counterparts, and they are likely to be
   a. Less assertive in resisting and reporting it
   b. More assertive in resisting and reporting it
   c. Equally assertive in resisting and reporting it
   d. More assertive in resisting, but less likely to report it

9. None of the *Fortune* 500 companies below has ever had a woman on the board of directors, except for which company?
   a. Microsoft                    b. Rite Aid
   c. Ocean Spray Cranberries      d. Rubbermaid

10. One of the most common complaints of employees with a physical disabling condition is
    a. They are constantly taken care of
    b. They are treated as though they are invisible
    c. They are asked to perform duties beyond their capabilities
    d. They are regularly asked about their condition

11. According to a 1993 American Bar Foundation study of bargaining at new car dealerships, the average profit that dealers made on an automobile was
    a. $225 from white male customers, $419 from black male customers
    b. $564 from white male customers, $1,665 from black male customers
    c. $540 from white male customers, $826 from black male customers
    d. $330 from white male customers, $380 from black male customers

12. Affirmative Action programs are designed to
    a. Give preference to female and minority candidates who may be somewhat less qualified in order to make their numbers in the workplace equal to white males
    b. Open access to potential employees who have previously been excluded from equal competition for jobs within particular organizations
    c. Fill a predetermined quota of women and minorities in an organization
    d. Have organizations look more affirmatively on women and minorities in job evaluations than they look upon white males.

13. An employer can be held responsible if a customer, contractor or other non-employee sexually harasses one of its own employees.
    a. True                        b. False

14. In one four-category description of the different "social styles" of people, (1) Analytic, (2) Driver, (3) Amiable, (4) Expressive, the most effective managers tend to be from
    a. The Analytic category
    b. The Driver category
    c. The Amiable category
    d. The Expressive category
    e. All of the above
15. Placing persons with disabilities in a separate seating area at public events is often experienced by people with disabilities as
    a. The same as segregation
    b. A reasonable accomodation
    c. Neither a nor b
    d. Both a and b
16. In the "Glass Ceiling" Report of the U.S. Department of Labor, women and minorities who were in higher management positions were almost always in
    a. Line positions such as operations and production
    b. Line positions such as sales
    c. Staff positions such as human resources and public relations
    d. Temporary positions
17. Between January of 1977 and August of 1991, no whites were executed for the killing of an African-American.
    a. True                           b. False
18. In 1994 what percentage of experts and sources named in business magazines and newspapers were women?
    a. 53%                            b. 29%
    c. 13%                            d. 4%
19. Which positive stereotype of Asian and Pacific Islander Americans is not a major barrier to their advancement into top leadership positions?
    a. They are good at science, engineering, and technology
    b. They are highly educated
    c. They are nonconfrontational
    d. All of the above
20. According to the 1995 Fact-Finding Report of the Federal Glass-Ceiling Commission, what are the three major differences that lead to discomfort in the workplace and, hence, discrimination?
    a. Cultural, gender, and color-based differences
    b. Socioeconomic, gender, and color-based differences
    c. Educational, cultural, and color-based differences

*(continued)*

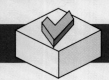

**21.** A Japanese-American male executive with a bachelor's degree who works for a private for-profit company earns on average how much more than his white counterpart?

    **a.** $22,400    **b.** $5,600    **c.** $13,800

    **d.** A Japanese male doesn't earn more than a white male

**22.** If maternity leave is controlled for, more men in senior management positions take leaves of absence than women at the same level.

    **a.** True                **b.** False

**23.** Over the past five years, the stock-market performance of firms that have good glass-ceiling records was approximately how many times higher than that of firms with poor glass-ceiling records?

    **a.** 9.7    **b.** 2.4    **c.** 0.5

    **d.** The stocks of companies with good glass-ceiling records did not perform better than the stocks of companies with poor ones.

**24.** The percentage of Americans with assets of $500,000 or more who are women is approximately

    **a.** 10%                **b.** 25%

    **c.** 40%                **d.** 65%

## SCORING

| | | | |
|---|---|---|---|
| **1.** c | **7.** d | **13.** a | **19.** b |
| **2.** e | **8.** d | **14.** e | **20.** a |
| **3.** a | **9.** d | **15.** d | **21.** a |
| **4.** d | **10.** d | **16.** c | **22.** a |
| **5.** a | **11.** b | **17.** a | **23.** b |
| **6.** a | **12.** b | **18.** c | **24.** c |

Give yourself 4 points for each correct response (for a total of 96 points). You get four points for just taking the assessment! Scoring is like a typical 100-point test. That is, 90 and above, you "aced" the assessment, meaning that you are well informed about diversity. Below 60 means that you are not as well informed as you could be about diversity issues in today's society. The key word is *informed*. Reading this text, as well as exposure to diversity issues in many of your classes and life experiences, will help to increase your awareness.

Source: D. P. Tulin and P. Watts, "What's Your Multicultural IQ?" *Executive Female* (May/June 1995), pp. 17–19. Used with permission of *Executive Female* magazine, the official publication of the National Association for Female Executives, (212) 477-2200.

Blending these three age groups will be required for supervisors to be effective. That is, supervisors will need to be trained to effectively deal with each group, and to respect the diversity of views that each offers.[18] Companies like the Travelers and the Hartford Insurance companies go to great lengths to train younger supervisors how to deal with older employees. Likewise, more mature supervisors are made aware of the different work attitudes younger workers may bring to the job. Inasmuch as work attitude conflict is natural between these groups, these companies have been successful in keeping problems to a minimum by helping the various groups learn about one another.[19]

## CHANGING HOW BUSINESS OPERATES

Where supervisors work today is changing. While in the past, big business dominated the American scene, that's not necessarily the case today. There has been more growth in small- and medium-sized companies during the past decade. It is these businesses that have been able to be more customer responsive. Nonetheless, big businesses are not throwing in the towel. Instead, to be more like their smaller counterparts, large businesses have been making some significant changes. The most obvious of these are downsizing, total quality management, and reengineering. Let's look at each of these and discuss how they will affect you on the job.

### WHY ARE ORGANIZATIONS DOING MORE WITH LESS?

American companies have been working to become "lean and mean" organizations. As a result of deregulation in certain industries (like the airlines), foreign competition, mergers, and takeovers, organizations have cut employees from their payrolls. In fact, by the mid 1990s, almost all Fortune 500 companies—like Sears, Kodak, IBM, and Toyota—had cut staff and reshaped their operations. In business terms, this action is called **downsizing.**

Organizations downsized to accomplish two primary goals: to create greater efficiency and reduce costs. In many cases this meant that they reduced the number of workers employed by the organization. This included employees at all levels, including supervisors. Organizations did not do this because it was fun for them. Many were forced into this action. Why? The world around them changed!

In order to deal effectively with factors in a rapidly changing business environment, such as increased global competition, companies had to be-

Downsizing
a reduction in the workforce and reshaping of operations to create lean and mean organizations. The goals of organizational downsizing are greater efficiency and reduced costs.

[18]L. Thornburg, "The Age Wave Hits: What Older Workers Want and Need," *HRMagazine* (February 1995), pp. 43–4.
[19]"Office Hours," *Fortune* (November 5, 1990), p. 184.

Downsizing efforts at IBM have resulted in supervisors having to become more responsive to employee needs. These IBM employees know they have more work in store for them, but their supervisor, Ted Childs (top center) recognizes he has to let each of his employees have some control over their daily work activities. He continually encourages them to do the best they can.

come more flexible about how work got done. Formal work rules that dominated bureaucracies didn't permit changes to occur fast enough. There were just too many people involved in making decisions—and in their implementation. In addition, workers in the organizations, may not have had the necessary skills to adapt to the changes in their jobs. In some cases, the organization had not planned ahead, or spent the money years ago, to ensure that employee skills would be up to date. As a result, someone outside the organization had to be hired to do the work. Companies found that it was sometimes cheaper to continue to do the work outside than it was to train and pay for a full-time employee. Thus, along with downsizing for flexibility's sake, came a realization that costs could be significantly cut by downsizing full-time staff resources.

## WHY THE EMPHASIS ON TOTAL QUALITY MANAGEMENT?

**Total quality management (TQM)** a philosophy of management that is driven by customer needs and expectations. Statistical control is used to reduce variability and result in uniform quality and predictable quantity of output.

There is a quality revolution taking place in both business and the public sector.[20] The generic term that has evolved to describe this revolution is **total quality management**, or **TQM** for short. It was inspired by a small group of quality experts, the most prominent of them being the late W. Edwards Deming.

An American, Deming found few managers in the United States interested in his ideas in the 1950s. Consequently, he went to Japan and began advising many top Japanese managers on how to improve their production

[20]M. Saskin and K. J. Kiser, *Total Quality Management* (Seabrook, MD: Ducochon Press, 1991).

effectiveness. Central to his management methods was the use of statistics to analyze variability in production processes. A well-managed organization, according to Deming, was one in which statistical control reduced variability and resulted in uniform quality and predictable quantity of output. That meant, from Deming's perspective, that the 64,233rd light bulb produced should have the same quality properties that the first one had. Deming developed a fourteen-point program for transforming organizations. Today, Deming's original program has been expanded into TQM—a philosophy of management that is driven by customer needs and expectations (see Exhibit 2–3). Importantly, the term *customer* in TQM is expanded beyond the traditional definition to include everyone who interacts with the organization's product or service either internally or externally. TQM encompasses employees and suppliers, as well as the people who buy the organization's products or services. The objective is to create an organization committed to continuous improvement.

TQM represents a counterpoint to earlier management theorists who believed that low costs were the only road to increased productivity. The American automobile industry, in fact, represents a classic case of what can go wrong when attention is focused solely on trying to keep costs down. Throughout the 1970s and 1980s, companies like GM, Ford, and

---

1. **Focus on the customer.** The customer includes not only outsiders who buy the organization's products or services, but also internal customers (such as shipping or accounts payable personnel) who interact with and serve others in the organization.

2. **Continuous Improvement.** TQM is a commitment to never being satisfied. "Very good" is not enough. Quality can always be improved.

3. **Improve the quality of everything the organization does.** TQM uses a very broad definition of quality. It relates not only to the final product but how the organization handles deliveries, how rapidly it responds to complaints, how politely the phones are answered, and the like.

4. **Measure Accurately.** TQM uses statistical techniques to measure every critical variable in the organization's operations. These are compared against standards or benchmarks to identify problems, trace them to their roots, and eliminate their causes.

5. **Involve Employees.** TQM involves the people on the line in the improvement process. Teams are widely used in TQM programs for finding and solving problems.

### EXHIBIT 2–3

The foundations of TQM.

Chrysler ended up building products that a large part of the car-buying public rejected. Moreover, when the costs of rejects, repairing shoddy work, product recalls, and expensive controls to identify quality problems were factored in, the American manufacturers actually were less productive than many foreign competitors. The Japanese demonstrated that it was possible for the highest quality manufacturers also to be among the lowest cost producers. Only recently have American auto manufacturers realized the importance of TQM and implemented many of its basic components, such as quality control groups, process improvement, teamwork, improved supplier relations, and listening to the needs and wants of customers. TQM is the recognition that continuous improvement in quality is necessary for an organization to compete effectively.

## HOW DOES REENGINEERING DIFFER FROM TQM?

Although TQM is a positive start in many organizations, it focuses on continuous improvement, or ongoing incremental change. Such action is intuitively appealing—the constant and permanent search to make things better. Companies, however, live in a time of rapid and dynamic change. As the elements around them change ever so quickly, a continuous improvement process may keep them behind the times.

The problem with continuous improvement is that it provides a false sense of security. It makes supervisors and managers feel like they're actively doing something positive, which is true. However, this may be the 1990s version of rearranging the deck chairs on the Titanic. Why? Unfortunately, ongoing incremental change puts off facing up to the possibility that what the organization may really need is radical or quantum change. This concept is now commonly referred to as **reengineering**.[21] Reengineering occurs when most of the work being done in an organization is evaluated and altered. It requires organizational members to rethink what work should be done, how it is to be done, and how to best implement these decisions. Reengineering efforts in companies like Federal Express, Bell Atlantic, and Vortex Industries, are designed to lead to improvements in production quality, speed, and customer service.[22]

If you read the preceding section closely, you may be asking yourself—aren't these authors contradicting what they said a few paragraphs ago about TQM? On the surface, it may appear so, but consider this: while TQM is important for organizations, and can lead to improvements for most, TQM may not always be the right thing initially. If what an organization is producing is outdated, a new improved version of the product may not be helpful to the company. Rather, major change is required. After

**Reengineering**
radical or quantum change that occurs when most of the work being done in an organization is evaluated, and then altered. Reengineering requires organizational members to rethink what work should be done, how it is to be done, and how to best implement these decisions.

[21]M. Hammer and J. Champy, *Reengineering the Corporation* (New York, NY: Haper-Collins, 1993).
[22]J. Byrne, "Reengineering: What Happened?" *Business Week* (January 30, 1995), p. 16.

that has occurred, then continually improving it (TQM) can have its rightful place. Let's see how this may be so.

Assume you are the supervisor responsible for implementing some type of change in your company's roller skate manufacturing process. If you take the continuous improvement approach, your frame of reference will be a high-toe leather shoe on top of a steel carriage, with four wooden wheels. Your continuous improvement program may lead you to focus on things like using a different grade of cowhide for the shoe, adding speed laces to the uppers, or using a different type of ball-bearing in the wheels. Of course, your new skate may be better than the one you previously made, but is that enough? Compare your action to that of a competitor who reengineers the process.

To begin, your competitor poses the following question: How does she design a skate that is safe and fun, that provides greater mobility, and that is fast? Starting from scratch, and not being constrained by her current manufacturing process, she completes her redesign with something that looks like today's popular inline skates. Instead of your new improved leather and metal skates, you are now competing against a molded boot, similar to that used in skiing. Your competitor's skate is better than one made from leather, and has no laces to tie. Additionally, it uses 4 to 6 high durability plastic wheels, which are placed inline for greater speed and mobility.

In this contrived example, both companies made progress. Which do you believe made the most progress given the dynamic environment they face? This hypothetical situation clearly reinforces why companies like Union Carbide, GTE, or Mutual Benefit Life opted for reengineering as opposed to incremental change.[23] It is imperative in today's business environment for all managers to consider the challenge of reengineering their organizational processes. Why? Because reengineering can lead to "major gains in cost, service, or time."[24] It is these kinds of gains that will take companies well into the 21st century.

## WHAT ARE THE SUPERVISORY IMPLICATIONS OF DOWNSIZING, TQM, AND REENGINEERING?

Although downsizing, total quality management, and reengineering are activities that are initiated at the top-management levels of an organization, they do have an affect on supervisors. Supervisors may be heavily involved in implementing the changes. They must be prepared to deal with the organizational issues these changes bring about. Let's look at some of the implications.

[23]T. A. Stewart, "Reengineering: The Hot New Managing Tool, " *Fortune* (August 23, 1993), pp. 41–43.
[24]Ibid, p. 42.

## DOWNSIZING AND SUPERVISORS

When an organization downsizes, the most obvious effect is that people lose their jobs. Therefore, a supervisor can expect certain things to occur. Employees—both those let go and the ones that remain—may get angry. Both sets of employees may perceive that the organization no longer cares about them. Even though the downsizing decision is made at higher levels of management, the supervisor may receive the brunt of this resentment. In some cases, the supervisor may have participated in deciding which individuals to let go, and which ones to keep, based on the organization's goals. After downsizing, employees who remain may be less loyal to the company.

An important challenge for supervisors will be motivating a workforce that feels less secure in their jobs and less committed to their employers. Corporate employees used to believe that their employers would reward their loyalty and good work with job security, generous benefits, and pay increases. By downsizing, companies have begun to discard traditional policies on job security, seniority, and compensation. These changes have resulted in a sharp decline in employee loyalty. As corporations have shown less commitment to employees, employees have shown less commitment to them. This impacts the supervisor's ability to motivate employees and maintain high productivity.

Downsizing may also cause increased competition among a supervisor's employees. If decisions are made to eliminate jobs based on a performance criterion, employees may be less likely to help one another. It may become every employee for him or her self. That behavior can defeat the team that a supervisor has built.

Finally, there are issues for the survivors that downsizing may foster. Unless the work processes have been revamped, major tasks of jobs that were cut may still be required. Usually that means increased workloads for the remaining employees. This can lead to longer work days, creating conflicts for employees between their work and personal lives. For the supervisor, this, too, can dramatically affect work unit productivity.

## TQM AND SUPERVISORS

Each supervisor must clearly define what quality means to the jobs in his or her unit. This needs to be communicated to every staff member. Each individual must then exert the needed effort to move toward "perfection." Supervisors and their employees must recognize that failing to do so could lead to unsatisfied customers taking their purchasing power to competitors. Should that happen, jobs in the unit might be in jeopardy.

The premise of TQM, or continuous improvement, can generate a positive outcome for supervisors and employees. Everyone involved may now have input into how work is best done. The foundation of TQM is built on

Downsizing, total quality management, reengineering, and technology. What do each of these have in common for supervisors? Each is bringing with it a new way for supervisors to work. Supervisors must continually keep abreast of what's happening around them. When changes occur in the workplace, they must be in positions to train and educate their employees on the latest equipment or methods the company is now using.

the participation of the people closest to the work. As such, TQM can eliminate many of the bottlenecks that have hampered work efforts in the past. TQM can help create more satisfying jobs—for both the supervisor and his or her employees.

## REENGINEERING AND SUPERVISORS

If you accept the premise that reengineering will change how businesses operate, it stands to reason that supervisors, too, will be directly affected. First of all, reengineering may leave some supervisors and employees confused and angry. When processes are restructured, some long-time work relationships may be severed.

Although reengineering has its skeptics, it can generate some benefits for supervisors. It may mean that they have an opportunity to learn new skills. They may now be working with the latest technology, supervising work teams, or having more decision-making authority. These are the same skills that may keep them marketable and help them move to another organization, should that time ever come. Finally, as these changes sweep across corporate America, supervisors may see changes in how they are paid. Under a reengineered work arrangement, supervisors and their employees may be in a better position to be compensated for the work they do and receive bonuses and incentives when they excel.

# THRIVING ON CHAOS

As a student, which one of the following scenarios do you find most appealing? *Scenario 1:* Semesters are 15 weeks long. Faculty members are required to provide, on the first day of each class, a course syllabus that specifies daily assignments, exact dates of examinations, and the precise percentage weights that various class activities count toward the final grade. College rules require instructors to hold classes only at the time specified in the class schedule. These rules also require instructors to grade assignments and return the results within one week from the time they're turned in. *Scenario 2:* Courses vary in length. When you sign up for a course, you don't know how long it will last. It might go for two weeks or thirty weeks. Furthermore, the instructor can end a course any time he or she wants, with no prior warning. The length of a class also changes each time it meets. Sometimes it lasts twenty minutes; other times it runs for three hours. Scheduling of the next class meeting is done by the instructor at the end of each class. Oh yes, the exams are all unannounced, so you have to be ready for a test at any time; and instructors rarely provide you with any significant feedback on the results of those exams.

If you're like most people, you chose Scenario 1. Why? Because it provides security through predictability. You know what to expect, and you can plan for it. It may, therefore, be disheartening for you to learn that the manager's world—including the supervisor's job—is increasingly looking a lot more like Scenario 2 than Scenario 1.

We propose that tomorrow's successful supervisors will be those who have learned to thrive on chaos. They will confront an environment in which change is taking place at an unprecedented rate. New competitors spring up overnight and old ones disappear through mergers, acquisitions, or failure to keep up with the changing marketplace. Downsized organizations mean fewer workers to complete the necessary work. Constant innovations in computer and telecommunications technologies are making communications instantaneous. These factors, combined with the globalization of product and financial markets, have created chaos. As a result, many traditional management practices—created for a world that was far more stable and predictable—no longer apply.

Successful supervisors must change too. They must be able to make sense out of a situation when everything appears futile. Supervisors must be able to turn disasters into opportunities. To do so, they must be more flexible in their styles, smarter in how they work, quicker in making decisions, more efficient in managing scarce resources, better at satisfying the customer, and more confident in enacting massive and revolutionary changes. As management writer Tom Peters captured in one of his best selling books: "Today's supervisors must be able to thrive on change and uncertainty."[25]

[25]T. Peters, *Thriving on Chaos: Handbook for a Management Revolution* (New York, NY: Knopf, 1987).

# THE GOOD AND PROFITABLE ORGANIZATION

Every organization has one simple goal. It wants to survive. Survival, though, may take on different forms. For many it means being profitable, while for others, it means continuing their work for the good of society. It is the former that oftentimes raises many questions. Can an organization operate in a manner that allows it to do the "right" thing and still make money? Although the answer is *yes*, the news headlines are filled with stories about organizations that may not operate in a manner that seems appropriate. For instance, if Dow Corning knew that its breast implants could have serious side effects for women if they leaked, should they have withdrawn the product before the courts made them? Should tobacco companies, like RJ Reynolds or Philip Morris, continue to sell billions of cigarettes when there is documented evidence that cigarette smoking may lead to serious medical problems or even death? We can't condemn such organizations. They are, after all, obeying the law—and that's all that is required of them! We assume that as long as businesses obey the law, they have a right to do whatever is necessary to ensure survival. We take this as a given. However, many organizations today are implementing policies and practices that focus on socially responsible behavior. Let's look at this phenomenon.

## WHAT IS A SOCIALLY RESPONSIBLE ORGANIZATION?

**Social responsibility** is an obligation organizations have to society. It means going beyond the law and profit making. Social responsibility tries to align organizational long-term goals with what is good for society. Society in this context refers to such groups as an organization's employees, customers, and the environment in which it operates.

We can understand social responsibility better if we compare it with two similar concepts: social obligation and social responsiveness (see Exhibit 2–4).[26] **Social obligation** is the foundation of a business's social involvement. A business has fulfilled its social obligation when it meets its economic and legal responsibilities and no more. It does the minimum that the law requires. In contrast to social obligation, both social responsibility and social responsiveness go beyond merely meeting basic economic and legal standards. **Social responsiveness** adds a moral obligation to do those things that make society better and not to do those that could make

[26]S. P. Sethi, "A Conceptual Framework for Environmental Analysis of Social Issues and Evaluation of Business Response Patterns," *Academy of Management Review* (January 1979), pp. 68–74; and Donna J. Wood, "Corporate Social Performance Revisited," *Academy of Management Review* (October 1991), pp. 703–8.

**Social responsibility** an obligation organizations have to pursue long-term goals that are good for society.

**Social obligation** the foundation of a business's social involvement. An organization's social obligation is fulfilled when it meets its economic and legal responsibilities.

**Social responsiveness** a process guided by social norms that required business to determine what is right or wrong and thus seek fundamental truths; an attempt to do those things that make society better and not to do those things that could make it worse.

**EXHIBIT 2–4**

Social obligation versus social responsiveness.

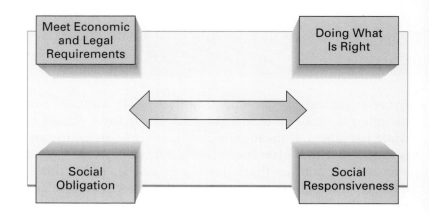

it worse. Social responsiveness, then, requires business to determine what is right or wrong and thus seek fundamental truths. Societal norms guide this process. Let's look at these two in an example to make them clearer.

When a company meets pollution control standards established by the federal government, or doesn't discriminate against employees on the basis of their race in a promotion decision, the organization is fulfilling its social obligation—and nothing more. Various laws say that employers may not pollute or be biased against certain groups, and this company is abiding by those laws. However, when a company packages its products in recycled paper or provides health care insurance for an employee's significant other, these firms are being socially responsive. How so? Although pressure may be coming from a number of societal groups, such businesses are providing something society desires—without having to be told to do so by law!

It's often easy for us to sit back and talk about a company being socially responsible. But what about when the "they" become "us?" Socially responsible behavior for individuals can be viewed from a perspective that we call ethics.

## How Do I Act Ethically?

Many people believe that our society is currently suffering a moral crisis. Behaviors that were once thought reprehensible—lying, cheating, misrepresenting, covering up mistakes—have become, in many people's eyes, common business practices. Products that can cause harm to their users still remain in the market. And males in one large organization have been alleged to have sexually harassed their female counterparts. Even college students seem to have become caught up in this wave. A Rutgers University study of more than 6000 students found that, among those anticipating careers in business, 76 percent admitted to having cheated on at least one test and 19 percent acknowledged having cheated on four or more tests.[27]

[27]R. Tetzeli, "Business Students Cheat Most," *Fortune* (July 1, 1991), p. 14.

How about in business—and more specifically the job of supervisor? What kinds of ethical issues might a supervisor face? Here are a few general questions related to supervisory ethics: Should you tell the truth all the time? Is it right to bend the rules to your company's advantage whenever you can? Does anything go, as long as you don't get caught? Now, consider a couple of specific cases: Is it ethical for one of your salespeople to offer a bribe to a purchasing agent as an inducement to buy? Is it wrong to use the company telephone for personal long distance calls? Is it ethical to ask your company secretary to type personal letters?

Supervisors face many ethical dilemmas. There are situations where they're required to define right and wrong conduct. By their comments and behavior, supervisors are a primary source for conveying an organization's ethical climate. For most employees, their supervisor is the only contact they have with management. As such, management's ethical standards are interpreted by employees through the actions of their supervisor. If supervisors take company supplies home, cheat on their expense accounts, or engage in similar practices, they set a tone in their work groups that is likely to undermine all the efforts by top management to create a corporate climate of high ethical standards.

In large companies such as American Express, Exxon, Sara Lee, and McDonnell Douglas, supervisors have a code of ethics to guide them as to what constitutes acceptable and unacceptable practices. **A code of ethics** is a formal document that states an organizations's primary values and the ethical rules it expects employees to follow. For instance, McDonnell Douglas's code of ethics instructs all employees to be law abiding in all activities, truthful and accurate in what they say and write, and to recognize

**Code of ethics**
a formal document that states an organization's primary values and the ethical rules it expects employees to follow.

Is what this supervisor is experiencing right? Should he be influenced by the actions of the other person. What will the organization think if he is influenced by this action? Moreover, is it ethical to make a decision that was influenced by something other than the issues at hand?

that high integrity sometimes requires the company to forego business opportunities.

As organizations put increased pressure on supervisors and employees to cut costs and increase productivity, ethical dilemmas are almost certain to increase. By what they say and do, supervisors contribute toward setting their organization's ethical standards. This is illustrated in comments from Robert Torres, a supervisor in the Tucson Police Department:

> *I tell my people that gratuities, in any form, are wrong. Take meals for example. A restaurant might offer my people half-priced meals because, they say, they like police officers. I believe there's a hidden agenda in everything. The reason they're giving you half-priced meals is because they want police officers and their vehicles there. Crooks aren't going to hit it. But basically they're buying our services for half the cost of a hamburger. If you have to arrest that restaurant manager, I guarantee you, he's going to come back and say, "Well, you eat at my restaurant at half price." What I tell my people is, "If I find out, we're going to have problems with it." I recommend to my people that, if it's the restaurant's policy to give half off the bill to officers, pay the additional amount in the tip. If it's a $4 hamburger and they charge you $2, put down a $3 tip.*

What individuals like Robert Torres want from their employees is for them to act ethically. What exactly is this thing we call ethics?

## What Is Ethics?

**Ethics**
rules or principles that define right and wrong conduct.

**Ethics** commonly refers to the rules or principles that define right and wrong conduct. People who lack a strong moral character are much less likely to do the wrong things if they are constrained by rules, policies, job descriptions, or strong cultural norms that frown on such behaviors. Conversely, very moral people can be corrupted by an organization and its culture that permit or encourage unethical practices. Consider an ethical situation alluded to previously—that of a purchasing agent taking a bribe. Taking a monetary bribe, we believe, is something almost everyone would consider unethical behavior. That's because it could also be an illegal activity. But what if the "bribe" is not as visible as money—or doesn't exist at all? For example, you are the supervisor of the purchasing department for a medium-sized hospital. You have several vendors who are making their best sales pitch to you in an effort to get your business. Vendor 1 makes his presentation to you, and leaves with you quite an attractive price list—given the large quantities you may be buying. Vendor 2 makes a similar presentation, and her company's prices are comparable. But, she also invites you and your friend to attend this coming weekend's San Francisco 49ers football game. It so happens that you are a big fan of football—but you rarely go to games simply because you can't get tickets. Do you go to the game with this vendor? Do you think it's okay to do so? After all, it's a football game. Furthermore, even if her company does get your business, their prices are, in fact, in line with the competing vendor.

The example above illustrates how ambiguity about what is ethical can be a problem for employees. Codes of ethics are an increasingly popular response for reducing that ambiguity.[28] It has been suggested that codes be specific enough to guide employees in what they're supposed to do. Unfortunately, you may not have such a policy to fall back on. In that case, you are going to have to respond in a way that you feel is appropriate—and deal with the consequences. Let's look at this more closely.

Suppose you are asked by your boss to fix prices with competitors and, at the same time, steal technology from the same groups you are colluding with. Your boss knows that in doing so, your organization can create an unbeatable market for its products and possibly run your competitors out of business. Also, if you do these things, you'll be rewarded handsomely—in fact, you may be put in charge of the operation.[29] What are your options? One option is to do what your boss has asked. After all, he's the boss, and he can make your life great or miserable. However, if you go to such extremes as price fixing or stealing "trade secrets," you might be criminally liable. You, not the manager, may face the charges. Even though you did it for the good of your organization, realize that the boss may not protect you if you get caught. In essence, your career may be tarnished.

Another option is to talk to your boss and register your displeasure with being asked to do this deed. It's doubtful that the request will be withdrawn, but at least you can state your position. You may also refuse to do what you've been asked to do. Of course, this refusal could create problems for you. You may feel that you need to go to organizational members in positions of higher authority. You may find that they are willing to help you, but, you cannot always count on that happening. Yet another option is to give the impression that you'll do what your boss asked, but never carry out the request. You might make up excuses that prices couldn't be fixed because other companies wouldn't agree to go along. In such an instance, you're hoping that the manager will "buy" your excuse, or simply forget to follow up on the request. Again, it's a risk you may be willing to take. Another downside to this option is that you are still committing an unethical act—lying to your boss.

Assuming that your boss continues to press you, you'll have another choice available to you. This, however, is the most extreme. If the request goes clearly against your ethics, and you cannot get any help from

[28]M. C. Matthews, "Codes of Ethics: Organizational Behavior and Misbehavior," in William C. Frederick and Lee E. Preston eds., *Business Ethics: Research Issues and Empirical Studies* (Greenwich, Conn.: JAI Press, 1990), pp. 99–122.

[29]This example is adapted from M. Whitcare, "My Life as a Corporate Mole for the FBI," *Fortune* (September 4, 1995), pp. 52–62.

## GUIDELINES FOR ACTING ETHICALLY

### ABOUT THE SKILL

Making ethical choices can often be difficult for supervisors. Obeying the law is mandatory, but acting ethically goes beyond mere compliance with the law. It means acting responsibly in those "grey" areas, where rules of right or wrong are ambiguous. What can you do to enhance your supervisory abilities in acting ethically? We offer some guidelines.

### STEPS IN PRACTICING THE SKILL

1. **Know your organization's policy on ethics.** Company policies on ethics, if they exist, describe what the organization perceives as ethical behavior and what it expects you to do. This policy will help you clarify what is permissible for you to do—the managerial discretion you have. It will become your code of ethics to follow.
2. **Understand the ethics policy.** Just having the policy in your hand does not guarantee that it will achieve what it is intended to do. You need to fully understand it. Ethical behavior is rarely a "cut and dry" process. With the help of the policy as a guiding light, you will have a basis from which to decide ethical issues in the organization. Even if a policy doesn't exist, there are several steps you can take when confronted with a difficult situation.
3. **Think before you act.** Ask yourself, why are you doing what you're about to do? What lead up to the problem? What is your true intention in taking some action? Is it

for a valid reason, or are there ulterior motives behind it—like demonstrating organizational loyalty? Will your action injure someone? Can you disclose to your manager or your family what you're going to do? Remember, it's your behavior that will be seen in your actions. You need to make sure that you are not doing something that will jeopardize your role as a manager, your organization, or your reputation.
4. **Ask yourself what-if questions.** When you think ahead about why you're doing something, you should also be asking yourself "what-if" questions. For example, the following questions may help you shape your actions: What if you make the wrong decision—what will happen to you? To your job? What if your actions were described, in detail, on your local news or in the newspaper? Would it bother or embarrass you or those around you? What if you get caught doing something unethical? Are you prepared to deal with the consequences?
5. **Seek opinions from others.** If it is something major that you must do, and you're uncertain about it, ask for advice from other managers. Maybe they've been in a similar situation and can give you the benefit of their experiences. If not, maybe they can just listen and act as a sounding board for you.
6. **Do what you truly believe is right.** You have a conscience and you are responsible for your behavior. Whatever you do, if you truly believe it is the right action to take, then what others say (or what the proverbial "Monday morning quarterbacks" say) is immaterial. You need to be true to your own internal ethical standards. Ask yourself: Can you live with what you've done? ■

individuals in the organization, you may have to think about quitting, or even going outside the organization to report what is happening. Sure, there are disadvantages to doing so, but at least you may have the comfort of knowing you've done the right thing.[30]

In situations involving ethics, its impossible to predict what you'll face. It helps if you prepare ahead of time and anticipate how you will handle ethical dilemmas (see Building a Supervisory Skill). The more you do to prepare, the easier it will be when and if that day arrives and you're asked to do something that "goes against your grain."

---

## Pop Quiz  (Are You Comprehending What You're Reading?)

5. When you find organizations with employees who are heterogeneous in terms of gender, race, ethnicity, sexual preference, or other characteristics,
   a. it indicates successful hiring practices exist in the organization
   b. you have workforce diversity
   c. you have an example of the diverse cultures found in the global village
   d. the teachings of Geert Hofstede are being followed
6. Why do organizations downsize?
7. Total quality management involves making radical changes in an organization in the attempt to maximize achieving its goals. Reengineering involves continuously improving an organization's operations and processes to make them more customer focused. True or False?
8. The rules or principles that define right and wrong conduct in an organization are referred to as
   a. corporate citizenry
   b. ethics
   c. social responsiveness
   d. none of the above

---

[30]Ronald Henkoff, "So Who is Mark Whitcare and Why Is He Saying These Things About ADM?" *Fortune* (September 4, 1995), p. 68.

# UNDERSTANDING THE BASICS

## SUMMARY

After reading this chapter, I can:

1. **Explain how globalization affects supervisors.** Globalization affects supervisors in many ways. The key factor is recognizing differences that exist among people from various cultures and understanding how these differences may block effective communications.

2. **Describe how technology is changing the supervisor's job.** Technology is changing the supervisor's job in several ways. Supervisors have immediate access to information that helps them in making decisions. Technological advancements assist supervisors who have employees in remote locations, reducing the need for face-to-face interaction with these individuals. On the other hand, effectively communicating with individuals in remote locations, as well as ensuring that performance objectives are being met, will become a major challenge for supervisors.

3. **Identify the significant changes that have occurred in the composition of the workforce.** Compared to years ago, when the workforce consisted primarily of white males, the workforce has become more diverse and will continue in this direction. Passage of federal legislation that prohibits employment discrimination, changing population demographics, and globalization of businesses have contributed to this change. The changing workforce means that supervisors will be interacting with people who are diverse in terms of gender, race, ethnicity, physical ability, sexual orientation and age—all of whom have different lifestyles, family needs, and work styles. The most significant implication for supervisors is the requirement of sensitivity to the differences in each individual. That means they must shift their philosophy from treating everyone alike to recognizing differences and responding to these differences in ways that will ensure employee retention and greater productivity.

4. **Explain why corporations downsize.** Corporate downsizing has occurred in response to global competition. It is an attempt by companies to become more responsive to customers and more efficient in their operations. The supervisory effect is twofold. First, supervisors must ensure that their skills and those of their employees are kept up to date. Employees whose skills become obsolete are more likely to be candidates for downsizing. Second, those who keep their jobs, will more than likely be doing the work of two or three people. This situation can create frustration, anxiety, and less motivation.

5. **Understand the concept of Total Quality Management and identify its goals.** TQM focuses on the customer, seeks continual improvement, strives to improve the quality of work, seeks accurate measurement, and involves employees.

6. **Describe why supervisors must be able to "thrive on chaos."** Supervisors will work in an environment in which change is taking place at an unprecedented rate. They must be more flexible in their styles, smarter in how they work, quicker in making decisions, more efficient in handling scarce resources, better at satisfying the customer, and more confident in enacting massive and revolutionary changes.

7. **Define ethics.** Ethics refers to rules or principles that define right or wrong con-

duct. In an organization, these rules or principles may be defined in a written code of ethics.

## REVIEWING YOUR KNOWLEDGE

1. Do you believe globalization has had the effect of making American organizations more responsive to their customers? Explain.
2. "Technology improvements sometimes hinder supervisory effectiveness." Do you agree or disagree? Support your position.
3. What is workforce diversity and what challenges does it create for supervisors?
4. What advice would you give to a friend who doesn't understand downsizing, but knows her company is going to be laying off employees in about three months?
5. Describe the difference between TQM and reengineering.
6. How can learning to manage chaos better prepare supervisors for their jobs in the next millennium?
7. Can organizations be socially responsible and still be profitable? If you think so, cite some examples of companies you believe fit this profile and describe what they are doing.
8. Is it ethical to cheat on an exam, if you know that it will not affect another student's grade, and you are guaranteed that you won't get caught? Why or why not?
9. Identify the characteristics and behaviors of what you would consider an ethical supervisor.

## ANSWERS TO THE POP QUIZZES

1. **False.** Just the opposite. The global village has made it nearly impossible to determine precisely where a company does business or from where its employees come. As such, generalizations like pop quiz question 1 and old stereotypes no longer apply.
2. **d. All of the above.** Statements a, b, and c are realistic "musts" for a supervisor to be successful in supervising employees from different cultures.
3. The biggest change required of you will be the recognition that employees from a collective culture are accustomed to having input into decisions that affect them at work. You will need to encourage and practice participative decision-making with these employees. In an individualistic culture, that is not the case—employees expect the supervisor to make many decisions unilaterally.
4. **b. Technology has increased the face-to-face interaction between supervisors and employees.** On the contrary, technology is creating situations where fewer face-to-face interactions between a supervisor and employee take place. Telecommuting, fax machines, computers, modems, e-mail, and the like are all contributing to this issue.
5. **b. You have workforce diversity.** This is the definition of workforce diversity as explained in the text.
6. Organizations downsize for a number of reasons, however, two goals appear to prevail. First, organizations attempt to create greater efficiency by eliminating work functions, layers in the organization, and

employees to enhance productivity. Second, by cutting staff and operations, organizations attempt to cut costs, thus saving the company money.

7. **False.** Just the opposite is true. TQM involves continuous improvements designed to make the organization more customer focused. Reengineering involves making radical changes in the organization's operations or processes.

8. **b. Ethics.** This is the definition of ethics presented in the text. ∎

## A CLASS EXERCISE: WORKING WITH DIVERSITY

In today's workforce, three generations coexist. There are the mature workers (born before 1946); the baby-boomers (born between 1946 and 1964); and the baby-busters, also called Generation Xers (born between 1964 and 1975). Each group has its own focus and holds different values.

Form three groups based on these age brackets. Group 1 will comprise the mature workers; group 2, the baby-boomers, and group 3, Generation Xers.

*Step 1:* Discuss your feelings about all three groups. To help frame your responses, the following questions can be used.

A. What do you believe each group:
- values in life?
- wants from their job?
- expects from their supervisor?
B. Now, identify two characteristics that best describe each group.

*Step 2:*
A. Each group will share its responses to the four questions above with the entire class.
B. What similarities and what differences exist between the views of the groups? Do these differences reflect how you see people differently? Discuss your responses.
C. Are the characteristics of your age bracket more positive for yourself than the characteristics you listed for the other two groups? What does this tell you about the perceptions of diverse workers?

## THINKING CRITICALLY

### CASE 2.A

### Bausch & Lomb Sets Its Sight

Bausch & Lomb, the Rochester, New York eyeware company, made some major changes that have a number of Western Maryland citizens seeing red. A Bausch & Lomb plant in the area, makers of sunglass lenses, has been targeted for closure. As a result, approximately 600 jobs will be lost.[31] Company representatives say that it has just gotten too expensive to maintain the plant in the Maryland area, and have decided to shift the operations to plants in San Antonio, Texas, and Hong Kong. Is Bausch & Lomb justified in its actions?

Clearly company officials have a right to manage the operations in the most profitable way they can. Moving to areas where employee pay is lower is one way to reduce costs. Therefore, from the "bottom line" perspective, these actions are warranted. Besides, the move follows on the heels of the ousting of the company's chief executive, who watched profits fall from $171.4 million in 1992 to $31.1 million in 1994.

Although the company has a right to shut down plants and eliminate jobs, Bausch & Lomb's action will create significant problems for employees and the surrounding community. The company is the largest employer in the region. When the biggest employer in an area makes such a change, it not only affects employees who will be laid off, it directly impacts other businesses. When income levels in

---

[31]Based on the story by Jay Hancock, "Made in the Shade No Longer," *The Sun: Business* (January 26, 1996), p. E1, E2.

a region drop significantly, fewer monies will be spent in the local economy. If nothing replaces this economic loss, serious problems may arise. For instance, restaurants that depended heavily on Bausch & Lomb employees' patronage may have to subsequently close because of a lack of business. Schools and other town-supported organizations could face a similar fate. Tax revenues could drop significantly, as many who are able will leave the area to find jobs elsewhere.

One reason for the company's actions relates to how much employees are paid in the Maryland plant. Jobs and employers in this area of Maryland are rare. When a company like Bausch & Lomb establishes an operation in the area, it is met with a skilled, dedicated, and committed work force. Because there are so few employers, employees stay with an organization for long periods of time; turnover is almost nonexistent. This long tenure is rewarded with annual pay increases. At the San Antonio plant turnover is significant, and new employees are hired at lower wage rates than the person who left the job. As a result of the longevity in Maryland, the average hourly wage rate is about 33 percent higher than it is in Texas, and even higher when compared to Hong Kong. Although employees in the Maryland plant make more money than their counterparts in Texas and Hong Kong, they've given the company something that other plants have not—highly-recognized quality products. Over the years, this Western Maryland plant has been recognized by several independent groups as producing some of the highest-quality sunglass lenses in the world. In fact, employees have been awarded a prestigious international designation of quality, something few organizations anywhere in the world achieve. Additionally, this Western Maryland plant received a produc-tivity award from the U.S. Government. Sadly, though, the buying public places less emphasis on quality of their sunglasses. Instead, purchases are made primarily on the basis of cost.

## RESPONDING TO THE CASE

1. What social responsibility, if any, do you believe Bausch & Lomb has to the citizens of this Western Maryland area?
2. Do you believe that companies should have a legal right to move to another area simply to cut costs, knowing it will create an economic hardship? Would you respond differently knowing that a company received special tax breaks from the state where it currently has its operations?

## CASE 2.B

### Banking with Interest

Anna Jackson has been with First National Bank of New York for six years. When Anna started working at First National, she was in high school and worked as a drive-in teller during the summer months. Anna joined First National for a number of reasons. First, she was offered a job. More importantly, the bank would pay for her college courses—so long as she worked at least 20 hours per week. Working her way through college, she has made many friends with both employees and customers. In fact, many of her customers know her so well, they ask for her when they bank at First National.

Anna has taken every opportunity for training that the bank has offered. Whenever a new process was implemented, or new technology was installed at the bank, Anna was one of the first individuals to sign up for training classes. Additionally, she carried 15 credit hours each semester to ensure that she could achieve her goal of graduating with a degree in economics in four years. Anna has so impressed the bank officials that she has been offered the opportunity to enter into the bank's branch management program. Surprisingly, shortly after graduating from college, Anna accepted a similar position with a competing bank at a comparable salary. In retrospect, this was the bank Anna wanted to work for all along, but it didn't offer college tuition reimbursement.

When Anna started in her new position, she inadvertently let her boss know that she had material she had collected while an employee at First National. He let her know that he was interested in seeing it. The information concerned the direction First National was moving toward over the next five years. In fact, one piece of data in the information packet Anna provided indicated that First National was establishing plans to offer several unique electronic banking services. Hearing this, top management at Anna's bank decided to imme-diately forge ahead with services similar to those that First National was planning to offer. Anna's bank simply did not want to lose its competitive position.

## RESPONDING TO THE CASE

1. Do you believe it was unethical for Anna to join First National Bank solely because the Bank would pay for her education? Support your position.
2. In the case, Anna inadvertently let her new employer know she had information about some First National plans. Was it ethical for this employer to request that information and use it in an attempt to beat First National to the market with new electronic banking services? Why or why not?
3. Would your response to question 2 change if you knew that Anna was hired because she was known to have been privy to such information and this was a way to obtain it? Explain. Had this been the case, did Anna act ethically in providing the requested information? Defend your position. ■

## PART I

### John Erickson
### Manager of A/V Services, Alliant Techsystems

John supervises a department of film/video producers, artists, photographers, and some support staff for Alliant. When John first assumed his position, he inherited a staff governed by preconceived notions. The former supervisor was controlling and judgmental. He had very traditional views of what makes an employee valuable. Women and people with technical school backgrounds were viewed as less valuable than male college graduates. John needed to assess the skills of his department without depending on past judgments.

During this period, Alliant was reorganizing and downsizing, and John was expected to reduce the size of his department. At the same time, demands for service were increasing. John needed to get the most from the people in his department and acquire new people who could adapt to the changing conditions.

1. What was the most important challenge that faced John Erickson when he became a supervisor? Do you think this challenge is typical for most supervisors (or organizations)? Why or why not?
2. How does a supervisor find the right talent for his or her department?
3. What are the elements that determine how the "right" people are hired for or are assigned to the "right" jobs?
4. How can the "right" talent be developed with existing employees and new hires?
5. What did John, as a supervisor, do to assure his department would be productive? How could his example be used by any supervisor?  ∎

# PART TWO

# PLANNING AND CONTROL

The foundation of supervision revolves around effectively planning and controlling the work to be done. In Part Two we'll discuss the major elements that facilitate establishing and attaining organizational and departmental goals. Once goals are established, supervisors must design and implement controls that will ensure that goals are met. Both the planning and the control functions require a high level of problem-solving and decision-making skills. Thus, we will examine these crucial supervisory skills as well.

Part Two contains three chapters:

3. ESTABLISHING GOALS

4. DESIGNING AND IMPLEMENTING CONTROLS

5. PROBLEM SOLVING AND DECISION MAKING

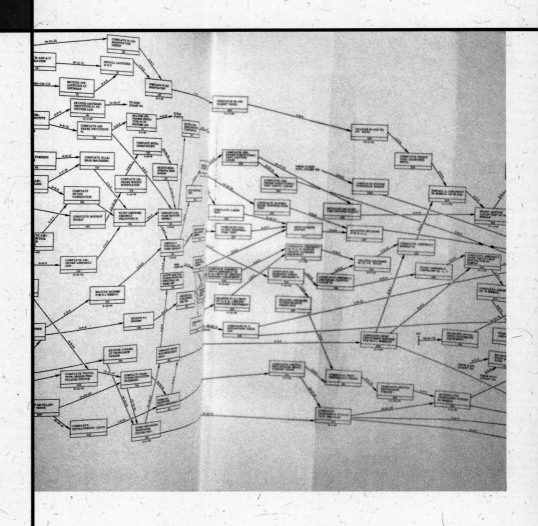

# LEARNING OBJECTIVES 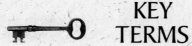 KEY TERMS

After reading this chapter, you should be able to:

1. Define productivity.
2. Describe how plans should link from the top to the bottom of an organization.
3. Contrast policies and rules.
4. Describe the Gantt chart.
5. Explain the information needed to create a PERT chart.
6. Describe the four ingredients common to MBO programs.

You should also be able to define these supervisory terms:

activities

budget

critical path

events

Gantt chart

intermediate-term plans

long-term plans

management by objectives (MBO)

PERT chart

policies

procedure

productivity

program

rule

scheduling

short-term plans

single-use plans

standing plans

strategic planning

tactical planning

# PERFORMING EFFECTIVELY

Jimmy Lai is a modern day rags-to-riches story.[1] Born in 1948, his early life was filled with poverty and despair. At age 12, he had to leave his family and flee to Hong Kong. Because Jimmy had little formal education, the only work he could find was laboring in sweat shops, making such garments as sweaters and gloves.

While Jimmy was unknowingly learning the clothing business, his low-paying job didn't provide him with enough money to pay for the basic necessities of life. He was often caught sleeping on work premises, for he couldn't afford a place to live. Jimmy didn't let such difficulties get the best of him. After all, he had only one way to go, and to him, that was up! He looked at this as an opportunity to better himself. He spent many of those long, cold, lonesome nights teaching himself English. Years later, his fluency with the language opened the doors for Lai to move up to supervisor of the garment factory. As a supervisor, Jimmy was able to travel abroad, gaining more insight about the knitwear business.

## INTRODUCTION

As mentioned in Chapter 1, planning encompasses defining an organization's objectives or goals, establishing the overall strategy for achieving those goals, and developing a comprehensive hierarchy of functions to integrate and coordinate activities. For our purposes, we'll treat the terms *objectives* and *goals* as interchangeable. Each is meant to convey some desired outcome that an organization, department, work group, or individual seeks to achieve.

## WHAT IS FORMAL PLANNING?

Does planning require that goals, strategies, and plans be written down? Ideally they should be, but they often aren't. In formal planning, specific goals are formulated, committed to writing, and made available to other organization members. Additionally, specific action programs exist in formal planning to define the path for the achievement of each goal.

[1]A. Tanzer, "Studying at the Feet of the Masters," *Forbes*, May 10, 1993, p. 43.

In 1981, Jimmy Lai started his own business—Giordano Holdings Ltd. In a dozen short years, his business has grown to over 600 shops (about 150 that he still personally supervises), selling a variety of expensive tee and polo shirts, sweaters, and jeans in Hong Kong, Japan, Southwest Asia, and China. Company sales net Jimmy about $20 million a year in profit.

How did Jimmy succeed in all these retail shops spread out over many miles? Lai has a system. In other words, he plans! He knows when inventories need to be replaced. He understands how many employees are needed to staff each store, with extra personnel on hand for peak sales periods. Jimmy also recognizes that each outlet store must maintain its profitability. He assists each store in this area by developing budgets and implementing procedures to ensure that budgets are controlled. ■

Many managers engage in informal planning. They have plans in their heads, but nothing is written down and there is little or no sharing of these plans with others. This probably occurs most often in small businesses where the owner-manager has a vision of where he or she wants to go and how to get there. In this chapter, when we use the term *planning* we will be referring to the formal variety. It is this formal planning that is most often required for an organization to be productive (see Something to Think About).

## PRODUCTIVITY

In almost any discussion of performance in an organization, the focus will eventually turn to the topic of productivity. Productivity, in essence, becomes the name of the game! This could refer to producing a product, like computer chips, or providing a service, like fixing the hard-disk drive when it has a problem. Yet, in a number of organizations—especially those that provide services—defining productivity can be very difficult. In some cases, it becomes a perceived, if not a real, impossibility. In today's organizations, an inability to determine what constitutes productivity is something that supervisors must avoid!

Formalized planning became very popular in the 1960s, and, for the most part, it still is today! It makes sense to establish some direction. After all, as the Cheshire cat said to Alice in the *Alice in Wonderland* story as she stood in the fork of the road, "If you don't know where you want to go, any road will take you there." Recently, critics have begun to challenge some of the basic assumptions underlying planning.

Some management experts believe that plans may create rigidity.[2] Formal planning efforts can lock organizational members into specific goals to be achieved within specific timetables. When these objectives are set, assumptions may have been made that the "world" won't change during the time period the objectives cover. That may be a faulty assumption. Nevertheless, rather than remaining flexible—and possibly scrapping the plan—some supervisors may continue to do things required to achieve the originally set objectives.

Other experts feel that formal plans can't replace intuition and creativity.[3] Formal planning efforts typically follow a specific methodology—making it a routine event. That can spell disaster for an organization. For instance, the rapid rise of Apple Computer Inc. in the late 1970s throughout the late 1980s, was attributed, in part, to the creativity and anticorporate attitudes of its cofounder, Steven Jobs. However, as the company grew, Jobs felt a need for more formalized management—something he was uncomfortable performing. He hired a CEO (Chief Executive Officer), who ultimately ousted Jobs from his own company. With Jobs' departure came increased organizational formality—the very thing Jobs despised so much because it hampered creativity. By 1996, this one-time leader of its industry had lost much of its creativity, and was struggling for survival.[4]

Finally, there's a perception that while formal planning may reinforce success, it may also lead to failure.[5] We have been taught that success breeds success. That's been an American "tradition." After all, if it's not broken, don't fix it. Right? Well, maybe not! Success may, in fact, breed failure in a changing world of work. It's tough to change or discard successful plans—leaving the comfort of what works for the anxiety of the unknown. Formal plans may provide a false sense of security, generating more confidence than is warranted. Consequently, supervisors often won't deliberately face that unknown until forced to do so by changes in the environment. Unfortunately, by then it may be too late!

So, given these facts, should we still plan formally? Is it worth it? What do you think?

[2]H. Mintzberg, *The Rise and Fall of Strategic Planning* (New York, NY: Free Press, 1994).
[3]Ibid.
[4]K. Rebello and P. Burrows, "The Fall of an American Icon," *Business Week*, Februrary 5, 1996, pp. 34–42.
[5]D. Miller, "The Architecture of Simplicity," *Academy of Management Review*, January 1993, pp. 116–138.

# WHAT IS PRODUCTIVITY?

In its simplest form, **productivity** can be expressed in the following ratio:

$$\text{Productivity} = \frac{\text{Outputs}}{\text{Labor} + \text{Capital} + \text{Materials}}$$

The above formula can be applied in its total form or broken down into subcategories.[6] Output per labor hour is perhaps the most common partial measure of productivity. Industrial engineers, who conduct time-and-motion studies in factories, are largely focused on generating increases in labor productivity. IBM's automated plant in Austin, Texas is an example of increasing productivity by substituting capital (i.e., machinery and equipment) for labor. Materials productivity is concerned with increasing the efficient use of material inputs and supplies. A meat-packing plant, as an illustrative case, improves its materials productivity when it finds additional uses for by-products that were previously treated as waste.

Productivity can also be applied at three different levels—the individual, the group, and the total organization. Word processing software, fax machines, and e-mail have made secretaries more productive by allowing them to generate more output during their work days. The use of teams has increased the productivity of many work groups at companies like Honeywell, Coors Brewing, and Aetna Life. Southwest Airlines is a more

**Productivity**
output per labor hour, best expressed by the formula Productivity = Output/Labor + Capital + Materials. Productivity can be applied to the individual, the group, and the total organization.

Companies like Ross Operating Valve Company are using technology to automate their production processes—and increase worker productivity. This supervisor is inspecting a circuit board that, when installed in machinery in his department, will eliminate many costly "man-hours" of production.

[6]E. E. Adam, Jr. and R. J. Ebert, *Production & Operations Management*, 5th Ed. (Englewood Cliffs, NJ: Prentice Hall, 1992), p. 46.

productive organization overall than rivals such as American Airlines or USAir because Southwest's cost per available-seat-mile is 30 to 60 percent lower than these competitors.

## WHY IS PRODUCTIVITY IMPORTANT TO THE U.S.?

For a number of years in the recent past, American productivity, as calculated by the federal government, was stagnant and, at times, decreasing. As little as a decade ago, the United States ranked eighth or ninth in terms of productivity for industrialized nations. Is that an accurate depiction of what is happening in the U.S. today? By all accounts, it appears that U.S. productivity is rising, targeted in the 3–4 percent range per year.[7] With this statistic, America has once again regained the top spot among industrialized nations. Much of this rise, however, has been attributed to downsizing and reengineering efforts in the early 1990s.[8] By reducing inefficiencies and introducing technological improvements, companies have been able to maintain or even increase production, all the while, employing fewer workers. American companies are also increasing productivity by becoming more quality and customer oriented.[9] The industries in which the United States is doing exceptionally well in relation to other industrialized nations are depicted in Exhibit 3–1.

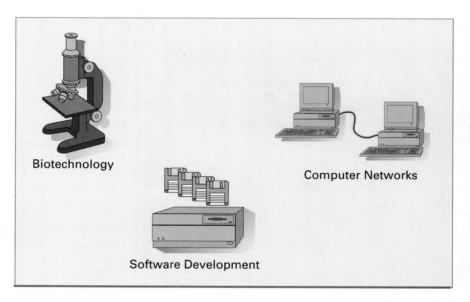

### EXHIBIT 3–1

Industries where the U.S. is number 1 in productivity.

[7]W. Kiechel, III, "When Management Regresses," *Fortune*, March 9, 1992, p. 157.
[8]Leading Economists Say Rise in Productivity, Built on Backs of Workers, Is Not Sustainable," *Work and Family: Newsbrief*, June 1996, p. 1; S. S. Roach, "Economics: Rethinking Productivity," *U. S. Investment Perspective*, May 8, 1996.
[9]A. Kupfer, "How American Industry Stacks Up," *Fortune*, March 9, 1992, p. 30.

What does all this fuss about productivity mean? In essence, having increased productivity makes the U.S. economy stronger. All economic indicators typically revolve around how much U.S. industries produce and sell—both at home and in the global village. Accordingly, when an industrialized nation like the U.S. has a strong productivity base, it creates jobs, enhances its production-dominance among industrialized nations, encourages job security for employees, and affords research and development efforts to continue finding ways to further productivity gains.

## PLANNING AND LEVEL IN THE ORGANIZATION

All managers, irrespective of their level in the organization, should plan. But the type of planning they do tends to vary with their level in the organization.

### WHAT IS THE BREADTH OF PLANNING?

The best way to describe planning is to look at it in two parts: strategic and tactical. **Strategic planning** covers the entire organization, includes the establishment of overall goals, and positions the organization's products or services against the competition (see Dealing with a Difficult Issue). Wal-Mart's strategy, for instance, is to build large stores in rural areas, offer an extensive selection of merchandise, provide the lowest prices, and then draw consumers from the many surrounding small towns.

**Tactical planning** covers the specific details on how overall goals are to be achieved. The Wal-Mart store manager in Fayetteville, Arkansas would be engaged in tactical planning when developing a quarterly expense budget or making out weekly employee work schedules.

For the most part, strategic planning is done by top-level managers; a supervisor's time is devoted to tactical planning. Both are important for an organization's success, but they are different in that one focuses on the big picture, while the other emphasizes the specifics within that big picture.

### HOW DO PLANNING TIME FRAMES DIFFER?

Planning often occurs in three time frames—short term, intermediate term, and long term.

**Short-term plans** are less than one year in length. **Intermediate-term plans** cover from one to five years. **Long-term plans** cover a period in excess of five years. A supervisor's planning horizon tends to emphasize the

**Strategic planning**
organizational planning that includes the establishment of overall goals, and positions an organization's products or services against the competition.

**Tactical planning**
organizational planning that provides specific details on how overall goals are to be achieved.

**Short-term plans**
plans that are less than one year in length.

**Long-term plans**
plans that cover a period in excess of 5 years.

**Intermediate-term plans**
plans that cover a period of one to 5 years.

## GATHERING COMPETITIVE INFORMATION

All businesses need to gather information about their competitors in an effort to plan effectively. For many, it's a game—but one that must be taken seriously. This might involve "surfing the Net" to see what new products are being released, or checking court record databases to determine what, if any, lawsuits or civil cases have been brought against a competitor. These are legitimate methods for obtaining "public information."

Some organizations pride themselves on being able to obtain competitive data in more unusual and somewhat questionable ways. They may call a competitor's office and ask questions about what the company is planning to do. Answers may not be forthcoming, but there's a chance the person on the other end of the line will be quite talkative. Other tactics may include buying some stock shares in a competitor's organization—thus getting annual reports and other information about the company that normally don't go to everyone. A company may even encourage one of its employees to take a job with a competitor—then quit and return to his or her old job after getting some "Company Private" data. Another method is to interview or hire individuals from a competing firm—who hopefully can bring with them a wealth of "inside" information.[10]

1. From your point of view, when does getting information about your competitor become corporate espionage?
2. If you were a supervisor in a Hershey's Chocolate plant, and were asked to get some information about Nestles', how would you go about it? What kinds of tactics would you use and how far would you go to get the data? Would your position change if you knew that getting some critical data could result in your receiving a $25,000 bonus?
3. Do you believe ethical guidelines should be established to deal with the process of obtaining valuable competitive data? Explain.

[10]See for example, H. G. DeYoung, "Thieves Among Us," *Industry Week* (June 17, 1996), pp. 12–16.

short-term: preparing plans for the next month, week, or day. People in middle-level managerial jobs, like regional sales directors, typically focus on one-to-three-year plans. Long-term planning tends to be done by the top executives such as vice presidents and above.

## How Are Plans and Managerial Levels Linked?

It is important to keep in mind that effective planning is integrated and co-ordinated throughout the organization. Long-term strategic planning sets the direction for all other planning. Once top management has defined the organization's overall strategy and goals and the general plan for getting there, then, in descending order, the other levels of the organization develop plans.

Exhibit 3–2 illustrates this linking of plans from the top to the bottom of an organization. The president, vice president, and other senior executives define the organization's overall strategy. Then upper-middle managers, such as regional sales directors, formulate their plans. This continues down to first-level supervisors. Ideally, these plans will be coordinated through joint participation. In the case of Exhibit 3–2, for instance, the Tucson territory manager would participate with other territory managers by providing information and ideas to the Arizona District Manager as she formulates plans for her entire district. If planning is properly linked, then the success-

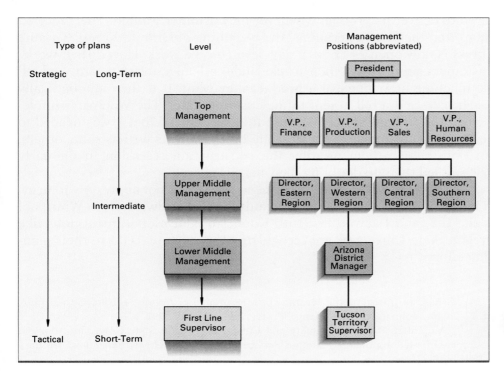

**EXHIBIT 3–2**

Planning and levels in the organization.

ful achievement of all the territory managers' goals should result in the Arizona District Manager achieving her goals. If all the district managers meet their goals, this should lead to the successful attainment of the regional sales manager's goals, and so on up each level in the organization.

## CAN TQM BE A HELP IN PLANNING?

An increasing number of organizations are applying Total Quality Management as a way to establish and achieve their strategic goals. As we discussed in Chapter 2, TQM focuses on quality and continuous improvement. To the degree that an organization can satisfy a customer's need for quality, it can differentiate itself from the competition and attract and hold a loyal customer base. To illustrate how TQM can be used to enhance planning efforts, let's look at the Watsonville, California Granite Rock Company—winners of a prestigious U.S. award for quality.

Granite Rock is a company that "produces and sells crushed stone, mixes concrete and asphalt products, and does some highway paving."[11] There didn't appear to be a serious need for Granite to change its operations. Nevertheless, its management team, headed by Bruce and Steve Woolpert, wouldn't sit still. They knew they had to continuously get to know their customers in terms of what quality meant to them. What they found was startling. They learned that each product line had special customer needs tied to it. For example, in its concrete operations, customers demanded "on-time delivery," which meant that Granite had to be prepared to deliver its product whenever the customer wanted. This required an around-the-clock operation—the beginning of Granite Xpress. Granite Xpress is now open 24 hours a day, seven days a week. How does it work? Customers simply drive their trucks under a loader, insert a card, and tell the machine how much of a product they want. It is then automatically dispensed—and a bill is sent to the customer later. The Woolpert's implemented this change simply because they recognized that it was needed to satisfy their customers. This strategic innovation, as well as some others, not only helped them weather the construction recession in the early 1990s, it led them to doubling their market share!

Using TQM for developing strategic goals does not apply only to firms in industries like Granite Rock. Organizations worldwide, from Whirlpool in the U.S. and Daewoo in South Korea, to educational institutions like Oregon State University, are recognizing the value of TQM in their planning efforts.[12]

[11]M. Barrier, "Learning the Meaning of Measurement," *Nation's Business*, June 1994, pp. 72–74; and John Case, "The Change Masters," *Inc.*, March 1992, p. 60.

[12]L. McMillen, "To Boost Quality and Cut Costs, Oregon State University Adopts a Customer-Oriented Approach to Campus Services," *Chronicle of Higher Education*, February 6, 1991, p. A-27.

# KEY PLANNING GUIDES

Once an organization's strategy and overall goals are in place, management will design additional plans to help guide decision makers. Some of these will be **standing plans.** Once designed, they can be used over and over again by managers faced with recurring activities. Others will be **single-use plans.** These are detailed courses of action used once or only occasionally to deal with problems that don't occur repeatedly. In this section we'll review the popular types of each.

**Standing plans**
plans that can be used over and over again by managers faced with recurring activities.

**Single-use plans**
detailed courses of action used once or only occasionally to deal with problems that don't occur repeatedly.

## WHAT ARE STANDING PLANS?

Standing plans allow managers to save time by handling similar situations in a predetermined and consistent manner. For example, when a supervisor has an employee who increasingly fails to show up for work, the problem can be handled more efficiently and consistently if a discipline procedure has been established in advance. Let's review the three major types of standing plans: policies, procedures, and rules.

### POLICIES

"We promote from within wherever possible." "Do whatever it takes to satisfy the customer." "Our employees should be paid competitive wages." These three statements are examples of **policies.** That is, they are broad guidelines for managerial action. Typically established by top management, they define the limits within which managers must stay as they make decisions.

**Policies**
broad guidelines for managerial action.

Supervisors rarely make policies. Rather, they interpret and apply them. Within the parameters that policies set, supervisors must use their judgment. For instance, the company policy that "our employees should be paid competitive wages" doesn't tell a supervisor what to pay a new employee. However, if the going rate in the community for this specific job is in the $9.20 to $10.50 an hour range, the company policy would clarify that offering a starting hourly rate of either $8.75 or $12.00 is not acceptable.

### PROCEDURES

The purchasing supervisor receives a request from the engineering department for five computer workstations. The purchasing supervisor checks to see if the requisition has been properly filled out and approved. If not, she sends the requisition back with a note explaining what is deficient. When the request is complete, the approximate costs are estimated. If the total exceeds $6500, which they do in this case, three bids must be obtained. If the total had been $6500 or less, only one vendor would need to have been identified and the order could have been placed.

The previous series of steps for responding to a recurring problem is an example of a **procedure.** Where procedures exist, managers only have to identify the problem. Once the problem is clear, so is the procedure to handle it. In contrast to policies, procedures are more specific; like policies, they provide consistency. By defining the steps that are to be taken and the order in which they are to be done, procedures provide a standardized way of responding to repetitive problems.

Supervisors follow procedures set by higher levels of management and also create their own procedures for their staff to follow. As conditions change and new problems surface that tend to be recurring, supervisors will develop standardized procedures for handling them. When the service department of a local Chevrolet dealership began accepting credit cards for payment, the department's supervisor had to create a procedure for processing such transactions and then carefully teach each step of the new procedure to all the service agents and cashier personnel.

### RULES

**A rule** is an explicit statement that tells a supervisor what he or she ought or ought not to do. Rules are frequently used by supervisors when they confront a recurring problem because they are simple to follow and ensure consistency. In the illustration described in the previous section, the $6500 cutoff rule simplifies the purchasing supervisor's decision about when to use multiple bids. Similarly, rules about lateness and absenteeism permit supervisors to make discipline decisions rapidly and with a high degree of fairness.

## What Are Single-Use Plans?

In contrast to the previous discussions of standing plans, single-use plans are designed for a specific activity or time period. The most popular types of these plans are programs, budgets, and schedules.

### PROGRAMS

Lynn Haskel got the news at a meeting on Monday morning. His company—Northwest Airlines—was going to lay off a thousand employees. As the baggage-handling supervisor for Northwest's Minneapolis hub, he was told to put together a reorganization plan that would allow his department to operate effectively with as many as 20 percent fewer workers. What Lynn developed was a **program**—a single-use set of plans for a specific major undertaking within the organization's overall goals. It included a list of

**Procedure**
a standardized way of responding to repetitive problems; they define the limits within which managers must stay as decisions are made.

**Rule**
explicit statements that tell supervisors what they ought or ought not to do.

**Program**
a single-use set of plans for a specific major undertaking within an organization's overall goals. Programs may be designed and overseen by top management or supervisors.

the most expendable employees, plans for new equipment, plans for re-designing the handling area, and suggested options for jobs that could be potentially combined.

All managers develop programs. A major program—like building a new manufacturing plant or merging two companies and consolidating their headquarters' staff—will tend to be designed and overseen by top management. It may extend over several years and may even require its own set of policies and procedures. Supervisors also frequently have to create programs for their departments. Some examples include the departmental reorganization at Northwest Airlines, mentioned previously; the creation of a comprehensive ad campaign by an advertising account supervisor for a new client; or the development by a regional sales supervisor for Hallmark of a training program to teach her staff a new phone-activated, computerized inventory system. Note the common thread through all these examples: They are nonrecurring undertakings that required a set of integrated plans to accomplish their objectives.

## BUDGETS

**Budgets** are numerical plans. They typically express anticipated results in dollar terms for a specific time period. For example, a department may budget $8000 this year for travel. Budgets may also be calculated in non-dollar terms, for example, employee hours, capacity utilization, or units of production. Budget may cover daily, weekly, monthly, quarterly, semi-annual, or annual periods.

**Budgets**
numerical plans that express anticipated results in dollar terms for a specific time period. They may act as planning guides as well as control devices.

Budgets are covered here as part of the planning process. However, they are also control devices. The preparation of a budget involves planning because it gives direction. The creation of a budget tells what activities are important and how resources should be allocated to each activity. A budget becomes a control mechanism when it provides standards against which resource consumption can be measured and compared.

If there is one type of plan in which almost every manager gets involved, it's the budget. Supervisors typically prepare their department's expense budget and submit it to the manager at the next higher level for review and approval (see Exhibit 3–3). Supervisors may also, depending on their needs, create budgets for employee work hours, revenue forecasts, or for capital expenditures like machinery and equipment. Once approved by higher management, these budgets set specific standards for supervisors and their departmental personnel to achieve.

## SCHEDULES

If you were to observe a group of supervisors or department managers for a few days, you would see them regularly detailing what activities have to be done, the order in which they are to be done, who is to do each, and

EXHIBIT 3–3

Department expense
budget.

## Department Expense Budget
### Calendar Year 1998

| ITEM | QUARTER | | | |
|---|---|---|---|---|
| | 1ST | 2ND | 3RD | 4TH |
| Salaries/Fixed | $23,600 | $23,600 | $23,600 | $23,600 |
| Salaries/Variable | 3,000 | 5,000 | 3,000 | 10,000 |
| Performance Bonuses | | | | 12,000 |
| Office Supplies | 800 | 800 | 800 | 800 |
| Photocopying | 1,000 | 1,000 | 1,000 | 1,000 |
| Telephone | 2,500 | 2,500 | 2,500 | 2,500 |
| Mail | 800 | 800 | 800 | 800 |
| Travel | 2,500 | 1,000 | 1,000 | 1,000 |
| Employee Development | 600 | 600 | 600 | 600 |
| Total Quarterly Expenses | $34,800 | $35,300 | $33,300 | $52,300 |

**Scheduling**
detailed planning of
activities to be done,
the order in which
they are to be done,
who is to do each ac-
tivity, and when the
activities are to be
completed.

**Gantt chart**
a bar chart with time
on the horizontal axis
and activities to be
scheduled on the verti-
cal axis. The chart
shows when tasks are
supposed to be done
and compares actual
progress on each task.

when they are to be completed. These supervisors are performing an activity called **scheduling.** Debbie Starr, an advertising supervisor at Della Femina McNamee, in Pittsburgh, considers scheduling one of her three biggest
challenges: "Many projects pass by my desk, so trying to decide which
should be finished first is no small task."

Two popular scheduling techniques that can help you prioritize activities and complete work on time are the Gantt chart and the PERT chart.
The **Gantt chart** was developed early in this century by an industrial engineer named Henry Gantt. The idea was inherently simple but has proved
extremely helpful in scheduling work activities. The Gantt chart is essentially a bar graph with time on the horizontal axis and activities to be
scheduled on the vertical axis. The bars show output, both planned and actual, over a period of time. The Gantt chart visually shows when tasks are
supposed to be done and compares that to the actual progress on each. As
we stated, it is a simple but important device that allows managers to detail easily what has yet to be done to complete a job or project and to assess
whether it is ahead, behind, or on schedule.

Exhibit 3–4 depicts a simplified Gantt chart that was developed for
producing a book by a manager in a publishing firm. Time is expressed in
months across the top of the chart. The major activities are listed down the
left side. The planning comes in deciding what activities need to be done to
get the book finished, the order in which they need to be done, and the
time that should be allocated to each activity. Where a box sits within a
time frame reflects its planned sequence. The shading represents actual
progress. The chart also becomes a control device when the supervisor
looks for deviations from the plan.

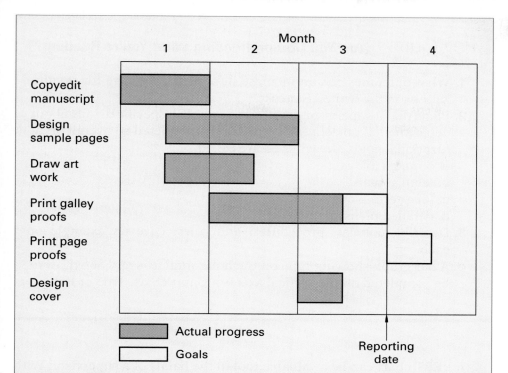

EXHIBIT 3–4
A sample Gantt chart.

Gantt charts are helpful as long as the activities being scheduled are few in number and independent of each other. But what if a supervisor had to plan a large project such as a departmental reorganization, the launching of a cost-reduction campaign, or the installation of a major piece of new equipment? Such projects often require coordinating hundreds of activities, some of which must be done simultaneously and some of which cannot begin until other activities have been completed. If you're constructing a building, for example, you obviously can't start erecting walls until the foundation is laid. How, then, can you schedule such a complex project? You could use a Program Evaluation and Review Technique (PERT) chart.

A **PERT chart** is a diagram that depicts the sequence of activities needed to complete a project and the time or costs associated with each activity. The PERT chart was originally developed in the late 1950s for coordinating the more than 3000 contractors and agencies working on the Polaris submarine weapon system.[13] This project was incredibly complicated, with hundreds of thousands of activities that had to be coordinated. PERT is reported to have cut two years off the completion date for the Polaris project.

**PERT chart**
a diagram that depicts the sequence of activities needed to complete a project and the time or costs associated with each activity.

[13]Cited in H. E. Fearon, *Fundamentals of Production/Operations Management*, 3rd Ed. (St. Paul, MN: West Publishing, 1986), p. 97.

1. What outcomes can an increase in productivity have for organizations in the United States?
2. Plans that a supervisor develops to establish specific details about departmental objectives that are to be completed so overall organizational goals are achieved are called
   a. strategic plans
   b. tactical plans
   c. long-term plans
   d. detailed plans
3. Describe policies, procedures, and rules. Give an example of each.
4. A bar graph showing time on the horizontal axis and activities to be completed on the vertical axis is a Gantt chart. True or False?

A PERT chart can be a valuable tool in the hands of a supervisor. With a PERT chart, a supervisor must think through what has to be done, determine which events depend on one another, and identify potential trouble spots. A PERT chart makes it easy to compare what effect alternative actions will have on scheduling and costs. Thus, PERT allows supervisors to monitor a project's progress, identify possible bottlenecks, and shift resources as necessary to keep the project on schedule.

To understand how to construct a PERT chart, you need to know three terms: *events, activities,* and *critical path.* Let's define these terms, outline the steps in the PERT process, and then work through an example.

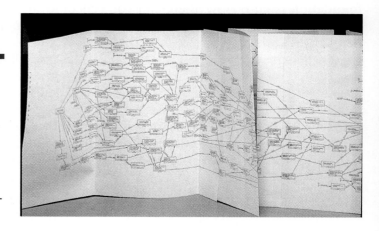

How are PERT charts used today? This photo shows a complex PERT chart used by the Grumman Corporation in the design and development of a missile system the company is working on for the U.S. Department of Defense.

**Events** are end points that represent the completion of major activities. **Activities** represent the time or resources required to progress from one event to another. The **critical path** is the longest or most time-consuming sequence of events and activities in a PERT chart.

Developing a PERT chart requires the supervisor to identify all key activities needed to complete a project, rank them in order of dependence, and estimate each activity's completion time. This can be translated into five specific steps:

1. Identify every significant activity that must be achieved for a project to be completed. The accomplishment of each activity results in a set of events or outcomes.
2. Determine the order in which these events must be completed.
3. Diagram the flow of activities from start to finish, identifying each activity and its relationship to all other activities. Use circles to indicate events and arrows to represent activities. This results in the diagram that we call the PERT chart.
4. Compute a time estimate for completing each activity.
5. Finally, using a PERT chart that contains time estimates for each activity, the supervisor can determine a schedule for the start and finish dates of each activity and for the entire project. Any delays that occur along the critical path require the most attention because they delay the entire project. That is, the critical path has no slack in it; therefore any delay along that path immediately translates into a delay in the final deadline for the completed project.

Now let's work through a simplified example. You're the production supervisor in the casting department at a Reynolds Metals aluminum mill in upstate New York. You have proposed and received approval from corporate management to replace one of three massive furnaces with a new, state-of-the-art, electronic furnace. This project will seriously disrupt the operations in your department, so you want to complete it as quickly and as smoothly as possible. You have carefully dissected the entire project into activities and events. Exhibit 3–5 outlines the major events in the furnace modernization project and your estimate of the expected time required to complete each activity. Exhibit 3–6 depicts the PERT chart based on the data in Exhibit 3–5.

Your PERT chart tells you that if everything goes as planned, it will take 21 weeks to complete the modernization program. This is calculated by tracing the chart's critical path: A-C-D-G-H-J-K. Any delay in completing the events along this path will delay the completion of the entire project. For example, if it took six weeks instead of four to get construction permits (event B), this would have no effect on the final

**Events**
end points that represent completion of major activities.

**Activities**
the time or resources required to progress from one event to another.

**Critical path**
the longest or most time-consuming sequence of events and activities in a PERT chart.

EXHIBIT 3–5

Data for the furnace modernization project.

| Event | Description | Expected Time (in weeks) | Preceding Event |
|-------|-------------|--------------------------|-----------------|
| A | Approve design | 8 | None |
| B | Get construction permits | 4 | None |
| C | Take bids on new furnace and its installation | 6 | A |
| D | Order new furnace and equipment | 1 | C |
| E | Remove old furnace | 2 | B |
| F | Prepare site | 3 | E |
| G | Install new furnace | 2 | D,F |
| H | Test new furnace | 1 | G |
| I | Train workers to handle new furnace | 2 | G |
| J | Final inspection by company and city officials | 2 | H |
| K | Bring furnace on-line into production flow | 1 | I,J |

completion date. Why? Because Start-B + B-E + E-F + F-G equals only eleven weeks, while Start-A + A-C + C-D + D-G equals seventeen weeks. However, if you wanted to cut the 21-week time frame, you would give attention to those activities along the critical path that could be speeded up.

## EXHIBIT 3–6

A PERT chart.

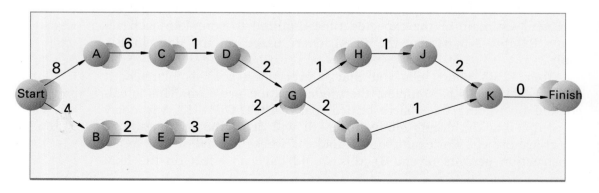

# MANAGEMENT BY OBJECTIVES

Many well-managed contemporary organizations use **management by objectives (MBO).** This is a system in which employees jointly determine specific performance objectives with their supervisors. Progress toward objectives is periodically reviewed, and rewards are allocated on the basis of this progress. Rather than using goals to control, MBO uses them to motivate people.

MBO makes objectives operational by devising a process by which they cascade down through the organization. The organization's overall objectives are translated into specific objectives for each succeeding level (for example, divisional, departmental, individual) in the organization. Because lower-unit managers jointly participate in setting their own goals, MBO works from the "bottom up" as well as the "top down" (see News Flash). The result is a hierarchy that links objectives at one level to those at the next level.

**Management by objectives (MBO)** a system by which employees jointly determine specific performance objectives with their supervisors, progress toward objectives is periodically reviewed, and rewards are allocated on the basis of this progress.

## SUPERVISORS AND TRADITIONAL GOAL SETTING

The traditional role of objectives in organizations was one of control imposed by top management. The president of a manufacturing firm would typically tell the production vice president what he expected manufacturing costs to be for the coming year. The president would tell the marketing vice president what level he expected sales to reach for the coming year. The plant manager would tell her maintenance supervisor how much his departmental budget would be. Then, at some later point, performance was evaluated to determine whether the assigned objectives had been achieved.

The central theme in traditional objective-setting was that objectives were set at the top and then broken down into subgoals for each level in the organization. It was a one-way process: The top imposed its standards on everyone below. This traditional perspective assumed that top management knew what was best because only it could see the "big picture."

In addition to being imposed from above, traditional objective-setting was often largely nonoperational. If top management defined the organization's objectives in broad terms such as achieving "sufficient profits" or "market leadership," these ambiguities had to be turned into specifics as the objectives filtered

*(con't)*

*(cont'd)*

down through the organization. At each level, managers would supply their own meaning to the goals. Specificity was achieved by each manager applying his or her own set of interpretations and biases. As shown in Exhibit 3–7, the result was that objectives lost clarity and unity as they made their way down from the top.

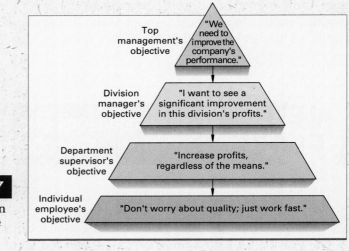

Top management's objective — "We need to improve the company's performance."

Division manager's objective — "I want to see a significant improvement in this division's profits."

Department supervisor's objective — "Increase profits, regardless of the means."

Individual employee's objective — "Don't worry about quality; just work fast."

### EXHIBIT 3–7

What may happen in traditional objective setting.

## WHAT IS THE KEY TO MAKING MBO EFFECTIVE?

There are four ingredients common to MBO programs. These are goal specificity, participative decision making, an explicit time period, and performance feedback. Let's look at each of these

### GOAL SPECIFICITY

The objectives in MBO should be specific statements of expected accomplishments. It's not adequate, for example, merely to state a desire to cut costs, improve service, or increase quality. Such desires have to be converted into tangible objectives that can be measured and evaluated. To cut departmental costs by seven percent, to improve service by ensuring that all telephone orders are processed within twenty-four hours of receipt, or to increase quality by keeping returns to less than one percent of sales are examples of specific objectives.

## PARTICIPATION

In MBO the objectives are not unilaterally set by the boss and assigned to employees, as was characteristic of traditional objective setting. Instead, MBO replaces these imposed goals with jointly determined goals. Together, the supervisor and employee choose the goals and agree on how they will be achieved and evaluated (see Building a Supervisory Skill).

## TIME LIMITS

Each objective has a concise time period in which it is to be completed. Typically, the time period is three months, six months, or a year. So, not only does everyone have specific objectives, but also a specific time period in which to accomplish them.

## PERFORMANCE FEEDBACK

The final ingredient in an MBO program is feedback on performance. MBO seeks to give continuous feedback on progress toward goals. Ideally, this is accomplished by ongoing feedback to individuals so they can monitor and correct their own actions. This is supplemented by periodic formal appraisal meetings in which supervisors and employees can review progress toward goals and further feedback can be provided.

Cheryl Munro Sharp, of London Life, participates with her boss in setting her department's goals. Goals are set on an annual basis, but she says, "We assess the major projects about once a month, just to make sure that we still agree on which projects take priority over others." In MBO terms, that's called ongoing feedback!

# BUILDING A SUPERVISORY SKILL

## SETTING GOALS

### ABOUT THE SKILL

We want to take the basic concepts of MBO and turn them into specific goal-setting skills that you can apply on the job. Effective goal-setting skills can be condensed to eight specific behaviors. When you follow all eight you will have mastered the skill of goal setting.

1. **Identify an employee's key job tasks.** Goal setting begins by defining what it is that you want your employees to accom-

plish. The best source for this information is each employee's up-to-date job description, if one is available. It details what task an employee is expected to perform, how these tasks are to be done, what outcomes the employee is responsible for achieving, and the like.

2. **Establish specific and challenging goals for each task.** This is self-explanatory. We should add that, if possible, these goals should be made public. When employees' goals are made public—announced in a group or posted for others to see—they seem to be more highly committed to them.

3. **Specify deadlines for each goal.** Again, as previously discussed, goals should include a specific time limit for accomplishment.

4. **Allow the employee to actively participate.** Employees are less likely to question or resist a process in which they actively participate than one that is imposed upon them from above.

5. **Prioritize goals.** When someone is given more than one goal, it is important to rank the goals in order of importance. The purpose of this step is to encourage the employee to take action and expend effort on each goal in proportion to its importance.

6. **Rate goals for difficulty and importance.** Goal setting should not encourage people to choose easy goals in order to ensure success. So goal setting needs to take into account the difficulty of the goals selected and whether individuals are emphasizing the right goals. When these ratings are combined with the actual level of goal achievement, you will have a more comprehensive assessment of overall goal performance. This procedure gives credit to individuals for trying difficult goals even if they don't fully achieve them.

7. **Build in feedback mechanisms to assess goal progress.** Ideally, feedback on goal progress should be self-generated rather than provided externally. When an employee is able to monitor his or her own progress, the feedback is less threatening and less likely to be perceived as part of a management control system.

8. **Commit rewards contingent on goal attainment.** Offering money, promotions, recognition, time off, or similar rewards to employees contingent on goal achievement is a powerful means to increase goal commitment. When the going gets tough on the road toward meeting a goal, people are prone to ask themselves, "What's in it for me?" Linking rewards to the achievement of goals helps employees to answer this question. ■

## WHY MIGHT MBO WORK FOR YOU?

There are several reasons why MBO works, and why it can help you be a more effective supervisor. First, it gives both you and your employees clarity and direction in your jobs. Your employees will know what's important to you in their jobs—and the specific outcomes by which their performance will be judged. Second, MBO increases your employees' involvement, commitment, and motivation. They'll feel more empowered because they will have the freedom to choose the means for achieving their objectives. That is, it's the goals that are important to you. How they do it is not the focal point. Additionally, providing regular feedback on their performance and tying rewards to the achievement of objectives acts to stimulate employee motivation. Finally, MBO can minimize the politics in performance appraisals and reward allocations. Subjective factors—like an employee's effort and attitude, or your prejudices—are replaced by objective measures of performance and rewards based on that performance.

# ASSESSING YOURSELF

## ARE YOU A GOOD GOAL SETTER?

For each of the following questions, check the answer that best describes your relationship with others—whether they are employees or others with whom you interact. Remember to respond as you have behaved or would behave, not as you think you should behave.

When I lead a project involving work of several individuals, others working with me have:

|  | *Usually* | *Sometimes* | *Seldom* |
|---|:---:|:---:|:---:|
| **1.** Specific and clear goals. | ○ | ○ | ○ |
| **2.** Goals for all key areas relating to their work. | ○ | ○ | ○ |
| **3.** Challenging but reasonable goals—work that is neither too hard nor too easy. | ○ | ○ | ○ |
| **4.** The opportunity to participate in setting their work efforts. | ○ | ○ | ○ |
| **5.** A say in deciding how to implement their goals. | ○ | ○ | ○ |
| **6.** Deadlines for getting their work done. | ○ | ○ | ○ |
| **7.** Sufficient skills and training to do their work. | ○ | ○ | ○ |
| **8.** Sufficient resources (i.e., time, money, equipment) to get their work done. | ○ | ○ | ○ |

*(continued)*

|  | Usually | Sometimes | Seldom |
|---|---|---|---|
| **9.** Feedback on how well they are progressing toward their goals. | ○ | ○ | ○ |
| **10.** Rewards (i.e., recognition, pay, promotions) given to them according to how well they do their jobs. | ○ | ○ | ○ |

## SCORING

For all questions, give yourself 3 points for "Usually," 2 points for "Sometimes," and 1 point for "Seldom." Sum up your total points. Scores of 26 or higher demonstrate a strong understanding of goal-setting techniques. A score of 21 to 25 indicates you can improve your goal-setting skills. Scores of 20 or less suggest that you have significant room for improvement.

## POP QUIZ  (Are You Comprehending What You're Reading?)

**5.** When would a PERT chart NOT provide much help?
  **a.** when sequencing is important
  **b.** for complicated jobs
  **c.** for independent projects
  **d.** for jobs with many steps involved
**6.** How does MBO assist in answering the question "What's in it for me?"
**7.** According to the philosophy of MBO,
  **a.** feedback occurs at the annual performance review
  **b.** goals follow a "top-down" approach
  **c.** goals typically are broad, general statements of intent
  **d.** constant feedback is provided
**8.** Goal setting should encourage employees to set easy goals so that their success can be assured. True or False?

## SUMMARY

After reading this chapter, I can:

1. **Define productivity.** Productivity is a relationship between outputs achieved and the inputs used in developing the outputs.

2. **Describe how plans should link from the top to the bottom of an organization.** Long-term strategic plans are set by top management. Then, each succeeding level down the organization develops its plans. Plans at each level should help to accomplish those for the level above and give direction for the level below.

3. **Contrast policies and rules.** Policies and rules are both standing plans. Policies are broad and leave room for managerial discretion, while rules are explicit statements that allow no discretion.

4. **Describe the Gantt chart.** The Gantt chart is a simple scheduling device. It is a bar graph with time on the horizontal axis and activities on the vertical axis. It shows planned and actual activities, and it allows supervisors to easily identify the status of a job or project.

5. **Explain the information needed to create a PERT chart.** To create a PERT chart, you need to identify all key activities needed to complete a project, their order of dependence, and an estimate of each activity's completion time.

6. **Describe the four ingredients common to MBO programs.** Four ingredients common to MBO programs are goal specificity, participative decision making, an explicit time period, and performance feedback.

## REVIEWING YOUR KNOWLEDGE

1. Why is productivity so important to organizations and their members?
2. Contrast the planning top managers do with that done by supervisors.
3. Explain how budgets are both a planning and a control device.
4. How might you use a Gantt chart to schedule a group term paper for a college class?
5. What are the implications of the critical path for PERT analysis?
6. Why has MBO proved so popular in organizations?

## ANSWERS TO THE POP QUIZ

1. Several outcomes can accrue to organizations, and to an entire economy, when productivity increases. Among them are creation of jobs, job security for employees, and support of research and development efforts to further productivity gains.

2. **b. tactical plans.** This is the definition of tactical plans and the distinction between strategic and tactical plans.

3. Policies are broad guidelines for managerial action. Typically established by top management, they define the limits within which managers must stay as they make decisions. For example, a policy might state that a supervisor can "sign-off" on purchases under $6500. A procedure defines the steps that are to be taken and the order in which they are to be done. They provide a standardized way of responding to repetitive problems. An example of a procedure would be the steps that supervisors are expected to follow when establish-

ing, completing, and submitting their unit's budget for the coming year. A rule is an explicit statement that tells a supervisor what he or she ought or ought not to do. An example of a rule would be an organization's statements about not permitting scrap materials to be taken home by employees.

4. **True.** This is the definition of a Gantt chart.

5. **c. for independent projects.** For a PERT chart to be effective, there must be interdependency, or relatedness of activities. If the activities are independent, no relationship exists among them. Accordingly, a PERT chart would not help in this situation.

6. MBO assists in answering the question "What's in it for me?" by showing the linkage of goal achievement and rewards. That is, money, promotions, recognition, time off, or similar rewards an employee receives is dependent on his or her meeting established work expectations.

7. **d. constant feedback is provided.** For MBO to function effectively, feedback must be continuous.

8. **False.** Setting easy goals defeats the purpose of goal setting. Instead, challenging goals should be set. The level of difficulty needs to be taken into account when reviewing/evaluating an employee's performance. ■

## A CLASS EXERCISE: SETTING GOALS

This is a role-play exercise. Break into groups of four to six students. One student in each group will assume the role of Lee, and one will assume the role of Whitney. The other students will serve as observers and evaluators.

Kelly Hobbs has recently been promoted to the position of operations supervisor at one of the largest branches of State Bank of New Hampshire. Her staff includes three project leaders, who report directly to her, and another 35 or so employees who work on these projects. One of these project leaders is responsible for directing the 15 tellers, while the other two direct customer relations and the computer functions. Kelly reports to the bank manager who, in turn, reports to the State Bank of New Hampshire's president.

Kelly has suggested to all three project leaders that they establish goals for themselves and their employees.

Lee Gordon, who is responsible for the tellers, has set up a meeting with the most senior teller, Whitney Millan, to begin the goal-setting process.

The objective of this exercise is to end up with a set of goals for Whitney. They might address issues such as prompt attention to customer needs, showing courtesy to customers, selling bank services like Christmas Club accounts and money market funds, keeping the cash drawer in balance, or taking bank-sponsored courses to improve skills.

This exercise should take no more than 15 minutes. When completed, the observers from each group should discuss with the entire class how their goal-setting session went. Focus specifically on the Building a Supervisory Skill section presented on pages 99–100 and any problems that surfaced.

## THINKING CRITICALLY

### CASE 3.A

## MBO in the U.S. Postal Service

Working for the U. S. Postal Service in Washington, D. C. is a new experience for Reginald Martin. When Reggie first started working for the Postal Service three years ago, he worked in a small Glyndon, Maryland office where he did nearly every job imaginable—from selling stamps and servicing postage meters at the counter to sorting letters and packages in the backroom. He knew all the postal office workers in Glyndon—including all the mail carriers!

In Washington, D.C., he has found that his job is much more specialized, but he will have the opportunity for career mobility and maybe even to become a supervisor. His supervisor, Chris McCafferty, has given Reggie a lot of support. Ms. McCafferty told him how important it is to learn about himself—what he likes to do, how he accomplishes work, and why he values certain things. Chris seems genuinely interested in her employees' professional growth and development and has implemented a Management By Objective program for her unit. In fact, Chris and Reggie will be sitting down next week to work out a personal and professional development plan that Reggie will follow during the next year.

Reggie is not exactly sure what the outcome of the meeting will be, but he is excited about setting some goals that will help him advance in his job. As a result of this new focus, he is beginning to give a lot of thought to what he wants out of life and how his immediate supervisor can help him achieve some of his goals.

## RESPONDING TO THE CASE

1. Outline the specific steps Ms. McCafferty should follow with Reggie to assure the MBO process works well.
2. As a good supervisor, what advice should Chris give to Reggie prior to the meeting?
3. What do you believe Reggie can expect to happen during the meeting and afterwards?
4. Divide into groups of three. Role play the meeting with one person playing the role of Ms. McCafferty, a second person playing the role of Reggie, and the third person recording observations. Share results, first by the observer, then Reggie, and finally Chris. From this exercise, what conclusions did you draw about the MBO process.

## CASE 3.B

### Using Plans at Sir Speedy Printing Services

Barry Williams has worked for Sir Speedy for five years. He now supervises five full-time employees and as many as 20 part-time employees who work from 2 to 15 hours a week. Sir Speedy is planning a promotion to bring more customers into the store during August, typically their slowest month of the year. The store will offer copying services at half price, 20 per-

cent off on all color copying and business card printing, and 10 percent off on custom printing on specialty paper or card stock. To promote the use of several of their computer graphics and desktop applications, the store will give 30 minutes free time to customers who purchase 30 minutes of desktop computer time.

The August promotion also will focus on creative ways to use color copiers and customized computer desktop applications. Barry plans to have his employees give short, creative demonstrations of color applications and software use. He decides that seven-minute demonstrations, repeated every 15 minutes, will be the best way to interest customers entering the store. With this schedule, Barry can run three different color applications each hour during his four-day promotion. He will also have eight different software application demonstrations during a two-hour period. In addition there are two touch-screen computers with five-minute general products videos from Sir Speedy that he can set up in strategic locations for customers to access at any time.

Seven of his part-time employees have been trained on the various applications; however, their schedules vary. Five of these part-time employees work 15 hours a week and the other two work 10 hours a week. The store's busiest hours are 11 A.M. to 1 P.M., 4 P.M. to 6 P.M., and 7:30 P.M. to 8:30 P.M. Barry thinks he will need at least three people to give demonstrations during these peak times.

Scheduling his employees to cover the demonstrations is a challenge. Barry knows that he will need some flexibility because of their availability, but he also knows that it would not be good to have the same person give more than three or four of the eight different software demonstrations. Also, he will need employees for store coverage.

## RESPONDING TO THE CASE

1. List and briefly describe several planning elements that Barry needs to consider in setting up his store promotion.
2. In planning Barry's promotion schedule:
   a. Identify the number of workers he will need during peak periods to cover the demonstrations.
   b. Determine the schedules each worker will have and what demonstrations each will be giving.
   c. Modify your list in question one as you find other areas which are important to the success of the promotion.
3. What alterations to Barry's original plan might be considered, now that you have looked at available workers and schedules?
4. What other elements are important to Barry in planning his promotion? Are there factors which have not been considered in his plan? If so, what are they? ■

# 4

# DESIGNING
# AND IMPLEMENTING
# CONTROLS

# LEARNING OBJECTIVES 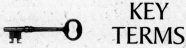 KEY TERMS

After reading this chapter, you should be able to:

1. Describe the control process.
2. Contrast two types of corrective action.
3. Compare preventive, concurrent, and corrective control.
4. Explain how a supervisor can reduce costs.
5. List the characteristics of an effective control system.
6. Explain potential negatives that controls can create.

You should also be able to define these supervisory terms:

basic corrective action

cause-effect diagrams

concurrent control

control process

control charts

control by exception

corrective control

flow charts

immediate corrective action

incident rate

just-in-time inventory systems

kanban

Occupational Safety and Health Act (OSHA)

preventive control

quality control

range of variation

scatter diagrams

# PERFORMING EFFECTIVELY

In the mid-1970s, America was going wild over motorcycles. Harley-Davidson, then owned by AMF Corp., responded by nearly tripling production to 75,000 units annually over a four-year period.[1] Along with this growth, however, came problems. Engineering and design of Harleys became dated. Quality deteriorated so much that more than half the cycles coming off the assembly line had missing parts, and dealers had to fix them before they could be sold. Harleys leaked oil, vibrated badly, and couldn't match the performance of the flawlessly built Japanese bikes. Hardcore Harley enthusiasts were willing to tolerate these inconveniences, but newcomers had no such devotion and bought Japanese bikes.

In 1973 Harley had 75 percent of the super-heavyweight market. By 1980 its market share had plummeted to less than 25 percent. AMF was fast losing confidence in Harley and sold the company in 1981.

Harley's new owner and supervisors worked together to introduce a number of new products, redesign and update the basic product line, and greatly improve the company's marketing programs. These actions would not have meant much if Harley hadn't also dramatically revised its pro-

## INTRODUCTION

You've completed your planning. You know your own department's objectives, and you've jointly set specific job objectives with all the people that report to you. Standing plans are in place. So, too, are your department's budgets and important schedules. Your next concern should be: how will I know if all my plans are being achieved? You won't, unless you've also developed controls!

As described in Chapter 1, controlling is the management function concerned with monitoring activities to ensure that they are being accomplished as planned and correcting any significant deviations. In this chapter, we want to show you how effective supervisors perform the controlling function. Specifically, we'll detail the control process, discuss the timing of controls, identify the major areas where supervisors concentrate their con-

[1]Based on "Harley Hogs the Spotlight," *Small Business Reports,* November 1994, p. 58; B. S. Moskal, "Born to Be Real," *Industry Week,* August 2, 1993, p. 58; "On the Road Again," ABC News 20/20, January 25, 1991; and "How Harley Beat Back the Japanese, *Fortune,* September 25, 1989, pp. 155–164.

duction and operations practices. The new supervisors visited Honda's assembly plant in Marysville, Ohio and realized what they were up against. In response, they initiated a number of changes on Harley's production floor. A new inventory system was introduced that eliminated mountains of costly inventory parts. They redesigned the entire production system, closely involving employees in planning and working out the details. Workers were taught statistical techniques for monitoring and controlling the quality of their own work. Supervisors even worked with the company's suppliers—as has long been done by Japanese manufacturers—to help them adopt the same efficiency and quality-improvement techniques that Harley had instituted in its plants.

Harley succeeded in pulling off one of America's most celebrated turnarounds. On the verge of bankruptcy in the early 1980s, ten years later Harley's share of the U.S. super-heavyweight market was almost 65 percent. The company was losing money in 1982, but now is highly profitable, thanks, in part, to well designed controls! ∎

trol activity, and describe the characteristics of effective controls. We'll also discuss some of the potentially undesirable side effects of controls that supervisors need to be on guard against.

## THE CONTROL PROCESS

The **control process** consists of three separate and distinct steps: (1) measure actual performance; (2) compare results with standards; and (3) take corrective action (see Exhibit 4–1). Before we discuss each of these steps, you should be aware that the control process assumes that standards of performance already exist. These standards are actually detailed in specific goals that you created in planning. So, planning must precede application of the control process.

If management by objectives is used, the MBO-derived objectives become the standards against which actual performance is compared. This is because MBO integrates planning and control by providing managers with a set of objectives or standards to be attained. If MBO is not practiced, then standards are the specific performance indicators that you use for

Control process
a three-step process that consists of: (1) measuring actual performance; (2) comparing results with standards; and (3) taking corrective action.

## EXHIBIT 4–1

The control process.

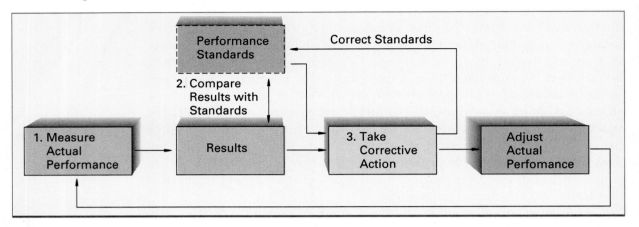

equipment utilization, resource usage, quality, employee productivity, and the like. These standards can be applied to individuals, teams, departments, or the entire organization. Some examples of popular performance standards include percent of plant capacity, number of units produced per work hour, average amount of scrap per unit produced, lost work days due to injuries, absence rates, return on investment, cost per unit sold, returns as a percent of sales, and total dollar sales per sales territory.

## HOW DO YOU MEASURE ACTUAL PERFORMANCE?

To determine what actual performance is, it is necessary to acquire information about it. The first step in control, then, is measuring. Let's consider both how we measure and what we measure.

### WAYS YOU MEASURE

Four common sources of information, used by supervisors to measure actual performance, are personal observation, statistical reports, oral reports, and written reports.

*Personal observation* provides firsthand, intimate knowledge of the actual activity. As such, it is probably the most widely used means by which supervisors assess actual performance. In fact, it has even acquired its own label—MBWA or Management by Walking Around. It permits intensive coverage, since minor as well as major performance activities can be observed. It also provides opportunities for the supervisor to "read between the lines." Personal observation can pick up verbal omissions, facial expressions, and tones of voice that may be missed by other methods.

This Tenneco Packaging Paper Mill supervisor is collecting data through the personal observation method. By walking around the plant facility, he's able to capture data that is used to keep his unit on track. Through his efforts, on-time paper product deliveries in his department have increased from 63 percent in 1991 to more than 91 percent in 1995.

The current wide use of computers in organizations has led to supervisors increasingly relying on *statistical reports* for measuring actual performance. This measuring device, however, is not limited to computer outputs. It also includes graphs, bar charts, and numerical displays of any form that supervisors may use for assessing performance.

Information can also be acquired through *oral reports,* that is, through conferences, meetings, and one-to-one conversations. The advantages of oral reports are that they are fast, allow for feedback, and permit language expression and tone of voice, as well as words themselves, to convey meaning.

Finally, actual performance can be measured by *written reports.* The strength of written reports is that they offer greater comprehensiveness and conciseness than is typically found in oral reports. They are also easier to catalog and reference. Written reports are often combined with statistical reports. They may also be used to precede or follow up oral reports.

## WHAT YOU MEASURE

What you measure is probably more critical to the control process than how you measure it. The selection of the wrong criteria can result in serious dysfunctional consequences (which we'll discuss later in this chapter). More importantly, what you measure determines, to a great extent, what employees will attempt to emphasize. For instance, suppose you're a supervisor in the accounting department of a large health-maintenance organization. You expect office staff to be at work at 8 A.M. Every morning, at precisely eight o'clock, you walk around the office to make sure everyone is in. What you typically find are purses and lunch bags on desks, open briefcases, coats over backs of chairs, and other physical evidence that your employees have arrived. But most of them are down in the cafeteria having coffee. Your employees make sure that they are at the office by 8 A.M., because you have a

## TOP-DOWN VERSUS BOTTOM UP BUDGETING

Where do budgets originate? For many traditional organizations, the answer points to one technique—top management tells organization members what their budgets will be!

Top-down budgeting originates at the upper-levels of the organization. Budgets are initiated, controlled, and directed by top management. This approach assumes top management is best able to allocate resources among alternative uses within the organization. These budgets are then given to middle-level and first-line supervisors whose responsibilities are to carry them out. This method has the advantage of simplifying the budgeting process and focusing attention on the organization's overall goals. However, the top-down approach has some huge disadvantages. It assumes that top management has comprehensive data on all activities within the organization. This assumption is rarely valid, especially in relatively large organizations. Since operating personnel and supervisors generally have no

input into their budgets, the top-down approach also does nothing to build support and commitment for budgets.

Many organizations today have moved to bottom-up budgeting where the initial budget requests are prepared by those who must implement them. Then they're sent up for approval to higher levels of management where modifications may be suggested. When differences occur, they're negotiated, and the process is followed upward until an organization-wide budget is developed. Essentially the bottom-up approach to budgeting has the opposite advantages and disadvantages of those initiated from the top. Because supervisors and other lower-level managers are more knowledgeable about their needs than are managers at the top, they are less likely to overlook important funding requirements. Supervisors are also much more likely to enthusiastically accept and try to meet budgets they have had a hand in shaping.

communication that this is an important control criterion. However, checking to make sure they're in doesn't mean that they're actually working.

Keep in mind that some control criteria are applicable to most supervisory situations while others are job specific. For instance, since all supervisors direct the activities of others, criteria such as employee satisfaction or absenteeism rates have universal application. Almost all supervisors also have budgets for their area of responsibility set in dollar costs (see News Flash). Keeping costs within budget, therefore, is a fairly common control measure. However, control criteria need to recognize the diversity of activities among supervisors. A production supervisor in a manufacturing plant might use measures of the quantity of units produced per day, units produced per labor hour, scrap per unit of output, or percent of rejects returned by customers. The supervisor of an administrative unit in a government agency might use number of document pages processed per day, number of orders processed per hour, or average time required to process service calls. Sales supervisors often use measures such as percent of market captured in a given territory, average dollar value per sale, or number of customer visits per salesperson. The key is that what you measure must be adjusted to fit the goals of your department.

## HOW DO YOU COMPARE RESULTS WITH STANDARDS?

The comparing step determines the degree of variation between actual performance and the standard. Some variation in performance can be expected in all activities; it is therefore critical to determine the acceptable **range of variation**.

Range of variation
variation in performance that can be expected in all activities.

### DETERMINING ACCEPTABLE RANGES

Deviations in excess of the acceptable range become significant and receive the supervisor's attention. In this comparison stage, you need to be concerned with the size and direction of the variation. An example should make this clearer.

Robin Coleson is the sales supervisor at Mueller Mercedes-Porsche in northern New Jersey. Robin prepares a report during the first week of each month that describes sales for the previous month, classified by model. Exhibit 4–2 displays both the standard (goal) and actual sales figures for the month in review.

Should Robin be concerned with the July performance? If he focused only on Mercedes' unit sales and Porsche's average dollar sales, the answer would be *No*. But there appears to be some significant deviations. Average sales prices on Mercedes were far below projection. A closer look at Exhibit 4–2 offers an explanation. The higher-priced "S" series cars weren't selling, while the lower-priced "C" and "E" series did better than expected. On the Porsche side, almost every model had disappointing sales.

EXHIBIT 4–2

Mueller Mercedes Porsche sales performance for July.

| Model | Goal | Actual | Over (under) |
|---|---|---|---|
| **Mercedes** | | | |
| C220 | 2 | 3 | 1 |
| C280 | 4 | 7 | 3 |
| E320 | 6 | 11 | 5 |
| E320C | 1 | 0 | (<1>) |
| E420 | 3 | 5 | (2) |
| S320 | 2 | 3 | (1) |
| S420 | 5 | 3 | (<2>) |
| S500 | 2 | 0 | (<2>) |
| S600 | 1 | 0 | (<1>) |
| SL320 | 2 | 1 | (<1>) |
| SL500 | 2 | 1 | (<1>) |
| Total units | 30 | 34 | |
| Total sales $ | 1,962,000 | 1,686,000 | |
| Average sales $ | 65,400 | 49,586 | |
| **Porsche** | | | |
| Carrera 2 Coupe | 4 | 2 | (2) |
| Carrera 2 Targa | 1 | 1 | - |
| Carrera 2 Cabriolet | 3 | 2 | (1) |
| Carrera 4 Coupe | 1 | 0 | (1) |
| 928 Coupe | 2 | 0 | (2) |
| 968 Coupe | 4 | 1 | (3) |
| 968 Cabriolet | 3 | 1 | (2) |
| Total units | 18 | 7 | |
| Total sales $ | 1,055,000 | 515,000 | |
| Average sales $ | 58,611 | 59,286 | |

Which performance deviations deserve Robin's attention? This depends on what Robin and his boss believe to be significant. How much tolerance should be allowed before corrective action is taken? The deviation on several models is very small and undoubtedly not worthy of special attention, for example, models where actual and standard were off by only one car. The shortages for the Mercedes S420 and S500 and Porsche Carrera 2, and 928 and 968 Coupes or the 968 Cabriolet may be more significant. That's a judgment Robin must make.

By the way, an error in understating sales can be as troublesome as an overstatement. For instance, are the strong sales for the Mercedes C and E models a one-month abnormality, or are these models increasing in popularity? Robin has concluded that the northern New Jersey economy is to blame. With some uncertainty about the economy and their job security, people appear to be moving to less expensive models. Reflecting national recessionary trends, sales of Porsche cars are down across the board. This example illustrates that both overvariance and undervariance may require corrective action.

Control is an important part of Mueller Mercedes-Porsche in northern New Jersey. Without it, sales supervisor Robin Coleson would have difficulty determining which car models are selling, and which ones are not. Armed with this information, Robin can determine what needs to be done to keep his department on track for reaching its goals.

## SOME SPECIAL MEASUREMENT TOOLS

Any discussion of how you measure would be incomplete without a discussion of the basic statistical techniques used to control variability. In this section, we'll describe the more popular statistical process control techniques.

*Cause and Effect Diagrams.* **Cause-effect diagrams** (also sometimes called fish-bone diagrams) are used to depict the causes of a certain problem and to group the causes according to common categories such as machinery, materials, methods, personnel, finances, or management.

As shown in Exhibit 4–3, these diagrams look somewhat like a fish bone, with the problem—the effect—defined as the head. On the "bones,"

**Cause-effect diagrams** diagrams used to depict the causes of a problem and to group them according to common categories such as machinery, methods, personnel, finances, or management.

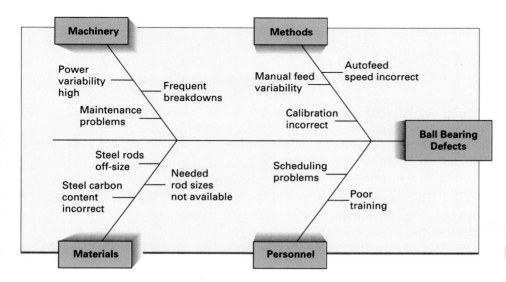

**EXHIBIT 4–3**

Example of a fish-bone diagram.

**Flow charts**
visual representations
of the sequence of
events for a particular
process that clarify
how things are being
done so inefficiencies
can be identified and
the process improved.

**Scatter diagrams**
diagrams that illus-
trate the relationship
between two variables
by visually depicting
correlations and possi-
ble cause-and-effect.

growing out of the "spine," are the possible causes of production problems. They're listed in order of possible occurrence. Cause-effect diagrams
provide guidance for analyzing the influence alternative courses of action
will have on a given problem.

*Flow Charts.* **Flow charts** are visual representations of the sequence of
events for a particular process. They clarify exactly how things are being
done so inefficiencies can be identified and the process improved. Exhibit
4–4 provides an illustration.

*Scatter Diagrams.* **Scatter diagrams** illustrate the relationship between
two variables such as height and weight or the hardness of a ball bearing

**EXAMPLE 4–4**

Example of a flow chart.
(Reprinted with permission of
the publisher. From *Putting
Total Quality Management to
Work*, p. 177, copyright © 1993
by Marshall Sashkin and Ken-
neth J. Kiser, Berrett-Koehler
Publishers, Inc., San Francisco,
CA. All rights reserved.)

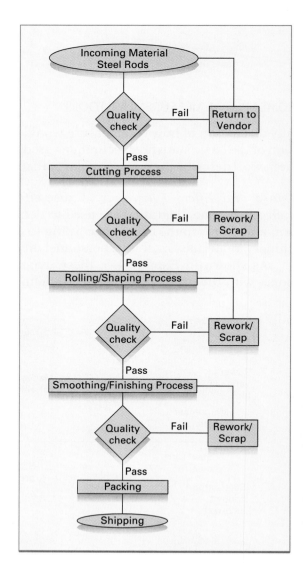

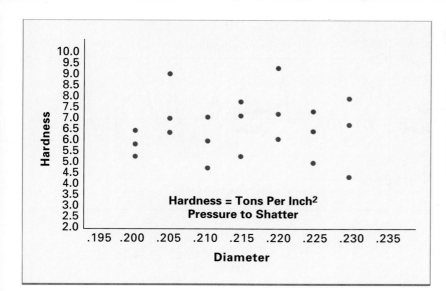

**EXHIBIT 4–5**

Example of a scatter diagram. (Reprinted with permission of the publisher. From *Putting Total Quality Management to Work*, p. 176, copyright © 1993 by Marshall Sashkin and Kenneth J. Kiser, Berrett-Koehler Publishers, Inc., San Francisco, CA. All rights reserved.)

and its diameter (see Exhibit 4–5). These diagrams visually depict correlations and possible cause-and-effect. So, for instance, a scatter diagram could reveal that the percentage of rejects increases as the size of production runs increase. This, in turn, might suggest the need to reduce production runs or reevaluate the process if quality is to be improved.

*Control Charts.* **Control charts** are the most sophisticated of the statistical techniques we'll describe. They are used to reflect variation in a system. Control charts reflect measurements of sample products averaged with statistically determined upper and lower limits. For instance, Coca Cola samples its one-liter bottles, after they're filled, to determine their exact quantity. This data is plotted on a control chart. It tells management when the filling equipment needs adjustment. As long as the process variables fall within the acceptable range, the system is said to be "in control" (see Exhibit 4–6). When a point falls outside the limits set, then the variation is unacceptable. Improvements in quality should, over time, result in a narrowing of the range between the upper and lower limits through elimination of common causes.

Control charts
run charts of sample averages with statistically determined upper and lower limits.

## WHEN SHOULD CORRECTIVE ACTION BE TAKEN?

The third and final step in the control process is the action that will correct the deviation. It will be an attempt either to adjust actual performance or to correct the standard, or both (refer back to Exhibit 4–1).

There are two distinct types of corrective action. One is immediate and deals predominantly with symptoms. The other is basic and delves into the

## EXHIBIT 4–6

Example of a control chart. (Reprinted with permission of the publisher. From *Putting Total Quality Management to Work*, p. 170, copyright © 1993 by Marshall Sashkin and Kenneth J. Kiser, Berrett-Koehler Publishers, Inc., San Francisco, CA. All rights reserved.)

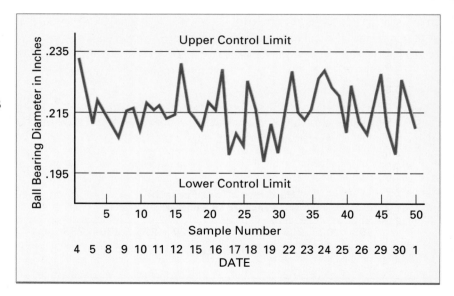

→ **Immediate corrective action**
action that adjusts something right now and gets things back on track.

→ **Basic corrective action**
action that asks how and why performance deviated.

causes. **Immediate corrective action** is often described as "putting out fires." It adjusts something right now and gets things back on track. **Basic corrective action** gets to the source of the deviation and seeks to adjust the differences permanently. It asks how and why performance deviated. Unfortunately, many supervisors rationalize that they don't have the time to

---

## POP QUIZ    (Are You Comprehending What You're Reading?)

1. The ultimate goal of any control system is the extent to which it leads to:
   a. cost savings
   b. more productivity
   c. more profits
   d. achieving goals
2. Explain how a fish-bone diagram is used for control.
3. Personal observation as a method for measuring performance is one of the most widely used means by which supervisors assess actual performance. True or False?
4. If a supervisor performs the job of an employee who has called in sick that day, the supervisor is
   a. performing immediate corrective action
   b. illustrating the role of an effective supervisor
   c. performing basic corrective action
   d. none of the above

take basic corrective action and therefore must be content to perpetually "put out fires." Effective supervisors recognize that they must find the time to analyze deviations and, in situations where the benefits justify such action, permanently correct significant differences between standard and actual performance.

Referring back to our Robin Coleson example, he might take basic corrective action on the positive deviation for the Mercedes C and E models. If sales have been greater than expected for the past several months, he might upgrade the standard for future months' sales of these models and increase his orders with the factory. The poor showing on all the Porsches and the upper-range Mercedes models might justify a number of actions—for instance, cutting back on orders of these cars, running a sales promotion to move the increased inventory, reworking the sales-commission plan to reward salespeople for selling Porsches and higher-priced Mercedes, and/or recommending an increase in his dealership's advertising budget.

## TYPES OF CONTROLS

Where, in the process, should you apply controls? You can implement controls before an activity commences, while the activity is going on, or after the fact. The first type is called preventive control, the second is concurrent control, and the last is corrective control (see Exhibit 4–7). There are also some special types of statistical controls that can be used.

### WHAT IS PREVENTIVE CONTROL?

There's an old saying: "An ounce of prevention is worth a pound of cure." Its message is that the best way to handle a deviation from standard is to see that it doesn't occur. Most supervisors understand that the most desirable type of control is **preventive control** because it anticipates and prevents undesirable outcomes.

Preventive control ⟵
a type of control that
anticipates and pre-
vents undesirable out-
comes.

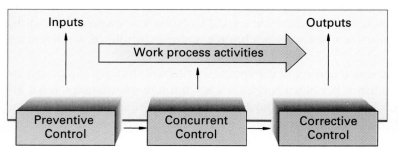

**EXHIBIT 4–7**
Three types of control.

→ **Concurrent control**
a type of control that takes place while an activity is in progress.

→ **Corrective control**
a type of control that provides feedback, after an activity is finished, in order to prevent future deviations.

What are some examples of preventive controls? Companies like McDonald's, Seagrams, and Southwest Airlines spend millions of dollars each year on preventive maintenance programs for their equipment with the sole purpose of avoiding breakdowns during operations. The National Collegiate Athletic Association (NCAA) requires that all college coaches under their jurisdiction take an exam on recruiting practices and violations. Coaches can't participate in recruiting athletes unless they get at least 80 percent on this exam. Other examples of preventive controls including hiring and training people in anticipation of new business, inspection of raw materials, practicing fire drills, and providing employees with company "code of ethics" cards to carry around in their wallets.

## WHEN ARE CONCURRENT CONTROLS USED?

As the name implies, **concurrent control** takes place while an activity is in progress. When control is enacted while the work is being done, you can correct problems before they get out of hand or become too costly.

Much of supervisors' day-to-day activities involve concurrent control. When they directly oversee the actions of employees, monitoring employees' work and correcting problems as they occur, concurrent control is taking place. While there is obviously some delay between the action and a supervisor's corrective response, the delay is essentially minimal. You'll find other examples of concurrent control on factory machinery and computers. Temperature, pressure, and similar gauges that are checked regularly during a production process, and which automatically send a signal to an operator that there is a problem, are examples of concurrent controls. So, too, are programs on computers that provide operators with an immediate response when an error is made. If the operator inputs the wrong command, the program will reject it and may even provide the correct command.

## WHAT IS CORRECTIVE CONTROL?

**Corrective control** provides feedback, after an activity is finished, in order to prevent any future deviations. Examples of corrective control include final inspection of finished goods, annual employee performance appraisals, financial audits, quarterly budget reports, and the like. The sales report that Robin Coleson at Mueller Mercedes-Porsche reviews each month, which we described earlier in this chapter, is an example of a corrective control.

The obvious shortcoming of corrective control is that, by the time you have the information, it's often too late. The damage or mistakes have already occurred. For instance, where information controls are weak, you may learn for the first time in August that your employees have already spent 110 percent of the department's annual photocopying budget. Nothing can be done to correct the over-expenditure in August. What corrective control does do is alert you that there is a problem. Then you can determine what went wrong and initiate basic corrective action.

## THE FOCUS OF CONTROL

What do supervisors control? Most of their control efforts are directed at one of five areas: costs, inventories, quality, and safety (see Exhibit 4–8). It's important too, to note that supervisors also control employee performance. Because performance evaluations are a critical component of managing your employees, we'll devote more space to that discussion in Chapter 8.

### WHAT COSTS SHOULD YOU CONTROL?

You are regularly under pressure to keep your costs in line. Let's look at the cost categories that you are likely to encounter and present a general program for cost reduction.

#### MAJOR COST CATEGORIES

The following list describes the major cost categories that supervisors come in contact with and need to monitor.

1. *Direct labor costs.* Expenditures for labor that are directly applied in the creation or delivery of the product or service. Examples: Machine operators in a factory or teachers in a school.

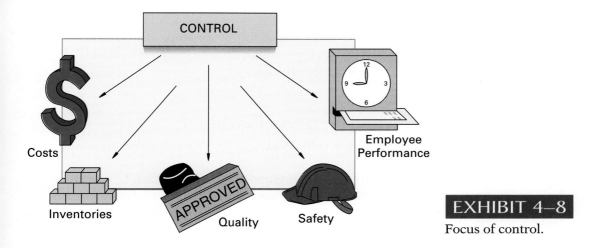

EXHIBIT 4–8

Focus of control.

2. *Indirect labor costs.* Expenditures for labor that are not directly applied in the creation or delivery of the product or service. Examples: Cost accountants, human resource recruiters, public relations specialists.

3. *Raw material costs.* Expenditures for materials that go directly into the creation of a product or service. Examples: Sheet steel at a Toyota plant or hamburger buns at a Wendy's.

4. *Supportive supplies costs.* Expenditures for necessary items that do not become part of the finished product or service. Examples: Cleaning compounds at the Toyota plant and photocopying costs at Aetna Life.

5. *Utility costs.* Expenditures for electricity, gas, water, and similar utilities. Example: Monthly electric bill for a regional office.

6. *Maintenance costs.* Material and labor expenditures incurred to repair and maintain equipment and facilities. Examples: Repair parts for equipment or jet engine maintenance technicians at Continental Airlines.

7. *Waste costs.* Expenditures for products, parts, or services that cannot be reused. Examples: Unsold french fries at Wendy's or scrap metal at a Maytag plant.

Typically, you will have a budget for each major cost category. By monitoring expenditures in each category, costs can be kept within your total budget plans (see Building a Supervisory Skill).

 # BUILDING A SUPERVISORY SKILL

## ESTABLISHING BUDGETS

### ABOUT THE SKILL

Budgets are an important component in running an effective department. If you've never been exposed to budgeting (other than your personal finances), developing a realistic budget can be difficult—especially the first few times. The following steps are designed to provide you with some guidance in developing an effective budget.

### STEPS IN PRACTICING THE SKILL

1. **Review the organization's overall strategy and goals.** Understanding your organization's strategy and goals will help you focus on where the overall organization is

going and your department's role in that plan.

2. **Determine your department's goals and the means to attaining them.** What activities will you do to reach your departmental goals and help the organization achieve its overall goals? What resources will you require to achieve these goals? Think in terms of things like staffing requirements, workloads, and the materials and equipment you'll need. This is also your opportunity to formulate new programs and propose new responsibilities for your department.

3. **Gather cost information.** You'll need accurate cost estimates of those resources you identified in Step 2. Old budgets may be of some help. But you'll also want to talk with your immediate boss, other supervisors, colleagues in similar positions, key employees, and other contacts you have developed inside and outside of your organization.

4. **Share your goals and cost estimates with your boss.** Your immediate boss will need to approve your budget, so his or her support is necessary. Discuss your goals, cost estimates, and other ideas with your immediate boss and key individuals in your organization before you include them in your budget. This will assure that they align with upper management's vision of your department's role and will build consensus for your proposed submission.

5. **Draw up your proposed budget.** Once your goals and costs are in place, constructing the actual budget is fairly mechanical. Be sure to show the linkage between your budget items and your departmental goals. You need to justify your requests and be prepared to explain and sell your budget to your immediate boss and other people in management. If there are other supervisors competing for some of the same resources that you want, your rationale will have to be especially strong.

6. **Be prepared to negotiate.** It's unlikely that your budget will be approved exactly as you submitted it. Be prepared to negotiate changes that management suggests; and revise your original budget. Recognize the politics in the budget process and negotiate from the perspective of building credits for future budgets. If certain projects aren't approved this time, use this point in the budget process to get some assurance that they will be reconsidered next time.

7. **Monitor your budget.** Once approved and implemented, you'll be judged on how well you manage your budget. Supervise by exception. Set variance targets that include both percentages and dollars. For instance, you could set a rule that says you'll investigate all monthly variances of 15 percent or larger where the actual dollar variance is $200 or more.

8. **Keep your boss informed of your progress.** Keep your immediate boss and other relevant parties advised on how you're doing in terms of meeting your budget. This is likely to help protect you if you exceed your budget for reasons beyond your control. Also, don't expect to be rewarded for underspending your budget. Underspending may indicate you need less money than you expected, and this could adversely affect your next budgeting cycle. ∎

## COST REDUCTION PROGRAMS

When costs are too high, you will more than likely be expected to implement a cost reduction program. Beginning in the late 1980s, U.S. corporations began a massive effort to reduce costs and improve their competitive position in relation to their global competitors. Much of this had a direct effect on supervisors. For instance, direct labor costs have been cut by automating jobs and redesigning work around teams that are more productive than individuals. Indirect labor costs have been slashed by laying off tens of thousands of support personnel in research, finance, human resources, and clerical functions. Budgets for training, travel, telephone calls, photocopying, computer software, office supplies, and similar expenditures have undergone significant cuts.

The following outlines a six-step program that can guide you in reducing costs in your department.[2]

1. *Improve methods.* Eliminate any unnecessary activities and introduce new work methods that can increase efficiency.
2. *Level the work flow.* Peaks and valleys in a work flow imply inefficiencies. By leveling the work flow, you can make do with fewer employees and cut down on overtime.
3. *Minimize waste.* Burning lights in unused areas, misuse of office supplies, idle employees, under-utilization of equipment, and wasteful use of raw materials add considerably to a supervisor's departmental costs.
4. *Install modern equipment.* Budget for new equipment to replace obsolete and worn-out machinery, computers, and the like.
5. *Invest in employee training.* People, like machines, can become obsolete if you allow their skills to become dated.
6. *Make cuts selectively.* Avoid across-the-board cuts. Some people and groups contribute significantly more than do others. Make cuts where they will generate the greatest efficiencies.

## WHY PAY ATTENTION TO INVENTORIES?

Supervisors are routinely responsible for ensuring that adequate inventories of materials and supplies are available for activities under their jurisdiction. For a shift supervisor at Burger King, that would include paper products, buns, burger patties, french fries, condiments, cooking utensils, cleaning supplies, and even proper change for the cash register. For a nursing supervisor at a hospital, that might mean things like pharmaceuticals, gloves, hypodermic needles, and bed linen.

The challenge in monitoring inventory cost is balancing the cost of maintaining inventories against the cost of running out of inventory. If ex-

[2]Based on J. J. Semrodek, Jr., "Nine Steps to Cost Control," *Supervisory Management,* April 1976, pp. 29–32.

cessive inventory is carried, money is needlessly tied up and unnecessary storage costs are incurred. Excessive inventory also adds to insurance premiums and taxes, and, of course, there are potential obsolescence costs. If Robin Coleson gets overstocked on Porsches and the new models begin to arrive, he might have to sell last year's models at below cost to get rid of them. If inventories drop too low, operations can be disrupted and sales lost. A stock-out of paper can bring a publisher's printing presses to a halt. If the Burger King supervisor fails to monitor his inventory of frozen French fries, he might find himself with some very disgruntled customers. Robin Coleson may also find that many Mercedes and Porsche customers will expect his dealership to have the model and color they want available immediately, or they'll take their business to another dealer.

A popular inventory technique that is sweeping across contemporary organizations is called **just-in-time (JIT) inventory systems.** Under JIT, inventory items arrive when they are needed in the production process instead of being stored in stock.[3] In Japan, JIT systems are called *kanban*. The derivation of the word gets to the essence of the just-in-time concept. **Kanban** is Japanese for "card" or "sign." Japanese suppliers ship parts to manufacturers in containers. Each container has a card, or kanban, slipped into a side pocket. When a production worker opens a container, he or she takes out the card and sends it back to the supplier. That initiates the shipping of a second container of parts that, ideally, reaches the production worker just as the last part in the first container is being used up. The ultimate goal of a JIT inventory system is to eliminate raw material inventories by coordinating production and supply deliveries precisely. When the system works as designed, it results in a number of positive benefits for a manufacturer: reduced inventories, reduced setup time, better work flow, shorter manufacturing time, less space consumption, and even higher quality. Of course, suppliers who can be depended on to deliver quality materials on time must be found. Because there are no inventories, there is no slack in the system to absorb defective materials or delays in shipments.

Just-in-time (JIT) inventory system
a system in which inventory items arrive when they are needed in the production process instead of being stored in stock. *See also* Kanban.

Kanban
In Japanese, a "card" or "sign." Shipped in a container, a kanban is returned to the supplier when the container is opened, initiating the shipment of a second container that arrives just as the first container is emptied.

## WHY THE FOCUS ON QUALITY?

With the possible exception of controlling costs, achieving high quality has become a primary focus of today's organizations. Many American products were criticized as being shoddy in quality compared to their Japanese and German counterparts. On the other hand, companies such as Maytag, Motorola, Ford, and Wal-Mart have thrived in the past decade by focusing on quality products or services. With this new emphasis has come increased demands on supervisors to engage in quality control.

[3]See, for instance, E. H. Hall, Jr., "Just-In-Time Management: A Critical Assessment," *Academy of Management Executive*, November 1989, pp. 315–18.

**Quality control**
identification of mistakes that may have occurred; monitoring quality to ensure that it meets some preestablished standard.

Historically, quality referred to achieving some preestablished standard for an organization's product or service. Today, quality has taken on a larger meaning. We introduced you to Total Quality Management in Chapter 2, describing it as a comprehensive, customer-focused program to continuously improve the quality of the organization's processes, products, and services. While TQM emphasizes actions to prevent mistakes, **quality control** emphasizes identifying mistakes that may have already occurred. Quality control continues to address monitoring quality—weight, strength, consistency, color, taste, reliability, finish, or any one of a myriad of quality characteristics—to ensure that it meets some preestablished standard.

Quality control is needed at multiple points in a process. It begins with the receipt of inputs. Are the raw materials satisfactory? Do new employees have the proper skills and abilities? It continues with work in process and all the steps up to the completion of the final product or service. Assessments at intermediate stages of the transformation process are typically part of quality control. Early detection of a defective part or process can save the cost of further work on the item.

A comprehensive quality control program would encompass preventive, concurrent, and corrective controls. For example, controls would inspect incoming raw materials, monitor operations while they are in progress, and include final inspection and rejection of unsatisfactory outputs. This same comprehensive program could be applied to services. For instance, a claims supervisor for State Farm could hire and train her people to make sure they fully understand their jobs, monitor their daily work flow to ensure it is done properly and on time, review completed claims for accuracy and thoroughness, and follow up with customers to determine their degree of satisfaction with the way their claims were handled.

## WHY THE EMPHASIS ON WORKPLACE SAFETY?

Barbara Fredericks considers safety a vital part of her job. Every morning, before her work crew arrives, she takes a tour of the warehouse. As a warehouse supervisor at Office Depot, she's looking for potential sources of accidents. She inspects the hand trucks, the forklifts, the ladders, and scaffolds. She checks the floor for loose tiles and grease. She looks over the merchandise to make sure it has been stacked properly. She makes notes about any merchandise that might be clogging aisles or walkways. During the day, when employees are working, she's always on the lookout for "accidents in the making"—for example, employees who handle equipment improperly or fail to follow company safety procedures.

As a supervisor, you have a legal responsibility to ensure that the workplace is free from unnecessary hazards and that working conditions are not harmful to employees' physical or mental health. Of course, accidents can and do happen, and the severity of these may surprise you. There are

Derrick Montgomery, safety supervisor for Maryland Pump Tank and Electric, works periodically to update his company's accident records. Through the use of computer-assisted programs, he's able to track where accidents have occurred, who's had them, and where potential training efforts are needed. In doing so, Derrick is abiding by the regulations established by OSHA.

approximately 10,000 reported work-related deaths and 2 million injuries each year in the United States. These occurrences result in more than 90 million days of lost productivity.[4] To put this in perspective, that's seven times the loss rate that occurs in Japan.[5] Heartless, then as it sounds, you must be concerned about safety and health if for no other reasons than unsafe and unhealthy work sites cost money. You're on the front line to prevent accidents from occurring. So another area where you need to focus your effort is both preventive and corrective safety controls.

## OCCUPATIONAL SAFETY AND HEALTH ACT

In 1970, Congress passed the **Occupational Safety and Health Act (OSHA)** "to assure so far as possible every working man and woman in the nation safe and healthful working conditions and to preserve our human resources" (see Exhibit 4–9). To enforce this law, the Occupational Safety and Health Administration was set up as part of the U.S. Department of Labor to inspect workplaces, penalize employers that don't meet standards, and provide health and safety consultation to firms.

OSHA has thousands of standards and regulations covering such diverse concerns as hazardous materials, personal protective equipment, machine guards, medical and first aid, fire protection, and materials handling

**Occupational Safety and Health Act (OSHA)**
a law that enforces, through standards and regulations, healthful working conditions and preservation of human resources.

[4]U.S. Department of Commerce, Bureau of the Census, *Statistical Abstracts of the United States: 1991*, Washington, D.C.: Government Printing Office, 1994, p. 434.

[5]"Falling Behind: The U.S. Is Losing the Job Safety War to Japan, Too," *Wall Street Journal*, May 16, 1992, p. A1.

# JOB SAFETY & HEALTH PROTECTION

The Occupational Safety and Health Act of 1970 Provides job safety and health protection for workers by promoting safe and healthful working conditions throughout the Nation. Provisions of the Act include the following:

## Employers

——All employers must furnish to employees employment and a place of employment free from recognized hazards that are causing or are likely to cause death or serious harm to employees. Employers must comply with occupational safety and health standards issued under the Act.

## Employees

——Employees must comply with all occupational safety and health standards, rules, regulations and orders issued under the Act that apply to their own actions and conduct on the job.
——The Occupational Safety and Health Administration (OSHA) of the U.S. Department of Labor has the primary responsibility for administering the Act. OSHA issues occupational safety and health standards, and its Compliance Safety and Health Officers conduct jobsite inspections to help ensure compliance with the Act.

## Inspection

——The Act requires that a representative of the employer and a representative authorized by the employees be given an opportunity to accompany the OSHA inspector for the purpose of aiding the inspection.
——Where there is no authorized employee representative, the OSHA Compliance Officer must consult with a reasonable number of employees concerning safety and health conditions in the workplace.

## Complaint

——Employees or their representatives have the right to file a complaint with the nearest OSHA office requesting an inspection if they believe unsafe or unhealthful conditions exist in their workplace. OSHA will withhold, on request, names of employees complaining.

——The Act provides that employees may not be discharged or discriminated against in any way for filing safety and health complaints or for otherwise exercising their rights under the Act.
——Employees who believe they have been discriminated against may file a complaint with their nearest OSHA office within 30 days of the alleged discriminatory action.

## Citation

——If upon inspection OSHA believes an employer has violated the Act, a citation alleging such violations will be issued to the employer. Each citation will specify a time period within which the alleged violation must be corrected.
——The OSHA citation must be prominently displayed at or near the place of alleged violation for three days, or until it is corrected, whichever is later, to warn employees of dangers that may exist there.

## Proposed Penalty

——The Act Provides for mandatory civil penalties against employers of up to $7,000 for each serious violation and for optional penalties of up to $7,000 for each nonserious violation. Penalties of up to $7,000 per day may be proposed for failure to correct violations within the proposed time period and for each day the violation continues beyond the prescribed abatement date. Also, any employer who willfully or repeatedly violates the Act may be assessed penalties of up to $70,000 for each such violation. A minimum penalty of $5,000 may be imposed for each willful violation. A violation of posting requirements can bring a penalty of up to $7,000.

——There are also provisions for criminal penalties. Any willful violation resulting in the death of any employee, upon conviction, is punishable by a fine of up to $250,000 (or $500,000 if the employer is a corporation), or by imprisonment for up to six months, or both. A second conviction of an employer doubles the possible term of imprisonment. Falsifying records, reports, or applications is punishable by a fine of $10,000 or up to six months in jail or both.

## Voluntary Activity

——While providing penalties for violations, the Act also encourages efforts by labor and management, before an OSHA inspection, to reduce workplace hazards voluntarily and to develop and improve safety and health programs in all workplaces and industries. OSHA's Voluntary Protection Programs recognize outstanding efforts of this nature.
——OSHA has published Safety and Health Program Management Guidelines to assist employers in establishing or perfecting programs to prevent or control employee exposure to workplace hazards. There are many public and private organizations that can provide information and assistance in this effort, if requested. Also, your local OSHA office can provide considerable help and advice on solving safety and health problems or can refer you to other sources for help such as training.

## Consultation

——Free assistance in identifying and correcting hazards and in improving safety and health management is available to employers, without citation or penalty, through OSHA-supported programs in each State. These programs are usually administered by the State Labor or Health department or a State university.

## Posting instructions

——Employers in States operating OSHA approved State Plans should obtain and post the State's equivalent poster.

*Under provisions of Title 29, Code of Federal Regulations, Part 1903.2(a)(1) employers must post this notice (or facsimile) in a conspicuous place where notices to employees are customarily posted.*

——More Information
——Additionl Information and copies of the Act, specific OSHA satety and Health standards, and other applicable regulations may be obtained from your employer or from the nearest OSHA Regional Office in the following locations:

| | |
|---|---|
| Atlanta, GA | (404) 347-3573 |
| Boston, MA | (617) 565-7164 |
| Chicago, IL | (312) 353-2220 |
| Dallas, TX | (214) 767-4731 |
| Denver, CO | (303) 844-3061 |
| Kansas City, MO | (816) 426-5861 |
| New York, NY | (212) 337-2378 |
| Philadelphia, PA | (215) 596-1201 |
| San Francisco, CA | (415) 744-6670 |
| Seattle, WA | (206) 442-5930 |

Washington, DC
1991 (Reprinted)
OSHA 2203

*Lynn Martin*

Lynn Martin, Secretary of Labor

## U.S. Department of Labor

Occupational Safety and Health Administration

---

## EXHIBIT 4–9

Government poster of OSHA regulations.

and equipment. You obviously can't be expected to know all of them, but you do need to be familiar with those relevant to your work unit. Because of OSHA's complexity, most companies generally have an individual or group of individuals—typically in the human resources, safety, or engineering department—who act as an information resource when you have questions.

OSHA places very specific responsibilities on supervisors for documenting injuries and illnesses. For instance, each occupational injury and illness that results in death, medical treatment other than first aid, loss of consciousness, restriction of work or motion, or transfer to another job must be recorded on a standardized form within six working days after learning of the injury or illness. In addition, supervisors are expected to participate in or oversee the training of their people to ensure they understand pertinent OSHA regulations. As a suprevisor, you may be asked to accompany OSHA officials during inspections of your work area.

## CAUSES OF ACCIDENT

What causes accidents? For the most part, they are caused by human error and unsafe working environments.

The primary cause of workplace accidents is employees who engage in unsafe behavior. They fail to wear safety glasses, use unsafe shortcuts to increase their output, take improper care of hazardous chemicals, or engage in horseplay around dangerous machinery. There are also some employees who are more likely than others to have accidents. These people tend to be forgetful, bored, stressed-out, or overly impulsive. This makes them more susceptible to accidents.

Barbara Fredericks' preventive safety controls at Office Depot focused on unsafe working conditions. No department is completely free from being the scene of an accident. However, certain environments increase the likelihood. Noises, poor lighting, and excessive heat or cold create distracting work environments. Disorganized and messy work stations can cause accidents. Lifting of materials is a frequent cause of back injuries. Power equipment creates high accident potential, as does improperly maintained equipment of any kind. Stairs, ladders, and scaffolds increase opportunities for people to fall. People who work for long periods of time on a computer are increasingly suffering from carpal-tunnel syndrome, which creates pain in the wrist and fingers.

## MEASURING ACCIDENTS

Consistent with our discussion of the control process, supervisors need to measure accident rates. How do you do that? It's done by calculating a company's incident rate.

The **incident rate** is a measure of the number of injuries, illnesses, or lost workdays in relation to a common base rate of 100 full-time employees. Say your department has 15 employees working 2000 hours a year (or

**Incident rate**
a measure of the number of injuries, illnesses, or lost workdays as it relates to a common base rate of 100 full-time employees.

30,000 hours) and that you have had three injuries in the department this year. To calculate your incident rate, use the following formula: (N/EH) × 200,000,[6] where (N) is the number of injuries, illnesses, and/or lost work days in a given year, (EH) is the total hours worked by all employees during the year, and 200,000 is the base hour rate equivalent (100 workers × 40 hours per week × 50 weeks per year). The calculation would look like the following: (3/30,000) × 200,000.[7] The incident rate would be 20. What does this 20 represent? That depends on a number of factors. If the organization is in the meat-packing industry where the industry average incident rate is 44.4, then they may be doing well. If however, they are in the insurance industry, where the industry incident rate is 2.4, the 20 indicates a serious problem.[8]

## ACCIDENT PREVENTION

If your accident data indicates a problem, what can you do? Here are some actions you might consider.

1. *Match people and jobs.* Factors such as visual skills and experience have been found to be related to increased accident rates on certain types of jobs. Moreover, when employees are undergoing personal problems or other sources of stress, their potential for accidents increases on some jobs. Rotating a person temporarily to a lower-risk job, for instance, should be considered if you think their personal problems might increase accident-proneness. Or restrict the activities of an employee who is temporarily accident-prone.

2. *Engineer the job and equipment.* The proper design of job activities, work devices, protective gear, and equipment can cut down on accidents and injuries. Office workers, for instance, are less likely to suffer back problems if their desk and chair arrangement is designed to their specific work activities and body movements.

3. *Educate and train employees.* Make sure your employees know the safety rules and incorporate accident prevention into training programs. Create safety awareness by posting highly visible signs that proclaim the importance of safety, use safety committees to identify and correct potential problems, and publicize safety statistics.

4. *Enforce safety standards.* The best rules and regulations will be ineffective in reducing accidents if they are not enforced. Make regular visits

[6]U.S. Department of Labor, Bureau of Labor Statistics, *A Brief Guide to Recordkeeping Requirements for Occupational Injuries and Illnesses*, Washington, D.C.: Government Printing Office, June 1986, p. 15.

[7]The number 30,000 reflects 15 employees working 40 hours per week for fifty weeks (15 × 40 × 50).

[8]Incident rates for both industries were reported in *Statistical Abstracts of the U.S.*, 1994, p. 434.

to the work floor and visually check to make sure safety standards are being maintained.

5. *Reward employees for safe performance.* Make sure employee safety is viewed as important and worthwhile. Provide incentives and awards for safe performance.

# WHAT ARE THE CHARACTERISTICS OF EFFECTIVE CONTROLS?

Effective control systems tend to have certain qualities in common. The importance of these characteristics vary with the situation, but the following can provide guidance to supervisors in designing their unit's control system.

## TIMELINESS

Controls should call attention to variations in time to prevent serious infringement on a unit's performance. The best information has little value if it is dated. Therefore, an effective control system must provide timely information.

## ECONOMY

A control system must be economically reasonable to operate. Any system of control has to justify the benefits that it gives in relation to the costs it incurs. To minimize costs, you should try to impose the least amount of control that is necessary to produce the desired results. The widespread use of computers, to a large extent, is due to their ability to provide timely and accurate information in a highly efficient manner.

## FLEXIBILITY

Effective controls must be flexible enough to adjust to adverse change or to take advantage of new opportunities. In today's dynamic and rapidly changing world, you should design control systems that can adjust to the changing nature of your departmental objectives, work assignments, and jobs tasks.

## UNDERSTANDABILITY

Controls that cannot be understood by those who have to use them are of little value. It is sometimes necessary, therefore, to substitute less complex controls for sophisticated devices. A control system that is difficult to understand can cause unnecessary mistakes and frustrate employees; it will eventually be ignored.

### REASONABLE CRITERIA

Consistent with our discussion of goals in the previous chapter, control standards must be reasonable and attainable. If they are too high or unreasonable, they no longer motivate. Since most employees don't want to risk being labeled incompetent for telling their bosses that they ask too much, employees may resort to unethical or illegal shortcuts. Controls should, therefore, enforce standards that are reasonable; they should challenge and stretch people to reach higher performance levels without being demotivating or encouraging deception.

### CRITICAL PLACEMENT

You can't control everything that goes on in your department. Even if you could, the benefits couldn't justify the costs. As a result, you should place controls on those factors that are critical to your unit's performance goals. Controls should cover the critical activities, operations, and events within your unit. That is, you should focus on where variations from standard are most likely to occur or where a variation would do the greatest harm. For instance, if your labor costs are $20,000 a month and postage costs are $50 a month, a 5 percent overrun in the former is more critical than a 20 percent overrun in the latter. Hence, you should establish controls for labor and a critical dollar allocation, whereas postage expenses would not appear to be critical.

### EMPHASIS ON THE EXCEPTION

**Control by exception**
a system that ensures that one is not overwhelmed by information on variations from standard.

Since you can't control all activities, you should place your control devices where they can call attention only to the exceptions. A **control by exception** system ensures that you are not overwhelmed by information on variations from standard. For instance, as an accounts receivable supervisor at a Sears store, you instruct your employees to inform you only when an account is 15 days past due. The fact that 90 percent of your customers pay their bills on time or no more than two weeks late means you can devote your attention to the 10 percent exceptions.

## CAN CONTROLS CREATE PROBLEMS?

Yes, controls can create their own problems. The introduction of controls come with potential negatives that need to be guarded against. These include employee resistance, misdirection of employee effort, and ethical dilemmas for supervisors concerning control devices. Let's take a brief look at each.

## EMPLOYEE RESISTANCE

Many individuals don't like to be told what to do or to feel that they're being "checked up on." When work performance is deficient, few people enjoy being criticized or corrected. The result is that employees often resist controls. They see their supervisor, daily production reports, performance appraisals, and similar control devices as evidence that their employer doesn't trust them.

Reality tells you that controls are a way of organizational life, because you have a responsibility to ensure that activities are going as planned. So what can you do to lessen this resistance?

First, wherever possible, encourage employee self-control (see Assessing Yourself). Once employees know their goals, give them the benefit of the doubt and leave them alone. Let them monitor and correct their own performance. Supplement this with regular communication so they can let you know what problems they've encountered and how they've solved them. The assumption with self-control is that employees are responsible, trustworthy, and capable of personally correcting any significant deviation from their goals. Only if this assumption proves incorrect do you need to introduce more formalized external control mechanisms.

When external controls are needed, there are some methods you can use to minimize employee resistance. Have employees participate in setting the standards. This lessens the likelihood that they'll view them as unrealistic or too demanding. Explain to employees how they will be evaluated. Surprisingly, the problem is often not the controls themselves that create resistance but the lack of understanding of how information will be gathered and how it will be used. Provide employees with regular feedback. Ambiguity causes stress and resistance. So let people know how they're doing. Finally, most people want the satisfaction that comes from doing their work better and want to avoid the pain and embarrassment that comes with discipline. As a result, supervisors should treat controls as devices for helping employees improve rather than for punishment.

## MISDIRECTION OF EFFORT

Three supervisors at a big General Motors truck plant in Flint, Michigan, installed a secret control box in an office to override the control panel that governed the speed of the assembly line.[9] The device allowed them to speed up the assembly line—a serious violation of GM's contract with the United Auto Workers. When caught, they explained that, while they knew what they had done was wrong, the pressure from higher-ups to meet unrealistic production goals was so great that they felt the secret control

[9]Cited in A. B. Carroll, "In Search of the Moral Manager," *Business Horizons*, March-April 1987, p. 7.

## HOW WILLING ARE YOU TO ENCOURAGE SELF-CONTROL?

For each of the following 18 statements, rate each on a scale of 1 to 5, where 5 represents strongly agree, 4 represents agree somewhat, 3 is neither agree nor disagree, 2 represents disagree somewhat, and 1 represents strongly disagree.

|  | Strongly Agree | | | Strongly Disagree | |
|---|---|---|---|---|---|
| **1.** I'd let others do more, but it appears the jobs never seem to get done the way I want them to be done. | 5 | 4 | 3 | (2) | 1 |
| **2.** I don't feel I have the time to explain to others what to do. | 5 | 4 | 3 | (2) | 1 |
| **3.** I carefully check on others' work without letting them know I'm doing it, so I can correct their mistakes if necessary, before they cause too many problems. | 5 | 4 | 3 | (2) | 1 |
| **4.** I let others control the whole job—giving them the opportunity to complete it without any of my involvement. Then I review the result. | 5 | 4 | 3 | 2 | (1) |
| **5.** When I have given clear instructions and the task isn't done right, I get upset. | 5 | 4 | 3 | (2) | 1 |
| **6.** I feel that others may lack the commitment I have. Any task I ask them to do won't get done as well as I'd do it. | 5 | 4 | 3 | (2) | 1 |
| **7.** I'd let others control things more, but I feel I can do the job better than the person I might have given the job to. | 5 | 4 | 3 | 2 | (1) |
| **8.** I'd let others control more, but if the individual I give this responsibility to does an incompetent job, I'll be severely criticized. | 5 | 4 | 3 | (2) | 1 |
| **9.** If I were to give up control, my job wouldn't be nearly as much fun. | 5 | 4 | 3 | 2 | (1) |
| **10.** When I give up control, I often find that the outcome is such that I end up doing the task over again myself. | 5 | 4 | 3 | 2 | (1) |
| **11.** I have not really found that giving up control saves any time. | 5 | 4 | 3 | 2 | (1) |

| | | | | | |
|---|---|---|---|---|---|
| **12.** I tell others exactly how something should be accomplished. | 5 | 4 | 3 | ②| 1 |
| **13.** I can't give up control as much as I'd like to because others lack the necessary experience. | 5 | 4 | 3 | ② | 1 |
| **14.** I feel that when I give up control, I lose control. | 5 | 4 | 3 | ② | 1 |
| **15.** I would give up control more, but I'm pretty much a perfectionist. | 5 | 4 | 3 | 2 | ① |
| **16.** I work longer hours than I should. | 5 | 4 | 3 | 2 | ① |
| **17.** I can give others the routine tasks, but I feel I must do nonroutine tasks myself. | 5 | 4 | 3 | 2 | ① |
| **18.** My own boss expects me to keep very close to all details of my job. | 5 | 4 | 3 | 2 | ① |

## SCORING

Total your score by adding the circled numbers for the 18 statements.

## WHAT THE INSTRUMENT MEANS

How much control you're willing to give up or share is directly related to how willing you are to assign this "authority" to others. Depending on your total score, the following interpretations can be made:

72–90 points = ineffective assignment of self-control
54–71 points = assigning self-control habits needs substantial improvement
36–53 points = assigning self-control habits are positive, but some improvement needed
18–35 points = superior assignment of self-control

Source:   Reprinted by permission of the publisher from *Management Review* May 1982 ©1982. American Management Association, New York. All rights reserved.

panel was the only way they could meet their targets. As described by one supervisor, senior GM executives would say (regarding the high production goals), "I don't care how you do it—just do it."

Did you ever notice that the people who work in government offices—for example, in departments that process motor vehicle licenses and building permits—often appear to not care much about the problems of taxpayers? They become so fixated on ensuring that every rule is followed

Employees in government offices like this one do want to perform well and serve their customers. Sometimes, however, they become so focused on ensuring that every rule is followed that they lose sight of what is really important in their job.

that they lose sight of the fact that their job is to serve the public, not hassle them!

These two examples illustrate another potential problem with controls: People may misdirect their efforts in order to look good on the control criteria. Because any control system has imperfections, problems occur when individuals or organizational units attempt to look good exclusively in terms of the control devices. In actuality, the result is dysfunctional in terms of the organization's goals. More often than not, this is caused by incomplete measures of performance. If the control system evaluates only the quantity of output, people will ignore quality. Similarly, if the system measures activities rather than results, people will spend their time attempting to look good on the activity measures.

What can you do to minimize this problem? Two things. First, make sure that control standards are reasonable. Very importantly, this should not merely be your perception. Your employees must believe that the standards are fair and within their capability. Second, you should select and evaluate criteria that are directly related to achievement of employee job goals. If the licensing supervisor in the motor vehicle office evaluates her people on their obedience to following rules, rather than on how effectively they serve the needs of clients, then her employees are not going to give much attention to satisfying clients. Finding the right criteria will often mean using a multiple set of standards. For instance, the goal of "serving clients" might require the licensing supervisor to evaluate her clerks on

**5.** Because a supervisor cannot control all activities, controls should be placed on _____ activities.
   **a.** risky
   **b.** risk-free
   **c.** critical
   **d.** complex

**6.** Explain what is meant by the term just-in-time inventory systems.

**7.** Quality control emphasizes actions to take to prevent mistakes; total quality management emphasizes identifying mistakes that may have already occurred.

**8.** Assume an organization has 1800 employees and has had 195 accidents reported over the past year. Calculate the accident incident rate for the organization.

criteria such as "greets all clients with a smile and friendly greeting," "answers all client questions without seeking outside assistance," and "solves the client's problems in one visit." In addition, the supervisor might set up a client comment box in her licensing department where individual employees could be praised or criticized on their service, and then use this feedback as one measure of how well employees are doing their jobs.

### ETHICS AND CONTROL DEVICES

Just because you can monitor the most minute details of an employee's work day doesn't mean you should. This has become a particularly sensitive issue in recent years, as sophisticated communication systems and computer software make it possible for a supervisor's control capability to potentially interfere with an employee's right to privacy.

Supervisors at General Electric's Answering Center record and review employees' handling of customer telephone inquiries. Supervisors of data-entry clerks at the Southern California Gas Company use computer software to count the clerks' keystrokes and calculate their daily productivity.[10] The technology now exists for "big brother" to directly and indirectly monitor employees. But is it ethical (see Dealing with a Difficult Issue)?

[10]Cited in G. Bylinsky, "How Companies Spy on Employees," *Fortune*, November 4, 1991, pp. 131–140.

### ARE SOME CONTROL SYSTEMS AN INVASION OF PRIVACY?

When do a supervisor's control efforts become an invasion of an employee's privacy? Consider the following:[11]

You have been a loyal employee of the Boston Sheraton Hotel. You just found out that you and a friend have been secretly videotaped while in the men's room off the hotel lobby. You were discussing a private matter (in addition to using the lavatory); now you feel like the hotel doesn't trust you.

If you work for Gateway 2000 in telephone sales, your phone conversations may be monitored. The company uses this monitoring to determine how well you're doing, and to identify where you may have areas for improvement. It could also be used to substantiate that you're not doing your job properly—and lead to your dismissal.

At Olivetti, all employees are given a "smart badge." These identification devices permit you access to various parts of the company. They can also be used to track your whereabouts. On one hand, knowing where you are assists in forwarding urgent messages to you. On the other, no matter where you are, Olivetti managers can track your location.

Are any of these practices described above an invasion of privacy? Moreover, when does a supervisor overstep the bounds of decency and privacy by silently (even covertly) scrutinizing the behavior of his or her employees?

[11]L. Smith, "What the Boss Knows About You," *Fortune*, August 9, 1993, pp. 88–93; Z. Schiller, and W. Konrad, "If You Light up on Sunday, Don't Come in on Monday," *Business Week*, August 26, 1991, pp. 68–72; and G. Bylinsky, "How Companies Spy on Employees," *Fortune*, November 4, 1991, pp. 131–140.

We have no absolute answer. It can be argued that this type of performance monitoring helps people do their jobs better. It enables supervisors to review employee performance and provide feedback that can improve the quality of the employees' work. At the very least, employees certainly should be aware that this monitoring is going on. Even then, studies have shown that stress-related complaints go up when employees know that somebody may be listening in on their phone calls.[12] This suggests that great care needs to be taken by supervisors as advanced technology expands their control capability.

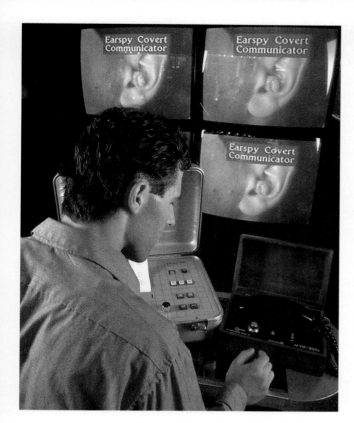

Just how far can supervisors go in monitoring their employees? Laws give them a lot of discretion. That means they can read an employee's e-mail or computer files, or even film them while they are on company premises! The real question, however, is just how much of an employee's privacy can be invaded.

## SUMMARY

After reading this chapter, I can:

1. **Describe the control process.** The control process consists of three separate and distinct steps: (1) measure actual performance; (2) compare results with standards; and (3) take corrective action.

2. **Contrast two types of corrective action.** There are two types of corrective action: immediate and basic. Immediate deals predominantly with symptoms. Basic corrective action looks for the cause of the deviation and seeks to adjust the differences permanently.

3. **Compare preventive, concurrent, and corrective control.** Preventive control is implemented before an activity begins. It anticipates and prevents undesirable outcomes. Concurrent control takes place while an activity is in progress. Corrective control is implemented after an activity is finished and facilitates prevention of future deviations.

4. **Explain how a supervisor can reduce costs.** Supervisors can reduce costs by improving work methods, leveling the work flow, reducing waste, installing more modern equipment, investing in employee training, and making selective cuts that will generate the greatest efficiencies.

5. **List the characteristics of an effective control system.** An effective control system should be timely; economical; flexible; understandable; have reasonable standards; be critically placed; and emphasize the exception.

6. **Explain potential negatives that controls can create.** Potential negatives include employee resistance; employees directing their efforts to the wrong activities; and ethical dilemmas created by advances in control technology.

## REVIEWING YOUR KNOWLEDGE

1. Why is it that what we measure may be more critical to the control process than how we measure it?
2. What constitutes an acceptable range of variation?
3. Which type of control is preferable—preventive, concurrent, or correctional? Why? What type do you think is most widely used in practice?
4. What is the challenge of monitoring inventory costs? Of implementing a just-in-time inventory system?
5. In terms of characteristics of an effective control system, where do you think most control systems fail? Why?
6. Why should a supervisor control "by exception?"
7. How can a supervisor lessen employee resistance to controls?
8. What can a supervisor do to minimize the problem of people trying to look good on control criteria?

## ANSWERS TO THE POP QUIZZES

1. **d. achieving goals.** This is a basic premise of control systems. They should be designed to ensure that goals are achieved.
2. Fish-bone diagrams are used to depict the causes of a certain problem and to group the causes according to common

categories such as machinery, materials, methods, personnel, finances, or management.

3. **True.** Personal observation is one of the most widely used means by which supervisors assess actual performance. It enables a supervisor to pick up verbal omissions, facial expressions, and tones of voice that may be missed by other methods.

4. **a. performing immediate corrective action.** This is the definition of immediate corrective action.

5. **c. critical.** Placing controls on critical activities is one of the elements of effective controls. It also enables a supervisor to focus on variations from standards that are most likely to occur or where a variation would do the greatest harm.

6. Just-in-time inventory systems involve having inventory items arrive when they are needed in the production process instead of being kept in stock.

7. **False.** Just the opposite. TQM emphasizes actions to take to prevent mistakes. Quality control emphasizes identifying mistakes that may have already occurred.

8. To calculate the incident rate, the formula (N/EH)/200,000 is used. In this problem, the following apply: (N) = 195; (EH) = $1800 \times 40 \times 50 = 3,600,000$. The incident rate is calculated as: $(195/3,600,000) \times 200,000 = $ **10.8.** ∎

## CLASS EXERCISE: DEVELOPING A BUDGET

You have recently been appointed advertising supervisor for a new monthly health magazine, *Today's Fitness*, being developed by the magazine division of the Rupert Murdoch organization. You were previously an advertising supervisor on one of the company's established magazines. You will report to the new magazine's publisher, Tom Morgan.

Estimates of first-year subscription sales for *Today's Fitness* are 125,000. Magazine stand sales should add another 40,000 a month to this number. Your concern is with developing advertising revenue for the magazine. You and Tom have set a goal of selling advertising space totaling $6 million during *Total Fitness's* first year. You think you can do this with a staff of about eight people. Since this is a completely new publication, there is no previous budget for your advertising group. You've been asked by Tom to submit a preliminary budget for your group.

Write up a report, not to exceed three pages in length: (1) Describe in detail how you would go about this assignment. For example, where would you get budget categories? Whom would you contact? (2) Present your best effort at creating a budget for your department. (Your instructor will inform you if this is to be turned in as a written assignment or discussed in class.)

## CASE 4.A

### Comparing Supervisory Controls

You will recall from reading this chapter that Robin Coleson is a sales supervisor at Mueller Mercedes-Porsche dealership in northern New Jersey. It is Robin's responsibility to project sales of the various models of cars, to correctly analyze the projections, and, in consultation with upper management, to identify appropriate action on deviations that are considered significant. You will remember that the slump in New Jersey's economy and job security fears were identified as major contributors to the slow sales at Mueller Mercedes-Porsche.

Robin's good friend, Jack Hurlan, is the maintenance and service supervisor at Mueller Mercedes-Porsche. Jack's main function is keeping customers happy by providing timely, quality maintenance and service to car buyers as well as repairing all models of Mercedes and Porsche vehicles on demand. Robin and Jack have found a lot of similar concerns and problems related to their jobs. They have also found that there are some direct relationships between their jobs. For example, when sales are down, usually there is an increase in maintenance and repair work.

External forces, such as the slow economy Robin identified as a contributor to poor sales, also is important to Jack. For example, not too long ago Porsche Cars North America, Inc. put out a recall notice about a cruise control defect relating to safety on all Porsche 911 Carrera 2 and 4 models between the years of 1989 and 1992. The notice stated that if the ball sockets on the cruise control linkage were to break, jamming could occur from loose parts, which might keep the engine from returning to idle.

Jack had a flood of calls from Porsche owners asking about the manufacturing problem. He also had a significant increase in business from 911 Porsche owners who wanted to have repairs made as soon as possible. The repair work was not difficult or too time consuming, but Jack had one mechanic on vacation and another was in the hospital for emergency surgery. Another part-time mechanic apprentice didn't show up for three days in a row, and Jack couldn't reach him by phone. To complicate matters, there was a major fire in one of the main parts-supply houses which provided most of the Porsche parts for Mueller. Jack had to make a quick decision to get parts from another supplier who was slow with shipments and frequently made shipping errors.

## RESPONDING TO THE CASE

1. Jack commented to Robin one day that he certainly believed in the saying, "When it rains, it pours." What do you believe he meant by this statement? How does it relate to supervisory controls?
2. Contrast the similarities and differences that Robin and Jack have in the control process.
3. Describe how the three types of controls might relate to both Robin's and Jack's jobs.
4. Make two lists (one for Robin and one for Jack) relating to the three major types of controls they need. Prioritize the controls as to their importance to the two supervisors. Will the priorities differ for each supervisor under other conditions? Why or why not? Discuss why this activity was difficult.

## CASE 4.B

### Control Measures at Frito Lay

All day long, each working day of the week, salespeople at Frito-Lay (a division of PepsiCo) punch information into their hand-held computers.[13] At the end of each workday, these salespeople download the collected information to computers at local sales offices or in their homes. This downloaded data is then transmitted to corporate headquarters in Dallas, Texas where within 24 hours it is made available to those who wish to review it. Information on 100 Frito-Lay product lines in 400,000 stores is available on computer screens in easy-to-read, color-coded charts: Red means a sales drop, yellow a slowdown, and green an advance. This system allows problems to be quickly identified and corrected.

Frito-Lay's control system helped the company solve a recent problem in San Antonio and Houston. Sales were slumping in area supermarkets. One supervisor turned on his computer, called up data for south Texas, and quickly isolated the cause. A regional competitor had introduced El Galindo, a white-corn tortilla chip. The chip was getting good word of mouth advertising, and store managers were

[13]J. Rothfeder and J. Bartimo, "How Software Is Making Food Sales a Piece of Cake," *Business Week*, July 2, 1990, pp. 54–55.

giving it more shelf space than Frito's traditional Tostitos tortilla chips. Using this information, the supervisor sprang into action. He worked with a product development team to produce a white-corn version of Tostitos. Within three months, a new product was on the shelves, and the company successfully won back lost market share. Interestingly, this control mechanism at Frito-Lay is relatively new. Before its installation, supervisors would have needed at least three months just to pinpoint the problem. But this new system gathers data daily from supermarkets, scans it for important clues about local trends, and warns executives about problems and opportunities in all of Frito-Lay's markets.

## RESPONDING TO THE CASE

1. Describe the type of control that Frito-Lay is using. Why do you think they've chosen this type of control system?
2. Identify instances in the case where Frito-Lay is using preventive and corrective controls. ■

# 5

# PROBLEM SOLVING
# AND DECISION MAKING

# LEARNING OBJECTIVES → KEY TERMS

After reading this chapter, you should be able to:

1. List the seven steps in the decision-making process.
2. Describe expected value analysis.
3. Contrast data with information.
4. Describe the four types of decision styles.
5. Explain three different ethical viewpoints.
6. Compare and contrast group decision and individual decision making.
7. List three techniques for improving group decision making.

You should also be able to define these supervisory terms:

attribute listing

brainstorming

data

decision trees

decision-making process

electronic meetings

end-users

expected value analysis

groupthink

information

justice view of ethics

lateral thinking

management information systems (MIS)

marginal analysis

nominal group technique

problem

rights view of ethics

synectics

utilitarian view of ethics

# PERFORMING EFFECTIVELY

Cathy Hughes is an individual on a mission.[1] Having spent several years studying broadcasting and working as a radio broadcaster, she dreamed of one day overseeing her own station. Cathy knew that to do this would be no easy task. There's a lot of information that must be gathered, and understood. For example, how does one go about getting FCC licensing? How does one obtain the necessary advertising to ensure an influx of revenues to operate the station? How does one select a program format so that a large listening audience can be generated—which in turn brings in more advertising dollars? Answers to such questions for Hughes meant dedicating herself to researching the facts, generating a data base, and making appropriate decisions. Once prepared, and building on her knowledge and experience, Cathy launched Radio One, Inc., competing for the ever-challenging weekday morning audience in the Baltimore-Washington area.

## INTRODUCTION

Decisions, decisions, decisions! One of your employees has been coming to work late recently and the quality of his work has fallen off. What do you do? You've got a vacancy in your department and your company's human resource representative has sent you six candidates. Which one do you choose? Several of your salespeople have told you that they're losing business to an innovative new product line introduced by one of your competitors. How do you respond?

As a supervisor, you are regularly confronted with problems that require decisions. For example, you help employees select goals, schedule workloads, and decide what information—and how much of it—to share with your boss. How do you learn to make good decisions? Are you born with some intuitive talent? Probably not! Sure, some of you, because of your intelligence, knowledge, and experience are able unconsciously to analyze problems; and that can result, over time, in an impressive trail of decisions. There are, however, some conscious decision-making techniques that anyone can use to become a more effective decision maker. We'll review a number of these techniques in this chapter.

[1]A. Williams, "Career Planning: Building on Strengths, Strengthening Weaknesses," *Black Collegian,* September/October 1993, p. 82–83.

To Cathy, building and supervising a successful company requires intuition, concrete plans, astute business savvy, and the ability to make timely and accurate decisions. And successful she has been. What helped her along the way? One of Cathy's most important decisions was to work in almost every job in the radio business that is required to bring a radio program to life. Doing so gave her complete information to work from, and gave her greater confidence when it came time to oversee such a risky venture.

For Cathy Hughes, supervisory ability is paying off. Given the success she is having, as measured by the large "tuned-in" audience each morning, Cathy is now making decisions to expand by adding more stations and reaching into new cities. ■

## THE DECISION-MAKING PROCESS

Let's begin by describing a rational and analytical way of looking at decisions. We call this approach the **decision-making process**. It's composed of seven steps (see also Exhibit 5–1).

1. Identify the ~~problem~~ concern
2. Collect relevant information
3. Develop alternatives
4. Evaluate each alternative
5. Select the best alternative
6. Implement the decision
7. Follow up and evaluate

To help illustrate this process, we'll work through a problem faced by Mike Reddman. Mike is head of operations at WJLA, a Fox affiliate in Richmond, Virginia. He has just received the news that the syndicated program he runs in the 7:30–8:00 p.m. time slot—Home Improvement—has been canceled by the syndicator. Let's look at how Mike handles this problem by working through the decision-making process.

**Decision-making process**
a seven-step process that provides a rational and analytical way of looking at decisions. The steps include identification of the problem; collection of rational information; development of alternatives; evaluation of alternatives; selection of the best alternative; implementation of the decision; and follow-up and evaluation.

# How Do You Identify the Problem?

**Problem**
a discrepancy between an existing and a desired state of affairs.

The decision-making process begins with the existence of a **problem** or, more specifically, a discrepancy between an existing and a desired state of affairs. For Mike Reddman, it's suddenly having a half-hour gap in his early-evening program schedule, which he wants filled with profitable, high-rated shows.

In the real world, problems don't always come with neon signs identifying themselves as such. Many of the problems you will confront aren't as obvious as Mike's dilemma. One of the most difficult chores in this stage, then, is separating symptoms from problems. Is a 5 percent decline in sales a problem? Or are declining sales merely a symptom of another problem, such as product obsolescence or an inadequate advertising budget? To use a medical analogy, aspirin doesn't deal with the problem of stress on the job, it merely relieves the headache symptom.

One last point: Solving the wrong problem perfectly is no better an outcome, and may be worse, than coming up with the wrong solution to the right problem! Correctly identifying what the real problem is, is not an easy task and should not be taken lightly.

# What Information Do You Need?

Once the problem has been identified, you need to gather the facts and information relevant to the problem. Why has it occurred now? How is it affecting productivity in your department? What, if any, organizational

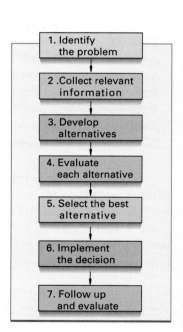

## EXHIBIT 5–1

The Decision-making process.

policies are relevant for dealing with this problem? What time limitations exist for solving it? What costs are involved?

In Mike's case, he'll need to find answers to questions such as: What were we paying the syndicator for the Home Improvement show? For how much longer will the syndicator provide new episodes? What are our competitors currently showing in the 7:30–8:00 p.m. time slot? What are the ratings of these shows? What contractual obligations do we have that would constrain our options to shuffle other programs into this slot?

## HOW DO YOU DEVELOP ALTERNATIVES?

Once you have collected the relevant information, it's now time to identify all possible alternatives. It is at this step in the decision process that you demonstrate your creativity (see Building a Supervisory Skill) by considering what alternatives exist beyond the obvious or those that may have been used previously.

Keep in mind that this step requires only identifying alternatives. No alternative—no matter how unusual or unconventional—should be discarded at this point. If an alternative isn't viable, you'll find out at the next stage. Also, avoid the tendency to stop searching for alternatives after only a couple have been identified. If you only see two or three choices, you probably haven't thought hard enough. Generally speaking, the more alternatives you can generate, the better your final solution will be. Why? Because your final choice can only be as good as the best alternative you've generated.

Mike Reddman, head of operations at WJLA, a Fox affiliate in Richmond, Virginia, spends a few moments with one of his news anchors. In his job, Mike has to make a number of decisions regarding how to provide the best programming possible.

What alternatives has Mike Reddman been able to develop? Here's what he came up with:

1. Buy a syndicated tabloid news show for this time slot. Hard Copy is available.
2. Buy the syndicated program Jeopardy.
3. Buy comedy reruns in syndication. Roseanne is available.
4. Move Entertainment Tonight from the 7:00 p.m. slot and fill the gap with expanded local news.
5. Create a local human-interest program—similar to Charleston Today, a program that he had developed at his previous job at a station in South Carolina.
6. Develop a new show around local college and professional sports teams.

 # BUILDING A SUPERVISORY SKILL

## BECOMING MORE CREATIVE

### ABOUT THE SKILL

Creativity is the ability to combine ideas in a unique way to make unusual associations between them. Each of us has the ability to be creative, yet some use their creativity more than others. Although creative people are sometimes referred to as "artsy" and difficult to describe, there are certain steps you can take in becoming more creative.[2]

### PRACTICING THE SKILL

1. **Think of yourself as creative.** Although it's a simple suggestion, research shows that if you think that you can't be creative, you won't be. Just as the little choo-choo train in the children's fable says, "I think I can", if we believe in ourselves, we can become more creative.

2. **Pay attention to your intuition.** Everyone has a subconscious mind that works well. Sometimes answers come when we least expect them. For example, when you are about to go to sleep, your relaxed mind sometimes comes up with solutions to problems you face. You need to listen to this intuition. In fact, many creative people keep a note pad near their bed and write down those "great" ideas when they come to them. That way, they are not forgotten.

3. **Move away from your comfort zone.** Every individual has a comfort zone in which certainty exists. But creativity and

[2]Adapted from J. Calano and J. Salzman, "Ten Ways to Fire Up Your Creativity," *Working Woman* (July 1989), pp. 94–95.

## ARE ALL ALTERNATIVES EQUAL?

The next step in the decision-making process is to evaluate all the strengths and weaknesses of each alternative. What will each cost? How long will each take to implement? What is the most favorable outcome you can expect from each? What is the most unfavorable outcome?

In this step, in particular, it is important to guard against biases. Undoubtedly some alternatives will have looked more attractive when they were first identified. Others, at first glance, may have seemed unrealistic or exceedingly risky. As a result, you may have a tendency to prematurely favor some outcomes over others and then bias your analysis accordingly. Try to put your initial prejudices on hold and evaluate each alternative as

the known often don't mix. To be creative, we need to move away from the status quo, and focus on something new.

4. **Engage in activities that put you outside your comfort zone.** Not only must we think differently, we need to do things differently. By engaging in activities that are different to us, we challenge ourselves. Learning to play a musical instrument or learning a foreign language, for example, opens the mind up and allows it to be challenged.

5. **Seek a change of scenery.** As humans, we are creatures of habit. Creative people force themselves out of their habits by changing their scenery. Going into a quiet and serene area where you can be alone with your thoughts is a good way to enhance creativity.

6. **Find several right answers.** Just as we set boundaries in rationality, we often seek solutions that are only good enough. Being creative means continuing to look for other solutions, even when you think you have solved the problem. A better,

more creative solution just might be found.

7. **Play your own devil's advocate.** Challenging yourself to defend your solutions helps you develop confidence in your creative efforts. Second guessing may also help you find more correct answers.

8. **Believe in finding a workable solution.** Like believing in yourself, you also need to believe in your ideas. If you don't think you can find a solution, one won't be found. Having a positive mental attitude, however, may become a self-fulfilling prophecy.

9. **Brainstorm with others.** Creativity is not an isolated activity. By bouncing ideas off of others, a synergistic effect occurs.

10. **Turn creative ideas into action.** Coming up with ideas is only half of the process. Once the ideas are generated, they must be implemented. Great ideas that remain in someone's mind, or on papers that no one reads, do little to expand one's creative abilities. ■

objectively as you can. Of course, no one is perfectly rational. However, you can improve the final outcome if you acknowledge your biases and overtly attempt to control them.

Exhibit 5–2 summarizes the highlights from Mike's evaluation of his six alternatives. By writing down key considerations—which in Mike's case are costs and audience market share—it is often easier for decision makers to compare alternatives.

## HOW DO YOU SELECT THE BEST ALTERNATIVE?

After analyzing the pros and cons for each alternative, it is time to select the best alternative. Of course, what's "best" will reflect any limitations or biases that you bring to the decision process. It depends on things

| Alternative | Estimated Weekly Cost | Estimated Market Share* | Strengths | Weaknesses |
|---|---|---|---|---|
| 1. Tabloid news show | $ 25,000 | 15-25 | Competition does well with *Hard Copy and American Journal* in this time slot. | High cost. Would leave little potential profit. Would split tabloid market further. |
| 2. Jeopardy | 16,000 | 8-12 | Known entity. | Low market potential. |
| 3. Comedy reruns | 30,000 | 20-35 | Could provide strong lead-in to 8:00 P.M. network programming. Might be perfect counter-programming move against competitor's tabloid shows. | High cost. Would leave almost no profit. |
| 4. Expand local news | 12-15,000 | 8-12 | Possible stop-gap measure. | Low potential. Not viable long-term solution. |
| 5. New human-interest show | 8-10,000 | 8-16 | Innovative. Nothing like this in our market. Could prove attractive to local advertisers. | Concept has failed in a number of major markets. |
| 6. New sports show | 6,000 | 6-20 | Unique. Nothing like this in our market. Build goodwill in community. Low cost. Strong appeal among 18-39 male market. | Risky. Is there a market for a half-hour of local sports coverage? |

\* Percent of those sets turned on which would be watching this show

## EXHIBIT 5–2

Evaluating alternatives.

like the comprehensiveness and accuracy of the information gathered in Step 2, your ingenuity in developing alternatives in Step 3, the degree of risk that you're willing to take, and the quality of your analysis in Step 4.

Mike's analysis led him to choose development of a new program focusing on local college and professional sports teams (Alternative 6). His logic went like this: "First of all, the syndicator advised us that they would produce Home Improvement through the end of the season. That meant I had ten weeks more of the show. I wanted to make my decision permanent, so I eliminated the option of expanding the local news. The payoff of going with Jeopardy didn't seem high enough to justify the cost. I think the tabloid news market is saturated in this time slot, so I passed on buying Hard Copy. We're in business to make money and, while I felt confident we could get the highest ratings in this time period with Roseanne, the cost was too high. That left developing a new human-interest or sports show. Of the two, I thought the sports-show alternative offered us the higher potential market share for the lower cost."

## How Do You Implement the Decision?

Even if you've made the proper choice, the decision may still fail if it is not implemented properly. This means you need to convey the decision to those affected and get their commitment to it. You'll specifically want to

Decisions are of little use until they are implemented. But implementation, at times, becomes an art. This supervisor uses a staff meeting to discuss the decisions that have been made and seeks assistance from her staff in putting these decisions into action.

assign responsibilities, allocate necessary resources, and clarify any deadlines (see Exhibit 5–3).

In Mike's case, he called a meeting of his programming staff, explained his decision and how he arrived at it, and encouraged discussion on any problems people anticipated. He then created a three-member departmental task force to develop the concept, prepare a format, and suggest key personnel for the program. He appointed one of the team members as the project leader and together they decided that the task force would make a formal presentation to Mike within three weeks.

### How Do You Follow Up and Evaluate?

The last phase in the decision-making process is to follow up and evaluate the outcomes of the decision. Did your choice accomplish the desired result? Did it correct the problem that you originally identified in Step 1? In Mike's decision, did he fill the time slot with a profitable, high-rated show? He hopes so, but he won't know the final answer until after the program has aired for a few months.

If the follow-up and evaluation indicate that the sought-after results weren't achieved, you'll want to review the decision process to see where you went wrong. You essentially have a brand new problem, and you should go completely through the decision process again with a fresh perspective.

## DECISION TOOLS

A number of tools and techniques have been developed over the years to help supervisors improve their decision-making capabilities. In this section, we'll present several of them.

# WHAT IS THE EXPECTED VALUE ANALYSIS?

The head of the skiing department at Dick's Sporting Goods store in Santa Fe is looking at several new brands of ski jackets. Given her space and budget limitations, she can only purchase one of these new brands to add to her selection. Which one should she choose?

**Expected value analysis** could help with this decision. It permits decision makers to place a monetary value on the various consequences likely to result from the selection of a particular course of action. The procedure is simple. You calculate the expected value of a particular alternative by weighting its possible outcomes by the probability (0 to 1.0, with 1.0 representing absolute certainty) of achieving the alternative, then summing up the totals derived from the weighting process.

Let's say our Dick's Sporting Goods supervisor is looking at three lines of ski jackets: Nike, Adidas, and Sunrise. She's constructed the payoff table in Exhibit 5–4 to summarize her analysis. Based on her past experience and personal judgment, she's calculated the potential yearly profit from each alternative and the probability of achieving that profit. The expected value of each alternative ranged from $6500 to $8800. Based on this analysis, the supervisor could anticipate the highest expected value by purchasing the Sunrise line of jackets.

**Expected value analysis**
a procedure that permits decision makers to place a monetary value on various consequences likely to result from the selection of a particular course of action.

| Alternative | Possible Outcome | Probability | Expected Value |
|---|---|---|---|
| Nike | $ 12,000 | 0.1 | $ 1,200 |
| | 8,000 | 0.7 | 5,600 |
| | 4,000 | 0.2 | 800 |
| | | | $ 7,600 |
| Adidas | $ 15,000 | 0.1 | $ 1,500 |
| | 10,000 | 0.2 | 2,000 |
| | 6,000 | 0.4 | 2,400 |
| | 2,000 | 0.3 | 600 |
| | | | $ 6,500 |
| Sunrise | $ 12,000 | 0.4 | $ 4,800 |
| | 8,000 | 0.4 | 3,200 |
| | 4,000 | 0.2 | 800 |
| | | | $ 8,800 |

**EXHIBIT 5–4**

Payoff table for ski jacket decision.

# How Are Decision Trees Useful?

**Decision trees** diagrams that analyze hiring, marketing, investment, equipment purchases, pricing, and similar decisions that involve a progression of decisions. Decision trees assign probabilities to each possible outcome and calculate payoffs for each decision path.

**Decision trees** are a useful way to analyze hiring, marketing, investment, equipment purchases, pricing, and similar decisions that involve a progression of decisions. They're called decision trees because, when diagrammed, they look a lot like a tree with branches. Typical decision trees encompass expected value analysis by assigning probabilities to each possible outcome and calculating payoffs for each decision path.

Exhibit 5–5 illustrates a decision facing Bart Rosen, the eastern region site-selection supervisor for a large bookstore chain. Bart supervises a small group of specialists who analyze potential locations and make store site recommendations to the eastern region's director. The lease on the company's store in Raleigh, North Carolina is expiring and the landlord has decided not to renew it. Bart and his group have to make a relocation recommendation to the regional director.

Bart's group has identified an excellent site in a nearby shopping mall. The mall owner has offered him two comparable locations: one with 12,000 square feet (the same as he has now) and the other a larger, 20,000 square-foot space. Bart has an initial decision to make about whether to recommend renting the larger or smaller location. If he chooses the larger space and the economy is strong, he estimates the store will make a $325,000 profit. However, if the economy is poor, the high operating costs of the larger store will mean only $50,000 in profit will be made. With the smaller store, he estimates the profit at $240,000 with a good economy and $130,000 with a poor one.

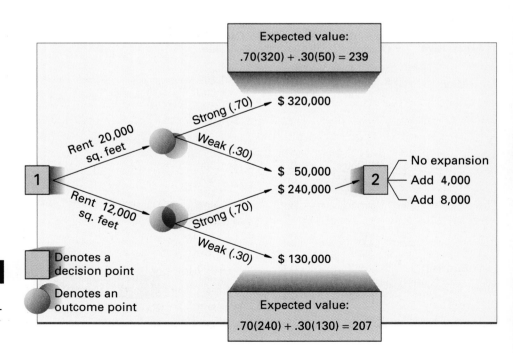

## EXHIBIT 5–5

Decision tree and expected values or renting a large or small retail space.

As you can see from Exhibit 5–5, the expected value for the larger store is $239,000 [(.70 × 320) + (.30 × 50)]. The expected value for the smaller store is $207,000 [(.70 × 240) + (.30 × 130)]. Given these results, Bart is planning to recommend the rental of the larger store space. But what if Bart wants to consider the implications of initially renting the smaller space and then possibly expanding if the economy picks up? He can extend the decision tree to include this second decision point. He has calculated three options: no expansion, adding 4,000 square feet, and adding 8,000 square feet. Following the approach used for Decision Point 1, he could calculate the profit potential by extending the branches on the tree and calculating expected values for the various options.

## WHAT IS THE MARGINAL ANALYSIS?

The concept of marginal, or incremental, analysis helps decision makers to optimize returns or minimize costs. **Marginal analysis** deals with the additional cost in a particular decision, rather than the average cost. For example, the operations supervisor for a large commercial dry cleaner wonders whether she should take on a new customer. She should consider not the total revenue and the total cost that would result after the order was taken, but rather what additional revenue would be generated by this particular order and what additional costs. If the incremental revenues exceed the incremental costs, total profits would be increased by accepting the order.

**Marginal analysis**
a method that helps decision makers optimize returns or minimize costs by dealing with the additional cost in a particular decision, rather than the average cost.

## WHAT BENEFIT DO YOU GET FROM MANAGEMENT INFORMATION SYSTEMS?

How can you improve your ability to collect the information needed for assessing problems and for accurately evaluating alternatives? The answer is: learn how to effectively use your organization's management information system.

A **management information system (MIS)** is a mechanism to provide you with needed and accurate information on a regular and timely basis. It can be manual or computer based, although recently almost all discussion on MIS focuses on computer-supported applications.

The term *system* in MIS implies order, arrangement, and purpose. Further, an MIS focuses specifically on providing you with information, not merely data. These two points are important and require elaboration.

A library provides a good analogy. Although it can contain millions of volumes, a library doesn't do users much good if they can't find what they want quickly. That's why libraries spend a lot of time cataloging their collections and ensuring that volumes are returned to their proper locations. Organizations today are like well-stocked libraries. There is no scarcity of data. The scarcity is in the ability to process it so that the right information

**Management information system (MIS)**
a mechanism that provides needed and accurate information on a regular and timely basis.

**Data**
raw, unanalyzed facts such as names, numbers, or quantities.

**Information**
analyzed and processed data.

**End-users**
users responsible for decision and control of systems.

is available to the right person when he or she needs it. A library is almost useless if it has the book you want, but you can't find it or it takes a week to retrieve it from storage. An MIS, on the other hand, has data organized in some meaningful way and can access the information in a reasonable amount of time. **Data** are raw, unanalyzed facts such as names, numbers, or quantities. As data, these facts are relatively useless to you. When data are analyzed and processed, they become **information**. An MIS collects data and turns it into relevant information for you to use.

Ten or fifteen years ago, supervisors essentially had two choices for getting the information they needed to make decisions. They could get it themselves through crude methods such as looking in files, making telephone calls, or asking questions in meetings. Sometimes, if they worked any place but the smallest organization, they could generally rely on reports generated by the organization's data processing specialist or centralized data processing department. Today, management information systems have become decentralized; that is, decisions and control of the systems have been pushed down to the users. With decentralization has come a major change—supervisors can now take responsibility for information control. They have become **end-users.** They can access the data they need and analyze it on their personal computers. As a result, today's supervisors need to be knowledgeable about their information needs and accept responsibility for their systems' operations.

The good news is that sophisticated management information systems dramatically improve the quantity and quality of information available to you, as well as the speed with which it can be obtained. On-line, real-time systems allow you to identify problems almost as they occur. Gone are the long delays between the appearance of a serious discrepancy and your

About twenty years ago, large mainframe computers drove an organization's MIS. Today, with the proliferation of desktop and laptop computers, supervisors have become end-users. That means they can access data and information from their offices and use that information to make decisions.

ability to find out about it. Database management programs allow you to look things up or get to the facts without either going to other people or digging through piles of paper. This reduces your dependence on others for data and makes fact gathering far more efficient. As a result, you can identify alternatives quickly, evaluate those alternatives by using a spreadsheet program, pose a series of what-if questions, and finally select the best alternative on the basis of answers to those questions.

## DECISION-MAKING STYLES

Each of you brings your own unique personality and experiences to the decisions you make. For instance, if you're someone who is basically conservative and uncomfortable with uncertainty, you're likely to value decision alternatives differently from someone who enjoys uncertainty and risk taking. These facts have led to research that has sought to identify individual decision styles.[3] To make the following discussion more personal, you might want to take ten minutes to complete the self-assessment (see Assessing Yourself).

[3]A. J. Rowe, J. D. Boulgarides, and M. R. McGrath, *Managerial Decision Making, Modules in Management Series,* Chicago, IL: SRA, 1994, pp. 18–22.

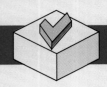

# ASSESSING YOURSELF

## INSTRUCTIONS

1. Use the following numbers to answer each question:
   8 - when the question is **MOST** like you.
   4 - when the question is **MODERATELY** like you.
   2 - when the question is **SLIGHTLY** like you.
   1 - when the question is **LEAST** like you.
2. Each of the numbers must be inserted in the box following the answers to each question.
3. DO NOT repeat any number on a given line.
4. For example, the numbers you might use to answer a given question could look as follows:
   8 2 1 4
5. Notice that each number has been used only once in the answers for a given question.
6. In answering the questions, think of how you **NORMALLY** act in your work situation.
7. Use the first thing that comes to your mind when answering the question.
8. There is no time limit in answering the questions and there are no right or wrong answers.
9. Your responses reflect how you feel about the questions and what you prefer to do, not what you think might be the right thing to do.

Please score the following questions based on the instruction given. Your score reflects *how you see yourself*, not what you believe is correct or desirable, as related to *your work situation*. It covers *typical decisions* that you make in your work environment.

| | I | | II | | III | | IV | |
|---|---|---|---|---|---|---|---|---|
| **1.** My prime objective is to: | Have a position with status | 1 | Be the best in my field | 8 | Achieve recognition for my work | 2 | Feel secure in my job | 4 |
| **2.** I enjoy jobs that: | Are technical & well defined | 2 | Have considerable variety | 4 | Allow independent action | 8 | Involve people | 1 |
| **3.** I expect people working for me to be: | Productive and fast | 4 | Highly capable | 2 | Commited and responsive | 8 | Receptive to suggestions | 1 |
| **4.** In my job, I look for: | Practical results | 1 | The best solutions | 4 | New approaches or ideas | 2 | Good working environment | 8 |
| **5.** I communicate best with others: | In a direct one to one basis | 8 | In writing | 2 | By having a group discussion | 4 | In a formal meeting | 1 |
| **6.** In my planning I emphasize: | Current problems | 8 | Meeting objectives | 2 | Future goals | 4 | Developing people's careers | 1 |
| **7.** When faced with solving a problem, I: | Rely on proven approaches | 2 | Apply careful analysis | 8 | Look for creative approaches | 4 | Rely on my feelings | 1 |
| **8.** When using information I prefer: | Specific facts | 2 | Accurate and complete data | 8 | Broad coverage of many options | 1 | Limited data which is easily understood | 4 |
| **9.** When I am not sure about what to do, I: | Rely on intuition | 1 | Search for facts | 4 | Look for a possible compromise | 2 | Wait before making a decision | 8 |
| **10.** Whenever possible I avoid: | Long debates | 1 | Incomplete work | 2 | Using numbers or formulas | 8 | Conflict with others | 4 |

| | I | | II | | III | | IV | |
|---|---|---|---|---|---|---|---|---|
| **11.** I am especially good at: | Remembering dates & facts | 8 | Solving difficult problems | 4 | Seeing many possibilities | 2 | Interacting with others | 1 |
| **12.** When time is important, I: | Decide & act quickly | 2 | Follow plans & priorities | 8 | Refuse to be pressured | 1 | Seek guidance or support | 4 |
| **13.** In social settings I generally: | Speak with others | 4 | Think about what is being said | 1 | Observe what is going on | 8 | Listen to the conversation | 2 |
| **14.** I am good at remembering: | People's names | 2 | Places we met | 1 | People's faces | 8 | People's personality | 4 |
| **15.** The work I do provides me: | The power to influence others | 1 | Challenging assignments | 4 | Achieving my personal goals | 8 | Acceptance by the group | 2 |
| **16.** I work well with those who are: | Energetic & ambitious | 2 | Self confident | 4 | Open minded | 1 | Polite and trusting | 8 |
| **17.** When under stress, I: | Become anxious | 8 | Concentrate on the problem | 2 | Become frustrated | 4 | Am forgetful | 1 |
| **18.** Others consider me: | Aggressive | 4 | Disciplined | 2 | Imaginative | 1 | Supportive | 8 |
| **19.** My decisions typically are: | Realistic and direct | 4 | Systematic or abstract | 1 | Broad & flexible | 8 | Sensitive to the needs of others | 2 |
| **20.** I dislike: | Losing control | 4 | Boring work | 2 | Following rules | 1 | Being rejected | 8 |

## SCORING THE DECISION-STYLE INVENTORY

**1.** Add the points of the four columns—I, II, III, IV.
**2.** The sum of the four columns should be 300 points. If your sum does not equal 300 points, check your addition and your answers.
**3.** Place your scores in the appropriate box—I, II, III, IV.

| ANALYTIC II | CONCEPTUAL III |
|---|---|
| 73 | 85 |
| **DIRECTIVE I** | **BEHAVIORAL IV** |
| 82 | 73 |

Source: A. J. Rowe, R. Mason, and K. Dickel, *Strategic Management and Business Policy.* Reading, MA: Addison-Wesley, 1982, p. 217, © Alan J. Rowe 1983. Reproduced by permission of Alan J. Rowe.

# WHAT ARE THE FOUR DECISION-MAKING STYLES?

The basic foundation for a decision-style model is the recognition that people differ along two dimensions. The first is their way of thinking. Some people are logical and rational. They process information serially. In contrast, some people are intuitive and creative. They perceive things as a whole. The other dimension addresses a person's tolerance for ambiguity. Some people have a high need to structure information in ways that minimize ambiguity, while others are able to process many thoughts at the same time. When these two dimensions are diagrammed, they form four styles of decision making (see Exhibit 5–6). These are: Directive, Analytic, Conceptual, and Behavioral.

### DIRECTIVE STYLE

People using the directive style have low tolerance for ambiguity and seek rationality. They are efficient and logical. Their efficiency concerns may result in them making decisions with minimal information and with assessing few alternatives. Directive-types make decisions fast and they focus on the short run.

### ANALYTIC STYLE

The analytic type has a much greater tolerance for ambiguity than do directive managers. This leads to the desire for more information and consideration of more alternatives than is true for directives. Analytic managers would be best characterized as careful decision makers with the ability to adapt or cope with new situations.

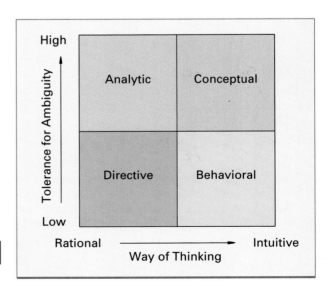

**EXHIBIT 5–6**

Decision-style model.

## CONCEPTUAL STYLE

Individuals with a conceptual style tend to be very broad in their outlook and consider many alternatives. Their focus is long range and they are very good at finding creative solutions to problems.

## BEHAVIORAL STYLE

The behavioral style characterizes decision makers who work well with others. They're concerned with the achievement of their employees. They're receptive to suggestions from others and rely heavily on meetings for communicating. This type of decision maker tries to avoid conflict and seek acceptance.

# WHAT'S THE POINT OF THESE FOUR DECISION-MAKING STYLES?

Although these four categories are distinct, most individuals have characteristics that fall into more than one. It's best to think in terms of an individual's dominant style and backup styles. While some people rely almost exclusively on their dominant style, more flexible individuals can make shifts depending on the situation. Referring to the self-assessment, the box with the highest score reflects your dominant style. The closer a person is to a score of 75 in each category, the greater flexibility he or she shows.

Business students, supervisors, and top executives tend to score highest in the analytic style. That's not surprising given the emphasis that formal education, particularly business education, gives to developing rational decision-making skills. For instance, courses in accounting, statistics, and finance all stress analytical thinking.

Focusing on decision styles can also be useful for helping you understand how two intelligent people, with access to the same information, can differ in the ways they approach decisions and the final choices they make. It can also explain conflicts between you and your employees (or others you come in contact with). For example, if you are a "directive" supervisor, you expect work to be performed rapidly. You may get frustrated by the slowness and deliberate actions of a conceptual or analytic employee. At the same time, if your style is "analytic," you might criticize a "decisive" employee for incomplete work or acting too hastily. As an "analytic," you may have great difficulty with your "behavioral" counterpart because of lack of understanding why feelings are used as the basis for decisions rather than rational logic.

# ETHICS IN DECISION MAKING

In Chapter 2, we introduced you to the topic of ethics, and described ways in which you can act ethically. Inherent in that discussion was the idea that when you are faced with ethical/unethical choices, you are faced with a problem (see Dealing with a Difficult Issue). Ethical concerns then become a part of your decision making. For instance, one alternative may generate a considerably higher financial return than the others, but it might be ethically questionable because it compromises employee safety. Let's look at this important issue in greater detail.

## WHAT ARE COMMON RATIONALIZATIONS?

Through the ages, people have developed some common rationalizations to justify questionable conduct.[4] These rationalizations provide some insights into why supervisors might make poor ethical choices.

*"It's not 'really' illegal or immoral."* Where is the line between being smart and being shady? Between an ingenious decision and an immoral one? Because this line is often ambiguous, people can rationalize that what they've

---

## DEALING WITH A DIFFICULT ISSUE

### HIRING A FRIEND?

In making hiring decisions, supervisors often face difficult issues. Take the following situation:

Your company is advertising for a new employee to work in your department. The person in this position will be important because the work directly affects the quality and quantity of your performance. One of your friends needs a job and you think he is qualified for the position. But you feel you *could* find better qualified and more experienced candidates if you keep looking.

What would you do? What might influence your decision? Would you tell your friend? How do you handle this sensitive situation?

---

[4]S. W. Gellerman, "Why 'Good' Managers Make Bad Ethical Choices," *Harvard Business Review,* July–August, 1986, p. 89.

done is not really wrong. If you put enough people in an ill-defined situation, some will conclude that whatever hasn't been labeled specifically as wrong must be OK. This is especially true if there are rich rewards for attaining certain goals, and the organization's appraisal system doesn't look too carefully at how those goals are achieved. The practice of profiting on a stock tip through insider information seems often to fall into this category.

*"It's in my (or the organization's) best interest."* The belief that unethical conduct is in a person's or an organization's best interests nearly always results from a narrow view of what those interests are. For instance, supervisors can come to believe that it's acceptable to bribe officials if the bribe results in the organization's getting a contract, or to falsify financial records if this improves their unit's performance record.

*"No one will find out."* The third rationalization accepts the wrongdoing but assumes that it will never be uncovered. Philosophers ponder, "If a tree falls in a forest and no one hears it, did it make a noise?" Some supervisors answer the analogous question, "If an unethical act is committed and no one knows it, is it wrong?" in the negative. This rationalization is often stimulated by inadequate controls, strong pressures to perform, the appraisal of performance results while ignoring the means by which they're achieved, the allocation of big salary increases and promotions to those who achieve these results, and the absence of punishment for those who get caught in wrongdoing.

*"Since it helps the organization, the organization will condone it and protect me."* This response represents loyalty gone berserk. Some supervisors come to believe that not only do the organization's interests override the laws and values of society, but also that the organization expects its employees to exhibit unqualified loyalty. Even if the supervisor is caught, he or she believes that the organization will support and reward him or her for showing loyalty. Supervisors who use this rationalization to justify unethical practices place the organization's good name in jeopardy. This rationalization has motivated some supervisors for defense contractors to justify labor mischarges, cost duplications, product substitutions, and other contract abuses. While supervisors should be expected to be loyal to the organization against competitors and detractors, that loyalty shouldn't put the organization above the law, common morality, or society itself.

# CAN YOU IDENTIFY THE THREE DIFFERENT VIEWS ON ETHICS?

In this section we want to present three different ethical positions. They can help us to see how individuals can make different decisions by using different ethical criteria (see Exhibit 5–7).

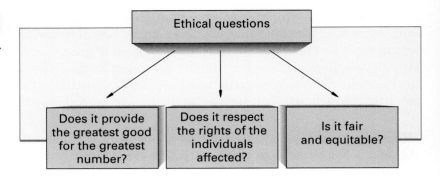

## EXHIBIT 5–7

Three views on ethics.

**Ethical questions**

- Does it provide the greatest good for the greatest number?
- Does it respect the rights of the individuals affected?
- Is it fair and equitable?

**Utilitarian view of ethics**
a view in which decisions are made solely on the basis of their outcomes or consequences.

## THE UTILITARIAN VIEW

The first is the **utilitarian view of ethics,** in which decisions are made solely on the basis of their outcomes or consequences. The goal of utilitarianism is to provide the greatest good for the greatest number. This view tends to dominate business decision making. Why? Because it's consistent with goals like efficiency, productivity, and high profits. By maximizing profits, for instance, a supervisor can argue that he or she is securing the greatest good for the greatest number.

**Rights view of ethics**
a view that calls on individuals to make decisions consistent with fundamental liberties and privileges as set forth in documents such as the Bill of Rights.

## THE RIGHTS VIEW

Another ethical perspective is the **rights view of ethics.** This calls on individuals to make decisions consistent with fundamental liberties and privileges as set forth in documents like the Bill of Rights. The rights view of ethics is concerned with respecting and protecting the basic rights of individuals; for example, the right to privacy, free speech, and due process. This position would protect employees who report unethical or illegal practices by their organization to the press or government agencies on the grounds of their right to free speech.

**Justice view of ethics**
a view that requires individuals to impose and enforce rules fairly and impartially so there is an equitable distribution of benefits and costs.

## THE JUSTICE VIEW

The final perspective is the **justice view of ethics.** This requires individuals to impose and enforce rules fairly and impartially so there is an equitable distribution of benefits and costs. Union members typically favor this view. It justifies paying people the same wage for a given job, regardless of performance differences, and it uses seniority as the criterion in making layoff decisions.

Each of these three perspectives has advantages and liabilities. The utilitarian view promotes efficiency and productivity, but it can result in ignoring the rights of some individuals, particularly those with minority representation in the organization. The rights perspective protects individuals from injury and is consistent with freedom and privacy, but it can create an overly legalistic work environment that hinders productivity and

efficiency. The justice perspective protects the interests of the under-represented and less powerful, but it can encourage a sense of entitlement that reduces risk taking, innovation, and productivity.

Even though each of these perspectives has its individual strengths and weaknesses, as we noted, individuals in business tend to focus on utilitarianism. But times are changing and so too must supervisors and other organizational members. New trends toward individual rights and social justice mean that supervisors need ethical standards based on nonutilitarian criteria. This is a solid challenge to today's supervisor because making decisions using criteria such as individual rights and social justice involves far more ambiguities than using utilitarian criteria such as effects on efficiency and profits.

## Is There a Guide to Acting Ethically?

There is no simple credo that we can provide that will ensure that you won't err in your ethical judgments. What we can offer are some questions that you can and should ask yourself when making important decisions and decisions with obvious ethical implications.[5]

1. How did this problem occur in the first place?
2. Would you define the problem differently if you stood on the other side of the fence?

[5]Adapted from L. L. Nash, "Ethics Without the Sermon," *Harvard Business Review,* November–December 1981, p. 81.

3. To whom and to what do you give your loyalty as a person and as a member of your organization?
4. What is your intention in making this decision?
5. What is the potential for your intentions to be misunderstood by others in the organization?
6. How does your intention compare with the probable result?
7. Whom could your decision injure?
8. Can you discuss the problem with the affected parties before you make the decision?
9. Are you confident that your position will be as valid over a long period of time as it seems now?
10. Could you disclose your decision to your boss or your immediate family?
11. How would you feel if your decision was described, in detail, on the front page of your local newspaper?

## GROUP DECISION MAKING

Decisions in organizations are increasingly being made by groups rather than by individuals. There seem to be at least two primary reasons for this. First is the desire to develop more and better alternatives. The adage "two heads are better than one" translates into groups being able to generate a greater number, and potentially a more creative set, of decision alternatives. Second, organizations are relying less on the historical idea that departments and other organizational units should be separate and independent decision units. To get the best ideas and to improve their implementation, organizations are increasingly turning to teams that cut across traditional departmental lines for decision making. This requires group decision-making techniques.

### What Are the Advantages of Group Decisions?

Individual and group decisions each have their own set of strengths. Neither is ideal for all situations. Let's begin, therefore, by reviewing the advantages that group decisions have over an individual decision maker (see Exhibit 5–8).

#### PROVIDES MORE COMPLETE INFORMATION

A group will bring a diversity of experience and perspective to the decision process that an individual, acting alone, cannot.

## EXHIBIT 5–8

The advantages and disadvantages of group decision making.

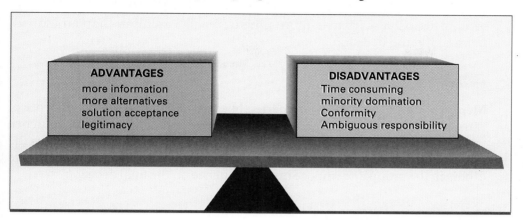

## GENERATES MORE ALTERNATIVES

Because groups have a greater quantity and diversity of information, they can identify more alternatives than can an individual.

## INCREASES ACCEPTANCE OF A SOLUTION

Many decisions fail after the final choice has been made because people do not accept the solution. If the people who will be affected by a certain solution and who will help implement it get to participate in the decision making itself, they will be more likely to accept the decision and to encourage others to accept it.

## INCREASES LEGITIMACY

The group decision-making process is consistent with democratic ideals and therefore may be perceived as more legitimate than decisions made by a single person.

## ARE THERE DISADVANTAGES TO GROUP DECISION MAKING?

If groups are so good, how did the phrase "A camel is a racehorse put together by a committee" become so popular? The answer, of course, is that group decisions are not without their drawbacks. The major disadvantages of group decision making are as follows.

## TIME CONSUMING

It takes time to assemble a group. Additionally, the interaction that takes place once the group is in place is frequently inefficient. The result is that groups almost always take more time to reach a solution than an individual making the decision alone.

## MINORITY DOMINATION

Members of a group are never perfectly equal. They may differ in terms of rank in the organization, experience, knowledge about the problem, influence with other members, verbal skills, assertiveness, and the like. This creates the opportunity for one or more members to use their advantages to dominate others in the group and impose undue influence on the final decision.

## PRESSURES TO CONFORM

There are social pressures in groups. The desire of group members to be accepted and considered assets to the group can quash any overt disagreement and encourage conformity among viewpoints. The withholding by group members of different views in order to appear in agreement is called **groupthink.**

**Groupthink**
withholding of differing views by group members in order to appear in agreement

## AMBIGUOUS RESPONSIBILITY

Group members share responsibility, but who is actually responsible for the final outcome? In an individual decision, it is clear who is responsible, but in a group decision the responsibility of any single member is watered down.

## IS THERE A GUIDE FOR WHEN TO USE GROUP DECISION MAKING?

When are groups better than individuals and vice versa? That depends on what you mean by better. Let's look at four criteria frequently associated with "better" decisions: accuracy, speed, creativity, and acceptance (see News Flash).

In terms of accuracy, group decisions tend to be more accurate. The evidence indicates that, on the average, groups make more accurate decisions than individuals. This doesn't mean, of course, that all groups outperform every individual. Rather, group decisions have been found to be more effective than those that would have been reached by the average individual in the group. However, they seldom are as good as the best individual.

If better is defined in terms of decision speed, individuals are superior. Group decision processes are characterized by give and take, which consumes time.

# NEWS FLASH!

## STIMULATING CREATIVE PROBLEM SOLVING

Regardless of your inherent creativity, there are techniques you can use to improve your ability as a creative problem solver. The more popular of these techniques include attribute listing, lateral thinking, and synectics.

**Attribute listing** is essentially individualized brainstorming. You isolate the major characteristics of traditional alternatives. Each major attribute of the alternative is then considered in turn, and is changed in every conceivable way. No ideas are rejected, no matter how ridiculous they may seem. Once this extensive list is completed, the constraints of the problem are imposed so as to leave only viable alternatives.

Creativity can be stimulated by replacing traditional vertical thinking with zig-zag or **lateral thinking.** Vertical thinking is highly rational. It is an orderly process, with each step following the previous step in an unbroken sequence. It must be correct at every step. Further, vertical thinking selects and deals only with what is relevant. In contrast, lateral thinking is thinking sideways: not developing a pattern but restructuring a pattern. It is not sequential. For example, you might tackle a problem from the solution end rather than the starting end, and back into various beginning states. A supervisor could, for instance, conceptualize what her department might look like in terms of tasks, people, and work layout in the year 2010—then back into various scenarios about how it got to look like that. Lateral thinking does not have to be correct at each step. It may be necessary to pass through a "wrong" area in order to reach a position from which the correct path may be visible. Finally, lateral thinking is not restricted to relevant information. It deliberately uses random or irrelevant information to bring about a new way of looking at the problem.

**Synectics** makes extensive use of analogies to make the strange familiar and the familiar strange. It operates on the assumption that most problems aren't new. The challenge is to view the problem in a new way. So you have to abandon familiar ways of viewing things. For instance, most of us think of hens laying eggs. But how many of us have considered that a hen is only an egg's way of making another egg? Obviously, this represents another way of looking at the situation.

Synectics makes extensive use of analogies to look for similarities between relationships or functions. These include personal, direct, and fantasy analogies.

**Attribute listing** individualized brainstorming; isolation of major characteristics of traditional alternatives, which are each considered in turn and changed in every conceivable way.

**Lateral thinking** sideways, nonsequential thinking.

**Synectics** use of analogies to look for similarities between relationships or functions.

A *personal analogy* requires personal identification. It requires that you put yourself into the problem. For example, assume that you're trying to conceive of new inner workings for a wristwatch. In order to stimulate your mind toward what alternatives may be available, imagine yourself inside the watch, actually viewing the mechanism. From this perspective you begin to see what things are relevant and what things are irrelevant to the inner workings of the timepiece. By putting yourself into the problem, you feel and react differently from the way you would if you were analyzing it from a distance.

The most popular analogy for developing new alternatives is the *direct analogy* in which you compare parallel facts, knowledge, or technology. For example, Alexander Graham Bell applied concepts that operate in the ear to his "talking box." He noticed that the massive bones in the ear are operated by a delicate, thin membrane. He wondered why, then, a thicker and stronger piece of membrane shouldn't move and cause a piece of steel to vibrate. Out of that analogy, the telephone was conceived.

With the *fantasy analogy*, you begin by assuming that anything you wish can in fact be operationalized. By starting out asking how you might like it to be, it is possible to back up and concoct an alternative that has never previously been thought of.

Decision quality can also be assessed in terms of the degree to which a solution demonstrates creativity. If creativity is important, groups tend to do better than individuals. This requires, however, that the forces that foster groupthink—pressure to repress doubts about the group's shared views, the validity of favored arguments, excessive desire by the group to give an appearance of consensus, and the assumption that silence or abstention by members is a "yes" vote—be constrained.

As noted previously, because group decisions have input from more people, they are likely to result in solutions that will have a higher degree of acceptance.

## HOW CAN YOU IMPROVE GROUP DECISION MAKING?

When members of a group meet face-to-face and interact with one another, they create the potential for groupthink. They can censor themselves and pressure other group members into agreement. Three ways of making group decision making more creative have been suggested: brainstorming, the nominal group technique, and electronic meetings.

## BRAINSTORMING

**Brainstorming** is a relatively simple technique for overcoming pressures for conformity that retard the development of creative alternatives.[6] It does this by utilizing an idea-generating process that specifically encourages any and all alternatives while withholding any criticism of those alternatives. In a typical brainstorming session, a half-dozen to a dozen people sit around a table. The group leader states the problem in a clear manner that is understood by all participants. Members then "freewheel" as many alternatives as they can in a given time. No criticism is allowed, and all the alternatives are recorded for later discussion and analysis. Brainstorming, however, is merely a process for generating ideas. The next method, the nominal group technique, goes further by helping groups arrive at a preferred solution.[7]

**Brainstorming**
a technique for overcoming pressures for conformity that retard the development of creative alternatives; an idea-generating process that specifically encourages alternatives while withholding criticism of those alternatives.

## NOMINAL GROUP TECHNIQUE

The **nominal group technique** restricts discussion during the decision-making process, hence the term. Group members must be present, as in a traditional committee meeting, but they are required to operate independently. The chief advantage of this technique is that it permits the group to meet formally but does not restrict independent thinking as so often happens in the traditional interacting group.

**Nominal group technique**
a technique that restricts discussion during the decision-making process.

## ELECTRONIC MEETINGS

The most recent approach to group decision making blends the nominal group technique with sophisticated computer technology.[8] It's called the **electronic meeting.**

Once the technology for the meeting is in place, the concept is simple. Participants may sit around a horseshoe-shaped table that is empty except

**Electronic meeting**
a group decision-making technique in which participants are positioned in front of computer terminals as issues are presented. Participants type responses onto computer screens as their anonymous comments and aggregate votes are displayed on a projection screen in the room.

[6]A. E. Osborn, Applied Imagination: Principles and Procedures of Creative Thinking (New York: Scribners, 1941).

[7]The following discussion is based on Andre L. Delbecq, A. H. Van de Ven, and D. H. Gustafson, *Group Techniques for Program Planning: A Guide to Nominal and Delphi Processes* (Glenview, Ill.: Scott, Foresman, 1975).

[8]See A. R. Dennis, J. E. George, L. M. Jessup, J. E. Nunamaker, Jr., and D. R. Vogel, "Information Technology to Support Group Work," *MIS Quarterly*, December 1988, pp. 591–619; D. W. Straub and R. A. Beauclair, "Current and Future Uses of Group Decision Support System Technology: Report on a Recent Empirical Study," *Journal of Management Information Systems*, Summer 1988, pp. 101–16; J. Bartimo, "At These Shouting Matches, No One Says a Word," *Business Week*, June 11, 1990, p. 78; and M. S. Poole, M. Holmes, and G. DeSanctis, "Conflict Management in a Computer-Supported Meeting Environment," *Management Science*, August 1991, pp. 926–53.

Companies like Minolta and IBM use electronic meetings to bring people from all over the world together to have input into decisions that are being made. This process permits anonymity, honesty, and speed. At IBM, more than 7000 employees have participated.

for a series of computer terminals—or they may be in remote sites with links to the computers. Issues are presented to participants who type their responses onto their computer screens. Individual comments, as well as aggregate votes, are displayed on a projection screen in the room.

The major advantages to electronic meetings are anonymity, honesty, and speed. Participants can anonymously type any message they want, and it will flash on the screen for all to see at the push of a board key. It also allows people to be brutally honest with no penalty. It's fast—chitchat is eliminated, discussions don't digress, and many participants (as many as 50) can "talk" at once without stepping on others' toes.

Experts claim that electronic meetings are as much as 55 percent faster than traditional face-to-face meetings.[9] Supervisors at Phelps Dodge Mining, for instance, used the approach to cut its annual planning meeting from several days down to twelve hours. However, there are drawbacks. Those who can type quickly can outshine those who may be verbally eloquent but are lousy typists; those with the best ideas don't get credit for them; and the process lacks the informational richness of face-to-face oral communication. This technology is currently only in its infancy. The future of group decision making is very likely to include extensive usage of electronic meetings.

[9]See William M. Bulkeley, "'Computizing' Dull Meetings Is Touted As an Antidote to the Mouth that Bored," *The Wall Street Journal,* January 28, 1992, p. B1.

**5.** A conceptual style of decision-making reflects an individual who
   **a.** thinks intuitively and has a low tolerance for ambiguity
   **b.** thinks rationally and has a high tolerance for ambiguity
   **c.** thinks intuitively and has a high tolerance for ambiguity
   **d.** thinks rationally and has a low tolerance for ambiguity
**6.** What is groupthink? What are its implications for decision making?
**7.** The justice view of ethics is concerned with respecting and protecting the basic freedoms of individuals, such as free speech and due process. True or False?
**8.** Group decisions will usually be superior to individual decisions except when
   **a.** speed is a concern
   **b.** accuracy is critical
   **c.** to minimize the tendency of groupthink
   **d.** flexibility is needed

## SUMMARY

After reading this chapter, I can:

1. **List the seven steps in the decision-making process.** The seven steps in the decision-making process are: (1) identify the problem; (2) collect relevant information; (3) develop alternatives; (4) evaluate each alternative; (5) select the best alternative; (6) implement the decision; (7) follow-up and evaluation.

2. **Describe expected value analysis.** Expected value analysis calculates the expected value of a particular alternative by weighting its possible outcomes by the probability of achieving the alternative, then summing up the totals derived from the weighting process.

3. **Contrast data with information.** Data are raw, unanalyzed facts. Data becomes information when it is analyzed and processed. It is information that is most relevant for making informed decisions.

4. **Describe the four types of decision styles.** The directive type is efficient and logical. The analytic type is careful, with the ability to adapt or cope with new situations. The conceptual type considers many alternatives and is good at coming up with creative solutions. The behavioral type emphasizes suggestions from others and conflict avoidance.

5. **Explain three different ethical viewpoints.** The utilitarian view of ethics makes decisions based on the greatest good for the greatest number. The rights view of ethics makes decisions consistent with fundamental liberties and privileges. The justice view of ethics seeks fairness and impartiality.

6. **Compare and contrast group decision and individual decision making.** The advantages of group decisions are more complete information, more alternatives, increased acceptance of a solution, and increased legitimacy.

7. **List three techniques for improving group decision making.** Three techniques for improving group decision making include brainstorming, nominal group technique, and electronic meetings.

## REVIEWING YOUR KNOWLEDGE

1. Contrast symptoms with problems. Give three examples.

2. In which step of the decision-making process do you think creativity would be most helpful? In which step would quantitative analysis tools be most helpful?

3. Calculate your estimated grade-point average this semester using expected value analysis.

4. What is meant by the expression "supervisors are increasingly becoming end-users in MIS"?

5. How might certain decision styles fit better with specific jobs? Give examples.

6. What rationalizations do people use to justify questionable conduct?

7. Which view of ethics dominates in business firms? Why?

8. When should supervisors use groups for decision making? When should they make the decisions themselves?

9. Contrast the nominal group technique and electronic meeting.

# ANSWERS TO THE POP QUIZZES

1. **c. recognizing a problem by comparison with past performance.** This question reinforces the importance of properly defining a problem. That is, a problem is a discrepancy between an existing and a desired state of affairs. Past performance sets standards against which current performance is compared.
2. Planning sets the standards against which a supervisor can compare actual performance. A significant variation from the plan represents a problem—which then requires a decision about how to correct it.
3. **False.** Solving the wrong problem is a waste of time. The first step in problem solving is to identify what the problem is. Solving the wrong problem can actually make the situation worse by creating new problems.
4. **b. the control function of management becomes important.** Follow up and evaluation involves determining if the problem has been corrected. This means that actual progress is again compared to the "standard." This is the fundamental activity of control.
5. **c. thinks intuitively and has a high tolerance for ambiguity.** This is the definition of conceptual decision-making style.
6. Groupthink is a term used to reflect the withholding by group members of different views in order to appear in agreement. It effects decision making by having pressure applied to group members so that doubts about the group's shared views are silenced; this silence is taken to mean a "yes" vote. Because of this pressure, poorer decisions may result.
7. **False.** This is the definition of the rights view of ethics. The justice view of ethics seeks fairness and impartiality.
8. **a. speed is a concern.** Responses b, c, and d are advantages of group decision making. Where speed is concerned, individuals perform better. Therefore, response (a) is the exception to the advantages of group decision making. ∎

## A CLASS EXERCISE: PROBLEM SOLVING ABC STYLE

Form into groups of four or five. You are a committee of employees at the ABC Television Network. This committee has been appointed to analyze the future of network television and to create a set of viable alternatives to assure the network's future.

The problem is this. In the 1960s, the three major television networks—ABC, CBS, and NBC—held better than 90 percent of the prime-time audience. By the early 1990s, that was down to less than 60 percent. Reasons for this decline included increased competition from cable stations, the new Fox Network, programming by nonnetwork-affiliated local stations, and video rentals. Further market erosion occurred as a result of efforts by companies like Time-Warner, Microsoft, and U.S. West to combine television sets, phone lines, and computers to create multimedia entertainment access in the home.

You have 30 minutes for your committee to develop a list of options for ABC. Be prepared to discuss (a) your top three recommendations, and (b) what your committee believes to be its most creative option.

## THINKING CRITICALLY

### CASE 5.A

### Helping Roger Kennedy Decide

When Roger Kennedy was promoted to assistant director of training at Alcoa, he had mixed feelings about the job. He knew he had the background to do the work. He had developed good interpersonal skills and was frequently called on to work on special assignments which required problem solving. He also had high grades in all his college coursework and especially liked his human resource management and psychology classes, where he frequently found herself in leadership roles. Most people would describe Roger as intelligent, resourceful, motivated, and hard working.

Roger was selected for the position by the training director. She knew Roger was energetic and creative—the two elements the training unit needed badly. Roger and his boss had numerous conversations about personnel training and they had similar ideas about what would stimulate and motivate workers. Why, then, did Roger have reservations about the training position? Roger would have to work with two other assistant directors who had been in their positions for four and nine years respectively. His boss also had been in the organization for nine years—all but two of those years in Roger's present position.

From the very beginning, Roger felt torn between wanting to forge ahead with new ideas that might ruffle some of the veterans' feathers, and trying to "fit in" by being more conservative in helping to implement the training model that had been in place for several years.

## RESPONDING TO THIS CASE

1. In his new job, how can Roger make good use of the knowledge he has about decision-making styles?
2. What can Roger do to learn more about his boss and his fellow assistant directors, to get them to consider some of his ideas about the direction training should take?

3. Based on the four decision-making styles, create a portfolio of famous people in leadership positions. Identify their dimensions and characteristics which make up their decision-making style.

# CASE 5.B

## Second Time Around

Rosalee Garcia is a supervisor at Second Time Around, a clothing resale shop located on Bainbridge Island in Washington state. Second Time Around has a good clientele—both from a seller's and buyer's viewpoint. Frequently the sellers who take their used clothing to Second Time Around have worn an outfit only once or twice. Buyers not only appreciate the like-new condition of the clothing, but the prices are excellent.

Rosalee has noticed that Becky Wilson, one of her salespersons, likes to try on some of the new consignment garments when they come into the store. It used to be that she took time to try on some of the clothing when the store was not terribly busy. However, now she is finding it is easier to "check out" some of the incoming merchandise by taking it home. More and more frequently she takes an outfit home to try on. Sometimes she buys the outfit at the 15 percent discount the store gives to employees for the merchandise they purchase. She returns to the store the things she doesn't buy, usually within a day or two, but always within a week.

Rosalee has noticed that some of the clothing Becky has taken home, looks like it may have been worn since the time it was brought into the store by the seller. Rosalee wonders if Becky is wearing an outfit and bringing it back. She wonders, too, if Becky is bringing all of the "borrowed" outfits back to the store. It is hard to know for sure, but Rosalee feels that some decisions have to be made about this growing perception of hers.

## RESPONDING TO THE CASE

1. What are some of the common rationalizations that Rosalee might have about this situation?
2. If you were in Rosalee's position, what course of action would you take to solve this problem? Who would benefit or lose from this course of action?
3. Assume that Becky was abusing her employee privilege. Discuss and apply the three different ethical views to this situation. Which position would you take? Defend your position.
4. Make a decision about what Rosalee should do to solve this problem. Then review the ethical decision guidelines on pages 171–172 and answer the 11 questions. After answering the 11 questions, would you make the same decision about the case? Why or why not? ∎

## Bonnie Patznick
## Satellite Lab Supervisor,
## Abbott-Northwestern Hospital

Bonnie had many year's experience as a lab technician, but no experience in supervision when she assumed this position. She has always worked in a hospital laboratory. Now she is responsible for six off-site laboratories, many of them inside clinics. In the hospital laboratory, quality controls are absolutely mandatory. To her surprise, Bonnie discovered that the satellite laboratories had very few quality controls. In fact, when she insisted that quality controls be run, her staff was amazed. Bonnie was a skilled lab technician, but she had always followed procedures. Now she had to set up her own.

New federal regulations supported the implementation of controls. Bonnie set up an internal control system. On a weekly or monthly basis, specimens are split and sent to the hospital laboratory for testing. She introduced external controls such as outside proficiency testing. Procedure manuals were created for each procedure. Bonnie's approach was proven successful during federal inspections.

The staff has accepted the new standards well. When they had a problem with a new freezer, it was the staff that first noted the discrepancies in their tests and reported them to Bonnie. When one staff person went on vacation and left a trainee in charge of some expensive equipment, the equipment malfunctioned. The trainee turned off the equipment on Friday afternoon. On Monday morning, it was no longer operating. When Bonnie arrived at the satellite laboratory she talked to the trainee. Bonnie determined that the trainee had not followed the procedure. Although the procedure manual existed, the trainee had never seen it. The experienced lab technician had left notes for the trainee to follow. Unfortunately, the notes were incorrect.

1. Why is it important to have quality controls? Justify implementing quality controls using the steps of the decision-making process.
2. If an organization has policies, procedures, and controls in place, why is it possible that a supervisor may view these differently than they are viewed by the employees? How were controls viewed by Bonnie?
3. Discuss the implications of the proper amount of supervision and the benefit of controls for all employees and an organization.
4. How can a system be developed for determining, implementing, and evaluating the controls within an organization? What place does planning have in developing such a system? ■

# PART THREE

# ORGANIZING, STAFFING, AND EMPLOYEE DEVELOPMENT

Part Three introduces you to effectively grouping employees in an organization. It emphasizes the different ways that employees can be organized to support achievement of departmental goals. The chapters in this part also focus on how to find qualified job candidates and how to develop them and keep their skills up to date. We will delve deeper into the topic of work goals as it relates to establishing employees' goals and evaluating them on their performance.

Part Three contains three chapters:

6. ORGANIZING AN EFFECTIVE DEPARTMENT

7. ACQUIRING THE RIGHT PEOPLE

8. APPRAISING EMPLOYEE PERFORMANCE

# 6

# ORGANIZING AN EFFECTIVE DEPARTMENT

# LEARNING OBJECTIVES 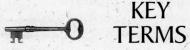 KEY TERMS

After reading this chapter, you should be able to:

1. Define organizing.
2. Describe why work specialization should increase economic efficiency.
3. Explain how the span of control affects an organization's structure.
4. Contrast line and staff authority.
5. Explain why organizations are increasingly becoming decentralized.
6. Describe what is meant by the term horizontal organization and how flatter structures can be beneficial.
7. Discuss the value of job descriptions.
8. Identify the four-step process of delegation.

You should also be able to define these supervisory terms:

accountability

authority

centralization

customer departmentalization

delegation

departmentalization

empowerment

functional authority

functional departmentalization

geographic departmentalization

horizontal structure

job description

line authority

organizing matrix

process departmentalization

product departmentalization

responsibility

simple structure

span of control

staff authority

unity of command

work specialization

# PERFORMING EFFECTIVELY

When you work for an organization, you, as well as those you supervise, are usually assigned to perform certain duties. These work tasks may encompass a wide variety of activities, or they may be narrowly defined to focus on a specific element of a work process. Understanding the way in which you and your employees are grouped together assists in clarifying what jobs entail, as well as partly indicating what you need to do to be successful performers. That's precisely what you can see at Pitney Bowes, a company that specializes in leasing postage equipment to businesses.

Supervisors at Pitney Bowes place workers in manufacturing positions based on their technical abilities. These workers have other responsibilities that go beyond simply performing their specialized tasks.

## INTRODUCTION

In the 1920s and 1930s, as organizations got bigger and more formal, supervisors felt a need to provide more coordination of activities and tighter control over operations. Early business researchers argued that formal bureaucracies would best serve the company—and that was true 60 or more years ago. These bureaucratic structures flourished. By the 1980s, the world began to change drastically. The global marketplace, rapid technological advancements, diversity in the workforce, and socioeconomic conditions made these formal bureaucracies inefficient for many businesses. As a result, since the late 1980s many organizations have restructured to be more customer and market oriented, and to increase productivity.

It is critical today for an organization to have the right structure. Although setting up the organization's structure is typically done by top management in an organization (or the owner in a small business), it is important for all organizational members to understand how these structures work. Why? Because you'll understand your job better if you know why you're "arranged" as you are. For example, How many people can you effectively supervise? When do you have authority to make a decision and when is it merely advice that you're providing? What tasks can you delegate to others? Will you supervise employees who produce a specific product? Will your department exist to serve a particular customer, a geographic region, or some combination of these? You'll see how to find the answers to questions like these in this chapter. We'll look at the tradi-

Specifically, they have the authority to make decisions that affect their work. If, in the process of building their postage-meters they encounter a problem, they have the right to stop production and fix the problem. Frankly, that may appear to be common sense. Yet in many organizations, this is not the case. In such a situation, workers would have to report to their supervisor that they are experiencing a problem, and have the supervisor handle the issue. Meanwhile, defective products continue down the assembly line.

In their postage-meter manufacturing plant in Connecticut, Pitney-Bowes has found that by redesigning their jobs and grouping employees into work teams, they have become more productive. ∎

tional components that go into developing an organization's structure, discuss the various ways that employees may be grouped, and look at how organizational structures change over time.

## WHAT IS ORGANIZING?

**Organizing** is arranging and grouping jobs, allocating resources, and assigning work in a department so that activities can be accomplished as planned. As mentioned above, the top management team in an organization typically establishes the overall organization structure. They'll determine, for instance, how many levels there will be from the top of the organization to the bottom, and the extent to which lower-level managers will have to follow formal rules and procedures in carrying out their jobs. In large corporations, it's not unusual for there to be five to eight levels from top to bottom; hundreds of departments; and dozens of manuals (for example, purchasing, personnel, accounting, engineering, maintenance, sales) that define procedures, rules, and policies within departments. Once the overall structure is in place, supervisors need to organize their individual departments. In this chapter, we'll show you how to do that.

Keep in mind that our discussion here concerns the formal arrangement of jobs and groups of jobs. These are defined by management. In addition, individuals and groups will develop informal alliances that are neither formally structured nor organizationally determined. Almost all employees in all organizations form these informal arrangements to meet their needs for social contact. We'll discuss informal groups in Chapter 12.

**Organizing**
arranging and grouping jobs, allocating resources, and assigning work so that activities can be accomplished as planned.

# BASIC ORGANIZING CONCEPTS

Every organization—large and small, profit and not-for profit, and so on—has a structure. Some of them, like that of Toyota or IBM, are more formalized. Others, like many small businesses, have structures that are less formalized and very simple. So what makes up this "thing" we work in? Let's look at what we call the organization structure.

The early writers in management developed a number of basic organizing principles which continue to offer valuable guidance to supervisors today.

## WHAT IS WORK SPECIALIZATION?

**Work specialization** the process of breaking down a job into a number of steps, with each step being completed by a separate individual.

**Work specialization** means that, rather than an entire job being done by one individual, it is broken down into a number of steps that are each completed by a separate individual. In essence, individuals specialize in doing part of an activity rather than the entire activity. Assembly-line production, in which each worker does the same standardized task over and over again, is an example of work specialization.

Up until very recently, designers of organizations have taken as an irrefutable law that increases in work specialization lead to increases in economic efficiencies. In most organizations, some tasks require highly developed skills; others can be performed by the untrained. If all workers

The advantages of work specialization are explicitly evident on an production line, such as this Avon cosmetic packaging plant. Each worker performs a narrow and standardized operation. This requires a limited range of skills and allows for increased efficiency.

were engaged in each step of, say, an organization's manufacturing process, all would have to have the skills necessary to perform the most demanding and the least demanding tasks. The result would be that, except when performing the most highly skilled or highly sophisticated tasks, employees would be working below their skill level. Since skilled workers are paid more than unskilled workers and their wages tend to reflect their higher level of skill, it is an inefficient usage of resources to pay highly skilled workers to do easy tasks.

Today, supervisors understand that while work specialization provides economic efficiencies, it is not an unending source of increased productivity. There is a point at which the problems from work specialization surface—things like boredom, fatigue, stress, low productivity, poor quality, increased absenteeism, and high turnover. Contemporary supervisors still use the work specialization concept in designing jobs. At the same time, they recognize that in an expanding number of situations, productivity, quality, and employee motivation can be increased by giving employees a variety of activities to do, allowing them to do a whole and complete piece of work, and putting them together into teams.

## WHAT IS THE SPAN OF CONTROL?

It is not very efficient for a supervisor to direct only one or two employees. Conversely, it's pretty obvious that the best of supervisors would be overwhelmed if he or she had to directly oversee several hundred people. This, then, brings up the **span of control** question: How many employees can a supervisor efficiently and effectively direct?

**Span of control**
the number of employees a supervisor can efficiently and effectively direct.

There is, unfortunately, no universal answer. For most supervisors, the optimum number is probably somewhere between five and thirty. Where, within that range, the exact span should be depends on a number of factors. How experienced and competent is the supervisor? The greater his or her abilities, the larger the number of employees that can be handled. What level of training and experience do employees have? The greater their abilities, the fewer demands they'll make on their supervisor— thus, a supervisor can directly oversee more employees. How complex are the employees' activities? The more difficult the employees' jobs, the more narrow the span of control. How many different types of jobs are under the supervisor's direction? The more varied the jobs, the more narrow the span. And how extensive are the department's formal rules and regulations? Supervisors can direct more people when employees can find solutions to their problems in organizational manuals rather than having to go to their immediate boss.

There is an important trend currently taking place in organizations. Spans of control are almost unanimously being expanded (see Exhibit 6–1). The reason is that this is a way for an organization to reduce costs. By doubling the span size, you cut the number of supervisors needed in

EXHIBIT 6–1

Contrasting spans of control.

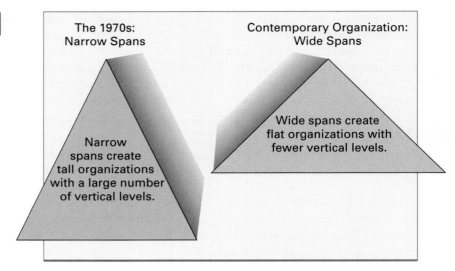

The 1970s: Narrow Spans

Contemporary Organization: Wide Spans

Narrow spans create tall organizations with a large number of vertical levels.

Wide spans create flat organizations with fewer vertical levels.

half. This, remember, is one of the basic premises of downsizing. Of course, this move to wider spans may not be effectively carried out without modifications in work assignments and improvements in skill levels. In order to make wider spans work, organizations may need to spend more on supervisory and employee training. They may also be able to redesign jobs around teams, so individuals can help each other solve problems without needing to go to their manager. For instance, Saturn organizes work around teams, and Saturn employees spend at least five percent of their time annually in training to facilitate team problem-solving.

Something else important is taking place in organizations that involves a supervisor's span of control. This is the increased use of telecommuting. Telecommuting allows employees to do their work at home on a computer that is linked to their office. Currently, more than six million people—at companies like Bank of America, Pacific Bell, and J.C. Penney—are telecommuting. The big plus in telecommuting is that it gives employees more flexibility. It frees them from the constraints of commuting and fixed hours and increases opportunities for meeting family responsibilities. For supervisors, telecommuting means supervising individuals they rarely see. Where it is being used, supervisors usually have a fairly wide span of control. This is because telecommuters tend to be skilled professionals and clerical employees—computer programmers, marketing specialists, financial analysts, and administrative support personnel—who typically make minimal demands on their supervisors. Additionally, because the supervisor's computer and the employee's computer are typically networked, supervisors often are able to communicate as well or better with telecommuters than with employees who are physically in their offices.

## What Is the Unity of Command?

The **unity of command** principle states that an employee should have one and only one supervisor to whom he or she is directly responsible. No employee should report to two or more people. Otherwise, he or she might have to cope with conflicting demands or priorities from several supervisors at once. If this happens, employees could be placed in a no-win situation, where whatever they do, they're possibly going to upset someone.

There are occasional times when an organization breaks the unity of command. It might be necessary, for instance, when a project team is created to work on a specific problem. Team members may report to their immediate supervisor and also to a team project leader. Another example is when a sales representative reports to both her immediate district supervisor and a marketing specialist in the home office, who is coordinating the introduction of a new product. Nevertheless, these are exceptions to the rule. They happen under special circumstances. For the most part, when allocating tasks to individuals or grouping assignments in your department, you should ensure that each employee has one boss, and only one boss, to whom he or she directly reports.

## What Is Authority?

**Authority** refers to rights inherent in a supervisory position to give orders and expect the orders to be obeyed. Each supervisory position has specific rights that incumbents acquire from their position's rank or title. Authority, therefore, relates to one's position within an organization and ignores the personal characteristics of the individual supervisor. People obey individuals in authority not because they like or respect them but because of the rights inherent in their position (see News Flash).

There are three different types of authority relations: line, staff, and functional (see Exhibit 6–2). The most straightforward and easiest to understand is **line authority.** This is the authority that gives the supervisor the right to direct the work of his or her employees and make certain decisions without consulting others.

**Staff authority** supports line authority by advising, servicing, and assisting, but it is typically limited. For instance, the assistant to the department head has staff authority. She acts as an extension of the department head. She can give advice and suggestions, but they needn't be obeyed. However, she may be given the authority to act for the department head. In such cases, she gives directives under the line authority of her boss. For instance, she might issue a memo and sign it: Joan Wilson for R.L. Dalton. In this instance, Wilson is only acting as an extension of Dalton. Staff authority allows Dalton to get more things done by having an assistant who can act on his behalf.

> **Unity of command**
> a principle that states that an employee should have one and only one supervisor to whom he or she is directly responsible.

> **Authority**
> rights inherent in a supervisory position to give orders and expect those orders to be obeyed.

> **Line authority**
> the authority that entitles a supervisor to direct the work of his or her direct reports and to make certain decisions without consulting others.

> **Staff authority**
> a limited authority that supports line authority by advising, servicing, and assisting.

Do people do what they are told—and not question those in a position of authority? Years ago in most businesses, that was a standard of operating. For many supervisors, this is what they expected—if not demanded! But just how far would someone go in obeying orders? Probably the best indication of an answer to this was a research project conducted years ago by a social psychologist at Yale University.[1] By the way, if you remember the opening of "Ghostbusters," a blockbuster movie in the mid-1980s, you have some insight into this research.

Subjects were placed in the role of a teacher in a learning experiment and told by the experimenter to administer a shock to a learner each time that learner made a mistake. The question was, would the subjects follow the commands of the experimenter? Would their willingness to comply decrease as the intensity of the shock was increased? To test these hypotheses, the researcher hired a set of subjects. Each was led to believe that the experiment was to investigate the effect of punishment on memory. Their job was to act as teachers and administer punishment whenever the learner made

a mistake on a learning test. Punishment in this case was administered by electric shock. The subject sat in front of a shock generator with thirty levels of shock, beginning at zero and progressing in 15-volt increments to a high of 450 volts. The range of these positions was from "slight shock" at 15 volts to "danger: severe shock" at 450 volts. To add realism to the experiment, the subjects received a sample shock of 45 volts and saw the learner strapped in an electric chair in an adjacent room. Of course, the learner was an actor, and the electric shocks were phony—but the subjects didn't know this.

The subjects were instructed to shock the learner each time he made a mistake. Subsequent mistakes would result in an increase in shock intensity. Throughout the experiment, the subject got verbal feedback from the learner. At 75 volts, the learner began to grunt and moan; at 150 volts, he demanded to be released from the experiment; at 180 volts he cried out that he could no longer stand the pain; and at 300 volts, he insisted he be let out because of a heart condition. After 300 volts, the learner did not respond to further questions.

Most subjects protested and,

[1]S. Milgram, *Obedience to Authority* (New York, NY: Harper & Row, 1974).

fearful they might kill the learner if the increased shocks were to bring on a heart attack, insisted they could not go on. But the experimenter responded by saying that they had to, that was their job. The majority of the subjects dissented, but dissension isn't synonymous with disobedience. Sixty-two percent of the subjects increased the shock level to the maximum of 450 volts. The average level of shock administered by the remaining 38 percent was nearly 370 volts— more than enough to kill even the strongest human!

What can we conclude from this experiment? Well, one obvious conclusion is that authority is a potent source of getting people to do things. Subjects in the experiment administered levels of shock far above that which they wanted to do. They did it because they were told they had to and in spite of the fact that they could have voluntarily walked out of the room anytime they wanted.

A third type of authority, **functional authority**, represents rights over individuals outside one's own direct areas of responsibility. For example, it is not unusual for a supervisor in a manufacturing plant to find that his immediate boss has line authority over him but that someone in corporate headquarters has functional authority over some of his activities and decisions. The supervisor in charge of the purchasing department at a Reynolds Metals plant in Alabama is responsible to that plant's manager and the corporate director of purchasing at the company's head office in Richmond, Virginia. Why, you might wonder, would the organization create positions of functional authority? After all, it breaks the unity of command principle by having people report to two bosses. The answer is: It can create efficiencies by permitting specialization of skills and improved coordination. Its major problem is overlapping relationships. This is typically resolved by clearly designating to an individual which activities his line boss has authority over and which activities are under the direction of someone else with functional authority. To follow up our purchasing example, the director in Richmond might have functional authority to specify corporate-wide purchasing policies on forms to be used and common procedures to be followed. All other aspects of the purchasing supervisor's job would be under the authority of the plant manager.

**Functional authority** rights over individuals outside one's own direct areas of responsibility.

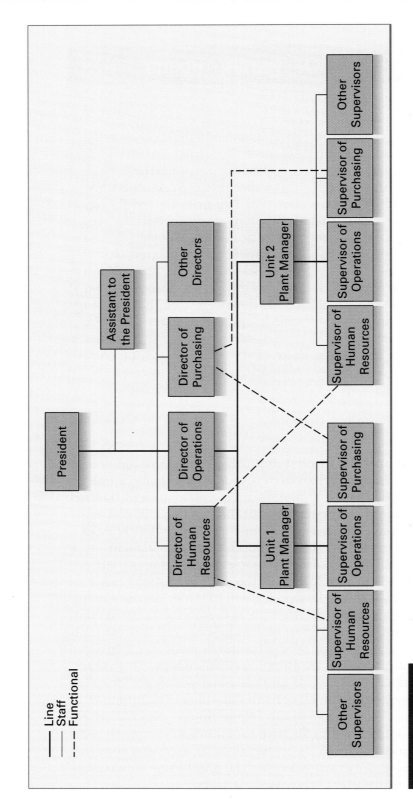

**Line**
**Staff**
**Functional**

**EXHIBIT 6–2**

Organization chart depicting line, staff, and functional authority relationships.

## HOW DO AUTHORITY AND RESPONSIBILITY DIFFER?

Supervisory jobs come with authority. They also come with **responsibility.** Supervisors are responsible for achieving their unit's goals, keeping costs within budget, following organizational policies, and motivating their employees. Authority without responsibility creates opportunities for abuse. For instance, if the supervisor isn't held responsible for motivating employees, he or she may become inclined to make excessive demands on an employee, resulting in that employee being injured on the job. Conversely, responsibility without authority creates frustration and the feeling of powerlessness. If you're held responsible for your territory's sales performance, you should have the authority to hire, reward, discipline, and fire the salespeople who work for you.

**Responsibility**
supervisory obligations such as achieving a unit's goals, keeping costs with budget, following organizational policies, and motivating employees.

## WHY MUST AUTHORITY AND RESPONSIBILITY BE EQUAL?

The previous analysis suggests the importance of equating authority and responsibility. When top management creates organizational units like divisions, regions, territories, and departments—and allocates supervisory personnel to each with specific goals and responsibilities—it must also give these supervisors enough authority to successfully carry out those responsibilities. The more ambitious and far-reaching the goals that a supervisor undertakes, the more authority he or she needs to be given.

# WHERE ARE DECISIONS MADE?

Where does decision making lie? The design of any organization requires top management to answer this question. If the answer is "with top management," you have centralized authority. With **centralization,** problems flow up to senior executives, who then choose the appropriate solution. Where top management pushes decision making down to lower levels, you have decentralized authority.

**Centralization**
decision-making responsibility in the hands of top management.

Twenty-five years ago, centralization ruled in most organizations. Why? Top management typically had the necessary critical information and the expertise to make most key decisions. Additionally, time was not a problem. If it took a couple of months for top management to get around to making a decision, there were minimal negative consequences. That's no longer true for most organizations. As jobs have become more complex, it's become nearly impossible for top managers to keep current and knowledgeable on everything going on in their organizations. Moreover, the dynamics of competition make it increasingly necessary for organizations to make decisions fast. Because speedy decision making and centralization are usually not compatible, top management in recent years has moved more toward decentralized decision making.

Several years back, a study of business people revealed that most had obeyed orders that they had found personally objectionable or unethical.[2] Far more thought-provoking was a survey taken among the general public near the end of the Vietnam War. In spite of public dismay over the actions of some military personnel during that war, about half the respondents said that they would have shot civilian men, women, and children in cold blood if they had been ordered to do so by their commanding officer.[3] More recently, a survey of U.S. supervisors revealed that there was a significant difference in the values, attitudes, and beliefs they personally held and what they encountered in the workplace.[4] And this is not simply a U.S. phenomenon. Supervisors around the world, in such places as the Pacific Rim, Europe, and India are all facing the same predicaments.

If you were asked to follow orders that you believed were unconscionable, would you comply? What if your boss asked you to destroy evidence that he or she had been stealing a great deal of money from the organization? What if the order were less serious, but you merely disagreed with them? For instance, if your boss asked you to bring him or her coffee each morning even though no such task is included in your job description? What would you do?

[2]S. N. Brenner and E. A. Molander, "Is the Ethics of Business Changing?" *Harvard Business Review*, January-February 1977, pp. 57–71.

[3]H. C. Kelman and L. H. Lawrence, "American Response to the Trial of Lt. William L. Calley," *Psychology Today*, June 1972, pp. 41–45.

[4]B. S. Moskal, "A Shadow Between Values and Reality," *Industry Week*, May 16, 1994, pp. 23–26.

Today, more than anytime in recent years, supervisors and operatives are being actively included in the decision-making process. As many organizations have cut costs and streamlined their organizational design to respond better to customer needs, they have pushed decision-making authority down to the lowest levels in the organization (see Building a Supervisory Skill). In this way, those people most familiar with a problem—and often those closest to it—are able to quickly size it up and solve it.

## HOW ARE EMPLOYEES GROUPED?

Early business experts argued that activities in the organization should be specialized and grouped into departments. Work specialization creates specialists who need coordination. This coordination is facilitated by putting specialists together in departments under the direction of a supervisor. Creation of these departments is typically based on the work functions being performed, the product or service being offered, the target

**1.** The idea that jobs should be broken down into the simplest of steps with one step generally assigned to each individual refers to
   **a.** span of control
   **b.** line authority
   **c.** chain of command
   **d.** none of the above

**2.** Describe the advantages and disadvantages of work specialization.

**3.** Early business experts believed top managers should have a larger span of control. True or False?

**4.** The *main* problem to be expected when the chain of command principle is ignored is that
   **a.** employees potentially have trouble coping with conflicting priorities and demands
   **b.** supervisors cannot keep abreast of what all their employees are doing
   **c.** decision making is slow
   **d.** there is not enough flexibility

customer or client, the geographic territory being covered, or the process being used to turn inputs into outputs. We call these groupings **departmentalization.** No single method of departmentalization was advocated by the early experts. The method or methods used should reflect the grouping that would best contribute to the attainment of the organization's objectives and the goals of individual units.

You find specialization throughout organizations. For instance, when a company appoints vice presidents for marketing, finance, production, and research, it is dividing up organizational activities by specialization. While major decisions such as what departments an organization will have and how they will interrelate are typically made by top management, supervisors still make organizing decisions. These decisions are confined to activities within their own areas of responsibility. As a result, supervisors need to understand various options for organizing their departments and grouping activities. These are, incidentally, the same options available to top managers when they are making decisions about the organization's overall structure. As a supervisor, you can departmentalize on the basis of work function, product or service, geographic territory, target customer or client, or the process being used to turn inputs into outputs.

**Departmentalization** grouping departments based on work functions, product or service, target customer or client, geographic territory, or the process used to turn inputs into outputs.

This department at Xerox groups employees by the work they do—or functional departmentalization. Each employee performs similar job tasks.

**Functional departmentalization** grouping activities into independent units based on functions performed.

**Product departmentalization** grouping activities into independent units based on problems or issues relating to a product.

## GROUPING BY FUNCTION

One of the most popular ways to group activities is by functions performed—**functional departmentalization.** When you see a company that separates engineering, accounting, manufacturing, human resources, and purchasing specialists into common departments, you have an example of departmentalizing by function (see Exhibit 6–3). Similarly, hospitals use this approach when they create departments devoted to research, patient care, accounting, and so forth.

Why is the functional department so popular? Because it most directly takes advantage of work specialization. By grouping jobs that are performed by people with the same kinds of training and experience, it is easier for people within the department to communicate with each other. It also makes it easier for the supervisor to coordinate activities since he or she will be overseeing activities that have a common component.

## GROUPING BY PRODUCT

Another way to departmentalize is by product. This means that each major product area in the organization is under the authority of a supervisor who is a specialist in, and responsible for, everything having to do with his or her product line.

In contrast to functional departments, **product departmentalization** creates relatively independent units. Any problem or issue that surfaces related to a product will fall under the responsibilities of that product's supervisor. This, in essence, captures a major advantage to organizing

## EXHIBIT 6–3

Functional departmentalization.

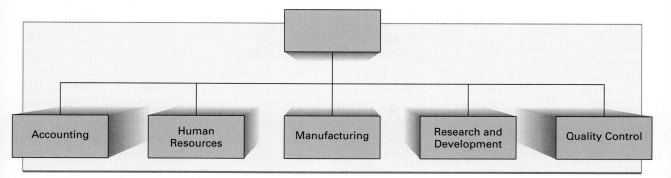

| Accounting | Human Resources | Manufacturing | Research and Development | Quality Control |

around products—it places ultimate responsibility for everything having to do with a specific product with one individual. Thus, eliminating the potential for "passing the buck."

Let's look at an example using a modified version of the structure at Procter & Gamble (see Exhibit 6–4). If sales of its Ultra Tide laundry detergent dropped suddenly, who would be responsible? If P&G were organized along functional lines, the Sales Department might blame the Advertising Department. The Advertising department could say the problem is due to the way the product's container is designed and blame the Packaging Design Department. The Packaging Design Department could say the problem is the lack of the detergent's strength and blame the Research and Development Department. This passing the blame around doesn't happen with product departmentalization. Any problems or decisions relating to Ultra Tide lie with its product group. It is their responsibility to find the cause of the sales decline and to correct it.

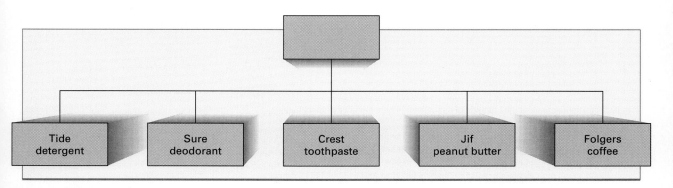

| Tide detergent | Sure deodorant | Crest toothpaste | Jif peanut butter | Folgers coffee |

## EXHIBIT 6–4

Product departmentalization.

## GROUPING BY GEOGRAPHY

**Geographic departmentalization** grouping activities into independent units based on geography or territory.

Another way to departmentalize is on the basis of geography or territory—called **geographic departmentalization.** This is particularly popular for sales and marketing units. For instance, Shell Oil Company's marketing operations are divided up into geographic regions: Eastern, Southern, Midwestern, Rocky Mountain, and Western (see Exhibit 6–5). You also see geographic departmentalization in large school districts when, for example, twelve high schools are organized so that each major area within the district is covered. When organizations set up international departments or divisions, they also are organizing around geography.

What's the advantage to this form of departmentalization? It puts decision-making authority close to where the work is being done. If activities are physically dispersed and different locations face different types of problems, organizations will want to ensure that the people who make the decisions understand those differences. Simon & Schuster Publishing, for example, has marketing units in Toronto, London, New Delhi, Singapore, and Rio de Janeiro to reflect the unique publishing needs of the Canadian, European, Indian, Asian, and South American markets, respectively.

## GROUPING BY CUSTOMER

The fastest growing form of departmentalizing is by customer. Why? Because contemporary companies are learning that success requires staying close to the customer. Organizations that lose touch with the changing needs of their diverse customer base aren't likely to be around five years from now. The primary force that has driven the growth of companies like MCI and Dell Computers has been carefully listening to and responding to the needs of their customers.

Where an organization has a diverse set of customers that can be grouped around common interests, concerns, or needs, then a customer

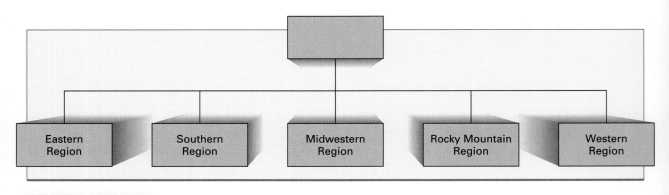

## EXHIBIT 6–5

Geographic departmentalization.

## EXHIBIT 6–6

Customer departmentalization.

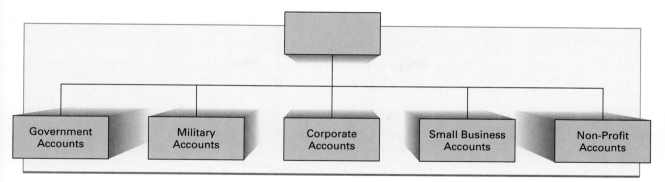

form of departmentalization makes sense. For instance, Electronic Data Systems Corp. provides supportive computer and information services to organizations. The needs of its clients such as the U.S. Army are different from those of the Social Security Administration, and both are still different from the needs of small businesses. So the EDS office in Washington D.C. is organized into an assortment of departments, grouped around common customer categories (see Exhibit 6–6). Other examples of **customer departmentalization** are universities that set up departments of evening studies or continuing education to cater to working and part-time students; and banks that separate commercial clients from individual customers.

Customer departmentalization grouping activities around common customer categories.

### GROUPING BY PROCESS

The final pure form of departmentalization is by process. Exhibit 6–7 shows the various production departments in a Reynolds Metals plant that manufactures aluminum tubing. The metal is cast in huge furnaces; sent

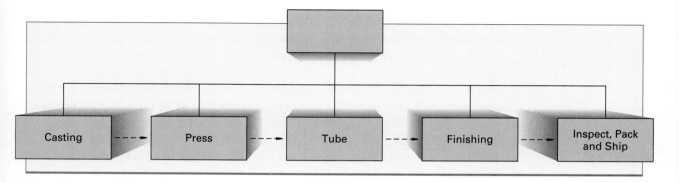

## EXHIBIT 6–7

Process departmentalization.

to the press department, where it is extruded into aluminum pipe; transferred to the tube mill, where it is stretched into various sizes and shapes of tubing; moved to finishing, where it is cut and cleaned; and finally arrives in the inspect, pack, and ship department. Since each process requires different skills and specialized equipment, this method offers a basis for the homogeneous categorizing of activities.

**Process departmentalization** can be applied to servicing customers as well as products. If you have ever been to a state motor vehicle office to get a driver's license, you probably went through several departments before receiving your license. In one state, applicants must go through three steps, each handled by a separate department: (1) validation, by the motor vehicles division; (2) processing, by the licensing department; and (3) payment collection, by the treasury department.

**Process departmentalization** grouping activities around a process; this method provides a basis for the homogeneous categorizing of activities.

## What is a Matrix Organization?

The functional department offers the advantages that accrue from work specialization. The product department has a greater focus on results but suffers from duplication of activities and resources. If the organization were completely organized around products—that is, if each product the company produced had its own supporting functional structure—the focus on results would again be high. Each product could have a product leader responsible for all activities related to that product. This, too, would result in redundancy, since each product would require its own set of functional specialists. Does any form combine the advantages of functional specialization with the focus and accountability that product departmentalization provides? The answer is yes, and it's called the **matrix**.

**Matrix**
a structure that weaves together elements of functional and product departmentalization.

The matrix structure creates a dual chain of command—explicitly breaking the principle of chain of command. Functional departmentalization is used to gain the economies of specialization. Overlaying the functional departments is a set of supervisors who are responsible for specific products, projects, or programs within the organization. (We'll use the terms products, projects, and programs interchangeably, since matrix structures can use any of the three). Exhibit 6–8 illustrates the matrix structure of an aerospace firm. Notice that along the top of the figure are the familiar functions of engineering, accounting, human resources, and so forth. Along the vertical dimension, however, have been added the various projects that the aerospace firm is currently working on. Each project is directed by a supervisor who staffs his or her project with people from the functional departments. The addition of the vertical dimension to the traditional functional departments, in effect, weaves together elements of functional and product departmentalization—hence the term *matrix*.

How does the matrix work? Employees in the matrix organization report to two bosses: their functional departmental supervisor and their

EXHIBIT 6–8

A matrix structure in an aerospace firm.

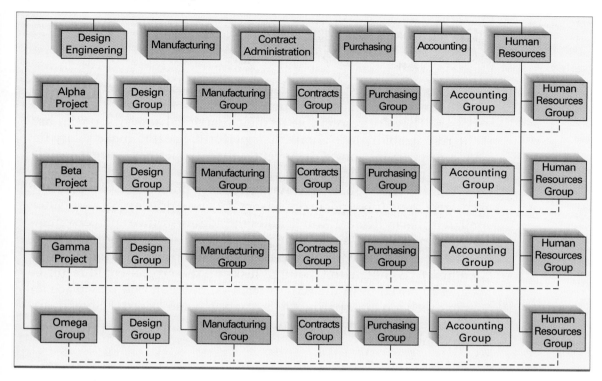

product or project supervisor (see Dealing with a Difficult Issue). The project supervisor has authority over the functional employees who are part of that supervisor's project team. The purchasing specialists, for instance, who are responsible for procurement activities on the Gamma project, are responsible to both the supervisor of purchasing and the Gamma project supervisor. Authority is shared between the two supervisors. Typically, this is done by giving the project supervisor authority over employees relative to the project's goals. However, decisions such as promotions, salary recommendations, and performance reviews remain the functional supervisor's responsibility. To work effectively, project and functional supervisors must communicate regularly and coordinate the demands upon their common employees.

The matrix creates an overall structure that possesses the strengths of both functional and product departmentalization, while avoiding the weaknesses of both. That is, the functional form's strength lies in putting like specialists together, which minimizes the number necessary, and it allows for the pooling and sharing of specialized resources across products. Its primary drawback is the difficulty in coordinating the tasks of the spe-

## DO MATRIX STRUCTURES CREATE CONFUSED EMPLOYEES?

Workers in matrix structures face a difficult issue that never arose in traditional organizational structures. That is, they have at least two bosses. They are responsible to their functional supervisor, who has the responsibility to evaluate their performance and make salary increase determinations. Concurrently, these employees are responsible to their project leader for specific project tasks.

In this situation, whose authority takes precedence? Do employees give their functional supervisor's requests priority because, after all, it is this individual who handles the administrative and personnel-related paperwork? Or is it the project leader—who is more involved with the employees on a day-to-day basis—who gets the "top-billing"? Failure to complete the required tasks on the project could result in being removed from the project team—a decision that may place an employee's job in jeopardy. Are both given equal priority? Should employees simply accept that they have to serve "two masters"? What do you think?

cialists so that their activities are completed on time and within the budget. The product form, on the other hand, has exactly the opposite benefits and disadvantages. It facilitates the coordination among specialists to achieve on-time completion and meet budget targets. Furthermore, it provides clear responsibility for all activities related to a product or project. But no one is responsible for the long-run technical development of the specialists, and this results in duplication of costs.

## WHY IS THERE MOVEMENT TO SIMPLER EMPLOYEE GROUPINGS?

Recall our discussion in Chapter 2 regarding the challenges businesses face. Two of these—downsizing and reengineering—are particularly relevant to today's organizing changes.[5] How? To answer, let's briefly review some facts regarding common structures. Many of the departmentaliza-

[5]R. Henkoff, "Getting Beyond Downsizing," *Fortune* (January 10, 1994), pp. 58–62.

Companies like Jack Singleton's Men's Clothing typify the majority of small businesses in the United States. Here, all employees report directly to Jack, who makes most of the decisions and coordinates all employee activity.

tions mentioned previously were highly complex and formalized, and decisions were made in a centralized fashion—resulting in rigid, oftentimes massive, multileveled structures. Although they were designed to promote efficiency, they did not lend themselves to adjust to the dynamic world around them. As a result, more emphasis today has been given to organizations that focus on simplicity. Let's look at what we mean by a simple structure.

If "bureaucracy" is the term that best describes most large organizations, "simple structure" is the one that best characterizes most small ones. A **simple structure** is defined more by what it is not than by what it is. It is not an elaborate structure.[6] If you see an organization that appears to have almost no structure, it is probably of the simple variety. By that we mean that it is low in complexity, has little formalization, and has its authority centralized in a single person. The simple structure is a "flat" organization; it usually has only two or three levels, employees who perform a variety of tasks, and one individual who makes most of the decisions.

The simple structure is most widely practiced in small businesses in which the manager and the owner are one and the same. This is illustrated in Exhibit 6–9—an organization chart for a men's clothing retail store. Jack Singleton owns and manages this store. Although Jack employs five full-time salespeople, a cashier, and part-time weekend help, he "runs the show."

The strengths of the simple structure should be obvious. Communications are efficient, accountability is clear, and it has flexibility to respond to the changing environment. One major weakness is that, in the past, it was only viewed as effective in small organizations. It became increasingly in-

**Simple structure**
a non-elaborate structure low in complexity, with little formalization, and with authority centralized in a single person; a "flat" organization with only two or three levels.

[6]Henry Mintzberg, *Structure in Fives: Designing Effective Organizations* (Englewood Cliffs, NJ: Prentice-Hall, Inc., 1983), p. 157.

## EXHIBIT 6–9

Jack Singleton's structure.

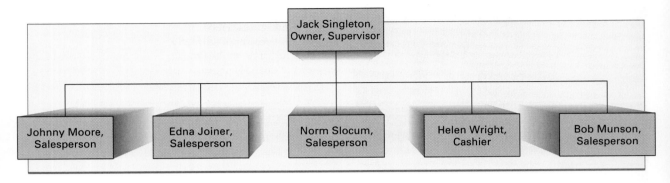

adequate as an organization grew because its low formalization and high centralization resulted in information overloads at the top. As size increased, decision making became slower and eventually came to a standstill as the single person in charge tried to continue making all the decisions. This often proved to be the undoing of many small businesses. The simple structure's other weakness is that it is risky: everything depends on one person. One heart attack, or a fatal auto accident on the way to work, can literally destroy the organization—for the only one who held the critical information is now gone. However, these weaknesses were not necessarily the fault of the simple structure. Rather, those in charge just couldn't give up the control that they had so enjoyed.

## ARE THERE SIMPLE-LIKE STRUCTURES FOR LARGER ORGANIZATIONS?

If there was one thing yesterday's organizations had in common, it was the rigid boundaries that separated employees from other parts of the organization. Employees were often segregated by the jobs they did and rarely interacted with others in different parts of the business. A select few ran the "show." That setup may no longer provide the best advantage in organizations. Some of those boundaries are being broken down, giving employees more interaction with others whom they count on for getting jobs done. In business today, we call this arrangement the horizontal structure.

### THE HORIZONTAL STRUCTURE

Before we begin this discussion, let's set the record straight. A horizontal structure is really nothing new. **Horizontal structures** are simply very flat structures—basically the same as what we called simple structures. What's

**Horizontal structures** very flat structures used in small businesses as well as giant companies in which job-related activities cut across all parts of the organization.

new about them, however, is that they are being used not only in small businesses, but in giant companies like AT&T, du Pont, General Electric, and Motorola.[7] Horizontal organizations, as the term implies, means job-related activities cut across all parts of the organization. Rather than having employees perform specialized jobs and work in departments with people who do similar tasks, they are grouped with other employees who have different skills—forming a work team. These individuals come together to work toward a common objective. They are given the authority to make the necessary decisions to do the work, and are held accountable for measurable outcomes.[8] Their jobs encompass the entire work to be completed, from beginning to end—rather than focusing on individualized job tasks.[9] In a horizontal structure, control shifts from those in management to supervisors and workers.

Working in a horizontal organization brings about other changes for supervisors. For instance, supervisors, reward employees for mastering multiple skills, rather than just a select few. The more they can do, the more valuable they are. Additionally, rather than being evaluated on the work one individual does, the rewards are based on how the team performs. In a horizontal organization, the supervisor's evaluations are no longer the only ones. Instead, employees are likely to be evaluated by anyone who has knowledge of their work. At General Electric, CEO Jack Welch has implemented what he calls a 360-degree appraisal process.[10] At GE, team members are evaluated by team leaders, peer members, other employees with whom they work—even customers. This evaluation system is becoming a model used in many large organizations.

## FITTING EMPLOYEE GROUPING TO THE SITUATION

Although the movement toward simple structures brings with it many strengths and may provide an exciting work atmosphere, keep one thing in mind. Simple structures must be used only where appropriate. The question then arises: When do the different groupings work best? In industries where efficiency of mass production is warranted, grouping employees by the jobs they perform may better serve the organization. The answer will depend on the environment in which you work.

Organizations group employees for a particular reason. They don't implement structures haphazardly for the fun of it. It's too expensive, and very difficult, to make these changes. When they do, you should learn from it. How so? Recognize what the structure is telling you as a supervisor. If grouping employees by the job performed appears to be the norm, then

---

[7]J. A. Byrne, "The Horizontal Corporation," *Business Week*, December 20, 1993, pp. 76–81.

[8]"A Master Class of Radical Change," *Fortune* (December 13, 1993), p. 83.

[9]Ibid, p. 88.

[10]Ibid.

your organization has made the decision that efficiency matters most. Therefore, to be successful in this element of your supervisory job, you need to focus on being efficient and continue refining your current skills. That may mean emphasizing work specialization for your employees—and yourself, too. In such an arrangement, you'll also be given clues on how best to make some of your decisions. You'll want to give greater weight to alternatives that are more cost effective, or provide greater output for a given input. Play to the strength of the employee grouping—that's usually what you'll be rewarded for.

In other employee groupings, similar guidelines can be found. Grouping by the product produced means that the "bigger" picture is most important. That is, achieving organizational goals is a "must," and the company is willing to use resources to do it.

## ORGANIZING YOUR EMPLOYEES

Once your departmental structure is in place, you need to organize the specific jobs of each of your employees. How do you do that? By identifying the tasks to be done, combining them into jobs, and then formalizing the process by creating job descriptions.

### How Do You Identify the Tasks to be Done?

You begin the process by making a list of all the specific tasks with which your department has been charged. These are the tasks that, when effectively accomplished, result in your department successfully achieving its goals. Exhibit 6–10 illustrates a partial list drawn up by a production supervisor in a large book publishing company.

It is unlikely that one person can do all the tasks that need to be accomplished. So the tasks need to be combined into individual jobs. Work specialization typically drives the creation of jobs. By specializing and grouping tasks by individuals, each person becomes more proficient at his or her job. So the book-production supervisor described previously will create specific jobs such as copyeditor, proofreader, photo editor, production coordinator, and designer.

In addition to grouping similar tasks you need to be sure that workloads within your department are balanced. Employee morale and productivity will suffer if some employees' jobs are significantly more difficult or time consuming than others. You should take into consideration the physical, mental, and time demands that the various tasks require to be accomplished, and use this information to help balance the workloads among department employees.

EXHIBIT 6–10

Partial listing of tasks in a book production department.

- Attend initial planning meeting with acquisition editor to launch a new book

- Contact with acquisition editors

- Contact with authors

- Contact with marketing personnel

- Contact with advertising group

- Contact with manufacturing buyers

- Develop production schedules for each book

- Design the internal layout of books and develop sample pages

- Draw up detailed design specifications for the computer; to be used for creating pages

- Have figures and tables drawn

- Design book covers

- Organize and direct weekly coordination meetings for each book

- Proof galleys and pages

## WHAT IS THE PURPOSE OF JOB DESCRIPTIONS?

A **job description** is a written statement of what a jobholder does, how the job is done, and why it is done. It typically portrays job duties, working conditions, and operating responsibilities. Exhibit 6–11 illustrates a job description for a production editor in a publishing company.

**Job description**
a written statement of job duties, working conditions, and operating responsibilities.

Why do you need to write job descriptions for each job under your jurisdiction? Two reasons. First, it provides you with a formal document describing what each one of your employees is supposed to be doing. It acts as a standard against which you can determine how well the employee is performing. This, in turn, can be used in the employee's performance appraisal, feedback, wage adjustment, and need-for-training decisions. Second, the job description helps employees learn their job duties and clarifies the results that you expect them to achieve. Information like this is crucial—especially when you empower your employees to perform certain duties that supervisors once performed.

EXHIBIT 6–11

A job description for a production editor in a publishing company.

Job Title: Project Production Editor

Department: College Book Editorial Production

Wage Category: Exempt

Reports to: Business Team Production Supervisor

Job Class: 7-12B

Job Statement:
    Performs and oversees editing work in the areas of book specifications, design, composition, printing, and binding. May carry a number of books at the same time. Works under general supervision. Incumbent exercises initiative and independent judgment in the performance of assigned tasks.

Job Duties:

1. Identifies activities to be completed, determines sequencing, and prepares a schedule for the ten-month process.

2. Performs or contracts-out copyediting of book manuscript.

3. Coordinates specification (size, color, paper, covers) and design (typefaces, art) with assigned designer. Coordinates preparation of galleys and pages with manufacturing buyers and compositor.

4. Distributes scheduling-status reports to acquisition editors and others as needed.

5. Acts as liaison with authors on all production issues.

6. Checks all permissions for completeness and accuracy.

7. Responsible for maintaining in-stock date set at initial launch meeting.

8. Performs related duties as assigned by team supervisor.

**Empowerment**
Increasing an employee's involvement in his or her work through greater participation in decisions and expanded responsibility for work outcomes.

## EMPOWERING OTHERS THROUGH DELEGATION

Contemporary supervisors need to learn to empower others. **Empowerment** means increasing your employees' involvement in their work through greater participation in decisions that control their work and by expanding responsibility for work outcomes. Two ways to empower people

## ARE YOU WILLING TO DELEGATE?

Think of times when you have been in charge of a group. This could be a full-time or part-time work situation, a student work group, or similar experience. Using this information as a frame of reference, complete the following questionnaire by recording how you feel about each statement according to this scale:[11]

**5** = Strongly disagree
**4** = Disagree
**3** = Neutral
**2** = Agree
**1** = Strongly agree

**When in charge of a group I find:**

1.  Most of the time other people are too inexperienced to do things, so I prefer to do them myself.　　5　4　3　2　1
2.  It often takes more time to explain things to others than to just do them myself.　　5　4　3　2　1
3.  Mistakes made by others are costly, so I don't assign much work to them.　　5　4　3　2　1
4.  Some things simply should not be delegated to others.　　5　4　3　2　1
5.  I often get quicker action by doing a job myself.　　5　4　3　2　1
6.  Many people are good only at very specific tasks, and thus can't be assigned additional responsibilities.　　5　4　3　2　1
7.  Many people are too busy to take on additional work.　　5　4　3　2　1
8.  Most people just aren't ready to handle additional responsibility.　　5　4　3　2　1
9.  In my position, I should be entitled to make my own decisions.　　5　4　3　2　1

[11]This self-assessment is adapted from L. Steinmetz and R. Todd, *First Line Management*, 4th ed (Homewood, IL: Irwin, 1986), pp. 64–67. Used with permission.

*(continued)*

### SCORING

This questionnaire gives you an idea of your willingness to empower others through delegation. Add up your score on the nine items. Possible total scores range from 9 to 45.

### WHAT THE ASSESSMENT MEANS

The higher your score, the more willing you are to delegate to others. A score of 36 or higher indicates a strong willingness to allow others to assume workplace responsibilities and exercise self control in their work. Scores in the 25 to 35 range imply serious reluctance to give up authority and control. Scores below 25 suggest considerable room for improvement in this area.

are to delegate authority to them and to redesign their jobs (see Assessing Yourself). In this section, we'll address delegation. In Chapter 9, we'll show you how to empower people through job design.

## WHAT IS DELEGATION?

There is no question that effective supervisors need to be able to delegate. Many supervisors find that this is hard for them. Why? They're typically afraid to give up control. "I like to do things myself," says Cheryl Munro Sharp of London Life, "because then I know it's done and I know it's done right." Lisa Flaherty of the Della Femina McNama advertising agency voiced a similar comment: "I have to learn to trust others. Sometimes I'm afraid to delegate the more important projects because I like to stay hands on." In this section, we want to show that delegation can actually increase your effectiveness and that, when done properly, still provides you control.

**Delegation**
allocation of duties, employee empowerment, assignment of responsibility, and creation of accountability.

**Delegation** is frequently depicted as a four-step process: (1) allocation of duties; (2) delegation of authority; (3) assignment of responsibility; and (4) creation of accountability. Let's look at each of these:

1. *Allocation of duties.* Duties are the tasks and activities that a manager desires to have someone else do. Before you can delegate authority, you must allocate to an employee the duties over which the authority extends.

2. *Delegation of authority.* The essence of the delegation process is empowering the employee to act for you. It is passing to the employee the formal rights to act on your behalf.

3. *Assignment of responsibility.* When authority is delegated, you must assign responsibility. That is, when you give someone "rights," you must also assign to that person a corresponding "obligation" to perform. Ask yourself: Did I give my employee enough authority to get the materials, the use of equipment, and the support from others necessary to get the job done?

4. *Creation of accountability.* To complete the delegation process, you must create accountability; that is, you must hold your employee answerable for properly carrying out his or her duties. So while responsibility means an employee is obliged to carry out assigned duties, **accountability** means that he or she has to perform the assignment in a satisfactory manner. Employees are responsible for the completion of tasks assigned to them and are accountable to you for the satisfactory performance of that work.

**Accountability**
the obligation to perform an assignment in a satisfactory manner.

## ISN'T DELEGATION ABDICATION?

If you dump tasks on an employee without clarifying exactly what is to be done, the range of the employee's discretion, the expected level of performance, when the tasks are to be completed, and similar concerns, you are abdicating responsibility and inviting trouble. But don't fall into the trap of assuming that, to avoid the appearance of abdicating, you should minimize delegation. Unfortunately, this is the approach taken by many new and inexperienced supervisors. Lacking confidence in their employees, or fearful that they will be criticized for their employees' mistakes, they try to do everything themselves.

It may very well be true that you're capable of doing the tasks you delegate to your employees better, faster, or with fewer mistakes. The catch is that your time and energy are scarce resources. It's not possible for you to do everything yourself. So you need to learn to delegate if you're going to be effective in your job (see Developing a Supervisory Skill). This suggests two important points. First, you should expect and accept some mistakes by your employees. It's part of delegation. Mistakes are often good learning experiences for your employees, as long as the costs of their mistakes are not excessive. Second, to ensure that the costs of mistakes don't exceed the value of the learning, you need to put adequate controls in place. Delegation without proper feedback controls that let you know when there are serious problems is abdication.

## DELEGATING

### ABOUT THE SKILL

In learning this skill, recognize that delegation is not the same as participation. In participative decision-making, there's a sharing of authority. With delegation, employees make decisions on their own. That's why delegation is such a vital component of empowering workers! A number of actions are recommended that when followed, can make you an effective delegator.

1. **Clarify the assignment.** The place to begin is to determine what is to be delegated and to whom. You need to identify the person best capable of doing the task, then determine if he or she has the time and motivation to do the job. Assuming you have a willing and able employee, it is your responsibility to provide clear information on what is being delegated, the results you expect, and any time or performance expectations you hold. Unless there is an overriding need to adhere to specific methods, you should delegate only the end results. That is, get agreement on what is to be done and the end results expected, but let the employee decide on the means. By focusing on goals and allowing the employee the freedom to use his or her own judgment as to how those goals are to be achieved, you increase trust between you and the employee, improve that employee's motivation, and enhance accountability for the results.

2. **Specify the employee's range of discretion.** Every act of delegation comes with constraints. You're delegating authority to act, but not unlimited authority. What you're delegating is authority to act on certain issues and, on those issues, within certain parameters. You need to specify what those parameters are so employees know, in no uncertain terms, the range of their discretion. When this has been successfully communicated, both you and the employee will have the same idea of the limits to the latter's authority and how far he or she can go without checking further with you. How much authority do you give an employee? In other words, how tight do you draw the parameters? The best answer is that you should allocate enough authority to allow the individual to successfully complete the task.

3. **Allow the employee to participate.** One of the best sources for determining how much authority will be necessary to accomplish a task is the employee who will be held accountable for that task. If you allow employees to participate in determining what is delegated, how much authority is needed to get the job done, and the standards by which they'll be judged, you increase employee motivation, satisfaction, and accountability for performance. Be aware, however, that participation can present its own set of potential problems, as a result of employees' self-interest and biases in evaluating their own abilities. Some employees, for example, are personally motivated to expand their authority beyond what they need and beyond what they are capable of handling. Allowing such people too much participation in deciding what tasks they should take on and how much authority they must have to complete those tasks can undermine the effectiveness of the delegation process.

4. **Inform others that delegation has occurred.** Delegation should not take place

in a vacuum. Not only do you and the employee need to know specifically what has been delegated and how much authority has been granted, anyone else who may be affected by the delegation act also needs to be informed. This includes people outside the organization as well as inside it. Essentially, you need to convey what has been delegated (the task and amount of authority) and to whom. If you fail to follow through on this step, the legitimacy of your employee's authority will probably be called into question. Failure to inform others makes conflicts likely and decreases the chances that your employee will be able to accomplish the delegated task efficiently.

5. **Establish feedback controls.** To delegate without instituting feedback controls is to invite problems. There is always the possibility that an employee will misuse the discretion that he or she has been delegated. The establishment of controls to monitor the employee's progress increases the likelihood that important problems will be identified early and that the task will be completed on time and to the desired specifications. Ideally, controls should be determined at the time of the initial assignment. Agree on a specific time for completion of the task, and then set progress dates when the employee will report back on how well

he or she is doing and any major problems that have surfaced. This can be supplemented with periodic spot checks to ensure that authority guidelines are not being abused, organization policies are being followed, proper procedures are being met, and the like. But too much of a good thing can be dysfunctional. If the controls are too constraining, the employee will be deprived of the opportunity to build self confidence and much of the motivational properties of delegation will be lost. A well-designed control system permits your employee to make small mistakes, but quickly alerts you when big mistakes are imminent.

6. **When problems surface, insist on recommendations from the employee.** Many supervisors fall into the trap of letting employees reverse the delegation process: The employee runs into a problem and then comes back to the supervisor for advice or a solution. Avoid being sucked into reverse delegation by insisting from the beginning that when employees want to discuss a problem with you, they come prepared with a recommendation. When you delegate downward, the employee's job includes making necessary decisions. Don't allow the employee to push decisions back upward to you. ■

**5.** When an insurance claims department groups all automobile collision claims employees under one supervisor, _____ is being demonstrated.

    **a.** functional departmentalization

    **b.** geographic departmentalization

    **c.** process departmentalization

    **d.** product departmentalization

**6.** Identify the five different ways in which you can departmentalize, or group, your employees.

**7.** A strength of the matrix structure is that it capitalizes on the accountability of product departmentalization and the efficiency of work specialization. True or False?

**8.** Which one of the following is not reflective of the term *job description?*

    **a.** A job description is a written statement of what a jobholder does.

    **b.** A job description involves allocation of duties, assignment of authority, responsibility, and accountability.

    **c.** A job description defines how and why a job is done.

    **d.** A job description typically portrays job duties and working conditions.

## SUMMARY

After reading this chapter, I can:

1. **Define organizing.** Organizing is arranging jobs and groups of jobs in a department so that activities can be accomplished as planned.
2. **Describe why work specialization should increase economic efficiency.** Work specialization increases economic efficiency by allocating the most difficult and complex tasks to those employees with the highest skill level and paying people less to do the less difficult and skilled tasks.
3. **Explain how the span of control affects an organization's structure.** The narrower the span of control, the more management levels are necessary to directly oversee activities. Wider spans create fewer managerial levels and flatter organization structures.
4. **Contrast line and staff authority.** Line authority refers to the right to direct the work of employees. Staff authority, on the other hand, advises, services, and assists line in accomplishing its job. Only line authority allows individuals to make decisions independently and without consulting others.
5. **Explain why organizations are increasingly becoming decentralized.** Organizations are becoming increasingly decentralized in order to meet competitive challenges through knowledgeable and rapid decision making.
6. **Describe what is meant by the term horizontal organization and how flatter structures can be beneficial.** The horizontal organization structure is flat. This means that job-related activities cut across all parts of the organization. Rather than having employees perform specialized jobs and work in departments with people who do similar tasks, they are grouped with other employees who have different skills—forming a work team. Horizontal structures can be beneficial because they are flexible and more adaptable to conditions external to the organization.
7. **Discuss the value of job descriptions.** Job descriptions: (a) provide supervisors with a formal document describing what the employee is supposed to be doing; (b) help employees learn their job duties; and (c) clarify the results that management expects.
8. **Identify the four-step process of delegation.** Delegation consists of: (1) allocation of duties; (2) delegation of authority; (3) assignment of responsibility; and (4) creation of accountability.

## REVIEWING YOUR KNOWLEDGE

1. What are the limitations, if any, to division of labor?
2. How might wider spans of control lead to cost reductions for an organization?
3. What is functional authority? Why would an organization use it?
4. What happens when authority and responsibility are out of balance?
5. What are the advantages of (a) product, (b) geographic, (c) customer, and (d) process departmentalization?
6. Why would an organization use a matrix structure?
7. What are the purposes of a job description?

8. Is delegation synonymous with abdication? Discuss.

# ANSWERS TO THE POP QUIZZES

1. **d. none of the above.** The idea that jobs should be broken down into the simplest of steps with one step generally assigned to each individual refers to **work specialization.**

2. **Describe the advantages and disadvantages of work specialization.** The advantages of work specialization relate to economic efficiencies. It makes efficient use of the wide range of skills that workers hold. Skills are developed through repetition. Less time is wasted, and training is also easier and less costly. The disadvantage of work specialization is that it can result in boredom, fatigue, stress, low productivity, poor quality, increased absence, and high turnover.

3. **False.** Early business experts believed top managers should have a smaller span of control.

4. **a. employees potentially have trouble coping with conflicting priorities and demands.** This is one element that early experts wanted to avoid when they identified chain of command. Conflicting priorities and demands create potential problems that can easily be avoided by having a specified chain of command.

5. **a. functional departmentalization.** This question focuses on grouping employees by work specialization.

6. You can group your employees on the basis of function (work being done), product (product or service being generated) customer (group served), geography (location of operations), or process (work flow).

7. **True.** This statement identifies the strengths of the matrix structure, which includes combining the strengths of functional departmentalization (work specialization) and product departmentalization (accountability).

8. **b. A job description involves allocation of duties, assignment of authority, responsibility, and accountability.** Response (b) is actually the process of delegation, and has little to do with defining the term job description. ■

## A Class Exercise: Learning to Delegate

This is a role-playing exercise. Break into groups of four to six students. One student in each group will assume the role of Chris Hall and one will assume the role of Dale Morgan. The other students will serve as observers and evaluators.

Students playing the role of Chris and Dale should read the situation and his or her respective role only. Observers should read the situation and both roles.

## THE SITUATION

Chris Hall is Director of Research and Development for a small pharmaceutical manufacturer. Chris has six direct reports: Sue Traynor (Chris's secretary), Dale Morgan (the laboratory supervisor), Todd Connor (quality standards supervisor), Linda Peters (patent coordination supervisor), Ruben Gomez (market coordination supervisor), and Marjorie England (senior project supervisor). Dale is the most senior of the five supervisors and is generally acknowledged as the chief candidate to replace Chris when Chris is promoted.

## CHRIS HALL'S ROLE

You have received your annual instructions from the CEO to develop next year's budget for your area. The task is relatively routine but takes quite a bit of time. In the past, you've always done the annual budget yourself. But this year, because your workload is exceptionally heavy, you've decided to try something different. You're going to assign budget preparation to one of your supervisors. The obvious choice is Dale Morgan. Dale has been with the company longest, is highly dependable, and, as your probable successor, is most likely to gain from the experience. The budget is due on your boss's desk in eight weeks. Last year it took you about thirty to thirty-five hours to complete. However, you had done a budget many times before. For a novice, it might take double that amount of time. The budget process is generally straightforward. You start with last year's budget and modify it to reflect inflation and changes in departmental objectives. All the data that Dale will need are in your files or can be obtained from your other supervisors. You have decided to walk over to Dale's office and inform him/her of your decision.

## DALE MORGAN'S ROLE

You like Chris Hall. You think Chris is a first-rate boss and you've learned a lot from him/her. You also consider yourself Chris's heir apparent. To better prepare yourself to take Chris's job, you'd like to take on more of Chris's responsibilities. Running the lab is a demanding job. You regularly come in around 7 a.m. and it's unusual for you to leave before 7 p.m. Four of the last five weekends, you've even come in on Saturday mornings to get your work done. But, within reasonable limits, you'd try to find the time to take on some of Chris's responsibilities. As you sit behind your desk reviewing a lab report, Chris walks into your office.

## THE WORK

This exercise should take no more than 10 to 15 minutes. When completed, representatives from each group should discuss with the entire class how their delegation exercise went. Focus specifically on the skill behaviors presented in Building a Supervisory Skill (p. 216–217) and any problems that surfaced.

## THINKING CRITICALLY

## CASE 6.A

### The Portland Museum of History and Fine Arts

Roger Gaylord is an environmental control supervisor for the Cincinnati Museum of History and Fine Arts. His main job responsibility is to assure that the lighting and air quality in the building remains constant at predetermined and prescribed levels for the priceless art and artifacts collections in the museum. He also sees to it that museum employees are comfortable working in their offices. He, in fact, maintains an interesting balancing act to assure the lighting, ventilation, air circulation, temperature, and humidity are appropriate for the Museum collections as well as for employees, storage areas, and equipment.

Some areas in the multistory building need more air conditioning than others. Some areas must be humidity- and heat-controlled. In still other areas, close monitoring is needed to assure that air quality and lighting is perfect to preserve the quality of the artwork that is displayed.

Roger constantly monitors the temperature controls to assure they are working prop-

erly. He also oversees other employees who install and maintain the lighting, heating, and air conditioning systems needed for the museum's special collections. His work is always closely coordinated with the building security manager.

## RESPONDING TO THE CASE

1. Explain how work specialization is important to Roger as a building environmental control supervisor.
2. What type of organizational structure does the Museum have? What are the strengths and weaknesses of this structure?
3. Discuss the factors that determine the size of Roger's span of control.
4. Why is the chain of command principle important to Roger as well as to the Museum?

## CASE 6.B

### East Carolina State Book Store

Betty Reynolds is a supervisor in the Book Store on the campus of East Carolina State University. Reporting to the book store manager, her main job responsibility is to supervise three individuals who are responsible for ancillary items—clothing, gifts, and novelty items—that the book store sells. To do this requires many activities. Betty's area is required to order these items for the book store. Each semester her department must decide what traditional items should be stocked and what specialty or seasonal items might be needed. To order goods, they are required to fill out a purchase order, identifying the number of items ordered and their costs. This purchase order is then filed until Betty receives the bill of sale that accompanies the invoice at delivery. When the goods arrive from various vendors, one of Betty's employees logs them into the bookstore's inventory system. An employee then checks the goods to see that the order is correct. When this has been verified, Betty signs off on the invoice and forwards it to the bookkeeper, who handles all monies in the book store. One of Betty's employees then unpacks the items and places them in a prearranged area of the stock room.

Unfortunately, just placing goods into inventory won't create a sale. Betty's department must set up displays on the book store floor. They must then continuously monitor the shelves and restock low supplies whenever necessary. During this time, Betty must also keep track of what goods have sold. She needs to have this information entered in her inventory system so that she does not run out of things that are selling. To track inventories, Betty receives cash register receipts twice daily during her shift. When a particular point is reached in remaining inventory, she can complete another purchase order—and start the process over again.

Betty is also required to meet weekly with other supervisors to coordinate a variety of activities. For example, she and the person responsible for textbooks meet to discuss space utilization. At times, like the beginning of a semester, more space is needed for textbook sales. After the first week of classes, the textbook space is reduced, enabling Betty's employees to set up more ancillary item displays. Similar meetings take place with the individuals responsible for snack and personal hygiene products, and office supplies and stationery.

## RESPONDING TO THE CASE

1. What type of departmentalization is evident in the employee grouping of Betty's department? Cite specific examples to support your point of view.
2. What are the strengths and weaknesses of this grouping?
3. If you were asked to decide how to best group employees and activities in the book store so that it is more efficient from a customer (student) standpoint, what would that grouping be like? Explain your position. ■

# 7

# ACQUIRING THE RIGHT PEOPLE

# LEARNING OBJECTIVES 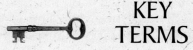 KEY TERMS

After reading this chapter, you should be able to:

1. Identify key laws and regulations affecting human resource practices.
2. Define the three steps in strategic human resource planning.
3. Explain the purpose of the job specification.
4. List the primary sources for recruiting job candidates.
5. Discuss the separate problems created by accept errors and reject errors.
6. Identify the strengths and weaknesses of the best-known selection devices.
7. Define what is meant by the terms *orientation, employee training,* and *employee development.*

You should also be able to define these supervisory terms:

accept errors

affirmative action

Age Discrimination in Employment Act of 1990

Americans with Disabilities Act

Civil Rights Act of 1964

Civil Rights Act of 1991

employee development

employee training

Equal Employment Opportunity Act

Family and Medical Leave Act
job specification

orientation

realistic job preview (RJP)

reject errors

reliability

sexual harassment

strategic human resource planning

validity

work sampling

# PERFORMING EFFECTIVELY

Becky Hannon dreamed of being successful.[1] As a risk taker, she wanted to pursue her individual interests. She ventured into her own business—TechSmart Inc., a Fort Hayes, Kansas Software Development company.

In the early days of her business, Becky made it a practice to hire family and friends. It wasn't that these individuals were the best qualified to do the jobs. Rather, many just wanted to help her—and Becky needed some workers. Before very long, a number of problems erupted. When certain tasks were needed—sometimes in a rush—some of her employees couldn't get the work done. Often, many weren't at work—they had either left work early, or simply decided to take the day off without notifying anyone. Compounding the problem was the fact that Becky didn't feel comfortable talking to these individuals about her dissatisfaction with their work behavior. She couldn't bring herself to "play" boss with people with whom she had a personal relationship. She didn't want to hurt anyone's feelings. As a result, the problems continued and were now threatening her company's survival. Becky felt she had no choice but to crack down on her haphazardly selected workforce. Of course, the employees reacted poorly. Several friends and family members quit. She regrets that her personal relationship with most of the people she hired is, at best, strained. ∎

## INTRODUCTION

Supervisors like Becky Hannon, by definition, oversee the work of other people. If these people lack skills, experience, or motivation, their work performance is sure to reflect it. Supervisors need to have qualified, high-performing people working for them. How do they find such people? When they have a vacancy to fill, what can they do to increase the probability that they'll hire a high-performing candidate from among the applicant pool?

In this chapter, we'll address a number of key personnel issues including employee recruitment, selection, and orientation and training. In the next chapter, we'll focus on another key element—appraising employee performance. First, let's consider the role of the human resources department in personnel decisions.

[1]This case is based on the article, by Michael P. Cronin and Stephanie Gruner, "Hiring: The Devil You Know?" *Inc.*, April 1994, p. 109.

## SUPERVISORS AND THE HUMAN RESOURCES DEPARTMENT

Some readers may be thinking, "Sure, personnel decisions like recruitment and selection are important, but aren't they made by personnel specialists in the human resources department? These aren't decisions that supervisors typically get involved in!"

It's true that large organizations have human resources departments. However, these people rarely make specific personnel decisions. Rather, as staff specialists, they help supervisors by writing and placing employment ads, screening applicants, and providing legal advice on personnel issues. The final decision, typically, is the supervisor's. Moreover, many small organizations don't have human resource departments. In such cases, supervisors typically have sole responsibility for hiring.

Every supervisor will be involved in staffing decisions. Regardless of the size of your organization or the presence of human resource specialists, there will be certain activities you need to understand. These include, at a minimum, human resource planning, conducting employment interviews, techniques for new-employee orientation, developing employees, and evaluating their performance. Also, very importantly, every supervisor must have a fundamental understanding of the current laws and regulations governing equal employment opportunity.

## UNDERSTANDING EQUAL EMPLOYMENT OPPORTUNITY (EEO)

Brad Coolidge had worked in the lumber business for more than 20 years, but he'd never held a management position before. About five months ago he was hired as a supervisor in the finishing department at a small Oregon lumber mill. When he recently had an opening in his department, he interviewed four candidates sent to him by the firm's human resources department. During an interview with one of the applicants, a female who was not made a job offer, he asked her a number of questions. Two of them were: "Are you married?" and "Do you have any children at home?" He didn't, however, ask those questions of the male candidates he interviewed. Brad learned today, from his boss, that this female applicant has filed an employment discrimination suit against him and the company. When Brad's boss asked if it was true that he had asked the woman about her marital status and whether she had children, Brad responded, "Sure. I was concerned she might miss work because of family responsibilities." Brad's

Today, most supervisors know that their hiring practices must meet the requirements of employment laws. As a result, rarely will you find a supervisor who blatantly excludes certain groups of people. This doesn't mean, however, that discrimination cannot occur. Employment practices that appear harmless may, in fact, keep certain people from having an equal chance. To see how this can happen, read the following situations that may arise in the employment process. After reading each one, check whether you feel it is a safe or a risky practice for an organization to be using. Dont' be concerned with whether you think the practice is legal or illegal. Just consider whether you believe it's okay to do, or whether it could create problems for the organization.

|  | Safe | Risky |
|---|---|---|
| 1. "Wanted: Recent college graduate to teach first grade in the local public school." | ☐ | ☐ |
| 2. A waiter in an exclusive restaurant was fired when his supervisor found out he tested positive for HIV. | ☐ | ☐ |
| 3. You want to take 12 weeks off without pay to care for your new child during the busiest part of your work year, and your supervisor denies the request. | ☐ | ☐ |
| 4. A Broadway theater hires a woman for the job of restroom attendant and assigns her to the men's restroom. | ☐ | ☐ |
| 5. A wheelchair-bound applicant is denied a job as a computer programmer. This 75-person company is on the 3rd floor and the building does not have elevators. Furthermore, door openings to offices are not wide enough for a wheelchair to pass safely—thus creating a safety hazard for the individual. | ☐ | ☐ |
| 6. The company policy states: "Applicants applying for jobs in the organization must have, at a minimum, a high school diploma." | ☐ | ☐ |
| 7. A pilot for Continental Airlines celebrates his 60th birthday. The following day, he is no longer permitted by his supervisor to fly the commercial flights he has been doing for the past 23 years. | ☐ | ☐ |
| 8. "Wanted: Sales rep to sell medical supplies to regional hospitals. The successful applicant must have five years of sales experience." | ☐ | ☐ |

boss was shocked. "Let me tell you something, Brad. Regardless of your intentions, you've just gotten yourself and this company into a heck of a mess!"

Brad Coolidge created problems by asking questions of women job candidates that he didn't ask of men, questions that, in fact, were not even job-relevant. In so doing, he has made himself and his employer potentially liable for damages.

This example illustrates the importance of every supervisor understanding the law and its effect on human resource practices. Large organizations will undoubtedly provide supervisors with specific guidelines to help ensure that they don't discriminate. They'll also probably have someone in the human resources department to provide advice when supervisors face uncertain situations. Supervisors in small organizations, where there are no formal guidelines or specialists to turn to, must keep abreast of current laws and make sure their hiring practices are in compliance with the laws. When in doubt, they should use outside lawyers or human resource consultants for advice. As we briefly review equal employment opportunity practices, remember that engaging in discrimination not only exposes you and your organization to potential liability, but also deprives you of hiring the most qualified applicant.

## WHAT LAWS PROTECT AGAINST EMPLOYMENT DISCRIMINATION?

Beginning in 1964 with the Civil Rights Act, there have been numerous federal laws and court decisions which affect employment practices (see Exhibit 7–1). In addition, many states and municipalities have passed laws that go beyond what the federal government requires. This section highlights the major federal laws dealing with employment discrimination with which you need to be familiar.

### CIVIL RIGHTS ACT OF 1964

The **Civil Rights Act of 1964** was divided into a number of parts, which are called Titles. For supervisors, Title VII is most important. It prohibits discrimination in hiring, firing, promoting, or privileges of employment based on race, religion, color, gender, or national origin. The law currently covers any organization with 15[2] or more employees and/or those which receive $50,000 or more in government monies. This minimum number of employees was meant to exclude the small, family-owned business.

It's impossible to overemphasize the importance of the Civil Rights Act. Prior to its passage, many employers blatantly discriminated against minorities and women when filling job vacancies. Qualified African-Americans, immigrants, and women were often passed over in favor of less qualified white males. Today, most of us take for granted that applicants should be judged on their ability to do a job—not the color of their skin, their religious beliefs, where they were born, or their gender. Not much more than a generation ago, this was not an accepted assumption.

**Civil Rights Act of 1964**
a law that prohibits discrimination in hiring, firing, promoting, and privileges of employment based on race, religion, color, gender, or national origin.

[2]The law, as originally passed, covered organizations with 25 or more employees.

## EXHIBIT 7–1

Major U.S. federal laws and regulations related to employment.

| Year | Law or Regulation | Description |
|------|-------------------|-------------|
| 1964 | Civil Rights Act, Title VII | Prohibits discrimination in hiring, firing, and promoting on the basis of race, color, religion, national origin, or gender (sex) |
| 1967 | Age Discrimination in Employment Act (amended 1978, 1986) | Prohibits age discrimination against employees. Prohibits forced retirement of most employees. |
| 1968 | Immigration Reform and Control Act | Prohibits unlawful employment and unfair immigration-related employment practices. |
| 1990 | American with Disabilities Act | Prohibits employers from discriminating against individuals with physical or mental disabilities or the chronically ill. Also requires organizations to reasonably accommodate these individuals. |
| 1991 | Civil Rights Act | Reaffirms and tightens prohibition of discrimination; permits individuals to sue for punitive damages in cases of intentional discrimination. |
| 1993 | Family and Medical Leave Act | Grants 12 weeks of unpaid leave each year to employees for the birth or adoption of a child, or the care of a spouse, child, or parent with a serious health condition; covers organizations with 50 or more employees. |

**Age Discrimination in Employment Act**
a law that prohibits discrimination against persons 40 years of age or older in any area of employment, including selection, because of age.

## AGE DISCRIMINATION IN EMPLOYMENT ACT OF 1967

Following the passage of the **Age Discrimination in Employment Act,** it is illegal to discriminate against persons 40 years of age or older in any area of employment, including selection, because of age. Furthermore, with the exception of a few jobs—like certain executive position—no one can be forced to retire at any age.

There is another exception, too. That's where an employer can show that advanced age may affect public safety. So, for example, American Airlines can reject the application of a 62-year-old for a pilot's position based on age and be within the law. We call such a requirement a *bonafide qualification.* However, as a manager of a retail store, you can't discriminate just because you want your sales staff to present a more youthful image or because you're concerned that older workers might miss more work due to health problems. If you do, you risk being in violation of the Age Discrimination Act.

The Age Discrimination in Employment Act prohibits employers from discriminating against individuals 40 years of age or older. This means that this recruiter must evaluate the candidate based on her qualifications to successfully perform the job—not based on her age!

## THE EQUAL EMPLOYMENT OPPORTUNITY ACT OF 1972

By the early 1970s, Congress realized that Title VII of the Civil Rights Act left a number of issues unclear. Most notably, there were few enforcement mechanisms available to uphold the law. To remedy this problem, Congress passed the **Equal Employment Opportunity Act**. This act established the Equal Employment Opportunity Commission (EEOC) to enforce the civil rights laws. It was given the power to sue organizations that failed to comply. It also expanded Title VII coverage to include state and local government employees and employers with 15 or more employees. Finally, it required employers to do more than just discontinue discriminatory practices. Employers were directed to actively develop a plan of action to correct areas of past discrimination. They were required to make an active effort to recruit, select, train, and promote members of protected groups. This is commonly referred to as **affirmative action**.

## THE AMERICANS WITH DISABILITIES ACT OF 1990

The passage of the **Americans with Disabilities Act** of 1990 sought to address discriminatory practices against the disabled. It protects the physically and mentally disabled—and even those with contagious diseases such as AIDS.

In addition to protecting the disabled from discrimination, this act requires employers to make reasonable accommodations to provide a qualified individual access to a job. A company may also be required to provide necessary technology, such as special hearing or reading equipment, to enable an individual to do his or her job.

## THE CIVIL RIGHTS ACT OF 1991

During the late 1980s, a number of Supreme Court decisions chipped away at the previous laws set up to protect against discrimination. In employer-employee discrimination disputes, the Court had increasingly taken the side of employers. For instance, one early interpretation of the Civil Rights Act was that the burden of proof fell on the employer to demonstrate that there was no discrimination when charges were brought. If an employer

**Equal Employment Opportunity Act**
a law that established the Equal Employment Opportunity Commission (EEOC) to enforce civil rights laws and gave it the power to sue organizations that failed to comply. It also expanded Title VII coverage and required employers to participate in affirmative action.

**Affirmative action**
legislation that requires employers to make an active effort to recruit, select, train, and promote members of protected groups.

**Americans with Disabilities Act**
a law that protects the physically and mentally disabled against discriminatory practices and requires employers to make reasonable accommodations to provide a qualified individual access to a job.

couldn't prove its innocence, then it was guilty. In the late 1980s, Supreme Court decisions changed that and put the burden of proof back on the employee.

Proponents of the 1964 legislation banded together to pass the **Civil Rights Act of 1991.** It restored much of the provisions lost to Supreme Court rulings. Specifically, it prohibits discrimination on the basis of race and prohibits racial harassment on the job; returns the burden of proof that discrimination did not occur back to the employer; reinforces the illegality of employers who make hiring, firing, or promotion decisions on the basis of race, ethnicity, gender, or religion; and permits women and religious minorities to seek punitive damages in intentional discrimination claims. For the first time, individuals claiming they have been intentionally discriminated against will be able to sue for damages.

### FAMILY AND MEDICAL LEAVE ACT OF 1993

One of the last laws passed that offers employment protection discrimination to employees is the **Family and Medical Leave Act** of 1993. The purpose of this Act was to provide employees in organizations with 50 or more employees the opportunity to take up to twelve weeks of unpaid leave each year for family matters—like the birth of a child, adoption, for their own illness, or to care for an ill family member.[3] Employees who take this leave are guaranteed their current job—or one equal to it—upon their return. Furthermore, during this period of unpaid leave, employees retain their current employer-offered health insurance.

## WHAT IS YOUR ROLE IN AFFIRMATIVE ACTION?

Many employers have formal affirmative action programs, with specific goals, to increase the number of women and minorities in their organizations. As a supervisor, you may be asked to actively pursue female and minority candidates and make a good faith effort to get them into the applicant pool.

Does this mean you have to hire an unqualified applicant in order to meet affirmative action goals? No! As we'll discuss shortly, before you begin looking to fill a position in your department, you need to know the skills, knowledge, and ability requirements of the job. If candi-dates meet these criteria, they are qualified. If your pool of job applicants doesn't include enough female and minority applicants, you should extend your search. For example you could place ads in papers contact organizations that are specifically targeted at women or minority-group members, send a notice of your job opening to the local disabled training center, or recruit

[3]F. G. Hermelin, "How Well is Family Leave Really Working?" *Working Woman*, September 1994, p. 9

Civil Rights Act of 1991
legislation that prohibits discrimination on the basis of race and prohibits racial harassment on the job; returns the burden of proof that discrimination did not occur back to the employer; reinforces the illegality of employers who make hiring, firing, or promotion decisions on the basis of race, ethnicity, gender, or religion; and permits women and religious minorities to seek punitive damages in intentional discriminatory claims.

Family and Medical Leave Act
a law that provides employees in organizations with 50 or more employees the opportunity to take up to twelve weeks of unpaid leave each year for family matters—such as childbirth, adoption, illness, or to care for an ill family member.

at educational institutions—but you are not required to hire any individual under this process. The objective of affirmative action is to eliminate discrimination by actively pursuing minorities and women; not to ensure the hiring of individuals from certain groups.

## DOES EEO GO BEYOND HIRING?

Most of what we've discussed in the previous few sections may have created a picture for you that EEO is most relevant in hiring decisions. Although much of the discussion of EEO typically focuses on the selection process, it goes beyond recruitment and selection of employees. It also addresses issues such as training and eliminating abusive work environments.

### EEO AND TRAINING OPPORTUNITIES

Are you making sure *all* of your employees have equal access to training? The Americans with Disabilities Act, for instance, makes it illegal to offer training courses at an off-site location that is inaccessible to disabled employees.

Do your employees need special training to learn to understand and work more effectively with individuals who are different from them? As the workforce becomes more culturally diverse, you will want to ensure that women, racial and ethnic minorities, homosexual employees, and any other group member who may be perceived as "different" is not treated prejudicially by others. This may require your employees to participate in awareness and sensitivity workshops to help them better understand and work with people who are unlike themselves.

### ELIMINATING SEXUAL HARASSMENT

Few workplace topics have received more attention in recent years than that of sexual harassment. Since 1980, U.S. courts generally have used guidelines from the Equal Employment Opportunity Commission to define sexual harassment. **Sexual harassment** generally encompasses anything of a sexual nature that involves requirements for getting a job, employment consequence (like a raise or promotion), or that creates an offensive or hostile work environment. This may include sexually suggestive remarks, unwanted touching and sexual advances, requests for sexual favors, and other verbal and physical conduct of a sexual nature.

In a 1993 ruling, the Supreme Court widened the test for sexual harassment under the civil rights law to whether comments or behavior in a work environment "would reasonably be perceived, and is perceived, as hostile or abusive." In so doing, employees need not show they have been psychologically damaged to prove sexual harassment in the workplace, merely that they are working in a hostile or abusive environment.

**Sexual harassment** anything of a sexual nature that is required for getting a job, has an employment consequence, or creates an offensive or hostile environment, including sexually suggestive remarks, unwanted touching, sexual advances, requests for sexual favors, and other verbal and physical conduct of a sexual nature.

From a supervisor's standpoint, sexual harassment is a growing concern because it intimidates employees, interferes with job performance, and exposes the organization to liability. To ensure that you do not have a hostile or abusive environment, you must establish a clear and strong position against sexual harassment. If your organization doesn't have a sexual harassment policy, then you need to establish one for your department. The policy should be reinforced by regular discussion sessions in which employees are reminded of the rule and carefully instructed that even the slightest sexual overture to another employee will not be tolerated. At AT&T, for instance, all employees have been specifically advised that they can be fired for making repeated unwelcome sexual advances, using sexually degrading words to describe someone, or displaying sexually offensive pictures or objects at work.

---

POP QUIZ  **(Are You Comprehending What You're Reading?)**

**1.** Which one of the following statements best reflects what is meant by the term affirmative action employer?
  **a.** The organization agrees to abide by employment laws.
  **b.** The organization actively seeks to hire women and minorities.
  **c.** The organization hires women and minorities but not white males.
  **d.** The organization hires women and minorities into the lowest level of the organization.
**2.** Under federal employment legislation, certain groups are protected. Identify the protected groups as designated by these laws.
**3.** Under the Age Discrimination in Employment Act, an employer can require an employee to retire after he or she has reached the age of 70. True or false?
**4.** Sexual harassment
  **a.** involves only physical conduct between male and female organizational members
  **b.** does not interfere with job performance
  **c.** holds the organization liable for the conduct of the supervisor
  **d.** is relevant only in large organizations

# DETERMINING STAFFING NEEDS

You've organized your department. You've identified the tasks that need to be done and grouped them into jobs. Now you've got to ensure that you'll have the right number and kinds of people to achieve your department's goals. We call this **strategic human resource planning** and it can be condensed into three steps: (1) assessing current human resources; (2) assessing future human resource needs; and (3) developing a program to meet future human resource needs.

## HOW DO YOU CONDUCT THE CURRENT ASSESSMENT?

Begin your assessment by reviewing your current human resource status. Your goal is to create a departmental human resource inventory.

The input for this report will be forms completed by your employees and filed in the human resources department. Increasingly, these files can be accessed by computer. This departmental inventory typically will include a list of your employees' names, education, training, prior employment, languages spoken, capabilities, and specialized skills. When completed, this inventory allows you to assess what talents and skills are available within your department. It lets you know what your individual employees can do.

## WHAT IS THE FUTURE ASSESSMENT?

Future human resource needs are determined by the organization's overall objectives and your departmental goals. The demand for the organization's overall human resources is a result of demand for the organization's products or services. On the basis of its estimate of total revenue, top management can attempt to establish the number and mix of human resources needed to reach these revenues. In some cases, the situation may be reversed. Where particular skills are necessary and in scarce supply, the availability of satisfactory human resources determine revenues. In recent years, this has been the case for Microsoft. This designer of computer software has more business opportunities than it can handle. Its primary limiting factor in building revenues has been its ability to locate and hire designers and programmers with the qualifications to write new software. In most cases, however, the overall organizational goals and the resulting revenue forecast provide the major input determining the organization's human resource requirements.

Based on forecasts provided by upper management, you can calculate their implications for your department's operations. What will be the increase or decrease in workload? What new or changing skills will be called for?

**Strategic human resource planning** the assessment of current human resources and future human resource needs, as well as the development of a program to meet all future human resource needs.

# How Do You Develop a Future Program?

After you've assessed both current capabilities and future needs, you'll be able to estimate shortages—both in number and kind—and to highlight areas in which your department will be overstaffed. Additionally, of course, your departmental projections will need to be combined with forecasts made by other supervisors in your organization and coordinated with the human resources department. This is important so that individuals with skills and capabilities that cut across departmental lines can be identified.

## FROM JOB DESCRIPTIONS TO JOB SPECIFICATIONS

**Job specification**
the minimum acceptable qualifications an incumbent must possess to perform a given job successfully.

You'll remember from the previous chapter that once your departmental structure is in place, the next step is to formalize the creation of specific jobs by creating job descriptions. These job descriptions tell employees what they're supposed to do. Another document, closely tied to the job description, is needed before you're ready to begin efforts at recruitment and selection. This document is the job specification.

The **job specification** states the minimum acceptable qualifications an incumbent must possess to perform a given job successfully. It identifies the knowledge, skills, and abilities needed to do the job effectively. In large organizations, job specifications are typically written by specialists in the human resources department with input from you. In smaller organizations, you may develop them yourself. An example of a job specification for a book production editor is shown in Exhibit 7–2.

What's the importance of the job specification? It's the standard against which job applicants will be compared. It keeps your attention fo-

"The first thing I look for in hiring is qualifications," says Mary Gasciogne at London Life. "Then it's just a gut feeling. I try to get a sense of how they will interact with the rest of the people. They have to be able to fit into the unit and get along with the rest of the employees."

**EXHIBIT 7–2**

Job Title: Project Production Editor

Department: College Book Editorial Production

Job Class: 7-12B

Education:
   Graduation from an accredited college or university with a
   specialization in creative writing, English, journalism, or equal.

Knowledge:
   No prior knowledge of book production necessary.

Abilities and skills:
   Ability to copyedit manuscripts; ability to organize and
   coordinate multiple projects simultaneously; ability to
   secure good working relationships with outside vendors;
   ability to meet deadlines; ability to express ideas clearly
   and concisely, orally and in writing; strong interpersonal
   skills; and skill in the use of Macintosh computers.

cused on the specific necessary and preferred qualifications for an individual to do a job effectively, and it assists you in determining whether candidates are qualified.

Once you've identified a vacancy in your department and have a job specification for that position, you can begin the search for the right candidate to fill that vacancy.

## RECRUITING CANDIDATES

If you have a departmental vacancy, where do you look to find potential candidates to fill it? In this section, we'll review the primary sources for job candidates.

### WHAT IS AN INTERNAL SEARCH?

Many organizations give preference to current employees for new openings. Employees like it because it gives them an advantage over outsiders in applying for lateral transfers and promotions. Internal candidates are sometimes preferred because detailed and accurate information on how the candidate did on prior jobs within the organization is readily available. While outside references are often vague and noncommittal, other individuals within your organization can typically provide the full history of an internal employee's performance record. In addition, internal candidates are already familiar with the organization. They, therefore, should take less time to adjust to a new job.

There are several drawbacks to relying on an internal search. First, it provides a limited set of candidates. You wouldn't want to hire a second-rate employee merely because he or she is there, when excellent candidates are available on the outside. Second, excessive reliance on internal search tends to perpetuate inbreeding. Internal candidates are less likely to bring new ideas and fresh perspectives to the job.

## ARE ADVERTISEMENTS EFFECTIVE?

The sign outside the plant reads: "Now Hiring Experienced Machinists." The newspaper advertisement reads: "Speech Pathologist. Large urban hospital is looking for a speech pathologist to join our rehabilitation group. M.A. and current state license required. Minimum of four years experience necessary. Salary to $48,000. Call Ms. Resnick at 579-5060."

Most of us have seen both types of advertisements. When an organization seeks to communicate to the public that it has a vacancy, advertisements are one of the most popular methods used. The higher the position is in the organization, or the more specialized the skills sought, the more widely dispersed the advertisement is likely to be. While the advertisement of blue-collar jobs is usually confined to the local daily newspaper or regional trade journals, the search for individuals with highly specialized technical skills might include advertisements in a national periodical.

Advertisements are an excellent means for disseminating information on a vacancy to a wide audience. Also, by careful selection of the medium for the ad, you can target specific minority groups or individuals with similar interests. The major drawback of advertisements is that, unless ads are very carefully worded, they tend to attract many unqualified candidates.

## WILL EMPLOYEE REFERRALS GENERATE QUALIFIED CANDIDATES?

One of the best sources of individuals who will perform effectively on the job is a recommendation from a current employee.[4] The reasons tend to be obvious. Employees will rarely recommend someone unless they believe that the person will perform adequately. Such a recommendation reflects

[4]A. Halcrow, "Employees Are Your Best Recruiters," *Personnel Journal*, November 1988, pp. 42–49.

on the recommender and, when someone's reputation is at stake, you can expect the recommendation to be based on relatively strong beliefs. Employee referrals may also have acquired more accurate information about their potential jobs. The recommender often gives the applicant more realistic information about the job than could be conveyed through employment agencies or newspaper advertisements. This information reduces unrealistic expectations and increases job survival. As a result of these preselection factors, employee referrals tend to be more acceptable applicants, to have a greater probability of accepting an offer if one is made, and, once employed, to have a higher job-survival rate.

There are, of course, some potentially negative features of employee referrals. For one thing, recommenders may confuse friendship with job-performance competence. Individuals often like to have their friends join them at their place of employment for social and even economic reasons. For example, they may be able to share rides to and from work. As a result, a current employee may recommend a friend for a position without giving unbiased consideration to the friend's job-related competence.

Employee referrals may also lead to nepotism; that is, hiring individuals who are related to persons already employed by the organization. The hiring of relatives is particularly widespread in family-owned organizations. While such actions do not necessarily align with the objective of hiring the most qualified applicant, interest in the organization and loyalty to it may be long-term advantages.

Finally, employee referrals may not help the organization in actively seeking minority and women candidates. Employees often refer someone who shares something with them—religion, demographics, race, etc. Accordingly, an organization that wants to increase the presence of protected groups must guard against over-reliance on employee referrals from members of nonprotected groups.

## WHAT ARE EMPLOYMENT AGENCIES?

There are two types of employment agencies: public and private. Let's take a look at each.

### PUBLIC AGENCIES

All states provide a public employment service. The main function of these agencies is closely tied in with unemployment benefits, since benefits are given only to individuals who are registered with their state employment agency.

Most public agencies tend to attract and list individuals who are unskilled or possess minimum training—although by no means is that the case every time. This, of course, does not reflect the agency's competence.

Rather, it reflects the image of public agencies. State agencies are perceived by prospective applicants as having few high-skilled jobs, and employers tend to see such agencies as having few high-skilled applicants. Therefore, public agencies tend to attract and place predominantly low-skilled workers. A public agency's image as perceived by both applicants and employers thus tends to result in a self-fulfilling prophesy. That is, few high-skilled individuals place their names with public agencies, and, similarly, few employers seeking individuals with high skills list their vacancies or inquire about applicants at state agencies.

## PRIVATE AGENCIES

Private agencies can be divided into three categories: full service agencies, temporary help services, and executive search firms. Since the last type has little relevance to supervisors—they specialize in placing middle-level and top-level executives—we'll focus on the other two.

The typical full-service private agency charges for its services. Their fees can be paid by the employer, the applicant, or on a shared basis. The perception is that private agencies offer positions and applicants of a higher caliber than those found at public agencies. In truth, they are more successful at finding professionals with high-level skills and experience. Private agencies also provide a more complete line of services. They advertise the position, they screen applicants against the criteria specified by the employer, and they usually provide a guarantee covering six months or a year as protection to the employer should the applicant not perform satisfactorily.

An increasingly popular type of private employment agency is the type that specializes in temporary employees. Organizations like Kelly and Manpower can be an excellent source of employees to fill part-time or short-term staffing needs. In the 1990s, as employers look for ways to increase their staffing flexibility and at the same time keep benefit costs down, the use of contingent workers hired through temporary help services is seen as a highly attractive alternative.

## How Do You Find Qualified Candidates in Educational Institutions?

Educational institutions at all levels offer opportunities for recruiting recent graduates. Most educational institutions operate placement services where prospective employers can review credentials and interview graduates; and many offer internship programs where you can find students who are looking for opportunities to practice on the job what they're learning. Whether the educational level required for the job involves a high school diploma, specific vocational training, or a college background with an associate, bachelor's, master's, or doctoral degree, educational institutions are an excellent source of potential employees for entry-level positions in organizations.

High schools or vocational-technical schools can provide blue-collar applicants; business or secretarial schools can provide white-collar staff; and two-year and four-year colleges and graduate schools can provide technical and professional personnel.

While educational institutions are usually viewed as sources of young, inexperienced entrants to the workforce, that's not necessarily the case today. It is not uncommon to find individuals with considerable work experience using an educational institution's placement service. They may be workers who have recently returned to school to upgrade their skills, completing second or advanced degrees, or alumni using their former school's placement center. With the downsizing that has occurred in the past decade, it's not unusual for experienced, mature workers to be enrolled in educational programs seeking to start new careers.

## How About Professional Organizations?

Many professional organizations, including labor unions, operate placement services for the benefit of their members and employers. The professional organizations include such varied occupations as accountants, industrial engineers, training specialists, and seafarers.

These organizations publish rosters of job vacancies and distribute these lists to members. It is also common practice to provide placement facilities at regional and national meetings where those looking for employment and companies looking for employees can find each other.

## Do Some Candidates Just Show Up?

"Walk-ins," whether they reach an employer by letter, telephone, or in person, can be a major source of prospective applicants. Although the qualifications of unsolicited applicants can depend on economic conditions, the organization's image, and the job seeker's perception of the types of jobs that might be available, this source does provide an excellent supply of applicants. Even if there are no particular openings when the applicant makes contact with the organization, the application can be kept on file for later needs.

Applications from individuals who are already employed can be referred to many months later and can provide applicants who (1) are interested in considering other employment opportunities and (2) regard the organization as a possible employer. Unsolicited applications made by unemployed individuals, however, generally have a short life. Those individuals who have adequate skills and who would be prime candidates for a

"I have total discretion over who is actually hired," says Jonathan Perkins, a supervisor at Simon & Schuster. In terms of locating applicants, that goes through the Human Resources Department. Our recruiters will place the ad in local papers, although they consult with me about which papers I think it should go in and the stated qualifications. We design the ad together. Yet, the recruiters, for the most part, bring in the applicants."

position in the organization if a position were available will usually find employment with some other organization that does have an opening. But in times of economic stagnation, excellent prospects are often unable to locate the type of job they desire and may stay actively looking in the job market for some time.

## ARE THERE OTHER SOURCES?

In the search for particular types of applicants, nontraditional sources should be considered. For example, Employ the Disabled associations can be a source of highly motivated workers; a Forty-Plus Club can be an excellent source of mature and experienced workers; and organizations like the National Organization for Women often provide placement services.

When you want to reach out and expand the diversity among applicants, sources might include National Urban League offices, local religious organizations, minority-oriented media, schools in the inner cities, local Hispanic and Asian-American organizations, and agencies dealing with ex-prisoners (see Dealing With a Difficult Issue).

## EMPLOYEE SELECTION

You've developed a pool of applicants. Now you need some method for screening the applicants and for identifying the most appropriate candidate. That screening method is the selection process.

## WHAT ARE THE FOUNDATIONS OF SELECTION?

Selection is a prediction exercise. It seeks to predict which applicants will be successful if hired. "Successful" in this case means performing well on the criteria the organization uses to evaluate employees. In filling a sales position, for example, the selection process should be able to predict which applicants will generate a high volume of sales for the company.

### PREDICTION

Consider for a moment, that any selection decision can result in four possible outcomes. As shown in Exhibit 7–3, two of these outcomes would indicate correct decisions, but two would indicate errors.

A decision is correct when the applicant was predicted to be successful and later proved to be successful on the job or when the applicant was predicted to be unsuccessful and would have performed accordingly if hired. In the former case, we have successfully accepted; in the latter case, we

## CAN YOU BE FAIR AND SUPPORT DIVERSITY, TOO?

As we saw in Chapter 2, our world of work is rapidly changing. With that change has come an influx of people from all parts of the globe into the jobs in the U.S. We've suggested that in order for each of us to be successful, we need to find ways to work with one another—regardless of race, religion, gender or nationality. In may respects, that means developing and practicing a sensitivity toward one another. Many organizations embrace this idea, but are they simply paying lip service to the issue? For can they truly be sensitive to individuals from different cultures when they require all of their employees to speak English only at the work site? First of all, is that legal? Generally, yes. At least that's what the Supreme Court has indicated.

At issue here are several items. On the one hand, supervisors have identified the need to have a common language spoken at the work site. They claim it is needed so they can communicate effectively with all employees—especially when safety matters are at stake. It is also a way for them to know if their employees are making fun of the organization, harassing other workers, or engaging in other inappropriate verbal behavior.

Nonetheless, workers in today's organizations speak different languages. It's estimated that about 32 million U.S. employees speak a language other than English. What about their need to speak their language, to communicate effectively with their peers, and their desire to maintain their cultural heritage? To them, being required to speak only English is discriminatory.

Should supervisors be permitted to require their employees to speak English only in the work place? What if it has nothing to do with work, nor does it create a safety hazard? Do you believe in the adage, "When in Rome, do as the Romans"—meaning that if people from around the globe want to work in the U.S., they need to adjust to the U. S. culture— including its language. What's your view on this hotly debated issue?

**Reject errors**
rejection of candidates who would later perform successfully on the job.

**Accept errors**
acceptance of candidates who would subsequently perform poorly on the job.

have successfully rejected. Thus the purpose of selection activities is to develop outcomes shown as "correct decision" in Exhibit 7–3.

Problems occur when we make errors by rejecting candidates who would perform successfully on the job (**reject errors**) or accepting those who subsequently perform poorly (**accept errors**). These problems are, un-

## EXHIBIT 7–3

Selection decision outcomes.

|  | Selection Decision | |
|---|---|---|
|  | Accept | Reject |
| **Successful** (Later Job Performance) | Correct decision | Reject error |
| **Unsuccessful** | Accept error | Correct decision |

fortunately, far from insignificant. Reject errors historically meant only that the costs of selection would be increased because more candidates would have to be screened. Today, however, selection techniques that result in reject errors can open the organization to charges of discrimination, especially if applicants from protected groups are disproportionately rejected. Accept errors, on the other hand, have very obvious costs to the organization, including the cost of training the employee, lost productivity, the cost of severance, and the subsequent costs of further recruiting and selection screening. The major thrust of any selection activity is, therefore, to reduce the probability of making reject errors or accept errors, while increasing the probability of making correct decisions.

## RELIABILITY

**Reliability**
an indication of whether a test or device measures the same thing consistently.

**Reliability** indicates whether the device measures the same thing consistently. For example, if a test is reliable, any single individual's score should remain fairly stable over time, assuming that the characteristics it is measuring are also stable.

The importance of reliability should be evident. No selection device can be effective if it is low in reliability. That is equivalent to weighing yourself everyday on an erratic scale. If the scale is unreliable—randomly fluctuating, say, ten to fifteen pounds every time you step on it—the results will not mean much. The same applies to selection devices. To be effective predictors, they must possess an acceptable level of consistency.

## VALIDITY

**Validity**
a proven relationship between a selection device and some relevant criterion.

Just because a selection device is reliable, doesn't make it proper to use. That's because any selection device that you use—such as application forms, tests, and interviews—must demonstrate **validity**. That is, there must be a proven relationship between the selection device and some relevant criterion. For example, the law prohibits you from using a test score as a selection device unless there is clear evidence that individuals with high scores on this test outperform, on the job, individuals with low test scores.

The burden is on you to support that any selection device you use to differentiate applicants is related to job performance. While you, for instance, can give applicants some sort of "paper and pencil" test and use the results to help make selection decisions, you must be prepared to demonstrate, if challenged, that this intelligence test is a valid measure. That is, you must be able to show that scores on the test are positively related to later job performance.

## What Selection Devices Are Available?

You can use a number of selection devices to reduce accept and reject errors. The best-known devices include an analysis of the prospect's completed application form, written and performance-simulation tests, interviews, background investigations, and in some cases a physical examination. Let's take a look at each of these devices, noting their respective strengths and weaknesses (see Exhibit 7–4).

## The Application Form

Almost all organizations require candidates to fill out some sort of an application. It may only be a form on which a prospect gives his or her name, address, and telephone number. At the other extreme, it might be a comprehensive personal history profile, detailing the applicant's activities, skills, and accomplishments.

## EXHIBIT 7–4

Dilbert's unique selection technique. (DILBERT® reprinted by permission of United Feature Syndicate Inc.)

Hard and relevant biographical data that can be verified—for example, rank in high school graduating class—have been shown to be valid measures of performance for some jobs.[5] Additionally, when application-form items have been appropriately weighted to reflect job relatedness—that is, allocating points to variables such as education and experience—the device has proven a valid predictor for such varied groups as salesclerks, engineers, factory workers, clerical employees, and technicians. Typically, only a couple of items on the application prove to be valid predictors, and then only for a specific job. Supervisors are encouraged to use weighted applications for selection purposes, but it is critical that application items be validated for each job and that the items be continually reviewed and updated to reflect changes in weights over time.

## WRITTEN TESTS

Typical written tests include tests of intelligence, aptitude, ability, and interest. Historically, these written tests were popular selection devices, but there has been a marked decline in their use over the past quarter-century. Why? Because these tests have frequently been characterized as discriminatory, and many organizations have been unable to demonstrate that they are job related. Sophisticated technology available today is making it easier to validate these tests, and they're making a comeback in the selection process.

Tests of intellectual ability, spatial and mechanical ability, perceptual accuracy, and motor ability have been shown to be moderately valid predictors for many semiskilled and unskilled operative jobs in industrial organizations.[6] However, remember the burden is on you to demonstrate that any test used is job related.

## PERFORMANCE SIMULATION TESTS

What better way to find out whether an applicant can do a job successfully than by having him or her do it? The logic of this question has resulted in increased usage of performance simulation tests. Undoubtedly, the enthusiasm for these tests lies in the fact that they are based on actual job behaviors rather than on surrogates. The best-known performance simulation test is called work sampling and it is designed for routine jobs.

**Work sampling** involves presenting applicants with a miniature replica of a job and letting them perform a task or set of tasks that are central to the job. Applicants demonstrate that they possess the necessary talents by actually doing the tasks. By carefully devising work samples,

**Work sampling**
the process of presenting applicants with a miniature replica of a job and letting them perform tasks that are central to the job.

[5]W. F. Casio, *Applied Psychology in Personnel Management*, 4th ed., (Englewood Cliffs, NJ: Prentice-Hall, Inc., 1991), p. 265.

[6]J. B. Miner, *Industrial and Organizational Psychology* (New York, NY: McGraw-Hill, 1991), pp. 504–511.

Manpower, the world's largest temporary help firm, tests applicants by using work sampling. Here the applicant is given the opportunity to demonstrate that he possesses certain computer skills that a potential employer needs.

supervisors can determine the knowledge, skills, and abilities needed for each job. Each work-sample element is then matched with a corresponding job-performance element. For instance, a work sample for a job that involves using a spreadsheet application would require applicants to demonstrate their proficiency with manipulating data on the spreadsheet.

The results from work-sample experiments have generally been impressive.[7] They have almost always yielded validity scores that are superior to those of written aptitude, personality, or intelligence tests.

## INTERVIEWS

The interview, along with the application form, is an almost universal selection device. Not many of us have ever gotten a job without one or more interviews. Unfortunately, interviews are typically poorly conducted and may result in distorted findings.[8] This doesn't mean that interviews can't provide valid and reliable selection information but, rather, that untrained interviewers tend to make common mistakes (see Assessing Yourself). Some of the problems include: interviewers often hold a stereotype of what represents a "good" applicant, they often tend to favor applicants who share the interviewer's own attitudes, the order in which applicants are interviewed often influences evaluations, the order in which information is elicited also influences evaluations, negative information is given unduly high weight, and interviewers forget much of the interviews' content within minutes after its conclusion.

[7]W. C. Borman and G. L. Hallman, "Observation Accuracy for Assessors of Work Sample Performance: Consistency Across Task and Individual Differences Correlates," *Journal of Applied Psychology*, February 1991, pp. 11–18.

[8]See R. L. Dipboye, *Selection Interviews: Process Perspectives* (Cincinnati, OH: South-Western, 1992), Chapter 2.

## DO YOU HAVE GOOD INTERVIEWING TECHNIQUES?

Below are eight questions regarding the interview process. Answer each question true or false.

**1.** It's risky to ask an applicant what foreign languages he or she can read, write, or speak fluently.        T    F

**2.** It's risky to ask an applicant about his or her past work experience.        T    F

**3.** It's risky to ask the full names of an applicant's brothers and sisters.        T    F

**4.** It's risky to ask an applicant what social clubs to which he or she belongs.        T    F

**5.** It's a good idea to tape record or take notes during an interview.        T    F

**6.** A good interviewer takes control of an interview and does most of the talking.        T    F

**7.** A good interviewer avoids asking questions that can be answered with a simple yes or no.        T    F

**8.** Early in the interview, you should provide the applicant with as much detail about the job being interviewed for as possible.        T    F

### SCORING

Questions 3, 4, 5, and 7 are true. Questions 1, 2, 6, and 8 are false. Total the number of correct responses you have.

### UNDERSTANDING THE ASSESSMENT

If you got seven or eight correct, you already have some understanding of how to conduct an effective selection interview. If you have fewer than seven correct, you need a better understanding of interviewing.

Interviews are widely used and tend to be given considerable weight in the final selection decision. As a result, you need to perfect your interviewing skills (see Building a Supervisory Skill).

## INTERVIEWING CANDIDATES

### About the Skill

Interviewing is difficult because it is, in effect, an art. Developing the art of the interview is to know what to do and how to do it. Then, it's a matter of practice so your interviewing skills don't become stale from lack of use.

### Steps in Practicing the Skill

1. **Review job description and job specification.** Reviewing pertinent information about the job provides valuable information about what you'll assess the candidate on. Furthermore, relevant job requirements help to eliminate interview bias.

2. **Prepare a structured set of questions to ask all applicants for the job.** By having a set of prepared questions, you ensure that the information you wish to elicit is attainable. Furthermore, by asking similar questions, you are able to better compare all candidates' answers to a common base.

3. **Prior to meeting a candidate, review his or her application form and resume.** Doing so helps you to create a complete picture of the candidate in terms of what is represented on the resume/application and what the job requires. You will also begin to identify areas to explore in the interview. Areas not clearly defined on the resume/application that are essential for your job should become a focal point in your discussion with the candidate.

4. **Open the interview by putting the applicant at ease and by providing a brief preview of the topics to be discussed.** Interviews are stressful for job candidates. By opening with small talk (e.g., the weather, or the traffic) you give the candidate time to adjust to the interview setting. By providing a preview of topics to come, you are giving the candidate an "agenda." This helps the candidate to begin framing what he or she will say in response to your questions.

5. **Ask your questions and listen carefully to the applicant's answers.** Select follow-up questions that naturally flow from the answers given. Focus on the responses as they relate to information you need to ensure that the candidate meets your job requirements. Any uncertainty you may have requires a follow-up question to further probe for the information.

6. **Close the interview by telling the applicant what's going to happen next.** Applicants are anxious about the status of your hiring decision. Be up-front with the candidate regarding others who will be interviewed and the remaining steps in the hiring process. If you plan to make a decision in two weeks or so, let the candidate know what you intend to do. Additionally, tell the applicant how you will respond to him or her about your decision.

7. **Write your evaluation of the applicant while the interview is still fresh in your mind.** Don't wait until the end of your day, after interviewing several candidates, to write your analysis of a candidate. Memory can fail you! The sooner you complete your write-up after an interview, the better chance you have for accurately recording what occurred in the interview. ■

## WHAT IS A BACKGROUND INVESTIGATION?

Background investigations include contacting former employers to confirm the candidate's work record and to obtain an appraisal of the applicant's work performance. It may also include contacting other job-related references, verifying educational accomplishments shown on the application, and checking credit references and criminal records.[9] The premise behind these investigations is that one can predict an individual's future behavior based on what he or she has done in the past.[10]

Several studies indicate that verifying "facts" given on the application form pays dividends. A significant percentage of job applicants—upward of 33 percent—exaggerate or misrepresent dates of employment, job titles, past salaries, or reasons for leaving a prior position.[11] Confirmation of hard data on the application with prior employers is therefore a worthwhile endeavor. Your organization must assess the liability that potential employees may create, and delve into their backgrounds in as much depth as necessary.[12] For example, daycare centers must go to great extremes to assure that potential employees do not pose a risk to the center's children. Failure to do the background check could prove detrimental to the organization should an unfortunate event occur—and the employee committing the act had a history of such behaviors.

## PHYSICAL EXAMINATION

For jobs that require certain physical requirements—e.g., police officers, airline pilots, train engineers, and stevedores—the physical examination has some validity. In most cases, nowadays, the physical examination is done for insurance purposes only. Great care must be taken to ensure that physical requirements are job related and do not discriminate. Physical requirements may not exclude persons with disabilities, when, in fact, such requirements do not affect job performance.

---

[9]"What Personnel Offices Really Stress in Hiring," *Wall Street Journal,* March 6, 1991; and "Responsible Background," ad in *HRMagazine,* February 1991, p. 50.

[10]See, for example, M. A. McDaniel, "Biographical Constructs for Predicting Employee Suitability," *Journal of Applied Psychology,* December 1989, pp. 964–970; and Michael Tadman, "The Past Predicts the Future," *Security Management,* July 1989, pp. 57–61.

[11]Commerce Clearing House, *Human Resource Management: Ideas and Trends* (May 17, 1992), p. 85.

[12]Norman D. Bates, "Understanding the Liability of Negligent Hiring," *Security Management Supplement,* July 1990, p. 7A.

# ORIENTATION, TRAINING, AND DEVELOPMENT

If you have handled the recruitment and selection duties properly, you should have hired competent individuals who can perform successfully. But successful performance requires more than possession of certain skills. New hires must adjust to their new surroundings and be trained to do the job in a manner consistent with the organization's objectives. To achieve these ends, you'll need to embark on two processes—orientation and training.

## How Do You Introduce New Hires to the Organization?

Once a job candidate has been selected, he or she needs to be introduced to the job and organization. This introduction is called **orientation.** The major objectives of orientation are to reduce the initial anxiety all new employees feel as they begin a new job; to familiarize new employees with the job, the work unit, and the organization as a whole; and to facilitate the outsider-insider transition. Job orientation expands on the information the employee obtained during the recruitment and selection stages. The new employee's specific duties and responsibilities are clarified, as well as how his or her performance will be evaluated. This is also the time to rectify any unrealistic expectations new employees might hold about the job (see News Flash). Work-unit orientation familiarizes the employee with the goals of the work unit, makes clear how his or her job contributes to the unit's goals, and includes introduction to coworkers. Organization orientation informs the new employee about the organization's objectives, history, philosophy, procedures, and rules. This should include relevant personnel policies such as work hours, pay procedures, overtime requirements, and benefits. A tour of the organization's physical facilities is often part of the organization orientation.

You have an obligation to make the integration of your new employee into the organization as smooth and as free of anxiety as possible. Successful orientation, whether formal or informal, results in an outsider-insider transition that makes the new member feel comfortable and fairly well adjusted, lowers the likelihood of poor work performance, and reduces the probability of a surprise resignation by the new employee only a week or two into the job.

Orientation
an expansion on information a new employee obtained during the recruitment and selection stages; an attempt to familiarize new employees with the job, the work unit, and the organization as a whole.

Supervisors who treat the recruiting and hiring of employees as if the applicants must be sold on the job and exposed only to an organization's positive characteristics set themselves up to have a work force that is dissatisfied and prone to high turnover.[13]

Every job applicant acquires, during the hiring process, a set of expectations about the company and about the job for which he or she is interviewing. When the information an applicant receives is excessively inflated, a number of things happen that have potentially negative effects on the company. First, mismatched applicants who would probably become dissatisfied with the job and quit soon would be less likely to withdraw from the search process. Second, the absence of accurate information builds unrealistic expectations. Consequently the new employees are likely to become quickly dissatisfied—leading to premature resignations. Third, new hires are prone to become disillusioned and less committed to the organization when they face the "harsh" realities of the job. In many cases, these individuals feel that they were duped or misled during the hiring process and, therefore, may become problem employees.

To increase job satisfaction among employees and reduce turnover, supervisors should provide a **realistic job preview (RJP)**. An RJP includes both positive and negative information about the job and the company. For example, in addition to the positive comments typically expressed in the interview, the candidate would be told of the downside of joining the company. He or she might be told that there are limited opportunities to talk to coworkers during work hours, that promotional advancement is slim, or that work hours fluctuate so erratically that employees may be required to work during typically off hours (nights and weekends). Applicants who have been given a more realistic job preview hold lower and more realistic job expectations for the jobs they'll be performing and are better able to cope with the job and its frustrating elements. The result is fewer unexpected resignations by new employees.

For supervisors, realistic job previews offer a major insight into the selection process. That is, retaining good people is as important as hiring them in the first place. Presenting only the positive aspects of a job to a job applicant may initially entice him or her to join the organization, but it may be an affiliation that both parties quickly regret.

[13]See, for example, S. L. Premack and J. P. Wanous, "A Meta-Analysis of Realistic Job Preview Experiments," *Journal of Applied Psychology*, November 1985, pp. 706–720.

# WHAT IS EMPLOYEE TRAINING?

On the whole, planes don't cause airline accidents, people do. Most collisions, crashes, and other mishaps—about 74 percent to be exact—result from errors by the pilot or air traffic controller or inadequate maintenance. Weather and structural failures cause only 15 percent of accidents.[14] We cite these statistics to illustrate the importance of training in the airline industry. These maintenance and human errors could be prevented or significantly reduced by better employee training.

**Employee training** involves changing employees' skills, knowledge, attitudes, and/or behavior.[15] This may mean changing what employees know, how they work, or their attitudes toward their jobs, coworkers, boss, and the organization. As a supervisor, you'll be responsible for deciding when your employees are in need of training and what form that training should take.

**Employee training** changing skills, knowledge, attitudes, or behavior of employees. Determination of training needs is made by supervisors.

Determining training needs typically involves generating answers to several questions (see Exhibit 7–5) . Using the leading questions in Exhibit 7–5, what kinds of signals can warn you that training may be necessary? The more obvious ones relate directly to productivity. That is, there may be indications that job performance is declining. This may include actual production numbers decreasing, lower quality, more accidents, and higher scrap or rejection rates. When you witness any of these outcomes, it often suggests that worker skills need to be fine-tuned. Of course, we're assuming here that the employee's performance decline was in no way related to lack of effort. You must also recognize that training may be required because of a "future" element. Changes that are being imposed on employees as a result of job design or a technological breakthrough also require training. For example, at XEL Corporation in Aurora, Colorado, supervisors and their bosses wanted to make the organization a premier producer of communica-

After new employees are hired, Robert Scott of Southwest Doors spends considerable time teaching them how to do their jobs. Here, Scott, and a skilled worker train a new employee.

[14]Cited in "The Five Factors that Make for Airline Accidents," *Fortune*, May 22, 1989, p. 80.
[15]R. G. Zalman, "The Basics of In-House Skills Training," *HRMagazine*, February 1991, p. 1.

## EXHIBIT 7–5

Determining training need.

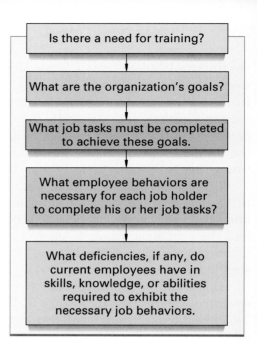

tions equipment. Unfortunately, many of the XEL employees lacked the necessary skills to work with new technologies, or even accept the autonomy managers wanted to give them.[16] Rather than "change" its entire workforce, XEL contracted with a local community college to provide training programs that would correct employee deficiencies. Having done so, companies like XEL view training proactively, as opposed to waiting and reacting to unsatisfactory performance conditions that may arise later.

### HOW ARE EMPLOYEES TRAINED?

Most training takes place on the job. This can be attributed to the simplicity of such methods and their usually lower cost. However, on-the-job training can disrupt the workplace and result in an increase in errors while learning takes place. Also, some skill training is too complex to learn on the job. In such cases, it should take place outside the work setting.

### WHAT ARE SOME OF THE TYPICAL METHODS USED?

There are many different types of training methods available for use in training employees. For the most part, however, we can classify them in two ways. That is, training programs can be viewed as on-the-job or off-the-job training methods. We have summarized the more popular of these training methods in Exhibit 7–6.

[16]M. P. Cronin, "Training: Asking Workers What They Want," *Inc.*, August 1994, p. 103.

EXHIBIT 7–6

| On-the-Job Training | Description |
|---|---|
| **Apprenticeship** | A time—typically two to five years—when an individual is under the guidance of a master worker to learn specific skills. |
| **Job Instruction Training** | A systematic approach to on-the-job training consisting of preparing the trainees by telling them about the job, presenting the instructions, having the trainees try the job to demonstrate their understanding, and placing trainees into the job under the lead of a resource person. |
| **Off-the-Job Training** | |
| **Classroom Lectures** | Lectures designed to communicate specific interpersonal, technical, or problem-solving skills. |
| **Multimedia** | Using various media productions to demonstrate specialized skills and deliver specific information. |
| **Simulation Exercises** | Training that occurs by actually performing the work. This may include case analysis, experiential exercises, role playing, or group decision making. |
| **Computer Based Training** | Simulating the work environment by programming a computer to imitate some of the realities of the job. |
| **Vestibule Training** | Training on actual equipment used on the job, but conducted away from the actual work setting—a simulated work station. |
| **Programmed Instruction** | Considering training materials into highly organized, logical sequences. May include computer methods, interactive video disks, or virtual reality simulations. |

Typical training methods.

## HOW CAN YOU ENSURE TRAINING IS WORKING?

It's relatively easy to offer a new training program. But training that is offered must be cost effective. You won't know if it is, unless you evaluate the training that's taking place. To keep the training ongoing, you must be able to show that the benefits gained by training outweigh the costs associated with providing the learning experience. Only by analyzing the outcomes training may have generated can effectiveness be determined.

Is there a way in which training programs are typically evaluated? Frequently, the following scenario takes place. Several individuals—usually representatives from the training department and a group of workers—are asked to critique a recently completed training program. If the comments are generally positive, the program gets a favorable evaluation. Based on that evaluation, the program continues, until something occurs which causes it to be changed or eliminated. These reactions, however, are questionable. The participants' opinions are often heavily influenced by factors that have little to do with actual training effectiveness—factors like difficulty, entertainment value, or personality of the instructor. Obviously, that's not the type of evaluation we're talking about. Rather, you must be certain that employee performance improves. Accordingly, training programs must be evaluated on some performance-based measures. This can be achieved by evaluating training based on how well employees can perform their jobs after they have received training; or on the differences found between pre- and post-training performance.

## HOW IS EMPLOYEE DEVELOPMENT DIFFERENT FROM EMPLOYEE TRAINING?

**Employee development** preparation of employees for future positions that require higher level skills, knowledge, or abilities.

In many organizations, the terms training and development are often used synonymously. In many respects, that may be correct. But employee development is different. Whereas employee training focuses its attention on the skills needed to do one's current job, **employee development** is more future oriented. That is, it deals with preparing employees for future positions that require higher level skills, knowledge, or abilities—like the analytical, human, conceptual, political, and specialized skills we introduced in Chapter 1 that all supervisors need. Although the methods of "delivering" employee development programs are similar to training methods, they focus more heavily on employees' personal growth.

It is important to consider one critical component of employee development in today's organizations. All employees, no matter what their level, can be developed. Historically, *development* was reserved for supervisory personnel, and those aspiring to be such. Although there's no question that development still must include preparing these individuals, downsizing, reengineering, and empowering has shown us that nonsupervisory personnel need such skills as planning, organizing, leading, and controlling, too. For instance, the use of work teams, giving workers the opportunity to participate in decision-making, and placing a greater emphasis on customer service and quality have all led to development being "pushed" down in the organization. Like training, development efforts must also be evaluated to ensure that the organization is getting "its money's worth."

**5.** A human resource inventory is

   **a.** a statement of what a current jobholder does, how it is to be done, and the accountabilites of the job

   **b.** a statement indicating employees' education, capabilities, and specialized skills

   **c.** a statement of the minimum qualifications required for job candidates to be successful on the job

   **d.** none of the above

**6.** What is the difference between reliability and validity? Is reliability alone sufficient for the selection process?

**7.** Negative information is frequently given more weight in an interview. True or False?

**8.** Which one of the following statements *best* reflects the difference between employee training and employee development?

   **a.** Employee training focuses on job skills needed for future positions. Employee development focuses on skills needed for current jobs.

   **b.** Employee development primarily involves off-the-job training methods. Employee training primarily involves on-the-job training methods.

   **c.** Employee training focuses on skills needed for current jobs. Employee development focuses on skills needed for future positions.

   **d.** Employee development focuses on current employees. Employee training focuses on potential job applicants.

## SUMMARY

After reading this chapter, I can:

1. **Identify key laws and regulations affecting human resource practices.** The Civil Rights Act of 1964, the Age Discrimination in Employment Act of 1967, the Equal Employment Opportunity Act of 1972, the Americans with Disabilities Act of 1990, the Civil Rights Act of 1991, and the Family and Medical Leave Act of 1993.

2. **Define the three steps in strategic human resource planning.** Assessing current human resources, assessing future human-resource needs, and developing a program to meet future human-resource needs.

3. **Explain the purpose of the job specification.** The job specification, which states the minimum acceptable qualifications that an incumbent needs in a job, guides supervisors in recruitment and selection by establishing the standard against which job applicants can be compared.

4. **List the primary sources for recruiting job candidates.** An internal search; advertisements; employee referrals; public and private employment agencies; schools, colleges, and universities; professional organizations; casual or unsolicited applicants; and nontraditional sources like disabled and women's organizations.

5. **Discuss the separate problems created by accept errors and reject errors.** Accept errors increase the costs to employers in the following areas: training, lost productivity, possible severance, and the recruiting and selection costs to find a replacement. Reject errors increase the number of candidates that must be screened. Additionally, they can subject the organization to charges of discrimination if members from protected groups are systematically rejected from jobs for which they are actually qualified.

6. **Identify the strengths and weaknesses of the best-known selection devices.** Hard and relevant data on an application form have been shown to provide valid information, but care must be taken not to ask for information that isn't job relevant. Some written tests demonstrate moderate validity, but they place a burden on management to support job relatedness. Work samplings are expensive but tend to yield high validity scores. Interviews are widely used and people have confidence in them, but they are typically poorly conducted and result in distorted findings. Verifying facts on an application form is a worthwhile endeavor. Physical exams as selection tools are relevant for only a small portion of jobs and care must be taken not to discriminate on the basis of physical requirements.

7. **Define what is meant by the terms *orientation, employee training,* and *employee development*.** Orientation involves introducing new employees to the organization and helping them adapt to their new surroundings. Employee training is a learning experience that seeks a relatively permanent change in employees such that their ability to perform on the job improves. Employee development, like employee training, seeks to make certain changes in employees. However, its focus is on developing skills for tomorrow's jobs, not skills to do today's job better.

# REVIEWING YOUR KNOWLEDGE

1. Discuss why supervisors need to know the basics of employee recruitment and selection.
2. Why is it important for every supervisor to understand equal employment opportunity laws?
3. Contrast job specifications with job descriptions.
4. How might advertisements be effective as a recruitment source?
5. Why are employee referrals considered one of the best sources for job applicants? What problems may arise from them?
6. Explain the importance of reliability and validity in a selection device.
7. Why are work samples more likely to be valid than written tests as selection devices?
8. Explain why a supervisor should provide a realistic job preview to a candidate and spend time orienting a new employee.
9. In what ways are employee training and employee development different?

# ANSWERS TO THE POP QUIZZES

1. **b. The organization actively seeks to hire women and minorities.** This response reflects the definition of affirmative action.
2. Protected groups under federal employment legislation include race, gender, religion, national origin, age (those over age 39), and the disabled.
3. **False.** Under the current terms of the Age Discrimination in Employment Act, an employer cannot require an employee to retire at any age. True, under certain conditions, retirement can be mandated, but those are the exceptions to the law.
4. **c. holds the organization liable for the conduct of the supervisor.** Anything of a sexual nature where it is a condition of employment, has an employment consequence, or creates an offensive or hostile environment is sexual harassment. Sexual harassment conduct by supervisors toward their employees can make the organization liable for their actions.
5. **b. a statement indicating employees' education, capabilities, and specialized skills.** This response reflects the definition of a human resource inventory.
6. Reliability reflects consistency. Validity reflects job relatedness. While a selection device can be consistently applied, it is risky if it doesn't measure something that is directly related to successful job performance.
7. **True.** Giving negative information undue weight in an interview is one of the problems that can lead to a distortion of interview findings.
8. **c. Employee training focuses on skills needed for current jobs. Employee development focuses on skills needed for future positions.** The question focuses on the time frame of each. ∎

## A CLASS EXERCISE

1. Break into groups of three.
2. Spend up to ten minutes, and write up to five challenging job-interview questions that you think would be relevant in the hiring of new college graduates for a sales management training program at Procter & Gamble. Each new hire will spend 18 to 24 months as a sales representative calling on retail grocers. After this training period, successful candidates can be expected to be promoted to the position of district sales supervisor.
3. Exchange your five questions with another group.
4. Each group should allocate one of the following roles to their three members: interviewer, applicant, and observer. The person playing the applicant should rough-out a brief resume of his or her background and experience, then give it to the interviewer.
5. Role-play a job interview. The interviewer should include, but not be limited to, the questions provided by the other group.
6. When completed, the observer should evaluate the interviewer's behaviors in terms of the skills presented in this section.

## CASE 7.A

### Hiring on the Internet

After you've planned effectively and grouped your employees accordingly, it's time to turn your attention to getting the right people. The jobs that have been identified, and their associated skills, point to very specific types of employees that you need. But these employees don't just magically appear. Instead, you must embark on an employment process of finding, hiring, and retaining qualified people.

That process starts when you notify the "public" that openings exist. You'll typically want to get your information out such that a large number of potentially qualified applicants respond. Then, after several interactions with the most promising of these candidates, people are hired. Those hired will be the ones who best demonstrate the skills, knowledge, and abilities to successfully perform the job.

Years ago, this entire process was dominated by paper and face-to-face interactions. Technology, today, is changing that. For individuals like Henry Liang, the job search has gone to the "Net."[17] Many jobs in organizations today are heavily influenced by technology. In fact, technology-related jobs in the U.S. grew by 320 percent in 1995, and that growth is predicted to continue through the turn of the century.[18] Accordingly, candidates must be able to demonstrate that they have the requisite skills and offer something special to organizations. Explaining qualifications in a letter to an employer often doesn't have the same effect as showing potential employers what you can do. When Henry, a University of Pennsylvania senior, wanted to let employers know he understood technology, he opted for an electronic resumé. By developing a Home Page on the Internet, Liang was able to refer potential employers to his Web page that he had designed. The electronic resumé, however, was only the beginning. Through the creation of links to

[17]M. Mannix, "A Paper Résumé? It's Passé," *U.S. News & World Report*, October 30, 1995, p. 90.

[18]"Hottest Corporate Jobs Are Unheard Of," *The Sun: Business*, February 11, 1996, p. E8. See also, Patrick Scheetz, "Best, Worst Majors for Job-Hunting Grads," *Employment Research Institute*, East Lansing, MI: Michigan State University, in *USA Today*, May 29, 1996, p. B11.

other Web pages, applicants like Henry can refer potential employers to a variety of Web sites that provide substantial data about him. For example, Liang can provide the details about the college he attended and his major course of study. He can also show some of his completed works or graphically highlight other pertinent data about his "fit" with the organization.

Although the use of the Internet for job hunting is still in its infancy, as more and more employers explore this technique, it's sure to gain momentum. For now, though, it's safe to say that a competitive advantage can be gained for highly technical jobs by using the Internet as a means of displaying one's skills.

## RESPONDING TO THE CASE

1. Describe the implications of job candidates placing resumés on the World Wide Web.
2. How can electronic resumés help you to identify that a job candidate possesses technical skills? How would you react if you found out that another person developed the candidate's Home Page? Explain.
3. Describe a selection process in which you can verify that a candidate, like Henry Liang, does possess the technical skill required for a job using the Internet.

## CASE 7.B

### Manpower, Inc.

When Anjali Gupta went to work for Manpower Inc., the temporary services agency, during the summer of her junior year in high school, she never dreamed that she would become a permanent Manpower employee, let alone a supervisor. At first her goal was to earn spending money for clothes and to go snow skiing. Her goal soon switched to paying her way to attend college, first on a part-time basis and then full time. When she was offered the Manpower supervisory position, her goal was to find a good permanent job.

By working a variety of temporary jobs that Manpower sent her to, she was able to evaluate many things about her temporary employers' places of business. She quickly identified the type of office where she liked to work and the type of people with whom she liked to interact. She liked to meet new people as well as work with a variety of personalities. She especially liked motivated, creative people who communicated with each other. She was partial to busy offices where change happened on a daily basis. She also liked to explore new software applications and find better and more productive tools to accomplish work.

It was no wonder that Manpower asked Anjali to work for them on a permanent basis! Anjali's working style was a perfect fit for them. In her new role of supervising the matching of temporary workers to temporary office placements, she found she needed some good assessment skills—of candidates seeking employment, of business needs, and the ability to effectively supervise a small staff of placement specialists.

## RESPONDING TO THE CASE

1. Why is it important for Anjali to know about the laws and regulations which affect human resource practices? Why should she understand them from an employee's view as well as from an employer's view?
2. Why is it important for Anjali to know how to determine staffing needs?

3. What are some of the recruiting methods Anjali might use to assure she has the right kind of employees to match the needs of the community? Explain why you selected one method over another.

4. Research the employment selection process of at least five businesses in your community. Ask such questions as: What type of and how much testing do they require? Is an application, work sample, or other similar material required? If so, what kind and for what purpose? How is the success of a potential applicant predicted? How important is the interview? The resumé? The follow-up letter or phone call? Who conducts the interviews and how long are they? Where does the final decision lie for hiring a new employee? What type of orientation and training is given to new hires? ■

# 8

# APPRAISING EMPLOYEE PERFORMANCE

# LEARNING OBJECTIVES  KEY TERMS

After reading this chapter, you should be able to:

1. Contrast the three purposes of the performance appraisal.
2. Differentiate formal and informal performance appraisals.
3. Describe key legal concerns in performance appraisals.
4. Identify the three most popular sets of criteria that supervisors appraise.
5. Contrast absolute and relative standards.
6. List human errors that can distort performance appraisal ratings.
7. Describe the purpose of employee counseling.

You should also be able to define these supervisory terms:

behaviorally-anchored rating scale (BARS)

central tendency error

checklist

critical incidents

employee counseling

extrinsic feedback

graphic rating scale

group order ranking

halo error

individual ranking

intrinsic feedback

leniency error

performance appraisal

recency error

similarity error

written essay

Most employees experience an evaluation of their job performance at least once a year. This may take the form of a five-minute, informal discussion between employees and their supervisors or a more elaborate, several-week process involving many specific steps. Irrespective of their degree of formality, employees generally see these evaluations as having some direct effect on their work lives. They may result in increased pay, a promotion, or assistance in personal or technical development areas for which the employee needs some training. As a result, any evaluation of employees' work can create an emotionally charged event. Consider what happened at Reich Engineering Services, a Durham, North Carolina engineering company.

The policy at Reich is that each employee is evaluated on the anniversary of his or her date of hire. Based on the evaluation, the supervisor makes a recommendation regarding an increase in the employee's hourly rate of pay. Fred Norris, the supervisor, has asked Adam Carrington to come to his office at 10 a.m. today. Although Adam thinks that it is time for his performance evaluation, he is not totally sure. He leaves his crew around 9:45, and heads for the office. When he arrives, Fred is in his office working on a standardized form used for evaluation. Adam sits quietly until Fred has finished. With the final touches complete, Fred begins his meeting. Let's eavesdrop on that conversation.

## INTRODUCTION

"I know it's wrong," remarked Fred Norris. "I know I should do more in terms of performance appraisals with my employees, but I don't. As long as my boss doesn't get on my case, I sort of ignore them. The reason is that when I do appraisals and give people feedback, we almost never agree. Everybody thinks they're doing an above average job. How can everybody be above average? If I believed their self-appraisals, I'd have only three kinds of people working for me—stars, all-stars, and super-stars!"

Fred Norris's comments—as well as his dealings with Adam— suggest why a lot of supervisors find appraising employee performance to be one of their most difficult tasks. In this chapter, we'll review the performance appraisal and provide you and the Fred Norrises of this world with some techniques that can make the appraisal and performance review a less traumatic experience.

**Fred:** Adam, glad you were able to make it here today. As you know, this is the anniversary of your hire date, and I am required to fill out an evaluation on you. Sorry I didn't have it done before you got here, it's been just one of those mornings. Well, let me see . . .

**Adam:** Fred, I've been through this five times before, so just give it to me. What's my raise? I'd really like to get back to my work crew. We're trying to finish up on that Beckley job—the builders want to start the excavation early next week.

**Fred:** Adam, there's more than just the pay increase. I want to talk about your performance. I believe, overall, you've done some good work, but you have some problem areas, too.

**Adam:** What do you mean problem areas? I've done my job better than most on my work crew. In fact, you've been using me to train our new field engineers.

**Fred:** Well Adam, that's your opinion. Yes, you're helping to train new field engineers, but I have had some complaints from them over the past few months. I think that needs to be addressed.

**Adam:** So get to the bottom line, Fred. What's my raise? Let's stop the ...

**Fred:** Okay, Adam, I am recommending a 50 cents an hour raise. I'd like for you to look over this evaluation, and sign it.

**Adam:** Just give me a pen, let me sign the paper, and I'll get out of here. ■

# THE PURPOSE OF EMPLOYEE PERFORMANCE APPRAISALS

Twenty years ago, the typical supervisor would sit down annually with his or her employees, individually, and critique their job performance. The purpose was to review how well they did toward achieving their work goals. Those employees who failed to achieve their goals found the performance appraisal to result in little more than their supervisor documenting a list of their shortcomings. Of course, since the performance appraisal is a key determinant in pay adjustments and promotion decisions, anything to do with appraising job performance struck fear into the hearts of employees. Not surprisingly, in this climate supervisors often wanted to avoid the whole appraisal process.

Today, effective supervisors treat the **performance appraisal** as an evaluation and development tool, as well as a formal legal document. It re-

**Performance appraisal**
a review of past performance that emphasizes positive accomplishments as well as deficiencies, and a means for helping employees improve future performance.

views past performance—emphasizing positive accomplishments as well as deficiencies. In addition, supervisors are using the performance appraisal as a means for helping employees improve future performance. If deficiencies are found, the supervisor can help employees draft a detailed plan to correct the situation. By emphasizing the future as well as the past, employees are less likely to respond defensively to performance feedback, and the appraisal process is more likely to motivate employees to correct their performance deficiencies. Finally, remember from the last chapter the issue of employee discrimination. Taking action against an employee for poor performance can create a problem if the problem is not well documented. The performance evaluation serves a vital purpose in providing the documentation necessary for any personnel action that is taken.

## WHEN SHOULD APPRAISALS OCCUR?

The performance appraisal is both a formal and an informal activity. Formal performance reviews should be conducted once a year at a minimum. Twice a year may even be better. Just as students don't like to have their entire course grade hanging on the results of one final exam, neither do employees relish having their careers depend on an annual review. Two formal reviews a year mean less "performance" will be appraised at each one, and lessen the tension employees often associate with the formal review.

The informal performance appraisal refers to the day-to-day assessment a supervisor makes of an employee's performance and the ongoing feedback the supervisor gives to the employee about that performance. The effective supervisor continually provides informal information to employees—commenting on the positive aspects of their work and pointing out problems when they surface. So while formal reviews may occur only once or twice a year, informal reviews should be taking place all the time. Moreover, when the informal feedback has been open and honest, the formal reviews will probably be less threatening to the employee and won't present any great surprises (see Assessing Yourself).

## YOUR ROLE IN PERFORMANCE APPRAISALS

How much latitude do supervisors have in the appraisal process? The larger your organization, the more likely it is that there will be standardized appraisal forms and formal procedures for you to follow. Even small companies tend to standardize some appraisal procedures in order to ensure that equal employment opportunity requirements are met.

## CONDUCTING THE APPRAISAL REVIEW INTERVIEW

For each of the following questions, check the answer that best describes your relationship with employees. Remember to respond as you have behaved or would behave, not as you think you should behave. If you have no supervisory experience, answer the questions imagining you are a supervisor.

When conducting an employee's performance appraisal review, I

| | Usually | Sometimes | Seldom |
|---|---|---|---|
| **1.** Try to put the employee at ease. | ○ | ○ | ○ |
| **2.** Make sure I fully understand the employee's job duties and responsibilities. | ○ | ○ | ○ |
| **3.** Encourage the employee to engage in self-evaluation. | ○ | ○ | ○ |
| **4.** Do most of the talking. | ○ | ○ | ○ |
| **5.** Avoid criticism. | ○ | ○ | ○ |
| **6.** Focus discussion on the employee's behavior rather than on his or her personal characteristics. | ○ | ○ | ○ |
| **7.** Use specific examples to support my judgments. | ○ | ○ | ○ |
| **8.** Try to get the appraisal over with as quickly as possible. | ○ | ○ | ○ |

## SCORING

For questions 1, 2, 3, 6, and 7, give yourself 3 points for "Usually," 2 points for "Sometimes," and 1 point for "Seldom." For questions 4, 5, and 8, give yourself 3 points for "Seldom," 2 points for "Sometimes," and 1 point for "Usually." Sum up your total points.

## WHAT THE ASSESSMENT MEANS

A score of 21 or higher indicates excellent performance-appraisal skills. Scores in the 16 to 20 range imply some deficiencies in this skill. Scores below 16 denote that you have considerable room for improvement.

## Will You Be the Sole Appraiser?

Most all employee performance appraisals are conducted by supervisors. However, a supervisor isn't always the sole source of pertinent information about employees' performance. In recent years, some organizations have added self-evaluations and peer evaluations to supplement those made by supervisors. Employees themselves often have valuable insights to provide. So, too, do their peers.

Self-evaluations get high marks from employees themselves. They tend to lessen employees' defensiveness about the appraisal process, and they make excellent vehicles for stimulating the job performance discussion. Self-evaluations tend to suffer from inflated assessments, so they should be used to enhance your evaluation rather than to replace it. The use of self-evaluations, however, is fully consistent with viewing performance appraisal as a developmental tool rather than for purely evaluative purposes.

There are some elements of an employee's job that peers are better at judging than you as a supervisor. In some jobs, for instance, you don't regularly observe an employee's work because your span of control is quite large or because of physical separation. In cases when work is largely built around teams, the team members are often better at evaluating each other, because they have a more comprehensive view of each member's job performance. In such instances, supplementing your appraisals with peer evaluations can increase the accuracy of the appraisal process.

## What Forms or Documentation Does the Organization Provide?

It is the unusual organization that doesn't require its supervisors to use a standardized form to guide them in doing performance appraisals. In some cases, top management or the human resources department will pro-

"At London Life, we do annual performance appraisals every October," says Cheryl Munro Sharp. "New employees get appraised after six months. That gives me a chance to talk to them about how they're doing on the job and identify any problems before they become serious."

vide an abbreviated form and allow considerable freedom in identifying and assessing job performance factors. At the other extreme, organizations provide detailed forms and instructions that all supervisors must follow (see, for example Exhibit 8–1).

Our point is that you rarely have complete discretion in evaluating your employees. Begin by reviewing any standard forms that your organization uses for appraisals. Familiarize yourself with the information you'll be expected to provide and make sure all of the people reporting to you—especially new employees—understand how and on what criteria they will be evaluated.

## HOW DO YOU SET PERFORMANCE EXPECTATIONS?

As a supervisor, you should be involved in determining performance standards for your employees. This ties back to the discussion of MBO and goal setting in Chapter 3.

Ideally, you and each employee should jointly review the employee's job, identify the processes and results needed, and then determine performance standards that will define how well the results are accomplished. Remember, before an employee's performance can be appraised, there must exist some standard against which the appraisal can be made. You must ensure that performance expectations have been defined for every employee and that employees fully understand these expectations.

## WHAT IS PERFORMANCE FEEDBACK?

Employees can receive performance feedback in one of two forms. It can be provided intrinsically by the work itself, or it can be given extrinsically by a supervisor or some other external source (see Building a Supervisory Skill).

In some jobs, employees regularly get feedback on how well they're doing because the feedback is built into the job. For example, a factory worker who assembles a CD player and tests it to determine if it operates properly gets self-generated feedback. Similarly, a freight clerk in a shipping department at a trucking company keeps an ongoing tally of the number of boxes he packs and the weight of each. At the end of the day, he totals the numbers and compares them to his daily goals. These calculations provide him with self-generated or **intrinsic feedback** on how he did that day.

**Extrinsic feedback** is provided to an employee by an outside source. If the factory worker routes the completed CD player on to a quality control inspector, who tests it for proper operation and makes needed adjustments, her performance feedback is extrinsic. If the freight clerk's shipping totals are calculated each day by his supervisor and posted on the department's bulletin board, his performance feedback is also extrinsic.

Intrinsic feedback
self-generated feedback.

Extrinsic feedback
feedback provided to an employee by an outside source.

## PRENTICE HALL NON-EXEMPT PERFORMANCE APPRAISAL

EMPLOYEE NAME: _____ TITLE: _____

REVIEW PERIOD: _____ — _____
Month/Year            Month/Year

SUPERVISOR'S NAME: _____ TITLE: _____

**SIMON & SCHUSTER
A VIACOM COMPANY**

## Writing the Appraisal Performance Ratings

**E  Exceptional** — Consistently exceeds expectations in major areas of responsibility.

**C  Commendable** — Performs the job as it is defined and exceeds expectations in some of the major areas of responsibility.

**I  Improvement Recommended** — Meets minimum requirements in most areas, but needs improvement in select areas of responsibility.

**U  Unsatisfactory** — Does not meet minimum performance requirements. Must improve if present position is to be maintained.

## PERFORMANCE FACTORS

Rate employee in each performance category. Include supporting examples for each performance factor.

E = EXCEPTIONAL
C = COMMENDABLE
I = IMPROVEMENT RECOMMENDED
U = UNSATISFACTORY

| Performance Factors | E | C | I | U | Comments and Supporting Examples |
|---|---|---|---|---|---|
| **Quality** Consider accuracy, comprehensiveness and orderliness of work | | | | | |
| **Quantity** Consider speed and volume of work produced | | | | | |
| **Initiative** Consider the ability to think independently with minimal direction and apply new concepts and techniques | | | | | |
| **Job Knowledge** Consider the understanding of the job and the ability to apply knowledge and skills effectively | | | | | |
| **Problem Solving/ Decision Making** Consider the ability to identify, analyze and solve problems, suggest viable alternatives and analyze impact of decisions before executing them | | | | | |
| **Judgment** Consider the ability to make logical and sound decisions and to know when to act independently or to seek assistance | | | | | |

| Performance Factors | E | C | I | U | Comments and Supporting Examples |
|---|---|---|---|---|---|
| **Punctuality** Consider adherence to the work schedule and promptness in notifying supervisor of absence | | | | | |
| **Planning and Organizational Skills** Consider the ability to establish priorities, maintain schedules and manage time effectively | | | | | |
| **Communication** Consider the ability to express oneself clearly, both verbally and in writing, and to listen well | | | | | |
| **Interpersonal Skills** Consider the ability to interact diplomatically and tactfully with internal and external contacts | | | | | |
| **Dependability** Consider adherence to the work schedule, the ability to maintain confidentiality, complete work under deadlines, follow through on assignments, and be reliable and flexible | | | | | |
| **Job Skills** Consider skills in areas such as typing/word processing, computer, telephone, etc. | | | | | |

### OVERALL PERFORMANCE RATING

__ Exceptional    __ Commendable    __ Improvement Recommended    __ Unsatisfactory

## EXHIBIT 8–1

Examples of employee appraisal forms.

## PERFORMANCE SUMMARY

I.  **Performance vs. Goals for Past Year:**

Describe how the employee met stated goals for past year and met additional goals if applicable.

II.  **Goals for Upcoming Year:**

List quantifiable goals with timetables for completion.

## PERFORMANCE SUMMARY

III.  **Strengths**

Identify employee unique strengths in relation to performance factors previously listed.

IV.  **Areas for Improvement**

Identify areas in which employee can focus to achieve improved performance.

## PERFORMANCE SUMMARY

V.  **Personal Growth and Development**

Describe activities to be undertaken that will maximize the employee's career development. These may include educational programs, counseling, on-the-job training, etc.

_____        _____
Supervisor's Signature                 Date

**EMPLOYEE'S COMMENTS**
Your comments are beneficial to the performance appraisal process. Additional comments may be attached on a separate page if desired.

**THE EVALUATION AND COMMENTS WERE DISCUSSED WITH THE EMPLOYEE**

| Employee's Signature and date | |
| --- | --- |
| Supervisor's Signature and date | Title |

# EXHIBIT 8–1
(Continued)

## CONDUCTING A PERFORMANCE EVALUATION

### ABOUT THE SKILL

Most contemporary discussions of the performance review advocate the problem-solving approach. We acknowledge our debt to this approach in developing many of the following guidelines.

### STEPS IN PRACTICING THE SKILL

1. **Schedule the formal appraisal review in advance and be prepared.** Many supervisors treat the entire performance appraisal as a lark. They put neither time nor thought into it. If a performance review is to be effective, planning must precede it. Review the employee's job description. Go over your rating sheet. Have you carefully considered the employee's strengths as well as weaknesses? Can you substantiate, with specific examples, all points of praise and criticism? Given your past experiences with the employee, what problems, if any, do you anticipate in the review? How do you plan to react to these problems?

2. **Put the employee at ease.** Regardless of your personal feelings about performance reviews—many supervisors feel uncomfortable judging others or fear that being honest will create resentment among their employees—you are responsible for creating a supportive climate for the employee. The performance review can be a traumatic experience for the best of employees. People don't like to hear their work criti-

cized. Then, too, many employees have little confidence that the organization's performance-appraisal system will accurately assess their contribution. Add the fact that people tend to overrate themselves and you have the ingredients for tension and confrontation. Recognize that the employee is probably uptight, so be supportive and understanding.

3. **Be sure that the employee understands the purpose of the appraisal review.** Is the review to be used for personnel decisions or to promote the employee's growth and development? The former purpose warrants focusing on the past, while the latter points to the future. In the problem-solving approach, the review is seen as an opportunity to provide recognition for those things the employee is doing well and to discuss any job-related problems that the employee may be experiencing. Regardless of the purpose, any uncertainty the employee may have about what will transpire during the review and the resulting consequences should be clarified at the start.

4. **Minimize threats.** You want to create a helpful and constructive climate. The review should not be an inquisition. You want to maximize encouragement and support, while minimizing threats.

5. **Obtain employee participation.** Effective performance reviews are characterized by high employee participation. Let the employee do the majority of the talking.

6. **Have the employee engage in self-evaluation.** Consistent with high participation, encourage the employee to evaluate his or her own performance. If the climate is supportive, the employee may even openly acknowledge performance problems you've identified, thus eliminating your need to raise them. Further, the employee may offer viable solutions to these

problems. By encouraging self-evaluation and being a good listener, you become a partner who is helping the employee perform better, rather than a "boss" who is looking for negatives to criticize.

7. **Criticize performance but not the person.** If you need to criticize, direct the criticism at specific job-related behaviors that negatively affect the employee's performance. Never criticize the employee. It's the person's performance that is unsatisfactory, not the person.

8. **Soften the tone when criticizing, but not the message.** Many of us find it difficult to criticize others. If you believe criticism is necessary, don't water down the message, don't dance around the issue, and certainly don't avoid discussing a problem in the hope that it'll just go away. State your criticism thoughtfully and show concern for the employee's feelings, but don't soften the message. Criticism is criticism, even if it's constructive. When you try to sell it as something else, you're liable to create ambiguity and misunderstanding.

9. **Don't exaggerate.** Many of us have a tendency to make extreme statements in order to make our point. Don't stretch the facts. If an employee has been late for four out of five recent meetings, don't say, "You're always late for meetings." Whenever possible, avoid absolutes like "always" or "never." Such terms encourage defensiveness and undermine your credibility. An employee only has to introduce one exception to your "always" or "never" statement to destroy the entire statement's validity.

10. **Use specific examples to support your ratings.** Document your employee's performance ratings with specific examples. This adds credibility to your ratings and helps employees to better understand what you mean by "good" and "bad" performance.

11. **Give positive as well as negative feedback.** No matter how poorly an employee is performing, he or she will have exhibited some strengths worthy of recognition. State what was done well and why it deserves recognition. What you want to avoid is turning the performance review into a totally negative feedback session. Of course, you want to avoid the other extreme, too: blanket praise when it isn't justified. If blanket praise is given, the employee is reinforced for mediocre as well as excellent behavior.

12. **Have the employee sum up the appraisal review.** As the review nears its conclusion, encourage the employee to summarize the discussion that has taken place. This gives your employee an opportunity to put the entire review into perspective. It will also tell you whether you have succeeded in clearly communicating your evaluation.

13. **Detail a future plan of action.** Where there are serious performance deficiencies, the final part of the review should be devoted to helping the employee draft a detailed, step-by-step plan to correct the situation. Your role should be supportive: "What can I do to provide assistance?" Do you need to make yourself more available to answer questions? Do you need to give the employee more freedom or responsibility? Would securing funds to send the employee to professional meetings, workshops, or training programs help? The object is to demonstrate your support for the employee by asking him or her where you can provide assistance and then committing to provide that assistance. In effect, you fulfill your partnership role by helping employees to clear the path on the road toward their goals. ■

You should provide your employees with ongoing extrinsic feedback, even if their jobs are rich in the intrinsic variety. This can be accomplished through informal performance reviews—ongoing comments that let an employee know how he or she is doing—and through formal performance reviews on a semiannual or annual basis.

## LEGAL ISSUES IN PERFORMANCE APPRAISALS

A great many lawsuits have arisen because supervisors said or did something that their employees believed adversely affected them. One supervisor told an employee that he had downgraded his evaluation because he had taken off work for religious holidays. An employee argued that her supervisor's appraisals were arbitrary and based on subjective judgments. Another employee was awarded damages because his supervisor failed to follow the company's performance appraisal policies and procedures.

Maybe the two most important legal facts you need to keep in mind concerning performance appraisals are: (1) performance appraisal policies and procedures, as set forth in organizational handbooks, are being increasingly construed by the courts as binding unilateral contracts; and (2) you must do everything possible to avoid the appearance of prejudice and discrimination.

Does your company have a published handbook that describes its performance appraisal procedures? If so, make sure you fully understand its contents. The courts, in most states, consider it a binding contract. The organization can be held accountable if those procedures are not followed or are followed improperly. If the handbook states, for instance, that appraisals must be performed annually or that managers will counsel employees to correct deficiencies, then you are obligated to fulfill these

Effective supervisors regularly document information on their employees performance. By doing so, Veronica London of Millerson's Office Supplies has support to show the unbiased nature of her appraisals, and documentation showing that the evaluation is based on job-related information.

commitments. On the other hand, the courts have generally supported giving supervisors a wide range of discretion, as long as fairness and equity are not compromised, when their organizations have no published performance appraisal policies.

The second point is a reminder that equal employment opportunity laws require that all human resource practices be bias-free—including employee performance appraisals. The appraisal criteria, methods, and documentation must be designed to ensure that they are job related. They must not create a different effect on women or minorities. Appraisal judgments must be neutral regarding an employee's race, color, religion, age, gender, or national origin. An increasing number of organizations are providing supervisory training in the mechanics of performance appraisal specifically to minimize the likelihood that discrimination might occur in the process (see Dealing with a Difficult Issue).

# DEALING WITH A DIFFICULT ISSUE

## THE FAULTY APPRAISAL

Most managers recognize the importance of effective performance appraisals in their organizations. Not only are they necessary for providing feedback to organizational members and for identifying areas of improvement, they do provide legal documentation.

Most managers also understand that performance evaluations need to meet EEO requirements. That is, they must be conducted in a way that is fair, and then should give everyone the same opportunities. But what about those instances when an appraisal is legal—yet involves a questionable practice. For example (assuming of course race or gender have no part in your rating), what if you deliberately evaluate an employee whom you like higher than one you dislike—even though the latter is the better performer? Likewise, what if you avoid identifying development areas for an employee so that his or her promotional advancements are limited?

In any appraisal system, two factors must exist—sincerity and honesty. However, these ethical elements don't appear in EEO regulations. Accordingly, can an organization have an effective performance appraisal system without sincerity and honesty being a vital part of it? Are "ethical" evaluations even possible? What do you think?

## APPRAISING APPROPRIATE CRITERIA

The criteria that you choose to appraise when evaluating employee performance will have a major influence on what employees do. In a public employment agency, which served workers seeking employment and employers seeking workers, employment interviewers were appraised by the number of interviews they conducted. Consistent with the thesis that the evaluating criteria influence behavior, employees emphasized the number of interviews conducted rather than the placement of clients in jobs.[1]

[1] P. M. Blau, *The Dynamics of Bureaucracy,* rev. ed. (Chicago, IL: University of Chicago Press, 1963).

The preceding example demonstrates the importance of criteria in performance appraisal. *What* should you appraise? The three most popular sets of criteria are individual task outcomes, behaviors, and traits.

## WHAT ARE INDIVIDUAL TASK OUTCOMES?

If ends count, rather than means, then you should evaluate an employee's task outcomes. Using task outcomes, a carpet cleaner might be judged on the number of square yards he or she was able to clean per day. A salesperson could be assessed on overall sales volume in his or her territory, dollar increase in sales, and number of new accounts established.

## WHAT BEHAVIORS MATTER?

Evaluating employees on behavior requires the opportunity to observe employees or devise a system for reporting to you on specific behavior criteria. Using the previous examples, behaviors of a carpet cleaner that could be used for performance-appraisal purposes might include promptness in reporting to work sites or thoroughness in cleaning equipment at the end of the work day. Pertinent salesperson behaviors could be average number of contact calls made per day or sick days used per year.

In many cases, it is difficult to identify specific outcomes that can be directly attributable to an employee's actions. This is particularly true of personnel in staff positions and individuals whose work assignments are intrinsically part of a group effort. In the latter case, the group's performance may be readily evaluated, but the contribution of each group member may be difficult or impossible to identify clearly. In such instances, it is not unusual to appraise the employee's behavior.

## IS EVALUATING TRAITS USEFUL?

When you rate people on the degree to which they are dependable, confident, aggressive, loyal, cooperative, and the like, you are judging traits. Experts seem to agree that traits are inferior to both task outcomes and behaviors as appraisal criteria.[2] The reason is that traits refer to potential predictors of performance, not performance itself. So the link between traits and job performance is often weak. Additionally, traits typically have a strong subjective component. What, for instance, does aggressive mean? Is it pushy, dominating, or assertive? Your evaluation of someone on this

---

[2]See, for example, M. J. Kavangh, "Evaluating Performance," in K. M. Rowland and G. R. Ferris, eds., *Personnel Management* (Boston, MA: Allyn & Bacon, 1982), pp. 187–226.

Many organizations still place a high importance on such traits as effort and dependability in their appraisal system. Without it, companies like Allied Equipment would not be able to meet production goals.

trait is largely determined by what the term means to you. Despite the drawbacks of traits as a criteria, they are still widely used in organizations for appraising employee performance.

## HOW DO YOU GATHER PERFORMANCE DATA?

Once performance standards have been set, expectations communicated, and appraisal criteria defined, you need to gather performance data. This is an activity every supervisor can and should do.

The best approach is to gather performance data on a continuous basis. Don't wait until a week or so before you are due to formally evaluate an employee to begin gathering your information. You should keep an ongoing file for each one of your employees, in which you record actual incidents (behaviors and/or outcomes) that affect his or her job success or failure. Such documentation reduces the potential for errors caused by over-reliance on recall of events and provides supportive evidence to back up your eventual ratings. Remember, too, that frequency of observation will improve the quality of the data you gather. The more opportunities you have to observe your employees' performance first hand, the more accurate your performance appraisals are likely to be.

# PERFORMANCE APPRAISAL METHODS

Once you have your data, you can begin your actual performance appraisals. If available, use the forms provided by the organization; otherwise, develop your own rating forms. The object is to replace the "global impression" each of us creates about someone else's overall performance with a systematic procedure for assessing performance. This systematic procedure increases the accuracy and consistency of results.

There are three different approaches for doing appraisals. Employees can be appraised against (1) absolute standards, (2) relative standards, or (3) objectives. No one approach is always best; each has its strengths and weaknesses. However, keep in mind that your choice may be dictated, or at least limited, by the human resource policies and procedures in your organization.

## WHAT ARE THE ABSOLUTE STANDARDS MEASUREMENTS?

The absolute standards measurement means that employees are not compared against any other person. Included in this group are the following methods: written essays, critical incidents, checklists, graphic rating scales, and behaviorally anchored rating scales.

### WRITTEN ESSAYS

Probably the simplest method of appraisal is to write a narrative describing an employee's strengths, weaknesses, past performance, potential, and suggestions for improvement. The **written essay** requires no complex forms or extensive training to complete. A drawback is that the results tend to reflect the ability of the writer. A good or bad appraisal may be determined as much by your writing style as by the employee's actual level of performance.

**Written essays** a written narrative describing an employee's strengths, weaknesses, past performance, potential, and suggestions for improvement.

### CRITICAL INCIDENTS

**Critical incidents** focus attention on those employee behaviors that are key in making the difference between executing a job effectively and executing it ineffectively. That is, you write down anecdotes that describe what the employee did that was especially effective or ineffective. The key here is that only specific behaviors, not vaguely defined personality traits, are cited. A list of critical incidents provides a rich set of examples from which the employee can be shown those behaviors that are desirable and those that call for improvement.

**Critical incidents** incidents that focus attention on employee behaviors that are key in making the difference between executing a job effectively and executing it ineffectively.

## CHECKLISTS

**Checklist**
a list of behavioral descriptions that are checked off when they apply to an employee.

With a **checklist,** you use a list of behavioral descriptions and check off those behaviors that apply to the employee. As Exhibit 8–2 illustrates, you merely go down the list and check off yes or no to each question. Checklists are quick, and relatively easy to administer. However, they have drawbacks. One drawback is their cost. Where an organization has a number of job categories, checklist items must be developed for each category. Second, simply checking yes or no provides little data for an employee—especially if you expect them to improve their work.

## GRAPHIC RATING SCALES

**Graphic rating scale**
a method of appraisal which uses a scale or continuum that best describes the employee, using factors such as quantity and quality of work, job knowledge, cooperation, loyalty, dependability, attendance, honesty, integrity, attitudes, and initiative.

One of the oldest and most popular methods of appraisal is the **graphic rating scale.** An example of some graphic rating scale items is shown in Exhibit 8–3.

Graphic rating scales can be used to assess factors such as quantity and quality of work, job knowledge, cooperation, loyalty, dependability, attendance, honesty, integrity, attitudes, and initiative. This method is most valid when subjective traits like loyalty or integrity are avoided, unless they can be defined in specific behavioral terms.

With the graphic rating scale, you go down the list of factors and note that point along the scale or continuum that best describes the employee. There are typically 5 to 10 points on the continuum. In the design of the graphic scale, the challenge is to ensure that both the factors evaluated and the scale points are clearly understood by the supervisor doing the rating.

|  | Yes | No |
|---|---|---|
| 1. Are supervisor's orders usually followed? | ____ | ____ |
| 2. Does the individual approach customers promptly? | ____ | ____ |
| 3. Does the individual suggest additional merchandise to customers? | ____ | ____ |
| 4. Does the individual keep busy when not servicing a customer? | ____ | ____ |
| 5. Does the individual lose his or her temper in public? | ____ | ____ |
| 6. Does the individual volunteer to help other employees? | ____ | ____ |

## EXHIBIT 8–2

Sample items from a checklist appraisal form.

# EXHIBIT 8–3

Example of graphic rating scale items.

| Performance Factor | Performance Rating | | | | |
|---|---|---|---|---|---|
| *Quality of Work* is the accuracy, skill, and completeness of work. | **1** Consistently unsatisfactory | **2** Occasionally unsatisfactory | **3** Consistently satisfactory | **4** Sometimes superior | **5** Consistently superior |
| *Quantity of work* is the volume of work done in a normal workday. | **1** Consistently unsatisfactory | **2** Occasionally unsatisfactory | **3** Consistently satisfactory | **4** Sometimes superior | **5** Consistently superior |
| *Job knowledge* is information pertinent to the job that an individual should have for satisfactory job performance. | **1** Poorly informed about work duties | **2** Occasionally unsatisfactory | **3** Can answer most questions about the job | **4** Understands all phases of the job | **5** Has complete mastery of all phases of the job |
| *Dependability* is following directions and company policies without supervision. | **1** Requires constant supervision | **2** Requires occasional follow-up | **3** Usually can be counted on | **4** Requires very little supervision | **5** Requires absolute minimum of supervision |

Why are graphic rating scales so popular? Though they don't provide the depth of information that essays or critical incidents do, they do have a number of advantages: they are less time consuming to develop and administer; they provide for quantitative aggregation and comparison; in contrast to the checklist, there is greater standardization of items so comparison with other employees in diverse job categories is possible. Furthermore, having this quantifiable assessment helps to support or defend supervisory personnel decisions when challenged.

## BEHAVIORALLY-ANCHORED RATING SCALES

**Behaviorally-anchored rating scales (BARS)** combine major elements from the critical-incident and graphic-rating scale approaches. You rate your employees based on items along a continuum, but the points are examples of actual behavior on the given job rather than general descriptions or traits.

Behaviorally-anchored rating scales specify definite, observable, and measurable job behaviors. Examples of job-related behaviors and per-

**Behaviorally-anchored rating scales (BARS)** scales that help a supervisor rate an employee based on items along a continuum; however, points are examples of actual behavior on a given job rather than general descriptions of traits.

formance dimensions are found by obtaining specific illustrations of effective and ineffective behavior for each performance dimension. These behavioral examples are then translated into a set of performance dimensions, each dimension having varying levels of performance. The results of this process are behavioral descriptions, such as anticipates, plans, executes, solves immediate problems, carries out orders, and handles emergency situations. Exhibit 8–4 provides an example of a BARS.

Studies conducted using BARS indicate that they tend to reduce rating errors. But its biggest plus may stem from the dimensions BARS generates rather than from any particular superiority of behavior over trait anchors. The process of developing the behavioral scales is valuable in and of itself for clarifying to both the employee and supervisor which behaviors mean good performance and which mean bad.

**EXHIBIT 8–4**

Sample bars for an employee relations specialist.
(*Source:* Reprinted from *Business Horizons,* August 1976. Copyright 1976 by the Foundation for the School of Business at Indiana University.)

Performance dimension scale development under BARS for the dimension "Ability to Absorb and Interept Policies for an Employee Relations Specialist."

**This employee relations specialist**

9 — Could be expected to serve as an information source concerning new and changed policies for others in the organization

Could be expected to be aware quickly of program changes and explain these to employees — 8

7 — Could be expected to reconcile conflicting policies and procedures correctly to meet HRM goals

Could be expected to recognize the need for additional information to gain a better understanding of policy changes — 6

5 — Could be expected to complete various HRM forms correctly after receiving instruction on them

Could be expected to require some help and practice in mastering new policies and procedures — 4

3 — Could be expected to know that there is always a problem, but go down many blind alleys before realizing they are wrong

Could be expected to incorrectly interpret guidelines, creating problems for line managers — 2

1 — Could be expected to be unable to learn new procedures even after repeated explanations

However, **BARS** is not without its drawbacks. It, too, suffers from the distortions inherent in most rating methods. BARS is also costly to develop, and to maintain.[3]

## HOW DO YOU USE RELATIVE STANDARDS?

In the second category of performance appraisals—relative standards—employees are compared against other employees in evaluating their performance. We'll discuss two relative methods: group order ranking and individual ranking.

### GROUP ORDER RANKING

**Group order ranking** requires you to place your employees into particular classifications, such as "top one-fifth" or "second one-fifth." If you have 20 employees, and you're using the group-order ranking method, only 4 of your employees can be in the top fifth, and, of course, 4 also must be relegated to the bottom fifth (Exhibit 8–5).

The advantage of this group ordering is that it prevents you from inflating employee evaluations so everyone looks good or equalizing the evaluations so everyone is rated near the average—outcomes that are not unusual with the graphic rating scale. The predominant disadvantages surface when the number of employees being compared is small. At the extreme, if you are looking at only 4 employees, all of whom may actually be excellent, you are forced to rank them into top quarter, second quarter, third quarter, and low quarter. Of course, as the sample size increases, the validity of relative scores as an accurate measure increases.

Another disadvantage, which plagues all relative measures, is the zero-sum consideration. This means that any change must add up to zero. If there are 12 employees in your department performing at different levels of effectiveness, by definition, 3 are in the top quartile, 3 are in the second quartile, and so forth. The sixth-best employee, for instance, would be in the second quartile. Ironically, if two of the workers in the third or fourth quartiles leave the department and are not replaced, then the sixth-best employee now falls into the third quartile. Because comparisons are relative, an employee who is mediocre may score high only because he or she is the "best of the worst." In contrast, an excellent performer who is matched against tough competition may be evaluated poorly, when in absolute terms his or her performance is outstanding.

**Group order ranking** placing employees into classifications, such as top one-fifth or second one-fifth. This method prevents a supervisor from inflating or equalizing employee evaluations.

[3]K. R. Murphy and V. A. Pardaffy, "Bias in Behaviorally Anchored Scales: Global or Scale Specific," *Journal of Applied Psychology*, April 1989, pp. 343–346; and M. J. Piotrowski, J. L. Barnes-Farrell, and F. H. Esris, "Behaviorally Anchored Bias: A Replication and Extension of Murphy and Constans," *Journal of Applied Psychology*, October 1988, pp. 827–828.

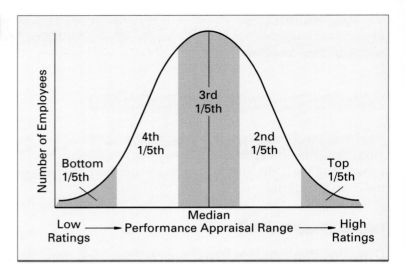

**EXHIBIT 8–5**

Group order ranking distribution.

### INDIVIDUAL RANKING

**Individual ranking** a method that requires supervisors to list all employees in order from highest to lowest performer.

The **individual ranking** method requires you to list all of your employees, in order, from the highest to lowest performer. In this method, only one can be "best." This method also assumes that differences between people are uniform. That is, in appraising 30 employees, it is assumed that the difference between the first and second employee is the same as that between the twenty-first and twenty-second. This method allows for no ties, which can be an advantage because it doesn't allow you to avoid confronting differences in performance levels. But its major drawback is that, in those situations where differences are small or nonexistent, this method magnifies and overemphasizes differences.

### OBJECTIVES

The final method for appraising performance is using objectives. This is essentially an application of management by objectives (MBO), introduced in Chapter 3.

Once you and your employee have established a set of tangible, verifiable, and measurable goals that encompass the key results he or she is expected to achieve, you have the standard in place against which the employee's performance can be assessed. At the end of the objective-setting period—which might be monthly, quarterly, semiannually, or annually—you and your employee can sit down and appraise how well he or she performed. If the objectives were carefully chosen to capture the essential performance dimensions in the employee's job and written so they can be readily measured, they should provide you with a fairly accurate appraisal of the employee's overall job performance.

## POTENTIAL PROBLEMS IN PERFORMANCE APPRAISALS

While you and your employer may seek to make the performance-appraisal process free from personal biases, prejudices, and idiosyncrasies, a number of potential problems can creep into the process. To the degree that the following factors are prevalent, an employee's performance appraisal is likely to be distorted.

### WHAT IS A LENIENCY ERROR?

Every appraiser has his or her own value system that acts as a standard against which appraisals are made. Relative to the true or actual performance an individual exhibits, some appraisers mark high and others low. The former is referred to as positive **leniency error**, and the latter as negative leniency error. When appraisers are positively lenient in their evaluations, an employee's performance becomes overstated, that is, rated higher than it actually should be. Similarly, a negative leniency error understates performance, giving the individual a lower appraisal than deserved.

**Leniency error**
positive or negative leniency that over- or understates performance, giving an individual a higher or lower appraisal than deserved.

If all employees in an organization were appraised by the same person, there would be no problem. Although there would be an error factor, it would be applied equally to everyone. The difficulty arises when we have different raters with different leniency errors making judgments. For example, assume that Jones and Smith are performing the same job for different supervisors, but they have absolutely identical job performance. If Jones's supervisor tends to err toward positive leniency, while Smith's supervisor errs toward negative leniency, we might be confronted with two dramatically different performance appraisals.

## HOW DO HALO ERRORS AFFECT APPRAISALS?

**Halo error**
a tendency to rate an individual high or low on all factors due to the impression of a high or low rating on some specific factor.

The **halo error** is a tendency to rate an individual high or low on all factors due to the impression of a high or low rating on some specific factor. For example, if an employee tends to be dependable, you might become biased toward that individual to the extent that you will rate him or her high on many desirable traits.

People who design teaching appraisal forms for college students to fill out to evaluate the effectiveness of their instructors each semester must confront the halo error. Students tend to rate a faculty member as outstanding on all criteria when they are particularly appreciative of a few things he or she does in the classroom. Similarly, a few bad habits—like showing up late for lecture, being slow in returning papers, or assigning an extremely demanding reading assignment—might result in students evaluating the instructor as "lousy" across the board.

How would you rate this individual? It's hard to say. If you rated him because he entertained you—rather than on how much you learned—you may be allowing the halo effect to cloud your appraisal.

## WHAT IS SIMILARITY ERROR?

When appraisers rate other people giving special consideration to those qualities that they perceive in themselves, they are making a **similarity error**. The supervisor who perceives himself as aggressive may evaluate others by looking for aggressiveness. Those who demonstrate this characteristic tend to benefit, while others are penalized.

Again, this error would tend to wash out if the same evaluator appraised all the people in the organization. However, multirater reliability obviously suffers when various evaluators are utilizing their own similarity criteria.

**Similarity error** rating others in a way that gives special consideration to qualities that appraisers perceive in themselves.

## WHAT IS RECENCY ERROR?

It's easier for most of us to remember vividly what happened yesterday than what happened six months ago. This creates the potential for the recency error to surface in performance appraisals.

The **recency error** results in evaluators recalling, and then giving greater importance to, employee job behaviors that have occurred near the end of the performance-measuring period. If you have to complete an appraisal form on each of your employees every June 1st, those accomplishments and mistakes that took place in May might tend to be remembered, while the behaviors exhibited during the previous November tend to be forgotten. Given the reality that we all have good days and bad days—even good and bad months—and that they don't occur at the same time for all employees, a semiannual or annual review may be significantly biased by employee behaviors just prior to your review.

**Recency error** rating others in a way that appraisers recall and give greater importance to employee job behaviors that have occurred near the end of the performance-measuring period.

## HOW DOES CENTRAL TENDENCY ERROR AFFECT APPRAISALS?

It's possible that, regardless of who the appraiser evaluates and what characteristics are used, the pattern of evaluation remains the same. It is also possible that a supervisor's ability to appraise objectively and accurately has been impeded by a failure to use the extremes of the appraising scale. This reluctance to assign extreme ratings, in either direction, is the **central tendency error**.

Raters who are prone to the central tendency error avoid the "excellent" category as well as the "unacceptable" category and assign all ratings around the "average" or midpoint range. For example, if you rate all employees as 3, on a 1 to 5 scale, then no differentiation among them exists. By suppressing differences, employees' work performances appear considerably more homogeneous than they really are.

**Central tendency error** appraisers' tendency to avoid the "excellent" category as well as the "unacceptable" category and assign all ratings around the "average" or midpoint range.

# ARE YOU INCLINED TO USE INFLATIONARY PRESSURES?

A clerical employee at a large insurance company was disappointed by the small salary increase she received following her recent performance review. After all, her supervisor had given her an 86 overall rating. She knew that the company's appraisal system defined "outstanding performance" as 90 and above, "good" as 80 to 89, "average" as 70 to 79, and "unacceptable" performance as anything below 70. This employee was really bewildered when she heard from some friends at work that her pay increase was below the company average. You can imagine her surprise when, after meeting with the assistant director for human resources, she learned that the "average" rating of clerical personnel in the company was 92!

This example illustrates a potential problem in appraisals— inflationary pressures. Here, you as a supervisor minimize differences among your employees and push all evaluations into the upper range of the rating scale. Inflationary pressures have always existed but have become more of a problem over the past three decades. As equality values have grown in importance, as well as fear of retribution from disgruntled employees who fail to achieve excellent appraisals, there has been a tendency for evaluators to be less rigorous and to reduce the negative repercussions from the appraisal process by generally inflating or upgrading evaluations.

# HOW CAN YOU OVERCOME THE HURDLES?

Just because there are potential hurdles to effective appraisals doesn't mean that supervisors should give up on the process. There are some things you can do to help overcome these hurdles.

## CONTINUALLY DOCUMENT EMPLOYEE PERFORMANCE

Keep a file for each of your employees and continually put notes into these files describing specific incidents of accomplishments and behaviors. Include dates and details. When time comes for you to conduct formal employee appraisals, you'll have a comprehensive history of each employee's performance record during the appraisal period. This will minimize the recency error, increase the accuracy of your ratings, and provide you with specific documentation to support your assessments.

## USE BEHAVIORALLY-BASED MEASURES

As we've noted previously, behaviorally-based measures are superior to those developed around traits. Many traits often considered to be related to good performance may, in fact, have little or no performance relationship. Traits like loyalty, initiative, courage, and reliability are intuitively appealing as desirable characteristics in employees. But the relevant question is: Are employees who are evaluated as high on these traits better performers than those who rate low? We can't answer that question. We know that there are employees who rate high on these characteristics and are poor performers. We can find others who are excellent performers but don't score well on traits such as these. Our conclusion is that traits like loyalty and initiative may be prized by organizations, but there is no evidence to support that certain traits will be adequate substitutes for performance in a large cross-section of jobs. Additionally, as we noted previously, traits suffer from weak agreement among multiple raters. What you consider "loyalty," I may not.

Behaviorally-based measures can deal with both of these objections. Because they deal with specific examples of performance—both good and bad—you avoid the problem of using inappropriate substitutes. Moreover, because you're evaluating specific behaviors, you increase the likelihood that two or more evaluators will see the same thing. You might consider a given employee as "friendly" while I rate her "standoffish." But when asked to rate her in terms of specific behaviors, we might both agree that she "frequently says 'good morning' to customers," "rarely gives advice or assistance to coworkers," and "almost always avoids idle chatter with coworkers."

## COMBINE ABSOLUTE AND RELATIVE STANDARDS

A major drawback to absolute standards is that they tend to be biased by inflationary pressures—evaluators lean toward packing their subjects into the high part of the rankings. On the other hand, relative standards suffer when there is little actual variability among the subjects.

The obvious solution is to consider using appraisal methods that combine absolute and relative standards. For example, you might want to use the graphic rating scale and the individual ranking method. It's much more meaningful to compare two employees' performance records when you know that Supervisor A gave Bob Carter an overall rating of 86, which ranked fourth in a department of 17; while Supervisor B also gave Tina Blackstone an 86 rating, but ranked her 12th in a department of 14. It's possible that Supervisor B has higher-performing employees than Supervisor A. Supervisor B's ratings may also suffer from inflationary pressures. By providing both absolute and relative assessments, it is easier to more accurately compare employees across departments.

## USE MULTIPLE RATERS

As the number of evaluators increases, the probability of attaining more accurate information increases. If rater error tends to follow a normal curve, an increase in the number of appraisers will tend to find the majority congregating about the middle. You see this approach being used in

Figure-skating performances are judged by using multiraters to increase accuracy. By dropping the highest and lowest scores from the final calculation, a better, more unbiased appraisal is achieved.

athletic competitions in such sports as diving, gymnastics, and figure skating. A set of evaluators judges a performance, the highest and lowest scores are dropped, and the final performance appraisal is made up from the cumulative scores of those remaining. The logic of multiple raters applies to organizations as well.

If an employee has had ten supervisors, nine having rated her excellent and one poor, the one poor appraisal takes on less importance. Multiple raters, therefore, increase reliability of results by tending to lessen the importance of rater personal biases like leniency, similarity, and central tendency errors.

## RATE SELECTIVELY

As an employee's direct supervisor, you are not always in a position to comprehensively appraise all the key aspects of that employee's performance. You should only rate in those areas in which you have significant job knowledge and have been able to observe, first-hand, the employee's job performance. If you appraise only those dimensions for which you are in a good position to rate, you make the performance appraisal a more valid process.

If there are important parts of an employee's job in which you aren't able to make accurate judgments, you should supplement your appraisal with self-appraisals, peer evaluations, or even customer appraisals, if that's more appropriate. A number of sales supervisors use customer input as part of their evaluation of sales representatives. Where supervisors have to be away from their work areas frequently, thus limiting their opportunities to observe their employees' job behavior, the use of peer reviews can improve the validity of the appraisal process.

## PARTICIPATE IN APPRAISAL TRAINING

Good appraisers aren't necessarily born. If your appraisal skills are deficient, you should participate in performance-appraisal training because there is evidence that training can make you a more accurate rater.

Common errors such as leniency and halo have been minimized or eliminated in workshops where supervisors practice observing and rating behaviors. These workshops typically run from one to three days, but allocating many hours to training may not always be necessary. One case has been cited where both halo and leniency errors were decreased immediately after exposing evaluators to explanatory training sessions lasting only five minutes.[4] However, the effects of training appear to diminish over time, which suggests the need for regular refresher sessions.

[4]H. J. Bernadin, "The Effects of Rater Training on Leniency and Halo Errors in Student Rating of Instructors," *Journal of Applied Psychology*, October 1975, pp. 550–555.

## PERFORMANCE APPRAISALS OF TEAMS

Performance-appraisal concepts have been almost exclusively developed with the individual employee as the focus point. This reflects the historic belief that individuals are the core building block around which organizations are built. Recently, as we've noted a number of times in this book, more and more organizations are restructuring themselves around teams (see News Flash).

## NEWS FLASH!

## PERFORMANCE APPRAISALS IN CONTEMPORARY ORGANIZATIONS

The foundation of the performance appraisal process is the concept that performance standards are clearly identified.[5] This fundamental fact implies that for workers to perform effectively, they must know and understand what is expected of them. This concept, however, applies only where clear job descriptions and specifications exist, and where variations to the job are minimal. In other words, conventional performance appraisals were designed to fit the needs of the traditional organization. But what happens to these when the organization is far from traditional? Let's look at some possibilities.

First, setting goals for an employee could become a thing of the past. Your workers may go from project to project, with the demands and requirements of their work rapidly changing. No formalized performance appraisal system may be able to capture the complexities of the jobs being done. Second, employees will likely have several bosses, not just you. Just who, then, will have the responsibility for the performance appraisal? It is more likely to be the team members themselves—setting their own goals and evaluating each other's performance. One can even speculate that this will take the format of an ongoing informal process, rather than some formal "ritual" held every twelve months.

All in all, while we surmise a drastic change in the performance appraisal process, it should not be interpreted that you will become less concerned with evaluating employee performance. On the contrary, individual performance will still matter most. The major difference is that employee performance information is likely to be collected from a number of sources—from anyone who's familiar with the employee's work.

[5]W. Bridges, "The End of the Job," *Fortune*, September 19, 1994, p. 64.

In team-based departments, job performance is a function of each individual's contribution to the team and his or her ability to be a good team player. Both of these performance dimensions are often better assessed by the team's members than by the team's supervisor. We suggest, therefore, that you include peer evaluations from team members in the performance appraisals of those whose jobs are inherently designed around team work. This enhances the autonomy of the team, reinforces the importance of cooperation, and increases the validity of the appraisal process. Additionally, you should consider the benefits of down playing individual contributions by substituting group performance measures. Where teams have clear responsibilities for achieving specific objectives, it makes more sense to appraise the team's overall performance than to focus on its individual members.

## NOW WHAT? RESPONDING TO PERFORMANCE PROBLEMS

Whenever one of your employees exhibits work behaviors that are inconsistent with the work environment (i.e., fighting, stealing, unexcused absences, and so forth) or is unable to perform his or her job satisfactorily, you must intervene. But before any intervention can begin, it is imperative for you to identify the problem. If you realize the performance problem is ability-related, your emphasis becomes one of encouraging training and development efforts. However, when the performance problem is desire-related, whether the unwillingness to correct the problem is voluntary or involuntary, **employee counseling** is the next logical approach.[6]

**Employee counseling** an emphasis on encouraging training and development efforts in a situation in which employee unwillingness or inability to perform his or her job satisfactorily is either voluntary or involuntary.

## WHAT DO YOU NEED TO KNOW ABOUT COUNSELING EMPLOYEES?

Although employee counseling processes differ, some fundamental steps should be followed when counseling an employee (see Exhibit 8–6).

### LISTEN TO WHAT THE EMPLOYEE HAS TO SAY

You can't effectively counsel others unless you listen to what they have to say.[7] Your actions should be tailored to the needs, demands, and personality of your employee. These factors can't be accurately assessed without active listening.

[6]J. Wisinski, "A Logical Approach to a Difficult Employee," *HR Focus*, January 1992, p. 9.
[7]G. D. Cook, "Employee Counseling Session," *Supervision*, August 1989, p. 3.

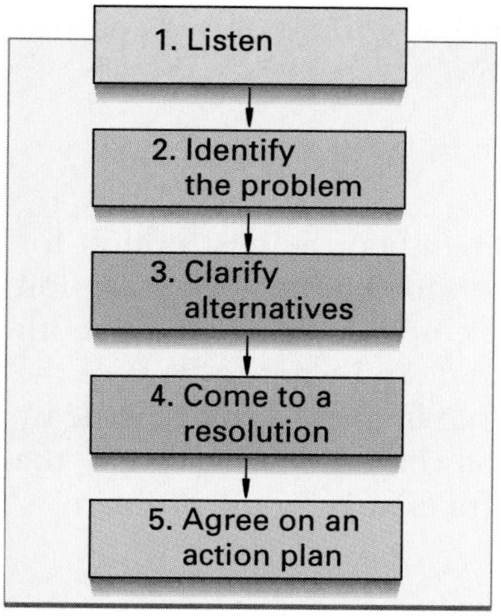

## EXHIBIT 8–6

The counseling process.

1. Listen
2. Identify the problem
3. Clarify alternatives
4. Come to a resolution
5. Agree on an action plan

When you sit down with your employee, demonstrate your willingness and desire to be helpful. Then, listen to what he or she has to say. Also, listen to what is not being said. How is the employee framing the problem? Who does the employee think is to blame? Are his or her emotions driving out rational thinking? Don't make judgments too quickly. Try to grasp the employee's perception of the situation without agreeing or disagreeing with that perception. At this point, it's not so important to determine whether the employee is right or wrong as it is to try to fully understand the problem from his or her point of view.

### IDENTIFY THE PROBLEM

After you've listened to your employee's initial assessment of the situation, begin the search to identify the problem and its causes. What does the employee think is the problem? Who or what is the cause? How is this problem affecting the employee? What, if any, responsibility is your employee taking for the problem? You must remember, though, you're attacking some behavior, not the employee!

### CLARIFY ALTERNATIVES

Problems come with options. In most cases there are a number of alternatives that can correct the problem. These need to be explored and clarified. This step is the place where a participative approach can be particularly valuable because you may see and know things that escape the employee. As a result, the merging of both your insights and the employee's can result in a larger number of quality options.

Once alternatives are identified, they need to be evaluated. What are the strengths and weaknesses of each? Again, two heads are better than one. Your goal should be to have the employee weigh the pluses and minuses of each course of action.

## COME TO A RESOLUTION

What's the best option for the employee? Remember, the best option for one employee is not necessarily the best option for another. The solution should reflect the unique characteristics of the employee. And ideally, both you and the employee will agree on the solution. You want to be sure the employee buys into the final choice, whether that final choice was made by you, the employee, or jointly. A terrific solution that's not accepted by the employee is unlikely to result in any meaningful change in the problem.

## AGREE ON AN ACTION PLAN

Finally, the employee needs to develop a concrete plan of action for implementing the solution. What, specifically, is the employee going to do? When will he or she do it? What resources, if any, will be needed?

It's usually a good idea to end a counseling session with the employee summarizing what has taken place and the specific actions he or she plans on taking. You should establish a follow-up point at some specific date in the future for reassessing the employee's progress. If a formal meeting isn't needed, request a short memo from the employee updating you on his or her progress. This can be effective as a reminder to the employee that progress is expected and as a control device for you to assess the employee's progress.

## IS YOUR ACTION ETHICAL?

What business do you have delving into an employee's personal life? That's a valid question and requires us to look at the ethics of counseling.

Employees bring a multitude of problems and frustrations from their personal lives to their jobs. They have difficulty finding quality day care for infants. A teenage child is expelled from high school. They have fights with their spouses. A family member suffers a nervous breakdown. They get behind in their bills and they're harassed by creditors. A close friend is seriously hurt in an automobile accident. A parent is diagnosed with Alzheimer's disease.

It may seem wise to keep your nose out of your employees' personal lives, but that is often unreasonable. Why? Because there is no clear demarcation that separates personal and work lives. Consider the following scenario involving one of your employees, Denise. Denise's son was arrested last night for possession of drugs. She spent most of the night with police and lawyers. Today, at work, she is tired and psychologically distant. She has trouble concentrating. Her mind is not on her job. It's naive to believe that employees can somehow leave their personal baggage at the door when they come to work each morning.

Employees have a right to privacy. However, when personal problems interfere with work performance, you should not consider it beyond your jurisdiction to inquire about the problem, offer yourself as an open ear, and genuinely seek to help with the problem. If your offer is rejected, don't push. If the employee understands how his or her personal problem is affecting work performance, and you make clear what the consequences will be if the work performance doesn't improve, you've reached the ethical limit of your involvement. If the employee is protective of his or her personal life, your rights as a supervisor don't extend to helping solve his or her personal problems. However, you do have the right and the obligation to make sure employees understand that if personal problems interfere with their work, they need to solve those personal problems—and you're there to help, if asked.

## SUMMARY

After reading this chapter, I can:

1. **Contrast the three purposes of the performance appraisal.** Performance appraisal is both an evaluation/development tool and a legal document. It reviews past performance to identify accomplishments and deficiencies; it offers a detailed plan to improve future performance through training and development. It also becomes a legal document that can be used to support/justify personnel actions.

2. **Differentiate formal and informal performance appraisals.** Formal performance appraisals are regular, planned meetings where the supervisor and employee discuss and review the latter's work performance. Informal performance appraisal is the day-to-day assessment a supervisor makes of an employee's performance and the ongoing feedback the supervisor gives to the employee about that performance.

3. **Describe key legal concerns in performance appraisals.** To minimize legal problems, supervisors should make sure that they carefully follow all performance-appraisal policies and procedures set forth in the organization's handbooks (if any) and make every effort to avoid prejudice and discrimination.

4. **Identify the three most popular sets of criteria that supervisors appraise.** The three most popular sets of criteria used by supervisors in appraisals are individual task outcomes, behaviors, and traits. The first two are almost always preferable to the third.

5. **Contrast absolute and relative standards.** Absolute standards compare the employee's performance against specific traits or behaviors rather than against other people. In contrast, relative standards compare employees against other employees.

6. **List human errors that can distort performance appraisal ratings.** Common human errors that can distort appraisals include leniency, halo, similarity, recency, central tendency, and inflationary pressures.

7. **Describe the purpose of employee counseling.** The purpose of employee counseling is to address performance problems where the deficiencies are desire-related.

## REVIEWING YOUR KNOWLEDGE

1. Why, in your opinion, do many supervisors dislike and even avoid giving employees performance feedback?

2. Contrast the advantages of supervisor-conducted appraisals, self-evaluations, and peer appraisals.

3. What is the relationship between goal setting and performance appraisal?

4. Contrast intrinsic and extrinsic feedback.

5. If appraising behaviors is superior to appraising traits, why do you think so many organizations evaluate their employees on criteria such as effort, loyalty, and dependability?

6. Do you believe formal performance appraisals can replace informal ones? Discuss.

7. Compare written essay appraisals with BARS.

8. Would human errors in the appraisal process be eliminated in small organizations where one person does all the appraisals? Explain.

9. What can a supervisor do to minimize distortions in the appraisal process?
10. Do you believe employee counseling is preferable to disciplining employees? Support your position.

# ANSWERS TO THE POP QUIZZES

1. **b. to determine if employees are in need of training.** One dimension of performance appraisals is to recognize weaknesses and use that information for employee training and development.
2. Intrinsic feedback involves getting information on performance on a daily basis. It is built into the job in terms of numbers produced, daily goals, and the like. Extrinsic feedback is provided to an employee by an outside source—such a supervisor, a quality inspector, or a customer.
3. **True.** This is one of the guiding principles of performance evaluations. It involves you and the employee, establishing standards that when accomplished, will lead to successful performance and departmental goal attainment.
4. **d. All of the above.** Each response deals with a particular documentation concern.

Having performance appraisal policies that are consistent and able to withstand review by external agencies; having bias free processes; and demonstrating that what is appraised and evaluated is job-related (c).

5. **c. There is probably no significant difference between the two employees.** Although a 92 is higher than a 90, the difference is relatively small. Accordingly, there is probably no significant difference between the two employees.
6. The six ways for reducing the barriers to effective performance appraisals include: (1) continually documenting employee performance; (2) using behaviorally-based measures; (3) combining absolute and relative standards; (4) using multiple raters; (5) rating selectively; and (6) participating in appraisal training.
7. **True.** This is one of the difficulties with using only traits. The reason is that traits refer to potential predictors of performance, not performance itself. Additionally, traits typically have a strong subjective component. They may mean different things to different people.
8. **b. employee counseling.** This question and response reflects the definition of employee counseling. ∎

## A Class Exercise: The Performance Appraisal

Break into pairs. One student will play the role of Dana (Employee Relations Supervisor); the other student will be Chris (Junior Research Analyst). Read only the character's role you are playing. Then take up to 15 minutes to conduct the role play.[8]

The person playing the role of Dana should consciously attempt to practice the appraisal-review skills described on pages 274 and 275 (Building a Supervisory Skill).

### DANA'S ROLE:

You are the Employee Relations Supervisor for a manufacturing firm. You are well thought of in the firm and have excellent rapport with your boss, the Vice President for Human Resources. Chris is a junior research analyst in your department. You know that Chris is reasonably good at his/her job. But you also know that Chris believes his/her job performance to be "outstanding," which isn't true. Chris is scheduled to have a performance review session with you in a few minutes, and you would like to establish clearer communication, as well as to convince Chris to adopt a less grandiose self-image. You believe that Chris is on the right track, but it will take him/her about two years to reach the stage at which he/she can be promoted to senior analyst. As for Chris's performance, you have received some good reports, as well as three letters of complaint. Chris prepared four research reports that you considered above average, but to keep him/her motivated and happy, you exaggerated and said they were "excellent." Maybe that was a mistake. You are worried about the impact on other employees, whose performance is nearly as good as Chris's, if Chris is promoted. Your plan is to set meaningful targets for Chris this year, evaluate his/her performance one or two years from now, and then recommend the promotion if it's deserved.

### CHRIS'S ROLE:

You are a junior research analyst in the Employee Relations Department of a manufacturing firm. Dana is your supervisor and head of the department. You know that you are one of the best performers in your department, and may even be the best. However, you were not promoted to senior analyst last year, even though you expected to be. You would like to be promoted this year. You expect your supervisor to raise some obstacles to your promotion. Dana is bound to mention three letters of complaint against you, for instance. Dana seems to point out only your errors. Up front, you plan to remind Dana that you wrote four research reports that Dana said were excellent. If Dana tries to delay your promotion unnecessarily, you plan to confront him/her and, if necessary, take the issue to Dana's boss, the Vice President for Human Resources. You think there have been many instances in which

---

[8]Based on S. Umapathy, "Teaching Behavioral Aspects of Performance Evaluation: An Experiential Approach," *The Accounting Review*, January 1985, pp. 107–108.

you were rated better on performance than your colleagues in the department. You have decided you will press your point of view firmly, but also rationally, in a professional manner. Dana has called you to his/her office. The subject: Your performance review. This role play begins as you enter Dana's office.

After the role play, both students should describe how the meeting went, highlighting the strengths and weaknesses of the performance appraisal.

## THINKING CRITICALLY

### CASE 8.A

### Jeannie Rice of Vanderbilt University

Jeannie Rice is a supervisor of buildings and property information at Vanderbilt University.[9] Like most individuals in her position, Jeannie felt she was doing her job to the best of her abilities. She was successful! She set department goals that supported the University's goals and, with the help of her employees, achieved them. There didn't appear to be anything unusual operating here, nor any underlying disagreements among her staff. Oh sure, there were trying times for Jeannie, but this is true for any supervisor. Jeannie's staff saw things differently. Most viewed Jeannie as being too demanding. She was creating a stressful work environment that was not only affecting Jeannie, herself, but many of those who had daily dealings with her.

As part of Jeannie's personal development plan, she was sent to the Center for Creative Leadership, where she was provided with numerous assessments and feedback instruments from her colleagues and employees. As a result of this feedback, a program was established for Jeannie to correct her behavior. One aspect was to return to her job and meet individually with her employees. There she shared the comments that were provided to her, and sought some clarification and elaboration. In many cases, however, employees began with statements such as "I didn't say that about you," or "You used to be that way." Fortunately, however, Jeannie was able to overcome this initial barrier, and delve deeper into the issues. As a result, Jeannie has changed the way she does business, and has created a more positive work climate for her employees. Jeannie is also a bit more relaxed now.

## RESPONDING TO THE CASE

1. Describe how getting feedback from her employees was useful to Jeannie.
2. Do you believe this kind of appraisal can work in most organizations? Explain. Describe some problems that may arise if the process gets off track.
3. Is it possible for this type of evaluation to work in a college classroom to evaluate your instructor? Explain your position.

[9]Adapted from B. O'Reilly, "360-Feedback Can Change Your Life," *Fortune,* October 17, 1994, p. 100.

## CASE 8.B

## Performance Appraisal at the Camera Shop

At the Camera Shop, formal performance appraisals are conducted annually. Each supervisor is expected to conduct a performance review for every employee during October—in time to recommend end-of-the-year employee bonuses. As a supervisor, it is essential that Chuck Martin take this responsibility seriously.

After Chuck and his area manager discuss the review for each employee in his store, Mr. Martin is expected to sit down with each employee individually to go over their performance review. He is expected to have the appraisal feedback meetings with his employees during November. This face-to-face meeting is important for each employee to get feedback about how Chuck views the employee's performance. The meeting also is designed to provide input to the employee to identify areas of performance that could be improved.

The company uses a standard form to evaluate employees. The form was developed by a group of employees representing all levels of workers in the company. It includes the following elements: job knowledge and skills; quality of work; productivity or quantity of work; following company policies and procedures; planning and organizing work; prioritizing work assignments; communication in speaking and writing; attitude toward job; teamwork and working with coworkers; cooperation and loyalty; adaptability to change; dependability and punctuality; and initiative and resourcefulness.

It is now time for Chuck Martin to evaluate his employees. He really doesn't like this aspect of his job because it is so hard to be objective. He distinctly remembers last year's meeting with his boss, Leslie Hines. Chuck can still hear her saying, "It is remarkable that all of your employees rate so high in all areas. How can this be?" Chuck knew that he had difficulty responding to her not-so-subtle way of telling him he was not adequately evaluating his personnel. He didn't want a repeat performance of that incident this year.

## RESPONDING TO THE CASE

1. Why do you think Chuck Martin is so concerned about his meeting with his area manager? Should he change his views about the ratings he uses to evaluate his employees? Why or why not?
2. What are some of the benefits Chuck Martin's employees get from their performance reviews? Drawbacks?
3. What could Chuck do to improve the performance evaluation process in his store?
4. What are the legal issues that need to be considered by Chuck Martin and other supervisors in conducting performance appraisals? Develop a list of guidelines Chuck could follow to avoid legal problems. ∎

## Mary Jo Romportl
## Teller Supervisor, Western Bank

Mary Jo was a teller at Western Bank before she was promoted to teller supervisor. There was dissension within the department. The former supervisor had personal problems and she seemed to bring many of those problems to work. She was cold and critical toward employees, and teamwork suffered. Most of the tellers felt they could not talk to their supervisor.

One of Mary Jo's first tasks was to build up the morale and teamwork in her department. She had serious problems with teamwork and absenteeism. None of the tellers wanted to work overtime. Customer service was very poor because the tellers suffered from poor attitudes.

1. What are the main goals Mary Jo has set for her department?
2. Do you think Mary Jo has set realistic goals? Why or why not?
3. Do you believe Mary Jo was the right person for the job? Explain what criteria might have been used to select her.
4. Why is it important to conduct an assessment of a team's effectiveness? What can be learned from it? Which role should a supervisor play in such an assessment?
5. Discuss the elements that need to be considered in developing a team employee performance appraisal system.

# STIMULATING INDIVIDUAL AND GROUP PERFORMANCE

If there is one thing common to employees wherever they work, it is the fact that they have a tendency to give their effort to those things that benefit them. Employees understand that they have to work—and work hard—but in doing so, they want something in return. They expect to work for supervisors who respect them, who keep them informed of things happening in the organization, and who can find a way to bring out their best.

Part Four contains three chapters:

# 9

# MOTIVATING YOUR EMPLOYEES

# LEARNING OBJECTIVES  KEY TERMS

After reading this chapter, you should be able to:

1. Define motivation.
2. Identify and define five personality characteristics relevant to understanding the behavior of employees at work.
3. Explain the elements and the focus of the three early theories of motivation.
4. Identify the characteristics that stimulate the achievement drive in high achievers.
5. Identify the three relationships in expectancy theory that determine an individual's level of effort.
6. List actions a supervisor can take to maximize employee motivation.

You should also be able to define these supervisory terms:

employee stock ownership programs

equity theory

expectancy theory

hierarchy of needs theory

hygiene factors

job design

job enrichment

locus of control

Machiavellianism

motivation

motivation-hygiene theory

need

need for achievement

pay-for-performance programs

reinforcement theory

risk propensity

self-esteem

self-monitoring

Theory X-Theory Y

What would you think about giving your employees substantial freedom to work as they wish—as long as they meet their goals? In essence, you'd be empowering all employees, giving them the flexibility in their schedules to do their work and eliminating the traditional "clock punching" practice. Do you think your employees would take advantage of the situation? Would you lose control? You won't find supervisors at the Fostoria, Ohio-based Roppe Corporation supporting that position.[1]

The Roppe Corporation produces rubber products (baseboards, stair treads, floor tiles, etc.). The company was generating annual sales in the $50 million range. Although this appears adequate and profitable, company officials knew they could do better. In fact, although sales growth appeared imminent with an upswing in the building economy in the mid-to-late 1990s, production employees were only producing at 75 percent of standard. That's because employees felt that by producing more to meet the quota, their bosses would merely increase the standard. As a result, the employees, after hitting the 75 percent range, just stopped working. So the supervisors tried an experiment. Employees were offered the following proposition. Production goals would be increased by 10 percent. When employees met the new standard, their hourly pay would also increase by

## INTRODUCTION

Sean Hartman is a hard-driving, competitive person. He gives a maximum effort on everything he does—at his job, on his summer softball team, in cleaning and waxing his classic 1963 Corvette. In contrast, his good friend Jim Cannon appears to have no discipline in his life. People who know him think he's lazy. While Jim is smart and highly capable, he has trouble holding a job because of his inability to put forth much sustained effort. Sean summed up his appraisal of Jim: "He can't stay with anything for more than a half-hour or so. He gets bored and distracted easily."

Supervisors like having Sean Hartman-types working for them. Such people are essentially self-motivated. You don't have to do much to get them to produce a full day's effort. The Jim Cannons of the world are another story. They're a supervisor's nightmare. It's a challenge to develop creative ways to motivate them.

[1]M. P. Cronin, "No More Clock Watchers," *Inc.*, February 1994, p. 83.

10 percent. Furthermore, although the standard would be set according to what time studies showed could be produced in eight hours of work, if the employees met the daily goals more quickly, they could go home—and still get eight hours of pay at the 10 percent increased level.

In less than one week, supervisors noticed a dramatic change. Employees increased their productivity (and the quality of the products) to meet the new standard. For example, the old standard for rubber baseboards was 26,000 feet per day per line. Typically workers made approximately 21,500 feet. Under this new plan, the goal was increased to 29,000 feet per day per line, and the workers produced every inch of it! That's a 35 percent increase over what they had been producing the week before! What's more, they did it in under seven hours and left for the day. Since implementation of the new goals, employees police themselves. Sabotage of machinery has disappeared. The machines don't suddenly break down after reaching 75 percent of standard. Supervisors also don't have to monitor the length of workers' breaks or lunch periods. Also, overtime for maintenance workers has significantly decreased. In fact, routine, preventive maintenance can often be performed between shifts now—especially when the employees leave early. ■

Most employees aren't like either Sean or Jim. They're more like Shelly Roberts. On some activities, Shelly is incredibly motivated. For example, she reads two or three romance novels a week and she gets up at 5:30 every morning and religiously runs three or four miles before showering and going to work. But at her sales job at the local Dick's sporting goods store, she seems bored and unmotivated. Most people are like Molly in that their levels of motivation vary across activities.

What can supervisors do to increase the motivation of people like Jim Cannon and Shelly Roberts? In this chapter, we'll provide you with some insights and tools that can help answer this question.

## WHAT IS MOTIVATION?

First, what do we mean by the term *motivation*? **Motivation** is the willingness to do something and is conditioned by this action's ability to satisfy some need for the individual. A **need**, in our terminology, means a physio-

**Motivation**
the willingness to do something conditioned by the action's ability to satisfy some need for the individual.

**Need**
a physiological or psychological deficiency that makes certain outcomes seem attractive.

## EXHIBIT 9–1

Needs and motivation.

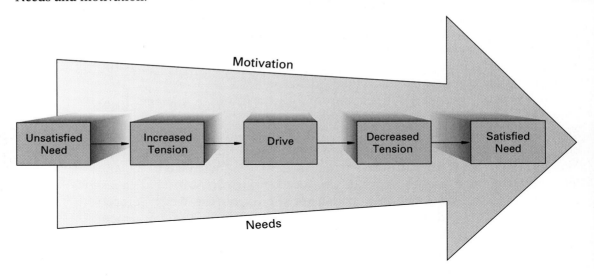

logical or psychological deficiency that makes certain outcomes seem attractive.

An unsatisfied need creates tension, which sets off a drive to satisfy that need (see Exhibit 9–1). The greater the tension, the greater the drive or effort will be required to reduce that tension. When we see employees working hard at some activity, we can conclude that they're driven by a desire to satisfy one or more needs that they value.

## UNDERSTANDING INDIVIDUAL DIFFERENCES

A common error that new supervisors often make is to assume that other people are like them. If they're ambitious, they think others are also ambitious. If they place a high value on spending evenings and weekends with their family, they assume that others feel the same way. These assumptions are big mistakes! People are different. What's important to us is not necessarily important to you. Not everybody, for instance, is driven by the desire for money. Yet, a lot of supervisors believe a bonus or the opportunity for a pay increase should make every employee want to work harder (see Something to Think About). If you're going to be successful in motivating people, you have to begin by accepting and trying to understand individual differences.

To make our point, let's look at personality. Most of us know people who are loud and aggressive. We know others who are quiet and passive. A number of personality characteristics have been singled out as having relevance to understanding the behavior and motivation of employees at work. Five specific personality traits have proven most powerful in explaining individual behavior in organizations. These are: locus of control, Machiavellianism, self-esteem, self-monitoring, and risk propensity. Let's look at these elements.

---

## SOMETHING TO THINK ABOUT *(and to promote class discussion)*

No one can know precisely what an employee is looking for in a job—or what you want, for that matter. That is, unless they ask. Sadly, that doesn't often happen. Instead, as supervisors, we often think we know what people want or need. To see how accurate you are, below are ten items that have often been cited in the literature as those things employees want at work. Rank each, from 1 to 10, regarding what you believe employees want. That is, a ranking of 1 is the most important thing you believe they want, 2 the second most important, and so on.

**What I Think They Want!**
**(Rankings)**
\_\_\_\_\_ Recognition for good work.
\_\_\_\_\_ Good wages.
\_\_\_\_\_ Employee Assistance Programs.
\_\_\_\_\_ Appropriate disciplinary procedures.
\_\_\_\_\_ A good work environment.
\_\_\_\_\_ Challenging work.
\_\_\_\_\_ A supervisor who's loyal to them.
\_\_\_\_\_ Job security.
\_\_\_\_\_ To participate in what affects them on their jobs.
\_\_\_\_\_ Promotion and growth opportunities.

Do you and your employees think alike in terms of their motivation needs? Research tells us that's not necessarily the case. Researcher Kenneth A. Kovach has identified the top ten rankings for employees in terms of their wants. Likewise, employers have also indicated what they think you want.

**What They Want**
  1. Challenging work.
  2. Recognition for good work.
  3. To participate in what affects them on their job.
  4. Job security.
  5. Good wages.

*(continued)*

6. Promotion and growth opportunities.
7. Good work environment.
8. A supervisor who's loyal to them.
9. Appropriate disciplinary procedures.
10. Employee Assistance Programs.

How close were you to the list compiled by the researcher? Where did you differ? Why do you believe this difference exists? Does it surprise you that research has shown that we as supervisors think our employees want something other than what we believe they want? What problems might that create for you?

*Source:* Adapted from Kenneth A. Kovach, "What Motivates Employees? Workers and Supervisors Give Different Answers," *Business Horizons*, September-October 1987, Table 2, p. 61. Reprinted from *Business Horizons*, September-October, Copyright 1987 by the Foundation for the School of Business at Indiana University. Used with permission.

## CAN PERSONALITY TYPES HELP PREDICT PRACTICAL WORK-RELATED BEHAVIORS?

**Locus of control**
the source of control over an individual's behavior.

Who has control over an individual's behavior? Some people believe that they control their own fate. Others see themselves as pawns of fate, believing that what happens to them in their lives is due to luck or chance. The **locus of control** in the first case is internal; these people believe that they control their destiny. In the second case it is external; these people believe that their lives are controlled by outside forces.[2] Studies tell us that employees who rate high in externality are less satisfied with their jobs, more alienated from the work setting, and less involved in their jobs than are internals. For instance, employees with an external locus of control may be less enthusiastic about their jobs because they believe that they have little personal influence on the outcome of their performance appraisals. If they get a poor appraisal, they're apt to blame it on their supervisor's prejudice, their coworkers, or other events outside their control.

**Machiavellianism**
a manipulative individual who believes ends can justify means.

The second characteristic is called **Machiavellianism** (Mach). It's named after Niccolo Machiavelli who wrote in the sixteenth century on how to gain and manipulate power. An individual exhibiting strong Machiavellian tendencies is manipulative and believes ends can justify means. Some might even see these people as ruthless. High Machs tend to be mo-

[2]See, for example, J. Fierman, "What's Luck Got To Do With It?" *Fortune*, October 16, 1995, p. 149.

These employees of the Petaluma, California-based Fantastic Foods Company recognize that their supervisors make every attempt to link their rewards to their work effort. One of Fantastic Foods' secrets is to let their employees know what is expected of them, hold them accountable for completing their tasks, and let them evaluate their own work. As a result of this freedom, and the learning environment, these employees have not only built their self-esteem, but have been energized to exert high levels of effort.

tivated on jobs that require bargaining (such as labor negotiator) or where there are substantial rewards for winning (as in commissioned sales). But they can get frustrated in jobs where there are specific rules that must be followed or where rewards are based more on using the proper means rather than on the achievement of outcomes.

People differ in the degree to which they like or dislike themselves. This trait is called **self-esteem.** Studies confirm that people high in self-esteem (SE) believe that they possess more of the ability they need in order to succeed at work. But the most significant finding on self-esteem is that low-SEs are more susceptible to external influence than are high-SEs. Low-SEs are dependent on the receipt of positive evaluations from others. As a result, they are more likely to seek approval from others and more prone to conform to the beliefs and behaviors of those they respect than are high-SEs.

Some individuals are very adaptable and can easily adjust their behavior to changing situations. Others are rigid and inflexible. The personality trait that captures this difference is called **self-monitoring.** Individuals high in self-monitoring show considerable adaptability in adjusting their behavior to external situational factors. They are highly sensitive to external cues and can behave differently in different situations. High self-monitors are capable of presenting striking contradictions between their public personas and their private selves. Low self-monitors can't disguise themselves this way. They tend to display their true feelings and beliefs in every situation. The evidence tells us that high self-monitors tend to pay closer attention to the behavior of others and are more capable of con-

**Self-esteem**
the degree to which individuals like or dislike themselves.

**Self-monitoring**
high self-monitors are adaptable in adjusting their behavior to external situational factors. and are capable of presenting striking contradictions between public personas and private selves. Low self-monitors tend to display their true feelings and beliefs in every situation.

forming than are low self-monitors. Additionally, because high self-monitors are flexible, they adjust better than low self-monitors to job situations that require individuals to play multiple roles in their work groups.

People differ in their willingness to take chances. Individuals with a high **risk propensity** make more rapid decisions and use less information in making their choices than low risk-propensity individuals. Not surprisingly, high-risk seekers tend to prefer, and are more satisfied in, jobs such as stockbroker or putting out fires on oil platforms.

**Risk propensity** willingness to take chances.

## How Can an Understanding of Personality Help You Be a More Effective Supervisor?

The major value of understanding personality differences probably lies in selection. You are likely to have higher performing and more satisfied employees if consideration is given to matching personality types with compatible jobs. In addition, there may be other benefits. By recognizing that people approach problem solving, decision making, and job interactions differently, you can better understand why, for instance, an employee is uncomfortable with making quick decisions or why an employee insists on gathering as much information as possible before addressing a problem. You can also anticipate that individuals with an external locus of control may be less satisfied with their jobs than internals and also that they may be less willing to accept responsibility for their actions.

## THE EARLY THEORIES OF MOTIVATION

Once we accept individual differences, we begin to understand why there is no single motivator that applies to all employees. Because people are complex, any attempt to explain their motivations will also tend to be complex. We see this in the number of approaches that have been taken in developing theories of employee motivation. In the following pages, we'll review the early theories, and the most popular of these approaches.

## How Do You Focus on Needs?

The most elementary approach to motivation was developed by Abraham Maslow.[3] He identified a set of basic needs, which he argued, were common to all individuals; and he said individuals should be evaluated in

---

[3]A. Maslow, *Motivation and Personality* (New York, NY: Harper and Row, 1954).

terms of the degree to which these needs are fulfilled. According to Maslow's **hierarchy of needs theory,** a satisfied need no longer creates tension and therefore doesn't motivate. The key to motivation then, at least according to Maslow, is to determine where an individual is along the needs hierarchy and focus motivation efforts at the point where needs become essentially unfulfilled.

Maslow proposed that within every human being there exists a hierarchy of five needs (see Exhibit 9–2). These needs are:

1. *Physiological*—includes hunger, thirst, shelter, sex, and other bodily needs.
2. *Safety*—includes security and protection from physical and emotional harm.
3. *Social*—includes affection, a sense of belonging, acceptance, and friendship.
4. *Esteem*—includes internal factors such as self-respect, autonomy, and achievement; and external factors such as status, recognition, and attention.
5. *Self-actualization*—the drive to become what one is capable of becoming; includes growth, achieving one's potential, and self-fulfillment.

**Hierarchy of needs theory**
a theory of Abraham Maslow that states that a satisfied need no longer creates tension and therefore doesn't motivate. Maslow believed that the key to motivation is to determine where an individual is along the needs hierarchy and focus motivation efforts at the point where needs become essentially unfulfilled.

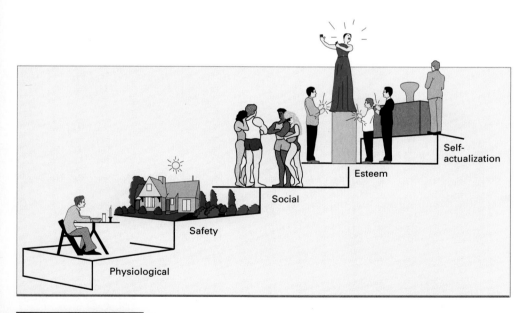

## EXHIBIT 9–2

Maslow's hierarchy of needs theory.
(*Source:* By permission of the Instructional Communications Centre. McGill University, Montreal, Canada.)

As each of these needs becomes substantially satisfied, the next need becomes dominant. In terms of Exhibit 9–2, the individual moves up the hierarchy. From the standpoint of motivation, the theory would say that although no need is every fully gratified, a substantially satisfied need no longer motivates.

A number of studies to test the validity of Maslow's theory have been made over the years. Generally, these studies have not been able to support the theory. We can't say, for example, that everyone's need structure is organized along the dimensions Maslow proposed. So, while this theory has been around for a long time and is certainly well known, it is probably not a very good guide for helping you motivate your employees.

**Theory X-Theory Y** a theory of Douglas McGregor that a supervisor's view of human nature is based on a certain grouping of assumptions and that he or she tends to mold behavior toward subordinates according to those assumptions.

## DO SUPERVISORS FOCUS ON THE NATURE OF PEOPLE?

Some supervisors believe that their employees are hard working, committed, and responsible. Others view their employees as essentially lazy, irresponsible, and lacking ambition. This observation led Douglas McGregor to propose his **Theory X-Theory Y** view of human nature and motivation.[4] McGregor argued that a supervisor's view of the nature of human beings is based on a certain grouping of assumptions, and that he or she tends to mold his or her behavior toward subordinates according to these assumptions.

Today, almost all permanently employed workers have their lower-order needs met. Retail clerks in Los Angeles, for instance, earn more than $9 an hour and have attractive health and security benefits provided by their employer.

[4]D. McGregor, *The Human Side of Enterprise* (New York, NY: McGraw-Hill, 1960).

Under Theory X, the four assumptions held by supervisors are:

1. Employees inherently dislike work and, whenever possible, will attempt to avoid it.
2. Since employees dislike work, they must be coerced, controlled, or threatened with punishment to achieve desired goals.
3. Employees will shirk responsibilities and seek formal direction whenever possible.
4. Most workers place security above all other factors associated with work, and will display little ambition.

In contrast to these negative views toward the nature of human beings, McGregor listed four other assumptions that he called Theory Y:

1. Employees can view work as being as natural as rest or play.
2. A person will exercise self-direction and self-control if he or she is committed to the objectives.
3. The average person can learn to accept, even seek, responsibility.
4. The ability to make good decisions is widely dispersed throughout the population, and not necessarily the sole province of supervisors.

What are the motivational implications of Theory X-Theory Y? McGregor argued that Theory Y assumptions were more valid than Theory X. As a result, he proposed ideas like participation in decision making, responsible and challenging jobs, and good group relations as approaches that would maximize an employee's job motivation.

Unfortunately, there is no evidence to confirm that either set of assumptions is valid, or that acceptance of Theory Y assumptions and altering one's actions accordingly will lead to more motivated workers. As will become evident later in this chapter, either Theory X or Theory Y assumptions may be appropriate in a particular situation.

## WHAT EFFECT DOES THE ORGANIZATION HAVE ON MOTIVATION?

"First, describe situations in which you felt exceptionally good about your job. Second, describe situations in which you felt exceptionally bad about your job." Beginning in the late 1950s, Frederick Herzberg asked these two questions of a number of workers. He then tabulated and categorized their responses. What he found was that the replies people gave when they felt good about their jobs were significantly different from the replies given when they felt bad. As shown in Exhibit 9–3, certain factors tend to be consistently related to job satisfaction (when they felt "good") and others to

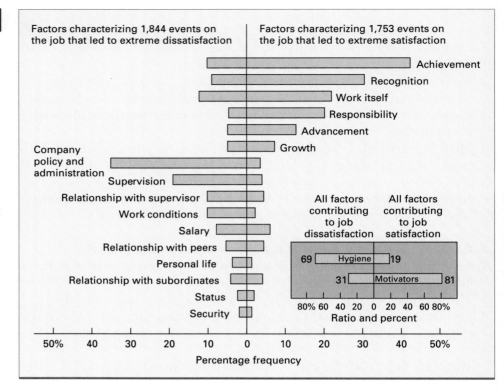

Factors characterizing 1,844 events on the job that led to extreme dissatisfaction

Factors characterizing 1,753 events on the job that led to extreme satisfaction

Achievement
Recognition
Work itself
Responsibility
Advancement
Growth
Company policy and administration
Supervision
Relationship with supervisor
Work conditions
Salary
Relationship with peers
Personal life
Relationship with subordinates
Status
Security

All factors contributing to job dissatisfaction

All factors contributing to job satisfaction

69 Hygiene 19
31 Motivators 81

80% 60 40 20 0 20 40 60 80%
Ratio and percent

50% 40 30 20 10 0 10 20 30 40 50%
Percentage frequency

job dissatisfaction (when they felt "bad"). Intrinsic factors such as achievement, recognition, the work itself, responsibility, and advancement seemed to be related to job satisfaction. When those questioned felt good about their work, they tended to attribute these factors to themselves. On the other hand, when they were dissatisfied, they tended to cite external factors, such as company policy and administration, supervision, interpersonal relations, and working conditions.

Herzberg took these results and formulated this **motivation-hygiene theory**.[5] He said the responses suggest that the opposite of satisfaction is not dissatisfaction, as was traditionally believed. Removing dissatisfying characteristics from a job does not necessarily make the job satisfying. Herzberg proposed that his findings indicate the existence of a dual continuum: the opposite of "Satisfaction" is "No Satisfaction," and the opposite of "Dissatisfaction" is "No Dissatisfaction" (see Exhibit 9–4).

According to Herzberg, the factors leading to job satisfaction are separate and distinct from those that lead to job dissatisfaction. Therefore, supervisors who seek to eliminate factors that can create job dissatisfaction may bring about peace, but not necessarily motivation. They will be pla-

**Motivation-hygiene theory**
a theory of Frederick Herzberg that the opposite of satisfaction is not "dissatisfaction" but "no satisfaction" and the opposite of dissatisfaction is not "satisfaction" but "no dissatisfaction."

[5]F. Herzberg, B. Mausner, and B. Snyderman, *The Motivation to Work* (New York, NY: John Wiley and Sons, 1959).

cating their employees rather than motivating them. As a result, such characteristics as company policy and administration, supervision, interpersonal relations, working conditions, and salary have been characterized by Herzberg as **hygiene factors.** When they're adequate, people will not be dissatisfied; however, neither will they be satisfied. If we want to motivate people on their jobs, Herzberg suggests emphasizing achievement, recognition, the work itself, responsibility, and growth. These are the characteristics that people find intrinsically rewarding.

**Hygiene factors** factors that lead to job dissatisfaction, such as company policy and administration, supervision, interpersonal relations, working conditions, and salary. The elimination of such factors, however, may not necessarily bring about worker satisfaction or motivation.

Convex Computer Corporation, a Texas-based supercomputer manufacturer with 1200 employees, applies motivation-hygiene theory in its employee recognition practices. Recognition for group and individual accomplishment is achieved in many ways. For instance, on a quarterly basis, the vice president of operations recognizes individuals who have been nominated by their supervisors as having gone "above and beyond the call of duty." Annually, individuals may nominate their peers for the Customer Service Award, which recognizes such categories as risk taking, innovation, cost reduction, and overall customer satisfaction. On the department level, recognition includes team or department T-shirts, coffee mugs, banners, and pictures. Supervisors have used movie tickets, Friday afternoon bowling get-togethers, time off, and cash awards to acknowledge such achievements as three months of defect-free assembly, five years of perfect attendance, and completing a project early.

The motivation-hygiene theory is important because it was the primary initiating force encouraging managers, beginning in the 1960s, to redesign jobs in order to make them more intrinsically interesting and challenging for employees. However, we should point out that the theory is concerned with job satisfaction rather than directly with motivation. That is, it seeks to predict what factors contribute to job satisfaction and dissatisfaction. A large body of research allows us to say, rather definitively, that

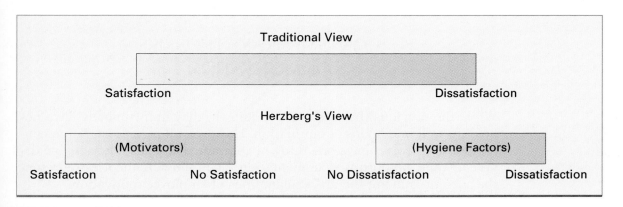

## EXHIBIT 9–4

Contrasting views of satisfaction-dissatisfaction.

satisfied workers are not necessarily motivated or productive workers.[6] High job satisfaction tends to result in reduced absenteeism and turnover, but the effect of satisfaction on productivity is minimal. Therefore, motivation-hygiene theory should be considered a more valuable guide for explaining an employee's level of job satisfaction than his or her level of motivation.

## CONTEMPORARY THEORIES OF MOTIVATION

While the previous theories are well known, they unfortunately have not held up well under close examination. However, all is not lost. Some contemporary theories have one thing in common: each has a reasonable degree of valid supporting documentation. The following theories represent the current "state-of-the-art" explanations of employee motivation.

[6]See R. A. Katzell, D. E. Thompson, and R. A. Guzzo, "How Job Satisfaction and Job Performance Are and Are Not Linked," in C. J. Cranny, P. C. Smith, and E. F. Stone, *Job Satisfaction* (New York, NY: Lexington Books, 1992), pp. 195–217.

# WHAT IS A FOCUS ON ACHIEVEMENT?

Some people have a compelling drive to succeed, but they are striving for personal achievement rather than the rewards of success. They have a desire to do something better or more efficiently than it has been done before. This drive is the need for achievement. Those people with a high **need for achievement** (nAch) are intrinsically motivated.[7] As you'll see, when high achievers are placed into jobs that stimulate their achievement drive, they are self-motivated and require little of your time or energy.

High achievers differentiate themselves from others by their desire to do things better. They seek situations where they can attain personal responsibility for finding solutions to problems. They look for rapid and unambiguous feedback on their performance so they can tell easily whether they are improving or not, and they set moderately challenging goals. High achievers are not gamblers; they dislike succeeding by chance. They prefer the challenge of working at a problem and accepting the personal responsibility for success or failure, rather than leaving the outcome to chance or the actions of others. They avoid what they perceive to be very easy or very difficult tasks.

High achievers perform best when they perceive their probability of success as being 0.5; that is, when they estimate that they have a 50-50 chance of success. They dislike gambling with high odds because they get no achievement satisfaction from accidental success. Similarly, they dislike low odds (high probability of success) because then there is no challenge to their skills. They like to set goals that require stretching themselves a little. When there is an approximately equal chance of success or failure, there is the optimum opportunity to experience feelings of accomplishment and satisfaction from their efforts.

What proportion of the workforce is made up of high achievers? In developed countries, the answer appears to be between 10 and 20 percent. The percentage is considerably lower in third-world countries. The reason is that the cultures of developed countries tend to socialize more people toward striving for personal achievement.

Based on an extensive amount of achievement research, we can draw three reasonably well-supported conclusions. First, individuals with a high nAch prefer job situations with personal responsibility, feedback, and an intermediate degree of risk. When these characteristics are prevalent, high achievers will be strongly motivated. The evidence consistently demonstrates, for instance, that high achievers are successful in entrepreneurial activities such as running their own businesses as well as in many sales positions. Second, a high need to achieve does not necessarily lead to being a good supervisor or manager, especially in large organizations. High nAch

**Need for achievement (nAch)**
a compelling drive to succeed; an intrinsic motivation to do something better or more efficiently than it has been done before.

[7]D. C. McClelland, *The Achieving Society* (New York, NY: Van Nostrand Reinhold, 1961).

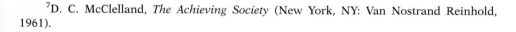

salespeople do not necessarily make good sales supervisors, and the good manager in a large organization does not typically have a high need to achieve. The reason seems to be that high achievers want to do things themselves rather than lead others toward accomplishments. Lastly, employees have been successfully trained to stimulate their achievement need. If a job calls for a high achiever, you can select a person with a high nAch or develop your own candidate through achievement training. Achievement training focuses on teaching people to act, talk, and think like high achievers by having them write stories emphasizing achievement, play simulation games that stimulate feelings of achievement, meet with successful entrepreneurs, and learn how to develop specific and challenging goals.

## How Can Reinforcement Help to Motivate Employees?

**Reinforcement theory**
a theory that states people will exert higher levels of effort in tasks that are reinforced. Reinforcers are consequences that, when immediately following a response, increase the probability that the behavior will be repeated.

**Reinforcement theory** states that people will exert higher levels of effort in tasks that are reinforced. Reinforcers are any consequence that, when immediately following a response, increases the probability that the behavior will be repeated. This would include piece-wage pay plans where workers are paid a fixed sum for each unit of production completed, giving prizes to employees for achieving perfect attendance, and complimenting employees when they do something nice for a customer.

The current popularity of pay-for-performance programs in organizations is clearly a direct response to the logic of reinforcement theory. Instead of compensating people on the basis of seniority, for example, paying people for performance outcomes increases their effort because the higher their performance the larger their compensation. But in its pure form, re-

Rewarding employees for certain performance measures can take on various meanings. Employees at Lincoln Electric, for example, are evaluated in part on how well they meet and exceed production goals—as well as on producing a quality product.

inforcement theory totally ignores the inner state of an individual and concentrates solely on what happens to a person when he or she takes some action. It's hard to believe that feelings, attitudes, expectations, and similar cognitive variables have no impact on behavior, but that's what reinforcement theory proposes. Our conclusion is that you should recognize that reinforcement undoubtedly has an important influence on motivation, but it is not the only influence.

## HOW IMPORTANT IS EQUITY?

Your company just hired someone new to work in your department, doing the same job you're doing. That person is essentially the same age as you, with almost identical educational qualifications and experience. The company is paying you $3800 a month (which you consider very competitive). How would you feel if you found out that the company is paying the new person—whose credentials are not one bit better than yours—$4100 a month? You'd probably be upset and angry. You'd probably think it wasn't fair. You're now likely to think you're underpaid. And you might direct your anger into actions like reducing your work effort, taking longer coffee breaks, or taking extra days off by calling in "sick."

Your reactions illustrate the role that equity plays in motivation (see News Flash). People make comparisons of their job inputs and outcomes relative to others, and inequities have a strong bearing on the degree of effort that employees exert.[8] **Equity theory** states that employees perceive what they can get from a job situation (outcomes) in relation to what they put into it (inputs), and then compare their input-outcome ratio with the input-outcome ratio of others. If they perceive their ratio to be equal to the relevant others with whom they compare themselves, a state of equity is said to exist. They feel their situation is fair—that justice prevails. If the ratios are unequal, inequity exists; that is, the employees tend to view themselves as underrewarded or overrewarded. When inequities occur, employees will attempt to correct them.

Equity theory recognizes that individuals are concerned not only with the absolute amount of rewards they receive for their efforts, but also with the relationship of this amount to what others receive (see Exhibit 9–5). Inputs such as effort, experience, education, and competence can be compared to outcomes such as salary levels, raises, recognition, and other factors. When people perceive an imbalance in their input-outcome ratio relative to others, tension is created. This tension provides the basis for motivation, as people strive for what they perceive as equity and fairness.

There is substantial evidence to confirm the equity thesis: Employee motivation is influenced significantly by relative rewards as well as absolute

Equity theory
a theory that states employees perceive what they can get from a job situation (outcomes) in relation to what they put into it (inputs), and then compare their input-outcome ratio with the input-output ratio of others.

[8]J. S. Adams, "Inequity in Social Exchanges," in L. Berkowitz (ed.), *Advances in Experimental Social Psychology*, Vol. 2 (New York, NY: Academic Press, 1965), pp. 267–300.

EXHIBIT 9–5

Equity theory.

| Individual outcomes | Compare with | Others' Outcomes |
|:---:|:---:|:---:|
| Individual inputs | | Others' inputs |

rewards. It helps to explain why, particularly when employees perceive themselves as underrewarded (we all seem to be pretty good at rationalizing being overrewarded), they may reduce their work effort, produce lower quality work, sabotage the system, skip work days, or even resign.

## DO EMPLOYEES REALLY GET WHAT THEY EXPECT?

**Expectancy theory**
a theory that argues that individuals analyze effort-performance, performance-reward, and rewards-personal goals relationships, and their level of effort depends on the strengths of their expectations that these relationships can be achieved.

The final perspective we'll present is an integrative approach to motivation. It focuses on expectations. Specifically, **expectancy theory** argues that individuals analyze three relationships: effort-performance, performance-rewards, and rewards-personal goals. Their level of effort depends on the strengths of their expectations that these relationships can be achieved.[9] According to expectancy theory, an employee will be motivated to exert a high level of effort when he or she believes that effort will lead to a good performance appraisal; that a good appraisal will lead to organizational rewards like a bonus, a salary increase, or a promotion; and that the rewards will satisfy the employee's personal goals. The theory is illustrated in Exhibit 9–6.

Expectancy theory has proven to provide a powerful explanation of employee motivation. It helps explain why a lot of workers aren't motivated on their jobs and merely do the minimum necessary to get by. This can be made clearer if we look at the theory's three relationships in a little more detail. We'll present them as questions which, if supervisors want to maximize employee motivation, need to be answered affirmatively by those employees.

First, *if I give a maximum effort, will it be recognized in my performance evaluation?* For a lot of employees, the answer is no. Why? Their skill level may be deficient, which means that no matter how hard they try, they're not likely to be a high performer. The company's performance appraisal system may be poorly designed—assessing traits, for example, rather than

[9]V. H. Vroom, *Work and Motivation* (New York, NY: John Wiley, 1964).

behaviors—making it difficult or impossible for the employee to achieve a strong evaluation. Still another possibility is that the employee, rightly or wrongly, perceives that her supervisor doesn't like her. As a result, she expects to get a poor appraisal regardless of her level of performance. These examples suggest that one possible source of low employee motivation is the belief, by the employee, that no matter how hard she works, the likelihood of getting a good performance appraisal is low.

Second, *if I get a good performance appraisal, will it lead to organizational rewards?* Many employees see the performance-reward relationship in their job as weak. The reason is that organizations reward a lot of things besides just performance. For example, when pay is allocated to employees based on factors such as seniority, being cooperative, or "kissing up" to the boss, employees are likely to see the performance-reward relationship as being weak and demotivating.

Last, *if I'm rewarded, are they the rewards that I find personally attractive?* The employee works hard in hope of getting a promotion, but gets a pay raise instead. Or the employee wants a more interesting and challenging job, but receives only a few words of praise. Unfortunately, many supervisors are limited in the rewards that they can distribute. This makes it difficult to tailor rewards to individual employees. Still other supervisors incorrectly assume that all employees want the same thing, thus overlooking the motivational effects of differentiating rewards. In either case, employee motivation is submaximized.

## How Do I Set an Atmosphere Where Employees Really Want to Work?

We've presented a number of approaches to motivation in this chapter. If you're a supervisor, concerned with motivating your employees, how do you apply the various concepts introduced? While there is no simple, all-

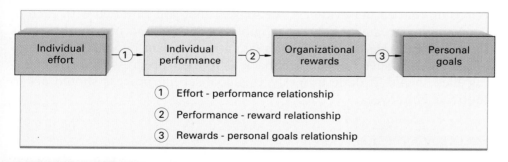

| Individual effort | → ① → | Individual performance | → ② → | Organizational rewards | → ③ → | Personal goals |

① Effort - performance relationship

② Performance - reward relationship

③ Rewards - personal goals relationship

## EXHIBIT 9–6
Expectancy theory.

encompassing set of guidelines, the essence of what we know about motivating employees is distilled in the following suggestions:

## RECOGNIZE INDIVIDUAL DIFFERENCES

If there is one thing we've learned over the years it's that employees are not the same. People have different needs. While you may be driven by the need for recognition, I may be far more concerned with satisfying my desire for security. We know that a minority of employees have a high need for achievement. But if one or more of the people working for you is a high achiever, make sure you design their jobs so as to provide them with the personal responsibility, feedback, and intermediate degree of risk that is most likely to provide them with motivation. Your job as a supervisor includes learning to recognize the dominant needs of each of your employees.

## MATCH PEOPLE TO JOBS

There is abundant evidence to support the idea that motivational benefits accrue from carefully matching people to jobs. Some people prefer routine work with repetitive tasks. While many people enjoy being part of a team, others do their best work when they're isolated from other people and able to do their jobs independently. When jobs differ in terms of autonomy, the variety of tasks to be done, the range of skills they demand, and the like, you should try to match employees to jobs that best fit with their capabilities and personal preferences.

## SET CHALLENGING GOALS

We talked about the importance of goals in Chapter 3. In that discussion, we showed how challenging goals can be a source of motivation. When people accept and are committed to a set of specific and difficult goals, they will work hard to achieve them. While we haven't directly addressed goals-as-motivators in this chapter, our earlier review of the evidence clearly indicates the power of goals in influencing employee behavior. Based on that earlier evidence, we suggest that you sit down with each of your employees and jointly set tangible, verifiable, and measurable goals for a specific time period. Then create a mechanism by which these employees will receive ongoing feedback as to their progress toward achieving these goals. If done properly, this goal-setting process should act to motivate employees.

## ENCOURAGE PARTICIPATION

Allowing employees to participate in decisions that affect them has been shown to increase their motivation. Participation is empowering. It allows people to take ownership of decisions. Examples of decisions in which em-

W. L. Gore & Associates, the maker of Gore-Tex fabrics, is a strong proponent of participation. All employees are encouraged to participate actively in all key decisions that affect them. Here, you see an actual production meeting in progress.

ployees might participate include setting work goals, choosing their own benefit packages, and selecting preferred work schedules and assignments. Participation, of course, should be at the option of the employee. No one should feel compelled to participate in decision making. While participation is associated with increasing employee commitment and motivation, consistent with our earlier discussion of individual differences, some people may prefer to waive their rights to participate in decisions that affect them. Those preferences should be heeded.

## INDIVIDUALIZE REWARDS

Since employees have different needs, what acts as a reinforcer for one may not work for another. You should use your knowledge of individual differences to individualize the rewards over which your have control. Some of the more obvious rewards that supervisors allocate include pay, job assignments, work hours, and the opportunity to participate in goal setting and decision making (see Dealing with a Difficult Issue).

## LINK REWARDS TO PERFORMANCE

In both reinforcement theory and expectancy theory, motivation is maximized when supervisors make rewards contingent on performance. To reward factors other than performance will only act to reinforce and encourage those other factors. Key rewards such as pay increases and promotions should be allocated for the attainment of the employee's specific goals. To maximize the impact of the reward contingencies, supervisors should look for ways to increase the visibility of rewards. Publicizing performance bonuses and allocating annual salary increases in a lump sum rather than spreading them out over the entire year are examples of actions that will make rewards more visible and potentially more motivating.

# DEALING WITH A DIFFICULT ISSUE

## REWARDING APPROPRIATE BEHAVIOR

You have just been hired as a supervisor at the San Diego-based Quality Travel Agency. When customers call to arrange travel plans, your employees look up airline flights, times, and fares on their computers. They help customers make travel reservations that work best for them. Customers also often want assistance in reserving rental cars or finding suitable hotel accommodations.

The car rental agencies and hotels frequently run contests for the sales representative who reserves the most cars for a particular firm or books the most clients for a specific hotel chain. The rewards for doing so are very attractive, too. One car rental firm offers to place employees' names in a monthly drawing to win $2500 if they book just 20 reservations. If they book a hundred in the same amount of time, they're eligible for a $10,000 prize. If they book 200 clients, they receive an-all expenses-paid, four-day Caribbean vacation for two. These incentives are attractive enough for your employees to "steer" customers toward those companies, even though they might not be the best or the cheapest for them. Yet, as the supervisor, you don't discourage participation in these programs. In fact, you view it as a bonus for your agency's hard work.

Do you believe that there is anything wrong with your firm doing business with these car rental and hotel firms that offer "kickbacks" to employees? What ethical issues do you see in this case for (a) you and (b) your customers? How could you design a performance reward system that would encourage employees to high levels of "bookings" while at the same time not compromise good ethical practices?

## CHECK FOR EQUITY

Rewards or outcomes should be perceived by employees as equaling the inputs they give. At a simplistic level, this should mean that experience, abilities, effort, and other obvious inputs should explain differences in pay, responsibility, and other obvious outcomes. The problem, however, is complicated by the fact that there are dozens of inputs and outcomes, and that employee groups place different degrees of importance on them. This suggests that one person's equity is another's inequity, so an ideal reward system should probably weight inputs differently in order to arrive at the proper rewards for each job.

## DON'T IGNORE MONEY!

Our last suggestion may seem incredibly obvious. But it's easy to get so caught up in setting goals or providing opportunities for participation that you forget that money is a major reason why most people work. The allocation of performance-based wage increases, piece-work bonuses, and other pay incentives are important in determining employee motivation. Maybe the best case for not overlooking money as a motivator is a review of eighty studies evaluating motivational methods and their impacts on employee productivity.[10] Goal setting alone produced, on average, a 16 percent increase in productivity; efforts to redesign jobs in order to make them more interesting and challenging yielded 8 to 16 percent increases; employee participation in decision making produced a median increase of less than one percent. In contrast, monetary incentives led to an average increase of 30 percent.

## CHALLENGES FOR TODAY'S SUPERVISORS

Today's supervisors have challenges in motivating their employees that their counterparts of 30 or 40 years ago didn't have. This is most evident when we look at some of the fastest growing employee subgroups.

### HOW DO YOU MOTIVATE A DIVERSIFIED WORKFORCE?

Jason Tinsley supervises a department of six workers in a Los Angeles steel-fabricating plant. Two of his employees are Latino, and the other four are African American, Pakistani, Korean, and a recent immigrant from the former Soviet Union. While several of Tinsley's people have strong communication skills, others speak very little English. They have different ideas on what constitutes a full day's work and the authority of a supervisor.

Diversity has become the norm in organizations. You are likely to supervise groups that include women, ethnic minorities, immigrants, physically disabled, senior citizens, and others from diverse groups. This diversity presents a number of motivation challenges. For instance, diverse group members often have different needs and expectations. If you're going to maximize motivation, you've got to understand and respond to this diversity (see News Flash).

The key word to guide you should be flexibility. Be ready to design work schedules, benefits, physical work settings, and the like to reflect your employees' varied needs. This might include offering child care, flexible work

---

[10]E. A. Locke and others, "The Relative Effectiveness of Four Methods of Motivating Employee Performance," in K. D. Duncan, M. M. Gruneberg, and D. Wallis, eds., *Changes in Working Life* (London: John Wiley, Ltd., 1980), pp. 363–83.

## MOTIVATING A DIVERSE WORKFORCE

The flexibility required in motivating a diverse workforce also means that you must be aware of *cultural* differences. The theories of motivation we have identified were developed largely by U.S. psychologists and validated by studying American workers. Therefore, these theories need to be modified for different cultures.[11]

For instance, the self-interest concept is consistent with capitalism and the extremely high value placed on oneself in countries such as the United States. Because almost all the motivation theories presented in this chapter are based on the self-interest motive, they should be applicable to employees in such countries as Great Britain and Australia, where capitalism and self-interest are highly valued. In more collective-oriented nations, such as Venezuela, Singapore, Japan, and Mexico, the individual's loyalty to the organization or society takes precedence over his or her self-interest. Employees in collective-oriented cultures should be more receptive to team-based job design, group goals, and group-performance evaluations. Reliance on the fear of being fired in such cultures is likely to be less effective, even if the laws in these countries allow managers to fire employees.

The need-for-achievement concept provides another example of a motivation theory with a

*(cont'd)*

[11]G. Hofstede, "Motivation, Leadership, and Organizations: Do American Theories Apply Abroad?" *Organizational Dynamics*, Summer 1980, p. 55.

hours, and job sharing for employees with family responsibilities. You might offer flexible leave policies for immigrants who want to return occasionally to their homelands. Or consider allowing employees who are going to school to be able to vary their work schedules from semester to semester.

## HOW DO YOU MOTIVATE LOW-PAY SERVICE WORKERS?

You're supervising counter workers at McDonald's, clerks at Blockbuster Video, orderlies in a hospital, or a building maintenance crew. These represent some of the fastest growing job categories in America. They also

## MOTIVATING A DIVERSE WORKFORCE

*(cont'd)*

U.S. bias. The view that a high need for achievement acts as an internal motivator presupposes the existence of two cultural characteristics: a willingness to accept a moderate degree of risk and a concern with performance. Results, however, of several recent studies among employees in countries other than the United States indicate that some aspects of motivation theory are transferable.[12] For instance, motivational techniques presented earlier in this chapter were shown to be effective in changing performance-related behaviors of Russian textile mill workers. However, we shouldn't assume that motivation concepts are universally applicable. The technique of recognizing and embarrassing the worst sales clerks by giving them awards—used by a large department store in Xian, China—may be effective in China.[13] But doing something that humiliates employees isn't likely to work in North America or Western Europe.

[12]D. H. B. Walsh, F. Luthens, and S. M. Sommer, "Organizational Behavior Modification Goes to Russia: Replicating an Experimental Analysis Across Cultures and Tasks," *Journal of Organizational Behavior Management*, Fall 1993, pp. 15–35; and J. R. Baum, et al., "Nationality and Work Role Interactions: A Cultural Contrast of Israel and U.S. Entrepreneurs' Versus Managers' Needs," *Journal of Business Venturing*, November 1993, pp. 499–512.

[13]A. Ignatius, "Now if Ms. Wong Insults a Customer, She Gets an Award," *Wall Street Journal*, January 24, 1989, p. A–1.

represent a major supervisory challenge: How do you motivate people in low-paying jobs that offer limited opportunities for advancement? In contrast to low-skill, blue-collar manufacturing jobs that paid $10 to $15 an hour in the 1960s, today's low-skill service jobs are paying $5 or $6 an hour—barely enough to satisfy basic needs and far from allowing the worker to move into the middle class.

So what can you do? Pay might be increased a bit, but significantly higher basic wages can't be passed on to consumers. The public isn't ready yet for the $10 Big Mac. So what you're left with are options such as offering job flexibility and variety, providing recognition, and capitalizing on the role of social support. Give employees flexibility in choosing their work hours. Increase variety by allowing them to change tasks and rotate among jobs. Build group cohesiveness, support, and commitment by encouraging employees to be part of a winning team.

## What Motivating Challenges Do Professionals Present?

How do you motivate the professional librarian, civil engineer, registered nurse, or lawyer? How do you get the most effort from the C.P.A. at Alexander and Alexander, the software programmer at Lotus, or the Dallas Cowboys football player making $5 million a year?

Professional employees provide a unique challenge in terms of motivation. Money, in an absolute sense, does not tend to be high on their need list. They tend to be sensitive to the design of their jobs. They're also more likely to attach their identity to their profession than to the organization that employs them.

Since professionals tend to be relatively well paid, money is more likely to be an equity issue than concern over its absolute amount. Many professionals are equity sensitive. They are prone to compare their salary, job assignments, benefit packages, office furnishings, and the like against others with whom they work and associate. A $5000 bonus tends to carry significantly more weight to a $25,000-a-year blue-collar worker than to the $75,000-a-year professional.

Professionals tend to place a high value on job factors such as autonomy, personal growth, recognition, and challenging work. Their motivation is closely tied to the degree to which their job satisfies these needs. Much of the upcoming discussion on designing motivating jobs is particularly relevant to professionals.

Finally, one characteristic that typically differentiates professional employees from others is that professionals put their allegiance to their field of expertise ahead of that to the organization. A corporate attorney who works for Mobil Oil will tend to see her identity more closely tied to the legal profession than to the Mobil Oil Corporation. This presents a challenge to supervisors because the rewards offered outside the organization often take precedent over those from within. For example, recognition by professional peers through articles in newsletters, awards, appointment to important committees, or election to a high-ranking office within the professional organization can be powerful motivators to the professional employee. But unfortunately, the typical supervisor has little influence over these outside sources of rewards.

---

"Librarians are professionals," says Susan Starr of the University of California at San Diego Library. "To motivate them, I tend to rely on professional development opportunities, travel, or projects that they find exciting."

## SHOULD EMPLOYEES BE PAID FOR PERFORMANCE OR TIME ON THE JOB?

What's in it for me? That's a question every person consciously or unconsciously asks before engaging in any form of behavior. Our knowledge of motivation tells us that people do what they do to satisfy some need. Before they do anything, therefore, they look for a payoff or reward. Although there may be many different rewards offered by organizations, most of us are concerned with earning an amount of money that allows us to satisfy our needs and wants. Because pay is an important variable in motivation as one type of reward, we need to look at how we can use pay to motivate high levels of employee performance. And this explains the intent and logic behind pay-for-performance programs.

**Pay-for-performance programs** are compensation plans that pay employees on the basis of some performance measure.[14] Piece-rate plans, gainsharing, wage incentive plans, profit sharing, and lump sum bonuses are examples of pay-for-performance programs.[15] What differentiates these forms of pay from the more traditional compensation plans is that instead of paying an employee for *time* on the job, pay is adjusted to reflect some performance measures. These performance measures might include such things as individual productivity, team or work group productivity, departmental productivity, or the overall organization's profits for a given period.

Performance-based compensation is probably most compatible with expectancy theory. That is, employees should perceive a strong relationship between their performance and the rewards they receive if motivation is to be maximized. If rewards are allocated solely on nonperformance factors—such as seniority, job title, or across-the-board cost-of-living raises—then employees are likely to reduce their efforts.[16]

Pay-for-performance programs are gaining in popularity in organizations. The growing popularity can be explained in terms of both motivation and cost control. From a motivation perspective, making some or all of a worker's pay conditional on performance measures focuses his or her attention and effort on that measure, then reinforces the continuation of that effort with rewards. However, if the employee, team, or the organization's performance declines, so too does the reward.[17] Thus, there's an incentive to keep efforts and motivation strong. For instance, employees at

Pay-for-performance programs compensation plans that pay employees on the basis of some performance measure.

---

[14]A. M. Dickinson and K. L. Gillette, "A Comparison of the Effects on Productivity: Piece-Rate Pay Versus Base Pay Plus Incentives," *Journal of Organizational Behavior Management*, Spring 1994, pp. 3–82.

[15]See, for example, D. Fenn, "Compensation: Bonuses That Make Sense," *Inc.*, March 1996, p. 95.

[16]G. Grib and S. O'Donnell, "Pay Plans that Reward Employee Achievement, *HRMagazine*, July 1995, pp. 49–50.

[17]"Compensation: Sales Managers as Team Players," *Inc.*, August 1994, p. 102.

Hallmark Cards, Inc., in Kansas City have up to 10 percent of their pay at risk. Depending on their productivity on such performance measures as customer satisfaction, retail sales, and profits, employees turn that 10 percent into rewards as high as 25 percent.[18] However, failure to reach the performance measures can result in the forfeiture of the 10 percent of salary placed at risk. Companies like Saturn, Steelcase, TRW, Hewlett-Packard, duPont, and Ameri-Tech use similar formulas where employee compensation is comprised of base and reward pay.[19] On the cost-savings side, performance-based bonuses and other incentive rewards avoid the fixed expense of permanent—and often annual—salary increases. The bonuses do not accrue to base salary, which means that the amount is not compounded in future years. As a result, they save the company money!

## How Can Employee Stock Ownership Plans Affect Motivation?

**Employee stock ownership plan (ESOP)**
a compensation program that allows employees to become part owners of an organization by receiving stock as a performance incentive.

Many companies are using employee stock ownership plans for improving and motivating employee performance. An **employee stock ownership plan** (ESOP) is a compensation program in which employees become part owners of the organization by receiving stock as a performance incentive. More than 10 million employees in such companies as United Airlines, British Petroleum, Avis, NationsBank, Pfizer, Owens Corning, Weirton Steel, and Starbucks participate in ESOPs.[20] Also, many ESOPs allow employees to purchase additional stocks at attractive, below-market prices. Under an ESOP, employees often are motivated to give more effort because it makes them owners who will share in any gains and losses. The fruits of their labors are no longer just going into the pockets of some unknown owners—the employees are the owners!

Do ESOPs positively affect productivity and employee satisfaction? The answer appears to be yes! The research on ESOPs indicates that they increase employee satisfaction and frequently result in higher performance.[21] However, other studies showed that productivity in organizations with ESOPs does increase, but the impact is greater the longer the ESOP has been in existence.[22] You shouldn't expect immediate increases

---

[18]D. Fenn, "Compensation: Goal-Driven Incentives," *Inc.*, August 1996, p. 91; and M. A. Verespej, "More Value for Compensation," *Industry Week*, June 17, 1996, p. 20.

[19]S. Overman, "Saturn Teams Working and Profiting," *HRMagazine*, March 1995, p. 72.

[20]K. Capell, "Options for Everyone," *Business Week*, July 22, 1996, pp. 80–88.

[21]See, for example, T. R. Stenhouse, "The Long and the Short of Gainsharing," *Academy of Management Executive*, Vol. 9, No. 1 (1995), pp. 77–78.

[22]S. A. Lee, "ESOP is a Powerful Tool to Align Employees with Corporate Goals," *Pension World*, April 1994, pp. 40–42.

in employee motivation and productivity if an ESOP is implemented. But over time, employee productivity and satisfaction should go up.

## DESIGNING MOTIVATING JOBS

One of the more important factors that influence an employee's motivational level is the structure of the work itself. Is there a lot of variety or is the job repetitive? Is the work closely supervised? Does the job allow the employee discretion? The answers to questions like these will have a major impact on the motivational properties inherent in the job and, hence, the level of productivity an employee can expect to achieve.

We use the term **job design** to refer to the way that tasks are combined to form complete jobs. Some jobs are routine because the tasks are standardized and repetitive; others are nonroutine. Some require a large number of varied and diverse skills; others are narrow in scope. Some jobs constrain the employee by requiring him or her to follow very precise procedures; others allow employees substantial freedom in how they do their work. The point is that jobs differ in the way tasks are combined, and these different combinations create a variety of job designs.

**Job design**
combining tasks to form complete jobs.

What are the key characteristics that define a job? There are five, and together they comprise the core dimensions of any job:[23]

1. *Skill variety:* The degree to which the job requires a variety of different activities, so the worker can use a number of different skills and talents.
2. *Task identity:* The degree to which the job requires completion of a whole and identifiable piece of work.
3. *Task significance:* The degree to which the job has a substantial impact on the lives or work of other people.
4. *Autonomy:* The degree to which the job provides substantial freedom, independence, and discretion to the individual in scheduling the work and in determining the procedures to be used in carrying it out.
5. *Feedback:* The degree to which carrying out the work activities required by the job results in the individual obtaining direct and clear information about the effectiveness of his or her performance.

Exhibit 9–7 offers examples of job activities that rate high and low for each characteristic. When these five characteristics are all present in a job,

| **Skill Variety** | |
|---|---|
| High variety | The owner-operator of a garage who does electrical repair, rebuilds engines, does body work, and interacts with customers |
| Low variety | A body shop worker who sprays paint eight hours a day |
| **Task Identity** | |
| High identity | A cabinet maker who designs a piece of furniture, selects the wood, builds the object, and finishes it to perfection |
| Low identity | A worker in a furniture factory who operates a lathe solely to make table legs |
| **Task Significance** | |
| High significance | Nursing the sick in a hospital intensive care unit |
| Low significance | Sweeping hospital floors |
| **Autonomy** | |
| High autonomy | A telephone installer who schedules his or her own work for the day, makes visits without supervision, and decides on the most effective techniques for a particular installation |
| Low autonomy | A telephone operator who must handle calls as they come according to a routine, highly specified procedure |
| **Feedback** | |
| High feedback | An electronics factory worker who assembles a radio and then tests it to determine if it operates properly |
| Low feedback | An electronics factory worker who assembles a radio and then routes it to a quality control inspector who tests it proper operation and makes needed adjustments |

## EXHIBIT 9–7

Examples of high and low job characteristics.

[23]J. R. Hackman and G. R. Oldham, "Motivation Through the Design of Work: Test of a Theory," *Organizational Behavior and Human Performance*, August 1976, pp. 250–279.

the job becomes enriched and potentially motivating. Notice we said "potentially motivating." Whether that potential is actualized is largely dependent on the employee's growth-need strength (see Assessing Yourself). Individuals with a high growth need are more likely to be motivated in enriched jobs than their counterparts with a low growth need.

**Job enrichment** increases the degree to which a worker controls the planning, execution, and evaluation of his or her work. An enriched job organizes tasks so as to allow the worker to do a complete activity, increases the employee's freedom and independence, increases responsibility, and provides feedback, so an individual will be able to assess and correct his or her own performance (see Building a Supervisory Skill).

**Job enrichment**
the degree to which a worker controls the planning, execution, and evaluation of his or her work.

# ASSESSING YOURSELF

## IS ENRICHMENT FOR YOU?

People differ in what they like and dislike in their jobs. Following are twelve pairs of jobs. For each pair, indicate which job you would prefer. Assume that everything else about the jobs is the same—pay attention only to the characteristics actually listed for each pair of jobs. If you prefer the job in the left-hand column (Column A), indicate how much you prefer it by putting a check mark in a space to the left of the Neutral point. If you prefer the job in the right-hand column (Column B), check one of the spaces to the right of Neutral. Check the Neutral blank only if you find the two jobs equally attractive or unattractive. Try to use the Neutral blank rarely.

### SCORING

This 12-item questionnaire taps the degree to which you have a strong versus weak desire to obtain growth satisfaction from your work. Each item on the questionnaire yields a score from 1 to 7. To obtain your individual growth-need strength score, average the twelve items as follows:

| | |
|---|---|
| #1, #2, #7, #8, #11, #12 (direct scoring) | [e.g. Strongly prefer A = 1, Neutral = 4 Strongly prefer B = 7] |
| #3, #4, #5, #6, #9, #10 (reverse scoring) | [e.g. Strongly prefer A = 7, Neutral = 4 Strongly prefer B = 1] |

*(continued)*

## WHAT THE ASSESSMENT MEANS

Average scores for typical respondents are close to the midpoint of 4.0. High scores suggest that you will respond to an enriched job. Low scores suggest that you wouldn't find enriched jobs satisfying or motivating.

### COLUMN A

**1.** A job that offers little or no challenge.

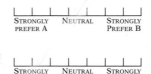

**2.** A job that pays very well.

**3.** A job that often requires you to make important decisions.

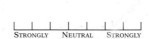

**4.** A job with little security in a somewhat unstable organization.

**5.** A job in which greater responsibility is given to those who do the best work.

**6.** A job with a supervisor who sometimes is highly critical.

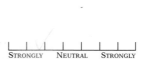

**7.** A very routine job.

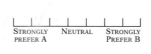

**8.** A job with a supervisor who respects you and treats you fairly.

### COLUMN B

A job that requires you to be completely isolated from coworkers.

A job that allows considerable opportunity to be creative and innovative.

A job in which there are many pleasant people to work with.

A job in which you have little or no opportunity to participate in decisions that affect your work.

A job in which greater responsibility is given to loyal employees who have the most *seniority*.

A job that does not require you to use much of your talent.

A job in which your coworkers are not very friendly.

A job that provides constant opportunities for you to learn new and interesting things.

**9.** A job that gives you a real chance to develop yourself personally.

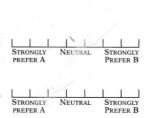

STRONGLY PREFER A · NEUTRAL · STRONGLY PREFER B

A job with excellent vacations and fringe benefits.

**10.** A job in which there is a real chance you could be laid off.

STRONGLY PREFER A · NEUTRAL · STRONGLY PREFER B

A job with very little chance to do challenging work.

**11.** A job with little freedom and independence to do your work in the way you think best.

STRONGLY PREFER A · NEUTRAL · STRONGLY PREFER B

A job with poor working conditions.

**12.** A job with very satisfying teamwork.

STRONGLY PREFER A · NEUTRAL · STRONGLY PREFER B

A job that allows you to use your skills and abilities to the fullest extent.

## DESIGNING JOBS

### ABOUT THE SKILL

As a supervisor, what can you do regarding job design to maximize your employees' performance? Based on the research, we suggest you improve the five core job dimensions.

### PRACTICING THE SKILL

1. **Combine tasks.** Put existing fractionalized tasks back together to form a new, larger module of work. This increases skill variety and task identity.
2. **Create natural work units.** Design tasks that form an identifiable and meaningful whole. This increases employee "ownership" of the work and encourages your employees to view their work as meaningful and important rather than as irrelevant and boring.

   [24]ibid.

3. **Establish client relationships.** The client is the user of the product or service that your employees work on. Wherever possible, you should establish direct relationships between your workers and their clients. This increases skill variety, autonomy, and feedback for the employees.
4. **Expand jobs vertically.** Vertical expansion means giving employees responsibilities and controls that were formerly reserved for you, the manager. It partially closes the gap between the "doing" and "controlling" aspects of the job, and it increases employee autonomy.
5. **Open feedback channels.** By increasing feedback, employees not only learn how well they are performing their jobs but also whether their performances are improving, deteriorating, or remaining at a constant level. Ideally, employees should receive performance feedback directly, as they do their jobs, rather than from you on an occasional basis.[24] ■

## SUMMARY

After reading this chapter, I can:

1. **Define motivation.** Motivation is the willingness to do something and is conditioned by this action's ability to satisfy some need for the individual.

2. **Identify and define five personality characteristics relevant to understanding the behavior of employees at work.** Five personality characteristics are: (1) locus of control— the degree to which people believe they are masters of their own fate; (2) Machiavellianism—the degree to which an individual is manipulative and believes ends can justify means; (3) self-esteem—an individual's degree of liking or disliking for himself or herself; (4) self-monitoring—an individual's ability to adjust his or her behavior to external, situational factors; and (5) risk propensity—the degree of an individual's willingness to take chances.

3. **Explain the elements and the focus of the three early theories of motivation.** Maslow focused on the self. Maslow's hierarchy of needs proposes there are five needs—physiological, safety, social, esteem, and self-actualization—and as each need is sequentially satisfied, the next need becomes dominant. McGregor focused on management's perception of the self. Theory X-Theory Y proposes two views of human nature, then argues that employees are essentially hard working, committed, and responsible. Therefore, to maximize

motivation, employees should be allowed to participate in decision making, given responsible and challenging jobs, and supervisors should strive to achieve good group relations among employees. Herzberg focused on the organization's effect on the self. According to motivation-hygiene theory, if you want to motivate employees, you have to emphasize achievement, recognition, the work itself, responsibility, and growth. These are the characteristics that people find intrinsically rewarding.

4. **Identify the characteristics that stimulate the achievement drive in high achievers.** High achievers prefer jobs that give them personal responsibility for finding solutions to problems, where they can receive rapid and unambiguous feedback on their performance, and where they can set moderately challenging goals.

5. **Identify the three relationships in expectancy theory that determine an individual's level of effort.** The three relationships in expectancy theory that determine an individual's level of effort are effort-performance, performance-rewards, and rewards-personal goals.

6. **List actions a supervisor can take to maximize employee motivation.** To maximize employee motivation, supervisors should recognize individual differences, match people to jobs, set challenging goals, encourage participation, individualize rewards, link rewards to performance, check for equity, and not ignore money.

*(continued)*

# REVIEWING YOUR KNOWLEDGE

## REVIEW AND DISCUSSION QUESTIONS

1. How does an unsatisfied need create motivation?
2. Contrast behavioral predictions about people with an internal versus an external locus of control.
3. Compare the assumptions of Theory X with Theory Y.
4. What is the importance of the dual-continuum in the motivation-hygiene theory?
5. What does a supervisor need to do to motivate a high achiever?
6. What role would money play in: (a) the hierarchy of needs theory; (b) motivation-hygiene theory; (c) equity theory; (d) expectancy theory; and (e) employees with a high nAch?
7. Describe expectancy theory.
8. What motivational challenges does a diversified work force create for supervisors?
9. Identify and explain the five core dimensions in a job.
10. How can a supervisor enrich a job?

## ANSWERS TO THE POP QUIZZES

1. **c. self-actualization needs.** Self-actualization in Maslow's theory means reaching one's full potential. "Being all you can be" reflects this attainment, and thus, the self-actualization needs.

2. Motivation is the willingness to exert high levels of effort in order to satisfy some individual need. The motivation process begins with an unsatisfied need, which creates tension and drives an individual to search for goals that, if attained, will satisfy the need and reduce the tension.

3. **False.** It's just the reverse. Theory X reflects the negative view of human nature, assuming that they dislike work. Theory Y, on the other hand, is basically a positive view of employees, assuming that they are creative.

4. **d. none of the above.** Motivation-hygiene theory factors that eliminate dissatisfaction are called **hygiene factors.**

5. **c. effort-performance linkage.** The degree to which an individual believes that working at a particular level will generate a desired outcome is reflective of the effort one must put forth in order to perform successfully.

6. In equity theory, individuals compare their job's inputs-outcomes ratio to those of relevant others. If they perceive that they are underrewarded, their work motivation declines. When individuals perceive that they are overrewarded, they often are motivated to work harder in order to justify their pay.

7. **True.** ESOPs enable employees to receive incentives that are directly tied to their performance. As "part owners," this incentive creates a motivational effect.

8. **d. flexibility.** Employees from diverse cultures have differing needs. To be able to motivate them, and meet their needs, supervisors must be flexible in their dealings with their workers. ∎

# PERFORMING YOUR JOB

## A Class Exercise: Designing Jobs at Citibank

Break into groups of four or five. You are a consulting team that has been hired by Citibank to help them solve a motivation/performance problem.

Citibank employs several hundred people in its back office who process all the company's financial transactions. These jobs have been split up so that each person performs a single, routine task over and over again. Employees have become dissatisfied with these mundane jobs, and this dissatisfaction shows in their work. Severe backlogs have developed, and error rates are unacceptably high. Your team's task is to (a) redesign these jobs in order to resolve these problems and (b) identify how these changes are likely to affect the jobs of supervisors in this department.

Your team has thirty minutes to complete this task. At the end, report orally to the class.

## Thinking Critically

### CASE 9.A

### Equity Theory in Practice

Undoubtedly, the past decade has been a difficult time for employees. Companies have restructured jobs and processes, resulting in thousands of workers being laid off. For the luckier ones who remain employed in these organization, pay levels were either held constant for several years (no raises given), or worse,

pay was cut. What effect did this have on employee motivation?

One researcher asked just that question. He studied the practices of three plants of a large midwest manufacturing organization.[25] Not unlike many manufacturing companies, this organization was struggling to survive. In an effort to do so, the company decided, among other things, to implement pay cuts for all its employees.

It's safe to say that no one expected workers to be happy about making less money. However, it was the supervisors' perception that a pay cut would cause less harm than eliminating several jobs altogether. In fact, by reducing pay levels, layoffs could be prevented. What happened next was clearly not the reaction anyone expected.

Employees did change their behaviors and attitudes toward the company. Sure, they were disgruntled, but they did more than complain. Employees began stealing from the company. Anything and everything that they could take was "looted". In fact, in two of the three plants, theft skyrocketed to unprecedented levels.

### Responding to the Case

1. Describe the behaviors (stealing) by these employees in terms of (a) their needs; (b) the organization's effect on them; (c) equating their inputs and outcomes; and (d) what employees expect from their employer.
2. What do you believe supervisors could have done differently to avert this "potential" problem?

[25] Based on J. Greenberg, "Employee Theft as a Reaction to Under Payment Inequity: The Hidden Costs of Pay Cuts," *Journal of Applied Psychology*, Vol 75, No. 5 (October 1990), pp. 561–568.

## CASE 9.B

## Motivating FormPac Employees

Have you ever heard of the FormPac Corporation? Probably not. But it's a good bet you've used one of their products. For instance, the paint tray at your local Home Depot was probably made by FormPac—as well as many of the containers that hold your favorite soda. The company, based in Sandusky, Ohio, is a major supplier of custom plastic products.[26] What's interesting about FormPac is that it has been rejuvenated over the past several years. Much of the credit for this goes to its employees. Of course many of FormPac's supervisors played important roles, too!

Many of the supervisors believed that employees should be rewarded for having a productive year. When the company exceeded its production and profit goals, they believed profits should be shared with employees. But FormPac's bonus program was ill-defined. No employee knew precisely what entered into the bonus "equation," nor did any have a clue of how much bonus they may get. In the past, the company president made these determinations. Then, in 1994, things started to sour. After FormPac lost a major account, and was heavily debt-ridden from building a new plant, no bonuses were given. Understandably, employees were puzzled. Some were even mad enough to become publicly vocal—claiming that the president had the money for bonuses, but was pocketing it all himself! That simply was not correct. Supervisors recognized why some of the employees were reacting this way—they had no information about how bonuses were awarded.

Then things changed. The bonus program was spelled out—a precise formula for individual bonuses to annual performance was established. The primary components of the formula were based on the company's financial statements; specifically, profits and monthly sales. Each month, supervisors would post in the cafeteria where the company stood on these two variables. This data enabled employees to compare their past work to the projected targets set by the company. In this manner, employees were able to see whether or not they were ahead of, even with, or below the targets. Additionally, posted next to the productivity trend data was a formula of how profits would be divided among the employees. Sixty percent of that amount would be divided among all employees, with the remaining 40 percent being split between hourly workers and supervisory personnel. While this "formula" provided the amount of money available in the pay-for-performance bonus pool, the specific amount any one employee would receive was based on a formula that factored in their wages and seniority—in an attempt to reward "loyalty and commitment, too."

FormPac's new variable pay-for-performance bonus plan has been an unqualified success. Employees have been earning bonuses in the range of 10 percent, while the company has enjoyed a 25 percent increase in profitability. In addition, FormPac's productivity has increased by more than 20 percent. As for the employees who are making this happen, they now understand how the bonus system works and their role in it.

---

[26]D. Fenn, "Compensation: Bonuses that Make Sense," *Inc.*, March 1996, p. 95.

## RESPONDING TO THE CASE

1. Explain the behavior of FormPac employees in terms of expectancy theory.
2. How has pay-for-performance helped the organization?
3. Do you believe a pay-for-performance plan can "backfire" in an organization when it incurs losses through no fault of employees? Explain your position. What would you build into a pay-for-performance program to safeguard against any employee backlash? ■

# 10

# PROVIDING EFFECTIVE LEADERSHIP

# LEARNING OBJECTIVES

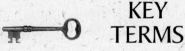 

# KEY TERMS

After reading this chapter, you should be able to:

1. Define leadership and describe the difference between a leader and a supervisor.
2. Identify the traits that may help you become a successful leader.
3. Define charisma and its key components.
4. Differentiate between task-centered and people-centered leadership behaviors.
5. Identify and describe three types of participative leadership styles.
6. Explain situational leadership.
7. Describe the leadership style differences between men and women.

You should also be able to define these supervisory terms:

autocratic leader

charismatic leader

consultative-participative leadership

credibility

democratic-participative leadership

free-reign leader

leadership

leadership traits

participative leadership

path-goal theory

people-centered leader

readiness

situational leadership

task-centered leader

transactional leader

trust

transformational leader

The concept of leadership has changed over the past 30 years. In the 1960s, when the majority of jobs were still in the manufacturing sector and less than 20 percent of the labor force had attended college, leaders were described in terms such as *strong, forceful, tough,* and *in charge.* Jobs and workers are different in the 1990s and so are leaders. The majority of today's workers are employed in the service sector. They're more likely to be working in an office than in a steel mill. Moreover, an increasing proportion of workers have been to college. They have ideas and opinions, and they expect to be able to express them. They have little tolerance for authoritarian leaders. Today, you're much more likely to hear leaders described in terms such as *visionary, enthusiastic, knowledgeable, coaching,* or *empowering.*

The shift we're describing has been widespread. Robert Torres of the Tucson Police Department described how leadership has changed in police

## UNDERSTANDING LEADERSHIP

**Leadership**
the ability an individual demonstrates to influence others to act in a particular way through direction, encouragement, sensitivity, consideration, and support.

**Leadership** is the ability you demonstrate when you influence others to act in a particular way. Through direction, encouragement, sensitivity, consideration, and support, you inspire your followers to accept challenges and achieve goals that may be viewed as difficult to achieve. As a leader, you're also someone who sees and can get the best out of others—helping them develop a sense of personal and professional accomplishment. Being a leader means building commitment to goal attainment among those being led, as well as a strong desire for them to continue following.

When you think of leaders, you may often view them as those individuals who are in charge of others. These would include you, as an authority over your employees, your boss, and anyone else who holds a position of power over you— like your professor in this class. Obviously, through a variety of actions, you and the others have the ability to influence. Yet, leadership goes frequently beyond formal positions. In fact, sometimes this person of power isn't around, yet leadership may still exist (see Dealing with a Difficult Issue). Let's look at these two issues.

work—a field where you might expect authoritarian leadership to still be pervasive. As Sergeant Torres explains, "I came from a military background. I learned the ropes in Vietnam, where my word was gospel. There, you ordered people to do what you wanted, and you expected compliance merely because you were the authority. It used to be that way in police work. My dad was a police officer, and I can remember when the sergeant said "jump," he jumped. It's different now. We have brought intelligence into the police department. The days of the 6'9", 400-pound authority figure are gone. We breed for brains rather than brawn. You have a group of men and women out there who are intellectually hungry. They want to know what things are happening and why. It's no longer acceptable for me to make decisions without having some input from my officers." ■

## ARE YOU A LEADER BECAUSE YOU'RE A SUPERVISOR?

Let's begin by clarifying the distinction between those who supervise others and those we call leaders. The two are frequently used to mean the same thing, but they do not.

Those who supervise others are appointed by the organization. They have legitimate power that allows them to reward and punish their employees. Their ability to influence employees is based on the formal authority inherent in their positions. In contrast, leaders may either be appointed or emerge from within a group. Leaders can influence others to perform beyond the actions dictated by formal authority.

Should all those who supervise others be leaders? Conversely, should all leaders be individuals who formally direct the activities of others? Because no one yet has been able to demonstrate through research or logical argument that leadership ability is a hindrance to those who supervise, we can state that anyone who supervises employees should ideally be a leader. However, not all leaders necessarily have the capabilities in other supervisory functions, and thus not all should have formal authority. Therefore when we refer to a leader in this chapter, we will be talking about anyone who is able to influence others.

# DEALING WITH A DIFFICULT ISSUE

## INFLUENCING WITHOUT POWER

Leadership is about your influence over others—especially in those instances where you don't have the formal authority over them—and the "power" you wield. The use or misuse of power can generate ethical questions about what's right or what's wrong. For instance, consider the following scenario.

Your boss has been dissatisfied with the way one of your fellow supervisors is handling a project. She has reassigned the project to you, but your colleague hasn't been told of this action. You've been told to work with this colleague to find out what he's already done, discuss any other necessary information that he might have, and to prepare a project report by the end of next month.

Your colleague is not giving you the information you need to even start, much less complete, the project. He finds your questions unusual. After all, it's his project, and he doesn't have time to stop and talk to you. That would delay him more—and jeopardize the success of his department. However, without this information, you won't be able to meet your deadline either. If that happens, you both may lose.

Do you see any problem in talking to your colleague and telling him the reason you're getting involved? How can you influence him in gaining his cooperation? What would you do in this situation?

## CAN THERE EVER BE "NO" LEADER?

Given that as a supervisor you should ideally be a leader, we would expect for leadership ability to be present. Nevertheless, that simply may not be the case. Although you have the formal authority to oversee employee activities, your leadership may be lacking. While that may not be the best of situations, can your employees survive if you provide little or no leadership? The answer is *yes*. In fact, leadership may not always be important. Many research studies have concluded that, in many situations, a leader's behavior may be irrelevant to goal attainment. That is, certain individual, job, and organizational factors can act as "substitutes for leadership." As a result, the "person in charge" has little influence on others.[1]

---

[1] For example, see J. P. Howell, D. E. Bowen, P. W. Dorfman, S. Kerr, and P. M. Podsakoff, "Substitutes for Leadership: Effective Alternatives to Ineffective Leadership," *Organizational Dynamics*, Summer 1990, pp. 21–38.

Employee characteristics such as experience, skill levels and training, "professional" orientation, or the need for autonomy, can neutralize the effect of leadership. These characteristics can replace the need for a leader's support. The drive to succeed in these cases comes from within. No external stimulus, therefore, is needed. Similarly, jobs that are well defined and routine require less leadership influence. In this case, employees know explicitly what is expected and how it is to be done. It generally doesn't take an inspirational leader to enforce compliance. Also, jobs that are intrinsically satisfying may place fewer demands on the need to be influenced. The job itself provides the influence to excel. Finally, organizational characteristics such as explicit and formalized goals, rigid rules and procedures, or cohesive work groups can act in the place of formal leadership.

Although the previous paragraph correctly cites instances where leadership is irrelevant, don't take this to mean that your leadership is not important in today's world of work. That simply would be an incorrect assumption. Rather, recognize that these "substitutions" are the exceptions. In most organizations, leadership is critical for organizational survival. That's why we will spend the rest of this chapter looking at what makes a good leader and the kinds of things they do.

## ARE YOU BORN TO LEAD?

Ask the average person on the street what comes to mind when he or she thinks of leadership. You're likely to get a list of qualities such as intelligence, charm, decisiveness, enthusiasm, strength, bravery, integrity, and self-confidence. In fact, these are probably some of the same characteristics you may have listed if you were asked that question. The responses that we get, in essence, represent **leadership traits**. The search for traits or characteristics that separate leaders from nonleaders, though done in a more sophisticated manner than an on-the-street survey, dominated the early research efforts in the study of leadership.

Is it possible to isolate one or more traits in individuals who are generally acknowledged to be able to influence others— people like Elizabeth Dole, Bill Clinton, Nelson Mandela, or Mother Theresa—that nonleaders do not possess? You may agree that these individuals meet the fundamental definition of a leader, but they represent individuals with completely different characteristics. If the concept of leadership traits was to prove valid, there would have to be identifiable characteristics that all leaders would be born with.

Leadership traits qualities such as intelligence, charm, decisiveness, enthusiasm, strength, bravery, integrity, and self-confidence.

# WHAT ARE THE TRAITS OF SUCCESSFUL LEADERS?

Research efforts at isolating specific traits resulted in a number of dead ends. Attempts failed to identify a set of traits that would always differentiate leaders from followers and effective leaders from ineffective leaders. Perhaps it was a bit optimistic to believe that a set of consistent and unique personality traits could apply across the board to all effective leaders—in such widely diverse organizations as McAfee Software, Jacksonville Jaguars, Archdiocese of Chicago, Dunkin' Donuts, Mutual of New York, or Toyota.

Attempts to identify traits consistently associated with those who are successful in influencing others has been more promising. For example, six traits on which leaders are seen to differ from nonleaders include: drive, the desire to influence others, honesty and moral character, self-confidence, intelligence, and relevant knowledge (see Exhibit 10–1).[2]

A person's *drive* reflects his or her desire to exert a high level of effort to complete a task. This type of individual often has a strong need to achieve and excel in what they do. Ambitious, this leader demonstrates high energy levels in his or her endless persistence in all activities. Furthermore, a person who has this drive frequently shows a willingness to take initiative. Leaders have a clear *desire to influence others*. Oftentimes, this desire to lead is viewed as a willingness to accept responsibility for a variety of tasks. A leader is also someone who builds trusting relationships with those he or she influences. This is done by being truthful and by showing a high consistency between spoken words and actions. In other words, others are more apt to be influenced by someone whom they view as *honest and having high moral character*.

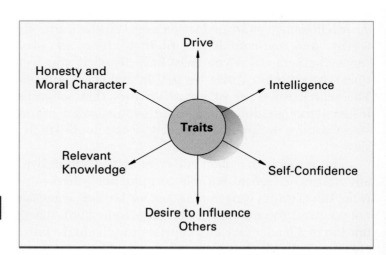

**EXHIBIT 10–1**

Six traits of effective leaders.

---

[2]S. A. Kirkpatrick and E. A. Locke, "Leadership: Do Traits Matter?" *Academy of Management Executive*, May 1991, pp. 48–60.

What traits characterize supervisory leaders? Research has identified six: drive, the desire to lead, honesty and integrity, self-confidence, intelligence, and job-related knowledge.

A person who leads is also someone who shows *self-confidence* in order to convince others of the correctness of goals and decisions. Employees, it has been shown, prefer to be influenced by individuals who are free of self-doubt. In other words, they are influenced more by a supervisor who has a strong belief as opposed to one who frequently waffles on decisions made. Influencing others requires a level of *intelligence*, too. To successfully influence others, one needs to be able to gather, synthesize, and interpret a lot of information. He or she must also be able to create a vision (a plan), communicate it in such a way that others understand it, solve problems, and make good decisions. Many of these "intelligence" requirements come from education and experience. Finally, an effective leader is someone who has a high degree of *relevant knowledge* about the department and the unit's employees. This in-depth knowledge assists the supervisor in making well-informed decisions, as well as understanding the implications those decisions have on others in the department.

## CAN YOU SEE THESE TRAITS THROUGH AN EXAMPLE?

Anyone who has ever watched cable television, seen the Atlanta Braves in a post-season play-off baseball game, or followed the meteoric rise of Turner Network Television, has probably heard the name of Ted Turner. In an American tradition, he is viewed as the epitome of leadership. Let's look at how he earned that reputation.

Each morning he is greeted by a sign on his desk. That sign reads "Either lead, follow, or get out of the way." In Turner's case, it's clear that he's chosen to lead. He has spent his entire adult life with a drive to take one bold risk after another—and succeeded when all the "experts" seemed assured that he'd fail.[3] Ted's ability to see opportunities that others haven't and to boldly "go for the victory" has differentiated him from many of his peers. He took over his family's nearly bankrupt billboard business in 1963 when he was twenty-four years old. Through his vision and "business smarts," he turned the company around in a few short years. He bought a small independent television station in Atlanta and confidently dubbed it the Super-Station. Building on his knowledge of the media and entertainment industries, he and his employees combined new satellite transmission technology with the unexploited cable television market. A year later he purchased the Atlanta Braves baseball team, then perennial losers, so that he'd have something to televise on his station besides old reruns of "Leave It to Beaver" and "Father Knows Best." Turner gambled everything when he ventured into a 24-hour news station. Although his critics laughed at his unconventional idea, it's Ted who's laughing now with the success of the highly praised Cable News Network (CNN). He proved them wrong again when he bought the rights to classic movies—colorizing them and showing them on his newly created Turner Network Television. In the end, Turner Broadcasting (his SuperStation vision) became a runaway media and entertainment success, and a sought-after merger partner, as it developed into an $8 billion empire.[4] Oh yes, the Braves have been perennial players in baseball playoffs since 1991—finally winning the World Series in 1995.

**Charismatic leader**
an individual with a compelling vision or sense of purpose, an ability to communicate that vision in clear terms that followers can understand, a demonstrated consistency and focus in pursuit of his or her vision, and an understanding of his or her own strengths.

## What Is this Thing Called Charisma?

What do people like Mary Kay Ash, Hillary Rodham Clinton, Michael Jordan, and Howard Stern have in common? They all have something in their personality construct that's called *charisma*. Charisma is a magnetism that inspires followers to go the "extra mile" to reach goals that are perceived as difficult or unpopular. Being charismatic, however, is not attributed to a single factor. Instead, it too, evolves from one's possession of several characteristics.[5]

Over the past two decades, several authors have attempted to identify those personal characteristics associated with the **charismatic leader.** Some of the earlier writings focused on such attributes as confidence level,

[3]See for example, S. N. Chakravarty, "What New Worlds To Conquer?" *Forbes*, January 1993, pp. 82-87.

[4]S. Bing, "The Smartest and Dumbest Moves of 1995," *Fortune*, January 15, 1996, p. 84; and "Ted Turner Emerges in a Different Light," *U.S. News & World Report*, September 11, 1995, pp. 48-51.

[5]See, for example, Patricia Sellers, "What Exactly is Charisma?" *Fortune*, January 15, 1996, p. 68–75.

dominance, and strong convictions in one's beliefs.[6] More charismatic dimensions were added when Warren Bennis, after studying ninety of the most effective and successful leaders in the United States, found that they had four common competencies. These included the individual's compelling vision or sense of purpose; an ability to communicate that vision in clear terms that their followers could readily understand; a demonstrated consistency and focus in the pursuit of their vision; and an understanding of their own strengths.[7] The most recent and comprehensive analysis, however, has been completed by two researchers from McGill University in Canada.[8] Among their conclusions (see Exhibit 10–2), they propose that charismatic leaders have an idealized goal that they want to achieve, and are able to communicate it to others in a way that they can understand. That goal, however, is something much different from the "status quo." It's a better "state" for the future, something that will significantly improve the way things are. Of course, the charismatic leader has a strong personal commitment to achieving that goal. This leadership trait also includes behaving in a way that is viewed as unconventional, or at best, out of the ordinary. That is, a charismatic leader often does things that come as a surprise to the followers. Herb Kelleher, CEO of Southwest Airlines, typifies this outrageous behavior. For instance, he's been known to appear in public dressed as the Easter Bunny. If that seems tame, consider the unconventional nature of his public address. At a speech at an exclusive Manhattan hotel delivered to members of a professional aviation group, for example, Kelleher began his talk by addressing two of the things he's proudest of. First, he said, he's "good at projectile vomiting." Naturally, his

The founder of Southwest Airlines, Herb Kelleher, provides the enthusiastic leadership that has made Southwest the only consistently profitable U.S. airline. His charisma has been widely appreciated by his employees.

[6]R. J. House, "A 1976 Theory of Charismatic Leadership," in J. G. Hunt and L. L. Larson, eds., *Leadership: The Cutting Edge* (Carbondale, IL: Southern Illinois University Press, 1977), pp. 189–207.

[7]W. Bennis, "The 4 Competencies of Leadership," *Training and Development Journal*, August 1984, pp. 15–19; see also Marshall Loeb, "Where Leaders Come From," *Fortune*, September 19, 1994, p. 241.

[8]J. C. Conger and R. N. Kanungo, "Behavioral Dimensions of Charismatic Leadership," in J. A. Conger, R. N. Kanungo and Associates, *Charismatic Leadership* (San Francisco, CA: Jossey-Bass, 1988), p. 79.

## EXHIBIT 10–2

Key characteristics of charismatic leaders. (*Source:* Conger, Jay A. and Kanungo, Rabindra N. "Behavioral Dimensions of Charasmatic Leadership," adaption as submitted of Table 1, p. 91. In J.A. Conger, R.N. Kanungo, and Associates, *Charasmatic Leadership: The Elusive Factor in Organizational Effectiveness.* Copyright 1988 Jossey-Bass Inc., Publishers.)

1. **Idealized goal.** Charismatic leaders have vision that proposes a future better than the status quo. The greater the disparity between this idealized goal and the status quo, the more likely that followers will attribute extraordinary vision to the leader.

2. **Ability to help others understand the goal.** They are able to clarify and state the vision in terms that are understandable to others. This explanation demonstrates an understanding of the followers' needs and, acts as a motivating force.

3. **Strong convictions about their goal.** Charismatic leaders are perceived as being strongly committed, and willing to take on high personal risk, incur high costs, and engage in self-sacrifice to achieve their vision.

4. **Behavior that is unconventional.** They engage in behavior that is perceived as being novel, out of the ordinary, and counter to norms. When successful, these behaviors evoke surprise and admiration in followers.

5. **Assertive and self-confident.** Charismatic leaders have complete confidence in their judgment and ability.

6. **High self-monitoring.** Supervisors who can easily adjust their behavior to different situations.

7. **Appearance as a change agent.** They are perceived as agents of radical change rather than as caretakers of the status quo.

second momentous event was the fact that he's "never had a really serious venereal disease."[9] Not your typical start to a state-of-the-business speech!

A charismatic leader is also assertive and self-confident. As previously noted, it is not surprising that a charismatic leader would have these traits. The individual's personal conviction and ability to convince others that he or she is leading them in the right direction provide followers with a sense that the leader knows best. After all, how many employees of a major airline would dare exhibit many of the "clowning antics" of their counterparts at Southwest? Few, unless their CEO, like Kelleher, believes that workers will be more productive in a "fun-filled" work environment.

In Chapter 9, we introduced the personality dimension called self-monitoring. As you'll recall, we described high self-monitors as individuals who can easily adjust their behavior to different situations. They can read verbal and nonverbal social cues and alter their behavior accordingly. This ability to be a "good actor" has been found to be associated with charismatic leadership (see Assessing Yourself). Because high self-monitors can accurately read a situation, understand the feelings of employees, and then exhibit behaviors that match employees' expectations, they tend to emerge as effective, and charismatic supervisors.[10]

[9]K. Labich, "Herb Kelleher: America's Best CEO," *Fortune,* May 2, 1994, p. 45.

[10]G. H. Dobbins and others, "The Role of Self-Monitoring and Gender on Leader Emergence: A Laboratory and Field Study," *Journal of Management,* September 1990, pp. 609–618.

## PROJECTING CHARISMA

Indicate the degree to which you think the following statements are true or false by circling the appropriate number; for example, if a statement is always true, you would circle the 5 next to that statement.

5 = Certainly, always true
4 = Generally true
3 = Somewhat true, but with exceptions
2 = Somewhat false, but with exceptions
1 = Generally false
0 = Certainly, always false

1. In social situations, I have the ability to alter my behavior if I feel that something else is called for.                     5    4    3    2    1    0

2. I am often able to read people's true emotions correctly through their eyes.        5    4    3    2    1    0

3. I have the ability to control the way I come across to people, depending on the impression I wish to give them.                  5    4    3    2    1    0

4. In conversations, I am sensitive to even the slightest change in the facial expression of the person I'm conversing with.                                      5    4    3    2    1    0

5. My powers of intuition are quite good when it comes to understanding others' emotions and motives.                        5    4    3    2    1    0

6. I can usually tell when others consider a joke in bad taste, even though they may laugh convincingly.                          5    4    3    2    1    0

7. When I feel that the image I am portraying isn't working, I can readily change it to something that does.             5    4    3    2    1    0

8. I can usually tell when I've said something inappropriate by reading the listener's eyes.                              5    4    3    2    1    0

9. I have trouble changing my behavior to suit different people and different situations.                                     5    4    3    2    1    0

*(continued)*

**10.** I have found that I can adjust my behavior to meet the requirements of any situation I find myself in.　　　　5　4　3　2　1　0

**11.** If someone is lying to me, I usually know it at once from that person's manner of expression.　　　　5　4　3　2　1　0

**12.** Even when it might be to my advantage, I have difficulty putting up a good front.　　　　5　4　3　2　1　0

**13.** Once I know what the situation calls for, it's easy for me to regulate my actions accordingly.　　　　5　4　3　2　1　0

## SCORING

This questionnaire measures your self-monitoring score. To obtain your total score, add up the numbers circled, except reverse scores for questions 9 and 12. On those, a circled 5 becomes a 0, 4 becomes 1, and so forth.

## WHAT THE ASSESSMENT MEANS

Scores of approximately 53 or higher indicate a high self-monitor. The lower your score, the greater your rigidity. This questionnaire can provide you with insights into your ability to project charisma. That's because the skill may require you to engage in behaviors that are not natural to you. The higher your score, the easier it should be for you to comfortably and effectively project behaviors associated with charismatic leadership.

Finally, a charismatic leader is often perceived as an agent of radical change. His or her refusal to be satisfied with the status quo means that everything is open for change. In the end, the vision, the conviction, and the unconventional nature of doing things leads to an admiration by the followers—and success for the charismatic leader.

What can be said about the charismatic leader's effect on his or her followers? There is an increasing support that there is a strong link between charismatic leadership and high performance and satisfaction among followers.[11] That is, people working for charismatic leaders are motivated to

[11] R. J. House, J. Woycke, and E. M. Fodor, "Charismatic and Noncharismatic Leaders: Differences in Behavior and Effectiveness," in Conger and Kanungo, *Charismatic Leadership*, pp. 103–104.

exert extra work effort and, because they like their leader, express greater satisfaction.

Although over the years traits of successful leaders have been identified, these traits alone are not adequate for entirely explaining leadership effectiveness. If they were, then leaders could be identified right from birth. While you may have been the natural line leader in kindergarten—exhibiting your influencing abilities at an early age—leading requires more. This is because the problem with focusing solely on traits is that it ignores the skills leaders must have, as well as the behaviors they must demonstrate in a number of situations. Fortunately, these latter two—skills and behaviors—are both learned! Therefore, it is more correct to say that leaders are made.

# HOW DO YOU BECOME A LEADER?

Whether or not you currently hold a formal position of authority over others, you can be in a position where you are able to influence others. Becoming a leader, however, requires certain skills (as well as possessing many of the traits described above). These are technical, conceptual, networking, and human relations skills. You're probably thinking you've heard these before. If you are, congratulations. You're paying close attention. Some of these are the competencies that effective supervisors need—as we discussed in Chapter 1. Because of their importance to leadership, let's look at them again—this time with an eye on leadership!

## WHY DOES A LEADER NEED TECHNICAL SKILLS?

It's a rare occurrence when you can influence others even though you have absolutely no idea of what they are doing. Although people may respect you as a person, when it comes to influencing them, they would like to believe you have the experience to make recommendations. This experience generally comes from your technical skills.

*Technical skills* are those tools, procedures, and techniques that are unique to your specialized situation. You need to "master" your job in your attempt to be viewed as a source of help—the "expert." Others generally won't come to you unless they need assistance. It's often the exceptions that they can't—or are ill-equipped to—handle. That's when they'll look to you for guidance. By having the technical skills, you're able to assist. But imagine if you didn't. You'd constantly have to ask someone else for the information. When you got it, you might be unable to adequately explain it to your employee who has requested it. At some point, employees may simply go around you, and talk directly to the "source" of the technical information. When that happens, you've lost some of your influence!

Pat Lancaster, second from left, demonstrates his leadership skills when he works with his employeees to find better ways to improve their department's production. As a result, their unit—which manufactures machines that wrap large items in plastic—has witnessed better production numbers and higher-quality units produced.

Emphasizing technical skills related to your job cannot be overstated. Those "in the know" do influence others. If you want "followers" to have confidence in your advice and the direction you give, they've got to perceive you as a technically competent supervisor.

## How Do Conceptual Skills Affect Your Leadership?

*Conceptual skills* refer to your mental ability to coordinate a variety of interests and activities. It means having the ability to think in the abstract, analyze lots of information, and make connections between the data. Earlier, we described an effective leader as someone who could create a vision. In order to do this, you must be able to think critically and conceptualize things regarding "how they could be."

Thinking conceptually is not as easy as you may believe. For some, it may be impossible! That's because to think conceptually, you must look at the infamous "big picture." Too many times, we get caught up in the daily grind, focusing our attention on the minute details. Not that focusing on the details isn't important. Without that, little may be accomplished. But setting long-term directions requires you to think about the future. It requires you to deal with the uncertainty and the risks of the unknown. To be a good leader, then, you must be able to make some sense out of this chaos and envision what can be.

# How Do Your Networking Skills Make You a Better Leader?

*Networking skills* refer to your ability to socialize and interact with outsiders—those not associated with your unit. As a leader, it's understood you cannot do everything by yourself. Obviously, if you did, you'd not be a leader, but rather a superworker! Therefore, you need to know where to go to get the things your followers need. This may mean "fighting" for more resources or establishing relationships outside of your area that will provide some benefit to your followers. Networking, if you're making the connection, means having good political skills. That's a point that shouldn't be overlooked.

Your employees will often look to you to provide them what they need to do an excellent job. If they can depend on you for providing them the tools (or running the interference they need), then you'll once again inspire a level of confidence in your employees. Your employees, too, will more likely respond better if they know you're willing to fight for them. Instead of finding 100 reasons why they can't do something, together you find one way that something different can be tried. You somehow muster the necessary resources and defend what "your people" are doing. In challenging employees to go beyond what they think they are capable of achieving, however, you know that mistakes will be made. When they are, you view them as a learning experience—and something from which to grow.

# What Role Do Human Relations Skills Play in Leadership?

*Human relation skills* focus on your ability to work with, understand, and motivate those around you. As you've been reading this book, these skills have been highlighted. Good human relations skills require you to be able to effectively communicate—especially your vision—with your employees and those outside of your unit. It also means listening to what they have to say. For a good leader is not a "know it all," but rather someone who freely accepts, and encourages involvement from his or her followers.

Human relations skills are those "people skills" that are frequently mentioned in today's discussion of effective supervision. It's the coaching, the facilitating, and supporting of others around you.[12] It's understanding yourself, and being confident in your abilities. It's your honesty in dealing with others and the values you live by. It's your confidence in knowing that by helping others succeed—and letting them get the credit—you're doing the right thing for them, the organization, and yourself. There's one aspect

---

[12]See, for example, S. Camminiti, "What Team Leaders Need To Know," *Fortune*, February 20, 1995, pp. 93-100.

that's almost a guarantee with respect to leadership. That is, if you fail as a leader, it most likely won't be because you lack technical skills. Rather, it's more likely that your followers, as well as others, have lost respect for you because of your lack of human relations skills. If that ever happens, your ability to influence others will be seriously impaired.

One of the interesting aspects of leadership is that traits and skills are difficult to detect by followers. As a result, they define your leadership by the behaviors they see in you. As the adage goes, "actions speak louder than words." It's what you do that matters. Therefore, you need to understand leadership behaviors.

## LEADERSHIP BEHAVIORS AND STYLES

The inability to explain leadership solely from traits and skills has led researchers to look at the behaviors and styles that specific leaders exhibited. Researchers wondered whether there was something unique in the behavior of effective leaders, and the style in which they practiced their "craft." For example, do leaders tend to be more participative than autocratic?

A number of studies looked at behavioral styles. The most comprehensive and replicated of the behavioral theories resulted from research that began at Ohio State University in the late 1940s.[13] This study (as well as others) sought to identify independent dimensions of leader behavior. Beginning with more than 1000 dimensions, they eventually narrowed the list down to two categories that accounted for most of the leadership behavior described by employees. These are best identified as task-centered, and employee-centered behaviors (see Exhibit 10–3).[14]

### WHAT IS TASK-CENTERED BEHAVIOR?

**Task-centered leader** an individual with a strong tendency to emphasize the technical or task aspects of a job.

**A task-centered leader** is an individual who has a strong tendency to emphasize the technical or task aspects of the job. This individual's major concern is ensuring that employees know precisely what is expected of them and providing any guidance necessary for goals to be met. Employees, as viewed by this leader, are a means to an end. That is, in order to achieve goals, employees have to do their jobs. As long as they do what is expected, this leader is happy.

[13]R. M. Stogdill and A. E. Coons, eds., *Leader Behavior: Its Description and Measurement*, Research Monograph No. 88 (Columbus, OH: Ohio State University, Bureau of Business Research, 1951).

[14]Ibid, and R. Kahn and D. Katz, "Leadership Practices in Relation to Productivity and Morale," in D. Cartwright and A. Zander, eds., *Group Dynamics: Research and Theory*, 2nd ed. (Elmsford, NY: Row, Paterson, 1960).

EXHIBIT 10–3

Supervisory leadership behaviors.

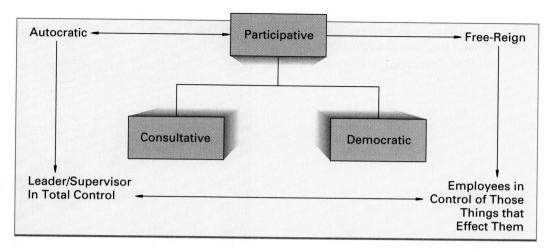

Calling a production-oriented person a leader may be somewhat of a misnomer. This individual may not lead in the classic sense, but simply ensures compliance with stated rules, regulations, and production goals. In motivational terms, a production-oriented leader is someone who frequently exhibits a Theory X orientation (see Chapter 9) or autocratic/authoritarian leadership style.

An **autocratic leader** is someone who can best be described as a task master. This individual leaves no doubt as to who's in charge, and who has the authority and power in the group. He or she makes all the decisions affecting the group and tells others what to do. This telling frequently happens in the form of orders—mandates that are expected to be followed. Failure to "obey" these orders usually results in some negative reinforcement at the hands of the authoritarian leader.

Obviously autocratic leadership is inappropriate in today's organization. Right? Well, maybe not. There are leaders in all types of organizations—business, government, and the military—that have found the autocratic style to work best.

**Autocratic leader**
a task master who leaves no doubt as to who's in charge, and who has the authority and power in the group.

## WHAT ARE PEOPLE-CENTERED BEHAVIORS?

A **people-centered leader** is someone who emphasizes interpersonal relations with those they lead. This leader takes a personal interest in the needs of his or her employees. A people-centered leader is concerned for employees' welfare. Interactions between this leader and his or her employees are characterized as trusting, friendly, and supportive. Furthermore, this leader is very sensitive to the concerns and feelings of

**People-centered leader**
an individual who emphasizes interpersonal relations with those he or she leads.

Would Indiana University basketball coach Bobby Knight's leadership style be effective in all situations? Although he's found success in using his task-centered style for winning basketball games, that doesn't imply that it would work elsewhere.

**Participative leadership**
the leadership style of an individual who actively seeks input from followers for many of the activities in the organization.

**Consultative participative leadership**
the leadership style of an individual who seeks input, hears the concerns and issues of the followers, but makes the final decision him- or herself, using input as an information-seeking exercise.

**Democratic participative leadership**
a leadership style that allows followers to have a say in what's decided.

**Free-reign leader**
an individual who gives employees total autonomy to make decisions that will affect them.

employees. Likewise, from a motivational point of view, a people-centered leader is one who exhibits more Theory Y (see Chapter 9) orientations. As a result, this individual often exhibits a *participative* (or democratic) *leadership* style.

A **participative leadership** style is one where input from followers is actively sought for many of the activities in the organization. This would mean that establishing plans, solving problems, and making decisions is not done solely by the supervisor. Instead, the entire work group participates. The only question that really remains is who has the final say. That is, participative leadership can be viewed from two perspectives. First is one where the leader seeks input, hears the concerns and issues of the followers, but makes the final decision him or herself. In this capacity, the leader is using the input as an information-seeking exercise. We call this **consultative-participative leadership.** On the other hand, a participative leader may allow the followers to have a "say" in what's decided. Here, decisions are made truly by the group. This is referred to as **democratic-participative leadership.**

Beyond participative leadership, there is one other behavioral leadership style. This is often referred to as free-reigning. A **free-reign** (or laissez-faire) **leader** is someone who gives employees total autonomy to make the decisions that will affect them. After establishing overall objectives and general guidelines, the employees are free to establish their own plans for achieving their goals. This is not meant to imply that there's a lack of leadership. Rather, it implies that the leader is removed from the day to day activities of the employees—but is always available to deal with the exceptions.

## POP QUIZ   (Are You Comprehending What You're Reading?)

1. Which one of the following statements about leadership is false?
   a. Sometimes formal leadership is irrelevant.
   b. All supervisors should be leaders.
   c. Leadership is the ability to influence others.
   d. All leaders should be supervisors.
2. Summarize the conclusions of trait theories of leadership.
3. A supervisor who gets input from his or her staff but makes the decision him- or herself would be classified as a democratic-participative leader. True or False?
4. Which one of the following characteristics is not associated with a supervisor who is regarded as a charismatic leader?
   a. A strong reliance on the authority of his or her position in the organization to influence others.
   b. A future vision of the organization.
   c. A strong commitment to the status quo.
   d. An agent of radical change.

## WHAT BEHAVIOR SHOULD YOU EXHIBIT?

In today's organizations, many employees appear to prefer to work for a supervisor with a people-centered leadership style. However, just because this style appears "friendlier" to employees, we cannot make a sweeping generalization that a people-centered leadership style will make you a more effective supervisor. There has actually been very little success in identifying consistent relationships between patterns of leadership behavior and successful organizational performance. Results vary. In some cases people-centered styles generate both high productivity and high follower satisfaction. However, in others, followers are happy, but productivity suffers. What sometimes is overlooked in trying to pinpoint one style over the other are the situational factors that influence effective leadership.

## EFFECTIVE LEADERSHIP

It became increasingly clear to those studying leadership that predicting leadership success involved something more complex than isolating a few traits or preferable behaviors. The failure to find answers led to a new focus on situational influences. The relationship between leadership style and effectiveness suggested that under condition *a*, style *X* would be appropriate, whereas style *Y* would be more suitable for condition *b*, and style *Z* for condition *c*. But what were the conditions *a*, *b*, *c*, and so forth? It was one thing to say that leadership effectiveness depended on the situation and another to be able to isolate those situational conditions. The key to many of these situational theories was their inclusion of followers.

## WHAT ARE THE KEY SITUATIONAL MODELS OF LEADERSHIP?

Several approaches to isolating key situational variables have proven more successful than others and, as a result, have gained wider recognition.[15] The first comprehensive model, developed by University of Washington Professor, Fred Fiedler, proposed that effective leadership is a function of a proper match between the leader's style of interacting with followers and the degree to which the situation gives control and influence to the leader.[16] According to Fiedler, a leader's style could be identified based on how the leader describes an individual he or she least enjoys working with. When a leader describes this person in favorable terms, this indicates that the leader is interested in good relationships. Accordingly, that leader's style would tend to be more people-centered. On the other hand, describing this least-preferred individual in unfavorable terms indicates more of a task-centered style. Fiedler felt that one's style is fixed. Using three situational factors (degree of respect for employees; structured jobs; and influence over the employment process) he identified eight situations where either the task- or people-centered styles would work best. That is, these situational factors would dictate which leadership style would be more effective (see Exhibit 10–4).

One of the more respected approaches to situational leadership was developed by Robert House. It is called the **path-goal theory** of leadership.[17] The basis of this model is that it is the leader's job to assist his or her followers in attaining their goals. This is done by providing the necessary direction and/or support to ensure that their goals are compatible

**Path-goal theory** the leader's job is to assist followers in overcoming obstacles in the way of attaining the goals by promoting the proper leadership style.

---

[15]For a good review of the Fielder Contingency Model, Path-Goal Theory, and Leader-Participation Model, see S. P. Robbins and D. A. De Cenzo, *Fundamentals of Management* (Englewood Cliffs, NJ: Prentice-Hall, Inc., 1995), pp. 300-306.

[16]F. E. Fiedler, *A Theory of Leadership Effectiveness* (New York, NY: McGraw-Hill, 1967).

[17]R. J. House and T. R. Mitchell, "Path-Goal Theory of Leadership," *Journal of Contemporary Business*, Autumn 1974, pp. 81-97.

# EXHIBIT 10-4

Fiedler's leadership findings.

| Situational Factors | I | II | III | IV | V | VI | VII | VIII |
|---|---|---|---|---|---|---|---|---|
| **Respect for Followers** | Good | Good | Good | Good | Poor | Poor | Poor | Poor |
| **Structured Jobs** | High | High | Low | Low | High | High | Low | Low |
| **Influence Over Employment Process** | Strong | Weak | Strong | Weak | Strong | Weak | Strong | Weak |
| **Preferred Leader Behavior** | Task | Task | Task | People | People | People | Task | Task |

Centered Behavior

with the overall objectives of the group or organization. The leader clarifies the path to help employees get from where they are to a point where they've achieved their goals—assisting them also by reducing potential roadblocks and pitfalls.

A few examples will illustrate how you can use the path-goal approach. If your employees have considerable experience and perceive themselves to have the ability to do their jobs, they don't need task-centered leadership. They know how to do their work, so people-centered leadership is appropriate. In contrast, new employees, those lacking confidence in their abilities, or those who are insecure will appreciate the help provided through task-centered leadership. Similarly, when an employee's job is unstructured and ambiguous, a task approach to leadership is appreciated. But if the employee has clear job goals, structured tasks, and a supportive work group that provides assistance, task-centered leadership will be seen as at least redundant and may even be perceived as overbearing and controlling.

In summary, path-goal theory demonstrates that employees are likely to be most productive and satisfied when their supervisor compensates for things lacking in either the employee or the work setting. However, the supervisor who spends time explaining tasks when those tasks are already clear or when the employee has the ability and experience to handle them without interference is likely to be ineffective. The employee will see this behavior as redundant or even insulting. The fundamental issue, then, is to adjust your style to the needs of your employees.

# How Can You Apply Situational Leadership?

**Situational leadership**
adjustment of a leadership style to specific situations to reflect employee needs.

**Readiness**
the ability and willingness of an employee to complete a task.

One model of leadership that has been getting much attention lately was proposed several years ago by Paul Hersey and Kenneth Blanchard. Called **situational leadership,** their emphasis on leadership focuses on leadership styles that adjust to specific situations.[18] Specifically, given that without employees there is no leader, situational leadership shows how you should adjust your leadership style to reflect employees' needs. That seemingly makes sense, and is being encouraged today in such organizations as Xerox, BankAmerica, and the military.[19]

Although similar in nature to Fiedler's theory, there are a couple of differences worth noting. First, situational leadership places much attention on what is called the **readiness** of employees. Readiness in this context reflects how able and willing an employee is to do a job. Hersey and Blanchard have identified four stages of follower readiness. These are:

R1: An employee is both unable and unwilling to do a job.
R2: An employee is unable to do the job, but willing to perform the necessary tasks.
R3: An employee is able to do the job, but unwilling to be told by a leader what to do.
R4: An employee is both able and willing to do the job.

A point should be made here concerning willingness. As defined, for example, in R1, an employee is unwilling to do something. This is not the same unwillingness that you would associate with being insubordinate. Rather, it's an unwillingness because that individual is not confident nor competent enough to do a job. You'll see how this works in a moment.

A second component of the model focuses on what you do as a leader. Given where an employee is in terms of readiness level, you'll exhibit a certain behavior. Behavior in this model is best reflective of the type of communications taking place. That is, task behavior can be seen as one-way communications—from you to an employee. Relationship behavior, on the other hand, reflects two-way communications—between you and the employee. Given that there are high and low degrees of these two behaviors that can exist, Hersey and Blanchard identified four specific leadership styles based on the maturity of the follower. Let's see how this model works

---

[18]P. Hersey and K. H. Blanchard, *Management of Organizational Behavior: Utilizing Human Resources,* 5th ed. (Englewood Cliffs, NJ: Prentice-Hall, Inc., 1988).

[19]Ibid., p. 171. For those who wish to look at both sides of the debate on the validity of situational leadership, you are encouraged to read W. R. Norris and R. P Vecchio, "Situational Leadership Theory: A Replication," *Group and Organization Management,* September 1992, pp. 331-342; and W. Blank, J. R. Weitzel, and S. G. Green, "A Test of the Situational Leadership Theory," *Personnel Psychology,* Autumn 1990, pp. 579-597.

by going through an example of a new employee in your department—and her first day on the job (see Exhibit 10–5).

When this employee first arrives at work, she is anxious. She's uncertain about what she is getting into and how to handle the job responsibilities. You feel that the employment process worked well in properly matching her to the job and orienting her to the organization. Now it's time to start what she was hired to do. Imagine if you were to just assign a list of tasks for her to complete and walk away! She would probably have some difficulty. Why? Because at this time, she's not ready (R1). It's doubtful she even knows the right questions to ask. Communications between you and the employee, at this point, need to be one-way. You need to tell her what to do and give her specific directions on how to do it. According to situational leadership, at this stage, you are using a *telling* style of leadership. But this new employee won't stay at R1 forever. After having been provided with ample directions and getting more familiar with the job, she's moving to stage R2.

At the R2 stage of work development, the employee is becoming more involved in her job, but she still lacks some ability. She's not fully trained as yet. She's asking questions about things she may not fully understand. She may question why certain things have to be done as you have asked. Accordingly, you may need to *sell* her on some of your ideas to get this employee to accept what you feel is necessary. At this point, high degrees of both one-way and two-way communications are happening simultaneously.

At some later point, this employee has become the expert on her job (R3). She knows her duties better than anybody, and she's beginning to put her special mark on things. You no longer need to tell her what to do, but

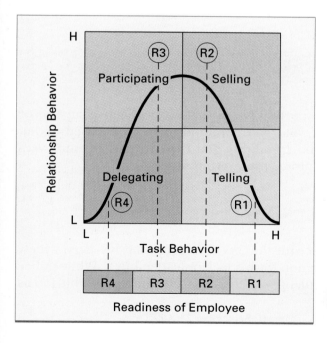

**EXHIBIT 10–5**

Situational leadership.

the reality is, you still need to be involved in what she's doing. She's just not to the point as yet where you feel comfortable leaving her totally alone. That's not an insult. It's just that you recognize that this employee still has some developing to do. Accordingly, you will best deal with this situation by being supportive of her and not being overly task-centered. Hersey and Blanchard refer to this as a *participating* style of leadership.

Finally, this employee has fully developed. She has your trust and can carry out her duties with little, if any, direction (R4). In this situation, she basically needs to be left alone. At this *delegating* stage of leadership, you simply assign the tasks and let her do her job. You now know—based on your appraisal of her performance—that she can and will get the job done. If she needs help, you're always available to deal with the exceptions.

An important aspect of situational leadership is that an employee can be in all four quadrants at the same time. To lead properly, you must be able to exhibit the correct leadership style given what each employee needs. If a seasoned employee is in stage R4, and gets a new assignment, you cannot assume that this employee is automatically at R4 for the new tasks. That simply may not be true. In fact, the employee may need to be clearly directed—and that implies a telling style of leadership. If that doesn't occur, problems may arise. On the other hand, if an employee has been at R4 for some time, and gets some additional assignments that require a telling style, problems will arise if that individual is treated like an R1 employee on all aspects of his or her job. All of a sudden, the employee is being told how to do what he or she has been doing for many months or years. That can have the effect of implying that you perceive the employee as not doing the job properly— which isn't true! The point is, you need to demonstrate a leadership style that's consistent with your employees' abilities (see News Flash).

## CONTEMPORARY LEADERSHIP ROLES

Let's turn our attention to important issues that every effective supervisor in the 1990s and beyond is, and will continue to be, concerned about. Specifically, how do you build credibility and trust with your employees and, how can you become a more empowering supervisor?

### DO CREDIBILITY AND TRUST REALLY MATTER?

Willie Williams, Chief of Police for the City of Los Angeles, has been widely criticized within his organization for his lack of leadership.[21] While police officers acknowledge the challenges Williams faced coming into his job as

[21]Based on a CBS "60 Minutes" segment, September 24, 1995.

# NATIONAL CULTURE COULD AFFECT YOUR LEADERSHIP STYLE

One general conclusion that surfaces from learning about leadership is that you shouldn't use any single leadership style in every case. Instead, you should adjust your style to the situation. Although not mentioned specifically in any of the theories we've presented, national culture is clearly an important situational variable in determining which leadership style will be most effective for you.

National culture affects leadership by way of your employees. You cannot choose your leadership styles at will. Rather, you are constrained by the cultural conditions your employees come to expect.[20] For example, an autocratic leadership style is more compatible with cultures where power is unequal, such as those found in Arab, Far Eastern, and Latin countries. This cultural "power"

ranking should be a good indicator of employees' willingness to accept participative leadership. Participation is likely to be most effective in cultures where power is more equally distributed—such as those in Norway, Finland, Denmark, and Sweden.

It's important to remember that most leadership theories were developed by North American researchers using North American subjects. The United States, Canada, and Scandinavian countries all rate below average on "power" criterion. This realization may help explain why our theories tend to favor more participative and empowering styles of leadership. Accordingly, you need to consider national culture as yet another contingency variable in determining your most effective leadership style.

[20]G. Hofstede, "Motivation, Leadership, and Organization: Do American Theories Apply Abroad?" *Organizational Dynamics* (Summer 1980), p. 57; and A. Ede, "Leadership and Decision Making: Management Styles and Culture," *Journal of Managerial Psychology* (July 1992), pp. 28–31.

an outsider—previously he was Chief of Police in Philadelphia—and his success at reducing crime, they claim he has lost their trust. "He lied and that's unforgivable," said one police officer. The main issue in question is whether Williams and his wife accepted free room and gratuities while staying in Las Vegas. He first denied the charge, then changed his story. As another officer put it, "I don't care if he got freebies or not. That's not the issue. The issue is he lied about it!" What lesson is there in the Willie

Williams story? The primary issue is that followers want leaders who are credible and whom they can trust. But what do these terms—*credibility* and *trust*—really mean?

## WHAT ARE CREDIBILITY AND TRUST?

The most dominant component of *credibility* is honesty. "Honesty is absolutely essential to leadership. If people are going to follow someone willingly, whether it be into battle or on the shop floor, they first want to assure themselves that the person is worthy of their trust."[22] In addition to honesty, credible supervisors have been found to be competent and inspiring. That is, they're capable and able to effectively communicate their confidence and enthusiasm to their employees. Employees judge their supervisors' **credibility** in terms of their honesty, competence, and ability to inspire.

Trust is so closely linked with the concept of credibility that the two terms are frequently used interchangeably. For instance, "The credibility check can reliably be simplified to just one question: Do I trust this person?"[23]

We define **trust** as the belief in the integrity, character, and ability of a leader. When employees trust their supervisor, they're willing to be vulnerable to their supervisor's actions because they're confident that their rights and interests won't be abused.[24] Recent evidence has identified five dimensions that underlie the concept of trust.[25] These include *integrity, competence, consistency, loyalty,* and *openness* (see Exhibit 10–6).

## WHY ARE CREDIBILITY AND TRUST IMPORTANT?

The top-rating of honesty as an identifying characteristic of admired supervisors indicates the importance of credibility and trust to leadership effectiveness.[26] This has probably always been true. However, recent changes in the workplace have reignited interest and concern with supervisors building trust.

The trend toward empowering employees and creating work teams has reduced or removed many of the traditional control mechanisms used to monitor employees.[27] For instance, employees are increasingly free to

**Credibility**
supervisory qualities of honesty, competence, and the ability to inspire.

**Trust**
the belief in the integrity, character, and ability of a leader.

---

[22]Ibid.

[23]Ibid., p. 37.

[24]Based on L. T. Hosmer, "Trust: The Connecting Link Between Organizational Theory and Philosophical Ethics," *Academy of Management Review*, April 1995, p. 393; and R. C. Mayer, J. H. Davis, and F. D. Shoorman, "An Integrative Model of Organizational Trust," *Academy of Management Review*, July 1995, p. 712.

[25]P. L. Schindler and C. C. Thomas, "The Structure of Interpersonal Trust in the Workplace," *Psychological Reports*, October 1993, pp. 563–573.

[26]T. A. Stewart, "The Nine Dilemmas Leaders Face," *Fortune*, March 18, 1996, p. 113.

[27]See for example, W. H. Miller, "Leadership at a Crossroads," *Industry Week*, August 19, 1996, pp. 43–44.

## EXHIBIT 10–6

Five dimensions of trust. (Source: Modified and reproduced with permission of authors and publishers from Schindler, P. L., & Thomas, C. C. The structure of interpersonal trust in the workplace. *Psychological Reports*, 1993, 73, 563–573 © Psychological Reports 1993.)

- Integrity: Honesty and truthfulness
- Competence: Technical and interpersonal knowledge and skills
- Consistency: Reliability, predictability, and good judgment in handling situations
- Loyalty: Willingness to protect and save face for a person
- Openness: Willingness to share ideas and information freely

schedule their own work, evaluate their own performance, and in some cases, even make their own team hiring decisions. Therefore, trust becomes critical. Employees have to trust supervisors to treat them fairly and supervisors have to trust employees to conscientiously fulfill their responsibilities.

Supervisors are increasingly having to lead others who are not in their direct line of authority—members of project teams, individuals who work for suppliers, customers, and people who represent other organizations through such arrangements as corporate partnerships. These situations don't allow supervisors to fall back on their formal positions to enact compliance. Many of the relationships, in fact, are dynamic. The ability to quickly develop trust may be crucial to the success of such relationships.

How can you build trust? We've listed several suggestions in Building a Supervisory Skill.

## WHAT IF YOU PLAY FAVORITES?

You would think that one way to undermine employees' trust in you would be for you to be seen as someone who plays favorites. In many cases you'd be right. But many supervisors, it appears, do play favorites.[29] That is, they don't treat all their employees in the same manner.

You're likely to have favorite employees who make up your "in" group. You'll have a special relationship with this small group. You'll trust them, give them a lot of your attention, and often give them special privileges. Not surprisingly, they'll perceive themselves as having preferred status. Be aware that this creation of a favored in-group can undermine your credibility, especially among those employees outside this in-group.

---

[29]D. Duchon, S. G. Green, and T. D. Taylor, "Vertical Dyad Linkage: A Longitudinal Assessment of Antecedents, Measures, and Consequences," *Journal of Applied Psychology*, February 1986, pp. 56–60.

## BUILDING TRUST

### ABOUT THE SKILL

Given the importance trust plays in the leadership role today, supervisors should actively seek to build trust among their employees. Here are some suggestions for achieving that goal.[28]

### PRACTICING THE SKILL

1. **Practice openness.** Mistrust comes as much from what people don't know as from what they do know. Openness leads to confidence and trust. Keep people informed, make the criteria on how decisions are made overtly clear, explain the rationale for your decisions, be candid about problems, and fully disclose relevant information.

2. **Be fair.** Before making decisions or taking actions, consider how others will perceive them in terms of objectivity and fairness. Give credit where it's due, be objective and impartial in performance appraisals, and pay attention to equity perceptions in reward distributions.

3. **Speak your feelings.** Supervisors who convey only hard facts come across as cold and distant. By sharing your feelings, others will see you as real and human. They'll know who you are and will increase their respect for you.

4. **Tell the truth.** If honesty is critical to credibility, you must be perceived as someone who tells the truth. Employees are more tolerant of learning something they "don't want to hear" than of finding of out that their leader lied to them.

5. **Show consistency.** Employees want predictability. Mistrust comes from not knowing what to expect. Take the time to think about your values and beliefs. Then let them consistently guide your decisions. When you know your central purpose, your actions will follow accordingly, and you'll project a consistency that earns trust.

6. **Fulfill your promises.** Trust requires that employees believe you're dependable. So you need to ensure that you keep your word. Promises made must be promises kept.

7. **Maintain confidences.** You trust those whom you believe to be discreet and whom you can rely on. Employees feel the same way. If they make themselves vulnerable by telling you something in confidence, they need to feel assured that you won't discuss it with others or betray that confidence. If employees perceive you as someone who leaks personal confidences or someone who can't be depended on, you won't be perceived as trustworthy.

8. **Demonstrate confidence.** Develop the admiration and respect of others by demonstrating technical and professional ability. Pay particular attention to developing and displaying your communication, negotiation, and other interpersonal skills. ∎

---

[28]This skills box is based on F. Bartolome, "Nobody Trusts the Boss Completely—Now What?" *Harvard Business Review,* March-April 1989, pp. 135–142; and J. K. Butler, Jr., "Toward Understanding and Measuring Conditions of Trust: Evolution of a Condition of Trust Inventory," *Journal of Management,* September 1991, pp. 643–663.

Be cautious of this tendency to create favorites in your department. You're human, so you'll naturally find some employees you feel closer to and with whom you'll want to be more open. What you need to think through is whether you want this favoritism to show. When this favored-employee status is granted to someone based on nonperformance criteria—for example, you share similar interests or common personality traits—it is likely to lessen your leadership effectiveness. However, it may have a place when you favor those employees who are high performers. In such cases, you are rewarding a behavior that you want to reinforce. Be careful when you follow this practice. Unless performance measures are objective and widely visible, you may be seen as arbitrary and unfair.

## HOW CAN YOU LEAD THROUGH EMPOWERMENT?

Several times in different sections of this text, we've stated that supervisors are increasingly leading by empowering their employees. Millions of individual employees and teams of employees are making key operating decisions that directly affect their work. They are developing budgets, scheduling workloads, controlling inventories, solving quality problems, evaluating their own performance, and so on—activities that until very recently were viewed exclusively as part of the supervisor's job.

The increased use of empowerment is being driven by two forces. First is the need for quick decisions by those people who are most knowledgeable about the issues. That requires, at times, moving decisions to employee levels. If organizations are to successfully compete in a dynamic global village, they have to be able to make decisions and implement changes quickly. Second is the reality that the downsizing and restructuring of organizations through the mid-1990s left many supervisors with considerably larger spans of control than they had earlier. In order to cope with the demands of an increased workload, supervisors have to empower their people. As a result, they are sharing power and responsibility with their employees.[30] This means their role is to show trust, provide vision, remove performance-blocking barriers, offer encouragement, motivate, and coach employees.[31]

Does this wholesale support of shared leadership appear strange given the attention paid earlier to contingency theories of leadership? If it doesn't, it should. Why? Because empowerment proponents are essentially advocating a noncontingent approach to leadership. That means they claim that empowerment will work anywhere. Such being the case, directive, task-oriented, autocratic leadership is out.

[30]L. Holpp, "Applied Empowerment," *Training*, February 1994, pp. 39–44.
[31]See, for example, R. Wellins and J. Worklan, "The Philadelphia Story," *Training*, March 1994, pp. 93–100.

The problem with this kind of thinking is that the current empowerment movement ignores the extent to which leadership can be shared and the conditions facilitating successful shared leadership. Because of factors such as downsizing, which results in the need for higher-level employee skills, commitment of organizations to continuous training, implementation of continuous improvement programs, and introduction of self managed teams, the need for shared leadership is increasing. But that is not true in all situations. Blanket acceptance of empowerment or any universal approach to leadership is inconsistent with the best and most current evidence we have on leadership.

## LEADERSHIP ISSUES TODAY

We'll finish this chapter by looking at two current debates surrounding leadership. These are differing leadership styles between men and women and the movement from transactional to transformational leadership.

### Do Men and Women Lead Differently?

Are there differences in leadership styles based on gender? Are men more effective leaders or does that honor belong to women? Just asking these questions is certain to evoke emotions on both sides of the debate. Before we attempt to respond to them, let's lay out one important fact. Although we want to know if women and men lead differently, the bottom line is that the two sexes are more alike than different in how they lead.[32] Much of this similarity is based on the fact that leaders, in spite of gender, perform similar activities in influencing others. That's their job, and both sexes do it equally well. This is similar to what can be said of nurses. Although the

---

### SOMETHING TO THINK ABOUT *(and to promote class discussion)*

Go to the library and find two or three recent articles that discuss the issue of gender differences in leadership. Summarize these articles. Then, respond to the following: Do you believe that in today's organizations both masculine and feminine approaches to leadership are equally important? Discuss. Also, explain how the situation one faces may affect one's leadership style.

---

[32]G. N. Powell, *Women and Men in Management*, 2nd ed. (Thousand Oaks, CA: Sage, 1993).

stereotypical nurse is a woman, men are equally effective—and success-ful—in this career choice. However, this is not a perfect picture where everything is the same. There are noted differences.

The most common difference lies in leadership styles. Women have a tendency to lead more so from a democratic style. This implies that they encourage participation of their followers and are willing to share their positional power with others. In addition, women tend to influence others best through their "charisma, expertise, contacts, and their interpersonal skills."[33] Men, on the other hand, tend to use a task-centered leadership style. Their directing of activities and reliance on their positional power to control the organization's activities tend to dominate how they influence others. Surprisingly, even this difference is blurred. All things considered, when a woman leads in a traditionally male-dominated job (like that of a police officer), she tends to lead in a manner that is more task-centered.[34]

Further compounding this issue is the changing role of supervisors in today's organizations. With more emphasis on teams, employee involvement, and interpersonal skills, democratic leadership styles are more in demand. Supervisors need to be more sensitive to their employees' needs,

Are Army leadership styles changing with the times? Previously, drill instructors—primarily men—were typically autocratic leaders. They gave orders and structured recruits' activities from sunrise to bed-time. They emphasized task accomplishment, accepting authority and obeying orders. The "new" Army still focuses on these, but is also taking into consideration factors like sensitivity training—things that are more frequently associated with women's leadership charac-teristics.

[33]S. P. Robbins. *Organizational Behavior: Concepts, Controversies, and Applications,* 7th ed. (Englewood Cliffs, NJ: Prentice-Hall, Inc., 1996), p. 441.
[34]Ibid.

be more open in their communications, and build more trusting relationships. Ironically, many of these are behaviors that women have typically grown up developing.

## WHAT ARE TRANSACTIONAL AND TRANSFORMATIONAL LEADERS?

The second issue is the interest in differentiating transformational leaders from transactional leaders.[35] As you'll see, because transformational leaders are also charismatic, there is some overlap between this topic and the preceding discussion on charismatic traits.

Most of the leadership models address **transactional leaders.** These leaders guide or motivate their employees in the direction of established goals by clarifying role and task requirements. There is another type of leader who inspires followers to transcend their own self-interests for the good of the organization. This leader is capable of having a profound and extraordinary effect on his or her followers. These are called **transformational leaders.** They pay attention to the concerns and developmental needs of employees; they change employees' awareness of issues by helping them to look at old problems in new ways; and they are able to excite, arouse, and inspire followers to put out extra effort to achieve group goals.

Transactional and transformational supervision should not be viewed as opposing approaches to getting things done.[36] Transformational supervision is built on top of transactional supervision. Transformational supervision produces levels of employee effort and performance that go beyond what would occur with a transactional approach alone. Moreover, transformational supervision is more than charisma. "The purely charismatic [leader] may want employees to adopt the charismatic's world view and go no further. The transformational supervisor will attempt to instill in employees the ability to question not only established views but eventually those established by the leader."[37]

The evidence supporting the superiority of transformational supervision over the transactional variety is overwhelmingly impressive. In summary, it indicates that transformational, as compared with transactional, supervision leads to lower turnover rates, higher productivity, and higher employee satisfaction.[38]

**Transactional leaders**
leaders who guide or motivate their employees in the direction of established goals by clarifying role and task requirements.

**Transformational leaders**
leaders who inspire followers to transcend self-interests for the good of the organization and who are capable of having a profound and extraordinary effect on his or her followers.

[35]B. M. Bass, "From Transactional to Transformational Leadership: Learning to Share the Vision," *Organizational Dynamics*, Winter 1990, pp. 19–31.

[36]See, for example, J. Seitzer and B. M. Bass, "Transformational Leadership: Beyond Initiation and Consideration," *Journal of Management*, December 1990, pp. 693–703.

[37]B. J. Avolio and B. M. Bass, "Transformational Leadership: Charisma and Beyond," working paper, School of Management, State University of New York, Binghamton (1995), p. 14.

[38]Bass and Avolio, "Developing Transformational Leadership."

**5.** According to situational leadership, when an employee is both unable and unwilling to perform the duties of his or her job, which supervisory leadership style would work best?

**a.** delegating

**b.** telling

**c.** selling

**d.** participating

**6.** Describe how credibility and trust affect leadership.

**7.** Empowering supervisors share power and responsibility with their employees. True or False?

**8.** Which one of the following statements about gender differences in leadership is correct?

**a.** There are no differences in leadership based on gender.

**b.** Women leaders have a tendency to lead using a directive leadership style.

**c.** Men have a tendency to use a leadership style that encourages participation of their followers.

**d.** None of the above statements about gender differences is correct.

## SUMMARY

After reading this chapter, I can:

1. **Define leadership and describe the difference between a leader and a supervisor.** Leadership is the ability to influence others. The main difference between a leader and a supervisor is that a supervisor is appointed. A supervisor has legitimate power that allows him or her to reward and punish. A supervisor's ability to influence is founded upon the formal authority inherent in his or her position. In contrast, a leader may either be appointed or emerge from within a group. A leader can influence others to perform beyond the actions dictated by formal authority.

2. **Identify the traits that may help you become a successful leader.** Six traits have been found on which leaders differ from nonleaders: drive, the desire to influence others, honesty and moral character, self-confidence, intelligence, and relevant knowledge. Yet, possession of these traits is no guarantee of leadership because they ignore situational factors.

3. **Define charisma and its key components.** Charisma is a magnetism that inspires employees to reach goals that are perceived as difficult or unpopular. Charismatic leaders are self-confident, possess a vision of a better future, have a strong belief in that vision, engage in unconventional behaviors, have a high degree of self-monitoring, and are perceived as agents of radical change.

4. **Differentiate between task-centered and people-centered leadership behaviors.** Task-centered leadership behaviors focus on the technical or task aspects of a job. People-centered leadership behaviors focus on interpersonal relations among the employees.

5. **Identify and describe three types of participative leadership styles.** The three types of participative leadership styles are consultative (seeking input from employees); democratic (giving employees a role in making decisions); and free-reign (giving employees total autonomy to make the decisions that affect them).

6. **Explain situational leadership.** Situational leadership involves adjusting one's leadership style to the readiness level of the employee for a given set of tasks. Given an employee's ability and willingness to do a specific job, a situational leader will use one of four leadership styles—telling, selling, participating, or delegating.

7. **Describe the leadership style differences between men and women.** Although there are some differences, the two are more alike than different in how they lead. The differences that do exist lie in leadership styles. Women tend to rely on charisma, expertise, and interpersonal skills to influence others. Men, on the other hand, tend to use positional power to direct and control organizational activities.

## REVIEWING YOUR KNOWLEDGE

1. "All supervisors should be leaders but, not all leaders should be supervisors." Do you agree or disagree? Support your position.
2. How is intelligence related to leadership?
3. What is charismatic leadership? Why might high self-monitors be more effective leaders? Discuss.

4. What's the difference between a task-centered and a people-centered supervisor? Which one do you believe employees would rather work for? Why? Which one would you prefer to work for? Explain.

5. Compare and contrast consultative, democratic, and free-reign styles of participative leadership.

6. How can supervisors be both flexible and consistent in their leadership styles? Aren't these contradictory? Explain.

7. How could a professor apply situational leadership with students in a classroom setting?

8. If leaders play favorites, is it good or bad for their department's performance? Discuss.

9. "Given the emphasis on caring for employees, women may be more effective supervisors." Do you agree or disagree? Support your position.

# ANSWERS TO THE POP QUIZZES

1. **d. All leaders should be leaders.** Leaders do not have to be supervisors, nor serve in any supervisory capacity whatsoever.

2. Six traits have been found on which leaders differ from nonleaders—drive, the desire to lead, honesty and integrity, self-confidence, intelligence, and job-relevant knowledge. Yet, possession of these traits is no guarantee of leadership because they ignore situational factors.

3. **False.** A supervisor who gets input from his or her staff but makes the decision him or herself would be classified as a consultative-participative leader.

4. **c. A strong commitment to the status quo.** A charismatic supervisor does what is necessary to make changes to move his or her department/organization forward. In doing so, this individual looks beyond the current state of events—the status quo.

5. **b. telling.** The unwillingness and inability to do the job reflects an employee in the R1 stage of readiness. Therefore the telling style of supervisory leadership would be best used.

6. Credibility and trust do influence leadership effectiveness. If employees do not view their supervisor as being honest, competent, consistent, loyal, open, and having the ability to inspire them, they may not have a strong sense of unity—nor a commitment to their jobs or the organization.

7. **True.** Empowering supervisors share power and responsibility with their employees. That's one of the basic concepts of empowering supervisors.

8. **d. None of the above statements about gender differences is correct.** Although men and women do, in some cases, demonstrate similar leadership styles, they are different in their style orientation. Women tend to use a leadership style that encourages participation of their followers. Men, on the other hand, have a tendency to lead using a directive leadership style. ■

## A Class Exercise: Projecting Charisma

The class is to break into pairs. Each member of the pair will practice exhibiting behaviors associated with charismatic leadership.

**Exercise 1:** Student A's task is to "lead" Student B through a new-student orientation to your college. The orientation should last about 10 to 15 minutes. Assume Student B is a new freshman and is unfamiliar with the campus. Remember, Student A should attempt to project himself or herself as charismatic.

**Exercise 2:** Student B's task is to "lead" Student A in a 10-to-15-minute program on how to study more effectively for college exams. Take a few minutes to think about what has worked well for you and assume that Student A is a new freshman and interested in improving his or her study habits. As with the first exercise, Student B should attempt to project himself or herself as charismatic.

When both exercises are complete, each pair should assess how well they did in projecting charisma and how they might improve.

## THINKING CRITICALLY

### CASE 10.A

## Roger Markus at Montreal Insurance Services

Roger Markus is twenty-two years old and will be receiving his B.S. degree in mathematics from Concordia University in Montreal at the end of this semester. He spent the past two summers working for Montreal Insurance Services (MIS), filling in on a number of different jobs while employees took their vacations. He's received and accepted an offer to join MIS as a supervisor in the policy renewal department on a permanent basis upon graduation.

Montreal Insurance Services is a large insurance company. In the headquarters office alone, where Roger will work, there are 11,000 employees. The company believes strongly in the personal development of its employees. This translates into a philosophy, flowing down from senior officials, of trust and respect for all MIS employees.

The job Roger will be assuming requires him to work with and supervise the activities of eighteen policy renewal representatives. The unit's job responsibility is to ensure that renewal notices are sent on current policies, to tabulate any changes in premiums from a standardized table, and to advise the sales division if a policy is to be canceled as a result of nonresponse to renewal notices.

Roger's department is composed of individuals ranging in age from 19 to 62 years of age. The median age is 38. The salary range for policy renewal representatives is $2480 to $3000 per month (in U.S. dollars). Roger will be replacing a long-time MIS employee, Peter

Finch. Peter is retiring after 37 years with MIS, the last 11 spent as the policy renewal supervisor. Because Roger spent a few weeks in Peter's department last summer, he's familiar with Peter's leadership style and knows most of the departmental employees. He anticipates no problems from any of his soon-to-be employees, except, possibly, for Uri Garavich. Uri is well into his forties, has been a policy renewal representative for over 16 years, and as one of the senior members of the department, carries a lot of weight with other employees. It may be important to note that Uri didn't apply for the supervisor's job Roger got. He simply didn't want the formal responsibility of being a supervisor—even though it would have meant about a 15 percent pay raise! He felt the job duties might interfere with his primary outside interest—coaching his son's ice hockey team. Nonetheless, Roger has concluded that his job could prove very difficult without Uri's support.

Roger is determined to get his leadership of the department off on the right foot. As a result, he's been doing a lot of thinking about the qualities of an effective supervisor.

## RESPONDING TO THE CASE

1. What critical factors will affect Roger's success as a leader? Do you believe these factors would be the same if success were defined as group satisfaction rather than group productivity?
2. Do you think that Roger can choose a leadership style? If so, describe the style you think would be most effective for him. If not, why?
3. What suggestions might you make to Roger to help him win the support of Uri Garavich? What factors may be important in determining the leadership style to use with Uri?

## CASE 10.B

### Max Richardson at Pennington Aviation

For a long time Diane Preston has been set on becoming an airplane mechanic. When Diane started working at Pennington Aviation as a mechanic apprentice, she was pleased to be able to start her career so early in life. Some of her friends had already gone on to college, but Diane wasn't particularly interested in going to school, especially if she could land a good job that she liked and that also paid well.

After becoming good friends with her Pennington Aviation supervisor, Max Richardson, Diane learned that she could aim for even higher career goals if she had some college experience. Diane really likes her job and wants to have a career in the airline business. In fact, she has decided to become an airplane mechanics supervisor, overseeing the crucial repairs that make aircraft safe for passengers.

Diane's focus on becoming a supervisor probably has come as a result of the influence of Max Richardson. Max is a very pleasant individual who is highly motivated. He's a natural at his job; he has extensive knowledge about airplane mechanics and is willing to share his expertise with his employees. He's a good teacher, and you can see that he is pleased when his workers can troubleshoot and solve complex problems on their own. Max gives credit to his workers, even when most everyone knows Max deserves the credit himself. Furthermore, Max is honest and trustworthy and gives Diane a lot of encouragement to reach her goals.

## RESPONDING TO THE CASE

1. What makes Max Richardson a good supervisor and a good leader? Identify his traditional and charismatic leadership traits.

2. Discuss Max's leadership style. Is his leadership task- or people-centered? Support your answer.

3. Some say that Max is a "born" leader. If he is, how can Diane possibly think she can go to college to "acquire" the skills she needs to be a good leader? ∎

# 11

# COMMUNICATING EFFECTIVELY

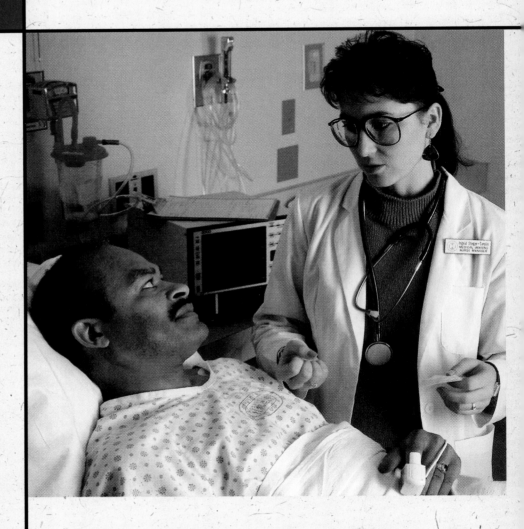

# LEARNING OBJECTIVES 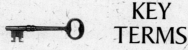 KEY TERMS

After reading this chapter, you should be able to

1. Define communication.
2. Contrast formal and informal communication.
3. Explain how electronic communications affect the supervisor's job.
4. List barriers to effective communication.
5. Describe techniques for overcoming communication barriers.
6. List the essential requirement for active listening.
7. Explain what behaviors are necessary for providing effective feedback.

You should also be able to define these supervisory terms

active listening

assertiveness training

body language

communication

formal communication

grapevine

informal communication

nonverbal communication

richness of information

roles

verbal intonation

# PERFORMING EFFECTIVELY

The following episodes occurred in one eight-hour day at a large Marriott hotel in Atlanta, Georgia.

Episode 1. The supervisor of convention sales, Jan Decker, was reviewing last quarter's sales report in preparation for a performance review with each of her three employees. Concerned particularly about Kim Wong's performance, Jan called Kim into her office.

"Kim, I just saw your last quarter's sales numbers. I thought we had agreed on a goal of six major conventions [1000 or more room nights] for the quarter. Now I'm looking at the data and it says you booked only four. What happened?"

"I don't understand the problem," Kim responded. "Six was our goal, a target. It was something we were trying to reach."

Clearly upset, Jan was trying to control her frustration. "Kim, six was our goal all right. But it wasn't some 'pie-in-the-sky' number. It was the minimum number of bookings we were counting on. You're responsible for getting us the big conventions. Ted and Dawn handle the smaller ones, but you know we rely on the big conventions to keep our occupancy rates up. I told Dave [the hotel's general manager and Jan's immediate boss] we'd book at least six big conventions in the second quarter. Now I've got to explain why we missed our goal!"

Episode 2. A memo had gone out a number of months previously from the hotel's director of human resources to all managers and supervisors. The topic of the memo was a change in the hotel's leave-without-pay pol-

## INTRODUCTION

The three episodes above demonstrate three facts about communication. First, words mean different things to different people. In this instance, to Jan Decker a goal meant a minimum level of attainment, while to Kim Wong it meant a maximum target that one tried to reach. Second, the initiation of a message is no assurance that it is received or understood as intended. Third, communications often become distorted as they are transmitted from person to person. As the marriage rumor illustrates, "facts" in messages can lose much of their accuracy as they are transmitted and translated.

These episodes illustrate potential communication problems for supervisors. The importance of effective communication for supervisors

icy. A complaint from the buyer in the Food and Beverage Department had just been received by the director of human resources. The employee's complaint was that his request for a two-week leave without pay to handle personal and financial problems related to the death of his mother had been denied by his supervisor. He felt his request was reasonable and should have been approved. Interestingly, the memo in question specifically stated that leaves of up to three weeks because of a death in the family were to be uniformly approved. When the human resources director called the Food and Beverage supervisor to follow up on the employee complaint, she was told by the supervisor, "I never knew there was a change of policy on leaves without pay."

Episode 3. The following conversation took place between two accounts payable clerks in the Accounting Department. "Did you hear the latest? The general manager's daughter is marrying some guy from Pittsburgh who's serving a five-year sentence for stealing."

"You're kidding?"

"No, I'm not kidding! I heard it this morning from Chuck in purchasing. Can you imagine the heartache the family must feel?"

This rumor had some basis in fact but was far from accurate. The truth was that, the previous week, the general manager had announced the engagement of his daughter to a football player with the Pittsburgh Steelers who had just signed a new five-year contract. ∎

can't be overemphasized for one specific reason: Everything a supervisor does involves communicating. Not some things, but everything! You can't make a decision without information, and that information has to be communicated. Once a decision is made, communication must again take place. Otherwise, no one will know you've made a decision. The best idea, the most creative suggestion, or the finest plan cannot take form without communication. Supervisors work with their employees, peers, immediate managers, people in other departments, customers, and others to get their own department's objectives accomplished; and the interactions with these various individuals all require communication of some type. The successful supervisor, therefore, needs effective communication skills. We are not suggesting, of course, that good communication skills alone make a successful supervisor. We can say, however, that ineffective communication skills can lead to a continuous stream of problems for the supervisor.

Communication involves the transfer of meaning. If no information or ideas have been conveyed, communication has not taken place. The speaker who is not heard or the writer who is not read does not communicate.

However, for communication to be successful, the meaning must not only be imparted, but also understood. A memo addressed to us in Farsi (a language of which we're totally ignorant), cannot be considered a communication until we have it translated. Therefore, **communication** is the transference and understanding of meaning. Perfect communication, if such a thing were possible, would exist when a transmitted thought or idea is perceived by the receiver exactly the same as it is envisioned by the sender. (See Exhibit 11–1.)

A final point before we move on: Good communication is often erroneously defined by the communicator as "agreement" instead of "clarity of understanding." If someone disagrees with us, many of us assume the person just didn't fully understand our position. In other words, many of us define good communication as having someone accept our views. But a person can understand very clearly what you mean and not agree with what you say. In fact, when a supervisor concludes that a lack of communication must exist because a conflict between two of her employees has continued for a prolonged time, a closer examination often reveals that there is plenty of effective communication going on. Each fully understands the other's position. The problem is one of equating effective communication with agreement.

**Communication**
the transference and understanding of meaning.

## EXHIBIT 11–1
What is communication?

# METHODS OF COMMUNICATION

Supervisors participate in two types of communication. One is **formal communication.** It addresses task-related issues and tends to follow the organization's authority chain. When supervisors give orders to an employee, provide advice to a work team in their department, are offered suggestions by employees, interact with other supervisors on a project, or respond to a request made by their boss, they are engaged in formal communication. Supervisors engage in formal communication through speech, written documents, electronic media, and nonverbal behavior. The other type is **informal communication.** This type of communication moves in any direction, skips authority levels, and is as likely to satisfy social needs as it is to facilitate task accomplishments.

**Formal communication** communication that addresses task-related issues and tends to follow the organization's authority chain.

**Informal communication** communication that moves in any direction, skips authority levels, and is as likely to satisfy social needs as it is to facilitate task accomplishments.

## How Do You Communicate Orally?

As a supervisor, you'll rely heavily on oral communication. Examples are when you meet one-on-one with an employee, give a speech to your department, engage in a problem-solving session with a group of employees, or talk on the phone to a disgruntled customer.

What are the advantages to oral communication? You can transmit information quickly through the spoken word, and oral communications include a nonverbal component which can enhance the message. A phone call, for instance, conveys not only words but tone and mood. Conversation in a one-on-one meeting further includes gestures and facial expressions. Additionally, today's supervisors are becoming increasingly aware that oral communications are not only an effective means for quickly conveying information, but that they have positive symbolic value as well. In contrast to a memo or electronic message, the spoken word is more personal. It conveys more intimacy and caring. As a result, some of the best supervisors rely extensively on oral communication even when the use of written or electronic channels would seem to be as effective. They have found, through experience, that reliance on oral communication tends to build trust with employees and creates a climate of openness and support (see Something to Think About)

## Why Do You Use Written Communication?

When your message is intended to be official, if it has long-term implications, or if it is highly complex, you'll want to convey it in written form. Introducing a new departmental procedure, for instance, should be conveyed in writing so there will be a permanent record to which all employees can refer. Providing a written summary to employees following

Do men and women communicate in the same way? The answer is no! The differences in communication styles between men and women may lead to some interesting insights. When men talk, they do so to emphasize status and independence; whereas women use it to create connections and intimacy. For instance, men frequently complain that women talk on and on about their problems. Women, however, criticize men for not listening. What's happening is that when a man hears a woman talking about a problem, he frequently asserts his desire for independence and control by providing solutions. Many women, in contrast, view conversing about a problem as a means to promote closeness. The woman presents the problem to gain support and connection—not to get the male's advice.

Because effective communication among the sexes is important to all supervisors for meeting departmental goals, how can you manage the diverse differences in communication style? To keep gender differences from becoming persistent barriers to effective communication requires acceptance, understanding, and a commitment to communicate adaptively across gender lines. Both men and women need to acknowledge that there are differences in communication styles, that one style isn't better than the other, and that it takes real effort to "talk" with each other successfully.

What do you think? Do men and women really communicate differently?

performance reviews is a good idea because it helps reduce misunderstandings and creates a formal record of what was discussed. Departmental reports that contain lots of detailed numbers and facts are best conveyed in writing because of their complexity.

The fact that written communications provide better documentation than the spoken word is both a plus and a minus. On the plus side, written documents provide a reliable "paper trail" for decisions or actions that are later called into question. They also reduce ambiguity for recipients. On the negative side, obsessive concern with documenting everything "in writing" leads to risk avoidance, decision paralysis, and creation of a highly politicized work environment. At the extreme, task accomplishment becomes subordinated to writing documents that "cover your rear" and make sure that no one person is held responsible for any questionable decision.

## IS ELECTRONIC COMMUNICATION MORE EFFICIENT?

Computers, microchips, and digitalization are dramatically increasing a supervisor's communication options. Today, you can rely on a number of sophisticated electronic media to carry your communications. These include electronic mail (e-mail), voice mail, electronic paging, cellular telephones, video conferencing, modem-based transmissions, and other forms of network-related communications.

Supervisors are increasingly using many of these technological advances. E-mail and voice-mail allow people to transmit messages twenty-four hours a day. When you're away from your office, others can leave messages for you to review on your return. For important and complex communications, a permanent record of e-mail messages can be obtained by merely printing out a hard copy. Cellular phones are dramatically changing the role of the telephone as a communication device. In the past, telephone numbers were attached to physical locations. Now, with cellular technology, the phone number attaches to mobile phones. You can be in constant contact with your employees, other supervisors, and key members in the organization, regardless of where they are physically located. Network-related communications also allows you to monitor the work of employees whose jobs are done on computers in remote locations, to participate in electronic meetings, and to communicate with suppliers and customers on interorganizational networks.

## HOW DOES NONVERBAL COMMUNICATION AFFECT YOUR COMMUNICATIONS?

Some of the most meaningful communications aren't spoken, written, or transmitted on a computer. These are **nonverbal communications.** A loud siren or a red light at an intersection tells you something without words. When you are conducting a training session, you don't need words to tell you that employees are bored when their eyes get glassy. Similarly, you can tell in an instant by your boss's body language and verbal intonations whether he's angry, upbeat, anxious, or distracted.

**Nonverbal communications** communications that are not spoken, written, or transmitted on a computer.

**Body language** refers to gestures, facial configurations, and other movements of the body. A snarled face, for example, says something different from a smile. Hand motions, facial expressions, and other gestures can communicate emotions or temperaments such as aggression, fear, shyness, arrogance, joy, and anger.

**Body language** gestures, facial configurations, and other movements of the body that communicate emotions or temperaments such as aggression, fear, shyness, arrogance, joy, and anger.

**Verbal intonation** refers to the emphasis someone gives to words or phrases. To illustrate how intonations can change the meaning of a message, consider the supervisor who asks a colleague a question. The colleague replies, "What do you mean by that?" The supervisor's reaction will vary, depending on the tone of the colleague's response. A soft, smooth tone creates a different meaning from one that is abrasive and puts a strong emphasis on the last word. Most of us would view the first intonation as coming from someone who sincerely sought clarification, whereas the second suggests that the person is aggressive or defensive.

**Verbal intonation** the emphasis an individual gives to words or phrases through speech.

The fact that every oral communication also has a nonverbal message cannot be overemphasized. Why? Because the nonverbal component is likely to carry the greatest impact. One study found that 55 percent of an oral message is derived from facial expression and physical posture, 38 percent from verbal intonations, and only 7 percent from the actual words

Words, either written or spoken, don't have to exist for meaning to be transferred. This sign tells you plenty. You know, for instance, that the picture on the lower left indicates the availability of restrooms. Other roadway services, too, are identified without so much as one word being spoken.

used.[1] Most of us know that animals respond to how we say something rather than what we say. Apparently, people aren't much different.

## What Is the Grapevine?

**Grapevine**
the means of communication by which most operative employees first hear about important changes introduced by organizational leaders; rumormill.

The **grapevine** is active in almost all organizations. In fact, studies typically find that the grapevine is the means of communication by which most operative employees first hear about important changes introduced by organizational leaders. It rates ahead of supervisors, official memoranda, and other formal sources.

Is the information that flows along the grapevine accurate? The evidence indicates that about 75 percent of what is carried is accurate.[2] But what conditions foster an active grapevine? What gets the rumor mill rolling?

It is frequently assumed that rumors start because they make titillating gossip. Such is rarely the case. Rumors have at least four purposes: to structure and reduce anxiety; to make sense of limited or fragmented information; to serve as a vehicle to organize group members, and possibly outsiders, into coalitions; and to signal a sender's status (I'm an insider

---

[1]A. Mehrabian, "Communication Without Words," *Psychology Today*, September 1968, pp. 53–55.

[2]K. Davis, cited in R. Rowan, "Where Did that Rumor Come From?" *Fortune*, August 13, 1979, p. 134.

and you're not) or power (I have the power to make you into an insider). Studies have found that rumors emerge as a response to situations that are important to us, where there is ambiguity, and under conditions that arouse anxiety. Work situations frequently contain these three elements, which explains why rumors flourish in organizations. The secrecy and competition that typically prevail in large organizations—around such issues as the appointment of new bosses, the relocation of offices, the realignment of work assignments, and layoffs—create conditions that encourage and sustain rumors on the grapevine. A rumor will persist either until the wants and expectations creating the uncertainty underlying the rumor are fulfilled or until the anxiety is reduced.

What can we conclude from this discussion? Certainly the grapevine is an important part of any group or organization's communication system and well worth understanding. Moreover, it's never going to be eliminated, so supervisors should use it in beneficial ways. Given that only a small set of employees typically passes information to more than one other person, you can analyze grapevine information and predict its flow (see Exhibit 11–2). Certain messages are likely to follow predictable patterns. You might even consider using the grapevine informally to transmit information to specific individuals by planting messages with key people who are active on the grapevine and are likely to find a given message worthy of passing on.

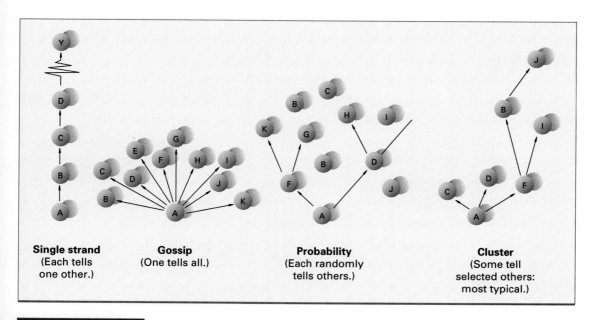

Single strand
(Each tells
one other.)

Gossip
(One tells all.)

Probability
(Each randomly
tells others.)

Cluster
(Some tell
selected others:
most typical.)

## EXHIBIT 11–2

Grapevine patterns. (*Source:* John W. Newstrom and Keith Davis, *Organizational Behavior: Human Behavior at Work,* 9th ed., New York: McGraw-Hill, 1993, p. 445. Reproduced with permission.)

You should not lose sight of the grapevine's value for identifying issues that employees consider important and that create anxiety among them. It acts as both a filter and feedback mechanism, picking up issues that employees consider relevant, and planting messages that employees want passed on to those "running" the organization. For instance, the grapevine can tap employee concerns. If the grapevine is hopping with a rumor of a mass layoff, and if you know the rumor is totally false, the message still has meaning. It reflects the fears and concerns of employees and, hence, should not be ignored.

## BARRIERS TO EFFECTIVE COMMUNICATION

As noted earlier, the goal of perfect communication is to transmit a thought or idea from a sender to a receiver so that it is perceived by the receiver exactly the same as it was envisioned by the sender. That goal is almost never achieved, because of distortions and other barriers. In this section, we want to describe some of the more serious barriers that hinder effective communication (see Exhibit 11–3). In the following section, we'll offer some suggestions for how to overcome these barriers.

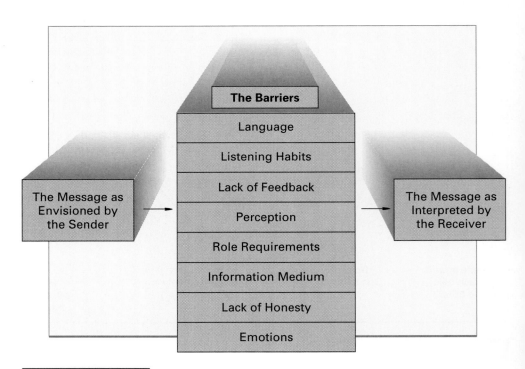

## EXHIBIT 11–3

Barriers to effective communication.

# How Does Language Affect Communications?

Words means different things to different people. Age, education, and cultural background are three of the more obvious variables that influence the language people use and the definitions they give to words. In an organization, employees usually come from diverse backgrounds. Furthermore, horizontal differentiation creates specialists who develop their own jargon or technical language. In large organizations, members are often widely dispersed geographically, and those in each locale will use terms and phrases that are unique to their area. Vertical differentiation can also cause language problems. For instance, differences in the meaning of words such as incentives and quotas occur at different levels of managerial personnel. Senior managers, for example, often speak about the need for incentives and quotas. Yet these terms have been found to imply manipulation and create resentment among supervisors.

The point is that while we may speak the same language (English), our use of that language is far from uniform. A knowledge of how each of us modifies the language would minimize communication difficulties. The problem is that you don't know how your various employees, peers, superiors, customers, and others with whom you interact have modified the language. Senders tend to assume that the words and terms they use mean the same to the receiver as they to do them. This, of course, is often incorrect and, thus, creates communication difficulties.

# What Did You Say?

Most of us hear, but we don't listen! Hearing is merely picking up sound vibrations. Listening is making sense out of what we hear. That is, listening requires paying attention, interpreting, and remembering what is being said.

Most of us are pretty poor listeners (see Assessing Yourself). At this point, it suffices to say that if you don't have good listening skills, you're not going to get the full message as the sender meant to convey it. For example, there are common flaws that many of us share regarding listening. We get distracted and end up hearing only parts of a message. Instead of listening for meaning, we listen to determine whether we agree or disagree with what's being said. We begin thinking about our response to what's being said rather than listening for the complete message. Each of these flaws in our listening habits contributes to messages being received differently from what the sender intended. We'll come back to active listening shortly.

## DO YOU LISTEN ACTIVELY?

Listening is difficult, and it's usually more satisfying to be on the offensive. That is, listening is often more tiring than talking. It demands intellectual effort and concentration. The average person speaks at a rate of about 150 words per minute, whereas we have the capacity to listen at the rate of over 1000 words per minute. The difference leaves idle time for the brain and opportunities for the mind to wander.

For each of the following questions, check the answer that best describes your listening habits.

|  | *Usually* | *Sometimes* | *Seldom* |
|---|---|---|---|
| **1.** I maintain eye contact with the speaker. | ○ | ○ | ○ |
| **2.** I determine whether a speaker's ideas are worthwhile solely by his or her appearance and delivery. | ○ | ○ | ○ |
| **3.** I try to align my thoughts and feelings with those of the speaker. | ○ | ○ | ○ |
| **4.** I listen for specific facts rather than for "the big picture." | ○ | ○ | ○ |
| **5.** I listen for both factual content and the underlying emotion. | ○ | ○ | ○ |
| **6.** I ask questions for clarification and understanding. | ○ | ○ | ○ |

## DID YOU GET MY MESSAGE?

Effective communication means the transference and understanding of meaning. But how do you know if someone has received your message and comprehended it in the way that you meant? The answer is: Use feedback. When you request that each member of your staff submit a specific report, receipt of the report is feedback. Likewise, when your instructor tests you on the material in this book, he or she gets feedback on your understanding of the text material and lectures.

When you fail to use feedback, you never know if the message has been received as intended. Thus, lack of feedback creates the potential for inaccuracies and distortions.

**7.** I withhold judgment of what the speaker is saying until he or she is finished.     ○      ○      ○

**8.** I make a conscious effort to evaluate the logic and consistency of what is being said.     ○      ○      ○

**9.** While listening, I think about what I'm going to say as soon as I have my chance.     ○      ○      ○

**10.** I try to have the last word.     ○      ○      ○

## SCORING

For questions 1, 3, 5, 6, 7, and 8, give yourself 3 points for Usually, 2 points for Sometimes, and 1 point for Seldom. For questions 2, 4, 9, and 10, give yourself three points for Seldom, 2 points for Sometimes, and 1 point for Usually. Sum up your total points.

## WHAT THE ASSESSMENT MEANS

A score of 27 or higher means you're a good listener. A score of 22 to 26 suggests you have some listening deficiencies. A score below 22 indicates that you have developed a number of bad listening habits.

## Do You See What I See?

Your attitudes, interests, past experiences, and expectations determine how you organize and interpret your surroundings. This explains how you can look at the same thing as someone else and perceive it differently (see Exhibit 11–4). In the communication process, the receiver selectively sees and hears messages based on his or her background and personal characteristics. The receiver also projects his or her interests and expectations into communications when interpreting them. Since senders and receivers of communications each bring their own set of perceptual biases, the messages they seek to transfer often are subject to distortions.

**EXHIBIT II–4**
What do you see? An old
woman or a young girl?

## WHAT DO ROLES HAVE TO DO WITH COMMUNICATIONS?

**Roles**
behavior patterns that
correspond to the po-
sitions individuals oc-
cupy in an
organization.

People in organizations play **roles.** They engage in behavior patterns that
go with the positions they occupy in the organization. Supervisory jobs,
for instance, come with role identities. Supervisors know they are supposed to be loyal to, and defend, their boss and the organization. Union
leaders' roles typically require loyalty to union goals such as improving
employee security. Marketing roles demand efforts to increase sales, while
the roles of people working in the credit department emphasize minimizing losses from bad debts.

As organizations impose different role requirements on different
members, they also create communication barriers. Each role comes with
its own jargon that sets the role off from others. Additionally, fulfilling
role requirements often requires individuals to selectively interpret events.
They hear and see the world consistent with their role requirements. The
result is that people in different roles often have difficulty communicating
with each other. Marketing people say they want to "increase sales." So,
too, do the people in credit. Except the marketing people want to sell
everything to anybody, while credit only wants to sell to those who are
credit worthy. Labor and company representatives have difficulty negotiating because their roles encompass very different language and interests. A lot of internal communication breakdowns in organizations are
merely individuals enacting behaviors consistent with the roles they are
playing.

# Is There a Preferred Information Medium?

The amount of information transmitted in a face-to-face conversation is considerably greater than that received from a flier posted on a bulletin board. The former offers multiple information cues (words, posture, facial expressions, gestures, intonations), immediate feedback, and the personal touch of "being there" that the flier doesn't. This reminds us that media differ in the **richness of information** they transmit. Exhibit 11–5 illustrates a hierarchy of information richness. The higher a medium rates in richness, the more information it is capable of transmitting.

Generally speaking, the more ambiguous and complicated the message, the more the sender should rely on a rich communication medium. For example, as a supervisor, if you want to share with your employees a major new product line that your company will be introducing—and which will affect everyone in your department—your communication is more likely to be effective in a face-to-face departmental meeting than through use of a memo. Why? Because this message is likely to initiate apprehension among employees and require clarification. In contrast, a modest change in tomorrow's departmental production schedule can be effectively communicated in a memo. Unfortunately, people in organizations don't always match the medium to the message and, thereby, create communication problems.

**Richness of information** a measure of the amount of information that is transmitted based on multiple information cues (words, posture, facial expressions, gestures, intonations), immediate feedback, and the personal touch.

# How Does Honesty Affect Communications?

A colleague asked you what you thought of the ideas he suggested in the recent team meeting in which you both participated. You thought his suggestions were weak, but you didn't tell him that. Rather, you

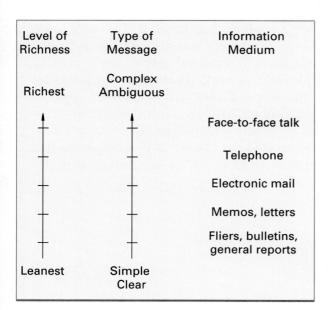

**EXHIBIT 11–5**
Hierarchy of information richness.

# DEALING WITH A DIFFICULT ISSUE

## SHOULD YOU TELL THE WHOLE TRUTH?

Effective communications in both your personal and work lives is built on the expectation that appropriate and accurate information is being given. In any communications encounter, people should be afforded the respect and dignity of being given complete and factual information. Under what circumstances then, is it appropriate to withhold information from someone?

One instance that calls for discretion in conveying information is when the issue of confidentially is involved. The decision to withhold confidential information is sometimes a must—especially at work. Take the situation where one of your employees has just been diagnosed with a treatable form of cancer. He's confided in you about the status of his health. He's also asked you not to say a word to anyone because he considers his health to be a personal matter.

Over the next few months, your employee is absent frequently, especially during his radiation treatments. Because of the circumstances surrounding his illness, you do not feel his absences are a major problem. In part, that's because some of his duties involve direct computer work, which he can do while at home and forward electronically to the appropriate people. You've also discretely divided the rest of his work among other employees in your work unit. Your employees, though, are wondering what is wrong. Many have come to you to you to find out. You simply, and politely, decline to discuss the issue about this employee with his coworkers. However, a number of them think that you're giving him preferential treatment, and they are ready to go to your boss to complain. You know if they only knew what was going on, they'd understand, but you can't reveal the reason for his absence. On the other hand, if some individuals begin to make trouble for you or this employee, this could create more problems for him. That's something he doesn't need right now in his life.

Is it ever appropriate to withhold or filter information in an organization? Should you tell your other employees the whole story? What do you think? Would your views change if this employee had a contagious disease and was working in close contact with his coworkers?

complimented his ideas and said how much they contributed to the final results.

A good deal of what passes as "poor communication" is nothing other than individuals purposely avoiding honesty and openness (see Dealing with a Difficult Issue). To avoid confrontations and hurting others' feelings, we frequently engage in practices such as conveying ambiguous messages, saying what we think others want to hear, or cutting off communication altogether.

Some people run from confrontation. They want everyone to like them. As such, they avoid communicating any messages they think might be displeasing to the receiver. What they end up doing is increasing tension and further hindering effective communication.

## CAN YOUR EMOTIONS HINDER COMMUNICATIONS?

How the receiver feels at the time of receipt of a message will influence how he or she interprets it. The same message received when you're angry or distraught is likely to be interpreted differently when you're in a neutral disposition. Extreme emotions such as jubilation or depression are most likely to hinder effective communication. In such instances, we are most prone to disregard our rational and objective thinking processes and substitute emotional judgments. These are also the times we're most likely to use inflammatory words or language that we later regret.

## HOW CAN YOU IMPROVE YOUR COMMUNICATION EFFECTIVENESS?

A few of the barriers we've described are part of organizational life and will never be fully eliminated. Perceptual and role differences, for example, should be recognized as barriers but are not easily corrected. However, most barriers to effective communication can be overcome. The following provides you with some guidance.

### THINK FIRST!

"Think before you speak!" That cliché can be expanded to include all forms of communication. Before you speak or write, ask yourself: What message am I trying to convey? Then ask: How can I organize and present my message so that it will achieve the desired outcome?

Most of us follow the "think first" dictate when writing a message. The formal and deliberate process of writing encourages thinking through what we want to say and how best to say it. The concept of "working on a draft" implies that the written document will be edited and revised. Few of

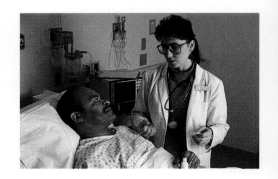

A nursing supervisor needs to adjust her language used when talking with a patient, from that used when talking to her medical staff.

us give anywhere near the same attention to our verbal communications. That's a mistake. Before you speak, make sure you know what you want to say. Then present your message in a logical and organized fashion so it will be clear and understood by your receiver.

### CONSTRAIN EMOTIONS

It would be naive to assume that you always communicate in a fully rational manner. Yet you know that emotions can severely cloud and distort the transference of meaning. If you are emotionally upset over an issue, you're more likely to misconstrue incoming messages and fail to clearly and accurately express your outgoing messages. What can you do? The simplest answer is to discontinue further communication until you have regained composure.

### LEARN TO LISTEN

We stated earlier that most of us are poor listeners. That doesn't mean, though, that we can't improve our listening skills. There are specific behaviors that have been found to be related to effective listening. We present those skills in the "Building a Supervisory Skill" box on pages 410-411.

### TAILOR LANGUAGE TO THE RECEIVER

Since language can be a barrier, you should choose words and structure your messages in ways that will be clear and understandable to the receiver. You need to simplify your language and consider the audience to whom the message is directed—so that the language will be tailored to the receivers. Remember, effective communication is achieved when a message is both received and understood (see News Flash). Understanding is improved by simplifying the language used in relation to the audience intended. For example, a nursing supervisor should always try to communicate to the staff in clear and easily understood terms. At the same time, the language used in messages to a patient should be purposely different from

It's important to recognize that communication isn't conducted in the same way around the world.[3] For example, compare countries that place a high value on individualism (such as the United States) with countries where the emphasis is on collectivism (such as Japan).[4]

Owing to the emphasis on the individual in countries such as the United States, communication patterns are individual-oriented and rather clearly spelled out. For instance, U.S. supervisors rely heavily on memoranda, announcements, position papers, and other formal forms of communication to stake out their positions in the organization. They also often hoard secret information in an attempt to promote their own advancement and as a way of inducing their employees to accept decisions and plans. For their own protection, lower-level employees also engage in this practice.

In collectivist countries such as Japan, there is more interaction for its own sake and a more informal manner of interpersonal contact. The Japanese manager, in contrast to U.S. managers, will engage in extensive verbal consultation over an issue first and will draw up a formal document later, only to outline the agreement that was made. Face-to-face communication is encouraged. Additionally, open communication is an inherent part of the Japanese work setting. Work spaces are open and crowded with individuals at different levels in the work hierarchy. In contrast, U.S. organizations emphasize authority, hierarchy, and formal lines of communication.

[3]See, for example, L. K. Larkey, "Toward a Theory of Communicative Interactions in Culturally Diverse Workgroups," *Academy of Management Review*, June 1996, pp. 463–491; R. V. Lindahl, "Automation Breaks the Language Barrier," *HRMagazine*, March 1996, pp. 79–82; D. Lindorff, "In Beijing the Long March Is Just Starting," *Business Week*, February 12, 1996, p. 68; and L. Miller, "Two Aspects of Japanese and American Coworker Interaction: Giving Instructions and Creating Rapport," *Journal of Applied Behavioral Science*, June 1995, pp. 141–161.

[4]Based on S. D. Saleh, "Relational Orientation and Organizational Functioning: A Cross-Cultural Perspective," *Canadian Journal of Administrative Sciences*, September 1987, pp. 276–293.

that used with the medical staff. Jargon can facilitate understanding when used with those who know what it means, but it can cause innumerable problems when used outside that group.

## MATCH WORDS AND ACTIONS

Actions speak louder than words. Therefore, it is important to watch your actions to make sure they align and reinforce the words that go along with them. We noted that nonverbal messages carry a great deal of weight. Given this fact, the effective supervisor watches his or her nonverbal cues to ensure that they too convey the message desired.

Remember, also, that as a supervisor, your employees will look at your behavior as a model. If your verbal comments are backed up by your actions, you will gain credibility and build trust. If, on the other hand, you say one thing and do another, your employees will ignore what you say and model themselves based on what you do. At the extreme, people stop listening because they no longer believe your words have credibility. Incidently, this is a problem that often plagues politicians.

## UTILIZE FEEDBACK

Many communication problems can be directly attributed to misunderstandings and inaccuracies. These are less likely to occur if you use feedback. This feedback can be verbal or nonverbal.

If you ask someone, "Did you understand what I said?" the response represents feedback. But feedback should include more than yes and no answers. You can ask a set of questions about a message in order to determine whether the message was received as intended. Better yet, you can ask the receiver to restate the message in his or her own words. If you then hear what was intended, understanding and accuracy should be enhanced. Feedback also includes subtler things than the direct asking of questions or summarizing of messages. General comments can give you a sense of the receiver's reaction to a message. Of course, performance appraisals, salary reviews, and promotions also represent forms of feedback.

Feedback does not have to be conveyed in words. The sales supervisor who sends out a staff directive describing a new monthly sales report that all sales personnel will need to complete receives feedback if some of the salespeople fail to turn in the new report. This feedback suggests that he or she needs to clarify further the initial directive. Similarly, when you give a speech to a group of people, you watch their eyes and look for other nonverbal clues to tell you whether they are getting your message or not. This may explain why television performers on comedy shows prefer to tape their programs in front of a live audience. Immediate laughter and applause, or their absence, convey to the performer whether the message is getting across as intended.

## PARTICIPATE IN ASSERTIVENESS TRAINING

Many people have no trouble asserting themselves. Being open and honest comes naturally to them. Some, in fact, are too assertive. They cross over the line to become aggressive and abrasive. Other individuals suffer from a constant fear of upsetting others and fall back on avoidance or ambiguous communication when they need to be open and assertive. Such people would benefit from participation in **assertiveness training.** An effective supervisor needn't always be assertive, but should be capable of being so when it's needed.

Assertiveness training is designed to make people more open and self-expressive. They confront issues in a straightforward manner. They say what they mean, but without being rude or thoughtless.

Individuals who take assertiveness training learn verbal and nonverbal behaviors which enhance their ability to communicate openly and unambiguously. These behaviors include direct and unambiguous language; the use of "I" statements and cooperative "we" statements; a strong, steady, audible voice; good eye contact; facial expressions matched to the message; an appropriately serious tone; and a comfortable but firm posture.

**Assertiveness training** a technique designed to make people more open and self-expressive, saying what they mean without being rude or thoughtless.

---

## POP QUIZ   (Are You Comprehending What You're Reading?)

1. Good communication does NOT require
   a. transference
   b. agreement
   c. understanding
   d. meaning
2. What value can a grapevine offer to a supervisor?
3. The advantage of oral communication is that it creates an accurate and permanent record of the communication that took place. True or False?
4. Communication is distorted when
   a. body language and verbal intonations are used
   b. e-mail is used, which lacks feedback opportunities
   c. body language and intonation are not aligned
   d. the information is complex

# A SPECIAL COMMUNICATION SKILL: ACTIVE LISTENING

**Active listening**
a technique that requires an individual to "get inside" a speaker's mind to understand the communication from the speaker's point of view.

Effective listening is active rather than passive. In passive listening, you're like a tape recorder. You absorb the information given. If the speaker provides you with a clear message and makes his or her delivery interesting enough to keep your attention, you'll probably get most of what the speaker is trying to communicate. But **active listening** requires you to "get inside" the speaker's mind so you can understand the communication from his or her point of view. As you'll see, active listening is hard work.[5] You have to concentrate, and you have to want to fully understand what a speaker is saying. Students who use active listening techniques for an entire fifty-minute lecture are as tired as their instructor when the lecture is over, because they've put as much energy into listening as the instructor puts into speaking.

There are four essential requirements for active listening. You need to listen with (1) intensity, (2) empathy, (3) acceptance, and (4) a willingness to take responsibility for completeness. Because listening presents the opportunity for the mind to wander, the active listener concentrates intensely on what the speaker is saying and tunes out thousands of miscellaneous thoughts (work deadlines, money, personal problems) that create distractions. What do active listeners do with their idle brain time? Summarize and integrate what has been said! They put each new bit of information into the context of what has preceded it.

Empathy requires you to put yourself in the speaker's shoes. Try to understand what the speaker wants to communicate rather than what you want to understand. Notice that empathy demands both knowledge of the speaker and flexibility on your part. Suspend your own thoughts and feelings and adjust what you see and feel to your speaker's world. In that way, you increase the likelihood that you will interpret the message being spoken in the way the speaker intended.

An active listener demonstrates acceptance. You listen objectively without judging content. This is no easy task. It is natural to be distracted by the content of what a speaker says, especially when you disagree with it. When you hear something you disagree with, you have a tendency to begin formulating mental arguments to counter what is being said. Of course, in doing so, you often miss the rest of the message. The challenge is to absorb what is being said and to withhold judgment on content until the speaker is finished.

The final ingredient of active listening is taking responsibility for completeness. That is, as an active listener, you do whatever is necessary to get the full intended meaning from the speaker's communication.

[5]R. McGarvey, "Now Hear This," *Entrepreneur*, June 1996, pp. 87–89.

# How Can You Develop Effective Listening Skills?

From a review of the literature on active listening, fourteen specific behaviors have been suggested (see Building a Supervisory Skill).[6] As you review these behaviors, ask yourself whether they describe your listening practices. If you're not currently using these techniques, there's no better time than right now to begin developing them.

## THE IMPORTANCE OF FEEDBACK SKILLS

Ask a supervisor about the feedback he or she gives to employees, and you're likely to get a qualified answer. If the feedback is positive, it's likely to be given promptly and enthusiastically. Negative feedback is often treated very differently. Like most of us, supervisors don't particularly enjoy communicating bad news. They fear offending or having to deal with the receiver's defensiveness. The result is that negative feedback is often avoided, delayed, or substantially distorted.[8] The purposes of this section are to show you the importance of providing both positive and negative feedback and to identify specific techniques to help make your feedback more effective.

## What's the Difference Between Positive and Negative Feedback?

We said that supervisors treat positive and negative feedback differently. So, too, do receivers. You need to understand this fact and adjust your feedback style accordingly.

Positive feedback is more readily and accurately perceived than negative feedback. Furthermore, while positive feedback is almost always accepted, you can expect negative feedback to meet resistance. Why? The logical answer appears to be that people want to hear good news and block out the rest. Positive feedback fits what most people wish to hear and already believe about themselves.

Does this mean, then, that you should avoid giving negative feedback? No! What it means is that you need to be aware of potential resistance and learn to use negative feedback in situations in which it's most likely to be accepted.[9] That is, negative feedback should be used when it's supported by hard data—numbers, specific examples, and the like.

[6]S. P. Robbins and P. L. Hunsaker, *Training in Interpersonal Skills: Tips for Managing People at Work,* 2nd ed. (Upper Saddle River, NJ: Prentice-Hall, Inc., 1996), pp. 37–39.
[8]C. Fisher, "Transmission of Positive and Negative Feedback to Subordinates," *Journal of Applied Psychology,* October 1979, pp. 433–540.
[9]F. Bartolome, "Teaching About Whether to Give Negative Feedback," *The Organizational Behavior Teaching Review,* Vol. 9, No. 2, 1986–1987, pp. 95–104.

## ACTIVE LISTENING

### ABOUT THE SKILL

To be effective in communications, you must listen actively. To do so requires you to concentrate and work at understanding just what is being said.

### STEPS IN PRACTICING THE SKILL

1. **Be motivated.** If you are unwilling to exert the effort to hear and understand, no amount of additional advice is likely to improve listening effectiveness. As we previously noted, active listening is hard work. So your first step toward becoming an effective listener is a willingness to make the effort.

2. **Make eye contact.** How do you feel when somebody doesn't look at you when you're speaking? If you're like most people, you're likely to interpret this as aloofness or disinterest. It's ironic that while "you listen with your ears, people judge whether you are listening by looking at your eyes."[7] Making eye contact with the speaker focuses your attention, reduces the likelihood that you will become distracted, and encourages the speaker.

3. **Show interest.** The effective listener shows interest in what is being said. How? Through nonverbal signals. Affirmative head nods and appropriate facial expressions, when added to good eye contact, convey to the speaker that you're listening.

4. **Avoid distracting actions.** The other side of showing interest is avoiding actions that suggest your mind is somewhere else. When listening, don't look at your watch, shuffle papers, play with your pencil, or engage in similar distractions. They make the speaker feel you're bored or uninterested. Maybe more importantly, they indicate that you aren't fully attentive and may be missing part of the message that the speaker wants to convey.

5. **Show empathy.** We said the active listener tries to understand what the speaker sees and feels by putting himself or herself in the speaker's shoes. However, don't project your own needs and intentions onto the speaker. When you do so, you're likely to hear what you want to hear. Instead, ask yourself: Who is this speaker and where is he coming from? What are his attitudes, interests, experiences, needs, and expectations?

6. **Take in the whole picture.** The effective listener interprets feelings and emotions as well as factual content. If you listen to words alone and ignore other vocal cues and nonverbal signals, you will miss a wealth of subtle messages. To test this point, read the script of a play. Then go and see that play live in a theater. The characters and the message take on a much richer meaning when you see the play acted on stage.

7. **Ask questions.** The critical listener analyzes what he or she hears and asks questions. This behavior provides clarification, ensures understanding, and assures the speaker that you're listening.

[7]P. L. Hunsaker and A. J. Alewssandra, *The Art of Managing People* (Englewood Cliffs, NJ: Prentice Hall, Inc., 1980), p. 123.

8. **Paraphrase.** Paraphrasing means restating what the speaker has said in your own words. Use phrases like: "What I hear you saying is . . ." or "Do you mean . . .?" Why rephrase what's already been said? Two reasons! First, it's an excellent control device to check on whether you're listening carefully. You can't paraphrase accurately if your mind is wandering or if you're thinking about what you're going to say next. Second, it's a control for accuracy. By rephrasing what the speaker has said in your own words and feeding it back to the speaker, you verify the accuracy of your understanding.

9. **Don't interrupt.** Let the speaker complete his or her thought before you try to respond. Don't try to second-guess where the speaker's thoughts are going. When the speaker is finished, you'll know it!

10. **Integrate what's being said.** Use your spare time while listening to better understand the speaker's ideas. Instead of treating each new piece of information as an independent entity, put the pieces together. Treat each part of the message as if it were an additional piece of a puzzle. By the time the speaker is done, instead of having ten unrelated bits of information, you'll have ten integrated pieces of information that form a comprehensive message. If you don't, you should ask the questions that will fill in the blanks.

11. **Don't overtalk.** Most of us would rather speak our own ideas than listen to what someone else says. Too many of us listen only because it's the price we have to pay to get people to let us talk. While talking may be more fun and silence may be uncomfortable, you can't talk and listen at the same time. The good listener recognizes this fact and doesn't overtalk.

12. **Confront your biases.** Evaluate the source of the message. Notice things like the speaker's credibility, appearance, vocabulary, and speech mannerisms, but don't let them distract you. For instance, all of us have "red flag" words that prompt our attention or cause us to draw premature conclusions. Examples might include terms like racist, gay, chauvinist, conservative, liberal, and feminist. Use information about the speaker to improve your understanding of what he or she has to say, but don't let your biases distort the message.

13. **Make smooth transitions between speaker and listener.** In most work situations, you're continually shifting back and forth between the roles of speaker and listener. The effective listener makes transitions smoothly from speaker to listener and back to speaker. From a listening perspective, this means concentrating on what a speaker has to say and practicing not thinking about what you're going to say as soon as you get your chance.

14. **Be natural.** An effective listener develops a style that is natural and authentic. Try not to become a compulsive listener. If you exaggerate eye contact, facial expressions, the asking of questions, showing of interest, and the like, you'll lose credibility. A good listener is not a manipulator. Use moderation and develop listening techniques that are effective and fit well with your interpersonal style. ■

This supervisor understands one of the cardinal rules of giving feedback. Praise, or positive feedback can be given in public—if the situation warrants it. Here with his employees he's congratulating them on a job well done. Negative feedback, however, should never be given publicly. Instead, it needs to be given in private.

## HOW DO YOU GIVE EFFECTIVE FEEDBACK?

There are six specific suggestions that we can make to help you become more effective in providing feedback. We'll discuss them below and summarize them in Exhibit 11–6.

### FOCUS ON SPECIFIC BEHAVIORS

Feedback should be specific rather than general. Avoid such statements as "You have a bad attitude" or "I'm really impressed with the good job you did." They're vague and, while they provide information, they don't tell the receiver enough to correct the "bad attitude" or on what basis you concluded that a "good job" has been done, so the person knows what behaviors to repeat.

### KEEP FEEDBACK IMPERSONAL

Feedback, particularly the negative kind, should be descriptive rather than judgmental or evaluative. No matter how upset you are, keep the feedback focused on job-related behaviors and never criticize someone personally because of an inappropriate action. Telling people they're incompetent,

• Focus on specific behaviors
• Keep feedback impersonal
• Keep feedback goal oriented
• Make feedback well timed
• Ensure understanding
• Direct negative feedback toward behavior that the receiver can control

## EXHIBIT 11–6

Suggestions for effective feedback.

lazy, or the like is almost always counterproductive. It provokes such an emotional reaction that the performance deviation itself is apt to be overlooked. When you're criticizing, remember that you're censuring job-related behavior, not the person. You might be tempted to tell someone he or she is rude and insensitive (which might just be true); however, that's hardly impersonal. It's better to say something more specific like, "You've interrupted me three times with questions that weren't urgent when you knew I was talking long distance to a customer in Brazil."

## KEEP FEEDBACK GOAL ORIENTED

Feedback should not be given primarily to "dump or unload" on another person. If you have to say something negative, make sure it's directed toward the receiver's goals. Ask yourself whom the feedback is supposed to help. If the answer is essentially you—"I've got something I just want to get off my chest"—bite your tongue and hold the comment. Such feedback undermines your credibility and lessens the meaning and influence of future feedback sessions.

## MAKE FEEDBACK WELL TIMED

Feedback is most meaningful to a receiver when there is a very short interval between his or her behavior and the receipt of feedback about that behavior. For example, a new employee who makes a mistake is more likely to respond to suggestions for improving right after the mistake or at the end of the work day—rather than during a performance review session six months later. If you have to spend time recreating a situation and refreshing someone's memory of it, the feedback you're providing is likely to be ineffective.[10] Moreover, if you're particularly concerned with changing behavior, delays in providing timely feedback on the undesirable actions lessens the likelihood that the feedback will be effective in bringing about the desired change. Of course, making feedback prompt merely for promptness's sake can backfire if you have insufficient information or if you're otherwise emotionally upset. In such instances, "well-timed" could mean "somewhat delayed."

*Ensure understanding.* Is your feedback concise and complete enough that the receiver clearly and fully understands your communication? Remember, that every successful communication requires both transference and understanding of meaning. If feedback is to be effective, you need to ensure that the receiver understands it. Consistent with our discussion of listening techniques, you should have the receiver rephrase the content of your feedback to find out whether it fully captured the meaning you intended.

[10]K. S. Verderber and R. F. Verderber, *Inter-Act: Using Interpersonal Communication Skills,* 4th ed. (Belmont, CA: Wadsworth, 1986).

## DIRECT NEGATIVE FEEDBACK

Negative feedback should be directed toward behavior the receiver can do something about. There's little value in reminding a person of some shortcoming over which he or she has no control. For instance, to criticize an employee who's late for work because she forgot to set her alarm clock is valid. To criticize her for being late for work when the subway she takes to work every day had a power failure, stranding her for 90 minutes, is pointless. There's nothing she could have done to correct what happened—short of finding a different means of traveling to work which may be unrealistic.

In addition, when negative feedback is given concerning something that the receiver can control, it might be a good idea to indicate specifically what can be done to improve the situation. This takes some of the sting out of the criticism and offers guidance to employees who understand the problem—but don't know how to resolve it.

---

POP QUIZ    **(Are You Comprehending What You're Reading?)**

**5.** What should active listeners do with idle brain time?
 **a.** summarize and integrate what has been said
 **b.** organize their schedules for the next few hours
 **c.** plan how to ask questions of the speaker
 **d.** rest and prepare to receive future communication
**6.** Identify the six elements of giving feedback.
**7.** Empathy in communications means you listen objectively without judging content. True or False?
**8.** The greatest value of feedback is that it
 **a.** forces the sender to think twice about what is communicated
 **b.** allows for further discussions between the sender and receiver
 **c.** is not necessary in written communication because the message is tangible and verifiable
 **d.** improves communication by reducing the chance of misunderstandings

---

## SUMMARY

After reading this chapter, I can:

1. **Define communication.** Communication is the transference and understanding of meaning.
2. **Contrast formal and informal communication.** Formal communication addresses task-related issues and tends to follow the organization's authority chain. Informal communication moves in any direction, skips authority levels, and is as likely to satisfy social needs as it is to facilitate task accomplishments.
3. **Explain how electronic communications affect the supervisor's job.** Electronic communications allow supervisors to transmit messages 24 hours a day and stay in constant contact with department members, other supervisors, and key members of the organization regardless of where they are physically located. Networks also allow supervisors to participate in electronic meetings and interact with key people outside the organization.
4. **List barriers to effective communication.** Barriers to effective communication include language differences, poor listening habits, lack of feedback, differences in perception, role requirements, poor choice of information medium, lack of honesty, and emotions.
5. **Describe techniques for overcoming communication barriers.** Techniques for overcoming communication barriers include thinking through what you want to say before communicating, constraining emotions, learning to listen, tailoring language to the receiver, matching words and

actions, utilizing feedback, and participating in assertiveness training.
6. **List the essential requirements for active listening.** The essential requirements for active listening are: (1) intensity, (2) empathy, (3) acceptance, and (4) a willingness to take responsibility for completeness.
7. **Explain what behaviors are necessary for providing effective feedback.** Behaviors that are necessary for providing effective feedback include focusing on specific behaviors; keeping feedback impersonal, goal-oriented, and well-timed; ensuring understanding; and directing negative feedback toward behavior that the recipient can control.

## REVIEWING YOUR KNOWLEDGE

1. "Everything a supervisor does involves communicating." Build an argument to support this statement.
2. Why isn't agreement necessarily a part of good communication?
3. When is a written communication preferable to an oral one?
4. Which type of communication method do you prefer to use at work when sending a message to someone else? Why? Is it the same preference when messages are being sent to you? Explain.
5. "Do what I say, not what I do." Analyze this phrase in terms of supervisors being effective communicators.
6. How can nonverbal messages be powerful communicators?
7. What use, if any, can the grapevine serve?
8. Can supervisors control the grapevine? Discuss.

9. Contrast passive and active listening.
10. Why are feedback skills so important to a supervisor's success?

# ANSWERS TO THE POP QUIZZES

1. **b. agreement.** Good communication involves transference of meaning—which enables understanding between the parties. It does not require agreement. In fact, two individuals can be in complete disagreement—yet still not be communicating.
2. The grapevine can indicate to a supervisor that employees perceive certain problems in the organization. Although the grapevine may not be totally accurate, information floating in the grapevine can be valuable to a supervisor.
3. **False. The advantage of oral communication is that it creates a chance for timely feedback.** An advantage of written communications is that it creates an accurate and permanent record of the communication that took place.
4. **c. body language and intonation are not aligned.** Effective communications requires that body language and intonation be aligned. Otherwise, they send mixed signals and create a barrier to effective communications.
5. **a. summarize and integrate what has been said.** This response is one of the basic elements of active listening.
6. The six elements of giving feedback are: (1) focus on specific behaviors; (2) keep feedback impersonal; (3) keep feedback goal oriented; (4) make feedback well timed; (5) ensure understanding; and (6) direct negative feedback toward behavior that the receiver can control.
7. **False.** Empathy in the communications process means trying to understand what the speaker wants to communicate rather than what you want to understand.
8. **d. improves communication by reducing the chance of misunderstandings.** Reducing the chance of misunderstandings—thus helping the transference of meaning—is the foundation of effective feedback. ■

## A CLASS EXERCISE: ACTIVE LISTENING DURING AN INTERVIEW

This is a role play to practice listening skills. Break into groups of three. One person will be the observer. He or she will evaluate the two other role players and provide feedback on their listening skills using the 14 points listed. The second person will take the role of Chris Humphries. Chris is a regional sales supervisor with Hershey's Chocolate, who is spending the month recruiting on college campuses. Chris joined Hershey's three years ago, directly out of college, and went through the company's marketing management training program. The third person in the group is Lee Pleasant. Lee is a college senior, graduating at the end of the semester.

**Note** to the role players: The role descriptions in this exercise establish each character. Follow the guidelines. Don't lie about or change the facts you're given but, within the guidelines, try to involve yourself in the character.

### Situation

Preliminary interview (in a college placement center) for a marketing management trainee position with Hershey's Chocolate. A brief job description and Lee's resume follow.

### Abbreviated Job Description

**Title:** Marketing Management Trainee— Chocolate Division
**Reports To:** Regional Sales Supervisor
**Duties and Responsibilities:** Completes formal training program at headquarters in Hershey, Pennsylvania. Thereupon:

- Calls on retail stores
- Introduces new products to store personnel
- Distributes sales promotion materials
- Stocks and arranges shelves in stores
- Takes sales orders
- Follows up on complaints or problems
- Completes all necessary sales reports

### Abbreviated Resume

**Name:** Lee Pleasant
**Age:** 22
**Education:** B.S. in Business; G.P.A. = 3.6 (out of 4.0). Major: Marketing. Minor: Economics.
**Work Experience:** Worked 15 hours a week during school and summer vacations at The Gap and at B. Dalton Bookseller
**Honors:** Dean's List (ranked in top 5 percent of business class).
**Other:** Intercollegiate tennis team (2-year letter winner); Vice President, College Marketing Club.

### Stop!

The observer should read both Chris and Lee's roles. The people playing Chris and Lee, however, should read only their own roles. After all have read their appropriate roles, begin the exercise. You have up to 15 minutes. When completed, the observer should provide feedback to both of the role players.

**Chris Humphries' Role:** You will be interviewing approximately 150 students over the next six weeks to fill four trainee positions. You're looking for candidates who are bright, articulate, ambitious, and have management potential. The Hershey's training program is 18 months in length. Trainees will be sales representatives calling on retail stores, and will spend the first six weeks taking formal classes at Hershey's head office. The compensation to start is $33,000 a year plus a car. You are to improvise other information as needed.

Examples of questions you might ask include: Where do you expect to be in five years? What's important to you in a job? What courses did you like best in college? Like least? What makes you think you would do well in this job?

**Lee Pleasant's Role:** Review your resumé. You are a very good student whose previous work experience has been limited to selling in retail stores part time while going to school and full time during the summers. This is your first interview with Hershey's, but you're very interested in their training program. Fill in any voids in information as you see fit.

CRITICAL THINKING

## CASE 11.A

# Communication Problems Can Be Deadly

At 7:40 p.m. on January 25, 1990, Avianca Flight 52 was cruising at 37,000 feet above the southern New Jersey coast.[11] The aircraft had enough fuel to last nearly two hours—a healthy cushion considering the plane was less than half an hour from touchdown at New York's Kennedy Airport. Then a series of delays began. First, at 8:00, the air traffic controllers at Kennedy told the pilots on Flight 52 that they would have to circle in a holding pattern because of heavy traffic. At 8:45, the Avianca copilot advised Kennedy that they were "running low on fuel." The controller at Kennedy acknowledged the message, but the plane was not cleared to land until 9:24. In the interim, the Avianca crew relayed no information to Kennedy that an emergency was imminent, yet the cockpit crew spoke worriedly among themselves about their dwindling fuel supplies.

Flight 52's first attempt to land at 9:24 was aborted. The plane had come in too low and poor visibility made a safe landing uncertain. When the Kennedy controllers gave Flight 52's pilot new instructions for a second attempt, the crew again mentioned that they were running low on fuel, but the pilot told the controllers that the newly assigned flight path was OK. At 9:32, two of Flight 52's engines lost power. A minute later, the other two cut off. The plane, out of fuel, crashed on Long Island at 9:34. All 73 people on board were killed.

When investigators reviewed the cockpit tapes and talked with the controllers involved, they learned that a communication breakdown caused this tragedy. A closer look at the events of that evening help to explain why a simple message was neither clearly transmitted nor adequately received. First, the pilots kept saying they were "running low on fuel." Traffic controllers told investigators that it is fairly common for pilots to use this phrase. In times of delay, controllers assume that everyone has a fuel problem. However, had the pilots uttered the words "fuel emergency," the controllers would have been obligated to direct the jet ahead of all others and clear it to land as soon as possible. As one controller put it, if a pilot "declares an emergency, all rules go out the window and we get the guy to the airport as quickly as possible." Unfortunately, the pilots of Flight 52 never used the word "emergency," so the people at Kennedy never understood the true nature of the pilots' problem.

[11]Case based on J. Cushman, "Avianca Flight 52: The Delays That Ended in Disaster," *New York Times*, February 5, 1990, p. B-1; and E. Weiner, "Right Word Is Crucial in Air Control," *New York Times*, February 29, 1990, p. B-5.

Second, the vocal tone of the pilots on Flight 52 didn't convey the severity or urgency of the fuel problem to the air traffic controllers. These controllers are trained to pick up subtle tones in a pilot's voice in such situations. While the crew of Flight 52 expressed considerable concern among themselves about the fuel problem, their voice tones in communicating to Kennedy were cool and professional. Finally, the culture and traditions of pilots and airport authorities may have made the pilot of Flight 52 reluctant to declare an emergency. A pilot's expertise and pride can be at stake in such a situation. Declaration of a formal emergency requires the pilot to complete a wealth of paperwork. Moreover, if a pilot has been found to be negligent in calculating how much fuel was needed for a flight, the Federal Aviation Administration can suspend his or her license. These negative reinforcers strongly discourage pilots from calling an emergency.

## RESPONDING TO THE CASE

1. Analyze the communications between pilots on Flight 52 and the traffic controllers at Kennedy Airport using the seven-step model presented in this chapter.
2. How could active listening skills have prevented this crash? Cite specific examples.
3. Avianca is a Columbian airline. A large number of flights into major world airports are foreign carriers. How is it possible for world air traffic controllers to be as generally effective as they are given that pilots and controllers may not share the same native language?

## CASE 11.B

### United Van Lines

Working as a dispatcher for United Van Lines was a fun job for Emily Banks. She had learned more about moving and the moving industry than she ever thought was possible. She knew when a person or business called United, it was important for the customer to know the company was concerned about the customer's needs. She knew it was important for all United employees to be dependable and to be concerned with details.

Emily was very serious about her training in packing, crating, and shipping. She didn't take lightly the company's policy about assuring a customer's move or storage needs were met. She, however, wasn't always taken seriously by her coworkers. Even her supervisor, Larry Carson, didn't seem to take her seriously. Was it because she liked to play practical jokes or maybe because she was close to getting her commercial trucking license? She really didn't know for sure. But she was looking forward to the day she could be "on the road" as a van driver, seeing all parts of the country and making some serious money.

Late one afternoon when Emily received a fax message, she didn't know what to think. The message read, "Ship cartons to RHill instead of Char in a parish." Was this a practical joke? It had to be! She tried to analyze the message. What was "Char in a parish"? It was quitting time and she would "catch up with the practical joker" sooner or later. She decided to ignore the message and go home.

Three days later, she was confronted by Mr. Carson. His voice was angry, "How could you possibly ignore an urgent request? Your negligence has cost the company time and money.

The Parkside Container Company in Charlotte, North Carolina had to purchase cartons from another company and was late meeting their deadline. Can't you be depended on to get a simple job done? It's way past time to get off your 'cutesy attitude' and pay attention to details. This is a place of business, not a place for satisfying your social needs. Well? . . ." Mr. Carson just stood there and glared at her. Emily was dumbfounded. Mr. Carson was so angry that Emily didn't think she could even respond.

(An explanation to the message is provided in question 3 below; however, it is recommended to answer questions 1 and 2 before referring to question #3.)

## RESPONDING TO THE CASE

1. Why do you believe Mr. Carson is so angry with Emily, who doesn't even know what he's talking about? What do you believe is contributing to Mr. Carson's harsh words?
2. What should Emily do to get at the root of the problem?
3. Here is the fax message explanation: The fax message that Emily received should have read, "Send cartons to Rock Hill, South Carolina instead of Charlotte. Anne Parrish" The sender of the message was "Anne Parrish." Anne Parrish works for Parkside Container Company. When Anne realized Parkside's carton order should go to Rock Hill instead of Charlotte—(about 20 miles separates the two towns), she tried to call United. Since it was late in the day and the United phone lines were busy, Anne sent a fax to United to be sure her message reached United before the end of the working day. Anne phoned the message to the information center at Parkside where a temporary worker typed it and sent the fax to United. Anne received the confirmation from the information center that the fax was sent and felt assured that United would reroute their carton order to Rock Hill the next day.

a. Discuss the problems that occurred in communications surrounding this incident.
b. Identify the communication methods that appeared to be ineffective in this communication.
c. Having a new perspective on the incident, what advice would you give to Mr. Carson? Emily? Ms. Parrish? ■

## Al Bunge
### Production QA Manager
### and Doris Dresson
### Controller, Josten's (Manufacturing)

The Josten's plant makes the molds (called tools) for rings the company produces. The plant switched to a work team approach a few years ago, and they have had great success with it. The plant employs 100 people, divided into five self-managed teams. The plant runs 24 hours a day, six days a week. Teams can include members from two or even three different shifts. They receive and process orders directly from customers. Each self-managed team has a designated leader.

Al and Doris supervise these teams together. Al is responsible for day-to-day production. Doris is responsible for budgeting, orders, and other tasks. They each attend team meetings and teams can address both of them with problems. Doris has more experience with products; Al has more experience with work teams.

In a team environment, cross-training is necessary. Vacations and absenteeism are managed by moving team members from one position to another. Cross-training helps when there is extra work or rush jobs. It helps team members understand different positions on the team, what functions the team can perform, and how a team can be reorganized or streamlined.

In a traditional factory, the supervisor would simply assign someone to be involved in cross-training. In a team environment, Al and Doris need to let the teams work out problems on their own.

Al and Doris had trouble convincing the teams to cross-train. Everyone was willing to train into a higher skill level, but employees with higher skill levels were unwilling to share their knowledge. Nobody wanted to learn a lower-level job. When the workload is heavy, there is little time to take trained team members off regular tasks to teach them a new skill.

1. Describe the pros and cons of self-managed teams; of cross-training.
2. What factors do you believe contribute to Al's and Doris's success as they manage their teams?
3. Which leadership traits are needed to manage a team? Which of these traits can you pick up from the story that Al and Doris have?
4. Explain why the supervisory approach used by Al and Doris does not violate this rule: Report to only one supervisor.
5. Contrast communications in the self-managed approach with a more traditional supervisory approach. ∎

# PART FIVE

# COPING WITH WORKPLACE DYNAMICS

If there is one thing common to most supervisors' jobs, it's the realization that things will never remain calm—at least for long. Supervisors know that problems arise, and they must be dealt with. So, too, must they deal with the dynamic change that takes place in organizations. They know that political factors can have a major effect on their success.

This part contains four chapters:

12. CONFLICT, POLITICS,
    AND NEGOTIATION

13. DEALING WITH CHANGE
    AND STRESS

14. DISCIPLINING EMPLOYEES

15. THE SUPERVISOR'S ROLE IN
    LABOR RELATIONS

# 12 CONFLICT, POLITICS, AND NEGOTIATION

# LEARNING OBJECTIVES

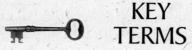 

# KEY TERMS

After reading this chapter, you should be able to:

1. Define conflict.
2. Identify the three general sources of conflict.
3. List the five basic techniques for resolving conflict.
4. Describe how a supervisor could stimulate conflict.
5. Define politicking.
6. Explain the existence of politics in organizations.
7. List specific guidelines for developing and improving political skills.
8. Contrast distributive and integrative bargaining.

You should also be able to define these supervisory terms:

accommodation

avoidance

collaboration

compromise

conflict

conflict management

culture

devil's advocate

distributive bargaining

forcing

integrative bargaining

mentor

negotiation

politicking

status

"I want him out of here," Arlene Parker, a production supervisor in the animation group at Walt Disney Studios, was yelling into the phone. "I've tried my best to work with him for two years. 'It ain't workin'.' You've got my recommendation and the paperwork. Transfer him, fire him, I don't care. We just can't get along!"

"Calm down, Arlene," came the voice from the other end. The voice belonged to Bill McKinley in the Human Resources Division. "I know you want Marvin out of your department. I'm doing my best. But it's not easy. He's been with the company for four years. His performance reviews haven't been bad. It's just personality differences between you two."

"You're darn right it's personality differences. He whines and complains all the time. He argues with every decision I make. He disrupts the department. I want him out of here! I don't care what you do with him, just get him out of my hair!"

"Arlene, listen to me," Bill pleaded. "I'm doing my best. But don't expect miracles. You may have to learn to live with Marvin Reynolds, at least for another four or five months."

"Over my dead body!" Arlene screamed into the phone, and then slammed down the receiver. ∎

## INTRODUCTION

Dealing with conflicts like that between Arlene Parker and Bill McKinley is a part of every supervisor's job. Those who learn how to manage conflict properly are likely to reap significant benefits. One study of a group of managers looked at 25 skill and personality factors to determine which, if any, were related to managerial success (defined in terms of ratings by one's boss, salary increases, and promotions).[1] Of the 25 measures, only one—the ability to handle conflict—was positively related to supervisory success.

In this chapter we'll define conflict, explore what brings it about, and examine the various ways you can handle it. Then we'll discuss organizational politics—why understanding politics is important for all supervisors and how you can make politics work for you. Finally, we'll conclude with some suggestions on how to be more successful at negotiation.

[1]J. Graves, "Successful Management and Organizational Muggings," In J. Papp, ed., *New Directions in Human Resource Management* (Englewood Cliffs, N.J.: Prentice Hall Inc., 1978).

**Conflict** is a process in which one party consciously interferes in the goal-achievement efforts of another party. This interference can be between a supervisor and a member of his or her department or between two operatives within a department. It might also exist between a supervisor and his or her boss, or involve interdepartmental parties, such as two supervisors in separate departments. In our opening dialogue, you saw evidence of two conflicts: one between Arlene Parker and Marvin Reynolds and the other between Arlene and Bill McKinley. The first is an intradepartmental conflict; the second is an interdepartmental conflict.

Conflict
a process in which one party consciously interferes in the goal-achieving efforts of another party.

## IS ALL CONFLICT BAD?

Most of us have grown up with the idea that all conflicts are bad. We were told not to argue with our parents or teachers, to get along with our brothers and sisters, and that countries spent billions of dollars on military outlays to preserve peace. But conflicts aren't all bad, especially in organizations.[2]

Conflict is a natural phenomenon of organizational life. It can't be completely eliminated. Why? Because (1) organizational members have different goals; (2) there are scarce resources, like budget allocations, which various people want and are willing to fight over; and (3) people in organizations don't all see things alike as a result of their diverse backgrounds, education, experiences, and interests. However, the existence of conflict in organizations has a positive side. It stimulates creativity, innovation, and change—and only through change can an organization adapt and survive (see Exhibit 12–1). A positive level of conflict in an organization supports disagreements, the open questioning of others, and challeng-

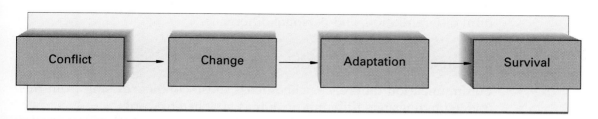

## EXHIBIT 12-1
The positive role of conflict.

[2]See Stephen P. Robbins, *Managing Organizational Conflict: A Nontraditional Approach* (Englewood Cliffs, N.J.: Prentice Hall Inc., 1974).

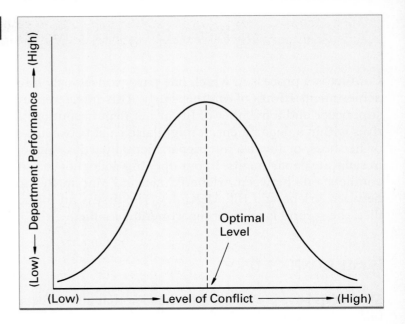

**EXHIBIT 12–2**

Conflict and department performance.

*(Graph: Department Performance (Low to High) on vertical axis, Level of Conflict (Low to High) on horizontal axis, showing a bell-shaped curve with "Optimal Level" marked at the peak)*

ing the status quo. If organizations were completely devoid of conflict, they would become apathetic, stagnant, and unresponsive to change.

You should look at conflict as having an up side as well as a down side. You should encourage enough conflict to keep your departments viable, self-critical, and creative. Of course, too much conflict is bad and should be reduced. Your goal should be to have enough conflict in your department to keep the unit responsive and innovative, but not so much as to hinder departmental performance (see Exhibit 12–2).

## WHERE DO CONFLICTS COME FROM?

Conflicts don't pop out of thin air. They have causes. These causes can be separated into three general categories: communication differences, structural differentiation, and personal differences.

### COMMUNICATION DIFFERENCES

Communication differences encompass those conflicts arising from misunderstandings and different meanings attached to words.

One of the major myths that most of us carry around with us is that poor communication is the reason for conflicts—"if we could just communicate with each other, we could eliminate our differences." Such a conclusion is not unreasonable, given the amount of time each of us spends communicating. Poor communication is certainly not the source of all conflicts, though there is considerable evidence to suggest that problems in the communication process act to retard collaboration and stimulate misunderstanding.

## STRUCTURAL DIFFERENTIATION

As we explained in Chapter 6, organizations are horizontally and vertically differentiated. Company officials divide up tasks, group common tasks into departments, and establish rules and regulations to facilitate standardized practices between departments.

This structural differentiation often causes conflicts. Individuals may disagree over goals, decision alternatives, performance criteria, and resource allocations. These conflicts, however, are not due to poor communication or personal hostility. Rather, they are rooted in the structure of the organization itself. The "goodies" that supervisors want—budgets, promotions, pay increases, additions to staff, office space, influence over decisions—are scarce resources that must be divvied up. The creation of horizontal units (departments) and vertical levels (the organizational hierarchy) brings about efficiencies through specialization and coordination but, at the same time, produces the potential for structural conflicts.

## PERSONAL DIFFERENCES

The third source of conflict is personal differences. These include value systems and personality characteristics that account for individual idiosyncrasies and differences.

Imagine the following situations. Your values emphasize developing close family ties, and our's focus on acquiring material possessions. An employee in your department thinks salary increases should be based on seniority. You think the criterion should be job performance. These value differences stimulate conflicts. Similarly, the chemistry between some peo-

Workforce diversity is likely to increase the incidents of conflicts based on communication and personal differences. Saturn Corporation makes differences a plus by using them to stimulate change and attack apathy.

ple makes it hard for them to work together. Factors like background, education, experience, and training mold each individual into a unique personality. Some personality types are attracted to each other, while some types are like the proverbial oil and water—they just don't mix. The result is that some people may be perceived by others as abrasive, hard to work with, untrustworthy, or strange. This creates interpersonal conflicts.

## How Do You Manage Conflict?

**Conflict management**
the application of resolution and stimulation techniques to achieve the optimum level of departmental conflict.

As a supervisor, you want to have the optimum level of conflict in your department. That means you need to manage it. You'll want to resolve conflict when it's too high and disrupting your department's performance. You'll want to stimulate conflict when it's too low. So **conflict management** is the application of resolution and stimulation techniques to achieve the optimum level of departmental conflict.

## What Resolution Techniques Can You Use?

What options do you have available to eliminate or reduce conflicts? You have five basic approaches or techniques for resolving conflict: avoidance, accommodation, force, compromise, and collaboration. As shown in Exhibit 12–3, they differ in terms of the emphasis they place on concern for others versus concern for oneself. Each technique has particular strengths and weaknesses and no one technique is ideal for every situation. You should consider each technique as a tool in your conflict-management tool chest. While you may be better at using some tools than others, the skilled supervisor knows what each tool can do and when it is likely to be most effective.

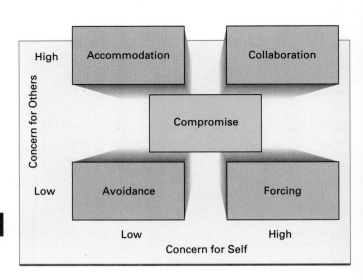

**EXHIBIT 12–3**

Basic techniques for resolving conflicts.

## AVOIDANCE

Sometimes **avoidance** is the best solution for you—just withdrawing from the conflict or ignoring its existence. When would that be? When the conflict you face is trivial, when emotions are running high and where time can help cool things down, or when the potential disruption from a more assertive action outweighs the benefits of resolution, avoidance can work best. The thing to be concerned about with this approach is that some supervisors believe that all conflicts can be ignored. These conflict avoiders are often very poor supervisors. They frustrate their employees and usually lose their respect. There are times when the best action is no action, but that shouldn't be the way you respond to every conflict.

**Avoidance**
withdrawal from a conflict or ignoring its existence.

## ACCOMMODATION

The goal of **accommodation** is to maintain harmonious relationships by placing another's needs and concerns above your own. You might, for example, yield to another person's position on an issue or try to defuse a conflict by focusing on points of agreement. This approach is most viable when the issue under dispute isn't that important to you or when you want to build up credits for later issues.

**Accommodation**
a method of maintaining harmonious relationships by placing others' needs and concerns above one's own.

## FORCING

With **forcing,** you attempt to satisfy your own needs at the expense of the other party. In organizations, this is most often illustrated by supervisors using their formal authority to resolve a dispute. The use of intimidation, majority-rule voting, or stubbornly refusing to give in on your position are other examples of force. Force works well (1) when you need a quick resolution, (2) on important issues where unpopular actions must be taken, and (3) where commitment by others to your solution is not critical.

**Forcing**
attempting to satisfy one's own needs at the expense of the other party.

## COMPROMISE

A **compromise** approach requires each party to give up something of value. This is typically the approach taken by management personnel and labor unions in negotiating a new labor contract. Supervisors also often use compromise to deal with interpersonal conflicts. For instance, a supervisor in a small printing company wanted one of his employees to come in over a weekend to finish an important project. The employee didn't want to spend his whole weekend at work. After considerable discussion, they arrived at a compromise solution: The employee would come in on Saturday only, the supervisor would also come in and help out, and the employee would get eight hours of overtime pay plus the following Friday off.

When should you look to compromise as an option? You do so when the party with whom you have the conflict has power about equal to yours,

**Compromise**
an approach to conflict that requires each party to give up something of value.

when it is desirable to achieve a temporary solution to a complex issue, or when time pressures demand an expedient solution.

## COLLABORATION

**Collaboration**
an approach to conflict that requires all parties seek to satisfy their interests.

The ultimate win-win solution is **collaboration.** All parties to the conflict seek to satisfy their interests. This technique is typically characterized by open and honest discussion among the parties, intensive listening to understand differences and identify areas of mutual agreement, and careful deliberation over a full range of alternatives to find a solution that is advantageous to all.

When is collaboration the best conflict approach for you? Collaboration is best used when time pressures are minimal, when all parties in the conflict seriously want a solution, and when the issue is too important to be compromised.

## WHICH CONFLICTS DO YOU HANDLE?

Not every conflict justifies your attention. Some might not be worth the effort; others might be unmanageable. Not every conflict is worth your time and effort to resolve. While avoidance might appear to be a "cop-out," it can sometimes be the most appropriate response. You can improve your overall management effectiveness, and your conflict-management skills in particular, by avoiding trivial conflicts. Choose your battles judiciously, saving your efforts for the ones that count.

Regardless of our desires, reality tells us that some conflicts are unmanageable.[3] When antagonisms are deeply rooted, when one or both parties wish to prolong a conflict, or when emotions run so high that constructive interaction is impossible, your efforts to manage the conflict are unlikely to meet with much success. Don't be lured into the naive belief that a good supervisor can resolve every conflict effectively. Some aren't worth the effort. Some are outside your realm of influence. Still others may be functional and, as such, are best left alone. Those you choose to handle, you need to know how to handle in the best way possible.

## HOW DO YOU CHOOSE THE APPROPRIATE RESOLUTION TECHNIQUE?

Given that you're familiar with your options, how should you proceed if you find you have a conflict that needs resolving? We've summarized them in Exhibit 12–4, and described them below.

[3]L. Greenhalgh, "Managing Conflict," *Sloan Management Review*, Summer 1986, pp. 45–51.

## EXHIBIT 12–4

Choosing the appropriate resolution technique: a guideline.

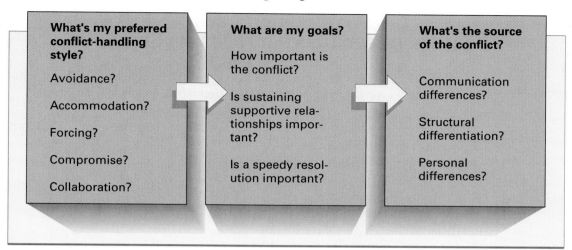

**What's my preferred conflict-handling style?**

Avoidance?

Accommodation?

Forcing?

Compromise?

Collaboration?

**What are my goals?**

How important is the conflict?

Is sustaining supportive relationships important?

Is a speedy resolution important?

**What's the source of the conflict?**

Communication differences?

Structural differentiation?

Personal differences?

Start by considering your preferred conflict-handling style (see Assessing Yourself). Each of us has a basic approach to handling conflict with which we feel most comfortable. Do you try to postpone dealing with conflicts, hoping they'll go away (avoidance)? Do you prefer soothing the other party's feelings so the disagreement doesn't damage your relationship (accommodation)? Are you stubborn and determined to get your way (forcing)? Do you look for middle-ground solutions (compromise)? Or maybe you prefer to sit down and discuss differences in order to find a solution that'll make everybody happy (collaboration).

Everyone has a basic resolution approach that reflects his or her personality. You should understand what yours is. Most people aren't held prisoner to their basic approach. They're flexible and can use different approaches if they need to. Unfortunately, some people are extremely rigid and incapable of adjusting their styles. These people are at a severe disadvantage because they can't use all of the resolution options. You should know your basic resolution style and try to show flexibility in using others. However, keep in mind that when push comes to shove, most of us fall back on our basic approach because it's the one we know best and feel most comfortable with.

## YOUR PREFERRED CONFLICT HANDLING STYLE

Instructions: Indicate how often you do the following—by checking usually, sometimes, or seldom—when you differ with someone.

|  | *Usually* | *Sometimes* | *Seldom* |
|---|:---:|:---:|:---:|
| **1.** I explore our differences, not backing down, but not imposing my view either. | O | O | O |
| **2.** I disagree openly, then invite more discussion about our differences. | O | O | O |
| **3.** I look for a mutually satisfactory solution. | O | O | O |
| **4.** Rather than let the other person make a decision without my input, I make sure I am heard and also that I hear the other out. | O | O | O |
| **5.** I agree to a middle ground rather than look for a completely satisfying solution. | O | O | O |
| **6.** I admit I am half wrong rather than explore our differences. | O | O | O |
| **7.** I have a reputation for meeting a person halfway. | O | O | O |
| **8.** I expect to get out about half of what I really want to say. | O | O | O |
| **9.** I give in totally rather than try to change another's opinion. | O | O | O |
| **10.** I put aside any controversial aspects of an issue. | O | O | O |
| **11.** I agree early on, rather than argue about a point. | O | O | O |
| **12.** I give in as soon as the other party gets emotional about an issue. | O | O | O |

**13.** I try to win the other person over.  ○ ○ ○
**14.** I work to come out victorious, no matter what.  ○ ○ ○
**15.** I never back away from a good argument.  ○ ○ ○
**16.** I would rather win than end up compromising.  ○ ○ ○

## SCORING

Total your choices as follows. Give yourself 5 points for "Usually;" 3 points for "sometimes;" and 1 point for "seldom." Then total them for each set of statements grouped as follows:

Set A:          Items 13–16          Set B:          Items 9–12
Set C:          Items 5–8            Set D.          Items 1–4.

## WHAT THE ASSESSMENT MEANS

Treat each set separately. A score of 17 or above on any set is considered high; scores of 12–16 are moderately high; scores of 8–11 are moderately low; and scores of 7 or less are considered low. Sets A, B, C, and D represent different conflict-resolution strategies.

A  =  Forcing: I win, you lose
B  =  Accommodation: I lose, you win
C  =  Compromise: Both you and I win some and lose some
D  =  Collaboration: Both you and I win

Everyone has a basic underlying conflict-handling style. Your score on this exercise indicates the strategy(ies) you rely on most [your highest score(s)].

The next thing you should look at is your goals. The best solution is closely intertwined with your definition of best. Three goals seemed to dominate our discussion of resolution approaches: the importance of the conflict, concern over maintaining long-term interpersonal relations, and the speed with which you need to resolve the conflict. All other things held constant, if the issue is critical to your unit's success, collaboration is preferred. If sustaining supportive relationships is important, the best approaches, in order of preference, are accommodation, collaboration, compromise, and avoidance. If it's crucial to resolve the conflict as quickly as possible, force, accommodation, and compromise—in that order—are preferred.

Lastly, you need to consider the source of the conflict. What works best depends, to a large degree, on the cause of the conflict. Communication-based conflicts revolve around misinformation and misunderstandings. Such conflicts lend themselves to collaboration. In contrast, conflicts based on personal differences arise out of disparities between the parties' values and personalities. Such conflicts are most susceptible to avoidance because these differences are often deeply entrenched. When you have to resolve conflicts rooted in personal differences, you'll frequently rely on force—not so much because it placates everyone involved, but because it works! The third category, structural conflicts, offers opportunities to use most of the conflict approaches.

This process of blending your personal style, your goals, and the source of the conflict should result in identifying the approach or set of approaches most likely to be effective for you in any specific conflict.

## How Do You Stimulate Conflict?

What about the other side of conflict management—situations that require supervisors to stimulate conflict? The notion of stimulating conflict is often difficult to accept. For almost all of us, the term conflict has a negative connotation, and the idea of purposely creating conflict seems to be counter to good supervisory practices. Few of us personally enjoy being in conflictive situations. Yet there are situations where an increase in conflict is constructive. Exhibit 12–5 provides a set of questions that can help you to determine if a situation might justify conflict stimulation. An affirmative answer to one or more of the questions in Exhibit 12–5 suggests that an increase in conflict might help your unit's performance.

We know a lot more about resolving conflict than stimulating it. However, the following are some suggestions you might want to consider if you find your department is in need of an increased level of conflict.

### USE COMMUNICATIONS

As far back as Franklin Roosevelt's administration, and probably before, the White House has consistently used communication to stimulate con-

1. Are you surrounded by "yes people"?
2. Are subordinates afraid to admit ignorance and uncertainties to you?
3. Do you and department members concentrate so hard on reaching a compromise that you lose sight of key values, long-term objectives, or the organization's welfare?
4. Do you believe that it is in your best interest to maintain the impression of peace and cooperation in your unit, regardless of the price?
5. Is there an excessive concern in your department not to hurt the feelings of others?
6. Do people in your department believe that popularity is more important for obtaining rewards than competence and high performance?
7. Is your department unduly unamored with obtaining consensus for all decisions?
8. Do employees show unusually high resistance to change?
9. Is there a lack of new ideas?
10. Is there an unusually low level of employee turnover?

**EXHIBIT 12–5**

Is conflict stimulation needed? (An affirmative answer to any or all of these questions suggests the need for conflict stimulation.) (*Source:* Adapted from Stephen P. Robbins, "'Conflict Management' and 'Conflict Resolution' Are Not Synonymous Terms," *California Management Review,* Winter 1978, p. 71.)

flict. Senior officials float trial balloons by "planting" possible decisions with the media through the infamous "reliable source" route. For example, the name of a prominent judge is leaked as a possible Supreme Court appointment. If the candidate survives the public scrutiny, his or her appointment is announced by the president. However, if the candidate is found lacking by the press, media, and public, the president's press secretary or other high-level official will make a formal statement such as, "At no time was this individual under consideration."

You can use rumors and ambiguous messages to stimulate conflict in your department. Information that some employees might be transferred, that serious budget cuts are coming, or that a layoff is possible can reduce apathy, stimulate new ideas, and force reevaluation—all positive outcomes as a result of increased conflict.

### BRING IN OUTSIDERS

A widely used method for shaking up a stagnant department is to bring in—either by hiring from outside or by internal transfer—individuals whose backgrounds, values, attitudes, or personalities differ from those of present members. One of the major benefits of the diversity movement (encouraging the hiring and promotion of people who are different) is that it can stimulate conflict and improve an organization's performance.

## RESTRUCTURE THE DEPARTMENT

We know that structural variables are a source of conflict. It is therefore only logical that you can look to structure as a conflict stimulation device. Centralizing decisions, realigning work groups, and increasing formalization are examples of structural devices that disrupt the status quo and act to increase conflict levels.

## APPOINT A DEVIL'S ADVOCATE

**Devil's advocate**
a person who purposely presents arguments that run counter to those opposed by the majority or against current practices.

A **devil's advocate** is a person who purposely presents arguments that run counter to those proposed by the majority or against current practices. He or she plays the role of the critic, even to the point of arguing against positions with which he or she actually agrees.

A devil's advocate acts as a check against groupthink and practices that have no better justification than "that's the way we've always done it around here." When thoughtfully listened to, the advocate can improve the quality of group decision making. On the other hand, others in the group often view advocates as time wasters; appointment of an advocate is almost certain to delay any decision process.

What would happen if conflict like this was evident in your department? If your boss viewed this as a negative reflection on your supervisory ability, you'd try to eliminate it at all costs. On the other hand, if you work for someone who believes that some conflict is positive and stimulates productivity, you might do what you can to have optimum levels of conflict.

# HOW CAUTIOUSLY SHOULD YOU PROCEED IN STIMULATING CONFLICT?

Even though there are situations where departmental performance can be enhanced through conflict stimulation, it may not be in your best career interests to use stimulation techniques.

If your organizational culture or your immediate superior views any kind of conflict in your department as a negative reflection on your supervisory performance, think twice before stimulating conflict or even allowing low levels of conflict to exist. Where company officials believe that all conflicts are bad, it's not uncommon for you to be evaluated on how peaceful and harmonious conditions are in your department. While a conflict-free climate tends to create stagnant and apathetic organizations, and eventually lower performance, it is important for your survival to adopt a conflict-management style that's compatible with your organization. In some cases, that might mean using only resolution techniques.

---

## POP QUIZ  (Are You Comprehending What You're Reading?)

1. Which one of the following best suggests the need for a manager to stimulate conflict?
   a. when a supervisor is surrounded by "yes people"
   b. when employees in a department lack specific expertise
   c. when the work unit is peaceful and cooperative
   d. when creativity and innovation are present
2. Describe why all conflict cannot be completely eliminated in organizations.
3. The ultimate win-win conflict resolution technique is accommodation, which seeks to satisfy each party's interests. True or False?
4. A person who purposely presents arguments that run counter to those proposed by the majority or against current practices is called a(n) _____ .
   a. conflict-stimulator
   b. devil's advocate
   c. external consultant
   d. all of the above

---

# UNDERSTANDING ORGANIZATIONAL POLITICS

"Don't use conflict-stimulation techniques, even if they would improve your department's performance, if your organization's senior management views all conflicts as bad." This summary of the previous paragraph acknowledges the political nature of organizations. You're not always rewarded for doing the right things. In the real world of organizations, the good guys don't always win. Demonstrating openness, trust, objectivity, support, and similar humane qualities in relationships with others doesn't always lead to improved supervisory performance. There will be times when, to get things done or to protect your interests against the maneuvering of others, you'll have to engage in politicking. Effective supervisors understand the political nature of organizations and adjust their actions accordingly (see Dealing with a Difficult Issue).

## WHAT IS POLITICS?

**Politicking**
the actions one can take to influence, or attempt to influence, the distribution of advantages and disadvantages within an organization.

Politics relates to who gets what, when, and how. **Politicking** is the actions you can take to influence, or attempt to influence, the distribution of advantages and disadvantages within your organization. Some examples of political behavior include withholding key information from decision makers, whistle-blowing, spreading rumors, leaking confidential information about organizational activities to the media, exchanging favors with others in the organization for mutual benefit, and lobbying on behalf of or against a particular individual or decision alternative.

One of the most interesting insights about politics is that what constitutes a political action is almost entirely a judgment call. Like beauty, politics is in the eye of the beholder. A behavior that one person labels "organizational politics" is very likely to be characterized as an instance of "effective supervision" by another. The fact is not that effective supervision is necessarily political, though in some cases it might be. Rather, a person's reference point determines what he or she classifies as organizational politics. Take a look at the labels in Exhibit 12–6 (on p. 442) that are used to describe the same activities.

## WHY IS THERE POLITICS IN ORGANIZATIONS?

Can you conceive of an organization that is free of politics? It's possible but most unlikely. Organizations are made up of individuals and groups with different values, goals, and interests. This sets up the potential for conflict over resources. Departmental budgets, space allocations, project

## TURNING IN A FRIEND

Imagine that you work in an organization with a trusted colleague. This individual has been part of your work life for several years now. When your department has met or exceeded its goals, your colleague has been there to congratulate you. More importantly, when you had some problems with employees, you turned to this friend for advice. Lately, though, you feel like your colleague has been putting you in an uncompromising position. Several times during the last two months, he's made comments to company officials about your inability to lead your "team." He's "leaked" information that your employees have problems with your supervisory style.

This morning, while having a cup of coffee with your friend, you noticed that he took some "unusual" pills. You know that your friend had a substance abuse problem years ago—but he had kicked the problem. Now his unusual behavior of late, coupled with his pending divorce, has you thinking that he may have "fallen off the wagon." You tried talking to him about your concerns, but he wouldn't listen.

Both of you work for an organization that has a very strict substance abuse policy. If anyone is suspected of abusing illegal substances, they must submit to a drug test. If that test is positive, the individual is suspended, with pay, for 60 days. During this time, the individual is required to attend daily a substance abuse clinic. At the conclusion of the suspension, another drug test is administered. If the result is negative, the employee may return to work; if positive, the individual is terminated.

While you aren't sure of the extent of your colleagues's problem (or if he truly has one at all), you do know both of you are competing for a promotion. One the one hand, you know that if you brought your suspicions to your boss's attention, she would investigate the situation. She might conclude, too, that his behavior and performance level has changed and request he take a drug test. Even if the drug test was negative, it might cast enough doubt to kill your coworker's chances for the promotion. On the other hand, this is your colleague, someone to whom you've turned for help in the past. When you really think about who's best for the promotion (not counting the performance problems of the past few months), even you have to admit he would be the better choice. He has more experience and has always been someone you went to for help.

So what do you do? Do you wait a while and confirm your suspicion? Or do you talk with your boss now? If it's the latter, are you taking political advantage of your colleague? What would you do in this situation?

## EXHIBIT 12–6

Is it politics or effective supervision?

| POLITICAL LABEL | | EFFECTIVE SUPERVISION LABEL |
|---|---|---|
| 1. Blaming others | or | Fixing responsibility |
| 2. Kissing up | or | Developing working relationships |
| 3. Apple - polishing | or | Demonstrating loyalty |
| 4. Passing the buck | or | Delegating authority |
| 5. Covering your rear | or | Documenting decisions |
| 6. Creating conflict | or | Encouraging change and innovation |
| 7. Forming coalitions | or | Facilitating teamwork |
| 8. Whistle blowing | or | Improving efficiency |
| 9. Nit picking | or | Meticulous attention to detail |
| 10. Scheming | or | Planning ahead |

responsibilities, and salary adjustments are just a few examples of the resources about which organizational members will disagree.

Resources in organizations are limited. This often turns potential conflict into real conflict. If resources were abundant, then all the various interests within the organization could satisfy their goals. Because resources are limited, not everyone's interests can be provided for. Further, whether true or not, gains by one individual or group are often perceived as being at the expense of others within the organization. These forces create a competition among members for the organization's limited resources.

Maybe the most important factor leading to politics within organizations is the realization that most of the "facts" that are used to allocate the limited resources are open to interpretation. What, for instance, is "good" performance? What's a "good" job? What's an "adequate" improvement? The coach of any National Football League team knows a quarterback rating of 88 is a high performer and one with a 23 rating is a poor performer. You don't need to be a football genius to know you should play the top quarterback and keep the lower rated one on the bench. But what if you have to choose between two quarterbacks who have ratings of 74 and 77? Then other factors—less objective ones—come into play: attitude, potential, ability to perform in the clutch, and so on.

Most supervisory decisions in organizations more closely resemble choosing between two fairly equally rated quarterbacks than deciding between a superstar and a bench warmer. It is in this large and ambiguous middle ground of organizational life—where the facts don't speak for themselves—that politics takes place.

Finally, because most decisions have to be made in a climate of ambiguity (where facts are rarely fully objective, and thus are open to interpretation), people within the organization will use whatever influence they can to taint the facts to support their goals and interests. That, of course, creates motivation for the activities we call politicking.

## CAN YOU PLAY POLITICS AND STILL BE ETHICAL?

All political actions are not necessarily unethical. To help guide you in differentiating ethical from unethical politicking, there are some questions you should consider. Exhibit 12–7 illustrates a decision tree to guide ethical actions. The first question you need to answer addresses self-interest versus organizational goals. Ethical actions are consistent with the organization's goals. Spreading untrue rumors about the safety of a new product introduced by your company, in order to make that product's design group look bad, is unethical. However, there may be nothing unethical if you, as a department head, exchange favors with your division's purchasing supervisor, in order to get a critical contract processed quickly.

The second question is concerned with the rights of other parties. If you went down to the mail room during your lunch hour and read through the mail directed to the purchasing supervisor (described in the previous paragraph) with the intent of "getting something on him" so he'd expedite your contract, you'd be acting unethically. You would have violated the purchasing supervisor's right to privacy.

The final question that needs to be addressed relates to whether the political activity conforms to standards of equity and justice. If you inflate the performance evaluation of a favored employee and deflate the evaluation of a disfavored employee, then use these evaluations to justify giving the former a big raise and nothing to the latter, you have treated the disfavored employee unfairly.

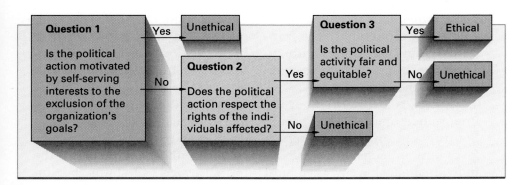

## EXHIBIT 12–7
Is a political action ethical?

# HOW DO YOU KNOW WHEN YOU SHOULD PLAY POLITICS?

Before you consider your political options in any situation, you need to evaluate that situation. The key situational factors are your organization's culture, the power of others, and your own power (see Building a Supervisory Skill).

## YOUR ORGANIZATION'S CULTURE

**Culture**
a set of underwritten norms that members of the organization accept and understand, and which guide their actions.

The place to begin is with assessing your organization's culture to determine which behaviors are desirable and which aren't.

Every organization has a system of shared meaning called its **culture.** This culture is a set of unwritten norms that members of the organization accept and understand, and which guide their actions. For example, some organizations' cultures encourage risk taking, accept conflicts and disagreements, allow employees a great deal of autonomy, and reward members according to performance criteria. Other organizations' cultures differ by 180 degrees: they punish risk taking, seek harmony and cooperation at any price, minimize opportunities for employees to show initiative, and allocate rewards to people according to such criteria as seniority, effort, or loyalty. The point is that every organization's culture is somewhat different, and if a political strategy is to succeed, it must be compatible with the culture (see News Flash).

# NEWS FLASH!     STATUS IN ORGANIZATIONS

**Status**
a social rank or the importance one has in a group.

Traditionally in organizations, those individuals who are politically shrewd often have the trimmings that go along with it. These are things that are grouped under the heading of status.

**Status** is a social rank or the importance one has in a group. Status is not something a person gives him or herself. Although an individual may have worked hard to achieve something, having status requires at least two people.

That is, someone else must view that individual as having a higher ranking (in some capacity) than he or she does. A supervisor's status may come from a number of sources. Generally these sources are grouped in two ways—formal and informal. Much of the discussion on power and politics, as well as authority, focuses on the formal aspects of status. For instance, the title supervisor carries a certain level of prestige with it.
*(continued)*

It implies you have the ability to direct others, and affect their work lives.

On the other hand, status may be informally conferred on a supervisor by characteristics such as education, age, skill, or experience. Anything a supervisor has can have status value if others evaluate it as such. Of course, just because status is informal does not mean that it is less important to a supervisor or that there is less agreement on whether or not one has it.

It is especially important in organizations to believe that the formal status system is fitting. That is, there should be fairness between perceived ranking and the status "symbols" given. If it is lacking, problems can arise between people in organizations.[4] Consider a situation where the supervisor of the quality control department has an office that is smaller, located in an isolated part of the organization, and is not as well furnished as a new employee just joining the unit. If one views importance in terms of the office and its furnishings,

then one might come to the conclusion that the new employee is more highly regarded than the supervisor. That's probably not the case! Yet, inconsistencies in status ranking have sent the wrong message.

Status may also have an effect on employees' willingness to work hard. For instance, imagine the potential for conflict if employees earn more than their supervisor—and that's not as unrealistic as one might think! That's because the supervisor may be paid a fixed salary and be ineligible for overtime pay. The employees, on the other hand, get paid on an hourly basis and, after working more than 40 hours in a week, earn time and one-half. If an employee works a lot of overtime, he or she could conceivably be making more money than the supervisor. That can easily be controlled if the supervisor simply stops overtime outright. However, in doing so, the supervisor may be losing sight of the goals of the department. In such a case, status got in the way of goal attainment!

[4]W. F. Whyte, "The Social Structure of the Restaurant," *American Journal of Sociology*, January 1954, pp. 302–308.

## THE POWER OF OTHERS

People are either powerful or they're not, right? Wrong! Power is differential. On some issues, a person may be very powerful. Yet that same person may be relatively powerless on other issues. What you need to do, therefore, is determine which individuals or groups will be powerful in a given situation.

Some people will have influence as a result of their formal position in the organization. That is probably the best place to begin your power assessment. What decision or issue do you want to influence? Who has formal authority to affect that issue? The answer to that is only the beginning. After determining who has formal authority, consider others—individuals, coalitions, departments—who may have a vested interest in the decision's outcome. Who might gain or lose as a result of one choice being selected over another? This helps to identify the power players— those motivated to engage in politicking. It also pinpoints your likely adversaries.

Now you need to specifically assess the power of each player or group of players. In addition to each one's formal authority, evaluate the resources each controls and his or her location in the organization. The control of scarce and important resources is a source of power in organizations. Control and access to key information, expert knowledge, and possession of special skills are examples of resources that may be scarce and important to the organization; hence, they become potential means of influencing organizational decisions. In addition, being in the right place in the organization can be a source of power. This explains, for example, the frequent power of secretaries. They are often in the direct flow of key information and control the access of others to their bosses.

Assess your boss's influence in any power analysis. What is his or her position on the issue under concern? For, against, or neutral? If it's for or against, how intense is your boss's stand? What is your boss's power status in the organization? Strong or weak? Answers to these questions can help you assess whether the support or opposition of your boss will be relevant.

These IBM software testers in Boca Raton, Florida reflect this office's informality. A new supervisor with effective political skills would adjust his or her dress and style to reflect the appropriate image.

## BECOMING POLITICALLY SMART

### ABOUT THE SKILL

Although there are few clear-cut ways of not getting involved in office politics, there are some suggestions that can be offered to help you in becoming politically smart. These recommendations, however, are not designed to teach you how to take advantage of someone else—or a given situation. Rather, they are intended to help you develop a personal profile, which can assist you if you find yourself in a political situation.

1. **Frame arguments in terms of organizational goals.** Effective politicking requires covering up self-interest. No matter that your objective is self-serving; all the arguments you marshal in support of it must be framed in terms of the benefits that will accrue to the organization. People whose actions appear to blatantly further their own interests at the expense of the organization's are almost universally denounced, are likely to lose influence, and often suffer the ultimate penalty of being expelled from the organization.

2. **Portray the proper image.** What others think about you is important to your political success. You need to understand the organization's culture and act accordingly. Accept and demonstrate the values, norms, and behaviors that the organization wants. Doing so shows that you know what is important for organizational survival. Portraying the proper image also increases your likelihood that when you do raise an issue, others may give it more legitimacy. An "outcast" who's always complaining rarely gets an audience—even if he or she is right.

3. **Gain control of organizational resources.** The control of organizational resources that are scarce and important is a source of power. Knowledge and expertise are particularly effective resources to control. They make you more valuable to the organization, and therefore more likely to gain security, advancement, and a receptive audience for your ideas.

4. **Make yourself appear indispensable.** Since we're dealing with appearances rather than objective facts, you can enhance your power by appearing to be indispensable. That is, you don't have to really be indispensable as long as key people in the organization believe that you are. If the prime decision makers believe there is no ready substitute for what you are giving the organization, they are likely to go to great lengths to ensure that your desires are satisfied. How do you make yourself appear indispensable? The most effective means is to develop expertise (through experience, contacts, secret techniques, and natural talents) that is perceived as critical to the organization's operations and that key decision makers believe no one else possesses to the extent that you do.

5. **Be visible.** Since the evaluation of supervisory effectiveness has a substantial subjective component, it is important that your boss and those in power in the organization be made aware of your contribution. If you are fortunate enough to have responsibilities that bring your accomplishments to the attention of others, it may not be necessary to take direct measures to increase your visibility. But your department may handle activities that are low in visi-

*(continued)*

bility, or your specific contribution may be indistinguishable because you're part of a team endeavor. In such cases—without creating the image of a braggart—you'll want to call attention to yourself by giving progress reports to your boss and others, being seen at social functions, being active in your professional associations, developing powerful allies who speak positively about your accomplishments, and similar tactics. Of course, the skilled politician actively and successfully lobbies to get those projects that will increase his or her visibility.

6. **Find a Mentor.** Nothing helps you avoid land mines better than someone who knows where the land mines are. Getting them to navigate your path makes things so much safer. In organizations, this navigator is called a mentor. A **mentor** is someone who is usually a more experienced and more senior member of the organization. They are usually already part of the "power" group, and their role is to be your support system. Mentors are also people who can vouch for you in the organization. They often are able to get you exposure to the power-brokers in the organization, and provide you advice on how to effectively maneuver through the system. From a political point of view, a mentor can act as a sounding-board for you, providing vital suggestions and feedback on how to survive and succeed.

7. **Develop powerful allies.** It helps to have powerful people in your camp. In addition to a mentor, you can cultivate contacts with potentially influential people above you and among other supervisors. They can provide you with important information that may not be available through normal channels. Additionally, there will be times when decisions will be made by those with the greatest support. Sometimes—though not always—there is strength in numbers. Having powerful allies can provide you with a coalition of support if and when you need it.

8. **Avoid tarnished individuals.** In almost every organization, there are fringe members whose status is questionable. Their performance and/or loyalty is under close scrutiny. Such individuals, while they are under the microscope, are "tainted." Carefully keep your distance from them. We all tend to judge others by the company they keep. Given the reality that effectiveness has a large subjective component, your own effectiveness might be called into question if you are perceived as being too closely associated with tainted people.

9. **Support your boss.** Your immediate future is in the hands of your current boss. Since he or she evaluates your performance, you will typically want to do whatever is necessary to have your boss on your side. You should make every effort to help your boss succeed and look good. Provide support if he or she is under siege and spend the time to find out what criteria will be used to assess your effectiveness. Don't undermine your boss. Don't speak negatively of him or her to others. If the individual is competent, visible, and in possession of a power base, she or he is likely to be on the way up in the organization. By being perceived as supportive, you increase the likelihood that you will be pulled along. ∎

## YOUR POWER

After looking at others' power, assess your own power base. What's your personal power? What power does your supervisory position in the organization provide? Where do you stand relative to others who hold power?

Your power can come from several sources. If you've got a charismatic personality, for instance, you can exert power because others will want to know your position on issues, your arguments will often be perceived as persuasive, and your position is likely to carry considerable weight in others' decisions. Another frequent source of power for supervisors is access to important information that others in the organization need.

**Mentor**
a more experienced and more senior member of the organization who can act as a sounding-board, providing vital suggestions and feedback on how to survive and succeed in the organization.

---

## SOMETHING TO THINK ABOUT *(and to promote class discussion)*

Gaining political power and building a power base in an organization is often fostered with the help of a mentor. In the past, however, most of those who were "supported" by an experienced, senior member of the organization often shared something in common. That is, they were usually male and white. But what about women, and people of color? What opportunities lie ahead for them to find and get this support?

Finding or getting a mentor is rarely easy. In fact, more often than not, you are approached by the other person. What can serve as the "attraction" to bring the two of you together? In the past, it was something a potential mentor saw in you—which was often something they saw in themselves years ago. But how can a male properly relate to a female or vice versa? How can individuals from different races or national origins identify with each other when there's no foundation of commonality between them? Unquestionably, these can be major issues—many of which we've highlighted in previous chapters. Organizations are attempting to bridge this gap. Many recognize that leaving it up to nature just won't work. There needs to be something in place such as special programs that promote senior members taking junior members under their wing. Yet, even when these programs exist, other problems still may arise. For example, is the male supervisor mentoring a younger female employee exhibiting appropriate mentoring behavior, or is she getting special treatment because she's a woman? If the two of them develop a close, personal work relationship is there a risk of crossing the line into sexual harassment?

Despite the potential difficulties diversity offers for mentoring, the fact remains that each of us needs this support. Therefore, if someone doesn't approach you, you must make every effort to find a mentor yourself. In either case, being mentored requires work on your part. That effort will only be magnified when your mentor is someone who has personal attributes different from yours.

What do you think about this diversity issue?

# NEGOTIATION

**Negotiation**
a process in which two or more parties who have different preferences and priorities must make a joint decision and come to an agreement.

We know that lawyers and auto sales people spend a significant amount of time on their jobs negotiating. So, too, do managers. They have to negotiate salaries for incoming employees, cut deals with their bosses, work out differences with their peers, and resolve conflicts with employees. For our purposes, we'll define **negotiation** as a process in which two or more parties who have different preferences must make a joint decision and come to an agreement. To achieve this goal, both parties typically use a bargaining strategy.

## HOW DO BARGAINING STRATEGIES DIFFER?

There are two general approaches to negotiation—distributive bargaining and integrative bargaining.[5] Let's see what's involved in each of these approaches.

You see a used car advertised for sale in the newspaper. It appears to be just what you've been looking for. You go out to see the car. It's great and you want it. The owner tells you the asking price. You don't want to pay that much. The two of you then negotiate over the price. The negotiating process you are engaging in is called **distributive bargaining.** Its most identifying feature is that it operates under zero-sum conditions. That is, any gain you make is at the expense of the other person, and vice versa. Referring to the used car example, every dollar you can get the seller to cut from the car's price is a dollar you save. Conversely, every dollar more he or she can get from you comes at your expense. Thus the essence of distributive bargaining is negotiating over who gets what share of a fixed pie.

**Distributive bargaining**
a negotiating process that operates under zero-sum conditions; any gain made is at the expense of the other person, and vice versa.

Probably the most widely cited example of distributive bargaining is in labor-management negotiations over wages and benefits (see chapter 15). Typically, labor's representatives come to the bargaining table determined to get as much as they can from management. Because every cent more that labor negotiates increases management's costs, each party bargains aggressively and often treats the other as an opponent who must be defeated.

In distributive bargaining, each party has a target point that defines what he or she would like to achieve. Each also has a resistance point that marks the lowest outcome that's acceptable (see Exhibit 12–8). The area between their resistance points is the settlement range. As long as there is some overlap in their aspiration ranges, there exists a settlement area where each one's aspirations can be met.

When engaged in distributive bargaining, your tactics should focus on trying to get your opponent to agree to your specific target point or to get as close to it as possible. Examples of such tactics are persuading your opponent

[5]R. E. Walton and R. B. McKersie, *A Behavioral Theory of Labor Negotiations: An Analysis of a Social Interaction System* (New York, NY: McGraw-Hill, 1965).

PART V COPING WITH WORKPLACE DYNAMICS

## EXHIBIT 12–8

Staking out the bargaining zone.

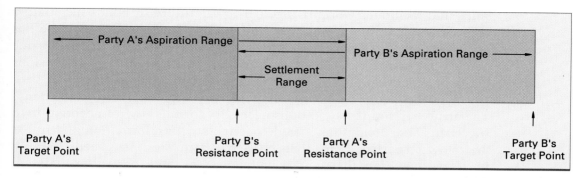

of the impossibility of getting to his or her target point and the advisability of accepting a settlement near yours; arguing that your target is fair, while your opponent's isn't; and attempting to get your opponent to feel emotionally generous toward you and thus accept an outcome close to your target point.

A sales representative for a women's sportswear manufacturer has just closed a $15,000 order from a small clothing retailer. The sales rep calls in the order to her firm's credit department. She is told that the firm can't approve credit to this customer because of a past slow-pay record. The next day, the sales rep and the firm's credit supervisor meet to discuss the problem. The sales rep doesn't want to lose the business. Neither does the credit supervisor, but he also doesn't want to get stuck with an uncollectible debt. The two openly review their options. After considerable discussion, they agree on a solution that meets both their needs. The credit supervisor will approve the sale, but the clothing store's owner will provide a bank guarantee that will assure payment if the bill isn't paid within sixty days.

The sales-credit negotiation is an example of **integrative bargaining.** In contrast to distributive bargaining, integrative problem solving operates

Integrative bargaining a negotiating process that operates under the assumption that there is at least one settlement that can create a win-win solution.

Who's one of the best distributive bargaining negotiators? It's Bill Richardson, U.S. Ambassador to the United Nations. He has negotiated with some of the most difficult negotiators in the world—like Saddam Hussein, Fidel Castro, and General Abachi of Nigeria. What's his trick? Richardson is a good listener, he prepares for the negotiations, and he gets to know what his "adversaries" want.

under the assumption that there is at least one settlement that can create a win-win solution. In general, integrative bargaining is preferable to distributive bargaining. Why? Because the former builds long-term relationships and facilitates working together in the future. It bonds negotiators and allows each to leave the bargaining table feeling that he or she has achieved a victory. Distributive bargaining, on the other hand, leaves one party a potential loser. It tends to build animosities and deepen divisions between people who have to work together on an ongoing basis.

Why, then, don't we see more integrative bargaining in organizations? The answer lies in the conditions necessary for this type of negotiation to succeed. These conditions include openness with information and frankness between parties; a sensitivity by each party to the other's needs; the ability to trust one another; and a willingness by both parties to maintain flexibility.[6] Because many organizational cultures and intraorganizational relationships are not characterized by openness, trust, and flexibility, it isn't surprising that negotiations often take on a win-at-any-cost dynamic. With that in mind, let's look at some suggestions for negotiating successfully.

---

## POP QUIZ    (Are You Comprehending What You're Reading?)

**5.** Which one of the following is not an example of political behavior that exists in an organization?
  **a.** leaking confidential information about organizational activities to the media
  **b.** using informal communications channels to expedite important messages
  **c.** whistle-blowing
  **d.** withholding key information from decision makers
**6.** What situational factors lead to office politics?
**7.** The most identifying feature of distributive bargaining is that it operates under zero-sum conditions. True or False?
**8.** The process in which two or more parties who have different preferences must make a joint decision to come to an agreement is called _____ .
  **a.** delegation
  **b.** empowerment
  **c.** conflict-handling
  **d.** none of the above

---

[6]K. W. Thomas, "Conflict and Negotiation Processes in Organizations," in M. D. Dunnette and L. M. Hough, eds. *Handbook of Industrial and Organizational Psychology*, 2nd ed., Vol. 3 (Palo Alto, CA: Consulting Psychologists Press, 1992), pp. 651–717.

# How Do You Develop Effective Negotiation Skills?

The essence of effective negotiation can be summarized in the following six recommendations.[7]

## CONSIDER THE OTHER PARTY'S SITUATION

Acquire as much information as you can about your opponent's interests and goals. What constituencies must he or she appease? What is his or her strategy? This information will help you understand your opponent's behavior, predict responses to your offers, and frame solutions in terms of the opponent's interests. Additionally, when you can anticipate your opponent's position, you are better equipped to counter his or her arguments with the facts and figures that support your position.

## HAVE A CONCRETE STRATEGY

Treat negotiation like a chess match. Expert chess players have a strategy. They know ahead of time how they will respond to any given situation. How strong is your situation and how important is the issue? Are you willing to split differences to achieve an early solution? If the issue is very important to you, is your position strong enough to let you play hardball and show little or no willingness to compromise? These are questions you should address before you begin bargaining.

## BEGIN WITH A POSITIVE OVERTURE

Studies on negotiation show that concessions tend to be reciprocated and lead to agreements. As a result, begin bargaining with a positive overture—perhaps a small concession—and then reciprocate your opponent's concessions.

## ADDRESS PROBLEMS, NOT PERSONALITIES

Concentrate on the negotiation issues, not on the personal characteristics of your opponent. When negotiations get tough, avoid the tendency to attack your opponent. It's your opponent's ideas or position that you disagree with, not him or her personally. Separate the people from the problem, and don't personalize differences.

---

[7]Based on R. Fisher and W. Ury, *Getting to Yes: Negotiating Agreement Without Giving In* (Boston, MA: Houghton Mifflin, 1981); J. A. Wall, Jr. and M. W. Blum, "Negotiations," *Journal of Management* (June 1991), pp. 295–296; and M. H. Bazerman and M. A. Neale, *Negotiating Rationally* (New York, NY: Free Press, 1992).

## PAY LITTLE ATTENTION TO INITIAL OFFERS

Treat an initial offer as merely a point of departure. Everyone has to have an initial position. These initial offers tend to be extreme and idealistic. Treat them as such.

## EMPHASIZE WIN-WIN SOLUTIONS

Bargainers often assume that their gain must come at the expense of the other party. As noted with integrative bargaining, that needn't be the case. There are often win-win solutions. Assuming a zero-sum game means missed opportunities for trade-offs that could benefit both sides. So if conditions are supportive, look for an integrative solution. Frame options in terms of your opponent's interests and look for solutions that can allow your opponent, as well as yourself, to declare a victory.

## SUMMARY

After reading this chapter, I can:

1. **Define conflict.** Conflict is a process in which one party consciously interferes in the goal-achievement efforts of another party.
2. **Identify the three general sources of conflict.** Conflicts generally come from one of three sources: communication differences, structural differentiation, or personal differences.
3. **List the five basic techniques for resolving conflict.** The five basic techniques for resolving conflict are avoidance, accommodation, force, compromise, and collaboration.
4. **Describe how a supervisor could stimulate conflict.** A supervisor could stimulate conflict by communicating ambiguous messages or planting rumors, bringing in outsiders with different backgrounds or personalities, restructuring the department, or appointing a devil's advocate.
5. **Define politicking.** Politicking is the actions you can take to influence, or attempt to influence, the distribution of advantages and disadvantages within your department.
6. **Explain the existence of politics in organizations.** Politics exist in organizations because individuals have different values, goals, and interests; organizational resources are limited; the criteria for allocating the limited resources are ambiguous; and individuals seek influence so they can shape the criteria to support their goals and interests.
7. **List specific guidelines for developing and improving political skills.** To develop and improve your political skills, frame arguments in terms of organizational goals, develop the right image, gain control of organizational resources, make yourself appear indispensable, be visible, get a mentor, develop powerful allies, avoid "tainted" members, and support your boss.
8. **Contrast distributive and integrative bargaining.** Distributive bargaining creates a win-lose situation because the object of negotiation is treated as fixed in amount. Integrative bargaining treats available resources as variable, and hence creates the potential for win-win solutions.

## REVIEWING YOUR KNOWLEDGE

1. How can conflict benefit an organization?
2. In what ways can an organization's structure create conflict?
3. What is conflict management?
4. When should you avoid conflict? When should you seek compromise?
5. What is a devil's advocate? How does an advocate effect conflict in a department?
6. Can an organization be free of politics? Explain.
7. Is it unethical to "play politics"? Discuss a situation where it is; and one where it is not.
8. How do you assess another person's power in an organization?
9. How can increased visibility enhance a person's power?
10. Assume you found an apartment that you wanted to rent and the ad said: "$550/month negotiable." What could you do to improve the likelihood that you would negotiate the lowest possible price?

# ANSWERS TO THE POP QUIZZES

1. **a. when a supervisor is surrounded by "yes people."** This is one of the items listed in Exhibit 12–5 which indicates a need to stimulate conflict. Response (b) indicates a need for training. And responses (c) and (d) are preferred unit characteristics.

2. **Describe why all conflict cannot be completely eliminated in organizations.** All conflict cannot be completely eliminated in organizations because it is a natural phenomenon of organizational life. That's because (1) organizational members have different goals; (2) there are scarce resources, like budget allocations, which various people want and are willing to fight over; and (3) people in organizations don't all see things alike as a result of their diverse backgrounds, education, experiences, and interests.

3. **False.** The ultimate win-win conflict resolution technique which seeks to satisfy each party's interests is **collaboration.**

4. **b. devil's advocate.** This is the definition of the actions of a devil's advocate.

5. **b. using informal communications channels to expedite important messages.** This choice was not identified as an example of political behavior. The other responses were examples.

6. Situational factors leading to office politics include individuals with different backgrounds and values, conflict over limited resources, and the realization that most of the "facts" that are used to allocate the limited resources are open to interpretation.

7. **True.** The most identifying feature of distributive bargaining is that it operates under zero-sum conditions. That is, any gain one makes is at the expense of the other person, and vice versa.

8. **d. none of the above.** The process in which two or more parties who have different preferences must make a joint decision to come to an agreement is called **negotiation.** ∎

## A Class Exercise: Negotiations

Break into pairs. This is a role-play exercise. One person will play the role of Terry, the department supervisor. The other person will play Dale, Terry's boss.

### The Situation

Terry and Dale work for Nike in Portland, Oregon. They are both former college runners who have worked for Nike for more than six years. Terry supervises a research laboratory. Dale is the manager of research and development. Dale has been Terry's boss for two years.

One of Terry's employees has greatly impressed Terry. This employee is Barbara Mitchell. Barbara was hired 11 months ago. She is 26 years old and holds a master's degree in mechanical engineering. Her entry-level salary was $42,500 a year. She was told by Terry that, in accordance with corporate policy, she would receive an initial performance evaluation at six months and a comprehensive review after one year. Based on her performance record, Barbara was told she could expect a salary adjustment at the time of the one-year evaluation.

Terry's evaluation of Barbara after six months was very positive. Terry commented on the long hours Barbara was putting in, her cooperative spirit, the fact that others in the lab enjoyed working with her, and that she was making an immediate positive impact on the project she had been assigned. Now that Barbara's first anniversary is coming up, Terry has again reviewed Barbara's performance. Terry thinks Barbara may be the best new person the R&D group has ever hired. After only a year, Terry has rated Barbara as the number three ranked performer in a department of eleven.

Salaries in the department vary greatly. Terry, for instance, has a basic salary of $67,000, plus eligibility for a bonus that might add another $8,000 to $11,000 a year. The salary range of the eleven department members is $36,400 to $61,350. The lowest salary is a recent hire with a bachelor's degree in physics. The two people that Terry has rated above Barbara earn base salaries of $49,700 and $53,350. They're both 31 years old and have been at Nike for three and four years, respectively. The median salary in Terry's department is $52,660.

**Terry's Role:** You want to give Barbara a big raise. While she's been with your unit only one year, she has proven to be an excellent addition to the department. You don't want to lose her. More importantly, she knows in general what other people in the department are earning and she thinks she's underpaid. The company typically gives one-year raises of 5 percent, although 10 percent is not unusual and 20 to 30 percent increases have been approved on occasion. You'd like to get Barbara as large an increase as Dale will approve.

**Dale's Role:** All your supervisors typically try to squeeze you for as much money as they can for their people. You understand this because you did the same thing when you were a supervisor. However, your boss wants to keep a lid on costs. He wants you to keep raises for recent hires generally in the 5 to 8 percent range. In fact, he's sent a memo to all managers and supervisors saying this. However, your boss is also very concerned with equity and paying people what they're worth. You feel assured that he will support any salary recommendation you make, as long as it can be justified. Your goal, consistent with cost reduction, is to keep salary increases as low as possible.

Terry has a meeting scheduled with Dale to discuss Barbara's performance review and salary adjustment. Take up to 15 minutes to conduct your negotiation. When your negotiation is complete, the class will compare the various negotiation strategies used and pair outcomes.

## Thinking Critically

### CASE 12.A

## Game Playing at the Cheese Factory

Mark Cummins is the supervisor of the night production line crew at Kraft Cheese. Mark has been in his position for four years and has learned a great deal about worker behavior. Some of his workers are self-motivated; others are lazy and need constant supervision to get an average amount of work done. Others he would classify as whistleblowers, nitpickers, and buck passers. He even has a couple of people who love to create conflict and seem to dream up ways to scheme against other workers and company officials.

Mark's crew compares favorably with the day crew in most of the indicators that are important to Kraft—quality, safety, employee turnover, and teamwork. It is the last element that bothers Mark the most because the other factors are so dependent upon teamwork. Mark feels he has to be on the lookout constantly for all the "gameplaying" his crew engages in, and he wonders how effective he really is in warding off conflict.

Mark has had some discussions about these problems with his night crew chief, Carol Lynch. Ms. Lynch has offered several worthwhile suggestions which have improved Mark's ability to resolve conflicts and deal with potential conflicts. When Ms. Lynch suggested Mark go with her to an upcoming seminar on "Politics and Conflict Resolution," Mark liked the idea. Mark doesn't want anything to do with organizational politics and hopes the seminar will teach him ways to avoid politicking.

## Responding to the Case

1. What can Mark and Carol hope to learn from the seminar about conflict and conflict management?
2. Assume they are told to assess their work environment's political landscape. What factors will they assess?
3. Assuming the seminar stresses guidelines for improving political skills, what advantage could the guidelines be to Mark? How might he implement the guidelines?
4. Identify some of the ways Mark could use politics to his advantage. Discuss the ethics of each suggestion you identified.

### CASE 12.B

## Ed Sapp's Promotion

Ed Sapp was flattered to be asked to become supervisor of the office staff at Home Video, Inc. Most of Ed's coworkers agreed that he was the right person to get the promotion. Ed got along with everyone. He was the "informal leader" among his six coworkers.

For example, when Carlos and Victoria would argue over how a customer's order should have been processed, it was Ed who would get "both sides of the story"—usually first from Carlos and then from Victoria. When John was unhappy about something or someone around the office—which was most of the time—John would turn to Ed for a sounding board. When Rose wanted some information about the "facts" of a rumor, she would go to Ed. Rose found Ed very level-headed about most situations. Ed and Rose had some good discussions, and she would frequently ask his opinion about a lot of things—from changes occurring in the organization, to conflicts within the office staff and among other employees in the store. Yes, Ed was the person for the job—even Mary and Leslie spoke up to say that Ed would be able to represent their interests to company officials better than any other person in the office. In her heart, however, Leslie really wanted the job for herself.

## RESPONDING TO THE CASE

1. Identify some of Ed's potential conflict problems in this case.
2. Apply the five basic conflict-resolution techniques to the conflicts you identified.
3. Do you think Ed will need to stimulate conflict in his department? Why or why not?
4. What are some of the ethical ways Ed can use politicking to his advantage? What pitfalls should he avoid that may have undertones of unethical politicking?
5. How do you think Ed's relationships will change with his coworkers when he becomes their supervisor? How should he prepare for this change? ■

# 13 DEALING WITH CHANGE AND STRESS

# LEARNING OBJECTIVES 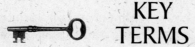 KEY TERMS

After reading this chapter, you should be able to:

1. Describe the traditional and contemporary views of change.
2. Explain why employees resist change.
3. Identify ways supervisors can reduce resistance to change.
4. List the steps a supervisor can use in changing negative employee attitudes.
5. Define stress.
6. Explain what causes work-related stress.
7. Contrast Type A and Type B behavior.

You should also be able to define these supervisory terms:

attitudes

change agent

change process

employee assistance programs (EAPs)

role ambiguity

role conflict

role overload

stress

Type A behavior

wellness programs

Type B behavior

Bill Collingsworth was a bit tired. He'd spent the previous night partying into the wee hours with a group of close friends from work. They were celebrating Bill's twentieth anniversary at the Alcoa plant in upstate New York. "I came to work here in July 1968, right out of college, as a metal roller. The supervisor at the time decided to retire several months later. Because of my education and background, I was offered the job. I've been in the job ever since."

When asked to recall how his job had changed over twenty years, he smiled. "Other than my title, I don't think anything is the same. In those early days, I had a secretary. She typed all my correspondence and made up the schedules and reports. Had to make three copies of everything—and she did that with carbon paper. Do you remember carbon paper? If I wanted to know the status of an order or whether a certain product was in inventory, I'd have to make a few calls. Like now, I spent a lot of time in meetings. But the meetings are different nowadays. And, of course, the people in my department are very different now. In 1970, I had six people reporting to me. All were high school graduates, many attending community college at night. I was the only one who had a college degree. My employees were paid hourly. They had to punch in and out on a time clock. They came to me frequently for solutions to problems they were experiencing on their jobs. I think most expected me to tell them what to do. Oh yeah, I almost forgot. We used to get this quarterly newsletter from the head honcho in New York. He'd describe all the things the company was planning to do. Now we have a closed-circuit television system throughout the company and the top brass put on question-and-answer sessions every Friday afternoon.

## INTRODUCTION

If it weren't for *change*, the supervisor's job would be relatively easy. Planning would be without problems because tomorrow would be no different from today. Given that the environment would be free from uncertainty, there would be no need to adapt. Decision making would be dramatically simplified because the outcome of each alternative could be predicted with almost certain accuracy. It would, indeed, simplify the supervisor's job if, for example, no new products were introduced, government regulations were never modified, technology never changed, or employees' needs didn't change.

It's a different world here today. I have no secretary. I do all my own correspondence and reports on my computer. The photocopier replaced carbon paper; then a few years back, e-mail replaced making paper copies. It used to take four days to get a physical order form from a sales office. We relied on the mail back then. Now we receive orders by fax—we have them minutes after the salesperson closes a deal. Twenty years ago, it would take a couple of phone calls and a half hour or more to check on the status of an order. It takes me about twenty seconds to do it now. Our information system tracks every order, and I can access that data from the computer here on my desk. While I still spend an hour or more every day in meetings, for most of them I never leave my office. Our computers are all networked, so we just do electronic meetings. But maybe the biggest change has to do with the people I work with. My boss and his boss all have graduate degrees. Everyone in my department is a college graduate. They're a lot smarter than the metal rollers we had twenty years ago. They want to be challenged more. I let them organize and monitor their own work. They're all paid on a monthly basis rather than hourly. They come and go as they wish. They're very responsible. If they need to work an hour or two extra or come in on Saturdays to get a project complete, they do it. Instead of telling them what to do, I'm basically here to coordinate production jobs, provide direction for the department, communicate with company officials, and help solve problems that my people need help with. I guess you could say I'm really their resource person." ■

However, change is an organizational reality. Handling change is an integral part of every supervisor's job. The forces that are "out there" simply demand it (see News Flash)!

## FORCES FOR CHANGE

In Chapter 2, we pointed out that there are both external and internal forces that constrain supervisors. These same forces also bring about the need for change. Let's briefly look at the factors that can create the need for change (see Exhibit 13–1).

# TECHNOLOGY CHANGES SEW THINGS UP

In 1978 French Rags was a $10 million-a-year business manufacturing women's knitwear.[1] From an outsider's perspective, the business looked healthy. French Rags products were being sold at leading department stores like Neiman Marcus, Bonwit Teller, and Bloomingdale's. However, inside the company it was known that many of these retailers were slow in paying for merchandise, which put financial pressures on French Rags' financial resources. Additionally, company officials were frustrated by department store buyers who were often choosing to sell just a few of the company's styles, sizes, and colors. They felt that their knitwear product line was only reaching a small percentage of its potential.

French Rags' financial and distribution problems were solved and the business was completely reshaped by two isolated events in 1989. First, company officials were introduced to an expert in knitting equipment who just happened to have acquired a German-made Stoll computerized knitting machine. The sleek Stoll knitting machine uses thousands of precisely angled needles to do things the old-fashioned way—one stitch at a time—while simultaneously churning out garments at a breathtaking pace. This one machine could produce as much as two dozen of French Rags' hand knitters. Second, the company's cash crunch forced officials to cut back production and sell only to the few stores that were willing to pay cash on delivery. One loyal customer, frustrated by not being able to buy her favored French Rags garments, called the company. On learning of French Rags' money problems, the customer said to company officials, "You bring your clothes to my house, and I know 20 people who'll buy them." Desperate, a company official went to the customer's home—and proceeded to take an order for $80,000 worth of products (with a 50 percent deposit).

These two events—the availability of a knitting expert with a computerized knitting machine and access to a new marketing channel—reinvented French Rags. Today, the company produces custom-made knitwear and sells

*(continued)*

[1] H. Plotkin, "Riches to Rags," *INC. Technology* (Summer 1995), pp 62–67.

it directly to customers. Its sales distribution system no longer includes retail stores. The sales force is now comprised of customers who sell goods out of their homes. The company supplies them with order forms, sample garments, and fabric snippets of 30 color choices. After customers make their selections and pick out their preferred color combinations, individual measurements are taken, a 50 percent down payment is secured, and the order form is faxed to the French Rags factory. It is at this point that French Rags' high-tech operation kicks into gear.

The company now owns 11 of the Stoll machines. Using custom software that produces knit-by-number templates for fast and easy switching from one garment to another and a Silicon Graphics workstation for designing the knitwear—when combined with the new, low-cost home distribution system—French Rags is able to produce quality, custom-made knitwear and sell it at off-the-rack prices. Using a personal computer, a software program produces portable templates with instructions about which color yarns should be loaded on which spools atop a knitting machine as the machine is about to knit a particular garment. An elaborate knit jacket that used to take a skilled craftsperson a day and a half to knit by hand can be produced on this equipment in less than an hour. Another jacket, in another style and color combination, can then be made in the following hour with a different knit-by-number template.

French Rags can offer its customers more than 50,000 possible style and color combinations, allowing them to wear custom-made outfits that fit perfectly and are exactly like no other. The company ships its merchandise directly to customers, usually within four to six weeks. Best of all, for a business that had consistently had money problems, French Rags no longer has to worry about carrying inventories or accounts receivables. As one company official noted, "We have no inventory problems because we have no inventory. Everything we make is presold."

## EXHIBIT 13–1

Forces of change.

| EXTERNAL | INTERNAL |
|---|---|
| • Marketplace | • Long Range Plans |
| • Government Regulations | • New Equipment |
| • Technology | • Work Force |
| • Economic Forces | • Compensation and Benefits |
| | • Employee Attitudes |

## WHAT ARE THE EXTERNAL FORCES CREATING A NEED FOR CHANGE?

The external forces that create the need for change come from various sources (see Assessing Yourself). In recent years, the marketplace has affected companies like Domino's Pizza by introducing new competition. For instance, Domino's must now contend with a host of new competitors like Pizza Hut and Little Caesar's, which recently have moved into the home-delivery market. Government laws and regulations are a frequent impetus for change. In 1990, the passage of the Americans with Disabilities Act required thousands of businesses to widen doorways, reconfigure restrooms, add ramps, and take other actions to improve accessibility. In the mid-1990s, the World Wide Web became a multifaceted vehicle for getting information and selling products.

Technology also creates the need for change. Recent developments in sophisticated equipment have created significant economies of scale for many organizations. At Charles Schwab (the discount brokerage firm), for example, new technology has given them the ability to process 20,000 mutual fund trades a day in 1996—compared to just 2,000 only two years

Labor-saving equipment, like the assembly-line robotics used at Honda, have replaced thousands of workers in building automobiles. Many auto workers fear such changes because they're afraid that their jobs might be—and have been—eliminated!

## HOW READY ARE YOU FOR COPING WITH WORK-RELATED CHANGE?

Instructions: Listed below are some statements a supervisor made about working in a large, successful corporation. If your job had these characteristics, how would you react to them? After each statement are five letters, A to E. Circle the letter that best describes how you think you would react according to the following scale:

**A**  I would enjoy this very much; it's completely acceptable.
**B**  This would be enjoyable and acceptable most of the time.
**C**  I'd have no reaction to this feature one way or another, or it would be about equally enjoyable and unpleasant.
**D**  This feature would be somewhat unpleasant for me.
**E**  This feature would be very unpleasant for me.

**1.** I regularly spend 30 to 40 percent of my time in meetings.  A  B  C  D  E

**2.** A year and a half ago, my job did not exist, and I have been essentially inventing it as I go along.  A  B  C  D  E

**3.** The responsibilities I either assume or am assigned consistently exceed the authority I have for discharging them.  A  B  C  D  E

**4.** At any given moment in my job, I have on the average about a dozen phone calls to be returned.  A  B  C  D  E

**5.** There seems to be very little relation in my job between the quality of my performance and my actual pay and benefits.  A  B  C  D  E

**6.** About two weeks a year of formal supervisory training is needed in my job just to stay current.  A  B  C  D  E

**7.** Because we have very effective equal employment opportunity (EEO) in my company and because it is thoroughly multinational, my job consistently brings me into close working contact at a professional level with people of many races, ethnic groups, and nationalities and of both sexes.  A  B  C  D  E

*(continued)*

8. There is no objective way to measure my effectiveness.     A     B     C     D     E

9. I report to three different bosses for different aspects of my job, and each has an equal say in my performance appraisal.     A     B     C     D     E

10. On average, about a third of my time is spent dealing with unexpected emergencies that force all scheduled work to be postponed.     A     B     C     D     E

11. When I have to have a meeting of the people who report to me, it takes my secretary most of a day to find a time when we are all available, and even then, I have yet to have a meeting where everyone is present for the entire meeting.     A     B     C     D     E

12. The college degree I earned in preparation for this type of work is now obsolete, and I probably should go back for another degree.     A     B     C     D     E

13. My job requires that I absorb 100–200 pages per week of technical materials.     A     B     C     D     E

14. I am out of town overnight at least one night per week.     A     B     C     D     E

15. My department is so interdependent with several other departments in the company that all distinctions about which departments are responsible for which tasks are quite arbitrary.     A     B     C     D     E

16. I will probably get a promotion in about a year to a job in another department that has most of these same characteristics.     A     B     C     D     E

17. During the period of my employment here, either the entire company or the department I worked in has been reorganized every year or so.     A     B     C     D     E

18. While there are several possible promotions I can see ahead of me, I have no real career path in an objective sense.     A     B     C     D     E

19. While there are several possible promotions I can see ahead of me, I think I have no realistic chance of getting to the top levels of the company.     A     B     C     D     E

20. While I have many ideas about how to make things work better, I have no direct influence on either the business policies or the personnel policies that govern my department.     A    B    C    D    E

21. My company has recently put in an "assessment center" where I and all other supervisors will be required to go through an extensive battery of psychological tests to assess our potential.     A    B    C    D    E

22. My company is a defendant in an antitrust suit, and if the case comes to trial, I will probably have to testify about some decisions that were made a few years ago.     A    B    C    D    E

23. Advanced computer and other electronic office technology is continually being introduced into my division, necessitating constant learning on my part.     A    B    C    D    E

24. The computer terminal and screen I have in my office can be monitored in my bosses' offices without my knowledge.     A    B    C    D    E

## SCORING

Give yourself 4 points for each "A," 3 points for each "B," 2 points for each "C," 1 point for each "D," and no point for each "E." Compute your total, and divide that score by 24. Round your answer to one decimal place.

## WHAT THE ASSESSMENT MEANS

While the results of this assessment are not intended to be more than suggestive, the higher your score, the more comfortable you appear to be with change. The test's author suggests analyzing scores as if they were grade point averages. In this way, a 4.0 average is an "A," a 2.0 is a "C," and scores below 1.0 "flunk." Using replies from nearly 500 students and individuals new to supervisory positions, the range of scores was found to be relatively narrow: between 1.0 and 2.2. The average score was between 1.5 and 1.6—a D+/C- sort of grade!

Source: Peter B. Vail, *Managing as a Performing Art: New Ideas for a World of Chaotic Change*, Exhibit 1, pp. 8–9. © 1989 Jossey-Bass, Inc., Publishers.

earlier.[2] The assembly line in many industries is undergoing dramatic changes as employers replace human labor with technologically advanced mechanical robots, and the fluctuation in labor markets is forcing managers to initiate changes. For instance, the shortage of software developers has required many software firms to redesign jobs and alter their reward and benefit packages.

Economic changes, of course, affect almost all of us. The dramatic increases in crude oil and gasoline prices in the spring of 1996 forced many U.S. companies that depended on fuel to transport their goods to increase prices, consolidate trips, or eliminate some delivery services. Meanwhile, in many parts of Europe where gasoline prices approach $4 (USD), increasing crude oil prices had very little effect.

## WHAT ARE THE INTERNAL FORCES CREATING A NEED FOR CHANGE?

In addition to the external forces noted previously, internal forces can also stimulate the need for change. These internal forces tend to originate primarily from the internal operations of the organization or from the impact of external changes.

When company officials redefine or modify the organization's strategy, they often introduce a host of changes. For example, when L'Oreal (the cosmetic maker) developed a new strategy of competing more aggressively in mass merchandising markets, organizational members had to change how the business operated—like reducing production costs to support mass marketing of products and increased research and development emphasis.[3] The introduction of new equipment represents another internal force for change. Employees may have their jobs redesigned, need to undergo training to operate the new equipment, or be required to establish new interaction patterns within their formal group. An organization's workforce is rarely static. Its composition changes in terms of age, education, gender, nationality, and so forth. In a stable organization where supervisors have been in their positions for years, there might be a need to restructure jobs in order to retain more ambitious employees, affording them more scheduling flexibility, and possibly, some upward mobility. The compensation and benefits systems might also need to be reworked to reflect the needs of a diverse workforce—and market forces where certain skills are in short supply. Employee attitudes, such as increased job dissatisfaction, may lead to increased absenteeism, more voluntary resignations,

[2]R. Mitchell, J. M. Laderman, L. N. Spiro, G. Smith, and S. Atchison, "The Schwab Revolution," *Business Week*, December 19, 1994, p. 91.
[3]S. Toy, "Can the Queen of Cosmetics Keep Her Crown?" *Business Week*, January 17, 1994, pp. 90–92.

and even strikes. Such events will, in turn, often lead to changes in company policies and practices.

## CAN YOU SERVE AS A CHANGE AGENT?

Changes within an organization need a catalyst. People who act as catalysts and assume the responsibility for overseeing the change process are called **change agents.**

    Any supervisor can be a change agent. The change agent can also be a nonmanager—for example, an internal staff specialist or outside consultant whose expertise is in change implementation. For major systemwide changes, company officials will often hire outside consultants to provide advice and assistance. Because they are from the outside, they often can offer an objective perspective usually lacking in insiders. However, outside consultants may be at a disadvantage because they have an inadequate understanding of the organization's history, culture, operating procedures, and personnel. Outside consultants are also prone to initiate more drastic changes than insiders—which can be either a benefit or a disadvantage—because they do not have to live with the repercussions after the change is implemented. In contrast, supervisors who act as change agents may be more thoughtful (and possibly more cautious) because they must live with the consequences of their actions (see Dealing with a Difficult Issue).

**Change agents**
people who act as catalysts and assume the responsibility for overseeing the change process.

---

## DEALING WITH A DIFFICULT ISSUE

### MAKING ORGANIZATIONAL CHANGES

When a supervisor, in cooperation with company officials, makes sweeping changes in his or her department, that effort is frequently called organization development (OD). Organization development interventions can produce change results that are frequently viewed as positive. Through the reliance on organizational member participation, these interventions can create openness and trust among coworkers—and respect for others. They can also result in helping employees understand that such organizational characteristics as risk taking and empowerment are desirable, and that "living" these characteristics can lead to better organizational performance.

    Supervisors involved in an OD effort oftentimes impose their value system on those involved in the intervention. This is particularly true when the catalyst for the intervention is coworker mistrust.

*(continued)*

---

## DEALING WITH A DIFFICULT ISSUE

To deal with this issue, a supervisor may bring all involved parties together to openly discuss their perceptions of the dilemma in an effort to resolve any problems that may exist. Although some supervisors are understanding of OD practices, sometimes they walk a very thin line between success and failure. That's because for personal issues to be resolved in the workplace, participants must disclose very sensitive information. In other words, these individuals must allow their privacy—namely their inner thoughts—to be "invaded." Even though every individual in such a setting can "refuse" to divulge certain information, doing so may carry with it negative ramifications. To its fullest extent, this avoidance could result in some adverse career impacts—lower performance appraisals, fewer pay increases, or even create career-threatening barriers.

On the other hand, active participation could lead to employees speaking their minds. But this, too, carries with it some risks. Saying what one truly believes could result in having that information used against them at a later time. For instance, imagine in such a setting an employee "publicly" challenges something his or her supervisor does—which this individual fully believes is detrimental to the department. This individual's "reward" for being open and honest could become purely punitive. Although at the time the supervisor may appear receptive to the feedback, he or she may "get even" later. In either case—participating or not—employees could be hurt. Even though the intent was to help overcome coworker mistrust, the end result may be more back stabbing, more hurt feelings, and more distance placed between the understandings of the participants.

What do you think about this issue? Do you believe coworkers can be "too open and honest" under this type of OD intervention? Moreover, what do you believe a supervisor can do to ensure that employees' rights will be protected when the intervention is designed to help rebuild constrained coworker relations?

## TWO VIEWS ON THE CHANGE PROCESS

We often use two very different ways to clarify the change process. The traditional way is to view the organization as a large ship crossing a calm sea. The ship's captain and crew know exactly where they're going because they've made the trip many times before. Change surfaces as the occasional storm, a brief distraction in an otherwise calm and predictable trip. The contemporary view sees the organization as a small raft navigating a raging river with uninterrupted white water rapids. Aboard the raft are half-a-dozen people who've never worked together before, who are totally unfamiliar with the river, who are unsure of their eventual destination, and, as if things weren't bad enough, who are traveling in the pitch-dark of night. In the contemporary view, change is a natural state, and directing change is a continual process.

These two ways of viewing change present very different approaches to understanding and responding to change. Let's take a closer look at each one.

## WHAT IS THE TRADITIONAL VIEW OF CHANGE?

Until very recently, the traditional view of change dominated the thinking of most individuals familiar with organizations. It is best illustrated in a three-step description of the **change process**[4] (see Exhibit 13–2). *Kurt Lewin*

According to this model, successful change requires unfreezing the status quo, changing to a new state, and refreezing the new state to make it permanent. The status quo can be considered an equilibrium state. To move from this equilibrium, unfreezing is necessary. It can be achieved in one of three ways:

1. The *driving forces,* which direct behavior away from the status quo, can be increased.
2. The *restraining forces,* which hinder movement from the existing equilibrium, can be decreased.
3. The two approaches can be combined.

Once unfreezing has been accomplished, the change itself can be implemented. However, the mere introduction of change does not ensure that it will take hold. The new situation, therefore, needs to be refrozen so that it can be sustained over time. Unless this last step is attended to, there is a strong chance that the change will be short-lived and employees will revert to the previous equilibrium state. The objective of refreezing, then,

**Change process** a model that allows for successful change by requiring unfreezing of the status quo (equilibrium state), changing to a new state, and refreezing the new change to make it permanent. Unfreezing the equilibrium state is achieved by (1) increasing driving forces; (2) decreasing restraining forces; or (3) combining these two approaches.

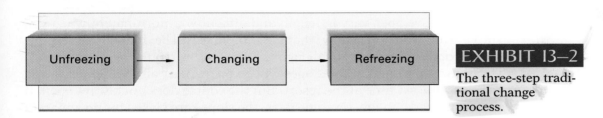

**EXHIBIT 13–2**

The three-step traditional change process.

[4]K. Lewin, *Field Theory in Social Science* (New York, NY: Harper & Row, 1951).

Change in a dynamic environment is often filled with uncertainty. Just like white-water rafters have to continuously maneuver to make it through the rapids, a supervisor, too, must be prepared to deal with unexpected issues.

is to stabilize the new situation by balancing the driving and restraining forces.

Note how this three-step process treats change as a break in the organization's equilibrium state. The status quo has been disturbed, and change is necessary to establish a new equilibrium state. This view might have been appropriate to the relatively calm environment that most organizations faced in the 1950s, 1960s, and early 1970s. But the traditional view of change is increasingly obsolete as a way to describe the kind of seas that current managers have to navigate.

## WHAT IS THE CONTEMPORARY VIEW OF CHANGE?

The contemporary view of change takes into consideration that environments are both uncertain and dynamic. To get a feeling for what directing change might be like when you have to continually maneuver in uninterrupted rapids, consider going on a ski trip and facing the following. Ski slopes that are open vary in length and difficulty. Unfortunately, when you start a "run," you don't know what the ski course will be. It might be a simple course, or one that is very challenging. Furthermore, you've planned your ski vacation assuming that the slopes will be open. After all, it's January—and that is prime ski time at the resort. But the course does not always open. If that is not bad enough, on some days, the slopes are closed for no apparent reason at all. Oh yes, there is one more thing. Lift ticket prices can change dramatically on the hour. And there is no apparent pattern to the price fluctuations. To succeed under these conditions, you would have to be incredibly flexible and be able to respond quickly to every changing condition. Those who were too slow, or too structured would have difficulty—and clearly no fun!

A growing number of supervisors are coming to accept that their job is much like what one might face on such a ski vacation. The stability and predictability of the traditional view of change may not exist. Disruptions in the status quo are not occasional and temporary, followed by a return to "calm waters." Many of today's supervisors never get out of the rapids. They face constant change, bordering on chaos. These supervisors are being forced to play a game they've never played before which is governed by rules that are created as the game progresses.[5]

## WILL YOU FACE A WORLD OF CONSTANT AND CHAOTIC CHANGE?

Every supervisor doesn't face a world of constant and chaotic change. However, the set of supervisors who don't is dwindling rapidly. Few supervisors today can treat change as the occasional disturbance in an otherwise peaceful world. Doing so can put you at great risk. Too much is changing too fast for anyone to be complacent. As business writer Tom Peters has aptly noted, the old saying "If it ain't broke, don't fix it" no longer applies. In its place, he suggests "If it ain't broke, you just haven't looked hard enough. Fix it anyway."[6]

## WHY DO PEOPLE RESIST CHANGE?

One of the most well-documented findings in the study of people at work is that individuals resist change. As one person once put it, "Most people hate any change that doesn't jingle in their pockets."

Resistance to change surfaces in many forms. It can be overt, implicit, immediate, or deferred. It is easiest for supervisors to deal with resistance when it is overt and immediate. For instance, a change is proposed and employees quickly respond by voicing complaints, engaging in a work slowdown, threatening to go on strike, or the like. The greater challenge is managing resistance that is implicit or deferred. Implicit resistance efforts are more subtle (loss of loyalty to the organization, loss of motivation to work, increased errors or mistakes, increased absenteeism due to "sickness"); hence more difficult to recognize. Similarly, deferred actions cloud

[5]See, for instance, T. Peters, *Thriving on Chaos* (New York, NY: Alfred A. Knopf, 1987).
[6]Ibid., p. 3.

## EXHIBIT 13–3

Why people resist change.

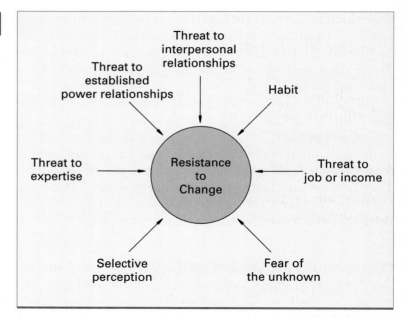

the link between the source of the resistance and the reaction to it. A change may produce what appears to be only a minimal reaction at the time it is initiated, but then resistance surfaces weeks, months, or even years later. A single change that in and of itself might have little impact can become the straw that breaks the camel's back. Reactions to change can build up and then explode in some response that seems totally out of proportion to the change action it follows. The resistance, of course, has merely been deferred and stockpiled. What surfaces is a response to an accumulation of previous changes.

So why do people resist change? There are a number of reasons (see Exhibit 13–3).

### HABITS

As human beings, we're creatures of habit. Life is complex enough; we don't need to consider the full range of options for the hundreds of decisions we have to make every day. To cope with this complexity, we all rely on habits or programmed responses. When confronted with change, this tendency to respond in our accustomed ways becomes a source of resistance. So when your department is moved to a new office building across town, it means your employees are likely to have to change many habits: waking up ten minutes earlier, taking a new set of streets to work, finding a new parking place, adjusting to the new office layout, developing a new lunch-time routine, and so on.

## THREATS TO JOBS AND INCOME

Employees often fear any change may reduce their job security or income. New labor-saving equipment, for instance, may be interpreted as the forerunner of layoffs. People are also often threatened by changes in job tasks or established work routines if they are fearful that they won't be able to perform them successfully. This is particularly threatening where pay is closely tied to productivity.

## FEAR OF THE UNKNOWN

Changes substitute ambiguity and uncertainty for the known, and human beings don't like ambiguity. If the introduction of a desktop publishing system by a small book publisher means that editorial people will have to learn to do their entire jobs on computers, some of these people may fear that they will be unable to learn the intricacies of the system. They may, therefore, develop a negative attitude toward working with desktop publishing or behave dysfunctionally—complaining, purposely working slowly, undermining department morale—if required to use the system.

## SELECTIVE PERCEPTION

Individuals shape the world through their perceptions. Once they have created this world, it resists change. So individuals are guilty of selectively processing what they see and hear in order to keep their perceptions intact. They often hear what they want to hear. They ignore information that challenges the world they've created. To return to the book editors who were faced with the introduction of desktop publishing, they may ignore the arguments that their supervisors make in explaining why the new equipment has been purchased or the potential benefits that the change will provide them.

## THREAT TO EXPERTISE

Changes in organizational policies and practices may threaten the expertise of specialized groups and departments. The introduction of personal computers, which allow supervisors access to information directly from a company's mainframe, is an example of a change that was strongly resisted by many information systems departments in the early 1980s. Why? Because decentralized end-user computing was a threat to the specialized skills held by those in the centralized information systems departments.

## THREAT TO ESTABLISHED POWER RELATIONSHIPS

Any redistribution of decision-making authority can threaten long-established power relationships within an organization. Efforts by company officials to empower operating employees or introduce self-directed work teams have frequently been met by resistance from supervisors who are threatened by a redistribution of power.

## THREAT TO INTERPERSONAL RELATIONSHIPS

Work is more than a means to earn a living. The interpersonal relationships that are part of a person's job often play an important role in satisfying the individual's social needs. We look forward to going to work to interact with coworkers and make friends. Change can be a threat to those relationships. Reorganizations, transfers, and restructuring of work layouts change the people that employees work with, report to, and regularly interact with. Since such changes are often seen as threats, they tend to be resisted.

---

### POP QUIZ    (Are You Comprehending What You're Reading?)

1. A number of your employees who ride the Metro subway show up for work one hour late every day. Attempts by them to leave their homes earlier do not work, given construction delays on an extension of the subway. You decide to allow these and other employees to start work one hour later. Of course, they work an hour later in the afternoon. What type of change did you make?
   a. people-oriented
   b. technological
   c. structural
   d. environmental
2. Explain the implications of Tom Peters' statement, "If it ain't broke, you just haven't looked hard enough. Fix it anyway."
3. The correct order of the traditional view of change is unfreezing—refreezing—changing. True or False?
4. The contemporary view of change
   a. is of little use to most organizations today
   b. is consistent with dynamic environmental forces
   c. involves unfreezing, change, and refreezing
   d. encourages individualism

---

# How Can You Overcome the Resistance to Change?

The resistance to change we've previously described can be overcome. We offer five specific techniques. Resistance is most likely to be eliminated when you implement all five of the techniques.

## BUILD TRUST

If employees trust and have confidence in you, they're less likely to be threatened by changes you propose. The implementation of self-directed work teams at Ocean Spray's Vero Beach, Florida processing plant initially met with considerable resistance because employees didn't trust supervisors. For years, supervisors hadn't trusted their employees to make decisions; then, all of a sudden, these same supervisors were telling workers to make their own decisions. It took more than a year for employees to accept responsibility for solving their own problems.

Trust takes a long time to develop. It's also very fragile; it can be destroyed easily. The ideas we offered in Chapter 10 should help you to build trust with your employees.

## OPEN CHANNELS OF COMMUNICATION

Resistance can be reduced through communicating with employees to help them see the logic of a change. When employees receive the full facts and get misunderstandings cleared up, resistance often fades. This explains why, for example, company officials at Apex Environmental allow any of its 100 employees to review the company's profit and loss statements and get questions answered about the firm's financial performance. Opening communication channels, however, will only be effective when there is a climate of trust and where the organization is truly concerned with the welfare of its employees. Improved communication is particularly effective in reducing threats created by ambiguity. For instance, when the grapevine is active with rumors of cutbacks and layoffs, honest and open communication of the true facts can be a calming force. Even if the news is bad, a clear message often wins points and opens people to accepting change. When communication is ambiguous and people are threatened, they often contrive scenarios that are considerably worse than the actual "bad news."

## INVOLVE YOUR EMPLOYEES

Organizations as varied as American Express, General Motors, Delmarva Power, and the U.S. Internal Revenue Service are asking employees to participate in planning of major change programs. Why? It's difficult for individuals to resist a change decision in which they participated. So solicit employee inputs early in the change process. When affected employees have been involved in a change from its beginning, they will usually actively support the change. No one wants to oppose something that he or she helped develop.

## PROVIDE INCENTIVES

Our last suggestion is to make sure that people see how supporting a change is in their best interests. What's the source of their resistance? What do you control that might overcome that resistance? Are they afraid they won't be able to do a new task? Provide them with new-skills training or maybe a short paid leave of absence so they'll have time to rethink their fears, calm down, and come to the realization that their concerns are unfounded. Similarly, layoffs can become opportunities for those who remain. Jobs can be redesigned to provide new challenges and responsibilities. A pay increase, a new title, flexible work hours, or increased job autonomy are additional examples of incentives that can help reduce resistance. Polaroid Corp., for instance, wants employees to broaden their skills and become more flexible. To encourage this, it offers pay premiums of up to 10 percent to employees who develop new skill competencies.

## DEAL WITH EMPLOYEE FEELINGS

**Attitudes**
evaluative statements or judgments concerning objects, people, or events.

"I hate my job." "My boss is insensitive to women." "I think the medical products we're producing make a real difference in people's lives." These employee statements are examples of **attitudes.** That is, they're evaluative statements or judgments concerning objects, people, or events. They reflect how people feel about something.

What can you do, as a supervisor, to change negative employee attitudes? We offer a five-step program based on the traditional change model (see Building a Supervisory Skill).

## CHANGING EMPLOYEE ATTITUDES

### ABOUT THE SKILL

Every employee has hundreds of attitudes on dozens of subjects. These attitudes affect department morale. Furthermore, employees tend to seek consistency between attitudes and behavior.

### STEPS IN PRACTICING THE SKILL

1. **Identify the Attitude You Want to Change.** The place to begin is to clearly identify the dysfunctional attitude. What specifically is it that you want to change?
2. **Determine What Sustains the Attitude.** Once a negative attitude is identified, you want to find out where it comes from. If you're going to change it, you need to know its source and what sustains it. Typically, attitudes grow out of (1) beliefs held by parents, teachers, and friends, which were communicated to us early in our lives; (2) previous experiences; (3) group pressures; or (4) incorrect information.
3. **Unfreeze the Attitude.** Once the roots of an undesirable attitude are clear, you can begin to weaken the assumptions that underlie it. You can, for instance, provide new information, clarify incorrect assumptions, provide opportunities for the employee to gain new experiences that will counter his or her prevailing attitude, or reorganize the formal work group if it's the source of the problem.
4. **Offer an Alternative Attitude.** It's not enough to unfreeze a current attitude. It must then be replaced with a substitute one.
5. **Refreeze the New Attitude.** Unless the new attitude is reinforced and supported, it's likely to fade over time. ■

## WORK-RELATED STRESS

For many employees change creates stress. A dynamic and uncertain environment characterized by restructurings, downsizings, empowerment, and the like, has created a large number of employees who are overworked and "stressed" out.[7] In this section, we'll review specifically what is meant

---

[7]See, for instance, "Workplace Stress is Rampant, Especially with the Recession," *The Wall Street Journal*, May 5, 1992, p. A1; and C. L. Cordes and T. W. Dougherty, "A Review and an Integration of Research on Job Burnout," *Academy of Management Review*, October 1993, pp. 621–656.

by the term *stress*, what causes it, how to identify it, and what supervisors can do to reduce the anxiety.

## WHAT IS STRESS?

**Stress**
something an individual feels when faced with opportunities, constraints, or commands perceived to be both uncertain and important. Stress can show itself in both positive and negative ways.

**Stress** is something you feel when you face opportunities, constraints, or demands which you perceive to be both uncertain and important.[8] Stress is a complex issue, so let us look at it more closely. Stress can show itself in both positive and negative ways. Stress is said to be positive when the situation offers someone an opportunity to gain something. For example, stress allows an athlete or entertainer to perform at his or her highest level in critical situations.

However, stress is more often associated with constraints or demands. Constraints are barriers that keep individuals from doing what they desire. If becoming a lawyer is your desire, yet, you've performed poorly on the Law School Admission Test, you may be not be accepted into law school. Constraints restrict individuals in ways that take control of a situation out of their hands. Demands, on the other hand, may cause people to give up something they want. If your boss is expecting you to turn in an important project the next morning—and it's not finished yet— the tickets just offered to you to attend the Super Bowl may have to be turned down. Thus, demands preoccupy your time and force you to shift priorities.

Constraints and demands can lead to potential stress. When they are coupled with uncertainty of the outcome and importance of the outcome, potential stress becomes actual stress. Performance evaluations are good examples of how stress may manifest itself. If a good performance appraisal can lead to a promotion, greater responsibility, a higher salary, stress may exist. Similarly, if a poor evaluation could keep one from getting these things, or could lead to some disciplinary action, stress, again, thrives. The key, though, is the uncertainty of the outcome, and its importance.

Being an air-traffic controller is a highly stressful job. One mistake can mean the death of hundreds of people. Stress in this situation is highly influenced by the importance of doing what is "right" in handling the job.

[8]Adapted from R. S. Schuler, "Definition and Conceptualization of Stress in Organizations," *Organizational Behavior and Human Performance* (April 1980), p. 189.

Regardless of the situation, a stressful condition exists only when there is doubt or uncertainty regarding whether the opportunity will be seized, whether the constraint is removed, or whether a loss will be avoided. That is, stress will be highest for individuals who think that winning or losing is a certainty. The importance of that outcome is also a critical factor. If winning or losing is unimportant, stress does not exist. As such, if one of your employees feels that keeping a job or earning a promotion are unimportant, he or she will experience little or no stress before a performance review.

## WHAT LEADS TO WORK-RELATED STRESS?

Work-related stress is brought about by both organizational and individual factors. As shown in Exhibit 13–4, these in turn are influenced by individual differences. That is, not all people in similar situations experience similar levels of stress.

### ORGANIZATIONAL FACTORS

There is no shortage of factors within the organization that can cause stress. Pressures to avoid errors or complete tasks in a limited time period, a demanding supervisor, and unpleasant coworkers are a few examples

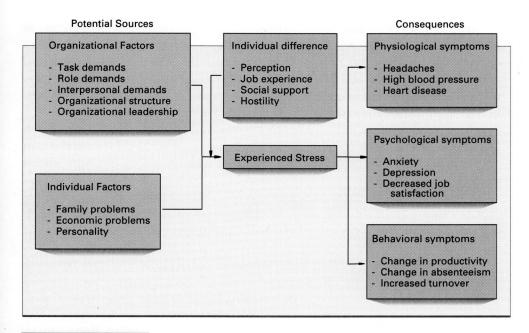

## EXHIBIT 13–4
Potential sources of stress.

## EXHIBIT 13-5

Primary causes of work-related stress. (*Source:* "Worries at Work," *Wall Street Journal*, April 7, 1988, p. 27. Reprinted by permission of Wall Street Journal, © 1988 Dow Jones & Company, Inc., all rights reserved worldwide.)

What factors cause the most stress on the job? A *Wall Street Journal* survey reported:

| Factor | Percentage Response |
|---|---|
| Not doing the kind of work I want to | 34 |
| Coping with current job | 30 |
| Working too hard | 28 |
| Colleagues at work | 21 |
| A difficult boss | 18 |

\* Percentages exceed 100 as a result of some multiple responses.

(see Exhibit 13–5). The discussion that follows organizes stress factors into five categories: task, role, and interpersonal demands; organization structure; and organizational leadership.

*Task demands* are factors related to an employee's job. They include the design of the person's job (autonomy, task variety, degree of automation), working conditions, and the physical work layout. Assembly lines can put pressure on people when their speed is perceived as excessive. The more interdependence between a person's tasks and the tasks of others, the more potential stress there is. Autonomy, on the other hand, tends to lessen stress. Jobs where temperatures, noise, or other working conditions are dangerous or undesirable can increase anxiety. So, too, can working in an overcrowded room or in a visible location where interruptions are constant.

*Role demands* relate to pressures placed on an employee as a function of the particular role he or she plays in the organization. **Role conflicts** create expectations that may be hard to reconcile or satisfy. **Role overload** is experienced when the employee is expected to do more than time permits. **Role ambiguity** is created when role expectations are not clearly understood and the employee is not sure what he or she is to do.

*Interpersonal demands* are pressures created by other employees. Lack of social support from colleagues and poor interpersonal relationships can cause considerable stress, especially among employees with a high social need.

*Organization structure* can increase stress. Excessive rules and an employee's lack of opportunity to participate in decisions that affect him or her are examples of structural variables that might be potential sources of stress.

*Organizational leadership* represents the managerial style of the organization's company officials. Some officials create a culture characterized by tension, fear, and anxiety. They establish unrealistic pressures to perform in the short run, impose excessively tight controls, and routinely fire employees who don't measure up. This style of leadership flows down through the organization to affect all employees.

**Role conflicts** expectations that may be hard to reconcile or satisfy.

**Role overload** pressure experienced when an employee is expected to do more than time permits.

**Role ambiguity** a situation created when role expectations are not clearly understood and the employee is not sure what he or she is to do.

## INDIVIDUAL FACTORS

The typical employee works about fifty hours a week. The experiences and problems that people encounter in those other 118 nonwork hours each week can spill over to the job. Our other category, then, encompasses factors in the employee's personal life. Primarily, these factors are *family issues, personal economic problems,* and *inherent personality characteristics.*

National surveys consistently show that people hold family and personal relationships dear. Marital difficulties, the breaking off of a relationship, discipline troubles with children, and relatives with serious illnesses are examples of relationship problems that create stress for employees and that aren't left at the front door when they arrive at work.

Economic problems created by individuals overextending their financial resources is another set of personal troubles that can create stress for employees and distract their attention from their work. Regardless of income level (people who make $90,000 a year seem to have as much trouble handling their finances as those who earn $23,000), some people are poor money handlers or have wants that always seem to exceed their earning capacity.

Recent studies have found that stress symptoms reported prior to beginning a job don't change much from that reported nine months later. This has led to the conclusion that some people may have an inherent tendency to accentuate negative aspects of the world in general. If true, then a significant individual factor influencing stress is a person's basic disposition. That is, stress symptoms expressed on the job may actually originate in the person's personality (See Something to Think About).

## ARE STRESS FACTORS ADDICTIVE?

A fact that tends to be overlooked when stress factors are reviewed individually is that stress is an additive phenomenon. Stress builds up. Each new and persistent stressor adds to an individual's stress level. A single stressor may seem relatively unimportant in and of itself, but if it is added to an already high level of stress, it can be "the straw that breaks the camel's back."

## INDIVIDUAL DIFFERENCES

Some people thrive on stressful situations, while others are overwhelmed by them. What is it that differentiates people in terms of their ability to handle stress? Four individual difference factors have been found to be important: perception, experience, social support, and hostility.

One person's fear that he'll lose his job because his company is laying off personnel may be perceived by another as an opportunity to get a large

Below are 20 statements. Use the following scale in responding to each statement:

4 = all the time
3 = often
2 = sometimes
1 = never

| | | | | | |
|---|---|---|---|---|---|
| 1. | I'm exhausted by daily demands at work, college, and home. | 4 | 3 | 2 | 1 |
| 2. | My stress is caused by outside forces beyond my control. | 4 | 3 | 2 | 1 |
| 3. | I'm trapped by circumstances that I just have to live with. | 4 | 3 | 2 | 1 |
| 4. | No matter how hard I work to stay on top of my schedule, I can't get caught up. | 4 | 3 | 2 | 1 |
| 5. | I have financial obligations that I can't seem to meet. | 4 | 3 | 2 | 1 |
| 6. | I dislike my work, but I can't take the risk of making a career change (or if not working: I dislike college, but can't take the risk of dropping out). | 4 | 3 | 2 | 1 |
| 7. | I'm dissatisfied with my personal relationships. | 4 | 3 | 2 | 1 |
| 8. | I feel responsible for the happiness of people around me. | 4 | 3 | 2 | 1 |
| 9. | I'm embarrassed to ask for help. | 4 | 3 | 2 | 1 |
| 10. | I don't know what I want out of life. | 4 | 3 | 2 | 1 |
| 11. | I'm disappointed that I have not achieved what I had hoped for. | 4 | 3 | 2 | 1 |
| 12. | No matter how much success I have, I feel empty. | 4 | 3 | 2 | 1 |
| 13. | If the people around me were more competent, I would feel happier. | 4 | 3 | 2 | 1 |
| 14. | People let me down. | 4 | 3 | 2 | 1 |
| 15. | I stew in my anger rather than express it. | 4 | 3 | 2 | 1 |
| 16. | I become enraged and resentful when I am hurt. | 4 | 3 | 2 | 1 |
| 17. | I can't take criticism. | 4 | 3 | 2 | 1 |
| 18. | I'm afraid I'll lose my job (or fail out of school). | 4 | 3 | 2 | 1 |
| 19. | I don't see the value of expressing sadness or grief. | 4 | 3 | 2 | 1 |
| 20. | I don't trust that things will work out. | 4 | 3 | 2 | 1 |

After rating each statement, total your score for the twenty items. Scores of 20–29 indicate a high degree of control, self-esteem, and low stress levels. Scores of 30–49 suggest that your occasional negative self-talk causes you to feel anxious in stressful situations, thus causing moderate levels of stress. Scores of 50-69 indicate a relatively high level of stress. This might indicate you feel trapped. Scores of 70 or more indicate very high stress levels—indicating life has become one crisis and struggle after another for you.

Using this questionnaire as a guide, describe the kinds of things that are causing stress in your life. How are you handling this stress? Do you feel successful? Why or why not? For those who have low stress, what tips could you offer to others for coping with the stress?

Source: From *Stress to Strength*, by Robert S. Eliot, M.D. © 1994 by Robert S. Eliot, M.D. Used by permission of Bantam Books, a division of Bantam Doubleday Dell Publishing Group, Inc.

severance allowance and start her own business. Similarly, what one employee perceives as an efficient and challenging work environment may be viewed as threatening and demanding by others. The potential for stress doesn't lie in objective conditions. Rather, it lies in an employee's perception and interpretation of those conditions.

Experience is said to be a great teacher. It can also be a great stress-reducer. Think back to your first date or your first few days in college. For most of us, the uncertainty and newness of these situations created stress. As we gained experience, that stress disappeared or at least significantly decreased. The same phenomenon seems to apply to work situations. Why? One explanation is the process of selective withdrawal. Voluntary turnover is more probable among people who experience more stress. Therefore, people who remain with the organization longer are those with more stress-resistant traits, or those who are more resistant to the stress characteristics of their organization. A second explanation is that people eventually develop coping mechanisms to deal with stress. Because this takes time, senior members of the organization are more likely to be fully adapted and experience less stress.

There is increasing evidence that social support—that is, collegial relationships with coworkers and supervisors—can buffer the impact of stress. The logic underlying this conclusion is that social support acts as a palliative, lessening the negative effects of even high-stress jobs.

For much of the 1970s and 1980s, a great deal of attention was directed at what became known as **Type A behavior** (see Exhibit 13–6). It was frequently seen as the primary individual difference factor in explaining who would be affected by stress. Type A behavior is characterized by feelings of a chronic sense of time urgency and by an excessive competitive drive. Type A's try to do more and more in less and less time. The opposite of Type A is **Type B behavior.** Type B's rarely suffer from time urgency or impatience. Until quite recently, it was believed that Type A's were more likely to experience stress on and off the job. A closer analysis of the evidence, however, has produced new conclusions. It's been found that only the hostility and anger associated with Type A behavior is actually associ-

**Type A behavior** behavior that is characterized by feelings of a chronic sense of time urgency and by an excessive competitive drive.

**Type B** behavior behavior that is the opposite of Type A behavior. Type B's never suffer from time urgency or impatience.

| Type A | Type B |
| --- | --- |
| Driven | Relaxed |
| Aggressive | Easy going |
| Competitive | Even tempered |
| Strong desire for achievement | Flexible |
| Impatient | Less time conscious |
| Irritated with non-type A types | Friendly |
| Resists change | Accepts change easily |

**EXHIBIT 13–6**

Type A and Type B behavioral characteristics

ated with the negative effects of stress. The chronically angry, suspicious, and mistrustful person is the one at risk of stressing out.

## What Are the Symptoms of Stress?

What signs indicate that an employee's stress level might be too high? There are three general ways that stress reveals itself. These include physiological, psychological, and behavioral symptoms.

Most of the early interest over stress focused heavily on health-related, or the *physiological* concerns. This was attributed to the realization that high stress levels result in changes in metabolism, increased heart and breathing rates, increased blood pressure, headaches, and increased risk of heart attacks. Because detecting many of these requires the skills of trained medical personnel, their immediate and direct relevance to supervisors is negligible.

Of greater importance to supervisors are psychological and behavioral symptoms of stress. It's these things that can be witnessed in the person. The *psychological symptoms* can be seen as increased tension and anxiety, boredom, and procrastination—which can all lead to productivity decreases. So too, can the *behaviorally-related symptoms*—changes in eating habits, increased smoking or substance consumption, rapid speech, or sleep disorders. The astute supervisor, upon witnessing such symptoms, does what he or she can to assist the employee in reducing stress levels.

## How Can Stress Be Reduced?

Reducing stress is one thing that presents a dilemma for supervisors. Some stress in organizations is absolutely necessary. Without it, there's no energy in people. Accordingly, whenever one considers stress reduction, what is at issue is reducing its dysfunctional aspects.

One of the first means of reducing stress is to make sure that employees are properly matched to their jobs—and that they understand the extent of their "authority." Furthermore, by letting employees know precisely what is expected of them, role conflict and ambiguity can be reduced. Redesigning jobs can also help ease work overload-related stressors. Employees should also have some input in those things that affect them. Their involvement and participation has been found to lessen stress.[9]

As a supervisor, you must recognize that no matter what you do to eliminate organizational stressors, some employees will still be "stressed-out." You simply have little or no control over the personal factors. You

[9]A. A. Brott, "New Approaches to Job Stress," *Nation's Business*, May 1994, pp. 81–82; and C. J. Bacher, "Workers Take Leave of Job Stress," *Personnel Journal*, January 1995, pp. 38–48.

also face an ethical issue when it is personal factors that are causing stress. That is, just how far can you intrude on an employee's personal life? To help deal with this issue, many companies have started employee assistance and wellness programs.

**Employee Assistance Programs (EAPs)** as they exist today are extensions of programs that began in companies in the 1940s. Companies like duPont, Standard Oil, and Kodak recognized that a number of their employees were experiencing problems with alcohol. To help their employees, special programs were implemented on the company's site to educate these workers on the dangers of alcohol and to help them overcome their "addiction." The idea behind these programs, which still holds today, is getting a productive employee back on the job as swiftly as possible. Since their early focus on alcoholic employees, EAPs have gone into new areas. One of the more notable areas is the use of EAPs to help control rising health care costs, especially in the areas of "mental health and substance abuse services."[10] For example, at Campbell's Soup Company, the com-

**Employee Assistance Programs (EAPs)** programs designed to act as a first stop for individuals seeking psychiatric or substance-abuse help, with the goal of getting productive employees back on the job as swiftly as possible

How does the Des Moines-based Principal Financial Group help its employees maintain healthy lives? One way is to provide them with a variety of wellness programs, including aerobic and weight machines, as well as fitness classes.

[10]"EAPs Evolve to Health Plan Gatekeeper," *Employee Benefit Plan Review*, February 1992, p. 18.

pany's **EAP** program is the first stop for individuals seeking psychiatric or substance-abuse help. By doing this, Campbell's was able to cut its health care insurance premiums by 28 percent.[11] Similar findings have occurred elsewhere as studies suggest that organizations that have EAPs save up to $5 for every EAP dollar spent.[12] That's a significant return on investment!

A **wellness program** is any type of program in an organization that is designed to keep employees healthy. These programs are varied, and may focus on such things as smoking cessation, weight control, stress management, physical fitness, nutrition education, high blood-pressure control, and so forth. In return, these programs are designed to help cut employer health costs, and lower absenteeism and turnover by preventing health and stress-related problems.[13] For instance, it is estimated that over a 10-year period, the Adolph Coors company saved several million dollars in decreased medical premium payments, reduced sick leave, and increased productivity.

**Wellness programs**
any type of program that is designed to keep employees healthy, focusing on such things as smoking cessation, weight control, stress management, physical fitness, nutrition education, high blood-pressure control, and so on.

## HEY, WHAT ABOUT ME?

How can you control the stress in your life and on your job? Are there some tips available to you? Sure there are. But you must recognize that stress is a fact of life and must be channeled properly. You, as well as your organization must find ways for reducing stress levels before they result in "something drastic." Although no clear-cut remedies are available for every case, there are some guidelines that you can follow.

### TAKE A GOOD LOOK AT YOURSELF

Have you stopped for a moment and assessed who you are? Are you susceptible to Type A characteristics? Do you know what causes you stress? One of the first things to do in managing your stress is finding out what you bring on yourself, and what creates stress in your life. Only then can you begin to think about making some worthwhile changes in your behavior. Self awareness is the initial key. Without it, controlling stress is difficult, at best.

[11]E. Stetzer, "Bringing Sanity to Mental Health Costs," *Business and Health*, February 1992, p. 72.

[12]See G. Nicholas, "How to Make Employee Assistance Programs More Productive," *Supervision*, July 1991, pp. 3–6; and "EAPs to the Rescue," *Employee Benefit Plan Review*, February 1991, pp. 26–27.

[13]L. Ingram, "Many Healthy Returns," *Entrepreneur*, September 1994, p. 84; H. Harrington, "Retiree Wellness Plan Cuts Health Costs," *Personnel Journal*, August 1990, p. 60.

5. For potential stress to become actual stress, which two conditions must exist?
   a. uncertainty and importance
   b. people and organizations
   c. certainty and importance
   d. uncertainty and risk
6. What are the three symptoms of stress? Which one is least important to detect in those one supervises?
7. Role conflict refers to a situation where jobs are ill-defined. True or False?
8. The main distinction between employee assistance programs and wellness programs is
   a. Employee assistance programs focus on helping employees prevent problems. Wellness programs focus on helping employees overcome their problems.
   b. Employee assistance programs focus on alcoholic employees. Wellness programs focus on substance abusers.
   c. Employee assistance programs return $5 for every $1 invested in them. Wellness programs return only $3 for every $1 invested in them.
   d. Employee assistance programs focus on helping employees overcome their problems. Wellness programs focus on helping employees prevent problems.

## BE FLEXIBLE

Tolerate life's curve balls. Realize that things happen, no matter what you do to prevent them. Accept that fact. Sure, some of them will be painful, but time will heal that pain—if you let it. Realize that no one is perfect, and we cannot expect nor demand perfection of ourselves. Oh sure, it's a good goal to shoot for, but if it doesn't happen, don't beat yourself up. There's a saying that goes something like this: "The way to a stress-free life is not to sweat the small stuff. Ninety-nine percent of life is small stuff." Save your anxiety for that one percent that really matters.

## BE POSITIVE

Here comes that positive attitude concept again. But it's true. How you see things contributes to your stress. There's no sense getting worked up about an employee who's submitted her resignation—even if you're counting on her to run a major project. After all, you're still alive, you're still the supervisor, and you have a job. Losing a valuable employee is not the end of the world. In fact, it may be a good reflection on you that you developed her to the point where she is now ready for a greater responsibility—even if it is out of your department!

## DON'T LET PEOPLE GET TO YOU

No one can upset you. Sure they can do things that may aggravate you, but only you can allow yourself to get upset. Let things bounce off of you. Giving people that kind of control over your body by pushing your blood pressure and heart rates up too frequently is harmful. Sooner or later, it may stay there. There's no reason to allow other individuals to bring you down with them. If that's where they want to be, let it be their choice, but you don't have to join them. Just walk away if need be.

## GET SOME EXERCISE

The medical community has shown that one of the greatest stress reducers is exercise. Do something other than sitting. Go for a walk, jog, swim, bicycle, wash the car, clean the house, or the like. Exert yourself in something you enjoy—other than watching the television or playing computer games.

## SEEK HELP FROM SOMEONE ELSE

The Bible says no one is an island. Each of us needs someone else. We need a special person—a friend, family member, counselor, clergy member, and the like—to talk to. Find someone who will actively listen to you and let you vent your frustrations. Share with them what's on your mind. Sometimes getting whatever it is off your chest is the best medicine. You and your special confidant may not be able to solve the matter, but at least you can relieve some of the stress you are facing. Keeping things in, and allowing them to fester inside you may only make matters worse. It could even lead to substance abuse.

## PLAN YOUR ACTIVITIES

Too many times, you may leave things to fate. You may not set schedules, or if you do, don't follow them as well as you should. You may put things off until later. And when later comes, you become overwhelmed. Planning activities helps you focus your attention on what needs to be done and when. Don't be so set in your schedule that if something unforeseen happens, you'll be thrown off. Remember, a plan is a plan, it is not cast in concrete. Planning is something Type A people do well. Frequently, their rigidity in driving the plan is what becomes a stressor to them. You work the plan, don't let the plan work you.

## SUMMARY

After reading this chapter, I can:

1. **Describe the traditional and contemporary views of change.** The traditional view of change treats change as a break in the organization's equilibrium state. Change is initiated and then stabilized at a new equilibrium. The contemporary view of change is that it is constant. Disequilibrium is the natural state.

2. **Explain why employees resist change.** Employees resist change out of habit, fear of the unknown, selective perception, or if they perceive the change as a threat to their job, income, expertise, established power relationships, or interpersonal relationships.

3. **Identify ways supervisors can reduce resistance to change.** Supervisors can reduce resistance by building trust, opening channels of communication, involving employees in the change decisions, providing incentives to employees for accepting change, and helping employees change their attitudes.

4. **List the steps a supervisor can use in changing negative employee attitudes.** The five steps in changing attitudes are: (a) identify the attitude you want to change; (b) determine what sustains the attitude; (c) unfreeze the attitude; (d) offer an alternative attitude; (e) refreeze the new attitude.

5. **Define stress.** Stress is something you feel when you face opportunities, constraints, or demands which you perceive to be both uncertain and important.

6. **Explain what causes work-related stress.** Stress comes from organizational factors like task and role demands, interpersonal demands, and structural variables; it can also be caused by individual factors like family problems, economic problems, and personality variables.

7. **Contrast Type A and Type B behavior.** Type A behavior is characterized by a chronic sense of time urgency and an excessive competitive drive. Type B behavior is the opposite—characterized by an absence of time urgency or impatience.

## REVIEWING YOUR KNOWLEDGE

1. Give several examples of environmental forces that might affect supervisors and require changes in a department.
2. Describe the traditional model of the change process. How does it differ from the contemporary view of change?
3. What signals or cues might tell you that an employee is resistant to a change you're planning on implementing?
4. How does an employee's perception relate to his or her resistance to change?
5. How can building trust lessen change resistance?
6. Why should supervisors be concerned with an employee's work-related attitudes?
7. What happens if an attitude change is not refrozen?
8. "All stress is bad." Do you agree or disagree with the statement? Discuss.
9. How can supervisors reduce employee stress?
10. Do you believe that you have the right to inquire about or try to help one of your employees deal with stresses that result from factors outside the job? Explain your position.

# ANSWERS TO THE POP QUIZZES

1. **c. structural.** Making this time change reflects a flexibility in work scheduling.
2. According to Tom Peters, supervisors must recognize that the work world is rapidly changing. Fighting to maintain the status quo may prove harmful to a department. Consequently, supervisors must continually look for ways to do things better, and more effectively—even those things that appear to work well now. The issue is: will it work well tomorrow given the "chaos" surrounding the department? Peters' quote implies that a supervisor must always be preparing for "tomorrow."
3. **False.** The correct order of the traditional view of change is unfreezing—changing—refreezing.
4. **b. is consistent with dynamic environmental forces.** The rapidly changing environmental forces often create a chaotic work environment, one similar to "shooting the rapids."
5. **a. uncertainty and importance.** These two elements are critical in creating stressful situations.
6. There are three general ways that stress reveals itself. These include physiological, psychological, and behavioral symptoms. Because detecting such things as changes in metabolism, increased heart and breathing rates, increased blood pressure, headaches, and increased risk of heart attacks requires the skills of trained medical personnel, the immediate and direct relevance of physiological stress symptoms to supervisors is negligible.
7. **False.** Role conflict refers to a situation where role expectations are hard to reconcile or satisfy.
8. **d. Employee assistance programs focus on helping employees overcome their problems. Wellness programs focus on helping employees prevent problems.** This distinction represents the main drive between both programs. ∎

## A CLASS EXERCISE: COPING WITH STRESS

Step 1: Complete the following questionnaire by circling one number in each line. To what extent does each fit as a description of you?

|  | VERY TRUE | QUITE TRUE | SOME-WHAT TRUE | NOT VERY TRUE | NOT AT ALL TRUE |
|---|---|---|---|---|---|
| 1. I "roll with the punches" when problems come up. | 1 | 2 | 3 | 4 | 5 |
| 2. I spend almost all of my time thinking about my work. | 5 | 4 | 3 | 2 | 1 |
| 3. I treat other people as individuals and care about their feelings and opinions. | 1 | 2 | 3 | 4 | 5 |
| 4. I recognize and accept my own limitations and assets. | 1 | 2 | 3 | 4 | 5 |
| 5. There are quite a few people I could describe as "good friends." | 1 | 2 | 3 | 4 | 5 |
| 6. I enjoy using my skills and abilities both on and off the job. | 1 | 2 | 3 | 4 | 5 |
| 7. I get bored easily. | 5 | 4 | 3 | 2 | 1 |
| 8. I enjoy meeting and talking with people who have different ways of thinking about the world. | 1 | 2 | 3 | 4 | 5 |
| 9. Often in my job, I "bite off more than I can chew." | 5 | 4 | 3 | 2 | 1 |
| 10. I'm usually very active on weekends with projects or recreation. | 1 | 2 | 3 | 4 | 5 |
| 11. I prefer working with people who are very much like myself. | 5 | 4 | 3 | 2 | 1 |
| 12. I work primarily because I have to survive, not necessarily because I enjoy what I do. | 5 | 4 | 3 | 2 | 1 |
| 13. I believe I have a realistic picture of my personal strengths and weaknesses. | 1 | 2 | 3 | 4 | 5 |
| 14. Often I get into arguments with people who don't think my way. | 5 | 4 | 3 | 2 | 1 |
| 15. Often I have trouble getting much done on my job. | 5 | 4 | 3 | 2 | 1 |
| 16. I'm interested in a lot of different topics | 1 | 2 | 3 | 4 | 5 |
| 17. I get upset when things don't go my way. | 5 | 4 | 3 | 2 | 1 |

| | VERY TRUE | QUITE TRUE | SOME-WHAT TRUE | NOT VERY TRUE | NOT AT ALL TRUE |
|---|---|---|---|---|---|
| 18. Often I'm not sure how I stand on a controversial topic. | 5 | 4 | 3 | 2 | 1 |
| 19. I'm usually able to find a way around anything that blocks me from an important goal. | 1 | 2 | 3 | 4 | 5 |
| 20. I often disagree with my boss or others at work. | 5 | 4 | 3 | 2 | 1 |

Step 2: Scoring and Interpretation. The author of this questionnaire believes that people who cope with stress effectively have five characteristics:

1. They know themselves well and accept their own strengths and weaknesses.
2. They have a variety of interests off the job, and they are not total "workaholics."
3. They exhibit a variety of reactions to stress, rather than always getting a headache or always becoming depressed.
4. They are accepting of others who have values or styles different from their own.
5. They are good at coping and are active and productive both on and off the job.

Add together the numbers you circled for the four questions contained in each of the five coping scales below.

| COPING SCALE | ADD TOGETHER YOUR RESPONSES TO THESE QUESTIONS | YOUR SCORE (WRITE IN) |
|---|---|---|
| 1. Knows self | 4, 9, 13, 18 | _____ |
| 2. Many interests | 2, 5, 7, 16 | _____ |
| 3. Variety of reactions | 1, 11, 17, 19 | _____ |
| 4. Accepts others' values | 3, 8, 14, 20 | _____ |
| 5. Active and productive | 6, 10, 12, 15 | _____ |

Now add the five scores together for your overall total score. Place that number here: _____

Scores on each of the five areas can vary between 5 and 20. Scores of 12 or above suggest that it might be useful to direct more attention to the area. The overall total score can range between 20 and 100. Scores of 60 or more suggest some general difficulty in coping on the dimensions covered.

Step 3: Break into groups of three or four. Compare your scale and total scores. Discuss what you might be able to do if your score is high.

Step 4: Have the two people in each group with the highest score and lowest score enact a role play. The person with the lowest score is the supervisor; the person with the highest is the employee. Assume that the supervisor has concluded that the employee seems to be acting strangely recently on his or her job. You think high stress may be part of the problem. Conduct a counseling session with the employee to discuss what you (the supervisor) might do to help the employee reduce his or her stress level.

Source: A. A. McLean, (1979). *Work Stress.* Reading, MA: Addison-Wesley, pp. 126–127. Copyright© 1976 by Management Decision Systems, Inc. Reprinted by permission.

## CRITICAL THINKING

### CASE 13.A

### Prentice Hall Moves to Upper Saddle River

Nearly from its beginning, Prentice Hall's College Division (the group that publishes textbooks and educational materials used in colleges and universities) had been located in Englewood Cliffs, New Jersey. This location proved convenient for a wide range of employees. Those who lived in New York City had only a 20-minute commute to work. Those who preferred to live in the suburban areas had more than a dozen small New Jersey communities from which to choose. Even those who preferred a rural lifestyle could find it within a 45-minute commute to work.

In the early 1990s, however, company officials determined that the organization had outgrown its facility in Englewood Cliffs. Attempts to obtain permits from local government officials to expand the facility were met with much resistance. As a result, the company bought the former headquarters of Western Union in Upper Saddle River, New Jersey. With some

remodeling to fit company needs, the College Division began operating in Upper Saddle River in June 1995.

The biggest issue facing supervisors concerning the move was the realization that hiring and retaining employees might be affected—especially in the advertising and design departments. That's because many of these employees lived in New York City. What was once a 20-minute commute from the city now took nearly an hour each way. Further compounding this was the realization that no public transportation was available. Going to work now required employees to have access to an automobile.

Linda Wilson supervises a small group at Prentice Hall that exclusively works on designing books. All six of her employees live in New York city. When Linda learned in the summer of 1994 of the move to Upper Saddle River, she immediately told her employees. Initially, news of the move appeared to have little effect. But as the date of the move drew nearer, rumors were rampant that almost all of her staff were looking for jobs in New York City.

## RESPONDING TO THE CASE

1. Why do you believe most of Linda Wilson's employees were resistant to the move? Describe the factors leading to this resistance.
2. Assume you are Linda Wilson. It's spring 1995. You don't want to lose any of the skilled and talented people you have on your staff. What specifically would you do?
3. Do you believe that company officials could have reduced some of the resistance to change—especially for those employees who lived in New York City? Explain.

## CASE 13.B

### Electronic Filings at Burke Accounting

Tax time is always the busiest time of the year for the accountants and most other employees at Burke and Company, one of the leading accounting firms in the Baltimore area. Dave Carroway, one of the supervisors of an information processing center at Burke, knows that the hassles of tax time will be rolling around soon. It is his job to ensure that the center's electronic equipment is serviced prior to their busy season. He must be certain he has the necessary materials and supplies that will be so crucial at this time. He also must hire part-time employees and schedule regular employees for longer hours.

Dave sees to it that work is scheduled, processed, and disseminated accurately and efficiently. Timing is vital because so many people depend on his department for production of the completed documents. As the tax deadline of April 15 for personal tax returns nears, there is no room for delays. Dave really likes his job, but it seems that tax time is becoming more and more stressful for him and his staff. It seems that during the tax-crunch period, absenteeism increases significantly among his employees— a problem which complicates departmental scheduling. He also thinks the annual tax time is becoming longer each year. Not only do employees talk about it more, more customers each year opt for the automatic filing extension. Most of the employees feel that the extra pay they can get with overtime doesn't reduce the pressures and stress that tax time brings with it.

### RESPONDING TO THE CASE

1. Describe why stress may be costly to the Burke firm; to its employees.
2. Discuss the factors which you believe are contributing to the building of stress among information processing center employees.
3. How does change enter into the situation described here?
4. What do you believe Dave can do to help to reduce the resistance to change? ∎

# 14  DISCIPLINING EMPLOYEES

# LEARNING OBJECTIVES 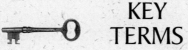 KEY TERMS

After reading this chapter, you should be able to

1. Define discipline.
2. Identify the four most common types of discipline problems.
3. List the typical steps in progressive discipline.
4. Explain the "hot stove" rule.
5. Describe the role of extenuating circumstances in applying discipline.
6. Explain the current status of the employment-at-will doctrine.
7. Describe how a collective bargaining agreement affects the disciplining of unionized employees.

You should be able to define these supervisory terms:

discipline

dismissal

employment-at-will

"hot stove" rule

positive discipline

progressive discipline

suspension

verbal warning

written warning

wrongful discharge

Regardless of how good a supervisor you are or how able and motivated the group of people in your department are, the hard truth is: at one time or another, you will have to discipline a problem employee. How effective you are in performing your disciplining skills—in the most extreme of circumstances—can literally have life or death consequences. A couple of examples can dramatize this statement.

A Federal Express employee, catching a ride with FedEx flight crew, was returning to headquarters for a disciplinary hearing regarding lying on his resume.[1] During the flight, for some unknown reason, the passenger attacked the flight crew with a hammer and spear he had brought aboard the plane. Only through extreme maneuvers was the pilot able to subdue the assailant and successfully land the plane.

The U.S. Postal Service seems to have had more than its share of disciplined employees taking drastic action against their supervisors. Shoot-

## INTRODUCTION

Any form of discipline can create fear or anger in employees. The supervisor who can make the discipline process less painful for the employee, who behaves with compassion and treats the employee with dignity, is likely to find that more severe forms of disciplinary action become unnecessary. In those cases where termination does occur, the employee is better able to handle it (see Assessing Yourself).

## THE DISCIPLINARY PROCESS

**Discipline**
actions taken by
supervisors to enforce
an organization's
standards and
regulations.

What specifically do we mean when we use the term **discipline** in the workplace? It refers to actions taken by a supervisor to enforce the organization's standards and regulations. It generally follows a typical sequence of four steps: verbal warning, written warning, suspension, and dismissal (see Exhibit 14–1).

---

[1]A. Toufexis, "Workers Who Fight Firing with Fire," *Time*, April 25, 1994, p. 35, and *L. A. Times*, April 9, 1994, p. A–31.

ings at a local post office by a recently disciplined employee, like the one upset over a disagreement about how paperwork was to be handled and another who disliked working for a woman, have become all too prevalent.[2]

Disciplinary action can be a traumatic experience for any employee. Disciplined employees are likely to become listless and depressed. In cases where they feel they've been stripped of their dignity, these employees may lash out in unpredictable and vicious ways. Unfortunately, many supervisors fail to understand the significant emotional impact that disciplinary action has on people. They incorrectly give people credit for being tougher than they really are. Some supervisors are downright thoughtless—they patronize the employee, fail to provide an adequate explanation, or deliver the message in an insensitive manner. ■

The mildest form of discipline is the **verbal warning**. A verbal warning is a temporary record of a reprimand which is placed in the supervisor's file. This verbal warning typically states the purpose, date, and outcome of the feedback session with you. If the verbal warning is effective, no further disciplinary action is needed. However, if an employee fails to improve their performance, they'll encounter more severe action—the written warning. The **written warning** is the first formal stage of the disciplinary procedure. This is because the written warning becomes part of an employee's official personnel file. In all other ways, however, the written warning is similar to the verbal warning. That is, the employee is advised in private of the violation, its effects, and potential consequences of future violations. Also, after a period of time if no further disciplinary problems arise, the warning is removed from your file.

A **suspension** or time off without pay may be the next disciplinary step, usually taken only if the prior two steps have not achieved the desired results—although exceptions do exist where suspension may be given without any prior verbal or written warning if the infraction is of a serious nature. Why would you suspend an employee? One reason is that a short lay-off, without pay, is potentially a rude awakening. It may convince the employee that you are serious and help him or her to fully understand and accept responsibility for following the organization's rules.

**Verbal warning**
a temporary record of a reprimand which is then placed in the supervisor's file.

**Written warning**
the first formal stage of the disciplinary procedure; the warning becomes part of an employee's official personnel file.

**Suspension**
time off without pay; this step is usually taken only if neither verbal nor written warnings have achieved desired results.

[2]Ibid.

## ARE YOU EFFECTIVE AT DISCIPLINING?

For each of the following statements, check the answer that best describes you. Remember to respond as you have behaved or would behave, not as you think you should behave. If you have no supervisory experience, answer the statements assuming you were a supervisor.

When disciplining an employee:

| | *Usually* | *Sometimes* | *Seldom* |
|---|---|---|---|
| **1.** I provide ample warning before taking formal action. | ○ | ○ | ○ |
| **2.** I wait for a pattern of infractions before calling it to the employee's attention. | ○ | ○ | ○ |
| **3.** Even after repeated offenses, I prefer informal discussion about correcting the problem rather than formal disciplinary action. | ○ | ○ | ○ |
| **4.** I delay confronting the employee about an infraction until his or her next performance appraisal review. | ○ | ○ | ○ |
| **5.** In discussing an infraction with the employee, my style and tone are serious. | ○ | ○ | ○ |
| **6.** I explicitly seek to allow the employee to explain his or her position. | ○ | ○ | ○ |
| **7.** I remain impartial in allocating punishment. | ○ | ○ | ○ |
| **8.** I allocate stronger penalties for repeated offenses. | ○ | ○ | ○ |

### SCORING

For questions 1, 5, 6, 7, and 8, give yourself 3 points for Usually, 2 points for Sometimes, and 1 point for Seldom. For questions 2, 3, and 4, give yourself 3 points for Seldom, 2 points for Sometimes, and 1 point for Usually.

### WHAT THE ASSESSMENT MEANS

Add up your total points. A score of 22 points or higher indicates excellent skills at disciplining. Scores in the 19 to 21 range suggest some deficiencies. Scores below 19 indicate considerable room for improvement.

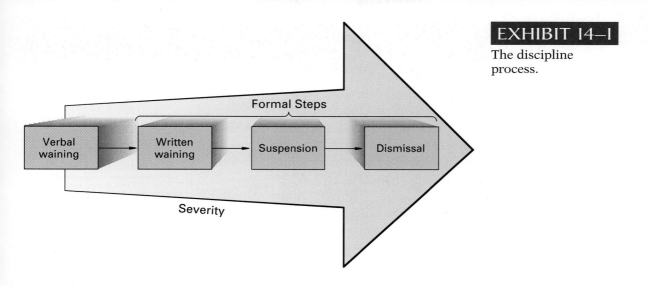

EXHIBIT 14–1

The discipline process.

Formal Steps

| Verbal waining | Written waining | Suspension | Dismissal |

Severity

Your ultimate disciplinary punishment is terminating employment. While **dismissal** is often used for the most serious offenses, it may be the only feasible alternative if your employee's behavior seriously interferes with a department or the organization's operation.

While many organizations may follow the process described above, recognize that it may be bypassed if an employee's behavior is extremely severe. For example, stealing or attacking another employee with intent to inflict serious harm, may result in immediate suspension or dismissal. Regardless of any action taken, however, discipline should be fair and consistent (see News Flash). That is, the punishment an employee receives should be appropriate for what he or she did, and others doing the same thing should be disciplined in a like manner.

**Dismissal**
termination of one's employment.

# NEWS FLASH!

## POSITIVE DISCIPLINE

Traditionally, discipline is generally regarded as negative—some punitive action taken against someone who has done something wrong. **Positive discipline,** however, removes the punitive nature from the discipline process. With the success it has had at such organizations as Union Carbide, there are some indications that it can change employees' views on the disci- *(con't)*

**Positive discipline**
a technique that attempts to reinforce the good work behaviors of an employee, while simultaneously emphasizing to the employee the problems created by undesirable performance.

pline process.[3] Positive discipline attempts to integrate the disciplinary process with the performance appraisal process. When problems arise, rather than promptly responding with a verbal warning (punitive), positive discipline attempts to get the employee back on track by helping him or her fully understand what the undesirable behavior was and the effect it had on the department. In other words, positive discipline attempts to reinforce the good work behaviors of the employee, while simultaneously emphasizing to the employee the problems created by the undesirable performance.

The positive discipline process typically follows three steps. These are *an oral reminder, a written reminder,* and *a decision-making leave.* An oral reminder serves as the initial formal phase of the discipline process. It is designed to identify what is causing the problem and attempts to correct it before it becomes worse. Notice, too, that the word "warning" is missing from this first step!

A written reminder occurs if the oral reminder was unsuccessful in achieving its goal. The written reminder once again reinforces what the employee problem is and what corrective action is necessary on the part of the employee. Furthermore, specific timetables are established which the employee must accept—and the consequences for failing to comply are spelled out. If the written reminder fails too, the employee is given a decision-making leave. Here, the employee is given time off from work—similar to suspension, but with pay—to think about whether or not they desire to continue to work for the company. This decision day is designed to give the employee a choice—either correct the problem behavior or separate from the company.

About now you might be thinking, what's really the difference between positive and negative discipline? It sounds more like a semantic issue. You might think so, but positive discipline goes a bit deeper. In positive discipline, while the supervisor remains in charge of the discipline process, it gives the employee the opportunity to change those things affecting his or her work. It also attempts to change this unwanted behavior with more caring and concern for the employee.

[3]C. A. B. Osigweh Yg and W. R. Hutchinson, "To Punish or Not to Punish? Managing Human Resources Through 'Positive Discipline,'" *Employee Relations*, March 1990, pp. 27–32.

# What Types of Discipline Problems Might You Face?

With very little difficulty, we could list several dozen or more infractions that supervisors might believe require disciplinary action. For simplicity's sake, we have classified the more frequent violations into four categories: attendance, on-the-job behaviors, dishonesty, and outside activities.

## ATTENDANCE

The most serious disciplinary problems facing supervisors undoubtedly involve attendance. Importantly, attendance problems appear to be even more widespread than those related to productivity (carelessness in doing work, neglect of duty, and not following established procedures).

## ON-THE-JOB BEHAVIORS

The second category of discipline problems covers on-the-job behaviors. This blanket label includes insubordination, horseplay, fighting, gambling, failure to use safety devices, carelessness, and two of the most widely discussed problems in organizations today—alcohol and drug abuse.

## DISHONESTY

Although it is not one of the more widespread employee problems confronting supervisors, dishonesty has traditionally resulted in the most severe disciplinary actions. It's a matter of trust. As a supervisor, you need to be able to trust your employees to do certain things, or to handle information properly. Lying, cheating, or other aspects of dishonesty simply destroy an employee's credibility—and your trust in him or her.

## OUTSIDE ACTIVITIES

This final problem category covers activities that employees engage in outside of work, but which either affect their on-the-job performance or generally reflect negatively on the organization's image. Included here are unauthorized strike activity, outside criminal activities, and working for a competing organization.

# Is Discipline Always the Solution?

Just because you have a problem with an employee, don't assume that discipline is the automatic answer. Before you consider disciplining an employee, be sure that the employee has both the ability and the influence to correct his or her behavior.

If an employee doesn't have the ability, that is, he or she can't perform, disciplinary action is not the answer. Some employee counseling is! Similarly, if there are external factors that block goal attainment and those are beyond the employee's control—things like inadequate equipment, disruptive colleagues, or excessive noise—discipline doesn't make much sense either. If an employee can perform but won't, then disciplinary action is called for. However, ability problems should be responded to with solutions like skill training, on-the-job coaching, job redesign, or a job transfer. Serious personal problems that interfere with work performance are typically best met with professional counseling, a medical referral, or those things addressed in employee assistance programs. Of course, if there are external obstacles in the employee's way, you should act to remove them. The point is that if the cause of an employee's problem is outside his or her control, then discipline is not the answer.

## BASIC TENETS OF DISCIPLINE

Based on decades of experience, supervisors have learned what works best when administering discipline. In this section, we'll review some of the lessons learned. We'll present the basic groundwork that needs to be laid prior to any punitive action, the importance of making discipline progressive, and how the "hot stove" rule can guide your actions (see Building a Supervisory Skill).

## DISCIPLINING AN EMPLOYEE

### ABOUT THE SKILL

Disciplining an employee is not an easy task. It is often painful for both parties involved. The following dozen principles, however, should guide you when you have to discipline an employee.

### STEPS IN PRACTICING THE SKILL:

1. **Before you accuse anyone, do your homework.** What happened? If you didn't personally see the infraction, investigate and verify any accusations made by others. Was it completely the employee's fault? If not, who or what else was involved? Did the employee know and understand the rule or regulation that was broken? Document the facts: date, time, place, individuals involved, mitigating circumstances, and the like.

2. **Was ample warning provided?** Before you take formal action, be sure you've provided the employee with reasonable previous warnings and that those warnings have been documented. Ask yourself: If challenged, will my action be defensible? Did I provide ample warning to the employee before taking formal action? It's very likely that applying stiffer punitive actions later on will be judged as unjust by the employee, an arbitrator, and the courts, if it is determined that these punitive actions could not be readily anticipated by the employee.

3. **Act in a timely fashion.** When you become aware of an infraction and it has been supported by your investigation, do something and do it quickly. Delay weakens the linkage between actions and consequences, sends the wrong message to others, undermines your credibility with your subordinates, creates doubt that any action will be taken, and invites repetition of the problem.

4. **Conduct the discipline session in private.** Praise employees in public but keep punishment private. Your objective is not to humiliate the violator. Public reprimands embarrass an employee and are unlikely to produce the change in behavior you desire.

5. **Adopt a calm and serious tone.** Many interpersonal situations are facilitated by a loose, informal, and relaxed manner on the part of a supervisor. The idea in such situations is to put the employee at ease. Administering discipline is not one of those situations. Avoid anger or other emotional responses, but convey your comments in a calm and serious tone. Do not try to lessen the tension by cracking jokes or making small talk. Such actions are only likely to confuse the employee because they send out conflicting signals.

6. **Be specific about the problem.** When you sit down with the employee, indicate that you have documentation and be specific about the problem. Define the violation in exact terms instead of just citing company regulations or the union contract. It's not the breaking of the rules per se that you want to convey concern over. It's the effect that the rule violation has on the work unit's performance. Explain why the behavior can't be continued by show-

ing how it specifically affects the employee's job performance, the unit's effectiveness, and the employee's coworkers.

7. **Keep it impersonal.** Criticism should be focused on the employee's behavior rather than on the individual personally. For instance, if an employee has been late for work several times, point out how this behavior has increased the workload of others or has lowered departmental morale. Don't criticize the person for being thoughtless or irresponsible.

8. **Get the employee's side of the story.** Regardless of what your investigation has revealed, and even if you have the proverbial "smoking gun" to support your accusations, due process demands that you give the employee the opportunity to explain his or her position. From the employee's perspective, what happened? Why did it happen? What was his or her perception of the rules, regulations, and circumstances? If there are significant discrepancies between your version of the violation and the employee's, you may need to do more investigating. Of course, you'll want to document your employee's response for the record.

9. **Keep control of the discussion.** In most interpersonal exchanges with employees, you want to encourage open dialogue. You want to give up control and create a climate of communication between equals. This won't work in administering discipline. Why? Violators are prone to use any allowed egalitarianism to put you on the defensive. In other words, if you don't take control, they will. Discipline, by definition, is an authority-based act. You are enforcing the organization's standards and regulations. So take control. Ask the employee for his or her side of the story. Get the facts. But don't let the employee interrupt you or divert you from your objective.

10. **Agree on how mistakes can be prevented next time.** Disciplining should include guidance and direction for correcting the problem. Let the employee state what he or she plans to do in the future to ensure that the violation isn't repeated. For serious violations, have the employee draft a step-by-step plan to change the problem behavior. Then set a timetable, with follow-up meetings in which progress can be evaluated.

11. **Select progressive disciplinary action and consider mitigating circumstances.** Choose a punishment that is appropriate to the crime. The punishment you select should be viewed as fair and consistent. Once you've arrived at your decision, tell the employee what the action will be, your reasons for taking it, and when it will be carried out.

12. **Fully document the disciplinary session.** To complete your disciplinary action, make sure that your ongoing documentation (what occurred, the results of your investigation, your initial warnings, the employee's explanation and responses, the discipline decision, and the consequences of further misconduct) is complete and accurate. This full documentation should be made part of the employee's permanent file. In addition, it's a good idea to give the employee a formal letter that highlights what was resolved during your discussion, specifics about the punishment, future expectations, and what actions you are prepared to take if the behavior isn't corrected or the violation is repeated. ∎

# How Do You Lay the Groundwork for Discipline?

Any disciplinary action you take should be perceived as fair and reasonable. This increases the likelihood that the employee will change his or her behavior to align with the organization's standards. Such action also prevents unnecessary legal entanglements. The foundation of a fair and reasonable disciplinary climate is created by ensuring that employees are given adequate advance notice of disciplining rules and that a proper investigation precedes any action.

## ADVANCE NOTICE

"The best surprise is no surprise." This phrase, used a number of years ago by a national hotel chain to describe their rooms and service, is a valid guide for supervisors when considering discipline. Employees have a right to know what is expected of them and the probable consequences should they fail to meet those expectations. They should also understand just how serious different types of offenses are. This information can be communicated in employee handbooks, company newsletters, posted rules, or labor contracts. It is always preferable to have these expectations in writing. This provides protection for you, the organization, and your employees.

## PROPER INVESTIGATION

Fair treatment of employees demands that a proper investigation precede any decision. Just like the American legal system, employees should be treated as innocent until proven guilty. Also importantly, no judgment should occur before all the relevant facts have been gathered.

As the employee's supervisor, you will typically be responsible for conducting the investigation. However, if the problem includes an interpersonal conflict between you and the employee, a neutral third party should be chosen to conduct the investigation.

The investigation should focus not only on the event that might lead to discipline but any related matters. This is important because these related concerns may reveal extenuating factors that will need to be considered. Of course, the employee must be notified of the offense with which he or she is being charged so that a defense can be prepared. Remember, you have an obligation to objectively listen to the employee's interpretation and explanation of the offense. A fair and objective investigation will include identification and interviewing of any witnesses and documentation of all evidence that is uncovered.

Failure to conduct a full and impartial investigation can carry high costs. A good employee may be unjustly punished, the trust of other em-

At London Life Insurance, employees are given three written warnings. This procedure is dictated by the procedures issued by the company's Human Resources Department.

ployees may be severely jeopardized, and you may place your organization under possible risk for financial damages should the employee file a lawsuit.

## How Do You Make Discipline Progressive?

**Progressive discipline** action that begins with a verbal warning, and then proceeds through written reprimands, suspension, and finally, in the most serious cases, dismissal.

Punishment should be applied in steps. That is, penalties should get progressively stronger if, or when, an offense is repeated. As we mentioned previously (see Exhibit 14–1), progressive disciplinary action begins with a verbal warning, and then proceeds through written reprimands, suspension, and finally, in the most serious cases, dismissal. At London Life Insurance, for example, employees are given three written warnings, followed by suspension or dismissal.

The logic underlying **progressive discipline** is twofold. First, stronger penalties for repeated offenses discourage repetition. Second, progressive discipline is consistent with court and arbitration rulings that mitigating factors (like length of service, past performance record, or ambiguous organizational policies) be considered when taking disciplinary action.

**"Hot stove" rule** a set of principles that can guide an individual in effectively disciplining an employee by demonstrating the analogy between touching a hot stove and administering discipline.

## What Is the "Hot Stove" Rule?

The **"hot stove" rule** is a frequently cited set of principles that can guide you in effectively disciplining an employee.[4] The name comes from the similarities between touching a hot stove and administering discipline (see Exhibit 14–2).

[4]D. McGregor, "Hot Stove Rules of Discipline," in G. Strauss and L. Sayles, eds., *Personnel: The Human Problems of Management* (Englewood Cliffs, NJ: Prentice-Hall, Inc., 1967).

## EXHIBIT 14–2

The "hot stove" rule.

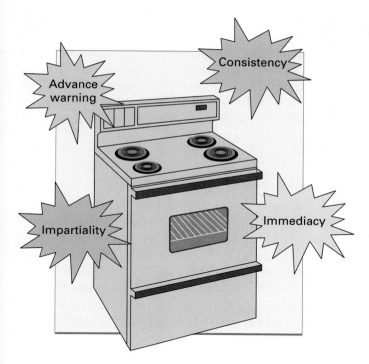

Both are painful, but the analogy goes further. When you touch a hot stove, you get an immediate response. The burn you receive is instantaneous, leaving no doubt in your mind about the cause and the effect. You have ample warning. You know what happens if you touch a red-hot stove. Further, the result is consistent. Every time you touch a hot stove, you get the same response—you get burned. Finally, the result is impartial. Regardless of who you are, if you touch a hot stove, you will be burned. The analogy with discipline should be apparent, but let's briefly expand on each of these four points since they are central tenets in developing your disciplining skills.

## IMMEDIACY

The impact of a disciplinary action will be reduced as the time between the infraction and the penalty's implementation lengthens. The more quickly the discipline follows the offense, the more likely it is that the employee will associate the discipline with the offense rather than with you as the imposer of the discipline. Therefore, it is best to begin the disciplinary process as soon as possible after you notice a violation. Of course, the immediacy requirement should not result in undue haste. Fair and objective treatment should not be compromised for expediency.

## ADVANCE WARNING

As we noted earlier, you have an obligation to give advance warning before initiating formal disciplinary action. This means the employee must be aware of the organization's rules and accept its standards of behavior. Disciplinary action is more likely to be interpreted as fair by employees when they have received clear warning that a given violation will lead to discipline and when they know what that discipline will be.

## CONSISTENCY

Fair treatment of employees demands that disciplinary action be consistent. If you enforce rule violations in an inconsistent manner, the rules will lose their impact. Morale will decline and employees will question your competence. Productivity will suffer as a result of employee insecurity and anxiety. Your employees will want to know the limits of permissible behavior and they will look to your actions for guidance. If Carl is reprimanded today for an action that he did last week, when nothing was said, these limits become blurry. Similarly, if Sara and Jean are both goofing around at their desks and only Sara is reprimanded, Sara is likely to question the fairness of the action. The point, then, is that discipline should be consistent. This need not result in treating everyone exactly alike, because that ignores mitigating circumstances. It does put the responsibility on you to clearly justify disciplinary actions that may appear inconsistent to employees.

## IMPARTIALITY

The last guideline that flows from the "hot stove" rule is to keep the discipline impartial. Penalties should be connected with a given violation, not with the personality of the violator. That is, discipline should be directed at what the employee has done, not at the employee personally. As a supervisor, you should make it clear that you are avoiding personal judgments about the employee's character. You are penalizing the rule violation, not the individual (see Something to Think About). All employees committing the violation can expect to be penalized. Further, once the penalty has been imposed, you must make every effort to forget the incident. You should attempt to treat the employee in the same manner you did prior to the infraction.

## WHAT FACTORS SHOULD YOU CONSIDER IN DISCIPLINE?

Defining what is "reasonable in relation to the offense" is one of the most challenging aspects of the discipline process. Why? Because infractions vary greatly in terms of severity. Suspending an employee is considerably

In Chapter 7, we discussed that supervisors do not choose employees at random. Rather, job applicants go through a series of selection devices to differentiate those who are likely to be successful performers from those who won't be. Accordingly, an effective hiring process should be designed to determine if job candidates "fit" into the organization. Fit, here, implies not only the ability to do the job but also the personality, work habits, and attitudes that the supervisor desires. Consequently, hiring should be recognized as one of the most widely used techniques by which supervisors can influence employee behavior. As a result, the hiring process should screen out those who think and act in ways that supervisors consider undesirable or inappropriate for successful performance.

Do you believe that an effective hiring process can significantly reduce employee performance problems later on? Can most "problems" be avoided by hiring smarter? What do you think?

more stringent than issuing a verbal warning. Similarly, the decision to fire someone—the organizational equivalent of the death penalty—is dramatically more punitive than a two-week suspension without pay. If you fail to recognize relevant extenuating factors and make the proper adjustments in the severity of penalties, you risk having your action perceived as unfair. The following factors—summarized in Exhibit 14–3—should be taken into consideration when applying negative discipline.

What should a disciplinary process be? It should be something that is reasonable and fair, and it should deal with the issues at hand. Decisions shouldn't be made until the inappropriate behavior has been investigated and the alleged wrongdoer has his or her say. As this symbol of justice typifies, an employee should be considered "innocent until proven guilty."

## EXHIBIT 14–3

Relevant factors determining the severity of penalties.

- Seriousness of the problem

- Duration of the problem

- Frequency and nature of the problem

- Employee's work history

- Extenuating circumstances

- Degree of warning

- History of the organization's discipline practices

- Implications for other employees

- Upper-management support

### SERIOUSNESS OF THE PROBLEM

How severe is the problem? Dishonesty, for example, is usually considered a more serious infraction than reporting to work 20 minutes late.

### DURATION OF THE PROBLEM

Have there been other discipline problems with this employee, and if so, over how long a time span? A first occurrence is usually viewed differently from a third or fourth offense.

### FREQUENCY AND NATURE OF THE PROBLEM

Is the current problem part of an emerging or continuing pattern of discipline infractions? Continual infractions may require a different type of discipline from that applied to isolated instances of misconduct.

### EMPLOYEE'S WORK HISTORY

How long has the employee worked for the organization, and what has been the quality of his or her performance? For many violations, the punishment will be less severe for those who have developed a strong track record.

### EXTENUATING CIRCUMSTANCES

Are there extenuating factors, such as influences outside the employee's control, that lessen the severity of the infraction? The employee who missed the plane for an important meeting because his wife went into labor with their first child is likely to have his violation assessed more leniently than would his peer who missed the same plane because he overslept.

## DEGREE OF WARNING

To what extent has the employee been previously warned about the offense? Did he or she know and understand the rule that was broken? As we have noted several times previously, discipline severity should reflect the degree of knowledge that the violator holds of the organization's standards of acceptable behavior. In addition, an organization that has formalized written rules governing employee conduct is more justified in aggressively enforcing violations than an organization whose rules are informal or vague.

## HISTORY OF THE ORGANIZATION'S DISCIPLINE PRACTICES

How have similar infractions been dealt with in the past within your department? Within the entire organization? Equitable treatment of employees must take into consideration precedents within the unit where the infraction occurs, as well as previous disciplinary actions taken in other units within the organization.

## IMPLICATIONS FOR OTHER EMPLOYEES

What impact will the discipline selected have on other workers in the unit? There is little point in taking a certain action against an employee if it will have a major dysfunctional effect on others within the unit. The result may be to convert a narrow and single disciplinary problem into a severe supervisory headache. Conversely, failure to impose discipline where it's justified can reduce departmental morale, undermine your credibility, and lessen employee concern with obeying the rules.

## COMPANY OFFICIAL SUPPORT

If a disciplined employee decides to appeal the case to a company official, will you have reasonable evidence to justify your decision? If you have the data to support your action, can you count on your boss backing you up? Your disciplinary actions aren't likely to carry much weight if violators believe that they can get your decision overridden.

## DISCIPLINE AND THE LAW

Making a mistake when disciplining an employee can have very serious repercussions for an organization. As a result, most large organizations have specific procedures that supervisors are required to follow. Supervisors typically are provided training in how to handle the discipline process. Moreover, they are encouraged to work closely with staff specialists in the human resources department. For instance, at American Express, supervisors are provided with detailed procedures to follow. One of the most important rules that supervisors are instructed to follow at American Express is to ensure that every action taken is documented in writing. If a supervisor at American Express believes that a problem employee may need to be fired, that supervisor is required to work closely with the human resources department to make sure all legal issues are addressed. In this section, we will briefly describe several legal issues you need to be aware of when considering discipline.

## WHAT IS EMPLOYMENT-AT-WILL?

**Employment-at-will**
a legal doctrine that defines an employer's rights to discipline or discharge an employee.

Beginning in the late 1800s, the major legal doctrine that defined an employer's rights to discipline or discharge an employee was the concept of **employment-at-will.** It stated that an employer could dismiss an employee "for good cause, no cause, or even for a cause morally wrong, without being guilty of a legal wrong."[5] The logic of employment-at-will was to equalize the employer-employee relationship. If employees could resign from their jobs whenever they pleased, why shouldn't employers have the same right?

Until about twenty-five years ago, the courts generally held to the employment-at-will doctrine. As a result, it was extremely hard for em-

Inappropriate disciplinary processes—real or perceived—can have a devastating effect. Here, this postal worker comforts a friend after a disgruntled colleague shot and killed two fellow postal employees in Escondido, California. Although the exact reasons for the shooting may never be known, such incidents have often occurred after some disciplinary action was taken against an employee.

[5]*Payne v. Western and Atlantic Railroad Co.*, 812 Tenn. 507 (1884). See also M. Leonard, "Challenges to the Termination-at-Will Doctrine," *Personnel Administrator,* February 1983, p. 49. (Quoted from L. E. Blades, *Columbia Law Review,* 67 (1967), p. 1405.)

ployees who felt they were unjustly fired to find redress through the courts. However, in recent years, the courts have been reinterpreting employee rights and employment-at-will. Of course, no supervisor can terminate an employee on the basis of race, religion, gender, national origin, age, or disability. Beyond these basic civil rights issues, jobs are increasingly being likened to private property—the argument being that individuals have a right to their jobs unless the organization can justify otherwise.

Today, should you fire an employee, you and your employer may end up in court defending yourselves against claims of **wrongful discharge** or that you improperly terminated the employee. All 50 states currently permit employees to sue their employer if they believe their termination was unjust. Almost 80 percent of the verdicts in these cases have come down in favor of the employee. Damage awards of $100,000 or more have not been uncommon.

Wrongful discharge improper or unjust termination of an employee.

As the courts have moved to protect an employee's right to his or her job, most organizations have responded by tightening up their hiring and discipline practices. They are carefully reviewing their hiring processes to remove any implied employment contracts. In the past, employment handbooks, interviewers, and supervisors often gave implied guarantees or promises about continued employment. The courts have interpreted such written and verbal statements as implied contracts that protect employees against termination. So, as a supervisor, you should be careful not to make any statement to any employee such as "we never lay people off here" or "you'll have a place with this company as long as you do your job."

The courts have also become increasingly concerned that, when an employee is terminated, the employee's rights have not been abused and that discipline has been fairly imposed. Proper documentation of all disciplining action is the best protection against employees who claim, "I never knew there was any problem," or, "I was treated unfairly." In addition, you will want to obey due process when taking any disciplinary action. This includes: (1) a presumption of innocence until reasonable proof of an employee's role in an offense is substantiated; (2) the right of the employee to be heard, and in some cases to be represented by another person; and (3) discipline that is reasonable in relation to the offense involved.

## CAN YOU DISCIPLINE A UNIONIZED EMPLOYEE?

What if your employees are unionized and protected by a contract? How does this affect the disciplinary process? Let's look at this issue.

Where employees belong to a union, there will be a collective bargaining agreement. This agreement, among other things, will outline rules governing the behavior of union members. It will also identify disciplinary procedures and clarify the steps members are to follow if they believe that they are receiving arbitrary or unfair treatment.

The collective bargaining agreement will typically define what represents a rule violation and what penalties are applicable. Keep in mind that the more serious actions—to suspend or dismiss an employee—usually can be expected to be vigorously opposed by both the employee and the union.

Most collective-bargaining agreements (1) stipulate that employees can only be disciplined for "just cause"; (2) provide a grievance procedure; and (3) afford opportunities for third-party review if employees believe they have been wronged. Disciplining unionized employees, therefore, tends to be a more quasilegal undertaking than the disciplining of nonunion employees. The bargaining contract, the existence of a grievance procedure, the right to have differences evaluated and resolved by a third party, and the whole quasilegal labor-management relationship all act to reduce your discretion as a supervisor in taking disciplinary action. We'll look at this "special" case of supervising in the next chapter.

---

## POP QUIZ  (Are You Comprehending What You're Reading?)

**5.** Which one of the following is *not* a recommended guideline in administering discipline?
   **a.** make it immediate
   **b.** make it progressive
   **c.** make it corrective
   **d.** make it visible

**6.** What are the two keys to the groundwork of the discipline process?

**7.** It is sometimes necessary to discipline an employee in public—especially when that employee's inappropriate actions were witnessed by other employees in the department. True or False?

**8.** The employment-at-will doctrine
   **a.** is no longer permitted in most states.
   **b.** means that an employer must have just cause for terminating an employee.
   **c.** was designed to equalize the employer-employee relationship.
   **d.** none of the above

---

## SUMMARY

After reading this chapter, I can:

1. **Define discipline.** Discipline refers to actions taken to enforce the organization's rules and standards.

2. **Identify the four most common types of discipline problems.** The most serious disciplinary problems facing supervisors are: (1) attendance issues such as absenteeism, tardiness, and abuse of sick leave; (2) on-the-job behaviors such as insubordination or substance abuse; (3) dishonesty; and (4) outside activities that affect on-the-job performance or reflect poorly on the organization.

3. **List the typical steps in progressive discipline.** The typical steps in progressive discipline are: (1) a verbal warning, (2) written reprimands, (3) suspension, and (4) dismissal.

4. **Explain the "hot stove" rule.** The "hot stove" rule states that discipline should be administered in the same way that people respond to touching a hot stove. The response should be immediate; there should be a warning; the result should be consistent; and the result should be impartial.

5. **Describe the role of extenuating circumstances in applying discipline.** Fairness demands that extenuating circumstances be considered before applying negative discipline. Factors such as the duration of the problem, the employee's work history, and past discipline practices in the organization are all legitimate factors that can influence the degree of disciplinary action.

6. **Explain the current status of the employment-at-will doctrine.** In recent years, the courts have been reinterpreting the employment-at-will doctrine. Employees may not always be terminated without cause. The courts are increasingly interpreting the right to hold a job like that of holding property.

7. **Describe how a collective bargaining agreement affects the disciplining of unionized employees.** In disciplining unionized employees, the bargaining contract, the existence of a grievance procedure, the right to have differences evaluated and resolved by a third party, and the entire quasilegal labor-management relationship all act to reduce a supervisor's range of discretion.

## REVIEWING YOUR KNOWLEDGE

1. "A good supervisor will never have to use discipline." Do you agree or disagree with this statement? Discuss.

2. Is punishment consistent with having confidence in employees? Discuss.

3. Describe what you would do if you practiced progressive discipline.

4. Why is it common for an organization to immediately dismiss a high-performing employee who lied about his or her educational qualifications on the job application but take less harsh action against an average employee who "calls in sick" and misses a day of work to go hunting? Do you believe this action is fair?

5. Why isn't discipline always the solution?

6. If you see a violation of an organizational rule by one of your employees with your own eyes, you do not have to investigate the "act." You simply go straight to discipline. Do you agree or disagree? Discuss.

7. Why is it so important to document, in writing, any disciplinary action you take against an employee?
8. What authority, if any, do you think human resource departments should have over a supervisor's disciplinary practices?
9. Contrast the advantages and disadvantages of the original employment-at-will doctrine.
10. What disciplinary process issues are different in a unionized department?

## ANSWERS TO THE POP QUIZZES

1. **b. written warning.** This is the first formal step of the discipline process because it is the first step in which a record of the discipline is placed in the employee's personnel file. The first step of the discipline process, the verbal warning, results in documentation which is informally kept in the supervisor's file on the employee.
2. The purpose of a suspension—a short layoff, typically without pay—is to create a rude awakening for the employee. It is designed to convince the employee that the supervisor is serious about the action being taken. Furthermore, it is designed to help the employee fully understand and accept responsibility for following the organization's rules.
3. **True.** This is the basic premise behind positive discipline.
4. **c. inability to do the job.** The inability to do the job is not the same thing as the lack of desire to do it. Inability to do a job is best dealt with through training—not discipline.
5. **d. make it visible.** All discipline should be handled privately. It's a matter of respecting the individual, even though disciplinary action is taking place.
6. The two keys to the groundwork to the discipline process are that the process is perceived as **fair and reasonable.**
7. **False.** All discipline should be conducted in private. The fact that the inappropriate behaviors were witnessed by other employees does not give the supervisor the freedom to discipline in public.
8. **c. was designed to equalize the employer-employee relationship.** The issue behind the employment-at-will doctrine was that an employee could resign at any time from his or her job. Therefore, employers should also have the same freedom to end the employment relationship should they desire. ■

## A CLASS EXERCISE: DISCIPLINING AN EMPLOYEE

The class should break into pairs. The following role play takes place between Chris Freedland (the supervisor) and Pat Marshall (the employee). One member of the pair will play the role of Chris; the other will play Pat. Each role player should read the following background material and then only his or her role. Do not read the other person's role. When you've both read your respective roles, begin the role play. This should take approximately ten to fifteen minutes to complete.

## BACKGROUND

Pat Marshall works on the quality inspection line at a toy manufacturing firm and has held the same job for two years. Pat's job is to inspect finished stuffed animals for defects, as they go down the conveyor belt toward the boxing and shipping department. Pat's supervisor, Chris Freedland, is new on the job. Chris was hired from another company and has been with the toy firm for only two weeks. Upon being hired, Chris called the entire quality inspection staff together and talked about his/her supervisory philosophy. One point Chris emphasized was the need for people to explicitly follow the company rules. Chris then proceeded to give a copy of the rules and procedures manual to everyone.

Pat's performance evaluations have been consistently good and Pat has no prior history of problems. Today Pat walked away from the conveyor belt for a few minutes without asking permission. Company rules state that assembly-line employees are not to leave their workstations unless they ask for and get permission from their supervisor. Pat has now returned to the conveyor belt.

## PAT MARSHALL'S ROLE

You left the conveyor belt—for what you thought was about five minutes—to check with your daughter's nursery school. You are a single parent and your daughter has been sick for the past few days. Although you left your workstation without asking permission, you didn't consider it a problem because everyone sometimes leaves their jobs on the line for a few minutes without getting permission. You like your job and, as a single parent, depend on your weekly paycheck to pay the bills. You're an emotional person. If challenged or reprimanded, you are prone to get very upset and become argumentative.

## CHRIS FREEDLAND'S ROLE

As a new supervisor, you are determined to do a good job. One problem that concerns you is that employees leave their workstations without asking permission. The previous supervisor apparently looked the other way and let employees break the rules. Well, no more! You're going to shape up the quality inspection department. You glanced at your watch when Pat left the conveyor belt—it was 10:20. Pat returned at 10:40.

To you, leaving a workstation without permission is serious for three reasons: (1) it increases the workload for others; (2) it means defective items have a lower probability of being caught; and (3) the company rule is well known and flouting it creates a breakdown in authority. You want to take disciplinary action with Pat. It is now 10:45—five minutes after Pat has returned to the line. Your office, which is only 30 feet from the conveyor line, provides privacy should you think this is necessary.

Use the steps presented in Building a Supervisory Skill (p. 509) as a guide for this exercise.

## CRITICAL THINKING

## CASE 14.A

### Discipline at the Post Office

Disciplining workers in the U.S. Postal System has taken on new meaning. In the past 15 years, there have been several incidents involving a disgruntled employee returning to the workplace seeking revenge. In each case, there has been one common link— the employee recently had been disciplined by his supervisor.

Investigations of these incidents point to a number of factors leading to the events. Workers are often faced with monotonous jobs— jobs that at times are extremely repetitive. Training for some of these postal employees may also be lacking, as much of that is contingent on the post office where one works. The volume of work also reveals that these employees' jobs never end. Transition from one day to the next occurs without ever finalizing many of the repetitive tasks. Then there is supervision, which postal workers feel leaves much to be desired. Employees are sometimes treated differently according to how well the supervisor likes them. Furthermore, those who are less favored by the supervisor receive most of the discipline. That appears consistent with reports that the disgruntled employees often come

"gunning" for their supervisor, whom they felt mistreated them.

### RESPONDING TO THE CASE

1. What role do you believe supervisors play in administering discipline in the post office? How can a supervisor who handles the process appropriately fend off potential repercussions?
2. In jobs that are monotonous and repetitive, do you believe a different disciplinary process should be developed—one that takes into account not only the work, but also the emotional side of employees? Explain your position.
3. In your opinion, can you ever eliminate most of the potential difficulties surrounding the discipline process that have lead to a number of the Post Office incidents? Discuss.

## CASE 14.B

### Brenda Miller at WalMart

Brenda Miller was an excellent greeter at the Norwalk, Connecticut Wal-Mart store. She greeted each person who walked through the front door as if that person was the only one who mattered to the company. Her friendly voice reflected exactly the same enthusiasm and sincerity when she answered the phone. Brenda gave personal attention to every visitor and caller—yes, she was a valued, conscientious ambassador for Wal-Mart.

As a matter of speaking, Brenda was one of the better performers that this Wal-Mart had.

Frequently she was the first contact customers had as they entered the store. Because of her kindness and outgoing nature, some customers stopped for a few moments just to chat with Brenda. Brenda's supervisor, Joan Thompson, was pleased that Brenda seemed so happy in her job. She would have to be sure to put a special notation on her performance review.

About two months later—sometime in early March—when Joan was having a conversation with two other store supervisors, they asked Joan if Brenda was okay. Brenda had been absent a lot lately and, when she was at work, her performance seemed to have fallen off. They indicated that some customers had even mentioned it to other store staff. In fact, in a couple of cases, several customers reported that Brenda was less than friendly when they entered the store.

Joan couldn't believe her ears. Brenda was busier than ever. She even volunteered for extra shifts when her replacement was unable to come to work. Yes, she did seem a bit pale and had taken off a few days from work, but the workload was always heavy during the holiday season. She seemed cheerful enough—how could anyone think something might be wrong? However, she had better talk with Brenda if others seemed to perceive there was a problem.

(Brenda's problem is identified in item #3 below; however, it is recommended that questions #1 and #2 be answered first before referring to #3.)

## RESPONDING TO THE CASE

1. What explanation might be offered as to why Joan was not seeing Brenda's work deteriorating as others did?

2. How can Joan find out if Brenda has a problem?

3. Problem: Brenda was an excellent employee, but was not challenged in her job. Because she didn't feel she had job security and her job didn't pay enough to support her, she responded to a newspaper ad seeking at-home direct mail representatives. As a direct mail representative she made follow-up phone calls for the direct mail company. At first she made only a few of the calls at work. When she found it easier to contact people during the day, she made more and more of her calls from the office. After all, she rationalized, she wasn't that busy at her job, everyone liked her work, and her supervisor wanted her to keep busy. One thing led to another and before she realized it, she was spending more time on the phone for her direct mail business than doing her work at WalMart. This way she also had more time to be with her friends during weekday evenings. Given these facts, what are some of the factors Joan should consider in disciplining Brenda? Discuss how the steps in progressive discipline are complicated by Joan not being "on top" of the situation earlier?

4. Are there any extenuating circumstances or other factors that would influence the type of action Joan should take in Brenda's case? If so, what are they? Why?

5. In groups of two or three, discuss the action Joan should take in this case. As each group shares its action plan with the class, the group should explain its reasons for their recommended plan of action. ∎

# 15

# THE SUPERVISOR'S ROLE IN LABOR RELATIONS

# LEARNING OBJECTIVES  KEY TERMS

After reading this chapter, you should be able to

1. Describe the current status of labor unions in the United States.
2. Explain the appeal of unions to employees.
3. Describe the importance of the National Labor Relations Act.
4. Identify the primary purpose of collective bargaining.
5. Explain the supervisor's role in contract administration.
6. Describe the steps for handling a grievance.

You should also be able to define these supervisory terms:

agency shop

arbitrator

bargaining unit

closed shop

collective bargaining

conciliation

dues checkoff

fact-finding

grievance procedure

interest arbitration

labor relations

Labor-Management Relations Act

lockout

maintenance of membership

management rights

mediation

National Labor Relations Act

National Labor Relations Board

open shop

spillover effect

strike

union

union shop

union steward

wildcat strike

Ron Thomas has been an assembly line supervisor at Saturn in Spring Hill, Tennessee for nearly eight years. Ron's job is to make sure his work crews produce Saturn automobiles in a safe and efficient manner. In a recent interview, Ron talked about his job and contrasted it to that of his brother, Bart, who works for a Fargo, North Dakota tree-cutting service. Bart is also a supervisor, but unlike Ron, Bart's employees don't belong to a union.

"Last week Bart and his family were down visiting. We were sitting in the living room and got around to comparing our jobs. Bart supervises a small group of tree trimmers. They meet at a central location every morning. Then Bart drives them to their various work locations. Bart's boss imposes very few rules on him or the work group. Bart has the major say-so in who he hires, how much they get paid, what tasks people should do, when they take breaks, and the like. If an employee gives him any trouble, he gives them a warning. If they don't shape up, he fires them. When they're working on a job, Bart runs the show. There is no question about who's the boss.

"The employees I oversee are all members of the United Auto Workers (UAW) union. They have a contract with Saturn (ala General Motors) that

## INTRODUCTION

As Ron Thomas vividly describes, supervising unionized workers is different from supervising nonunionized employees. In this chapter, we'll discuss why employees join unions, review the key labor laws you need to know about, and then consider the role that supervisors play in labor matters.

## WHAT IS LABOR RELATIONS?

**Labor relations**
all activities within a company that involve dealing with a union and its members.

**Union**
an organization that represents workers and seeks to protect their interests through collective bargaining.

**Labor relations** includes all the activities within a company that involve dealing with a union and its members. But what is a union? We can best answer that by stating that a **union** is an organization that represents workers and seeks to protect their interests through collective bargaining.

covers just about anything that could come up. For instance, although our contract gives employees some discretion to make their own decisions, I can't tie a part of the employees' pay to quality and productivity. Furthermore, all of my employees are protected from layoffs due to economic downturns. Consequently, I have little control over the number of employees in my unit. Things like this are negotiated at the time of the contract by union and company representatives.

"And it's easier to get Congress to pass a tax cut than it is for me to terminate one of my employees. I have to fill out dozens of forms and the employees have all kinds of appeal procedures. Bart told me that he fired one of his employees because he caught him drinking hard liquor during his afternoon break. The guy had been warned once about the company's rule about no drinking on the job. If one of my people were caught drinking, I'd be required to issue three written warnings, then if the employee still didn't shape up, he'd be sent for counseling. Even if the employee continued with his drinking problem, it would take six or nine months to go through all the appeals that the union contract provides before the person would actually be terminated." ∎

The beginnings of unionization in the United States can be traced back to the late 1700s. Unions at that time were comprised of skilled craftpersons—like carpenters, and shoemakers—whose primary objective was to enhance job security, maintain fair wages, and assist members and their families in the event of a member's illness or death. The early days of unionization were not easy ones, however, for union members. Most of their activities were severely impeded by the court's adoption of the English criminal conspiracy doctrine, which stated that any attempt by workers to band together with the objective of negotiating with an employer was considered to be a criminal conspiracy. This ruling continued until 1842, when in the Massachusetts State Court case of *Commonwealth v. Hunt,* it was ruled that unions were not considered an illegal entity. However, this case did not legalize unionization. It simply overturned the use of imposing the criminal conspiracy doctrine in labor-management matters.

It would be nearly another 100 years before unions as we know them today would exist. Through years of legal challenges, changing public opinion for and against unions, and political lobbying, unions finally got their full freedom to exist, represent workers, and negotiate over wages, hours, and terms and conditions of employment. During this fight for existence, problems among various unions arose. Specifically, unions originally were built around skilled workers. Workers who possessed those skills were encouraged to join a certain union. In fact, the *American Federation of Labor*, today part of the AFL-CIO, was founded to organize skilled workers in a number of industries. The unskilled workers, however, were by and large left out—until the founding of the *Congress of Industrial Workers* (CIO). The CIO was built on the premise that it would represent all eligible workers from a particular company or industry regardless of their occupation or skill level. This internal dispute between the AFL and the CIO lasted for 20 years until they joined forces in forming the AFL-CIO in 1955 to promote the mutual interests of all workers.

Unions exist in most industrialized nations—such as Sweden, Great Britain, Italy, Germany, Japan, Spain, France, and the United States (see Exhibit 15–1).[1] Today, only about 11 percent of the U.S. private sector workforce is unionized.[2] As little as 50 years ago, however, almost 1 in 3 workers belonged to a union. Union membership in the U.S., as a percent of the civilian workforce, has been declining. A number of factors have contributed to this decline. The economic sectors where union strength has traditionally been greatest—particularly blue collar manufacturing jobs in the automobile, steel, rubber, and chemical industries—have significantly cut their American workforces. Many of these jobs have been eliminated through automation or exported to countries with lower labor costs. The growth in the labor force since the late 1960s has been among women, professionals, government employees, and service workers— groups that have been more resistant to labor's effort to organize them. Unions have also suffered directly as a result of their own success. Labor union growth in the 1930s and 1940s was largely a result of responding to the depressed status of the American working class. As unions succeeded in raising wages and improving working conditions, the reasons for their very existence became less obvious.

The fact that only about one in nine Americans belongs to a union or that union membership has been declining for many years should not be interpreted as implying that unions have little influence in the American workplace. We're still talking about an organized group of millions of members. In many key industries (for instance, mining, construction, railroads, and trucking) the majority of workers are unionized. Most importantly, we can't overlook the **spillover effect**. Successes made by unions at the negotiating table spill over to influence the wages, working conditions, and terms of employment for workers who are not unionized. For example, the wages, hours, and working conditions of nonunion employees at a

**Spillover effect** successes made by unions through negotiations that spill over to influence the wages, working conditions, and terms of employment for nonunion workers.

[1]"European News in Brief," *Facts on File* (Chicago, IL: Rand McNally Corporation, 1993), p. 672.
[2]"Why Labor Keeps Losing," *Fortune* (July 11, 1994), p. 178.

EXHIBIT 15–1

| Country | Percent of Civilian Employees Unionized |
|---|---|
| Sweden | 81 |
| Great Britain | 39 |
| Italy | 34 |
| Germany | 32 |
| Japan | 20 |
| Spain | 11 |
| United States | 11 |
| France | 10 |

Percent of unioniza-
tion in industrialized
nations. (*Source:*
"European" News in
Brief, *Facts on File,*
(Chicago, IL: Rand
McNally Corpora-
tion, 1993), p. 672.)

Columbia, Maryland meat packing plant may be affected by an agreement reached between the United Auto Workers and General Motors at GM's Baltimore minivan facility.

## Why Would Your Employees Want to Join a Union?

What do employees seek to gain when they join a union? The answer to this question varies with the individual and the union context, but the following captures the most common reasons.

### HIGHER WAGES AND BENEFITS

There's power and strength in numbers. As a result, unions sometimes are able to obtain higher wages and benefit packages for their members than these employees would be able to negotiate individually. One or two employees walking off the job over a wage dispute is unlikely to significantly affect most businesses, but hundreds of workers going out on strike can temporarily disrupt or even close down a company. Additionally, professional bargainers employed by the union may be able to negotiate more skillfully than any individual could on his or her own behalf.

### GREATER JOB SECURITY

Unions provide members with a sense of independence from management's power to arbitrarily hire, promote, or fire. The collective bargaining contract will stipulate rules that apply to all members, thus providing fairer and more uniform treatment. For example, after a lengthy strike involving the Teamsters Union and the Giant Food Company, an agreement was reached between the parties that guarantees Teamsters' union members life-long job security—regardless of external factors affecting the company.

### INFLUENCE WORK RULES

Where a union exists, workers are provided with an opportunity to participate in determining the conditions under which they work, and they have an effective channel through which they can protest conditions they believe are unfair. Therefore, a union is not only a representative of the worker but also provides rules that define channels in which complaints and concerns of workers can be registered. Grievance procedures and rights to third-party arbitration of disputes are examples of practices that are typically defined and regulated as a result of union efforts.

### COMPULSORY MEMBERSHIP

Many labor agreements require that individuals must join the union or at least pay dues if they want to keep their jobs. We'll come back to these compulsory membership actions shortly.

### BEING UPSET WITH YOU

In spite of the reasons why employees join a union, there appears to be one common factor—you, the supervisor. If employees are upset with the way you handle problems, upset over how you disciplined one of their co-workers, and the like, they are likely to seek help from a union. In fact, research has shown that when employees vote to unionize, it's often a vote

What types of workers are more likely to join a union? Traditionally, blue collar workers—like these coal miners in West Virginia—were the most likely candidates. As such, they have worked under the presence of a negotiated labor agreement.

against their immediate supervisor rather than a vote in support of a particular union.

## WHAT LABOR LEGISLATION DO YOU NEED TO KNOW ABOUT?

You don't need to be a labor lawyer to deal with legal issues surrounding union-management relations. But there are some basic U.S. laws with which you need to be familiar. These include the National Labor Relations Act, the Labor-Management Relations Act, and right-to-work laws.

### THE NATIONAL LABOR RELATIONS ACT

Prior to the mid-1930s, the U.S. courts were generally antiunion. The legal environment was almost entirely on management's side. For instance, companies could legally fire workers for joining unions, force them to sign a pledge not to join a union as a condition of employment, require them to belong to company unions, and spy on them to cut off any antagonistic union organizing efforts before they began.

All that changed with the passage of the **National Labor Relations Act**—more frequently called the Wagner Act—in 1935. The Wagner Act guaranteed workers the right to organize and join unions, to bargain collectively, and to act in concert in pursuit of their objectives. In terms of collective bargaining, the act specifically required management to bargain in good faith over rates of pay, wages, hours of employment, or other conditions of employment. Over the years, this mandate has been steadily broadened by the courts to additionally include items such as Christmas bonuses, pensions, information on plant shutdowns, and subcontracting work out to other firms.

The Wagner Act specifically prohibited employers from the following. Committing any of these is considered an unfair labor practice on the part of the company.

1. Interfering with, restraining, or coercing employees in the exercise of the rights to join unions and bargain collectively.
2. Dominating or interfering with the formation or administration of any labor organization.
3. Discriminating against anyone because of union activity.
4. Discharging or otherwise discriminating against any employee for filing charges or giving testimony under the act.
5. Refusing to bargain collectively with the representatives chosen by the employees.

National Labor Relations Act (Wagner Act) a law that guarantees workers the right to organize and join unions, to bargain collectively, and to act in concert in pursuit of their objectives.

**National Labor Relations Board (NLRB)**
a group given primary responsibility for conducting elections to determine union representation and to interpret and apply the law against unfair labor practices.

**Labor-Management Relations Act (Taft-Hartley Act)**
a law passed in 1947 that specified unfair union labor practices and declared the closed shop to be illegal.

To administer this law, the **National Labor Relations Board (NLRB)** was established. This board was given primary responsibility for conducting elections to determine union representation and to interpret and apply the law against unfair labor practices.

## THE LABOR-MANAGEMENT RELATIONS ACT

The Wagner Act shifted the pendulum of power to favor unions. By the mid-1940s, following a number of post-World War II strikes, the public and Congress came to believe that labor unions had become too powerful. Some believed that something had to be done to lessen unions' clout. That something was the passage of the **Labor-Management Relations Act** of 1947 or what is more typically referred to as the Taft-Hartley Act.

The major purpose of the Taft-Hartley Act was to specify unfair union labor practices. For instance, it stated that it was an unfair labor practice for unions to:

1. Restrain or coerce employees in joining the union or to coerce the employer in selecting bargaining or grievance representatives.
2. Discriminate against an employee to whom union membership had been denied or to cause an employer to discriminate against an employee.
3. Refuse to bargain collectively.
4. Engage in strikes and boycotts for purposes deemed illegal by the act.
5. Charge excessive or discriminatory fees or dues under union-shop contracts.

**Closed shop**
an illegal practice favored by unions that contractually binds employers to hire only workers who are already members of the union.

Additionally, Taft-Hartley declared the **closed shop** to be illegal. This was a practice, favored by unions, which contractually bound employers to hire only workers who were already members of the union. Until Taft-Hartley's passage, the closed shop was dominant in labor contracts. By declaring it illegal, Taft-Hartley significantly reduced the power of unions. Taft-Hartley also set forth procedures that would allow workers to decertify, or vote out, their union representative.

## RIGHT-TO-WORK LAWS

The power of a union to organize employees in your firm is largely dependent on your state's legal position toward unions. Currently, 21 states (see Exhibit 15–2) have passed right-to-work laws. These laws forbid compulsory union membership. That is, in right-to-work states, employees are free to choose whether or not to join the union. If they don't join, they are not required to pay union dues.

As you might expect, unions don't look favorably on right-to-work legislation. They regard it as antiunion since employees aren't required to pay union dues but still obtain union benefits.

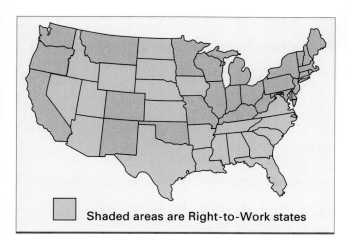

**EXHIBIT 15–2**
Right-to-work states.

Shaded areas are Right-to-Work states

As a supervisor, a union's influence on you and your employees is likely to be far less if you're in a right-to-work state than if your employer has negotiated a union-shop agreement. In the latter case, all employees covered by the collective bargaining agreement must, after a 30- to 60-day grace period, join the union or forfeit their jobs.

## IS ALL LABOR-MANAGEMENT INTERACTION CONFRONTATIONAL?

Historically, the relationship between labor and management was built on conflict. The interests of labor and management were seen basically at odds—each treating the other as the opposition. But times have somewhat changed. Management has become increasingly aware that successful efforts to increase productivity, improve quality, and lower costs require employee involvement and commitment. Similarly, some labor unions have come to recognize that they can help their members more by cooperating with management rather than fighting them.

Unfortunately, current U.S. labor laws, passed in an era of mistrust and antagonism between labor and management, have become barriers to their becoming cooperative partners. As a case in point, the National Labor Relations Act was passed in 1935 to encourage collective bargaining and to balance workers' power against that of management.[3] That legislation also sought to eliminate the then widespread practice of firms setting up company unions for the sole purpose of undermining efforts of outside unions

[3]"Teamwork for Employees and Managers (TEAM) Act," *HR Legislative Fact Sheet* (June 1996), pp. 28–29; and Randall Hanson, Rebecca I. Porterfield, and Kathleen Ames, "Employee Empowerment at Risk: Effects of Recent NLRB Rulings," *Academy of Management Executive*, Vol. 9, No. 2 (1995), pp. 45–56.

organizing their employees. So the law prohibits employers form creating or supporting a "labor organization." Ironically, labor laws—like the National Labor Relations Act—are now working against management and labor cooperation. For instance, the National Labor Relations Board ruled against two firms—Electromation Inc., a small Indiana electrical components manufacturer, and a Du Pont chemical plant in New Jersey—that had set up worker committees and empowered them to handle issues like pay and plant safety. The NLRB ruled that in both instances management dominated the formation and operation of the groups, which met the broad definition of labor organizations and thus behaved as company-run unions.

Although this issue is the subject of Congressional debate,[4] the current legal environment doesn't prohibit employee-involvement programs in the

---

[4]Legislation, called the "Teamwork for Employees and Managers (TEAM) Act" has been proposed in both the House of Representatives and the Senate. The Act, as proposed, was designed to "permit employers and employees to establish and maintain employee involvement programs—including various approaches to problem-solving, communication enhancement, and productivity improvement programs." In May 1996, the Act was passed in the House, and sent to the Senate for approval. By a vote of 53–46, the Senate approved the Act in principle, but did not agree to some of its language. Accordingly, the bill returned to the House for its review. Whatever that outcome, it is important to note that President Clinton has publicly stated he would veto any such bill if it came to the White House for his signature. ["Teamwork for Employees and Managers (TEAM) Act." *HR Legislative Fact Sheet* (June 1996), pp. 28–29.]

EXHIBIT 15–3

An affirmative response to any one of the following questions may mean that an employee involvement program violates national labor law.

1. Does management dominate the employee involvement program by controlling its formation, setting its goals, or deciding how it operates?

2. Does the employee involvement program address issues affecting other, non-involved, employees?

3. Does the employee involvement program deal with traditional bargaining issues such as wages and working conditions?

4. Does the employee involvement program deal with any supervisors or company officials on any issue?

When an employee involvement program may be illegal in a unionized setting. (*Source:* Reprinted from January 25, 1993 issue of Business Week by special permission. © 1997 by McGraw-Hill companies.)

U.S. Rather, to comply with the law, management is required to give its employee-involvement programs independence. That is, when such programs become dominated by management, they're likely to be interpreted as groups that perform some functions of labor unions but are controlled by management. What kinds of actions would indicate that an employee-involvement program is *not* dominated by management? Some examples might include choosing program members through secret ballot elections, giving program members wide latitude in deciding what issues to deal with, permitting members to meet apart from management, and specifying that program members are not susceptible to dissolution by management whim. The key theme labor laws appear to be conveying is that where employee involvement programs are introduced, members must have the power to make decisions and act independent of management. Exhibit 15–3 suggests some key questions that might indicate where an employee involvement program violates national labor law.

## A QUICK REVIEW OF LABOR RELATIONS

Unions don't just appear overnight. Rather, they represent employees in an organization often after a lengthy, and in many instances, hard-fought process. Once they are "certified," the collective bargaining process begins. Exhibit 15–4 depicts a simplistic flow of the labor relations process. As a supervisor, you won't typically be directly involved initially in the labor-relations process. You will, however, be affected by the process and outcome. This section will describe things you can and cannot legally do dur-

## EXHIBIT 15–4

The labor relations process.

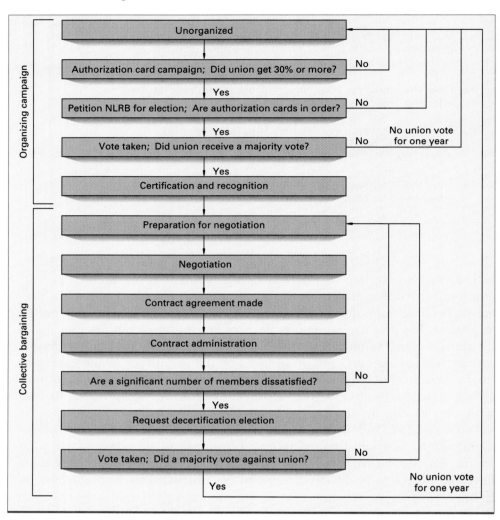

ing the period when a union is attempting to organize employees in your company; it will also show how you play a major part in the administration of the final union contract. This is why you need a basic understanding of labor relations.

## How Are Employees Organized?

Efforts to organize a group of employees may begin when employee representatives ask union officials to visit the employees' organization and solicit members or when the union itself initiates a membership drive. Either way, the law requires that a union must secure signed authorization cards from at least 30 percent of the employees that it desires to represent. If the 30 percent goal is achieved,[5] either the union or management will file a petition with the National Labor Relations Board requesting a representation election.

When the NLRB receives the required number of authorization cards, it evaluates them, verifies that legal requirements have been satisfied, and then clarifies the appropriate **bargaining unit,** that is, it identifies which employees the union will represent if it wins the election.

Bargaining unit
employees a union will represent if it wins an election.

A secret-ballot election is usually called within 25 days after the NLRB receives the authorization cards. If the union gets a majority in this election—50 percent of those voting, plus one vote—the NLRB certifies the union and recognizes it as the exclusive bargaining representative for all employees within the specified bargaining unit. Should the union fail to get a majority, another election cannot be held for one year.

Occasionally, employees become dissatisfied with a certified union. In such instances, employees may request a decertification election by the NLRB. If a majority of the members vote for decertification, the union is out. However, recognize two things about decertification: First, most union contracts forbid them during the contract's term. Second, union members cannot decertify today and bring in another union tomorrow. At least one year must transpire between votes.

## What Can't You Do During
## an Organizing Campaign?

When a union is attempting to organize your employees, there are a number of things that you can and can't do. Because under labor laws the "can'ts" get most attention, we'll focus our attention on them. Probably the easiest way to address these can'ts is to think of the acronym TIPS.

The "T" in TIPS stands for threaten. It is an unfair labor practice to threaten employees for exercising their right to consider joining a union. Any attempts on your part to intimidate employees—like saying you'll fire them for being sympathetic to the union's cause—is illegal. If any such action is deemed to be extensive to the point that it unduly influenced the election, the NLRB can nullify the election results and certify a union as the employees' bargaining agent.

"I" stands for interrogate. You cannot pry information out of any employee about what's happening with the union organizing campaign. It's

[5]While the NLRB requires 30 percent of the potential bargaining unit to sign authorization cards, unions typically will not seek a vote unless significantly more—upwards of 75 percent—sign the authorization cards. In doing so the union increases its chance of winning the election from 8 percent with only 30 percent of the authorization cards signed, to 60 percent with 75 percent signed. [J. Wimberely, "Union Elections," *Commerce Clearing House: Human Resources Management—Ideas and Trends,* February 15, 1990, p. 35.]

tempting, because so much of the initial union campaign effort is "under-ground," hidden from your sight. Even though you suspect something, you cannot question any employees about their actions. However, if in the normal course of daily events, an employee freely talks to you about the union campaign, you have every right to listen. You just cannot ask probing questions to obtain information that you may use against the union drive.

You also cannot "Promise employees anything for remaining nonunion. Telling them that you will give them a pay raise, or provide some other "reward" for voting against unionization is an unfair labor practice. Finally, you cannot "S"py on employees. This one is not as applicable today as it was 50 years ago, but it still has supervisory ramifications. Decades ago, the company literally owned the town—the company buildings, the town school, church, grocery store, recreation facility, and the like. When union organizers came to town and tried to have meetings, company officials would attempt to "spy" on them by claiming that it was company property and officials had the right to be on their own property. The courts did rule differently, and the effect is the same—you cannot spy on union organizing efforts that take place off your company premises. Of course, anything that happens at work is "free game," and you have every right to observe the activities (see Something to Think About).

## Ok, the Union Won, What Now?

**Collective bargaining** a process for negotiating a union contract and for administrating the contract after it has been negotiated. It includes preparing to negotiate, the actual contract negotiations, and administering the contract after it has been ratified.

After a union has been certified—meaning it won the election and was successful in organizing a group of workers—the collective bargaining process commences. **Collective bargaining** is a process for negotiating a union contract and for administrating the contract after it has been negotiated. It includes preparing to negotiate, the actual contract negotiations, and administering the contract after it has been ratified.[6]

The people who do the negotiating for both the union and the company are referred to as the negotiations teams. The company's representatives will often depend on the size of the organization. In a small firm, for instance, bargaining is probably done by the president—and probably some other staff the president feels are necessary participants. In larger organizations, there is usually an industrial relations expert. In such cases, you can expect the company to be represented by the senior official for industrial relations, other company executives, and company lawyers—with support provided by legal and economic specialists in wage and salary administration, labor law, benefits, and so forth.

On the union side, you typically can expect to see a bargaining team made up of an officer of the local union, local shop stewards, and some representation from the union. Again, as with the company, representation

[6]This section is based on D. A. De Cenzo and S. P. Robbins, *Human Resource Management,* 5th ed. (New York, NY: John Wiley & Sons, Inc., 1996), pp. 494–497.

You recognize that your employees are not happy over the recent events in your organization. Company officials made significant personnel cuts, restructured the reporting relationships due to the elimination of several offices, and have announced that pay increases will not be forthcoming this year. You know there have been rumblings among your employees, but you never expected it to lead to a union organizing drive. After all, you've had a respectful relationship with your employees over the past several years.

Yet, late this morning, you noticed union literature on your parking lot. You also have witnessed something "hush-hush" going on between employees. In fact, one of your employees has mentioned that he overheard several coworkers talking about joining a union. Not wanting to take any chances, you contact your boss, who contacts the company's attorney. The attorney suggests that the company take some immediate steps. First of all, information is sent to employees telling about all the good things the company has done and how supervisors value employee input. The company's official position is that they prefer to solve problems one-on-one rather than through a third party. Unfortunately, these actions appear to be having little effect on the union activity around the work site.

Company officials call a meeting of all employees late one afternoon. They explain to employees that although it is their right to pursue a union, they feel it is only right for them to "set the record straight." Employees are told that when a union organizes employees, there is historically an increase in administrative costs incurred by the company. In the financial shape the organization is in, if it were to incur more costs, it might create significant financial hardships. Accordingly, if the organizing drive is successful, and if costs go up, there will be no other choice than to close the business and move to another state where costs won't be so high.

When the election is held, more than 65 percent of the employees vote to remain nonunion. The company has been successful in averting an organizing drive. But at what expense? Company officials spent a lot of money during the organizing campaign, and left the impression that they would close down the facility if the union election ultimately added to administrative costs.

Were these efforts on the part of your company legal? Absolutely! Were they ethical? Were they in the best interest of the company or the employees? How do you feel?

---

is modified to reflect the size of the bargaining unit. If negotiations involve a contract that will cover 50,000 employees at company locations throughout the United States, the team will be dominated by several union officers, with a strong supporting cast of economic and legal experts employed by the union. In a small firm or for local negotiations covering special issues at the plant level for a nationwide organization, bargaining representatives for the union might be the local officers and a few specially elected committee members.

Watching over these two sides is a third party—government. In addition to providing the rules under which the company and labor bargain, government provides a watchful eye on the two parties to ensure the rules are followed. It stands ready to intervene if an agreement on acceptable terms cannot be reached, or if the impasse undermines the nation's well-being.

While there are a number of groups involved in collective bargaining, our discussion will focus on labor and the company. After all, it is the labor and company negotiating teams that buckle down and hammer out the contract.

## PREPARING TO NEGOTIATE

Once a union has been certified as the bargaining unit (the organizing effort), both union and management begin the ongoing activity of preparing for negotiations. We refer to this as an ongoing activity because ideally it should begin as soon as the previous contract is agreed upon or union certification is achieved. Realistically, it probably begins anywhere from one to six months before the current contract expires. We can consider the preparation for negotiation as composed of three activities: fact gathering, goal setting, and strategy development. Recognize that while we'll look at preparation from the company's perspective, unions are preparing in a similar fashion.

Information is acquired from both internal and external sources. Internal data include grievance and accident records; employee performance reports; overtime figures; and reports on transfers, turnover, and absenteeism. External information should include statistics on the current economy, both at local and national levels; economic forecasts for the short and intermediate terms; copies of recently negotiated contracts by the adversary union to determine what issues the union considers important; data on the communities in which the company operates—cost of living; changes in cost of living, terms of recently negotiated labor contracts, and statistics on the labor market; and industry labor statistics to see what terms other organizations, employing similar types of personnel, are negotiating.

This information tells company officials where they stand, what similar organizations are doing, and what they can anticipate from the economy in the near term. These data are then used to determine what company officials can expect to achieve in the negotiation. What can they expect the union to ask for? What is management prepared to concede?

With homework done, information in hand, and tentative goals established, company officials must put together the most difficult part of the bargaining preparation activities—strategy for dealing with the union's demands. This includes assessing the union's power and specific tactics. But not all unions bargain from equal power bases. The labor market, economic conditions, rates of inflation, and recent contract settlements all affect the degree of union influence. The company's ability to tolerate a strike is also crucial. If demand for the company's product or service has been high, management may be reluctant to absorb a strike, even one of short duration. On the other hand, if business has been slow, company officials may be considerably less willing to concede to union demands and may be prepared to accept a lengthy strike. That is precisely what Caterpillar faced as it "forced" a lengthy strike with the United Automobile Workers representing thousands of its workers. It worked so well that John Deere is employing the same strategy in its negotiations with the UAW.[7] Consequently, variations in power factors will affect the tactics used in bargaining.

## NEGOTIATING THE CONTRACT

Negotiation customarily begins with the union delivering to company officials a long list of demands. By presenting extreme demands, the union creates significant room for trading in later stages of the negotiation. It also disguises the union's real position, leaving management to determine which demands are adamantly sought, which are moderately sought, and which the union is prepared to quickly abandon. Examples of recent demands made by unions in negotiations include an immediate increase in the hourly wage, special adjustments for skilled workers, cost-of-living adjustments, early retirement, free dental care, free psychiatric care, improved quality of work life, increased relief time off the assembly line, more paid holidays, extended vacations, a shorter work week, and a guaranteed annual wage.

A long list of demands often fulfills the internal political needs of the union. By seeming to back numerous wishes of the union's members, union administrators appear to be satisfying the needs of the many factions within the membership. In reality, however, these demands will be scaled down or abandoned if the union's negotiators believe it is expedient to do so. Not surprisingly, company officials' initial response is usually just as extreme—that is, company officials counter by offering little more (or even nothing more) than the terms of the previous contract. It is not unusual for company officials to begin by proposing a reduction in benefits and demanding that the union reduce or eliminate some of their work rules, such as job transfer or outsourcing work.

These initial proposals are then considered by each party. This is a time of exploration—each trying to clarify the others' proposals and to organize arguments against them. At some point, agreement is reached between the negotiating parties. But the process doesn't stop there. Although the chief negotiator can bind the company to the agreement made, the union chief negotiator doesn't have the same "authority." Rather, a con-

[7]See, for example, "Caterpillar Strike," *USA Today*, June 22, 1994, p. B–1; and K. Kelly, "Why the Talks at Deere Hit Bedrock," *Business Week*, October 31, 1994, p. 48.

**Management rights**
in negotiations, issues that are specific to management.

tract is not binding until the union members, called the rank and file, vote to ratify the contract.

Irrespective of how negotiations proceed, there are several issues that are specific to each group. For the company, we refer to these as **management rights;** for the union, union security arrangements.

Under national labor laws, company officials and the union must negotiate over wages, hours, and terms and conditions of employment. Although this covers a wide array of topics, everything outside of these mandatory items is considered management rights. Even though a unionized work force may exist, company officials still retain their right to run the business. This means that they are not responsible for negotiating over such items as products to produce and sell, selling prices, the size of its workforce, or the location of operations. In other words, company officials have the right to make unilateral decisions about those issues without having to consult or negotiate with the union. Unions, on the other hand, desire to achieve a position where more and more is open to negotiations. Just because something is a management right does not mean that it can never be part of negotiations. If company officials desire, they may take something that is rightfully theirs and place it into negotiations. When, and if that occurs, it is then removed from the "management right" category, and will remain so until subsequent negotiations remove it from the contract. It is important to note, however, that under no circumstances are company officials required to discuss such issues with the union. Furthermore, the company cannot be found "guilty" of negotiating in bad faith for failing to entertain discussions on management rights issues.

When one considers the importance of security arrangements to unions—importance brought about in terms of numbers and guaranteed income—it is no wonder that such emphasis is placed on achieving a union security arrangement that best suits their goals. Such arrangements range from compulsory membership in the union to giving employees the freedom in choosing to join the union. The various types of union security arrangements—the union shop, the agency shop, and the right-to-work shop, as well as some special provisions under the realm of union security arrangements—are discussed below and summarized in Exhibit 15–5.

The most powerful relationship legally available (except in right-to-work states) to a union is a **union shop.** This arrangement stipulates that employers, while free to hire whomever they choose, may retain only union members. That is, all employees hired into positions covered under the terms of a collective-bargaining agreement must, after a specified probationary period of typically 30 to 60 days, join the union or forfeit their jobs.

**Union shop**
an arrangement which stipulates that employers, while free to hire whomever they choose, may retain only union members.

**Agency shop**
an agreement that requires nonunion employees to pay the union a sum of money equal to union fees and dues as a condition of continuing employment.

An agreement that requires nonunion employees to pay the union a sum of money equal to union fees and dues as a condition of continuing employment is referred to as an **agency shop.** This arrangement was designed as a compromise between the union's desire to eliminate the "free rider" and company officials' desire to make union membership voluntary.

EXHIBIT 15–5

Union security arrangements (and related elements).

| Union Shop | Strongest of the union security arrangements. Mandates employees join the union within a specified period of time—or forfeit their jobs. Union shops are illegal in right-to-work states. |
|---|---|
| Agency Shop | Membership is not compulsory, but non-union workers in the bargaining unit must still pay union dues. These workers do have the right to demand that their monies be used for collective bargaining purposes only. Like the union shop, the agency shop is illegal in right-to-work states. |
| Open Shop | The weakest form of union security. Workers are free to choose to join the union or not. Those that do join must pay union dues. Those that do not join do not have to pay dues. Leaving the union typically can only occur during an escape period at the expiration of a contract. In right-to-work states, the open shop is the only permissible union security arrangement. |
| Maintenance of Membership | In an open shop, membership is required for the duration of an existing contract. |
| Dues Checkoff | Involves the employer deducting union dues directly from a union member's pay check. The employer collects the money and forwards a check to the union treasurer. Management typically offers this service free of charge to the union. |

In such a case, if for whatever reason workers decide not to join the union (e.g., religious beliefs, values, etc.), they still must pay dues. Because workers will receive the benefits negotiated by the union, they must pay their fair share. However, a 1988 Supreme Court ruling upheld union members' claims that although they are forced to pay union dues, those dues must be specifically used for collective bargaining purposes only—not for political lobbying.[8]

The least desirable form of union security, from a union perspective, is the **open shop.** This is an arrangement in which joining a union is totally voluntary. Those who do not join are not required to pay union dues or any associated fees. For workers who do join, there is typically a maintenance of membership clause in the existing contract that dictates certain provisions. Specifically, a **maintenance of membership** agreement states that should employees join the union, they are compelled to remain in the union for the duration of the existing contract. When the contract expires, most maintenance of membership agreements provide an escape clause—a short inter-

**Open shop** an arrangement in which joining a union is totally voluntary.

**Maintenance of membership** an agreement which states that should employees join the union, they are compelled to remain in the union for the duration of the existing contract. Such an agreement often provides an escape clause in which employees may choose to withdraw their membership from the union without penalty.

[8]*Communication Workers of America v. Beck,* U. S. Supreme Court, 109LC (1988).

**Dues checkoff**
a provision that often exists in union security arrangements whereby an employer withholds union dues from members' paychecks.

val of time, usually ten days to two weeks—in which employees may choose to withdraw their membership from the union without penalty.

A provision that often exists in union security arrangements is a process called the **dues checkoff**. A dues checkoff occurs when the employer withholds union dues from the members' paychecks. Similar to other pay withholdings, the employer collects the dues money and sends it to the union. There are a number of reasons why employers provide this service, and a reason why the union would permit them to do so. Collecting dues takes time, so a dues checkoff reduces the "downtime" by eliminating the need for the shop steward to go around to collect dues. Furthermore, recognizing that union dues are the primary source of income for the union, having knowledge of how much money there is in the union treasury can provide company officials with some insight as to whether or not a union is financially strong enough to endure a strike. Given these facts, why would a union agree to such a procedure? Simply, the answer lies in guaranteed revenues! By letting the company deduct dues from a member's pay-check, the union is assured of receiving their monies. Excuses from members that they don't have their money, or will pay next week, are eliminated!

## CONTRACT ADMINISTRATION

Once a contract is agreed upon and ratified, it must be administered. In terms of contract administration, four stages must be carried out. These are: (1) getting the information agreed to out to all union members and management personnel; (2) implementing the contract; (3) interpreting the contract and grievance resolution; and (4) monitoring activities during the contract period.[9]

In terms of providing information to all concerned, both parties must ensure that changes in contract language are spelled out. For example, the most obvious would be hourly rate changes. Company officials must make sure the payroll system is adjusted to the new rates as set in the contract. But it goes beyond just pay: changes in work rules, hours, and the like must be communicated. If both sides agree to mandatory overtime, something that was not in existence before, all must be informed of how it will work. As a supervisor, this information is critical for you. Furthermore, neither the union nor the company can simply hand a copy of the contract to each organization member and expect it to be understood. It will be necessary to hold meetings to explain the new terms of the agreement.

Probably the most important element of contract administration relates to spelling out a procedure for handling contractual disputes. Almost all collective-bargaining agreements contain formal procedures to be used

[9]Adapted from M. Bowers and D. A. De Cenzo, *Essentials of Labor Relations* (Englewood Cliffs, NJ: Prentice-Hall, Inc., 1992), p. 101–114.

Supervisors in the NYU library need to know contract administration because the University's librarians are unionized. Every three years, when the contract is renegotiated, supervisors meet with someone from the personnel office, and changes in the contract are described—as well as their effect on the supervisors' jobs.

in resolving grievances of the interpretation and application of the contract. We'll come back to this important topic shortly.

In our discussion of preparation for negotiations, we stated that both company and union need to gather various data. One of the most abundant databases for both sides is information kept on a current contract. By monitoring activities, company and union can assess how effective the current contract was, when problem areas or conflicts arose, and what changes might need to be made in subsequent negotiations.

## WHAT IS YOUR ROLE IN LABOR RELATIONS?

Now let's turn our attention to the various demands placed on you as a supervisor as a result of labor-management relations.

### ORGANIZING DRIVES

If your employees aren't currently unionized, you may experience going through a union organizing drive. If that happens, be very careful about what you say and do. Remember, the law is clear in stating that you can't threaten, intimidate, promise, or spy on employees in order to get them to vote against the union.

Because you are the closest level of management to the workers, you represent the best source of information about intentions and actions. So pay attention. If you see that union-organizing activities are taking place among employees, report your observations to your boss or to the human resources department. Early detection can allow your company to plan a proper response.

Exhibit 15–6 provides a list of guidelines to lessen the likelihood that you'll break the law or hinder your company's response to the union's or-

## EXHIBIT 15-6

Supervisory guidelines during a union organizing campaign.

- If your employees ask for your opinion on unionization, respond in a neutral manner. For example, " I really have no position on the issue. Do what you think is best."

- You can prohibit union organizing activities in your work place during work hours only if they interfere with work operations.

- You can prohibit outside union organizers from distributing union information in the work place.

- Employees have the right to distribute union information to other employees during break and lunch periods.

- Don't question employees publicity or privately about union-organizing activities. For example, " Are you planning to go to that union rally this weekend? " But if an employee freely tells you about the activities, you may listen.

- Don't spy on employees' union activities for example, by standing in the lunchroom to see who is distributing prounion literature.

- Don't make any threats or promises that are related to the possibility of unionization. For example, " If this union effort suceeds, upper management is seriously thinking about closing down this plant. But if it's defeated, they plan to push through an immediate wage increase.

- Don't discriminate against any employee who is involved in the unionization effort.

- Be on the lookout for efforts by the union to coerce employees to join its ranks. This is illegal. If you see this occurring, report it to your boss or the human resources department. Your company may want to file a complaint against the union with the NLRB.

ganizing effort. You are free to express your views and opinions about unions to your employees, but the law forbids you from interfering in your employees' right to choose a union to represent them. Because the line is often vague about where your free speech becomes interference, you've got to be cautious.

### NEGOTIATION

You typically play a minor part in the actual negotiation of the contract. Basic responsibility for this activity lies with specialists in the human resource department and top management.

Your role during the negotiation period tends to be limited to that of a resource person. You may be called on to provide your organization's negotiators with departmental information on past problems with work-shift schedules, seniority rights, transfers, discipline, or ambiguous terminology in the current contract. This suggests that it is important for you to keep careful records of labor problems you experience during the current contract period so that these problems can be addressed during the next contract negotiation.

## CONTRACT ADMINISTRATION

Once a formal agreement is in place, you must operate your department within the framework established by that contract. This means that you must fully understand all the "fine print" in the contract—and you need to make sure departmental members have the contract information, too. Large and small organizations alike will hold supervisory training sessions and meetings to help you understand the contract and clarify new provisions. You'll be given a copy of the agreement to study, an opportunity to get questions answered, and procedures to follow when problems arise.

Why do organizations give so much emphasis to ensuring that you know and understand the contract? Because you are the primary link between management and the employees. For the typical unionized employee, you may be his or her sole contact with management. What you say and do, then, largely determines the labor-management climate in the organization. If you misinterpret a contract provision, treat an employee unfairly, or engage in a similar contract violation, the consequences for you and the company could be immediate or postponed until the next negotiation. The union's representatives will be keeping track of these incidents and they'll use them to help win concessions in the next contract.

Keep in mind that working under a labor contract and supervising unionized employees does not take away your rights to make decisions or manage your people. What it does is spell out limitations to your authority and establish procedures for employees to challenge any action you take that they see as a violation of the labor agreement. For instance, you can still assign work schedules, make job transfers, and discipline problem employees—except you must do so within the framework defined in the labor contract.

Remember, too, that the labor contract is a bilateral agreement. It also specifies responsibilities for employees and procedures you can use when employees fail to comply with provisions in the contract. Thus the labor agreement constrains employees as well as management.

## WHO IS THIS PERSON CALLED THE UNION STEWARD?

The **union steward** in your department is essentially to the union what you are to the company. Just as you're there to protect the rights of management, he or she is an employee who is the elected representative of the employees in your work unit, and is there to protect the rights of the union members.

**Union steward**
an employee who is the elected representative of the employees in a work unit, and is there to protect the rights of union members.

What authority does a union steward have in running your department? Very little to none! The steward cannot tell you or any employee what to do. The only authority stewards have is to give advice. They can offer advice to you and employees as to their understanding of how the contract limits your actions.

Just because union stewards have limited formal authority doesn't mean they can't be troublesome. Poor relations with your steward is likely to result in increased challenges to your actions and increased grievance filings. Getting along with your union steward tends to make your life at work a lot more pleasant.

The role of steward comes with certain expectations from employees. The steward is their representative. He or she is elected to protect their rights. To keep in their employees' good graces, then, you have to expect the stewards' loyalties to lie with their constituents. That doesn't mean, however, that you can't attempt to minimize hostilities with your steward. The best means for developing a cooperative relationship is to show respect for the steward and to keep him or her informed of problems you're having and of any changes that will affect the people in your department. A good supervisor-steward relationship can allow problems to be resolved quickly in the department and avoid the stress and cost associated with a lengthy dispute.

## WHAT IF NEGOTIATIONS REACH AN IMPASSE?

**Strike**
an action where employees leave their jobs and refuse to return to work until a contract has been signed.

**Lockout**
a company action equivalent to a strike; when management denies unionized employees access to their jobs.

Sometimes representatives of management and labor cannot reach an agreement on a new contract. When this happens, the union may choose to call a strike. In a **strike,** employees leave their jobs and refuse to come to work until a contract has been signed. Realize, too, that there's a company equivalent to a strike. It's called a **lockout.** That is when management denies unionized employees access to their jobs (see News Flash).

Historically in the United States, the strike was a potent weapon. By withholding labor, the union could impose financial hardships on an employer. However, beginning in the early 1980s, strikes began to lose much of their potency. For one thing, public sentiment supporting their use by unions has declined. More importantly, management in recent years has become much more aggressive in replacing striking workers. A strike by flight attendants at American Airlines in November 1993 didn't completely stop American from flying. Although many flights had to be cancelled, supervisors and other employees with flight-attendant training temporarily took some of their places. A few years earlier, when TWA flight attendants participated in a lengthy strike against their employer, TWA's management went out and recruited replacements. The present law allows management to replace striking workers, although unions have made new federal legislation that would bar companies from hiring permanent replacements for strikers a high priority (see Dealing with a Difficult Issue).

Although strikes (and lockouts) are very visible outcomes of one aspect of labor-management relationships, few individuals truly understand the difference between having the right to strike and using a strike successfully.[10] In a sense, the distinction is similar to having the right to vote and actually voting. The right exists in both instances; however, a number of factors may intervene to preclude the actual exercise of this right. Consequently, several questions should be considered before a strike or a lockout is called. These include:

1. Is the issue important enough to one party or the other that they will strike (or lockout) over it?

2. How long is it reasonable to expect the strike or lockout to last?

3. What, if any support, will either party get from external sources?

4. Will strikers likely be replaced?

5. Is there a stockpile of inventories?

6. Will a strike or lockout cause the company to go out of business?

7. How will the public respond to the strike or lockout?

[10]Ibid., pp. 123–124.

**Conciliation**
an impasse resolution technique that states that the role of the third party is to keep the negotiations ongoing and to act as a go-between.

**Mediation**
an impasse resolution technique where a mediator attempts to pull together the common ground that exists, and makes settlement recommendations for overcoming the barriers that exist between two sides in a conflict.

When labor and management cannot reach a satisfactory agreement themselves, they may need the assistance of an objective third-party individual. This assistance comes in the form of conciliation and mediation, fact-finding, or interest arbitration.

**Conciliation** and **mediation** are two very closely related impasse resolution techniques. Both are techniques whereby a neutral third party attempts to get labor and management to resolve their differences. Under conciliation, however, the role of the third party is to keep the negotiations ongoing. In other words, this individual is a go-between—advocating a voluntary means through which both sides can continue negotiating. Mediation, on the other hand, goes one step further. The mediator attempts to pull together the common ground that exists and make settlement recommendations for overcoming the barriers that exist between the two sides. A mediator's suggestions, however, are only advisory. That means that the suggestions are not binding on either party.

## REPLACING STRIKING WORKERS

Inherent in collective-bargaining negotiations is an opportunity for either side to generate a power base that may sway negotiations in their favor. For example, when labor shortages exist, or when inventories are in short supply, a strike by the union could have serious ramifications for the company. Likewise, when the situation is reversed—and the company has the upper hand—it could easily lock out the union to achieve its negotiation's goals. In fact, both the Wagner and Taft-Hartley Acts saw to it that the playing field was to be as fair as possible, by requiring both sides to negotiate in good faith and permitting impasses if they should be warranted.

For decades, this scenario played itself out over and over again. Timing of a contract's expiration proved critical for both sides. For example, in the coal industry, having a contract expire just before the winter months—when coal is needed in greater supply for heating and electricity—worked to the union's advantage, unless the coal companies stockpiled enough coal to carry them through a lengthy winter strike. This game, although serious to both sides, never appeared to be anything more than bargaining strategies; one that could show how serious both sides were. And even though a Supreme Court case from 1938, NLRB v. MacKay Radio, gave employers the right to hire replacement workers for those engaged in an economic strike, seldom was that used. In fact, often to settle a strike, and for the organization to get back its skilled workforce, one stipulation would be that all replacement workers be "let go."

In the early 1980s, this began to change. When President Ronald Reagan fired striking air-traffic controllers and hired replacements, businesses began to realize the weapon they had at their disposal. Some organizations, like Caterpillar, the National Football League, and John Deere, realized that using replacement workers could be to their advantage. The union members either came back to work on company terms or they simply lost their jobs. Period.

Undoubtedly, in any strike situation, company officials have the right to keep their doors open and to keep producing what they sell. Often that may mean using supervisory personnel in place of striking workers, or in some cases, bringing in replacements. But does a law that permits replacement workers undermine the intent of national labor law? Does it create an unfair advantage for the company in that it could play hardball just to break the union? Should a striker replacement bill (which would prevent permanent replacement workers from being hired) be passed? Should striking workers' jobs be protected while they exercise their rights under the Wagner Act? What do you think?

**Fact-finding** is a technique whereby a neutral third-party individual conducts a hearing to gather evidence from both labor and management. The fact-finder then renders a decision as to how he or she views an appropriate settlement. Similar to mediation, the fact-finder's recommendations are only suggestions—they, too, are not binding on either party. The final impasse resolution technique is called **interest arbitration.** Under interest arbitration, generally a panel of three individuals—one neutral and one each from the union and management—hears testimony from both sides. After the hearing, the panel renders a decision on how to settle the current contract negotiation dispute. If all three members of the panel are unanimous in their decision, that decision may be binding on both parties. Interest arbitration is found more frequently in public-sector collective bargaining; its use in private-sector labor disputes is rare.

As a supervisor, there is little you can do to directly resolve a strike. However, if your employees go out on strike, you may be called on to assume an increased number of nonsupervisory tasks in order to keep the business going. If management decides to replace striking workers, you will have to train and orient the new employees.

A more troublesome situation for supervisors is the **wildcat strike.** This is an illegal strike where employees refuse to work during the term of a binding contract. These can be brought about by a number of factors, but they usually involve ambiguities in the current contract. For instance, employee concerns over management's right to contract out (or outsource)

**Fact-finding**
a technique whereby a neutral third-party individual conducts a hearing to gather evidence from both labor and management.

**Interest arbitration**
arbitration in which a panel of three individuals hears testimony from both sides and renders a decision on how to settle the current contract negotiation dispute.

**Wildcat strike**
an illegal strike where employees refuse to work during the term of a binding contract, often due to ambiguities in the current contract.

These iron workers walk the picket line over a labor dispute. Unable to reach agreement in negotiations, they decided to withhold their labor in the form of a strike.

## EXHIBIT 15–7

Supervisory guidelines
for handling wildcat
strikes. *Source:* L. W.
Rue, and L. L. Byars,
*Supervision: Key Link
to Productivity,* 4th ed.
(Homewood, IL:
Richard D. Irwin,
1993), p. 325. Used
with permission.

- Stay on the job.
- Notify higher management by telephone or messenger.
- Carefully record the events as they happen.
- Pay strict attention to who the leaders are and record their behavior.
- Record any lack of action by union officials.
- Report all information as fully and as soon as possible to higher management.
- Encourage employees to go back to work.
- Ask union officials to instruct employees to go back to work.
- Don't discuss the cause of the strike.
- Don't make any agreements or say anything that might imply permission to leave work.
- Make it clear that management will discuss the issue when all of the employees are back at work.

some assembly work has resulted in wildcat strikes at several electronic-component manufacturers. The key point to remember is that wildcat strikes are illegal. Grievance procedures exist precisely to settle such differences. Should you find yourself in the middle of a wildcat strike, Exhibit 15–7 provides you with some guidelines to follow.

## HANDLING GRIEVANCES

We've used the term *grievance* at several points in this chapter. But how do you go about handling one? Of all the activities that supervisors of unionized employees get involved in, none are more important than the handling of grievances. In this section, we'll help you develop your grievance-handling skills (see Assessing Yourself).

Almost all collective bargaining agreements contain formal procedures to be used in resolving disputes surrounding the interpretation and application of the contract. Collectively these are called **grievance procedures.** These procedures are typically designed to resolve disputes as quickly as possible and at the lowest level in the organization. Whenever possible, then, you are encouraged to resolve employee grievances without involving upper levels of management and senior union officials.

**Grievance procedures** procedures designed to resolve disputes as quickly as possible and at the lowest level in the organization.

Consistent with this belief that grievances should be handled at the lowest level possible in the organization, the typical grievance procedure looks like Exhibit 15–8. An employee's first efforts should be directed at attempting to resolve the complaint with you. If the employee is dissatisfied with your response, the grievance typically escalates through the following stages: you and the union steward discuss the complaint; you and a labor specialist from the human resources department discuss the complaint

## ARE YOU AN EFFECTIVE GRIEVANCE-HANDLER?

Answer each of the following questions as you have or would behave, not as you think you should behave. Use the following scale:

SA: strongly agree
A:  agree
U:  undecided
D:  disagree
SD: strongly disagree

| | SA | A | U | D | SD |
|---|---|---|---|---|---|
| **1.** If an employee has a grievance, the first thing I do is review the relevant clause in the union contract. | — | — | — | — | — |
| **2.** As soon as an employee informs me of a grievance, to avoid escalation I specifically provide him or her with management's side of the story. | — | — | — | — | — |
| **3.** If I'm unsure about wording or an interpretation in the contract, I contact a labor specialist in the organization for counsel. | — | — | — | — | — |
| **4.** I make sure I get all the facts pertinent to the dispute, regardless of how much time it may take. | — | — | — | — | — |
| **5.** I avoid letting personalities or personal preferences influence my decision on a grievance. | — | — | — | — | — |
| **6.** If a grievance has merit, I assume I have the authority to take immediate corrective action. | — | — | — | — | — |
| **7.** I keep comprehensive records on every grievance in expectation that my decision will be appealed. | — | — | — | — | — |

*(continued)*

## SCORING:

For questions 3, 5, and 7, give yourself five points for SA, four points for A, 3 points for U, 2 points for D, and 1 point for SD. For questions 1, 2, 4, and 6, reverse the scoring (one point for SA, 2 points for A, 3 points for U, 4 points for D, and five points for SD). Add up your total score.

## WHAT THE ASSESSMENT MEANS

The range will be between 7 and 35. Scores of 30 and above indicate good grievance-handling skills. Scores of 25 to 29 indicate room for improvement. Scores of less than 25 suggest a strong need to work on these skills.

**Arbitrator**
an impartial third party to a dispute who will hear the case and make a ruling.

with the chief union steward or union grievance committee; the facilities manager and the labor specialist meets with the union grievance committee; the organization's top management meet with the union grievance committee and a representative of the national union to try to work out a solution. If the grievance still cannot be resolved, the dispute may be referred to an impartial third-party **arbitrator** who will hear the case and make a ruling. This is called grievance or rights arbitration.

In practice, 98 percent of all collective-bargaining agreements provide for arbitration as the final step in an impasse. Grievance arbitration usually focuses on one of two issues—contract interpretation and discipline and discharge. The party that is claiming that the contract language has been improperly interpreted has the burden to go forward in presenting its case. In discipline and discharge cases, because the action was initiated by the company, the company officials have the burden to show that they had just cause. As for who pays the arbitrator, it's often dependent on who's raising the issue. More often, though, the labor agreement will stipulate who pays, or how the costs of arbitration will be divided.

The previous discussion describes the overall grievance procedure. Our concern here is in building supervisory skills. So we need to address a more specific question: How should you, as a supervisor, respond if an employee or union steward presents a formal grievance? We offer you the following guidelines in *Building a Supervisory Skill.*

EXHIBIT 15–8

A typical grievance procedure.

Step 5 | Arbitration

Step 4 | Organization's Top Management | Union Grievance Committee and Representative from National Union

Step 3 | Facilities Manager and Labor Specialist | Union Grievance Committee

Step 2 | Supervisor and Labor Specialist | Chief Steward or Union Grievance Committee

Step 1 | Supervisor | Union Steward

Employee with Grievance

☐ Management representatives

☐ Union representatives

The grievance procedure is essentially a formal appeals system. It is designed to protect an employee's rights. Your judgment may be overruled at a higher level. But that's OK. If you've followed the contract's procedures, made your decision in good faith, and carefully documented your actions, you've correctly fulfilled your obligations in the grievance procedure.

## HANDLING GRIEVANCES

### ABOUT THE SKILL

As the first person involved in the dispute, there are certain actions you can take to help resolve the problem.

### STEPS IN PRACTICING THE SKILL:

1. **Listen to the employee's complaint.** Don't be defensive and don't take the complaint personally. Employees regularly have grievances and you're the first contact point in the process that represents the organization. Calmly listen to the employee's complaint. Keep an open mind. Very importantly at this stage, don't argue with the employee. What you want to do is gain understanding.

2. **Investigate to get the facts.** You want to separate facts from opinions. Is the situation, as presented by the employee, complete and factual? Interview any key people who may be able to verify the employee's claims. Review all pertinent documents. Go over the clauses in the labor contract that apply to the employee's complaint. If you're unsure about the contract's language or how a relevant clause should be interpreted, get counsel from a labor specialist in your human resources department. Getting assistance isn't a sign of ignorance. You're not a legal specialist, so don't pretend to be one.

3. **Make your decision and explain it clearly.** You need to complete your investi-

gation promptly so that you can reach your decision in a relatively short period of time. Why? Because most labor agreements specify a definite time period within which a grievance must be answered. If you determine that the grievance is unfounded, verbally give the employee and union steward your interpretation. Be sure to back up your decision with specific reasons for denying the grievance, citing evidence from your investigation and/or language from the contract. You should then follow up the verbal answer with a written response. If the grievance has merit, provide a written response to the employee and union steward stating this fact. Additionally, you should describe the corrective action you plan to take. Before you write this response, be sure that your remedy is consistent with established practices, doesn't set any new precedents, and is within your authority. When in doubt, get approval from your boss or a manager in human resources. You want to be very careful about making individual exceptions to past practices. This might seem like an easy way to make the grievance disappear, but you could end up setting a precedent that might seriously hurt the organization in future contract negotiations or in future arbitration decisions.

4. **Keep records and documents.** It's important to document everything you do relating to a grievance. Remember that the labor agreement is a binding, legal contract. As such, formality is important. You have to follow the language of the contract. To protect yourself and the organization against charges that you have not followed the contract as intended, you must keep all

the records that you've accumulated on every grievance.

5. **Be prepared for appeals.** If you rule against the employee, you should expect the employee or the union steward to appeal your decision to a higher level. Be prepared to be questioned by union officials and various labor specialists from your organization's human resource group. Don't let this shake you, and don't let an employee or union representative's threat of appeal influence your decision. ■

---

POP QUIZ **(Are You Comprehending What You're Reading?)**

**5.** Which one of the following is not part of the collective bargaining process?
   **a.** interpretation of a written agreement
   **b.** negotiations of a written agreement
   **c.** approval of a written agreement by the NLRB
   **d.** administration of a written agreement
**6.** Bargaining in good faith means that the company and labor union must negotiate until they've reached an agreement acceptable to both parties. True or False?
**7.** Explain what is meant by the terms *conciliation, mediation,* and *fact-finding.* When are any of the three used?
**8.** The procedure used in resolving disputes surrounding the interpretation and application of the contract is called _____ .
   **a.** the grievance procedure
   **b.** interest arbitration
   **c.** a strike or a lockout
   **d.** none of the above

## SUMMARY

After reading this chapter, I can:

1. **Describe the current status of labor unions in the United States.** The overall percentage of the labor force that belongs to a union has been declining since the mid-1950s. Currently it is down to approximately 11 percent of the civilian work force. However, this decline should not be interpreted as implying that labor union influence has declined similarly. Labor unions still represent the majority of workers in many key industries. Additionally, wages and benefits won by labor unions typically spill over to influence the wages and benefits of nonunionized employees.

2. **Explain the appeal of unions to employees.** Unions are appealing to employees because their power offers the promise of higher wages and benefits, greater job security, and increased opportunities to influence work rules.

3. **Describe the importance of the National Labor Relations Act.** The National Labor Relations Act dramatically changed the power distribution between management and labor. This act guaranteed workers the right to organize and join unions, to bargain collectively, and to act in concert in pursuit of their objectives. This act, in essence, legitimated the legality of unions and stimulated the active organizing of employees by labor unions.

4. **Identify the primary purpose of collective bargaining.** The primary purpose of collective bargaining is to negotiate a union contract and spell out the terms for administering that contract.

5. **Explain the supervisor's role in contract administration.** The supervisor plays a very important role in contract administration. He or she needs to know the details of the contract in order to interpret it and carry out its procedures. What supervisors say and do largely determines the labor-management climate in the organization.

6. **Describe the steps for handling a grievance.** The steps involved in handling a grievance are: 1) listen to the employee's complaint; 2) investigate to get the facts; 3) make your decision and explain it clearly; 4) keep records and documents; and 5) be prepared for appeals.

## REVIEWING YOUR KNOWLEDGE

1. What might explain the decline in union membership over the past 35 years?
2. How does a union shop and an open shop differ?
3. Why was the Labor-Management Relations Act important?
4. Describe the supervisor's role in a union's organizing effort.
5. "An employer might not want to stifle a union organizing effort. In fact, an employer might want to encourage his employees to join a union." Provide an argument in support of this statement. Then provide an argument against this statement.
6. What is collective bargaining?
7. Describe the typical steps in the grievance procedure process.
8. Explain the difference between a strike and a lockout.

9. How would the existence of a union and a collective-bargaining contract affect (a) employee recruitment and selection, (b) compensation, and (c) discipline?
10. Do you believe supervisors should be able to join a union? Explain. What reasons do you believe they may have for wanting to join?

## ANSWERS TO THE POP QUIZZES

1. **b. good supervision.** Where supervision and supervisory practices are "good," there's less likely a chance for a successful union organizing campaign.
2. Because in a right-to-work state, compulsory union membership is illegal. Right-to-work states permit freedom of choice when it comes to unionization.
3. **True.** Like Pop Quiz question 1, where supervision is good, the likelihood of having a union is low; where supervisory practices are poor, a union is likely to be encouraged to represent the workers.
4. **c. it established unfair labor practices on the part of unions.** It was the Labor-Management Relations Act (Taft-Hartley) that identified union unfair labor practices.

5. **c. approval of a written agreement by the NLRB.** The NLRB does not approve labor-management agreements. Final approval of a contract is the province of the rank-and-file members who are to ratify a contract before it is binding.
6. **False.** Bargaining in good faith means that the company and labor union must negotiate in an attempt to reach an agreement acceptable to both parties. Reaching an agreement is not guaranteed, however.
7. Conciliation, mediation, and fact-finding are three impasse resolution techniques. Conciliation and mediation involve a neutral third party who attempts to get labor and management to resolve their differences. Fact-finding is a technique whereby a neutral third-party individual conducts a hearing to gather evidence from both labor and management. The fact-finder then renders a decision as to how he or she views an appropriate settlement. Suggestions from all three techniques, however, are not binding on either party.
8. **a. the grievance procedure.** This is the definition of the process used in labor-management relationships to resolve disputes surrounding the interpretation and application of the contract. ■

## A CLASS EXERCISE:
## HANDLING A GRIEVANCE

Break the class into groups of three. This role play requires one person to play the role of the supervisor (Chris), another to play the role of the employee (Pat), and the third to play the union steward (C.J.).

All players should read the following scenario and the excerpt from the union's contract. Then you are to role-play a meeting in Chris's office. This role play should take no more than 15 minutes.

## SCENARIO

The head of security guards has recently been focusing attention on the removal of illegal substances from the company's workplace. One morning last week, the guard suspected the possession of a controlled substance by an employee, Pat Brandon. The guard, noticing Pat placing a bag in his/her personal locker, searched the locker for drugs. The guard found a variety of pills, some of which he thought were nonprescription amphetamines. As Pat was leaving work for the day, the security guard stopped him/her and requested Pat to empty the contents of the bag. Pat was not told why the request was being made. Pat refused to honor the request, stormed out the door, and left the company premises. Pat was informed the next morning that he/she was being terminated for refusing to obey the legitimate order of a plant security guard.

Chris has just gone into a meeting with Pat and C.J. Chris wishes to enforce management's decision to terminate Pat and justify the reason for it. C.J. and Pat, on the other hand, claim this action is a violation of the contract.

Relevant Contract Language: The following is extracted from the union-management contract:

An employee who fails to maintain proper standards of conduct at all times, or who violates any of the following rules, shall subject him or herself to disciplinary action:

Rule 4. Bringing illegal substances or intoxicating liquors onto company premises, using or possessing these on company property, or reporting to work under the influence is strictly prohibited.

Rule 11. Refusal to follow supervisory orders, or in any way act insubordinate to any company agent, is strictly prohibited.

For the role of Chris, you may want to use the grievance handling skills suggested in the Building a Supervisory Skills section (p. 558) as a guideline.

## THINKING CRITICALLY

## CASE 15.A

### Caterpillar Steamrolls
### Its Union

Caterpillar, the manufacturer of large earth-moving equipment, was willing to face a long-term strike as it discontinued negotiations with the United Automobile Workers (UAW). Ironically, company officials didn't appear to be concerned about the strike. In fact, many company officials viewed it as creating some company advantages. For instance, because the construction industry was in a recession, Caterpillar had a lot of equipment in inventory.

Having a strike meant that inventory could be reduced—as well as reducing payroll costs. Furthermore, any worker who struck faced the potential of losing his or her job permanently.[11]

You would think that in a confrontational situation like this, union members would have rallied the "troops" to fight the company. That was not always the case. Some union employees crossed the picket line—returning to work without a labor agreement to protect them. Many did so because they felt that if they didn't, they'd lose their jobs. Period!

To help stop this internal union dissension, the UAW agreed to have all its members return to work if Caterpillar officials would stop hiring replacements. As a result, about 12,000 workers returned to their jobs, ending almost a six-month walk-out.

## RESPONDING TO THE CASE

1. Describe the relationship between Caterpillar and the UAW. Do you believe such a relationship is conducive to a long-term, lasting working relationship? Explain.
2. Do you believe the threat of replacing strikers will impede cooperation between unions and management? Explain your position.
3. Why do you think the unionized workers at Caterpillar agreed to return to work without a labor contract? Do you think that having these employees working without a contract is a scheme to eliminate the UAW as the employees bargaining agent? Discuss.

[11]A. Kupfer, "Caterpillar's Union Fallout," *Fortune*, May 18, 1992, p. 16.

## CASE 15.B

### Conoco Provides Labor-Management Training

Charlene Lyons works at Conoco Inc., where a significant reorganization has recently taken place. A large number of employees took reassignments, some even in other parts of the world. The numerous changes that have been made in the operations of this oil and gas giant have created the need for more training, especially labor-management relations training for supervisors.

Ms. Lyons is the director of labor relations who has helped to develop and administer the policies of the organization. She is particularly adept at warding off and diffusing employee grievances as well as negotiating contracts that will benefit management and employees alike. She frequently gives workshops to unit supervisors about changes in labor legislation, how such laws affect Conoco's employees and company officials, and promoting effective labor-management relations for the good of the organization.

In less than a month, Ms. Lyons will begin a training session for several new Conoco supervisors. Charlene has provided each supervisor with the basic labor relations policies and procedures manuals for the company. Jason, Ginny, and Tom are three Conoco supervisors who will receive training. Each has been recently promoted from within the company. They all have several common concerns, two of which are the increased concern by company officials with raising productivity and promoting an atmosphere to avoid employee grievances.

## RESPONDING TO THE CASE

1. What do these new supervisors need to know about the labor relations and the collective-bargaining process?

2. Describe the various roles a supervisor may have in labor matters (such as organizing drives, negotiations, contract administration, and so on). ∎

## Jan Homan,
## Maintenance Manager, Metropolitan
## Transit Commission

Jan supervises two kinds of workers—mechanics and cleaners. According to the union, a supervisor can ask an employee to perform tasks at or below his or her level. Because the Metropolitan Transit Commission (MTC) sometimes has a shortage of cleaners, Jan will ask the mechanics to clean the buses. One morning Jan called in mechanics on overtime to do repairs. At the same time, some buses needed to be cleaned. Because all cleaners were busy, Jan asked a mechanic on overtime to clean the buses. A cleaner filed a grievance with the union. He claimed it was unfair to call in mechanics to do a cleaner's job.

Jan and the MTC maintained that they had the right to ask the mechanic to clean the bus. It had been an emergency situation. The bus needed to go out and there were no cleaners available. The problem was taken to the third level of grievance proceedings in front of the MTC's Chief Administrator.

1. What is Jan Holman's main source of conflict? Why?
2. What are some of the problems and challenges Jan Holman faces as he considers implementing change at the MTC? What do you consider his biggest challenge and why?
3. When are problems and conflicts within a unionized organization handled differently than in a non-unionized business? In such cases, are supervisors expected to solve all problems that arise? Why or why not?
4. What course of action may be necessary when a formal grievance is filed within a unionized organization? What role, if any, does the supervisor assume in such action? How does this apply to Jan Holman's situation?
5. What can a supervisor do to help employees reduce conflict and stress, cope with change, and improve their working environment? Which of these "solutions" would be helpful to Jan Holman and his employees? ∎

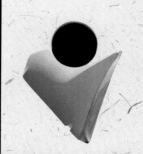

# PART SIX

# PERSONAL DEVELOPMENT

You have now had the opportunity to explore a variety of topics related to supervising employees. You should have a better understanding of what this job entails and what skills you need to be successful in the job. You have considered the importance of motivating your employees, as well as being an effective leader—especially during a time of rapid change.

A common thread in many of the discussions throughout this text was the element of how each of your actions may affect your career. In this part we will look at your quest to achieve your career goals.

Part Six contains one chapter:

16.   Building Your Career

# 16 BUILDING YOUR CAREER

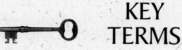

# LEARNING OBJECTIVES

# KEY TERMS

After reading this chapter, you should be able to:

1. Define what is meant by the term *career*.
2. Explain why traditional career paths are disappearing.
3. Identify your basic talents and strengths.
4. Describe your interests.
5. Match your individual personality to an organizational culture.
6. Define your career goals.
7. List five steps for better time management.

You should also be able to define these supervisory terms:

career

lifelong learning

personal career planning

plateauing

time management

What do those born between 1946 and 1964 have going for their careers? The title "baby-boomer"? Being part of a time in U.S. history where unprecedented growth catapulted many of their careers? Sure, both of these things, but this generation of workers cannot rest on their past "successes." What about the twenty-somethings—the Generation Xers? In spite of the reputation that precedes their generation, they're making some headway on the job scene. Consider the story of Robb Gaynor, a 29-year-old manager at Charles Schwab & Company.[1] Robb Gaynor is quite representative of Generation Xers. One stereotype of this group of individuals is that they are underachievers who have poor work habits and low ambitions. Robb fit that role exceptionally well. He attended four colleges, hopping from one to another in an effort to "find" himself. For Robb, finding who he was, though, didn't involve college. He dropped out permanently. He jumped from job to job before he finally accepted a position with a

## INTRODUCTION

**Career**
a sequence of job positions occupied by a person during his or her lifetime.

What is a career? The term **career** has a number of meanings. In popular usage, it can mean advancement ("his career is progressing nicely"), a profession ("she has chosen a career in medicine"), or a lifelong sequence of jobs ("his career has included fifteen jobs in six different organizations"). For our purposes, we define a career as the sequence of positions occupied by a person during his or her lifetime. By this definition, it is apparent that we all have, or will have, careers. Moreover, the concept is as relevant to transient unskilled laborers as to engineers or physicians.

Many of you are currently pursuing, or plan to pursue, a career that involves directing the activities of others. That typically begins with a supervisory job. Success as a supervisor is almost always a prerequisite to assuming positions of greater responsibility in an organization.

Are you well suited to a career in supervising others? What type of organization is best matched to your particular supervisory style and most likely to lead to your being successful? What can you do to better prepare yourself for an increasingly changing and uncertain world? Finally, how can you help achieve all these things by effectively using your time? We'll try to answer these questions in the remainder of this chapter.

[1]P. Sellers, "Don't Call Me Slacker," *Fortune*, December 12, 1994, pp. 181–182.

Charles Schwab discount brokerage firm in San Francisco. Even on this job, Gaynor didn't conform to the baby boomers' ideal work ethic. In fact, Robb leaves his job some afternoons to go to his favorite sunny place to fish. Even his personal affairs appear somewhat messed up to the well-organized boomers. Robb has often missed paying his monthly electric bill and has been late in his car payments about 25 percent of the time. Does he fit the Generation X stereotype perfectly? Maybe, but who should care! In spite of Robb's personal demeanor, he's also the "fastest rising star under age 30" in the Charles Schwab organization.

For anyone who does business with Charles Schwab, one thing may be noteworthy. It's an electronic trading process called Schwablink. Gaynor developed and supervises this system for the company, and over the past few years, it has helped Schwab add billions of dollars in assets. ■

## THE TRADITIONAL CAREER PATH

Traditional career paths meant that an individual progressed through a sequence of positions with increasing responsibilities. The traditional career path is characterized by relative predictability, upward vertical movement, and the organization taking responsibility for your career development (see News Flash).

Exhibit 16–1 illustrates a traditional career path that many college graduates of the early 1960s might have experienced. Graduating at age 21 or 22, with a degree in business and little or no work experience, they went to work for large corporations like General Motors, Shell Oil, Alcoa, IBM, or Procter & Gamble. Along with 50 or more other young graduates, these new employees were put into the company's management training program. Trainees would begin in one department, for example, production control, and proceed in lock-step fashion from department to department for two or three years. Never staying in any department for more than four to six months, the trainees got to see many different facets of the company and were able to find the area where they and the company believed each could make the largest contribution. Companies treated their trainees as soft clay, to be shaped into the type of person whose skills and supervisory style fit their corporate mold. General Motors, for instance, sought conservative people who could sublimate their individuality to the larger corpo-

## EXHIBIT 16–1
Traditional career paths.

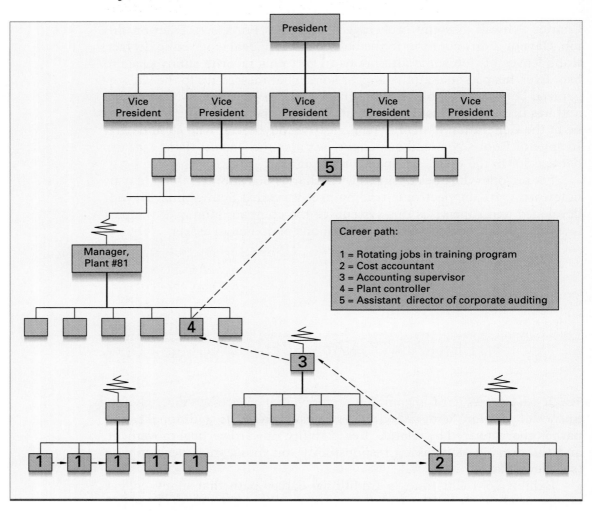

Career path:

1 = Rotating jobs in training program
2 = Cost accountant
3 = Accounting supervisor
4 = Plant controller
5 = Assistant director of corporate auditing

rate team. Committees made the key decisions at GM; individual stars were discouraged.

Once assigned to a specific department, the employee began a relatively standardized series of promotions within a functional area. So the IBM trainee, who decided to focus on finance, might start as a cost accountant at a plant in upstate New York. From there he or she might be transferred to a California plant as an accounting supervisor, then to another location as a plant controller, and so on—as far as this individual's technical, supervisory, and political skills would carry him or her. Some people, of course, reached plateaus along the way. They were rarely fired; instead, further promotion opportunities just disappeared.

Previously, one of the most popular ways of analyzing and discussing careers was to view them as a series of stages.[2] Progression from the beginning of a career to its end was viewed as a natural occurrence that happened to most individuals. This included a five-stage model that applied to most people during their adult years, regardless of the type of job they did. If this model is applicable today, it's among a small set of growing companies.

Most individuals begin to form ideas about their careers during their elementary and secondary school years. Their careers begin to wind down as they reach retirement age. The stages that most individuals will go through during these years are *exploration, establishment, mid-career, late career,* and *decline.* These stages, and the challenges they bring are shown in Exhibit 16–2.

The age ranges for each of the five stages in Exhibit 16–2 are provided as general guidelines. They should not be interpreted as ages when events must occur. So, for example, someone who makes a career change to another line of work at age 47 will have many of the same establishment-stage concerns as someone starting at age 21.

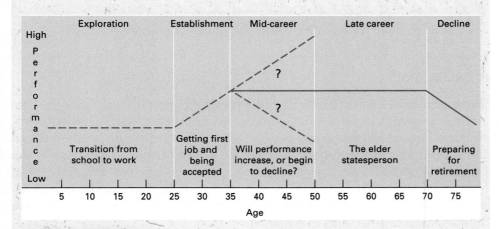

## EXHIBIT 16–2

Traditional career stages.

[2]See, for example, D. E. Super, *The Psychology of Careers* (New York, NY: Harper & Row, 1957); E. Schein, *Career Dynamics: Matching Individual and Organizational Needs* (Reading, MA: Addison Wesley, 1978); and D. J. Levinson, C. N. Darrow, E. B. Klein, M. H. Levinson, and B. McKee, *A Man's Life* (New York, NY: Knopf, 1978).

The tall pyramid shape of these large corporations meant there were lots of promotion opportunities. Additionally, rapid growth and expansion further opened the doors to continuous promotions. The traditional career path allowed people to spend their work lives in only one or two organizations and eliminated the need for them to worry about their future. The company's human resources group (then called the personnel department) developed replacement charts, succession tracking systems, and individual career progression plans. Responsibility for career development essentially fell on the company rather than on the individual employee.

## IS THE TRADITIONAL CAREER PATH ALIVE AND WELL TODAY?

Some large corporations still have formal supervisory training programs for new college graduates. There are also some current employees who will experience a relatively uninterrupted ascent up a single organization's corporate hierarchy. However, such corporations and employees are increasingly rare. More common today are corporations which have cut costs by reducing layers of supervisory personnel; widening spans of control; and significantly shrinking, and in some cases eliminating, entry-level management training programs. As a result, you should not expect to follow the traditional career path we've previously described. More likely, you'll pursue a different path, one which will be characterized by unpredictability, lateral and interorganizational moves, occasional bouts of stagnation, and the continual need for educational updating and retraining. Finally, you must be prepared to do what's necessary on your own to advance your career (see Assessing Yourself). We'll offer some guidelines later in this chapter.

### UNPREDICTABILITY

The traditional career path offered predictability. This was possible because companies faced relatively stable environments. In the 1960s, for instance, General Motors' competition essentially came from only Ford and Chrysler. Established brand names like Chevrolet, Buick, Oldsmobile, Cadillac, and GMC Truck—plus strong customer loyalty—assured GM of high sales year after year. With nearly a 50 percent share of the U.S. automobile market, GM could offer its supervisory personnel a stable, predictable, and upward career path.

Today, GM faces aggressive competition from dozens of automakers. Consumers demand high quality, innovative features, and maximum value for their dollar. In this competitive world, GM is no longer able to pass along its inefficiencies or higher development and production costs to consumers. So GM has had to restructure its organization. It has cut tens of thousands of jobs and reorganized the work of those whose jobs remain.

## How Do You Define Life Success?

Instructions: Rate the following 42 statements according to the scale below:

5 = Always Important
4 = Very Often Important
3 = Fairly Often Important
2 = Occasionally Important
1 = Never Important

| | | | | | |
|---|---|---|---|---|---|
| **1.** Getting others to do what I want | 5 | 4 | 3 | ②  | 1 |
| **2.** Having inner peace and contentment | ⑤ | 4 | 3 | 2 | 1 |
| **3.** Having a happy marriage | 5 | 4 | 3 | 2 | 1 |
| **4.** Having economic security | 5 | 4 | 3 | ② | 1 |
| **5.** Being committed to my organization | 5 | ④ | 3 | 2 | 1 |
| **6.** Being able to give help, assistance, advice, and support to others | 5 | 4 | 3 | 2 | ① |
| **7.** Having a job that pays more than peers earn | 5 | 4 | 3 | 2 | ① |
| **8.** Being a good parent | ⑤ | 4 | 3 | 2 | 1 |
| **9.** Having good job benefits | 5 | 4 | ③ | 2 | 1 |
| **10.** Having a rewarding family life | ⑤ | 4 | 3 | 2 | 1 |
| **11.** Raising children to be independent adults | ⑤ | 4 | 3 | 2 | 1 |
| **12.** Having people work for me | 5 | 4 | 3 | 2 | ① |
| **13.** Being accepted at work | ⑤ | 4 | 3 | 2 | 1 |
| **14.** Enjoying my nonwork activities | ⑤ | 4 | 3 | 2 | 1 |
| **15.** Making or doing things that are useful to society | ⑤ | 4 | 3 | 2 | 1 |
| **16.** Having high income and the resulting benefits | 5 | 4 | 3 | ② | 1 |
| **17.** Having a sense of personal worth | ⑤ | 4 | 3 | 2 | 1 |
| **18.** Contributing to society | ⑤ | 4 | 3 | 2 | 1 |
| **19.** Having long-term job security | 5 | 4 | 3 | ② | 1 |
| **20.** Having children | 5 | 4 | 3 | ② | 1 |
| **21.** Getting good performance evaluations | ⑤ | 4 | 3 | 2 | 1 |
| **22.** Having opportunities for personal creativity | ⑤ | 4 | 3 | 2 | 1 |
| **23.** Being competent | ⑤ | 4 | 3 | 2 | ① |
| **24.** Having public recognition | 5 | 4 | 3 | 2 | ① |
| **25.** Having children who are successful emotionally and professionally | ⑤ | 4 | 3 | 2 | 1 |
| **26.** Having influence over others | 5 | 4 | 3 | ② | ① |
| **27.** Being happy with my private life | ⑤ | 4 | 3 | 2 | 1 |
| **28.** Earning regular salary increases | 5 | 4 | ③ | 2 | 1 |
| **29.** Having personal satisfaction | ⑤ | 4 | 3 | 2 | 1 |

*(continued)*

| | | | | | |
|---|---|---|---|---|---|
| **30.** | Improving the well-being of the work force | 5 | 4 | 3 | 2 | 1 |
| **31.** | Having a stable marriage | 5 | 4 | 3 | 2 | 1 |
| **32.** | Having the confidence of my bosses | 5 | 4 | 3 | 2 | 1 |
| **33.** | Having the resources to help others | 5 | 4 | 3 | 2 | 1 |
| **34.** | Being in a high-status occupation | 5 | 4 | 3 | 2 | 1 |
| **35.** | Being able to make a difference in something | 5 | 4 | 3 | 2 | 1 |
| **36.** | Having money to buy or do anything | 5 | 4 | 3 | 2 | 1 |
| **37.** | Being satisfied with my job | 5 | 4 | 3 | 2 | 1 |
| **38.** | Having self-respect | 5 | 4 | 3 | 2 | 1 |
| **39.** | Helping others to achieve | 5 | 4 | 3 | 2 | 1 |
| **40.** | Having personal happiness | 5 | 4 | 3 | 2 | 1 |
| **41.** | Being able to provide quality education for my children | 5 | 4 | 3 | 2 | 1 |
| **42.** | Making a contribution to society | 5 | 4 | 3 | 2 | 1 |

## SCORING

This questionnaire taps six dimensions of life success. These are the achievement of status and wealth, contribution to society, good family relationships, personal fulfillment, professional fulfillment, and security. Calculate your scores as follows: Add your total scores, then divide by the number of items in each category to determine a mean score on each dimension.

| STATUS AND WEALTH | CONTRIBUTION TO SOCIETY | FAMILY RELATIONSHIPS | PERSONAL FULFILLMENT |
|---|---|---|---|
| 1. 2 | 6. 5 | 3. 5 | 2. 5 |
| 7. 1 | 15. 5 | 8. 5 | 14. 5 |
| 12. 1 | 18. 5 | 10. 5 | 17. 5 |
| 16. 2 | 22. 5 | 11. 5 | 23. 5 |
| 24. 1 | 33. 5 | 20. 2 | 27. 3 |
| 26. 2 | 35. 5 | 25. 5 | 29. 5 |
| 34. 1 | 39. 5 | 31. 5 | 38. 5 |
| 36. 3 | 42. 5 | 41. 5 | 40. 3 |
| 13 Total | 45 Total | 37 Total | 45 Total |
| 1.625 Total/8 | 5 Total/8 | 4.625 Total/8 | 5 Total/8 |
| ___ Mean | ___ Mean | ___ Mean | ___ Mean |

**PROFESSIONAL FULFILLMENT**

5. _4_
13. _5_
21. _5_
32. _5_
37. _5_
_24_ Total
_4.8_ Total/5
____ Mean

**SECURITY**

4. _2_
9. _3_
19. _2_
28. _3_
30. _5_
_15_ Total
_3_ Total/5
____ Mean

## WHAT THE ASSESSMENT MEANS

The higher your score on any one dimension, the greater the importance you place on that criterion. Those things that are important to you, then, must be considered when choosing a career. For instance, if family relationships are important to you, then you want to work in an organization and to have a career where both your personal and professional life can be combined. Jobs that do not offer what you want, or don't lead to helping you "achieve your life success" can create problems for you.

You can also compare your scores with the following norms based on surveys of supervisory personnel.

| Dimension | Females (n = 439) | Males (n = 317) |
|---|---|---|
| Status/Wealth | 3.48 | 3.65 |
| Social Contribution | 4.04 | 4.07 |
| Family Relationships | 4.44 | 4.28 |
| Personal Fulfillment | 4.60 | 4.43 |
| Professional Fulfillment | 4.21 | 4.15 |
| Security | 4.30 | 4.21 |

Source: Barbara Parker and Leonard H. Chusmir, *Development and Validation of Life Success Measures Scale* (Miami, FLA: Florida International University, 1991). Used with permission.

What has taken place at GM has gone on at almost every major corporation in the world. Continual efforts at cost cutting and reorganization have eliminated the traditional "management" career path. In fact, career paths in large corporations are increasingly looking like those in small business, where rapid change and uncertainty create a wide range of diverse career paths.

## LATERAL AND INTERORGANIZATIONAL MOVES

In the traditional career path, individuals expected a sequence of steady promotions. In companies like GM or IBM, it was not unusual for supervisory personnel to get promoted every two to three years. Success, in fact, was defined more by the speed of one's promotions than the promotions themselves. Except during early training, lateral transfers were perceived as nearly equivalent to a demotion.

In today's organization, your career is very likely to include a number of lateral moves. New challenges will come from taking on different rather than greater responsibilities. In addition, the restructuring and downsizing that corporations have undergone during the past decade have reduced the loyalty bonds that previously held employees to organizations. As corporations have shown less commitment to employees, employees have shown less commitment to them. So while your father or grandfather may have spent his entire working career with one employer, you're likely to change employers as conditions change and new opportunities arise.

## PLATEAUING

**Plateauing**
little likelihood of any further upward movement in a career with a current employer.

Reduced promotion opportunities translate into increased career **plateauing**. After only one or two promotions, employees are increasingly finding that there is not likely to be any further upward movement in their career with their current employer.

Plateauing is increasingly becoming a way of life for many supervisors. In the traditional career path, plateauing occurred, but it usually didn't hit until the individual reached his or her late 40s or early 50s. Nowadays,

The traditional career path historically began for college graduates with a visit to their career placement center. From there, they joined an organization, specialized in a particular area of the company, and worked at climbing the organizational ladder.

many supervisors are plateauing as early as their mid-20s. Downsizing, fewer supervisory levels in the organization, less turnover in the senior ranks, and fewer job opportunities elsewhere have made plateauing a fact of life for millions of supervisors and middle-level managers.

Ambitious employees will be finding new paths to job satisfaction and personal growth. Success is less likely to be defined solely in terms of promotions. Jobs will be redesigned to increase diversity and challenge. Regular lateral moves will become commonplace. Compensation plans will be reworked to pay people more on their contribution than on their title. And we can expect to see many employees turning more attention toward their families or hobbies as a means of finding life gratification.

## SKILL UPDATING

The usable life span of your skills is rapidly shrinking. The computer skills you learned five years ago have become obsolete. Recently enacted laws affecting disabled employees and "family rights" require supervisors to change some of their practices. Corporate efforts at empowering employees means supervisors need to learn empowerment skills. The changing work force demands that supervisors learn how to manage diversity. Organizations implementing continuous improvement programs expect their supervisors to understand its techniques and methods (see Exhibit 16–3).

Future success in supervisory positions will require individuals to pursue **lifelong learning**. You'll be expected to read extensively and keep current on new supervisory concepts, business practices, and changes in your industry. You'll regularly attend company seminars, industry workshops, and evening college classes to upgrade your skills. You may even need to take occasional leaves of absence from work in order to go back to school for advanced certificates and degrees.

**Lifelong learning**
continuing education through attendance at company seminars, industry workshops, and evening college classes to upgrades one's skills as well as self-education on new supervisory concepts, business practices, and changes in one's industry.

## EXHIBIT 16–3

Ziggy learns a lesson. (Drawing by Wilson. © 1993 Ziggy and Friends. By permission of Universal Press Syndicate.)

# WHY MUST YOU TAKE CONTROL OF YOUR CAREER?

While career development has been an important topic in business-related courses for the past three decades, we have witnessed some drastic changes over the years. Years ago, career development programs were designed to assist you in advancing your work life. Its focus was to provide the necessary information and assessment in helping you realize your career goals. Career development was also a way for the organization to attract and retain highly talented personnel. But those events are all but disappearing in today's contemporary organizations—for many of the reasons we mentioned previously—downsizing, restructuring, and reengineering. As a result, one significant conclusion can be drawn about career development. You are responsible for your career—not the organization! Some three million employees have learned that the hard way over the past few years.[3] As one supervisor aptly put it, "I've got to look out for Number One. No one else is going to."

How do you take control of your own career? The next section provides a detailed guide for helping you do personal career development.

---

## POP QUIZ  (Are You Comprehending What You're Reading?)

1. Which one of the following is not considered part of the definition of a career?
   a. advancement
   b. profession
   c. position
   d. lifelong sequence of jobs
2. The traditional career path often resulted in individuals progressing through a sequence of positions with increasing responsibilities in the same organization. True or False?
3. Identify the five traditional stages of careers.
4. Which one of the of the following was not identified as a cause hindering the traditional career path?
   a. company responsibility for development employees' careers
   b. unpredictability
   c. more emphasis on lateral moves
   d. continual need for educational updating and retraining

---

[3]"Three Million U.S. Jobs Cut in Seven Years," *Manpower Argus* (Milwaukee, WI: Manpower, March 1996), p. 3.

# PERSONAL CAREER DEVELOPMENT

Personal career planning can provide no guarantees that you will optimize your career potential. However, many years ago, a wise individual suggested that "opportunity knocks two or three times in every person's life. The difference between those who are able to take advantage of these opportunities and those who aren't is preparation." Further, another person said, "the person we typically call 'lucky' is usually just someone who was ready when the right situation came around." **Personal career planning** can prepare you to be ready when opportunity does knock.

**Personal career planning**
preparing oneself for future work opportunities by examining one's talents and strengths, needs and interests, and the corporate culture in which one would best fit.

## WHAT ARE YOUR TALENTS AND STRENGTHS?

The place to begin is by assessing your basic strengths. What is it that you do best? What skill or skills do you excel at? Writing, speaking, concentrating, interacting with people, organizing things, and logical reasoning are just a few skills to consider. Exhibit 16–4 provides a list that might help you. You might also reflect on classes in school where you did particularly well and comments from friends or relatives as to where they thought your talents lay.

Everyone has something that he or she does better than other things. What's yours? The idea here is to play off your strengths.

## WHAT ARE YOUR NEEDS AND INTERESTS?

Next, determine what it is you like to do. Forget, for a moment, what you're good at and think about what "really excites you." Do you like to talk to people? Participate in sports? Read? Explain things to others? Research subjects? Do something risky?

If nothing comes immediately to mind, think back over previous courses you've taken in school or past work experiences that you found particularly interesting. You might also find Exhibit 16–5 helpful. It identifies six personality types and the characteristics associated with each. Which one of these best describes you? You might also want to check out the career counseling center at your college. Many of them offer "personality assessments," like the one featured in Exhibit 16–5, that provide you insight into your interests.

**Analytical skills:** Comparing, evaluating, and understanding complex problems or situations

**Interpersonal communication skills:** Speaking with clarity, clarifying misunderstandings, and listening effectively

**Making presentations:** Presenting ideas to groups of people with a clear and logical presentation

**Writing skills:** Writing with clarity and conciseness

**Manipulating data and numbers:** Processing information and numbers skillfully; handling budgets and statistical reports

**Entrepreneurial skills and innovation:** Recognizing and seizing opportunities for new ideas or products, creating new services or processes or products

**Leading and managing others:** Inspiring others, assessing others' abilities, delegating effectively, motivating others to achieve a set of goals

**Learning skills:** Grasping new information quickly, using common sense to deal with new situations, using feedback effectively

**Team membership skills:** Working well on teams and committees, incorporating a variety of perspectives toward a common goal

**Conflict resolution skills:** Dealing with differences, confronting other effectively

**Human development skills:** Encouraging, guiding, and evaluating others; explaining and/or demonstrating new ideas or skills, creating an environment for learning and growth

## How Do You Merge Your Strengths and Interests?

The next step in career development is to merge what you do best with what you like to do (see Exhibit 16–6).

If you're a good writer but like to be left alone, maybe your life's work should be as a novelist or researcher. If your strength is writing but you like to interact with people, maybe you should consider journalism. Think about linking jobs with your strengths and preferences. For example, supervisors need analytical, interpersonal, leading, and team skills. Conventional and social personalities are also probably better matched to a supervisory career than are artistic types. If you're good at organizing things, supervision may be right for you—or a career as a library cata-

| TYPE | PERSONALITY CHARACTERISTICS |
|---|---|
| **Realistic:** Prefers physical activities that require skills, strength, and coordination | Shy, genuine, persistent, stable, conforming, practical |
| **Investigative:** Prefers activities that involve thinking, organizing, and understanding | Analytical, original, curious, independent |
| **Social:** Prefers activities that involve helping and developing others | Sociable, friendly, cooperative, understanding |
| **Conventional:** Prefers rule-regulated, orderly, and unambiguous activities | Conforming, efficient, practical unimaginative, inflexible |
| **Enterprising:** Prefers verbal activities where there are opportunities to influence others and attain power | Self-confident, ambitious, energetic, domineering |
| **Artistic:** Prefers ambiguous and unsystematic activities that allow creative expression | Imaginitive, disorderly, idealistic, emotional, impractical |

**EXHIBIT 16–5**

Job personality types. (*Source:* Reproduced by special permission of the Publisher, Psychological Assessment Resources, Inc., from *Making Vocational Choices,* copyright © 1973, 1985, 1992 by Psychological Assessment Resources, Inc. All rights reserved.)

loguer. If you like sports, coaching is a possibility. If you like to explain things, you'd probably find a great deal of satisfaction in teaching; or you might combine this with an interest in supervision by pursuing a career in educational administration. These examples only break the surface of potential job opportunities. Keep in mind that the Dictionary of Occupational Titles, published by the federal government, lists over 30,000 job titles!

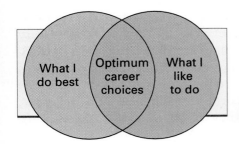

**EXHIBIT 16–6**

Merging strengths and interests.

# What Type of Organization Fits You Best?

Once you've got a set of jobs that you think you'd like and also do well at, ask yourself: Where do I want to work? There is a popular myth that a good employee or supervisor will succeed anywhere. In truth, you can do a job in one organization and be considered a superstar and do the same job in another organization and be rated "a poor performer." Why? Because organizations value different types of attitudes and behaviors. You increase the chances of your contribution being positively valued by an organization if you properly match your talents and personality to that organization. You need to choose organizations whose size and culture fit your style.

## SIZE

Working in a large organization with thousands of employees is different from working in a small one. Large ones tend to have more job specialization, more rules and regulations, more fixed duties, and more formal communication channels. Additionally, large organizations generally provide fewer opportunities for supervisors and operative employees to participate in decision making, less proximity and identification with the organization's goals, and less ability to see the link between individual effort and the final goods or services the organization produces.

Noting these differences is not meant to imply that small organizations are better places to work or have happier employees. In reality, some people find themselves more comfortable working in large bureaucracies while others prefer smaller, less formal organizations.

## ORGANIZATION CULTURE

The better the match between your personal style and the culture of your employing organization, the more likely you are to receive favorable performance reviews and rewards such as pay raises and promotions. Given this reality, a critical decision in your career plans is choosing employers where there is a good individual-organization fit.

What is organizational culture? As briefly described in previous chapters, it's the organization's personality. It's a set of characteristics that distinguishes one organization from another. The culture at MCI is very informal and risk-taking. The company values employees who are individualistic, independent, self-directed, and aggressive. In contrast, employees at Walt Disney theme parks are expected to maintain the uniform "Disney look." The company standardizes appearance, language, and behavior; and good employees at Disneyland, Disney World, and Euro Disney are people who behave exactly as they're instructed.

Exhibit 16–7 presents a labeling typology for classifying organizational cultures.[4] An *academy* is the place for steady climbers who want to thoroughly master each new job they hold. These companies like to recruit recent college graduates, provide them with much special training, and then carefully steer them through a myriad of specialized jobs within a particular function. These cultures, incidentally, were the primary reasons underlying the traditional career path. Companies that typify the academy culture include IBM, General Motors, and Procter & Gamble.

A *club* places high value on fitting in, loyalty, and commitment. Seniority is the key at clubs. Age and experience count. In contrast to an academy, the club grooms supervisory personnel as generalists. Examples of clubs are United Parcel Service, the Bell operating phone companies, government agencies, and the military.

*Baseball teams* are entrepreneurially-oriented havens for risk takers and innovators. They seek out talented people of all ages and experiences, then reward them for what they produce. Because they offer huge financial incentives and great freedom to their star performers, job hopping among these organizations is commonplace. Organizations that fit the baseball team description are common in accounting, law, investment banking, consulting, advertising, software development, and bioresearch.

While baseball teams prize inventiveness, *fortresses* are preoccupied with survival (see Dealing with a Difficult Issue). Many were once academies, clubs, or baseball teams, but fell on hard times and are now seeking to reverse their sagging fortunes. Fortresses offer little job security, yet they can be exciting places to work for those who like the challenge of a

| Type | Description |
|---|---|
| Academy | Employees stay within a narrow functional specialty and are promoted after they thoroughly master a new job. |
| Club | Employees are trained as generalists and are promoted on the basis of seniority. |
| Baseball team | Employees are rewarded for what they produce; risk-taking and innovation are highly valued. |
| Fortress | These cultures are preoccupied with survival, offer little job security, and reward employees who can reverse the organization's sagging fortunes. |

**EXHIBIT 16–7**

Four types of organizational cultures.

[4]C. Hymowitz, "Which Culture Fits You?" *Wall Street Journal*, July 17, 1989, p. B–1.

## WILL ONLY THE STRONG SURVIVE?

In the animal kingdom, there's a saying that only the strong survive. In the wild, the animal that is the quickest, or the strongest, has the advantage at being toward the top of the "food chain." Being more powerful or the swiftest, then, is handsomely rewarded. But what about humans? Is survival in our world based on being the strongest?

Many cases can be built to support this premise. Military strength has been shown to help a nation defend itself or avert invasions by an opposing country. Professional sports, as well as the entertainment industry, reinforce that being very competitive has its advantages. Those who want it more—who have the strongest desire to climb to the top—frequently succeed. And this success is often achieved at the expense of someone else's mistakes. Take a football running back who fumbles deep in his own end of the field. As a result of his misfortune, the opponent has now received great field position. This is not a result of their great ability to move the ball down field. Rather, it's because they capitalized on an opponent's mistake.

Obviously in professional sports, or even military matters, there's a good reason behind this behavior. It's how the "game" is played. Can this be applied to organizations where their is competition for positions of responsibility or for generating a good "bottom line?" Does one have to be *overly* competitive? Can you achieve your career goals by working with others as opposed to being out for yourself? If you help others succeed, do you believe you'll be overrun by those who are willing to take advantage of your kindness? Does acting in an ethical manner have a justifiably right place when your career is at stake? Or does ethics matter when everything else is in place—like the "bottom line" being met. What do you think?

turnaround. Fortress organizations include large retailers, hotels, and oil and natural gas exploration firms.

Research has shown that each of these four cultural types tends to attract certain personalities. The personality-organizational culture match affects how far and how easily a person will move up the hierarchial ranks. For instance, a risk taker will thrive at a baseball team, but fall flat on his or her face at an academy. Job offers, performance appraisals, and promotions are strongly influenced by the individual-organization fit, that is, whether the attitudes and behavior of the applicant or employee are compatible with the culture of the organization. Additionally, employee satisfaction will be significantly higher when there is a good match between individual needs and the culture.

## What Are Your Career Goals?

Once you understand your strengths and interests and the type of organization that fits you best, you need to address your career goals. Where do you want to be in five years? Ten years? Twenty years?

In today's rapidly changing work place, very specific goals are likely to be limiting as well as widely off-target. Things are changing too fast to make detailed goals very meaningful. What you need are goals that can give your career direction. Identify the general type of job you want, the size of the organization, the appropriate culture, approximate responsibilities, preferred geographic location, and the like. So, for instance, you might set a ten-year goal to hold a supervisory position in a small but fast-growing biotechnology firm, where performance rather than seniority is valued, located in the southeastern part of the United States. These goals would contrast sharply with the comparable ten-year goals your counterpart might have set back in the early 1970s—to be a branch official or higher at a Citizens & Southern office within a thirty-mile radius of Atlanta.

## Where Are You Now?

Before you can define the path that will get you to your goals, you need to take stock of where you are now. What is your level of education? How much work experience do you have? What are your skill strengths and weaknesses? As part of this assessment, if you're preparing for a career in supervision, take a moment to complete the supervisory inventory in Exhibit 16–8. This provides a summary of the skills you've been introduced to in this book and a quick checklist of your competency level for each.

## How Do You Reach Your Goals?

The final issue you need to address in personal career development is laying out a plan that will help you achieve your goals. The journey of a thousand miles begins with the first step. Once you know where you want to go, you have to take the initiative to begin that journey. Remember, don't count on your boss or organization to take responsibility for your career. If they offer assistance, great. But you're far less likely to be disappointed and far more likely to achieve your goals if you treat career planning as a self-development project.

## EXHIBIT 16–8

Supervisory skills inventory.

| | LEVEL OF COMPETENCE | | |
|---|---|---|---|
| **Skill** | **Weak** | **Needs Improvement** | **Strong** |
| Goal setting | ☐ | ☐ | ☐ |
| Budgeting | ☐ | ☐ | ☐ |
| Creative problem - solving | ☐ | ☐ | ☐ |
| Developing control charts | ☐ | ☐ | ☐ |
| Empowering others through delegation | ☐ | ☐ | ☐ |
| Employment interviewing | ☐ | ☐ | ☐ |
| Conducting the performance appraisal interview | ☐ | ☐ | ☐ |
| Coaching | ☐ | ☐ | ☐ |
| Designing motivating jobs | ☐ | ☐ | ☐ |
| Projecting Charisma | ☐ | ☐ | ☐ |
| Active listening | ☐ | ☐ | ☐ |
| Conducting a group meeting | ☐ | ☐ | ☐ |
| Negotiating | ☐ | ☐ | ☐ |
| Stress reduction | ☐ | ☐ | ☐ |
| Counseling | ☐ | ☐ | ☐ |
| Disciplining | ☐ | ☐ | ☐ |
| Handling grievances | ☐ | ☐ | ☐ |

## SELECT YOUR FIRST JOB JUDICIOUSLY

All first jobs are not alike. Where you begin in the organization has an important effect on your subsequent career progress. Specifically, evidence suggests that if you have a choice, you should select a powerful department as the place to start your supervisory career.[5] A power department is one where crucial and important organizational decisions are made. If you start out in departments that are high in power within the organizations, you're more likely to advance rapidly throughout your career.

## DO GOOD WORK

Good work performance is a necessary (but not sufficient) condition for career success. The marginal performer may be rewarded in the short term, but his or her weaknesses are bound to surface eventually and cut off career advancement. Your good work performance is no guarantee of success, but without it, the probability of a successful career is low.

[5]J. E. Sheridan, J. W. Slocum, Jr., R. Buda, and R. C. Thompson, "Effects of Corporate Sponsorship and Departmental Power on Career Tournaments," *Academy of Management Journal* (September 1990), pp. 578–602.

## PRESENT THE RIGHT IMAGE

Assuming that your work performance is in line with other successful supervisors, the ability to align your image with that sought by the organization is certain to be interpreted positively. You should assess the organization's culture so you can determine what the organization wants and values. Then you need to project that image in terms of style of dress; organizational relationships that you should and should not cultivate; whether you should project a risk-taking or risk-averse stance; the leadership style you should use; whether you should avoid, tolerate, or encourage conflict; the importance of getting along well with others; and so forth.

## LEARN THE POWER STRUCTURE

The authority relationships defined by the organization's formal structure, as shown by an organizational chart, explain only part of the influence patterns within an organization. It is of equal or greater importance to know and understand the organization's power structure. You need to learn "who's really in charge, who has the goods on whom, what are the major debts and dependencies"—all things that won't be reflected in neat boxes on the organization chart. Once you have this knowledge, you can work within the power structure with more skill and ease.[6]

## GAIN CONTROL OF ORGANIZATIONAL RESOURCES

The control of scarce and important organizational resources is a source of power. Knowledge and expertise are particularly effective resources to control. They make you more valuable to the organization and therefore more likely to gain job security and advancement.

## STAY VISIBLE

Because the evaluation of supervisory effectiveness can be very subjective, it is important that your boss and those in power in the organization be made aware of your contributions. If you're fortunate enough to have a job that brings your accomplishments to the attention of others, taking direct measures to increase your visibility might not be needed. However, your job may require you to handle activities that are low in visibility, or your specific contribution may be indistinguishable because you're part of a group endeavor. In such cases, without creating the image of a braggart, you'll want to call attention to yourself by giving progress reports to your boss and others. Other tactics include being seen at social functions, being

[6]C. Perrow, *Complex Organizations: A Critical Essay* (Glenwood, IL: Scott, Foresman, 1972), p. 43.

active in professional associations, and developing powerful allies who speak positively of you.

### DON'T STAY TOO LONG IN YOUR FIRST JOB

The evidence indicates that, given a choice between staying in your first supervisory job until you've "really made a difference" or accepting an early transfer to a new job assignment, you should go for the early transfer. By moving quickly through different jobs, you signal to others that you're on the fast track. This, then, often becomes a self-fulling prophecy. The message for you is to start fast by seeking early transfers or promotions from your first supervisory job.

### FIND A MENTOR

A *mentor* is someone from whom you can learn and who can encourage and help you. The evidence indicates that finding a sponsor who is part of the organization's power core is essential for you to make it to top levels of management.[7]

### SUPPORT YOUR BOSS

Your immediate future is in the hands of your current boss. He or she evaluates your performance, and you're unlikely to have enough power to successfully challenge this manager. Therefore, you should make the effort to help your boss succeed, be supportive if your boss is under siege from other organizational members, and find out what he or she will be using to assess your work effectiveness. Don't undermine your boss. Don't speak negatively of your boss to others. If your boss is competent, visible, and in possession of a power base, he or she is likely to be on the way up in the organization. Being perceived as supportive, you might find yourself pulled along too. If your boss's performance is poor and his or her power is low, you need to transfer to another unit. A mentor may be able to help you arrange this. It's hard to have your competence recognized or your positive performance evaluation taken seriously if your boss is perceived as incompetent.

### STAY MOBILE

You're likely to move up more rapidly if you indicate your willingness to move to different geographical locations and across functional lines within the organization. Career advancement may also be facilitated by your will-

[7]G. F. Dreher and R. A. Ash, "A Comparative Study of Mentoring Among Men and Women in Managerial, Professional, and Technical Positions," *Journal of Applied Psychology* (October 1990), pp. 539–546.

ingness to change organizations. Working in a slow-growth, stagnant, or declining organization makes mobility even more important to you.

## THINK LATERALLY

The suggestion to think laterally acknowledges the changing world of business. Because of organizational restructurings and downsizings, there are fewer rungs on the promotion ladder in many large organizations. To survive in this environment, it's a good idea to think in terms of lateral career moves.[8] It's important to recognize a point previously mentioned—that lateral movers in the 1960s and 1970s were presumed to be mediocre performers. That presumption doesn't hold today. Lateral shifts are now a viable career consideration. They give you a wider range of experiences, which enhances your long-term mobility. In addition, these moves can help energize you by making your work more interesting and satisfying. So if you're not moving ahead in your organization, consider a lateral move internally or a lateral shift to another organization.

## FOCUS ON ACQUIRING AND UPGRADING SKILLS

Organizations need employees who can readily adapt to the demands of the rapidly changing marketplace. By focusing on skills that you currently have and continuing to learn new skills, you can establish your value to the organization. It is employees who don't add value to an organization whose jobs (and career advancement) are in jeopardy.

## WORK HARD AT DEVELOPING A NETWORK

Our final suggestion is based on the recognition that having a network of friends, colleagues, neighbors, customers, suppliers, etc., can be a useful tool for career development. If you spend some time cultivating relation-

How do you keep your career goals from stalemating? One way is to recognize that you're never too old to go back to school. In today's work environment, you'll likely have to return to educational settings to enhance your skills and your credentials.

[8]D. T. Hall and Associates, *The Career is Dead—Long Live the Career: A Relational Approach to Careers* (San Francisco, CA: Jossey-Bass, 1996).

ships and contacts throughout your industry and community, you'll be prepared if "worse comes to worse" and your current job is eliminated. Even if your job is in no danger of being cut, having a network can prove beneficial in getting things done.

## A SPECIAL CAREER DEVELOPMENT AID: TIME MANAGEMENT SKILLS

What is time? It's something that can be your best friend in that it gives you an opportunity to accomplish your goals—career or otherwise. Of course it can also be your biggest enemy, for there never appears to be enough of it to get everything done. Time therefore, is a scarce resource. If it's wasted, it can never be replaced. Time, too, can never be saved. When a second passes, it's gone forever.

**Time management**
a tool any individual can use to schedule his or her time effectively; a self-discipline that keeps an individual's attention focused on those things that need to be accomplished.

**Time management** is a tool any individual can use to schedule his or her time effectively. It's a way of planning your personal activities. Time management is also a self discipline that keeps your attention focused on those things that need to be accomplished. Unfortunately, there are no hard and fast rules for managing time that will work in every case. A perfect solution has yet to be found—if one could ever be. Nonetheless, there are several time management techniques that can make you a better time manager (see Building a Supervisory Skill).

Remember, time management is not something that generally comes easy. It takes a dedicated effort to be a good time manager. Individuals who are good at this technique often appear to have more time than others. They don't! After all, what they face is the same 24-hour constraint everyone else faces in a day. What they do have going for them, however, is that they know how to use those 24 hours more effectively. They understand whether they are more productive in the mornings or in the evening. By knowing your productivity cycle, you should schedule your most important activities when you are able to give them the most effort.

Good time managers also know how to minimize disruptions. There are a number of time constraints, called time wasters, that will steal a person's time (see Something to Think About). These include interruptions, phone calls, and the like. During your most productive time, you need to insulate yourself from the time wasters. Go somewhere, if possible, where you won't be disturbed. Have calls screened, or let them roll over to the answering machine. Close your door to keep interruptions to a minimum. Obviously, the degree of insulating yourself will depend on your organization's policies, your boss, and your employees. However, you must attempt to protect your productive time at all costs. Remember though, if you are interrupted, take it in stride. Deal with the issue, then return to your task as soon as you can.

## TECHNIQUES FOR MANAGING YOUR TIME

### ABOUT THE SKILL

The essence of time management is to use your time effectively. This means you must know the goal you want to accomplish, the required activities that, when accomplished, will help you meet your goal, and the urgency of each activity.

### PRACTICING THE SKILL

1. **Identify your objectives.** What specific objectives have you set for yourself or for your unit? If you work in an organization where MBO, or some variation of goal setting exists, these objectives may already exist.

2. **Prioritize your objectives.** Not all objectives you have are equally important. Given limitations that exist on your time, you want to give highest priority to those objectives that are most important.

3. **List the activities that must be done to accomplish your objectives.** Planning is really the key here. You must identify the specific actions you need to take to achieve your goals. Write these activities down in a notebook, on a calendar, or use a computer-generated schedule. These activities become your "To Do" list. Your "To Do" list

should cover, at a minimum, those things that need to be done over the next few days. The list should be reviewed throughout the day, updated where necessary, and items completed should be crossed out.

4. **Prioritize your "To Do" list.** This step involves imposing a second set of priorities. Here, you need to emphasize both importance and urgency. If the activity is not important, you should consider delegating it to someone else below you. If it's not urgent, it can usually wait. Completing this step helps you to identify those activities you *must* do, activities you *should* do, those you'll do *when you can,* and activities that you can *get others to do for you.*

5. **Schedule your Day.** After prioritizing your activities, develop a daily plan. Each morning (or the night prior) identify what you want to accomplish during the day. This list should identify a manageable number of things you want to do during the day. Work first on any activity that you must do. Then follow with those you should do, and so forth. Be realistic in your schedule. Given the nature of your activities, you may be unable to complete everything. The key, however, is to concentrate on the "must do's", making sure they do get done. Fifteen minutes here, a half-hour there adds up in getting a "must do" done. Don't be pulled into working on the "when you can" activities because they are easier to accomplish. You'll be spending time on activities that really won't add to your effectiveness. ∎

Below are listed many of the typical reasons supervisors cite as time wasters. Check all those that apply to you in both Column A and Column B.

| *Column A* | *Column B* |
|---|---|
| _____ Interruptions | _____ Procrastination |
| _____ Attending meetings | _____ Too much work to do |
| _____ Drop-in visitors | _____ Complete easy tasks first |
| _____ Telephone calls | _____ Messy desk |
| _____ Red tape | _____ Unnecessary mail |
| _____ Unclear expectations | _____ Can't say no |
| _____ Lack of clear goals | _____ Failure to listen |
| _____ Lack of help | _____ Waiting for others |
| _____ Unrealistic time estimates | _____ Lack of self-discipline |
| _____ Too many bosses | _____ Visual distractions |
| _____ Lack of motivation | _____ Misplaced items |

After you've checked those that apply, study your time wasters. Is there anything in common you can find?

Irrespective of what you checked, did you see any similarities between the columns? If you observe closely, you probably found that Column A are those things that waste your time but are not in your direct control. In Column B are time wasters we bring on ourselves. Unfortunately, time management isn't that simple. Contrary to what most of us want to believe, every item in both columns is within our control. Many of those things in Column A which we shrug off as impossible to deal with, can be dealt with properly. That's the purpose of good time management.

How would you address your time wasters? How will you face these issues? What will you do to correct your time management "problems"?

Finally, as a supervisor, you'll be attending many meetings. If it's your meeting, have a reason for it. Meeting just to meet is usually a waste of time. Set an agenda for the meeting describing its purpose and what you want to accomplish. Then stick to it. Efficiently run meetings are time effective. If it's not your meeting, request an agenda if one isn't sent. If you're able, find out why you need to attend. Maybe someone on your staff could represent you. If that's not possible, attempt to attend only the part of the meeting that requires your presence. If that fails, just go. Don't fret it, don't waste more time chit-chatting after the meeting. Do what you need to do, then return to your priority tasks!

**5.** Which one of the following would reflect a characteristic of a "club" organizational culture?
   **a.** loyalty and commitment
   **b.** entrepreneurial spirit
   **c.** specialized jobs
   **d.** survival
**6.** Why is career planning important?
**7.** Starting out in a department that is high in power within the organization often hinders your career growth. True or False?
**8.** Which one of the following is recommended as the final step in time management?
   **a.** prioritizing objectives
   **b.** listing goals
   **c.** listing the activities that will accomplish your objectives
   **d.** preparation of a daily plan

## SUMMARY

After reading this chapter, I can:

1. **Define what is meant by the term *career*.** A career is a sequence of positions occupied by a person during his or her lifetime.
2. **Explain why traditional career paths are disappearing.** The traditional career path is disappearing because organizations have cut costs by reducing layers of the hierarchy, widening spans of control, and cutting back on entry-level supervisory programs. The new career path is characterized by unpredictability, lateral and interorganizational moves, occasional bouts of plateauing, the continual need for educational updating and retraining, and personal assumption of responsibility for career planning.
3. **Identify your basic talents and strengths.** Since everyone has specific talents and strengths, there is no common answer. Examples include writing, speaking, concentrating, interacting with people, organizing things, and reasoning.
4. **Describe your interests.** You can identify your interests by looking at courses you've taken in school or past work experiences that you found particularly interesting.
5. **Match your individual personality to an organizational culture.** Make sure the culture of any organization you choose to work for fits well with your style and personality. The better the match, the more likely you are to receive favorable performance reviews and rewards such as pay raises and promotions.
6. **Define your career goals.** You should define career goals for five, ten, and twenty years into the future. These goals should be more directional than specific.
7. **List five steps for better time management.** Five steps for better time management include: (1) identify your objectives; (2) prioritize your objectives; (3) list the activities that must be done to accomplish your objectives; (4) prioritize your "To Do" list; and (5) schedule your day.

## REVIEWING YOUR KNOWLEDGE

1. Can you plan a career with any degree of certainty? Discuss.
2. Do you think the decline of the traditional career path increases or decreases organizational politics? Explain.
3. What can an employee do if he or she faces a mid-career plateau?
4. Why must employees assume personal responsibility for their career planning?
5. List six personality types and describe each. Which fits you best? How can this knowledge be beneficial to you?
6. For each of the six personality types, identify a job that you think would be a good match.
7. "Most people would prefer to work in a medium- to large-sized organization." Build an argument to support this statement, then negate that argument.
8. Contrast the four types of organizational cultures. Which one do you prefer, and why?
9. How can you assess how well you are currently managing your time?

# ANSWERS TO THE POP QUIZZES

1. **c. position.** The specific job one holds is not necessarily a component of one's career. The other three are dimensions identified as part of the definition of a career.
2. **True.** This statement reflects the predictability that was associated with traditional career pathing.
3. The five traditional stages of careers are: exploration, establishment, mid-career, late career, and decline.
4. **a. company responsibility for developing employees' careers.** On the contrary, it is the employee, not the company, that is responsible for ensuring career goals are met.
5. **a. loyalty and commitment.** Entrepreneurial spirit is more associated with a "baseball" culture; specialized jobs with an academy culture; and survival with a fortress culture.
6. Career planning is important because it can prepare you to be ready when career opportunities present themselves.
7. **False.** Starting out in a department that is high in power has the opposite effect. That is, you're more likely to advance rapidly throughout your career.
8. **d. preparation of a daily plan.** This step follows the others, which are broader in perspective. ■

## A CLASS EXERCISE: MANAGING YOUR TIME AND MONEY

Have you ever thought much about how you spend your time and money in a typical week? Do you know who or what "wastes" your time? How about where you've spent your money? Can you account for your expenditures? Or has your money just disappeared?

For this exercise, develop a time log for each day for the next week. Starting at 7:00 a.m. and in 15 minute increments, list what you do, and who you interact with until 11:00 p.m. Fill in each time period as it ends—don't let it wait until later and attempt to complete it by memory. In a similar fashion, develop an expense budget, listing all your expenditures that occur during the week.

When you have tracked data for the week, review the seven time logs and the expense budgets. Develop responses to the following questions. In the time logs, can you identify: a) when you are most productive? and b) your "time wasters?" Are there consistencies in the time wasters—time, place, individual?

Do a similar analysis of your expenditures. What have you spent most of your money on? Do you tend to spend your money on "things" you need or do you find yourself impulse buying? Do you believe that having a weekly budget could benefit you in managing your money? Explain.

After you've compiled this data, exchange papers with two classmates. Look for similarities between what they identified and your list. Make two recommendations for each group member that could help them manage their time and their money better. Share these with the group. Discuss your reactions to their recommendations and answer any questions they may have about the recommendations you've made. Finally, as a group, discuss what changes you are willing to make in terms of better managing your time and money.

## CRITICAL THINKING

## CASE 16.A

## Michael Giles Cleans Up

What makes a person change his or her career aspirations after working long and hard to achieve a goal? That's a question many have posed to Michael Giles, Founder of Quick-Wash-Dry Clean USA.[9] Michael Giles has been the "talk of the town" of late. A graduate of the prestigious Columbia Law School, Michael was able to write his own ticket after graduation. He was in such demand that he could have accepted numerous job offers presented to him. The one, though, that intrigued him most was an offer from IBM.

IBM offered Giles a position as a marketing representative in the Washington, D.C. area. Starting him at $160,000, Michael appeared to have it all—a good income, a great house in a distinguished neighborhood, and a future with the organization that had no boundary. But none of this was apparently enough for Giles. Sure, he liked his lifestyle, but he felt he wasn't giving anything back to the community. He was particularly concerned about black residents who lived in deplorable

[9]Drawn from Lee Smith, "Landing that First Real Job," *Fortune*, May 16, 1994, p. 94; and William Echikson, "Young Americans Go Abroad and Strike it Rich," *Fortune*, October 17, 1994, p. 186.

conditions in South Africa. So at age 35, Michael quit his IBM job and moved to Soweto, a small South-African township just outside of Johannesburg. There he took up residence in an area where there was no running water, nor any of the creature comforts most U.S. citizens are accustomed to. Needless to say, everyone thought Michael had flipped!

But there's more to the Giles story than a high potential employee leaving corporate America. His value system and beliefs led him to try to make the world a better place for disadvantaged people. He believed he could be successful in this world and help others at the same time. In his quest, Giles sought a loan from the Overseas Private Investment Corporation to start the Quick-Wash-Dry Clean USA Corporation. Michael's company is building coin-operated laundromats to provide laundry services to most of South Africa's black community. In doing so, he's making a profit. More importantly, he's making water available to areas that never had it before and developing sewage systems for the first time in many locations. For Michael Giles, this is the sweet smell of success!

## RESPONDING TO THE CASE

1. What do you think went into Michael Giles' decision to leave a promising career at IBM and move to Soweto?
2. Do you think IBM could have done anything to change Michael's mind and have him reconsider leaving the company?
3. How has Giles demonstrated a spirituality in his career decision to start Quick-Wash-Dry Clean USA?

# CASE 16.B

## Jackie Zaleski Looks for Career Insights

Jackie Zaleski, an industrial supervision major, is in her final semester at Rockland Community College. Jackie will graduate in the top five percent of her class. While attending RCC, she has worked part-time in the information technology division of a large industrial supply company. Jackie is married and has two small children. Her husband works full time for the county government.

When Jackie started her studies at RCC, one of her business professors, Dr. Jerry Flynn, suggested that she get a part-time job even though she would have to juggle her studies and work. He also recommended Jackie plan some leisure and social time into her life—a truly difficult balancing act for Jackie.

In the first class Jackie took with Dr. Flynn, he assigned several interesting projects: a) researching the facts about an industry where you might want to start your working career; b) arranging for an interview with a firm where you might like to work; c) developing a personal career development plan; and d) creating a placement file at RCC.

Dr. Flynn's class projects were time-consuming, and some of Jackie's classmates didn't take them too seriously. Some students completed the requirements and did just the minimum to get a grade. Unlike Jackie, some students felt the assignments were "busy work," even though Dr. Flynn stressed the importance of their potential and long-term value.

Jackie can relate to the potential value of the assignments, since she has a second interview next week with a vice president of a company where she hopes to land a supervisory position when she finishes school. The vice president is a friend of the supervisor Jackie interviewed for her class. Both the vice president and the supervisor are active members of the Society for Human Resource Management (SHRM). Jackie was introduced to the vice president at one of the Society for Human Resource Management monthly meetings she has been attending regularly. Jackie wishes there was some way she could tell entering students the importance of taking their schoolwork and assignments seriously.

## RESPONDING TO THE CASE

1. Form groups of three to four students. When Jackie did the background research on a company where she interviewed a supervisor, what information was essential for her to gather? What questions do you think Jackie asked in the interview? Share your "lists" with classmates.

2. Of what benefit to item #1 was the personal career plan that Jackie developed? What elements should Jackie's plan include to be of optimum value to her? Why?

3. As Jackie learned more and more about herself, she discovered it was important to match her individual personality to an organizational culture. Why? How does this apply to you?

4. Jackie is one interview away from a full-time job. She also has made some excellent networking contacts, and she is enjoying her affiliation with SHRM. What conclusions can you draw from these statements that would be good advice you could follow in planning your career? ■

## Andrea Gurley
### Associate Director, Skills Survival Institute

Andrea is the supervisor at a nonprofit day care center for at-risk children. She was lead teacher in the preschool program. When Andrea was promoted to supervisor, another lead teacher, who had many years of experience, resented it. The teacher did not want to take orders from Andrea and she criticized Andrea to other staff members.

When the lead teacher was asked to reorganize her program in order for the center to renew its state licensing, additional resentment was evident. Andrea knew that the state wanted a dynamic play area set up in the teacher's classroom. The teacher did not agree.

Andrea called team meetings to present these proposals to the staff. She wanted the staff to support the changes. The lead teacher made sarcastic comments during the meeting, undermining Andrea's authority. Andrea knew that the lead teacher was wonderful with the children. Because she was afraid the teacher would quit, Andrea did not confront the woman directly. Instead, Andrea called in an outside consultant to analyze the center's physical set-up. The outside consultant made the same recommendations that Andrea had made about the play area. The lead teacher still refused to make the changes.

1. What are some of the problems that face an employee who is promoted to a leadership position?
2. How can the new supervisor overcome some of the problems encountered in the case?
3. What can new supervisors do to prepare themselves for their new careers?
4. What are some of the ways a new supervisor can gain the trust, respect, and confidence of other employees? Why is this necessary for a supervisor who has newly-gained authority? ■

# GLOSSARY

**Accept errors.** acceptance of candidates who would subsequently perform poorly on the job.

**Accommodation.** a method of maintaining harmonious relationships by placing others' needs and concerns above one's own.

**Accountability.** the obligation to perform an assignment in a satisfactory manner.

**Active listening.** a technique that requires an individual to "get inside" a speaker's mind to understand the communication from the speaker's point of view.

**Activities.** the time or resources required to progress from one event to another.

**Affirmative action.** legislation that requires employers to make an active effort to recruit, select, train, and promote members of protected groups.

**Age Discrimination in Employment Act.** a law that prohibits discrimination against persons 40 years of age or older in any area of employment, including selection, because of age.

**Agency shop.** an agreement that requires non-union employees to pay the union a sum of money equal to union fees and dues as a condition of continuing employment.

**Americans with Disabilities Act.** a law that protects the physically and mentally disabled against discriminatory practices and requires employers to make reasonable accommodations to provide a qualified individual access to a job.

**Arbitrator.** an impartial third party to a dispute who will hear the case and make a ruling.

**Assertiveness training.** a technique designed to make people more open and self-expressive, saying what they mean without being rude or thoughtless.

**Attitudes.** evaluative statements or judgments concerning objects, people, or events.

**Attribute listing.** individualized brainstorming; isolation of major characteristics of traditional alternatives, which are each considered in turn and changed in every conceivable way.

**Authority.** rights inherent in a supervisory position to give orders and expect those orders to be obeyed.

**Autocratic leader.** a task master who leaves no doubt as to who's in charge, and who has the authority and power in the group.

**Avoidance.** withdrawal from a conflict or ignoring its existence.

**Baby-boomers.** the largest group in the workforce; they are regarded as the career climbers—at the right place at the right time. Mature workers view them as unrealistic in their views and workaholics.

**Baby-busters.** a group of workers less committed, less rule-bound, and more into self-gratification, with an intolerance of baby-boomers and their attitudes. They are viewed as selfish and not willing to play by the rules.

**Bargaining unit.** employees a union will represent if it wins an election.

**Basic corrective action.** action that asks how and why performance deviated.

**Behaviorally-anchored rating scales (BARS).** scales that help a supervisor rate an employee based on items along a continuum; however, points are examples of actual behavior on a given job rather than general descriptions or traits.

**Body language.** gestures, facial configurations, and other movements of the body that communicate emotions or temperaments such as aggression, fear, shyness, arrogance, joy, and anger.

**Brainstorming.** a technique for overcoming pressures for conformity that retard the development of creative alternatives; an idea-generating process that specifically encourages alternatives while withholding criticism of those alternatives.

**Budget.** numerical plans that express anticipated results in dollar terms for a specific time period. They may act as planning guides as well as control devices.

**Career.** a sequence of job positions occupied by a person during his or her lifetime.

**Cause-effect diagrams.** diagrams used to depict the causes of a problem and to group them according to common categories such as machinery, methods, personnel, finances, or management.

**Central tendency error.** appraisers' tendency to avoid the "excellent" category as well as the "unacceptable" category and assign all ratings around the "average" or midpoint range.

**Centralization.** decision-making responsibility in the hands of top management.

**Chain of command.** a principle that states that an employee should have one and only one supervisor to whom he or she is directly responsible.

**Change agents.** people who act as catalysts and assume the responsibility for overseeing the change process.

**Change process.** a model that allows for successful change by requiring unfreezing of the status quo (equilibrium state), changing to a new state, and refreezing the new change to make it permanent. Unfreezing the equilibrium state is achieved by (1) increasing driving forces; (2) decreasing restraining forces; or (3) combining these two approaches.

**Charismatic leader.** an individual with a compelling vision or sense of purpose, an ability to communicate that vision in clear terms that followers can understand, a demonstrated consistency and focus in pursuit of his or her vision, and an understanding of his or her own strengths.

**Checklist.** a list of behavioral descriptions that are checked off when they apply to an employee.

**Civil Rights Act of 1964.** a law that prohibits discrimination in hiring, firing, promoting, and privileges of employment based on race, religion, color, gender, or national origin.

**Civil Rights Act of 1991.** legislation that prohibits discrimination on the basis of race and prohibits racial harassment on the job; returns the burden of proof that discrimination did not occur back to the employer; reinforces the illegality of employers who make hiring, firing, or promotion decisions on the basis of race, ethnicity, gender, or religion; and permits women and religious minorities to seek punitive damages in intentional discriminatory claims.

**Closed shop.** an illegal practice favored by unions that contractually binds employers to hire only workers who are already members of the union.

**Code of ethics.** a formal document that states an organization's primary values and the ethical rules it expects employees to follow.

**Collaboration.** an approach to conflict that requires all parties seek to satisfy their interests.

**Collective bargaining.** a process for negotiating a union contract and for administrating the contract after it has been negotiated. It includes preparing to negotiate, the actual contract negotiations, and administering the contract after it has been ratified.

**Communication.** the transference and understanding of meaning.

**Compromise.** an approach to conflict that requires each party to give up something of value.

**Conceptual competence.** the mental ability to analyze and diagnose complex situations.

**Conciliation.** an impasse resolution technique that states that the role of the third party is to keep the negotiations ongoing and to act as a go-between.

**Concurrent control.** a type of control that takes place while an activity is in progress.

**Conflict.** a process in which one party consciously interferes in the goal-achieving efforts of another party.

**Conflict management.** the application of resolution and stimulation techniques to achieve the optimum level of departmental conflict.

**Consultative participative leadership.** the leadership style of an individual who seeks input, hears the concerns and issues of the followers, but makes the final decision him- or herself, using input as an information-seeking exercise.

**Control by exception.** a system that ensures that one is not overwhelmed by information on variations from standard.

**Control charts.** run charts of sample averages with statistically determined upper and lower limits.

**Control process.** a three-step process that consists of: (1) measuring actual performance; (2) comparing results with standards; and (3) taking corrective action.

**Controlling.** monitoring an organization's performance and comparing performance with previously set goals. If significant deviations exist, getting the organization back on track.

**Corrective control.** a type of control that provides feedback, after an activity is finished, in order to prevent future deviations.

**Credibility.** supervisor qualities of honesty, competence, and the ability to inspire.

**Critical incidents.** incidents that focus attention on employee behaviors that are key in making the difference between executing a job effectively and executing it ineffectively.

**Critical path.** the longest or most time-consuming sequence of events and activities in a PERT chart.

**Cultural environments.** values, morals, customs, and laws of countries.

**Culture.** a set of underwritten norms that members of the organization accept and understand, and which guide their actions.

**Customer departmentalization.** grouping activities around common customer categories.

**Data.** raw, unanalyzed facts such as names, numbers, or quantities.

**Decision trees.** diagrams that analyze hiring, marketing, investment, equipment purchases, pricing, and similar decisions that involve a progression of decisions. Decision trees assign probabilities to each possible outcome and calculate payoffs for each decision path.

**Decision-making process.** a seven-step process that provides a rational and analytical way of looking at decisions. The steps include identification of the problem; collection of rational information; development of alternatives; evaluation of alternatives; selection of the best alternative; implementation of the decision; and follow-up and evaluation.

**Delegation.** allocation of duties, employee empowerment, assignment of responsibility, and creation of accountability.

**Democratic participative leadership.** a leadership style that allows followers to have a say in what's decided.

**Departmentalization.** grouping departments based on work functions, product or service, target customer or client, geographic territory, or the process used to turn inputs into outputs.

**Devil's advocate.** a person who purposely presents arguments that run counter to those opposed by the majority or against current practices.

**Discipline.** actions taken by supervisors to enforce an organization's standards and regulations.

**Dismissal.** termination of one's employment.

**Distributive bargaining.** a negotiating process that operates under zero-sum conditions; any gain made is at the expense of the other person, and vice versa.

**Downsizing.** a reduction in the workforce and reshaping of operations to create "lean and mean" organizations. The goals of organizational downsizing are greater efficiency and reduced costs.

**Dues checkoff.** a provision that often exists in union security arrangements whereby an employer withholds union dues from members' paychecks.

**Effectiveness.** doing a task right; goal attainment.

**Efficiency.** doing a task right; also refers to the relationship between inputs and outputs.

**Electronic meeting.** a group decision-making technique in which participants are positioned in front of computer terminals as issues are presented. Participants type responses onto computer screens as their anonymous comments and aggregate votes are displayed on a projection screen in the room.

**Employee Assistance Programs (EAPs).** programs designed to act as a first stop for individuals seeking psychiatric or substance-abuse help, with the goal of getting productive employees back on the job as swiftly as possible

**Employee counseling.** an emphasis on encouraging training and development efforts in a situation in which employee unwillingness or inability to perform his or her job satisfactorily is either voluntary or involuntary.

**Employee development.** preparation of employees for future positions that require higher level skills, knowledge, or abilities.

**Employee stock ownership plan (ESOP).** a compensation program that allows employees to become part owners of an organization by receiving stock as a performance incentive.

**Employee training.** changing skills, knowledge, attitudes, or behavior of employees. Determination of training needs is made by supervisors.

**Employment-at-will.** a legal doctrine that defines an employer's rights to discipline or discharge an employee.

**Empowerment.** Increasing an employee's involvement in his or her work through greater participation in decisions and expanded responsibility for work outcomes.

**End-users.** users responsible for decision and control of systems.

**Equal Employment Opportunity Act.** a law that established the Equal Employment Opportunity Commission (EEOC) to enforce civil rights laws and gave it the power to sue organizations that failed to comply. It also expanded Title VII coverage and required employers to participate in affirmative action.

**Equity theory.** a theory that states employees perceive what they can get from a job situation (outcomes) in relation to what they put into it (inputs), and then compare their input-outcome ratio with the input-output ratio of others.

**Ethics.** rules or principles that define right and wrong conduct.

**Events.** end points that represent completion of major activities.

**Expectancy theory.** a theory that argues that individuals analyze effort-performance, performance-reward, and rewards-personal goals relationships, and their level of effort depends on the strengths of their expectations that these relationships can be achieved.

**Expected value analysis.** a procedure that permits decision makers to place a monetary value on various consequences likely to result from the selection of a particular course of action.

**Extrinsic feedback.** feedback provided to an employee by an outside source.

**Fact-finding.** a technique whereby a neutral third-party individual conducts a hearing to gather evidence from both labor and management.

**Family and Medical Leave Act.** a law that provides employees in organizations with 50 or more employees the opportunity to take up to twelve weeks of unpaid leave each year for family matters—such as childbirth, adoption, illness, or to care for an ill family member.

**First-level managers.** managers that represent the first level in the management hierarchy.

**Flow charts.** visual representations of the sequence of events for a particular process that clarify how things are being done so inefficiencies can be identified and the process improved.

**Forcing.** attempting to satisfy one's own needs at the expense of the other party.

**Formal communication.** communication that addresses task-related issues and tends to follow the organization's authority chain.

**Free-reign leader.** an individual who gives employees total autonomy to make decisions that will affect them.

**Functional authority.** rights over individuals outside one's own direct areas of responsibility.

**Functional departmentalization.** grouping activities into independent units based on functions performed.

**Gantt chart.** a bar chart with time on the horizontal axis and activities to be scheduled on the vertical axis. The chart shows when tasks are supposed to be done and compares actual progress on each task.

**Geographic departmentalization.** grouping activities into independent units based on geography or territory.

**Grapevine.** the means of communication by which most operative employees first hear about important changes introduced by organizational leaders; rumormill.

**Graphic rating scale.** a method of appraisal which uses a scale or continuum that best describes the employee, using factors such as quantity and quality of work, job knowledge, cooperation, loyalty, dependability, attendance, honesty, integrity, attitudes, and initiative.

**Grievance procedures.** procedures designed to resolve disputes as quickly as possible and at the lowest level in the organization.

**Group order ranking.** placing employees into classifications, such as "top one-fifth" or "second one-fifth." This method prevents a supervisor from inflating or equalizing employee evaluations.

**Groupthink.** withholding of differing views by group members in order to appear in agreement.

**Halo error.** a tendency to rate an individual high or low on all factors due to the impression of a high or low rating on some specific factor.

**Hierarchy of needs theory.** a theory of Abraham Maslow that states that a satisfied need no longer creates tension and therefore doesn't motivate. Maslow believed that the key to motivation is to determine where an individual is along the needs hierarchy and focus motivation efforts at the point where needs become essentially unfulfilled.

**Horizontal structures.** very flat structures used in small businesses as well as giant companies in which job-related activities cut across all parts of the organization.

**"Hot stove" rule.** a set of principles that can guide an individual in effectively disciplining an employee by demonstrating the analogy between touching a hot stove and administering discipline.

**Immediate corrective action.** action that adjusts something right now and gets things back on track.

**Incident rate.** a measure of the number of injuries, illnesses, or lost workdays as it relates to a common base rate of 100 full-time employees.

**Individual ranking.** a method that requires supervisors to list all employees in order from highest to lowest performer.

**Informal communication.** communication that moves in any direction, skips authority levels, and is as likely to satisfy social needs as it is to facilitate task accomplishments.

**Information.** analyzed and processed data.

**Integrative bargaining.** a negotiating process that operates under the assumption that there is at least one settlement that can create a win-win solution.

**Interest arbitration.** arbitration in which a panel of three individuals hears testimony from both sides and renders a decision on how to settle the current contract negotiation dispute.

**Intermediate-term plans.** plans that cover a period of one to 5 years.

**Interpersonal competence.** the ability to work with, understand, communicate with, and motivate other people, both individually and in groups.

**Intrinsic feedback.** self-generated feedback.

**Job description.** a written statement of job duties, working conditions, and operating responsibilities.

**Job design.** combining tasks to form complete jobs.

**Job enrichment.** the degree to which a worker controls the planning, execution, and evaluation of his or her work.

**Job specification.** the minimum acceptable qualifications an incumbent must possess to perform a given job successfully.

**Just-in-time (JIT) inventory system.** a system in which inventory items arrive when they are needed in the production process instead of being stored in stock. *See also* Kanban.

**Justice view of ethics.** a view that requires individuals to impose and enforce rules fairly and impartially so there is an equitable distribution of benefits and costs.

**Kanban.** In Japanese, a "card" or "sign." Shipped in a container, a kanban is returned to the supplier when the container is opened, initiating the shipment of a second container that arrives just as the first container is emptied.

**Labor relations.** all activities within a company that involve dealing with a union and its members.

**Labor-Management Relations Act (Taft-Hartley Act).** a law passed in 1947 that specified unfair union labor practices and declared the closed shop to be illegal.

**Lateral thinking.** sideways, nonsequential thinking.

**Leadership.** the ability an individual demonstrates to influence others to act in a particular way through direction, encouragement, sensitivity, consideration, and support.

**Leadership traits.** qualities such as intelligence, charm, decisiveness, enthusiasm, strength, bravery, integrity, and self-confidence.

**Leading.** motivation of employees, direction of activities of others, selection of the most effective communication channel, and resolution of conflicts among members.

**Leniency error.** positive or negative leniency that over- or understates performance, giving an individual a higher or lower appraisal than deserved.

**Lifelong learning.** continuing education through attendance at company seminars, industry workshops, and evening college classes to upgrades one's skills as well as self-education on new supervisory concepts, business practices, and changes in one's industry.

**Line authority.** the authority that entitles a supervisor to direct the work of his or her direct reports and to make certain decisions without consulting others.

**Lockout.** a company action equivalent to a strike; when management denies unionized employees access to their jobs.

**Locus of control.** the source of control over an individual's behavior.

**Long-term plans.** plans that cover a period in excess of 5 years.

**Machiavellianism.** a manipulative individual who believes ends can justify means.

**Maintenance of membership.** an agreement which states that should employees join the union, they are compelled to remain in the union for the duration of the existing contract. Such an agreement often provides an escape clause in which employees may choose to withdraw their membership from the union without penalty.

**Management.** the process of getting things done, effectively and efficiently, through and with other.

**Management by objectives (MBO).** a system by which employees jointly determine specific performance objectives with their supervisors, progress toward objectives is periodically reviewed, and rewards are allocated on the basis of this progress.

**Management functions.** planning, organizing, leading, and controlling.

**Management information system (MIS).** a mechanism that provides needed and accurate information on a regular and timely basis.

**Management rights.** in negotiations, issues that are specific to management.

**Marginal analysis.** a method that helps decision makers optimize returns or minimize costs by dealing with the additional cost in a particular decision, rather than the average cost.

**Matrix.** a structure that weaves together elements of functional and product departmentalization.

**Mature workers.** a group of workers born prior to 1946 who are security oriented and have a committed work ethic.

**Mediation.** an impasse resolution technique where a mediator attempts to pull together the common ground that exists, and makes settlement recommendations for overcoming the barriers that exist between two sides in a conflict.

**Mentor.** a more experienced and more senior member of the organization who can act as a sounding-board, providing vital suggestions and feedback on how to survive and succeed in the organization.

**Middle managers.** all employees below the top-management level who manage other managers. These managers are responsible for establishing and meeting specific departmental or unit goals set by top management.

**Motivation.** the willingness to do something conditioned by the action's ability to satisfy some need for the individual.

**Motivation-hygiene theory.** a theory of Frederick Herzberg that the opposite of satisfaction is not "dissatisfaction" but "no satisfaction" and the opposite of dissatisfaction is not "satisfaction" but "no dissatisfaction."

**National Labor Relations Act (Wagner Act).** a law that guarantees workers the right to organize and join unions, to bargain collectively, and to act in concert in pursuit of their objectives.

**National Labor Relations Board (NLRB).** a group given primary responsibility for conducting elections to determine union representation and to interpret and apply the law against unfair labor practices.

**Need.** a physiological or psychological deficiency that makes certain outcomes seem attractive.

**Need for achievement (nAch).** a compelling drive to succeed; an intrinsic motivation to do something better or more efficiently than it has been done before.

**Negotiation.** a process in which two or more parties who have different preferences and priorities must make a joint decision and come to an agreement.

**Nominal group technique.** a technique that restricts discussion during the decision-making process.

**Nonverbal communications.** communications that are not spoken, written, or transmitted on a computer.

**Occupational Safety and Health Act (OSHA).** a law that enforces, through standards and regulations, healthful working conditions and preservation of human resources.

**Open shop.** an arrangement in which joining a union is totally voluntary.

**Organization.** a systematic grouping of people brought together to accomplish some specific purpose.

**Operative employees.** employees who physically produce an organization's goods and services by working on specific tasks.

**Organizing.** arranging and grouping jobs, allocating resources, and assigning work so that activities can be accomplished as planned.

**Orientation.** an expansion on information a new employee obtained during the recruitment and selection stages; an attempt to familiarize new employees with the job, the work unit, and the organization as a whole.

**Parochialism.** seeing things solely through one's own eyes and within one's own perspectives; believing that what we do is best.

**Participative leadership.** the leadership style of an individual who actively seeks input from followers for many of the activities in the organization.

**Path-goal theory.** the leader's job is to assist followers in overcoming obstacles in the way of attaining their goals by providing the proper leadership style.

**Pay-for-performance programs.** compensation plans that pay employees on the basis of some performance measure.

**People-centered leader.** an individual who emphasizes interpersonal relations with those he or she leads.

**People.** *See also* Process; Efficiency; Effectiveness.

**Performance appraisal.** a review of past performance that emphasizes positive accomplishments as well as deficiencies, and a means for helping employees improve future performance.

**Personal career planning.** preparing oneself for future work opportunities by examining one's talents and strengths, needs and interests, and the corporate culture in which one would best fit.

**PERT chart.** a diagram that depicts the sequence of activities needed to complete a project and the time or costs associated with each activity.

**Planning.** defining an organization's goals, establishing an overall strategy for achieving these goals, and developing a comprehensive hierarchy of plans to integrate and coordinate activities.

**Plateauing.** little likelihood of any further upward movement in a career with a current employer.

**Policies.** broad guidelines for managerial action.

**Political competence.** a supervisor's ability to enhance his or her power, build a power base, and establish the "right" connections in the organization.

**Politicking.** the actions one can take to influence, or attempt to influence, the distribution of advantages and disadvantages within an organization.

**Positive discipline.** a technique that attempts to reinforce the good work behaviors of an employee, while simultaneously emphasizing to the employee the problems created by undesirable performance.

**Preventive control.** a type of control that anticipates and prevents undesirable outcomes.

**Problem.** a discrepancy between an existing and a desired state of affairs.

**Procedure.** a standardized way of responding to repetitive problems; they define the limits within which managers must stay as decisions are made.

**Process.** the primary activities supervisors perform.

**Process departmentalization.** grouping activities around a process; this method provides a basis for the homogeneous categorizing of activities.

**Product departmentalization.** grouping activities into independent units based on problems or issues relating to a product.

**Productivity.** output per labor hour, best expressed by the formula Productivity = Output/Labor + Capital + Materials. Productivity can be applied to the individual, the group, and the total organization.

**Program.** a single-use set of plans for a specific major undertaking within an organization's overall goals. Programs may be designed and overseen by top management or supervisors.

**Progressive discipline.** action that begins with a verbal warning, and then proceeds through written reprimands, suspension, and finally, in the most serious cases, dismissal.

**Quality control.** identification of mistakes that may have occurred; monitoring quality to ensure that it meets some preestablished standard.

**Range of variation.** variation in performance that can be expected in all activities.

**Readiness.** the ability and willingness of an employee to complete a task.

**Recency error.** rating others in a way that appraisers recall and give greater importance to employee job behaviors that have occurred near the end of the performance-measuring period.

**Reengineering.** radical or quantum change that occurs when most of the work being done in an organization is evaluated, and then altered. Reengineering requires organizational members to rethink what work should be done, how it is to be done, and how to best implement these decisions.

**Reinforcement theory.** a theory that states people will exert higher levels of effort in tasks that are reinforced. Reinforcers are consequences that, when immediately following a response, increase the probability that the behavior will be repeated.

**Reject errors.** rejection of candidates who would later perform successfully on the job.

**Reliability.** an indication of whether a test or device measures the same thing consistently.

**Responsibility.** supervisory obligations such as achieving a unit's goals, keeping costs within budget, following organizational policies, and motivating employees.

**Richness of information.** a measure of the amount of information that is transmitted based on multiple information cues (words, posture, facial expressions, gestures, intonations), immediate feedback, and the personal touch.

**Rights view of ethics.** a view that calls on individuals to make decisions consistent with fundamental liberties and privileges as set forth in documents such as the Bill of Rights.

**Risk propensity.** willingness to take chances.

**Role ambiguity.** a situation created when role expectations are not clearly understood and the employee is not sure what he or she is to do.

**Role conflicts.** expectations that may hard to reconcile or satisfy.

**Role overload.** pressure experienced when an employee is expected to do more than time permits.

**Roles.** behavior patterns that correspond to the positions individuals occupy in an organization.

**Rule.** explicit statements that tell supervisors what they ought or ought not to do.

**Scatter diagrams.** diagrams that illustrate the relationship between two variables by visually depicting correlations and possible cause-and-effect.

**Scheduling.** detailed planning of activities to be done, the order in which they are to be done, who is to do each activity, and when the activities are to be completed.

**Self-esteem.** the degree to which individuals like or dislike themselves.

**Self-monitoring.** high self-monitors are adaptable in adjusting their behavior to external situational factors, and are capable of presenting striking contradictions between public personas and private selves. Low self-monitors tend to display their true feelings and beliefs in every situation.

**Sexual harassment.** anything of a sexual nature that is required for getting a job, has an employment consequence, or creates an offensive or hostile environment, including sexually suggestive remarks, unwanted touching, sexual advances, requests for sexual favors, and other verbal and physical conduct of a sexual nature.

**Short-term plans.** plans that are less than one year in length.

**Similarity error.** rating others in a way that gives special consideration to qualities that appraisers perceive in themselves.

**Simple structure.** a non-elaborate structure low in complexity, with little formalization, and with authority centralized in a single person; a "flat" organization with only two or three levels.

**Single-use plans.** detailed courses of action used once or only occasionally to deal with problems that don't occur repeatedly.

**Situational leadership.** adjustment of a leadership style to specific situations to reflect employee needs.

**Skill.** the ability to demonstrate a system and sequence of behavior that is functionally related to attaining a performance goal.

**Social obligation.** the foundation of a business's social involvement. An organization's social obligation is fulfilled when it meets its economic and legal responsibilities.

**Social responsibility.** an obligation organizations have to pursue long-term goals that are good for society.

**Social responsiveness.** a process guided by social norms that require business to determine what is right or wrong and thus seek fundamental truths; an attempt to do those things that make society better and not to do those things that could make it worse.

**Span of control.** the number of employees a supervisor can efficiently and effectively direct.

**Spillover effect.** successes made by unions through negotiations that spill over to influence the wages, working conditions, and terms of employment for nonunion workers.

**Staff authority.** a limited authority that supports line authority by advising, servicing, and assisting.

**Standing plans.** plans that can be used over and over again by managers faced with recurring activities.

**Status.** a social rank or the importance one has in a group.

**Strategic planning.** organizational planning that includes the establishment of overall goals, and positions an organization's products or services against the competition.

**Stress.** something an individual feels when faced with opportunities, constraints, or commands perceived to be both uncertain and important. Stress can show itself in both positive and negative ways.

**Strike.** an action where employees leave their jobs and refuse to return to work until a contract has been signed.

**Supervisors.** part of an organization's management team, supervisors oversee the work of operative employees and are the only managers who don't manage other managers. *See also* First-level managers.

**Supervisory competencies.** conceptual, interpersonal, technical, and political capabilities.

**Suspension.** time off without pay; this step is usually taken only if neither verbal nor written warnings have achieved desired results.

**Synectics.** use of analogies to look for similarities between relationships or functions.

**Tactical planning.** organizational planning that provides specific details on how overall goals are to be achieved.

**Task-centered leader.** an individual with a strong tendency to emphasize the technical or task aspects of a job.

**Technical competence.** the ability to apply specialized knowledge or expertise.

**Technology.** any high-tech equipment, tools, or operating methods that are designed to make work more efficient.

**Telecommuting.** linking a worker's remote computer and modem with coworkers and management at an office.

**Theory X-Theory Y.** a theory of Douglas McGregor that a supervisor's view of human nature is based on a certain grouping of assumptions and that he or she tends to mold behavior toward subordinates according to those assumptions.

**Time management.** a tool any individual can use to schedule his or her time effectively; a self-discipline that keeps an individual's attention focused on those things that need to be accomplished.

**Top management.** a group of people responsible for establishing an organization's overall objectives and developing the policies to achieve those objectives.

**Total quality management (TQM).** a philosophy of management that is driven by customer needs and expectations. Statistical control is used to reduce variability and result in uniform quality and predictable quantity of output.

**Transactional leaders.** leaders who guide or motivate their employees in the direction of established goals by clarifying role and task requirements.

**Transformational leaders.** leaders who inspire followers to transcend self-interests for the good of the organization and who are capable of having a profound and extraordinary effect on his or her followers.

**Trust.** the belief in the integrity, character, and ability of a leader.

**Type A behavior.** behavior that is characterized by feelings of a chronic sense of time urgency and by an excessive competitive drive.

**Type B behavior.** behavior that is the opposite of Type A behavior. Type B's never suffer from time urgency or impatience.

**Union.** an organization that represents workers and seeks to protect their interests through collective bargaining.

**Union shop.** an arrangement which stipulates that employers, while free to hire whomever they choose, may retain only union members.

**Union steward.** an employee who is the elected representative of the employees in a work unit, and is there to protect the rights of union members.

**Utilitarian view of ethics.** a view in which decisions are made solely on the basis of their outcomes or consequences.

**Validity.** a proven relationship between a selection device and some relevant criterion.

**Verbal intonation.** the emphasis an individual gives to words or phrases through speech.

**Verbal warning.** a temporary record of a reprimand which is then placed in the supervisor's file.

**Wellness programs.** any type of program that is designed to keep employees healthy, focusing on such things as smoking cessation, weight control, stress management, physical fitness, nutrition education, high blood-pressure control, and so on.

**Wildcat strike.** an illegal strike where employees refuse to work during the term of a binding contract, often due to ambiguities in the current contract.

**Work sampling.** the process of presenting applicants with a miniature replica of a job and letting them perform tasks that are central to the job.

**Work specialization.** the process of breaking down a job into a number of steps, with each step being completed by a separate individual.

**Workforce diversity.** the composition of the workforce to include males, females, whites, blacks, Hispanics, Asians, Native Americans, the disabled, homosexuals, heterosexuals, the elderly, and so on.

**Written essays.** a written narrative describing an employee's strengths, weaknesses, past performance, potential, and suggestions for improvement.

**Written warning.** the first formal stage of the disciplinary procedure; the warning becomes part of an employee's official personnel file.

**Wrongful discharge.** improper or unjust termination of an employee.

# INDEX